CHILD WELFARE IN CANADA

This book is published in cooperation with the National Welfare Grants Program, Social Development and Education Group, Human Resources Development Canada.

CHILD WELFARE IN CANADA

Research and Policy Implications

Edited by
Joe Hudson *(The University of Calgary)*
and
Burt Galaway *(University of Manitoba)*

THOMPSON EDUCATIONAL PUBLISHING, INC.
Toronto

Orders may be sent to:

Canada
14 Ripley Avenue, Suite 105
Toronto, Ontario
M6S 3N9

For faster delivery, please send your order by telephone or fax to:
Tel (416) 766–2763 / Fax (416) 766–0398

Canadian Cataloguing in Publication Data

Main entry under title:
Child welfare in Canada : research and policy implications
Includes bibliographical references.
ISBN 1-55077-071-3

1. Child welfare - Canada. 2. Child welfare - Government policy - Canada.
3. Children - Legal status, laws, etc. - Canada. I. Hudson, Joe.
II. Galaway, Burt, 1937- .

HV745.A6C45 1995 362.7'0971 C95-930419-3

Cover: A Wreath of Flowers by William Brymner, National Gallery of Canada.

Printed and bound in Canada.
1 2 3 4 97 96 95

Table of Contents

PART 2 :
SUPPORT AND PREVENTION PROGRAMMING

PART 3:
FOSTER CARE PROGRAMMING

PART 4: ADOPTIONS PROGRAMMING

PART 5: CHILD WELFARE SERVICE EXPERIENCES AND OUTCOMES

PART 6: A RESEARCH AGENDA

Acknowledgements

Earlier versions of the papers presented in this volume were developed for a Research and Policy Symposium funded by National Welfare Grants, Human Resources Development Canada. The symposium was co-sponsored by The University of Calgary Faculty of Social Work and the University of Manitoba Faculty of Social Work. We extend our deepest appreciation to Fran McIninch and David Thornton of National Welfare Grants for their support, encouragement, and assistance in planning both the Symposium and this publication. The book is only possible because of the hard work of the authors whose papers are presented here. We thank them for their efforts and appreciate the spirit of cooperation as we worked under tight timelines. A special word of thanks is due to many people whose hard work was essential to the production of this volume. Diane Dennis, Research Associate, University of Calgary, Faculty of Social Work (Edmonton Division), prepared volumes of correspondence and other materials in preparation for the Symposium. Claudette Cormier of the University of Manitoba Faculty of Social Work was responsible for manuscript production and Patricia Turenne did French-to-English translations for the work. Finally, we appreciate the assistance of Keith Thompson, Thompson Educational Publishing, who helped move this from manuscript to book form. This volume is a collaborative responsibility and would not have been possible without the assistance of many people. Ideas and points of view expressed in the chapters, however, are solely the responsibility of the various authors. Materials presented in this volume do not necessarily represent the policies or views of National Welfare Grants or the sponsoring organizations.

Foreword

Child welfare systems are being strained and stretched under the major social and economic changes taking place here and around the globe. Decision makers are struggling to develop policies and programs which better meet the needs of children and families while budgets are shrinking and deficits loom. Research based, policy-relevant information is crucial as they strive to make the best decisions.

This book is the result of a national Research/Policy Symposium on Child Welfare held in Alberta, Canada, May 10–14, 1994. This symposium, the third supported by National Welfare Grants, brought together 39 researchers and 33 decision makers including representatives of advocacy and consumer groups. The researchers came from Canada, the United States, Britain, New Zealand, and Norway. Senior policy makers came from the Canadian federal, provincial, and territorial governments as well as from the voluntary sector. The symposium was an opportunity for researchers, decision makers and service and consumer representatives to meet and interact around four issues in child welfare: the organization and delivery of child welfare services; support and prevention programming; foster care and adoption; the child welfare service experience and outcomes. This book presents and critically assesses the current state of research on the above key issues, identifies the policy implications, and provides a research agenda for the future.

The symposium was funded and co-sponsored by the National Welfare Grants Division, Social Development and Education Group, Human Resources Development Canada. I am very pleased with both the outcome of the symposium and with this book and extend my appreciation to the symposium's organizing group all of whom contributed to its positive outcome. Joe Hudson, Faculty of Social Work, the University of Calgary, and Burt Galaway, Faculty of Social Work, University of Manitoba co-directed the workshop and Fran McIninch of National Welfare Grants identified symposium themes and the researchers and decision makers who participated in the symposium.

We believe this book will make a significant contribution to the development of new thinking on child welfare issues and the application of innovative ways of meeting the needs of vulnerable children and families. It will be of vital interest to a variety of audiences including decision makers in and out of government, practitioners, researchers, students, advocacy groups, and youth and families who are struggling with these issues. I commend all those associated with this book and the symposium for their commitment and dedication to creating a society which values children and supports families.

David Thornton, Ph.D., *Director, National Welfare Grants*
Human Resources Development Canada

Contributors

Backe-Hansen, Elisabeth. Research Coordinator/researcher, Norwegian Institute of Child Welfare Research, Oslo, Norway.

Bagley, Christopher. Faculty of Social Work, The University of Calgary, Calgary, Alberta.

Bloomberg, Laura. Assistant Director, Institute on Community Integration, University of Minnesota, U.S.A.

Bone, Norman. West Region Child and Family Services, Keeseekoowenin First Nation, Elphinstone, Manitoba.

Bullock, Roger. Dartington Social Research Unit, Totnes, England.

Burford, Gale. Associate Professor, School of Social Work, Memorial University of Newfoundland, St. John's, Newfoundland.

Cameron, Gary. Director, Centre for Social Welfare Studies, Faculty of Social Work, Wilfrid Laurier University, Waterloo, Ontario.

Cameron, Sylvie. Doctoral Student, École de service social, Université de Montréal, Québec.

Chamberland, Claire. Full Professor, École de service social, Université de Montréal, Montréal, Québec.

Cohen, Joyce S. Professor of Social Work Practice, Faculty of Social Work, University of Toronto, Toronto, Ontario.

Dallaire, Nicole. Doctoral Student, Applied Social Science, Université de Montréal, Montréal, Québec.

Durst, Douglas. Associate Professor, Faculty of Social Work, University of Regina, Regina, Saskatchewan.

Fuchs, Don. Dean, Faculty of Social Work, University of Manitoba, Winnipeg, Manitoba.

Gabor, Peter. Professor, Faculty of Social Work, The University of Calgary (Lethbridge Division), Lethbridge, Alberta.

Galaway, Burt. Professor, Faculty of Social Work, University of Manitoba, Winnipeg, Manitoba.

Geoffrion, Suzanne. Executive Director, Children's Aid Society of the County of Lanark, Perth, Ontario.

Gorlick, Carolyne A. Associate Professor, School of Social Work, Kings College, The University of Western Ontario, London, Ontario.

Hébert, Jacques. Associate Professor, Département de travail social, Université du Québec à Montréal, Montréal, Québec.

Hill, Malcolm. Senior Lecturer, Department of Social Policy and Social Work, University of Glasgow, Glasgow, Scotland.

Hudson, Joe. Professor, Faculty of Social Work, The University of Calgary, Calgary, Alberta.

Jackson, Sonia. Professor of Applied Social Studies, University of Wales, Swansea, United Kingdom.

Kérisit, Michèle. Professor, École de service social, Université d'Ottawa, Ottawa, Ontario.

Kufeldt, Kathleen. Chair in Child Protection, School of Social Work, Memorial University of Newfoundland, St. John's, Newfoundland.

Lafrance, John. Children's Advocate, Alberta Family and Social Services, Edmonton, Alberta.

Longclaws, Lyle. Child Protection Centre, Children's Hospital, Winnipeg, Manitoba.

Lovell, Madeline. Assistant Professor, Sociology Department, Seattle University, Seattle, Washington.

Maxwell, Gabrielle M. Senior Researcher, Office of the Commissioner for Children and Institute of Criminology, Victoria University of Wellington, Wellington, New Zealand.

Morris, Allison. Director, Institute of Criminology, Victoria University of Wellington, Wellington, New Zealand.

McDonald, Josephine. Community Researcher, Miawpukek Mi'kamawey Mawi'omi, Council of the Conne River Micmacs, Conne River Reserve, Micmac Territory, Newfoundland.

McKenzie, Brad. Associate Professor, Faculty of Social Work, University of Manitoba, Winnipeg, Manitoba.

McPhee, Debra. Doctoral Student, Faculty of Social Work, University of Toronto, Toronto, Ontario.

Nutter, Richard W. Associate Professor, Faculty of Social Work (Edmonton Division), The University of Calgary, Edmonton, Alberta.

Pecora, Peter J. Manager of Research, The Casey Family Program, and Associate Professor, School of Social Work, University of Washington, Seattle, Washington, U.S.A.

Pennell, Joan. Associate Professor, School of Social Work, Memorial University of Newfoundland, St. John's, Newfoundland.

Rich, Cecilia. Community Researcher, Department of Social Development, Innu Nation, Sheshatshit, Nitassinan/Labrador.

Richardson, Gordon. Faculty of Social Work, University of Manitoba, Winnipeg, Manitoba.

Rosenbluth, David. Director, Research and Evaluation Branch, Saskatchewan Social Services, Regina, Saskatchewan.

Scarth, Sandra. Executive Director, Child Welfare League of Canada, Ottawa, Ontario.

Seidl, Esther. West Region Child and Family Services, Winnipeg, Manitoba.

Silva-Wayne, Susan. Instructor, Faculty of Social Work, Wilfrid Laurier University, Waterloo, Ontario.

St-Amand, Nérée. Professor, École de service social, Université d'Ottawa, Ottawa, Ontario.

Swift, Karen. Assistant Professor, School of Social Work, McGill University, Montréal, Québec.

Tam, Kwok Kwan. Doctoral Candidate, Faculty of Social Work, University of Toronto, Toronto, Ontario.

Thériault, Evariste. Social Research Consultant, National Welfare Grants, Ottawa, Ontario.

Thomlison, Barbara. Associate Professor, Faculty of Social Work, The University of Calgary, Calgary, Alberta.

Thompson, A.H. (Gus). Mental Health Division, Edmonton, Alberta.

Trocmé, Nico. Assistant Professor, Faculty of Social Work, University of Toronto, Toronto, Ontario.

Westhues, Anne. Associate Professor, Faculty of Social Work, Wilfrid Laurier University, Waterloo, Ontario.

Wharf, Brian. Professor, Faculty of Human and Social Development, University of Victoria, Victoria, British Columbia.

Introduction: Child Welfare as Competence Building

Joe Hudson and Burt Galaway

This book presents a set of original papers dealing with contemporary Canadian child welfare research, identifies public policy implications, and proposes an agenda for future research. The material is organized in five sections. The first section deals with research on the organization and delivery of child welfare services. The sections following present research on support and prevention services, foster care, adoption, and child welfare service experiences and outcomes. Each section concludes with a summary chapter identifying major themes, suggesting key policy implications, and proposing a research agenda for future work. The final chapter presents a comprehensive research agenda for Canadian child welfare research. Three major themes are addressed throughout—empowering and strengthening families, building and strengthening communities and social support networks, and providing family and cultural continuity for children.

Empowering and Strengthening Families

This theme relates to the renewed appreciation of what it means to belong to a family, the variety of services that can be brought to bear for families in need, and the strengths and resources that families can offer. Emphasis is on allocating child welfare resources to maintain families with the focus of helping work placed on the family unit, rather than the individuals involved, whether children, parents or foster parents. Brian Wharf as well as Douglas Durst, Josephine McDonald and Cecilia Rich make the point that adequate resources are not often made available to families and as a result children are placed in care. To address this type of situation Peter Pecora describes the variety of family-based services that have been established with the aims of promoting child development and healthy family functioning, assisting families and children in need, and protecting abused and neglected children. Pecora emphasizes the point that family based services are just one of an array of services that must be available to support families. Without a broad network of family support available in communities, families may not be able to maintain gains made as a result of receiving family-based services, and children may be vulnerable to continued abuse or neglect. Laura Bloomberg also addresses this theme in her description of the Hennepin County School/Human Services Redesign Initiative with its focus on delivering a comprehensive set of services to meet the multiple needs of families. Gary Cameron and Don Fuchs also describe approaches to supporting troubled families to reduce abuse and neglect and out-of-home placement. The focus in all of these approaches is on working with the family as a service unit.

Family group conferences offer a particularly promising method of involving families. The use of family group conferences originated in New Zealand; its use with youthful offenders in that country is described by Gabrielle Maxwell and Allison Morris, while Gale Burford and Joan Pennell report on a Newfoundland replication in which family group conferences are used in situations of child abuse and neglect. Family group conferences entail a shift in assumptions about the way child welfare services are planned and provided, away from a deficit or pathology model to an ecological model emphasizing the strengths of families, their adaptability, and the importance of parent-child relationships. Emphasis is given to promoting parental competence, providing opportunities for learning skills, and moving away from identifying the faults, treatment needs, pathologies or perceived deficiencies of parents. While parents and young persons may well have emotional difficulties which may need to be addressed, intra-psychic matters are not the exclusive focus of helping work. Service planning should build on family strengths and resources. This includes a more optimistic view of the ability of people to overcome difficulties in their lives. One implication of this is stopping the practice of filling up case records with one-sided information emphasizing client pathologies. For every deficiency, a strength should be presented to give a more balanced view of the person described.

The importance of involving families and empowering them is also addressed by Wharf who makes the point that there is a very clear relationship between being poor and being involved in the child welfare system. Providing psychotherapy to poor people is not likely to have much effect on their living conditions. Carolyne Gorlick also emphasizes the importance of listening to families and providing resources to aid poor families in their child rearing work. Fuchs and Cameron note that poverty can reduce the social resources available to families; social isolation is often a result of material deficiencies and sustained attention must be given to family needs for income, housing, food, clothing, jobs, and social support.

The theme of empowering families also appears in relation to adoption and foster family care work. Christopher Bagley and Ann Westhues and Joyce Cohen report research on adoption outcomes including cross cultural adoptions. This work suggests that efforts to empower and strengthen adoptive families can result in stable environments in which young people may develop as contributing citizens of Canadian society. In a similar vein, Gord Richardson and his colleagues and Kathleen Kufeldt describe research related to the concept of inclusive care in which birth parents become active participants in decision-making with their children who may be in out-of-home care. Roger Bullock notes some of the problems of children returning home from care and the importance of assisting families in maintaining a role and place within the family for the absent child.

Running through the chapters by Fuchs, Cameron, Bagley, Westhues and Cohen, Gorlick, Burford and Pennell, and Maxwell and Morris is an emphasis on the strengths of people and the resources in their environment they can use to deal with their problems. Burford and Pennell characterize this by noting that the family must be respected for its expertise. In contrast with this emphasis on strengths is the all-too-common concern with deficits or treatment needs. This view can lead to unimaginative programming because clients are seen as incapable of participating in, or benefiting from, helping efforts calling on their strengths and capabilities. Burford and Pennell give an illustration of this when they note that referrals to their Family Group Decision-Making Project were slow in coming because child welfare workers viewed families as having so many deficiencies that they never expected them to be responsible for planning for themselves. Similar views toward families were apparently held in New Zealand when setting up family group conferences and have proved groundless. Maxwell and Morris note that families almost always attend the family group conferences and can develop plans for dealing with their youthful offenders.

Nico Trocmé, Kwok Kwan Tam, and Debra McPhee offer another perspective on family empowerment. The analysis of a database of child maltreatment investigations in Ontario found that severity of maltreatment is the most powerful predictor of case substantiation when an allegation of child abuse is made. On the basis of this work they suggest that social workers can reliably determine when cases should and should not be substantiated. The challenge for practice, then, is to link decision making to providing the types of services that empower families. This is addressed by Michèle Kérisit and Nérée St-Amand who identify methods of supporting family and community empowerment and reconfiguring power relationships between community workers and families. Offering people respect and opportunities for involvement in making decisions can help them overcome the isolation that results when officials of the child welfare system take sole responsibility. Families and children become partners in service planning and delivery, not passive recipients. This approach can instill a sense of hope and personal control rather than robbing people of their sense of worth and responsibility for themselves and their families. Wharf explicitly notes that sharing power and dealing with clients and staff as partners is a key to changing the way child welfare services are organized and delivered.

Building and Strengthening Communities and Social Support Networks

Several chapters note the importance of families belonging to a community and the important role of social networks in providing emotional support. As Cameron and Fuchs note, local residents should be participants, planners, and managers of community services including activities to strengthen and improve the environment. Their work underscores the point that attention needs to be given to working to support and strengthen social support networks and less with doing direct treatment. In her research, Susan Silva-Wayne found that a mentor or pathfinder within the community was a necessary condition to assist young people, often from very disadvantaged backgrounds, make the successful transition from public care to adulthood.

An empowering approach to a neighbourhood or community aims at strengthening self-help and enhancing problem-solving capacities. Social isolation and the absence of informal helping systems such as extended families, churches, clubs, groups of friends, can play a key role in child abuse and neglect. But these networks can be reinvigorated within the neighbourhood. Giving help, as well as receiving it, can empower people and strengthen their sense of self worth. The chapters by Fuchs, Cameron, Burford and Pennell, Kérisit and St-Amand, and Dallaire and her colleagues all illustrate the point that a variety of helping arrangements can be used to enhance social support networks and empower people to take responsibility for dealing with their problems. These different empowering approaches all use the services of professionals but their role is one of facilitating, brokering, and consulting, rather than serving in the role of an expert who has taken up the task of solving the problems of a family, neighbourhood, or community.

The importance of appreciating the institutions and traditions—the culture—that bring people together in communities runs through many of these chapters. Local institutions are the medium through which people learn and grow and an appreciation of diverse cultural backgrounds is critical to a well functioning child welfare system. The design of service programs requires sensitivity to cultural difference, the ability to identify with different perspectives and to incorporate these into the way services are organized and delivered. Many clients in the child welfare system are ethnic minorities and unless practitioners have an appreciation of their cultures and develop skills in working with them, the services are not likely to be experienced as helpful. Respect for different cultural backgrounds is fundamental and from respect can come creative solutions to child welfare problems. The family group conferences were developed in response to Maori culture in New Zealand. The Family Group Decision-Making Project in Labrador and Newfoundland described by Burford and Pennell illustrates culturally appropriate procedures used in culturally appropriate settings to provide culturally appropriate services. Brad McKenzie, Esther Seidl and Norman Bone suggest that building community support includes developing culturally appropriate standards for child welfare services delivered by First Nations; they describe a process of involving First Nations communities in the development of their own child welfare standards.

John Lafrance also deals with empowerment in his description of research on the views held by senior provincial child welfare administrators about citizen involvement. While Lafrance found that most senior administrators supported citizen involvement, the reasons given for this support varied according to the two types of administrators identified. Bureaucratic norms, such as those for efficiency, orderliness, and hierarchical control, conflict with the demands of community systems emphasizing such norms as intimacy, personal relationships, and loyalty. Nicole Dallaire and her colleagues did an extensive review of prevention projects in the Montréal area, some of which were located in public institutions and others in the private sector; they found that incorporating empowerment into practice was practically non-existent in the institutional sector and, further, was poorly developed in the community projects. A key question then becomes how to move child welfare officials toward greater citizen and client involvement and power sharing. Durst, McDonald and Rich in their case study of the efforts of two First Nations communities to gain control of their child welfare services, see empowered leadership as one of the keys.

Providing Family and Cultural Continuity for Children

Increased effort is being given to maintaining and strengthening attachments between young people in state care and their families and cultures. Foster families are increasingly being viewed as temporary or relatively permanent extensions of the birth family, rather than as a replacement of it. When the child comes into care, the boundaries of the birth family are changed to incorporate the foster family. Birth parents and other relatives are expected to have on-going responsibilities and involvement with foster families and the children. From this perspective, the foster parents become care-givers, sharing responsibilities for the child within the extended family that has been formed. Birth parents are empowered by making them participants in the placement of their child and in the life of the foster family. The value placed on this type of arrangement is described by Kathleen Kufeldt and, with specific reference to First Nations communities, by McKenzie, Seidl and Bone.

The primary means for maintaining parental attachment in foster care is visiting. Visits are the core of the placement and amount to opportunities for birth parents to act in a parental role. The central premise of birth parents visiting children in foster care is that the child's experience of family connection is a fundamental ingredient of the growing sense of self, personal significance, and identity. The critical concern is the maintenance of the child's and the birth family's mutual connections so that the child grows up at least emotionally connected to his birth family. Gord Richardson and his colleagues provide detailed information about visiting and other birth parent participation policies and practices in treatment foster care programs in the United Kingdom and North America. The key question addressed is the extent to which program policies about birth parent involvement are reflected in program practices. Program policies tend to emphasize the importance of birth parent participation but the practice lags somewhat behind. Chapters by Richard Nutter and his colleagues, Barbara Thomlison, and Kathleen Kufeldt also deal with birth parent visits in foster care and all emphasize the positive relationship between visits and return home.

The importance of cultural respect is particularly significant in Canada, especially for the Native population. Bagley, McKenzie and colleagues, and Rosenbluth and colleagues note that cross-racial and cross-cultural placement of children in adoptions and foster family care has too often involved a profound loss of racial and cultural ties and amounted to cutting off relationships with the birth and extended family for Native young persons. Removing young Native children from their homes and relocating them to culturally alien environments can have serious implications for their identity development. The young people all too often become marginalized between cultural groups, without feelings of belonging to either. Unable to identify with their natural families, they are not likely to have an appreciation of their cultural heritage. The identity problems, poor self image and cultural alienation experienced by adolescent Native foster children can then be manifested in alcohol and drug abuse, conflict with the law or school system, depression, and suicide. Many of these difficulties in living become exaggerated as the young people move into adulthood. The young people are deprived of role models for child rearing practices and the sense of impermanence experienced as a result of having been moved from one placement to another can impair their ability as adults to let themselves trust others and develop close personal ties.

Native children who have been separated from their families and reservations for an extended period of time and then return to the reservation are often unable to speak their tribal language. They are likely to have different life styles and possess different views of the world as a result of being raised in white families. This can make returning to the reservation difficult. The psychological stress experienced by these young persons during their return home can be particularly difficult in terms of socially and emotionally reintegrating with their families and communities. Evidence of the disastrous effects that separating Natives from their cultures can have is most dramatically illustrated in Canada by residential schools. These institutional settings separated young persons from their birth and extended families, friends, and culture for long periods of time in ghetto-like environments, isolated from both the Native community and the larger white society. The chapters by McKenzie, Seidl, and Bone as well as Durst, McDonald, and Rich note that the schools are now credited with having produced a generation of parents raised in institutional environments and lacking an understanding of culturally appropriate child rearing techniques.

These chapters bring out a number of implications for the child welfare system. One is that children should not be separated from their families, except as a last resort. Rosenbluth makes clear that in the Province of Saskatchewan, Native children have been apprehended less as a result of direct physical abuse by parents and more as a result of neglect. Key questions then become what is the meaning of neglect within a Native community and whether child welfare authorities can do a better job raising children than the parents, extended family, or home community. Child welfare practitioners may well be ignorant of Native cultures, misinterpret their child rearing practices, or fail to recognize the importance of the extended family in the Native community. Having taken responsibility for raising the young Native people, the state may itself be carrying out a systematic form of child abuse with these young people. The chapters by Burford and Pennell, Maxwell and Morris, Fuchs, and Cameron describe the use of family group meetings and formal and informal supports as a way of mobilizing the relationships and resources within and around the family to prevent children coming into care. If separation is required, then as McKenzie, Seidl, and Bone note, every attempt should be made to place the child with extended family members or, failing that, another Native family in the same community.

Cultural and familial continuity for children also extends to planning for their discharge from public care. Roger Bullock notes the difficulty families have in maintaining a role and physical space for a child who has been removed and, unless these are assured, the child may have difficulty reintegrating with the family. Thomlison's research suggests the importance of explicit planning for the child to return home if the child is to be discharged to a family setting. The concept of inclusive care developed by Kathleen Kufeldt, and which underlies the research by Richardson and his colleagues, provide a framework by which continuity is assured during and after placement. Continuity is also important for children who emerge from state care into interdependent adult living.

Silva-Wayne's study of a group of young people who had successfully made the transition to adulthood notes that the presence of community supports and the continuity of relationship with a mentor or pathfinder was essential for their relatively successful transition to adulthood.

Moving Practices and Policy Toward Empowerment and Competence Building

Research reported in these chapters suggest the need for a major reorientation of child welfare practice and policy. Brian Wharf calls for a power sharing with clients, Gorlick calls for listening to the people served, and the Family Group Conference approach described by Maxwell and Morris and Burford and Pennell illustrate one useful method of involving parents as partners in decision making. This same theme is developed in relation to children who are placed in out of home care by Kufeldt, Richardson and his colleagues, and Thomlison. Reports by Fuchs and Cameron illustrate the importance of developing informal social supports, while Kérisit and St-Amand's work suggests some ways to reconfigure the power relationships between workers and families. But there seems to be little in terms of creative programming and power sharing to assist families and neighborhoods in addressing the problems they are encountering and to assure some cultural and familial continuity for children. Work by Dallaire and her colleagues suggests that empowerment and prevention practices are practically non-existent in public programs and are present, but not well developed, in programs provided by smaller alternative agencies.

Attention must be given to ways and means of shifting child welfare practice, and the policies that support practice, in the direction of empowering and supporting families and communities and in developing informal systems of social support. If the practices of established, mainline agencies cannot be changed, then policies may need to be pursued to systematically transfer resources from these agencies to smaller, alternative agencies that may be more flexible in the types of services provided. Both the research by Kérisit and St-Amand as well as Dallaire and her colleagues suggests that smaller alternative agencies do hold more promise in delivering empowering and preventive services, even though their funding is in constant jeopardy. One step in this direction may be the development of Aboriginal agencies to assume responsibility for services in reserve communities as discussed by Durst and his colleagues and by McKenzie and his colleagues.

A minor theme which emerges in the chapters is the need to coordinate and integrate services. Wharf calls for this, although he is unable to identify any integrated service projects that demonstratively improve the quality of services. While the need for service integration has been a consistent theme in social services over the last 50 years, the concept of service integration needs careful examination in terms of whether it will in fact empower families and communities or have the effect of empowering professionals and organizations by limiting choice and access to services. The costs of coordinating and integrating services must be carefully reviewed in light of the historic evidence that service integration projects have tended to fall apart and have not produced any documented evidence of improvement of either quality or quantity of services to clients. Perhaps it is time to abandon discussions of service integration and focus instead on choice and empowerment of families and communities.

Finally one must ask the fundamental question regarding the central purpose for providing child welfare services. Too often we avoid the obvious. The work of Sonia Jackson moves us in this direction. She suggests that when the state intervenes and assumes responsibility for children, services must be evaluated in terms of whether or not the child is being provided the services and supports that any good parent would provide. She reports on a program in the United Kingdom to assess the outcomes of state intervention in terms of whether or not the child's health, education, identity, family and social relationships, social presentation, emotional and behavioral development, and self-care skills needs are being met. Given that the purpose of child welfare is to provide what any good parent would provide in situations where parents are unavailable or unable to do so, a next step is using this standard to evaluate both public and private child welfare programs.

Direction for program evaluation research is given in these chapters including:

- The involvement and collaboration of a variety of persons in planning and conducting the research work (Bloomberg; McKenzie, Seidl, Bone; Burford and Pennell; Durst, McDonald and Rich).
- Research carried out in service of policy and programming with clear practice implications (Bullock; Jackson; Kufeldt; Burford and Pennell; Backe-Hansen).
- Research aimed at understanding the complex situations so often characteristic of child welfare practice, policy and programming efforts; data collection efforts that get close enough to the people and events studied to understand in depth the details of what goes on; research aimed at representing accurately the points of view that people hold about the world they experience (Bullock; Gorlick; Jackson; Silva-Wayne; Kufeldt; Lafrance).
- Research that demonstrates sensitivity to cultural practices, including the use of community-based researchers with an appreciation of cultural traditions (Maxwell and Morris; Burford and Pennell; McKenzie, Seidl, and Bone; Durst, McDonald and Rich).
- Use of an inductive approach in which patterns emerge from the data, rather than testing pre-determined hypothesis; emphasizing a process of discovery, of learning what is happening and identifying emerging patterns (Bullock; Jackson; Kufeldt; Silva-Wayne; Backe-Hansen).
- Research carried out in natural settings, real world situations that unfold naturally with no control exercised by the investigator (Jackson; Cameron; Fuchs; Bullock; Kufeldt).
- An emphasis on processes, how activities take place and particularly the interactions between people and their environments. The ecological relationships in which people are implicated is emphasized, as opposed to a linear cause and effect model. The collection of descriptive information about how programs and policies unfold, the experiences of clients

within programs (Bullock; Bloomberg; Backe-Hansen; Maxwell and Morris).

- An emphasis on qualitative data collected on the basis of relatively small samples selected purposefully (Silva-Wayne; Gorlick; Backe-Hansen; Bullock).
- The use of flexible research designs in which data collection methods are adapted to the unfolding situation encountered by the investigator so that new leads are pursued as they emerge in the research process (Bullock; Kufeldt; Cameron; Jackson).

1

ORGANIZING AND DELIVERING CHILD WELFARE SERVICES

1

Organizing and Delivering Child Welfare Services: The Contributions of Research

Brian Wharf

This chapter presents an overview of the state of knowledge about organizing and delivering child welfare services in Canada. The paper is organized in four sections. The first section draws on research to identify and describe the clients of child welfare. The second examines the enterprise of child welfare: the legislation and policies that guide child welfare, the structural arrangements of the agencies which provide services, and the modes of practice of front line staff. The third addresses the ubiquitous issue of coordination and integration of child welfare services. The final section suggests some strategies for change based largely on the experience of an ongoing action research project (Callahan, Lumb & Wharf, 1994).

Child welfare has always been a "poor people's social service system" (Meyer, 1985 p. 101). Indeed in most Canadian provinces child welfare is a poor *woman's* social service system and yet policies and practice are blind to this dominating characteristic of the enterprise. Clients of child welfare agencies are poor, live in substandard housing in unsafe neighbourhoods, and lack control over their lives. A line of fault exists between policy and the needs of clients. Preoccupation with organization, delivery, and modes of practice issues has resulted in failure to honour the age old social work principle of starting "where the client is." This practice dictum predates but is entirely consistent with a "backward mapping approach" to the development of policy (Elmore, 1980). Backward mapping starts the policy process with the client and with the staff who have the closest relationship with and knowledge of the client's circumstances. Failing to observe this principle and approach to policy development has resulted in an oxymoronic system of services. An American observer notes, "In many states a family's access to child welfare services is contingent on their failure to pass the test of parental adequacy as administered by the very state agency charged with helping them" (Morris-Bilotti, 1992, p. 6).

Research and Clients

In this chapter research is defined in a way that departs from the usual understanding of the word, but is uniquely suited to research into the organization and delivery of services:

> After all, "re-search" is, as the word implies, a process of looking again; of being curious; of being interested in surprising patterns; of being able to reflect upon

> what happens in a systematic fashion and, above all, of having the confidence to adopt a critical attitude towards conventional wisdom, accepted practice or current fashion. Good research does not have to be complicated or necessarily expensive; but making it simple calls for considerable thought about how to pose pertinent yet uncomplicated questions (Parker, 1985, p. 5).

Given this interpretation of research, reports and reviews which lack an empirical data base but reflect on existing pieces of information and search for new explanations are considered here to be research. Thus the work of Leroy Pelton (1994), who has figured prominently in the debate about the connections between poverty and child neglect and abuse, is given the same attention as more formal inquiries into the state of child welfare such as the CELDIC report (1970), the Best Practice Survey of the Laidlaw Foundation (Clutterbuck, 1990), and the empirical work of the Ontario Child Health Study (Offord, 1987).

Knowing the needs of clients served by child welfare agencies is the first step in assessing organizational and delivery issues. Agencies operate in a vacuum without an intimate knowledge of client circumstances and yet such information is not always collected by child welfare agencies. For example, the intake sheet completed by child welfare workers in the province of British Columbia following a complaint of neglect or abuse does not require workers to record factual information regarding income, employment, housing, and neighbourhood conditions. As a consequence of the Empowering Women project, one Office in the Ministry of Social Services now collects this information and the client profile reveals that 80% of the clients are single parent women and 75% are in receipt of social assistance (Callahan, Lumb, & Wharf, 1994).

This profile of clients is consistent with those reported in other inquiries. Twenty years ago The National Council on Welfare reported that "one fundamental characteristic of the child welfare system has not changed appreciably over the years: its clients are still overwhelmingly drawn from the ranks of Canada's poor" (National Council on Welfare, 1975, p. 2). More recently the Institute for the Prevention of Child Abuse conducted a nationwide study which found that child abuse was regarded as a serious problem by more respondents in the lowest socio-economic group than any other group (Kitchen, 1991, p. 8). A comprehensive inquiry into child welfare in B.C. identified poverty as "the number one problem facing families, children and youth today" (Community Panel, 1992, p. 9). And a major metropolitan child welfare agency reported "that 83% of the families which it served in 1988 had incomes below the Statistics Canada low-income cut off lines and that an additional 11% of its clientele was economically vulnerable" (Kitchen, 1991, p. 8). The results of inquiries in Canada are virtually identical to those of major investigations in the U.S.:

> There is overwhelming and remarkably consistent evidence—obtained across a variety of definitions and methodologies and from studies performed at different time periods—that poverty and low income are related strongly to child abuse and neglect and to severity of child maltreatment. Even though most impoverished parents do not abuse or neglect their children, children from impoverished and low-income families are vastly over represented in the incidence of child abuse and neglect. This strong relationship holds not only for child abuse and neglect in general but for their every identified from including emotional abuse, emotional neglect and sexual abuse. (Pelton, 1993, p. 17)

The above studies refer to the connections between poverty and the clients of child welfare agencies. The connections are reinforced when the consequences of growing up poor are considered. There is a rich literature which documents the impact of poverty on the physical, mental health, and educational development of children (Kitchen, et al., 1991). Children in poor families begin life with low birth rates (Shah, 1987), suffer more from chronic health problems than non poor children, higher rates of psychiatric disorders than other children (Offord, 1989), and drop out of school at double the rate of the non poor (Ross and Shillington, 1990). The impact of growing up poor is captured in interviews with young parents:

> They grew up angry, blaming their parents for not providing for them. Going to school without proper clothing or school supplies they were targets of bigotry and discrimination that increased with every year of their young lives. And, worst of all, they said—worse than the deprivation and discrimination and the thousand and one other injuries and insults that go with being poor—poverty left then with unshakable feelings of being neglected, unloved and worthless. (Community Panel, 1991, p. 9)

Many of these poor children grow into adults who feel neglected, unloved and worthless, particularly if they have left school at an early age, have experienced poor health, have not been able to locate decent employment, live in substandard housing, and rely on the inadequate provisions of social assistance for income. When these adults become parents the cycle is repeated. The typical label attached to clients who come to the attention of child welfare agencies is "multi-problem." In turn the range of problems they experience leads them into contact with a number of agencies and inevitably to the cry for coordination!

Gender is a crucial aspect of the connection between poverty and child welfare. A study in B.C. points out that half the children taken into care in 1988 were from single parent families, 95% of these families had incomes under $20,000, and 72% were in receipt of social assistance (Campbell, 1991). Further, neglect accounted for 70% of the children taken into care.

> The picture that emerges is striking. A major group of clients whose children are coming into care in the child welfare system are very poor women on social assistance who are charged with neglecting their children ... The care of children also suffers, not just because their mothers have fewer economic resources but because mothers are unable to protect them from violence (Callahan, 1993, p. 183).

The poverty-ridden lives of women and particularly of single parent women is reported by a number of studies (National Council on Welfare, 1990; Hudson and Galaway, 1992).

Adherence to the principle of beginning where the client is and to the backward mapping approach to policy in child welfare leads to the conclusion that single parent women living in poverty are the single largest group of clients being served by child welfare agencies. Policy and practice, however, are not informed by this evidence. Instead, all involved in the child welfare enterprise—researchers, policy makers and practitioners—have accepted poverty as a given, have assumed nothing can be done to alter this given, and have focused energies on organizing and reorganizing services and on refining professionals' skills.

Research and the Organization of Services

Organizational matters refer to legislation, policies, structures and modes of practice—to the bundle which makes up the child welfare agency. One recent inquiry reveals a remarkable consistency in child welfare legislation in Canada (Herringer, 1992); child welfare legislation is residual. It seeks to protect children from neglect and abuse after the event and does little to ensure that these conditions do not occur. Child welfare legislation has been anchored in the principle of least intrusiveness, but ironically, by not intervening until neglect or abuse has occurred, residual legislation virtually ensures that the intervention will be intrusive. On the other hand, services acquired to support and strengthen families are not intrusive. However, provincial governments have shrunk from incorporating a range of preventive services into legislation, and no province has to this date adopted the New Zealand innovation of family panels (Burford & Pennell, 1994; Maxwell & Morris, 1994).

Other reviews have focused on services provided by agencies. One review established ten best practice criteria and then conducted a nation wide search of child welfare agencies (Clutterbuck et al., 1990). The criteria included empowering practice, self determination, contextual awareness and structural analysis, mutual interdependence, demonstrated outcomes, cultural sensitivity, and preventive orientation. Thirty-nine exemplary practice models were identified: 19 agencies provided services to families living in poverty, 15 to First Nation families, and 6 to children in foster care. All of these best practice models were distinguished by their commitment to a mission and by involving clients in the provision of service. But the public child welfare agencies were missing from their list; not a single provincial ministry or Children's Aid Society qualified. The uncomfortable conclusion is that the mainstream child welfare enterprise is lacking in innovation, in commitment to a mission, and in capacity to involve clients. This conclusion is reinforced by an investigation into the state of child welfare in B.C. A panel appointed by the Minister of Social Services toured the province, heard submissions from a wide variety of sources, and conducted original research. The panel reported:

> Families told us of being frightened and threatened by a child welfare structure they thought should have provided help and support. Families also told us that all too often problems had to reach crisis proportions before help could be obtained. Young people said the experience of being moved from home into government care was like going from the frying pan into the fire. Ministry staff, service providers and caregivers described to us the feelings of frustration and isolation. They said the system is focused on symptoms, not on the underlying causes, of the problems facing families and children (Community Panel, 1992, p. 3).

Other studies have focused attention on the internal operating structures of child welfare agencies. One review conducted by the Auditor General of B.C. on the Ministry of Social Services was severely critical of the work environment in the Ministry:

> Although the nature of the work is difficult in itself and staff morale can be greatly tested in the field of child welfare we found that staff dissatisfaction lay mostly with the work environment rather than with the work itself ... Forty per cent of social workers and 45% of district supervisors indicated that they are experiencing job related stress ... When asked if the ministry delivered social services efficiently, 61% of social workers and 44% of district supervisors said it did not (Auditor General of British Columbia 1992, pp. 63–66).

There is a hefty literature on the industrialization of social work practice and on the failure of large bureaucracies to respond in a sympathetic way to the needs of clients (Weatherley, 1980; Fabricant, 1985; Davies & Shragge, 1990; Callahan, 1993). These critiques suggest that the organizational structures devised in Canada to provide child welfare services are inappropriate and ineffectual.

Mode of practice is the third ingredient of organizational matters. There is substantial agreement that practice has been dominated by investigations into child neglect and abuse (Community Panel, 1993; Kamerman & Kahn, 1993). The volume of complaints has risen dramatically over the past decade. In British Columbia complaints jumped from 3,500 to 32,000 between 1980 and 1990. Responding to this number of complaints has driven out the time and attention needed for family counselling, community work, and a variety of preventive programs. Yet, over half of the complaints result in no further attention, one quarter are referred to other agencies, and only the remaining quarter receive some form of service from the Ministry (Ministry of Social Services, n.d.). The experience in B.C. parallels that of the U.S. where "most child welfare activities of public child welfare agencies are largely directed toward the problem of child abuse and neglect" (Kamerman & Kahn, 1990, p. 10)

Research and the Interorganizational Scene

The multitude of problems that face the typical child welfare client and the narrowness of the boundaries of child welfare agencies results in clients requiring services from a number of agencies. One response is to simply let clients "shop around," and this is often what happens. But this reality is seen as unsatisfactory by many policy makers, professionals, and clients. Hence there is a continuing cry for "one-stop shopping centres" or some other form of integrated services. In Canada the search for coordination has taken many forms: local level service teams, the case manager strategy, service protocols, multi service centres, and the folding together of previously separate agencies.

The search has been conducted by numerous inquiries ranging from community studies to provincial and national inquiries. One of the earliest and most comprehensive studies is the CELDIC inquiry which was sponsored by seven national organizations, took 5 years to complete and provided policy makers with a daunting list of 144 recommendations. But despite the breadth of concerns the issue which dominates the CELDIC report is the lack of coordination. "The multiplicity of unrelated services seems to us to be the number one problem in providing assistance to children with emotional and learning disorders" (CELDIC, 1971, p. 294). The report proposed that "comprehensive community personal care services be established in each local community, units to serve populations of between 25000—50,000 and that there be set up a community services board to promote and plan the establishment of a comprehensive and coordinated network of personal care services" (CELDIC, 1971,p. 476). This recommendation has not been implemented in any province except Québec and in an *ad hoc* fashion in a number of communities in Ontario and Manitoba. The lack of attention to implementation has not deterred other groups, from Royal Commissions to local level task forces, from pursuing the same issue and arriving at essentially the same conclusion—that services are not coordinated and should be. The calls for reform have differed slightly from integration of human service ministries into a combined single ministry (Ombudsman, B.C., 1990) to integration of human service agencies at a regional level (Advisory Committee on Children's Services, 1990).

Canadian interest in integration pales by comparison with the United States. The extent of the interest is such that a National Centre for Service Integration has been established to provide a clearing house for state and local agencies interested in learning about approaches to integration. An annotated bibliography published by the Centre reviews 53 attempts to integrate services at both state and local levels (Chaudry, et al., 1993). This bibliography identifies barriers to integration, discusses and analyses models, but is silent with respect to the impact on clients. Only one annotation (Schorr, 1988) claims that services to clients improved, but this book reviews innovations in practice rather than experiments in integrating services. Two comprehensive inquiries into the results of service integration reach similar and pessimistic appraisals:

> We should know by now that services alone will not cure poverty or rebuild a sense of community. A low-income family seeking help to find housing will not be helped by services if no housing is available at a price the family can afford. Job training does not help when there are no jobs. Drug treatment is a drop in the ocean when there is a tidal wave of drugs on the street. Tutoring services will not make up for schools that do not teach. The problems of the street will engulf even the most sophisticated multi service centre if that initiative is taken in isolation (Edelman & Radin,1991, p. 13).

The second inquiry focused attention on the differences in outcomes between reforms which amalgamated state agencies into a single department and those which concentrated on coordination at the local level. Their conclusions are striking:

> The Congress and federal executive agency officials seeking to reshape the human service delivery system are faced with a 30 years history of marginal success. Efforts designed to effect broad and fundamental changes in the way human service agencies organize and delivery health, education and social services face large barriers. When exploring ways to improve at-risk families' access to health and social service Congress may wish to promote service oriented efforts like Head Start. This approach focused at the point of delivery and adapted to local conditions is a more realistic approach to improving service delivery—particularly in the short term given current fiscal constraints (General Accounting Office,1992, p. 8).

The Impact of Research on Policy and Practice

The preceding discussion has argued that there is an abundance of research on the characteristics of clients of child welfare agencies. Further, a number of research inquiries and practice innovations have reached similar findings with respect to organizing and delivering child welfare services. It is clear that effective services are characterized by accessibility with respect to geographic location, by a welcoming and non stigmatizing attitude, by being client centred, and by offering a comprehensive range of services (Jones, 1985; Kamerman & Kahn, 1990; MacKenzie, 1991). In addition, innovative approaches including mutual aid and intensive family based services have produced positive outcomes (Cameron, 1992; Pecora, 1993). But innovations in practice and in the delivery of services remain on the periphery and do not characterize the mainstream child welfare enterprise, and in addition innovative approaches to the resolution of personal troubles has not spilled over into the public issues facing clients. These innovations may buffer clients from the impact of poverty and other public issues but they do little to ensure that the children of child welfare families will not face the same issues as adults. How can research in the Parkerian sense guide future reforms for organizing and delivering child welfare services?

Experience of the Empowering Women project confirms that child welfare legislation, policy, and organizational structures have combined to produce an approach to practice which disempowers workers and clients (Callahan, Lumb, & Wharf, 1994). Clients are viewed as cases to manage, as inadequate in parenting and budgeting skills, or as emotionally crippled. All of these client roles lead to dependency and require that workers train people into being clients. Mullins (1994) describes the process of creating clients as follows:

> The Risk/Need Management Tool rather than enhancing service delivery to families at risk will further detract from addressing the true needs of families and increase the rift between workers and clients. The ideological and theoretical framework of the Risk/Need instrument does not allow workers to start where the client is but requires workers to start from an already existing belief about child neglect that may have nothing to with what the client sees as the problem. The role of the worker who is supposed to be an advocate and supporter of the family is now co-opted to ensure that the client is "worked up" to conform to what we expect of neglectful parents (pp. 8–9).

In turn the labelling of clients as cases, inadequate or sick, has led in an inexorable fashion to the professional responses of a case manager responsible for coordinating services, a teacher of skills, and a therapist providing expert counselling. Action research suggests that these labels are built on faulty assumptions (Cochrane, 1988; Callahan, et al., 1994). Clients are not cases to be managed; to see people in this light dehumanizes them. Clients with inadequate resources require more resources rather than training in budgeting. Viewing clients beset by both personal troubles and public issues as emotionally unstable distorts their reality.

A re-search view sees clients as "harassed parents doing their best to cope under difficult circumstances with very limited access to support and resources" (Hern, 1993, p. 2). This view of clients treats them as partners, as individuals who are expert in knowing their situation and its difficulties, and as individuals who can contribute to the resolution of these difficulties. Re-search in the Empowering Women project has developed an approach to practice which shares power with clients and pushes workers to take a critical and reflective stance to both policy and practice. Policy is seen not so much as a regulation to be faithfully put into place, but as a guide to practice which can be improved by contributions from both workers and clients.

A power shared approach to practice will not result in substantial improvements in the poverty-ridden lives of clients. Why then is it seen as a preferred approach? First, the approach acknowledges and respects the reality of client situations. It names poverty and poor housing as problems and does not transform these public issues into personal troubles. It recognizes that clients, like most parents, care about their children, but unlike other parents do not have the resources to care for them (Swift, 1991).

Second, the clients who have participated in project report that the power shared approach gives them a place in the sun. While this is admittedly a still somewhat shady place, their participation as partners has increased their self confidence. They have organized and staffed an information office complete with a computer and policy manuals on social assistance and child welfare and have taken a leadership role in developing a community Women's Resource Centre. They relish invitations to speak at staff meetings as experts on poverty; they now read and sign off on worker recordings and have an assured place at conferences held to discuss their situation and future. While their poverty situation has not changed appreciably, they are now more aware of the benefits and programs available through the Ministry and from other community agencies. As a consequence some have obtained additional benefits. They feel more in control of their lives and have hopes and plans for their future since they no longer have to rely totally on workers for information.

Third, the power shared approach not only rejects the investigative approach to practice, it also rejects the corporate approach to managing the child welfare enterprise. It calls for sharing the power between management and line staff in organizations characterized by:

1. An emphasis on people. People are challenged and developed, they are given power to act and to use their judgment.
2. Participative leadership. Leadership is not authoritarian but participative wherever possible.
3. Innovative work styles. Staff reflect on their performance. They seek to solve problems creatively.
4. Strong client orientation. These organizations focus strongly on their client deriving satisfaction from serving the client rather than the bureaucracy.
5. A mindset that seeks optimum performance. People hold values that drive them to seek improvement in their organization's performance (Brodtrick, 1991, pp. 18–19).

The power shared approach is consistent with the backward mapping approach to the development of policy and extends this to a policy community approach. Policy communities involve all affected in the policy making process and ensures that the assumptions and concerns of those who traditionally dominated the policy process are balanced by the standpoint of clients and line workers.

Finally the power shared approach calls for identifying the proper balance between private troubles and public issues (Mills, 1959). It acknowledges that some troubles affecting clients are personal and must be dealt with on a personal level. But it also recognizes that some issues are public and are beyond the control of individuals. Drawing attention to public issues requires that child welfare workers and agencies become "a window into the needs of many families who lack information and access to help. It is a fundamental child welfare task to convey what is seen in this window to the appropriate legislative, administrative, judicial and professional bodies for purposes of redress" (Pecora et al., 1992, p. 30). Most involved in the child welfare enterprise have shrunk from the daunting task of opening the window.

Opening the window requires that child welfare agencies take on a social reporting function. A consequence of doing this at a local level has substantially changed the culture of one office. No longer can the issues of poverty and single parenthood be avoided when the evidence is published on a monthly basis. Similar reports at provincial and national levels will provide accurate information about the clients of child welfare to the public and to policy makers. In British Columbia the provincial officer of health is required to present a report on the health of citizens of the province. Why not a similar state of the province report on children, particularly those served by child welfare agencies?

Opening the window requires a backward mapping approach to child welfare policy. Beginning where the clients are will increase appreciation of the impact of poverty and will begin a process of casting around for innovative solutions to the dominant issue of poverty and single parent women. We might examine current conceptions of work, and, stripped of the contaminating effects of tradition and conventional wisdom, ask why child care should not be defined as work and as work requiring a wage from the public purse (Wharf, 1993). We might have the temerity to ask why it is deemed appropriate to build weapons of destruction from the public purse and not to establish public day care centres.

Future research as re-search will benefit from action and participatory research projects that replicate the power shared approach to practice. We will benefit from evaluation studies of these and other innovative modes of practice. We will benefit from cross community comparisons of localities served by community based and governed multi-service centres and other localities where traditional patterns of service obtain. We will benefit from community based inquiries that elicit the opinions of clients and citizens about their priorities for child welfare services. We will benefit from demonstration projects which examine significant issues such as the desirability of separating the protection/investigation function from the function of providing support and advocacy. Perhaps, above all, we will benefit from re-search that examines and tracks the efforts of social movements to redress the fundamental inequities in the distribution of wealth and income in Canada.

The writer wishes to acknowledge the assistance of Sheila Wallace for a comprehensive review of the literature on service integration and the perceptive comments on drafts of the paper.

References

Advisory committee on children's services (1980). *Children first.* Toronto: Queen's Printer for Ontario.

Auditor General of British Columbia. (1992). *Managing professional resources.* Victoria, British Columbia: unpublished paper.

Brodtrick, O. (1981). A second look at the well performing organization. In McDavid, J.C. & Marson, D.B. (Eds.), *The well performing government organization.* Ottawa: The Institute of Public Administration of Canada.

Burford, G., & Pennell, J. (1995). *Family group decision making: An innovation in child and family welfare.* In J. Hudson & B. Galaway (Eds.), *Canadian Child Welfare: Research and policy implications.* Toronto: Thompson Education Publishing.

Callahan, M. (1993). The administrative and practice context: Perspectives from the front line. In B. Wharf (Ed.), *Rethinking child welfare in Canada.* Toronto: McClelland and Stewart.

Callahan, M., Lumb, C., & Wharf, B. (1994). *Strengthening families by empowering women.* Ministry of Social Services. Victoria, British Columbia.

Campbell, J. (1991). *An analysis of variables in child protection apprehension and judicial dispositions in British Columbia welfare practice.* Unpublished master's thesis. Vancouver: University of British Columbia.

Chaudry, A., Maurer, K., Oshinsky, C., & Mackie, J. (1993). *Service integration: An annotated bibliography.* New York: National Centre for Service Integration.

Clutterbuck, P. , Davis, E., Novick, M., & Volpe, R. (1990). *Best practice survey.* A review prepared for the Children at risk Sub-Committee of the Laidlaw Foundation, Toronto.

Cochrane, M. (1988). Between cause and effect: The ecology of program impacts. In A. Pence (Ed.), *Ecological research with children and families.* New York: Teachers College Press.

Commission on Emotional and Learning Disorders in Children (CELDIC) (1970). *One million children.* Toronto: Leonard Crainford.

Community Panel, Family and Children's Services Legislative Review in British Columbia (1992).

Making Changes: A place to start. British Columbia: Ministry of Social Services.

Davies, L., & Shragge, E. (Eds.) (1990). *Bureaucracy and community.* Montréal: Black Rose Books.

Edelman, P. , & Radin, B. (1991). *Serving children and families effectively: How can the past help chart the future.* Washington, D.C.: Institute for Educational Leadership.

Elmore, R. (1982). Backward mapping: Implementation research and policy decisions. In W. Williams, (Ed.), *Studying implementation.* New Jersey: Chatham House Press.

Fabricant, M. (1985). The industrialization of social work practice. *Social work,* 30(5), 389–395.

Hern, R. (1994). *Western communities family and children's services.* Unpublished paper. Victoria, British Columbia.

Herringer, B. (1989). *Major features of child protection legislation in Canada.* School of Social Work, University of Victoria, Victoria, British Columbia.

Hudson, J., & Galaway, B. (1993). *Single parent families: Perspectives on research and policy.* Toronto: Thompson Educational Publishing.

Jones, M. A. (1985). *A second chance for families: five years later follow-up of a program to prevent foster care.* New York: Child Welfare League of America.

Kamerman, S., & Kahn, A. (1990). If CPS is driving child welfare—where do we go from here? *Public Welfare, 48*(1), 9–13.

Kitchen, B., Mitchell, A., Clutterbuck, P. , & Novick, M. (1991). *Unequal futures: The legacies of child poverty in Canada.* Toronto: The Child Poverty Action Group and the Social Planning Council of Metropolitan Toronto.

Maxwell, G. M., & Morris, A. (1995). *Deciding about justice for young people in New Zealand: The involvement of families, victims and culture.* In J. Hudson & B. Galaway (Eds.), *Child Welfare in Canada: Research and policy implications.* Toronto: Thompson Educational Publishing.

McKenzie, B. (1991). Decentralization in Winnipeg: Assessing the effects of community-based child welfare services. *Canadian Review of Social Policy,* 27, 57–60.

Meyer, C. (1985). The institutional context of child welfare. In J. Laird & A. Hartman (Eds.), *A handbook of child welfare.* New York: The Free Press.

Mills, C. W. (1959). *The sociological imagination.* Oxford University Press.

Ministry of Social Services (nd). *An overview of family and children's services, 1990/91.* Victoria: Family and Children's Services Division and Research, Evaluation and Statistics Division.

Morris-Bilotti, S. (1991). *Is an integrated child centred, family focused community based prevention system possible?* Springfield, Illinois: State Department of Children and Family Services.

Mullins, G. (1994). *Child and family services risk/need assessment policy: Implications for practice.* Unpublished Paper. Faculty of Human and Social Development, University of Victoria, Victoria, British Columbia.

National Council on Welfare (1979). *In the best interests of the child.* Ottawa: Author.

National Council on Welfare (1990). *Women and poverty revisited.* Ottawa: Author.

Office of the Ombudsman (1990). *Public services to children, youth and their families in British Columbia: The need for integration.* Public Report No. 22. Victoria, British Columbia: Author.

Offord, D. R. (1987). *Ontario child health study.* Toronto: Ministry of Community and Social Services.

Parker, R. (1989). Themes and variations. In B. C. Kahon (Ed.), *Child care: Research, policy and practice.* London: Hodder and Staughton.

Pecora, P. , Whittaker, J., & Maluccio, A. (1992). *The child welfare challenge.* New York: Aldine de Gruyter.

Pelton, L. (1994). Is poverty a key contributor to child maltreatment? Yes!. In E. Gambrill & T. Stein (Eds.), *Controversial issues in child welfare.* Boston: Allyn and Bacon.

Ross, D., & Shillington, R. (1990). Child poverty and poor educational attainment: the economic costs and implications for society. In Standing Senate Committee on Social Affairs, Science and Technology, *Children in poverty: Toward a better future.* Ottawa: Minister of Supply and Services.

Schorr, L. (1988). *Within our reach: Breaking the cycle of disadvantage.* New York: Anchor Press.

Shah, C., Kahan, M., & Krauser, J. (1987). The health of children of low-income families. *Canadian Medical Association Journal, 137*, 485–490.

Swift, K. (1991). Contradictions in child welfare: neglect and responsibility. In C. Baines, P. Evans, & S. Neysmith (Eds.), *Women's caring*. Toronto: McClelland and Stewart.

United States General Accounting Office (1992). *Integrating human services: Linking at-risk families with services is more successful than system reform efforts.* Washington, DC: U.S. Government Printing Office.

Volpe, R. (1989). *Poverty and child abuse: A review of selected literature.* Toronto: The Institute for the Prevention of Child Abuse.

Weatherley, R., Kottwitz, C.B., Lishner, D., Reid, K., Roset, G., & Wong, G. Accountability of social service workers at the front line. *Social service review, 54*(4), 556–571.

Wharf, B. (Ed.). (1993). *Rethinking child welfare in Canada.* Toronto: McClelland and Stewart.

2

Bridging the Gap: An Exploration of Social Service Administrators' Perspectives on Citizen Involvement in Social Welfare Programs

John Lafrance

Much of the literature in public administration, political science, and social work encourages the involvement of communities and citizens in the development and delivery of human services programs (Besharov, 1975; Bjur, 1977; Cooper, 1985; DeSario & Langston, 1987; Kweit & Kweit, 1981). Citizen participation is called for in response to perceived bureaucratic insularity and insensitivity, in the hope that it will introduce alternative views, reduce impersonality, and bring about increased familiarity with the problems and needs of client populations and communities (Davis, 1973). The nature of bureaucracies and the logical positivist approach utilized in the training of professionals, however, has created a negative perspective toward citizen involvement. This perspective may, in turn, adversely impact the nature and quality of public human services.

Large public bureaucracies have an uneven performance record and often exclude citizens from participation. Over thirty years ago Cohen (1960) pointed out that one of the greatest changes in human services had been an increase in formal organizational structures with the accompanying paraphernalia of professionalism, regulations, and bureaucracy. William James foresaw some of the dangers that accompanied the creation of formal organizations and suggested that most human institutions, because of the purely technical and professional manner in which they come to be administered, can become obstacles to the very purposes which their founders had in view, and can easily get out of touch with human life (Cohen, 1960).

The social services in general, and child welfare in particular, have fulfilled James' prediction. Child welfare agencies deal with some of the most intimate aspects of the lives of citizens, namely the relationships which exist within families as well as between families and communities. Yet, the bulk of their service modalities appear to be primarily based on technical and professional considerations (Kammerman & Kahn, 1989). A community is characterized by the quality and scope of its educational, health, and welfare institutions. When these are used and supported by citizens, then democratic society is in good health. Sieder (1960) cautions that when responsibility for the institutional life of the community is relegated entirely to employed officials, whether in the public or private sector, a precious part of our heritage is lost and services fail to achieve their full potential.

This chapter reports research which explores the views of public officials about citizen participation. These officials are increasingly subject to societal criticism for having assumed responsibilities that many now believe belong to the community. The perspectives of public managers are important factors to consider in efforts to involve citizens in publicly operated social service programs (Clayton & Gilbert, 1971). The study focused on the receptivity of social services administrators to the participation of citizens in the development and delivery of social services, in particular, child welfare programs. This study explored their opinions and experiences with both volunteers and citizen advisory groups, the two predominant approaches for involving citizens in planning and delivery of social services. Researchers have paid relatively little attention to the roles, attitudes, and perspectives of administrators who work at the nexus of organizational and community systems. Without their cooperation, organizations cannot succeed in creating viable partnership arrangements with communities. Yet government bears the final responsibility for public-private partnerships and should initiate such undertakings (Cooper, 1985). The views of public administrators are a key consideration to implementing this approach.

Methodology

Thirty senior administrators responsible for planning and delivering social service programs in British Columbia, Alberta, and Saskatchewan were interviewed. Executive management in each province nominated five administrators reputed to be community oriented and five reputed to be internally focused according to pre-selected criteria. One set of administrators was expected to have a reputation for working closely with the community (community oriented administrators), while the other set was judged to be equally competent, but were believed to concentrate their efforts on internal matters (internally focused administrators). Demographic factors, such as the education or experience of potential participants, were not restricted but each administrator was expected to hold mid to upper level operational responsibility for planning and delivering services to a designated geographic or program area. The final sample consisted of fifteen administrators who were reputed to be community oriented and fifteen who were reputed to be internally focused. Most were relatively highly educated males who had majored in social work. These administrators were seasoned and occupationally stable and were serving in senior level administrative and/or policy posts. Many had served in a number of program areas; their experience in the social services extended back two to three decades. The vast majority worked in regional or district offices where they officially represented their organization at the community level.

The study was exploratory and descriptive. This design was considered relevant for this study because empirical information concerning the perspectives and attitudes of bureaucrats toward the participation of citizens in the work of social service agencies is limited. The study concentrated on the acquisition of qualitative information. The data collection instrument was an interview schedule consisting of open ended questions that guided personal interviews with the administrators. It was designed to provide the respondents with an opportunity to reflect upon and share their perspectives regarding the involvement of citizens in social services programs. The information collected was tape recorded, supplemented by extensive note taking, and transcribed into a computer software program for qualitative data analysis. Transcripts were analyzed for recurring themes and response patterns. This type of qualitative analysis places emphasis on critical thinking, and invokes a spiral of growing knowledge, leading to new findings and new information that are grounded in experience (Glaser & Straus, 1975; Morgan, 1988). This information was expected to help develop a conceptual map by which to compare the perspectives of community oriented and internally focused administrators. The administrators were asked about (1) their previous experiences with volunteers and citizen advisory groups; (2) the organizational factors that influence the citizen-departmental relationship; (3) the community factors that influence the citizen-departmental relationship; (4) the costs and benefits, the advantages and disadvantages of citizen participation in social service programs; and (5) the future that citizen participation should take in their organizations.

Findings

Most respondents supported the concept of citizen involvement in organizational affairs, but their reasons varied with their orientation to the community. The major differences in managerial styles of the administrators are summarized in Table 2.1. The differentiation between craftsmen and artisans helps to illustrate the major difference between community oriented and internally focused administrators (Havassey, 1990). Community oriented administrators (CO) exhibited characteristics that have been ascribed to the artisan, while the internally focused (IF) exhibited characteristics associated with craftsman. The craftsman possesses the skills and knowledge to efficiently produce standardized, interchangeable products. These products are predictable and effective when the circumstances or needs tend to be uniform. Artisans complement this ability with a greater sensitivity to emerging needs and requirements, and are able to apply their knowledge and skills contextually in situations that require idiosyncratic responses. The artisans in the CO group were oriented to the achievement of the organizations' mission. The craftsmen in the IF group favoured relationships with citizens that would ensure organizational survival, leading one to conclude that they could be foul-weather friends (McNair, 1983) who could forego such relationships when they were no longer useful.

Many respondents acknowledged that citizen involvement could improve organizational productivity. The CO administrators ascribed greater importance to the actual process in which they were engaged. The IF administrators seemed to value concrete outcomes, and were particularly concerned with the amount of effort necessary to produce benefits. They were most satisfied when minimal efforts on their part produced maximum returns. The CO administrators expressed concerns about the impact of citizen involvement on clients, fearing at times that volunteers might take advantage of more vulnerable clients. The IF administrators tended to be more concerned about the potential impact such involvements might have on the organization.

The CO administrators seemed more visionary than their internally focused counterparts, whose responses tended to be far more pragmatic. The visionaries in the CO group seemed more responsive to emotional appeals that were

Table 2.1: Comparison of Community Oriented and Internally Focused Administrators

Community Oriented	Internally Focused
Artisan	**Craftsman**
Process Oriented	Outcome Oriented
Client Oriented	System Oriented
Mission oriented	Maintenance oriented
Visionary	**Pragmatic**
Ideological	Technological
Risk Taker	Risk Avoider
Passionate	Detached

ideologically driven. The pragmatists in the IF group, on the other hand, were attracted to rational appeals that provided the technology needed to involve citizens in their activities. Contrary to their more internally focused colleagues, the visionary CO group seemed more open to risk in their search for increased levels of partnership with citizens. The more pragmatic IF group was oriented toward control and risk aversion, preferring to involve citizens who could be co-opted into the achievement of organizational objectives. The visionaries in the CO group described their experiences with citizens with zeal and an almost palpable sense of excitement. The pragmatic IF group, on the other hand, described their experiences with citizens in detached and almost neutral terms. The descriptions of their worst experiences was with a note of resignation that seemed to indicate that one could hardly have expected anything different.

A recurring theme was the perception that many social services organizations were isolated from the community. Some administrators attributed this isolation to the inexorable assumption of community decision making and responsibilities by government over the years. Internally focused administrators tended to blame isolation on the hierarchy, stating that local community relationships were good, but the overall isolation of their organizations complicated efforts to work with the community. Community oriented administrators were more introspective, reflecting on what could have been done differently in the past and what future actions would make a difference. Some considered the situation to be beyond their control, while others sought to influence it. Further research is needed to uncover what factors might have led to such widely varying conclusions, and what might be a more realistic perspective.

Administrators who supported the need to involve citizens had different motives. Some suggested that it was worthwhile because citizens had resources that could be useful in fulfilling organizational missions. Others sought greater interdependence with community groups in order to fulfil their common objectives. Some administrators supported the involvement of citizens at a philosophical level because it seemed to be the right thing to do. Others were more likely to support the notion because they had concluded that it was becoming necessary for organizational survival. Further exploration of these perspectives may assist organizations to develop more relevant inducements for administrators to engage their communities.

Discussion and Conclusions

The interview guide contained a large number of questions that sometimes pre-empted a detailed exploration of interesting side-issues. This resulted in less in-depth discussion than might have been desirable. It would have been useful to compensate for this deficiency with follow-up interviews with specific individuals, or to conduct focus groups to explore specific areas of interest. The researcher had faced many of the same issues and challenges as the participants, leading to the possibility of bias and over-identification with their situation. The researcher's personal acquaintance with many of the Alberta respondents may also have contributed to the potential for bias. Such reputational knowledge can be an advantage and a disadvantage. A deep and long-lived familiarity with the culture under study can potentially dull an investigator's powers of observation and analysis (McCracken, 1988). On the other hand, it may also provide the investigator with an extraordinarily intimate acquaintance with the object of study, generating a "fineness of touch and delicacy of insight" (McCracken, 1988, p. 32). Generalizability of the study is limited because of the small sample size and a failure to randomly select from the population of administrators.

One of the critical issues for public child welfare programs is whether they can develop new roles and functions in response to new and rapidly increasing service needs at a time when resources and community support are decreasing. In order to begin the process of change, they must open new lines of communication and develop relationships with various community systems such as local agencies, special interest groups, churches, schools and neighbourhoods. Most child welfare systems, forged in the Weberian model of organizational bureaucracy, find it difficult to live up to calls for community participation. Their very nature as bureaucracies can create significant obstacles to the development of collaborative relationships with community systems. The tools provided by current technology may be inadequate for the tasks that lie ahead. The tools usually considered in the bureaucratic paradigm consist of complex structures and frameworks, staff, resources, and power to effect change. Yet, in many ways, these are the antitheses of prevailing values and the approaches utilized by local communities. Different tools and processes may be needed if bureaucracies are to actively participate in the promotion of increased levels of community ownership and control of programs that serve them.

The diverse and even conflicting features of bureaucracies and communities can create difficult situations for administrators who function at the nexus of such systems (Litwak, 1970; Warren, 1978; Berger & Neuhaus, 1984). Officials who have been socialized to a Weberian model of administration, which prizes efficiency and orderliness, are likely to find it difficult to consider the demands of community systems which emphasize intimacy, relationships, and personal loyalty. The top-down authority and control orientations of distant bureaucracies may constrain the capacity of local communities to solve many of their problems. Administrators are considered an important element in changing these types of power relationships and re-establishing greater balance *vis à vis* the roles of communities and governmental bureaucracies. The administrators in this sample candidly discussed the personal and professional dilemmas that they encountered in their dealings with local communities while representing their organizations. These administrators experienced difficulties as they attempted to reconcile the conflicting values, assumptions, and priorities of horizontal and vertical systems. Respondents suggested that the struggles of administrators to maintain the present societal compact, while making the adjustments necessary to move into new modes of operation, deserve serious attention. Administrators emphasized the importance of attending to both ideological and technological prerequisites for change. Most administrators reported that they wished their superiors would enunciate and then actively support the ideology associated with greater community ownership and control. Many had experienced false starts in the past, as departmental citizen participation initiatives ebbed and flowed. This led many to insist on concrete manifestations of organizational commitment in the form of specific and tangible resources and help, before they would fully engage in initiatives with their communities.

Survival and maintenance are dominant organizational values. Organizations will do everything in their power to protect their core functions and mission. Couchman (1992) concludes that innovative approaches to the delivery of human services are rarely adopted if changes to core functions are proposed. This signals some of the difficulties that organizations could anticipate if citizens were to propose changes that required dramatic modifications to core functions. The examples of citizen participation utilized in this study were limited to activities that remain largely under bureaucratic control and required no change in core functions. If trends favouring greater autonomy and authority for communities continue, and efforts at building sustainable communities become more widely accepted societal objectives, then both communities and higher levels of government will be challenged to find news ways of working together.

There are few readily adoptable models available to help pave the way toward increased levels of citizen participation and control. Promising suggestions advanced by respondents were that superiors could model appropriate behaviours and staff who are skilled in working with communities could become mentors for others in their organizations. Many observed that most organizations did not provide any inducements or guidance to administrators for involving citizens in their activities. A number of administrators concluded that task-environments dominated by citizens were indeed fraught with risk for those who ventured into these relatively uncharted waters. Organizations place staff in difficult situations when they ask them to work closely with citizens. Many administrators suggested that few organizational rewards are provided and considerable risks are entailed for those who involve citizens; their reluctance to go should come as no surprise.

References

Berger P. L. & Neuhaus, R. J. (1984). *To empower people: The role of mediating structures in public policy.* Washington, D.C.: American Enterprise Institute for Public Policy Research.

Besharov, D. J. (1975). Building a community response to child abuse and mistreatment. *Children Today, 4,* 5.

Bjur, W. E. (1983). *Coproduction: Some refinements on an emerging concept.* Unpublished Manuscript. University of Southern California. School of Public Administration, 135–149.

Clayton, R., & Gilbert, R. (1971). Perspectives for public managers: Their implications for public service delivery systems. *Public Management, 53*(1), 9–12.

Cohen, N. E. (Ed.) (1960). *The Citizen volunteer: His responsibility, role, and opportunity in modern society.* New York: Harper & Brothers.

Cooper, T. L. (1979). The hidden price tag: Participation costs and health planning. *American Journal of Public Health, 69*(4), 368–374.

Cooper, T. L. (1985). The public-private continuum: Interdependence in a democratic society. *Public Budgeting and Finance*, Autumn, 112–119.

Couchman, R. (1992). The politics of resistance to change in innovative Programming. *The Philanthropist, 11*(3).

Davis, J. (1973). Citizen control in a bureaucratic society: Some questions and skeptical notes. In V. Jones (Ed.), *Neighbourhood control in the 1970s.* New York: Chandler

DeSario, J., & Langton S. (Eds.) (1987). *Citizen participation in public decision making*. New York: Greenwood Press.

Glaser, B. G., & Straus, A. L. (1975). *The discovery of grounded theory: Strategies for qualitative research.* Chicago: Aldine.

Havassey, H. M. (1990). Effective second-story bureaucrats: Mastering the paradox of diversity. *Social Work, 35*(2), 103–109.

Kammerman, S., & Kahn, A. J. (1989). *Social services for children, youth, and families in the United States.* New York: Columbia University Press.

Kweit, M. G., & Kweit, R. W. (1981). *Implementing citizen participation in a bureaucratic society: A contingency approach.* New York: Praeger Publications.

Kweit, M. G., & Kweit, R. W. (1987). The politics of policy analysis: The role of citizen participation in analytic decision making. In J. Desario & S. Langston (Eds.), *Citizen participation in public decision making*. New York: Greenwood Press.

Litwak, E. (1970). Community participation in bureaucratic organizations: Principles and strategies. *Interchange, 1*(4), 44–60.

McCracken, G. (1988). *The long interview.* Newbury Park: Sage Publications.

McNair, R. H. (1983). Citizen participants in public bureaucracies: Foul weather friends. *Administration and Society, 14*(4), 507–524.

Morgan, D. L. (1988). *Focus groups as qualitative research.* Newbury Park: Sage Publications.

Patton, M. Q. (1980). *Qualitative evaluation methods.* Beverly Hills: Sage Publications.

Sieder, V. (1960). The citizen volunteer in historical perspective. In N. E. Cohen (Ed.), *The citizen volunteer: His responsibility, role, and opportunity in modern society.* New York: Harper & Brothers.

Strauss, A., & Corbin, J. (1990). *Basics of qualitative research: Grounded theory procedures and techniques.* Newbury Park: Sage Publications.

Tichy, N. (1983). *Managing strategic change.* New York: Wiley.

Warren, R. (1978). *The community in America.* Chicago: Rand McNally College Publishing Company.

3

Correlates of Substantiation of Maltreatment in Child Welfare Investigations

Nico Trocmé, Kwok Kwan Tam, and Debra McPhee

North American child welfare services are facing spiralling reports of suspected child abuse and neglect with increasingly limited resources. In many jurisdictions child welfare agencies have been reduced to conducting investigations with very limited funds remaining to provide protection and services (Kammerman & Kahn, 1990). Some argue that the growing volume of reports and investigations reflects a failure to develop clear enough reporting and investigation criteria, and that the children with the greatest needs are not being effectively targeted (Besharov, 1990; Hutchinson, 1990; Lindsey, 1991a). Concern about the subjectivity of child welfare intervention decisions has arisen as a result of studies that have found that factors such as source of referral, geographic location, family income, and race appear to have more influence on case dispositions than do severity of harm, nature of maltreatment, and family functioning.

Research on predictors of child welfare intervention decisions have been conducted at all points in the decision-making process: reporting suspected maltreatment (Hampton & Newberger, 1985; Hampton, 1987; Ards & Harrell, 1993), screening reports (Hutchinson, 1989), case substantiation (Groenveld & Giovannoni, 1977; Zuravin & Watson, 1987; Eckenrode, Munsch, Powers & Doris, 1988; Giovannoni, 1989; Winefield & Bradley, 1992), provision of services (Giovannoni & Becerra, 1982; Wolock, 1982; Johnson & L'Esperance, 1984), deciding to take cases to child welfare court or criminal court (Giovannoni & Becerra, 1982; Tjaden & Thoennes, 1992), assessing risk of placement (Berry, 1991), removal of children from their homes (Runyan, Gould, Trost, & Loda, 1981; Miller, Shireman, Burke & Brown, 1982; Katz, Hampton, Newberger, Bowles & Snyder, 1986; Seaberg, 1988; Lindsey, 1991b), selecting types of placement (Schwab, Bruce & McRoy, 1985; Knapp, Baines, Bryson & Lewis, 1987), and returning children home (Segal & Schwartz, 1985; Seaberg & Tolley, 1986). Some studies have failed to find evidence that a consistent set of criteria are applied (Runyan et al., 1981; Miller et al., 1982; Katz et al., 1986; Lindsey, 1991b). When predictor variables are identified they appear to reflect case processing factors, such as source of referral (Groenveld & Giovannoni, 1977; Miller et al., 1982) or geographic location (Runyan, 1981; Wolock, 1982; Eckenrode et al. 1988), rather than factors related to the severity of maltreatment and the level of future risk to the child (Runyan et al., 1981; Katz et al., 1986; Johnson & L'Esperance, 1984). In addition, some studies have found evidence of marked class and race bias (Hampton & Newberger, 1985; Lindsey, 1991b). A growing number of studies, however, have been more successful in identifying decision-making practices that do reflect severity of maltreatment and other clinical risk factors (Seaberg & Tolley, 1986; Zuravin et al., 1987; Seaberg, 1988; Giovannoni, 1989; Tjaden & Thoennes, 1992; Winefield & Bradley, 1992). These differences can be attributed in part to the closer attention paid to measuring severity of maltreatment and controlling for its effects on other related factors, such as source of referral.

The importance of controlling for the effects of severity of maltreatment is particularly clear in studies of case substantiation decisions. Groenveld and Giovannoni (1977) completed the first large case record study (N=2,400) of factors related to case substantiation. They examined three types of predictor variables: variables describing the incident, variables describing the child and family, and variables describing case processing. Their analysis indicated that the best predictors of case disposition were case processing variables rather than severity of maltreatment. They found in particular that cases referred by the police were more likely to be substantiated than were cases referred by other sources. Unfortunately, because the study was based on a case file analysis, the authors were restricted to a limited range of proxy measures in considering the effects of severity of maltreatment (e.g. medical care required). The influence of source of referral was examined in a second case file study of a representative sample of 1,874 maltreatment investigations (Eckenrode et al., 1987). This study found that source of report (professional vs. nonprofessional) as well as race were strong predictors of case substantiation. However, no measure of severity of maltreatment was included in the analysis.

In contrast, studies that factor in the effects of severity of maltreatment have found that the influence of case processing variables, such as source of referral, is mediated by severity of maltreatment. Zuravin and colleagues (1987) compared anonymous reports to reports from professionals and nonprofessionals by analyzing case records from a random sample of 1,207 child maltreatment reports in Baltimore. While they found that anonymous reports were least likely to be substantiated, and professional reports most likely to be substantiated, they also found that anonymous reports involved significantly less severe cases of maltreatment. Giovannoni (1989) collected information directly from investigating child protection workers for a sample of 1,156 reports. Severity of injury and form of maltreatment were strong predictors of substantiation, whereas source of report was not. A study of computer records from 3,228 reports made in Australia also found that severity of maltreatment was the strongest predictor of substantiation, and that when severity of maltreatment was controlled, source of report was not associated with case substantiation (Winefield & Bradley, 1992).

The present study provides an opportunity to further examine the relationship between severity of maltreatment and case processing factors in a representative sample of Ontario child welfare investigations. As with the Giovannoni (1989) and the Winefield and Bradley (1992) studies, data were collected directly from investigating workers, avoiding many of the coding problems encountered in case file studies. A significant advantage with the Ontario data base is that it includes a broad spectrum of maltreatment, family background, and case processing variables that allow for a more detailed analysis of the complex array of factors considered in conducting child maltreatment investigations. The data base includes information on five types of case disposition: substantiation, provision of services, placement in care, child welfare court applications, and laying criminal charges. The present analysis focuses on case substantiation. The relative contribution of three sets of variables on substantiation rates are analyzed: variables relating to the nature and severity of maltreatment; family background variables, such as family structure, race, and parent mental health; and case processing variables, such as agency size and location, and worker experience. The primary hypothesis tested is that severity of maltreatment plays a central role in determining case substantiation, and that the effect of case processing variables is mediated by severity of maltreatment.

Methods

Sample

The study is based on a secondary analysis of data collected for the Ontario Incidence Study (Trocmé, McPhee, Tam, & Hay, 1994). The primary objective of the OIS was to estimate the incidence of reported child maltreatment, and to describe the characteristics of these cases. The OIS collected child maltreatment investigation data directly from intake workers in a sample of 15 randomly selected Ontario child welfare agencies stratified by size and geography location. All* families and children assessed for service during the study period (March to June 1993) were eligible for inclusion. The estimated participation rate was over 85%, and the completion rate on all items but two was over 90% (95% on all case disposition variables). OIS data forms were collected on a total of 2,950 families. Sixty percent of these families (N=1,898) were specifically investigated because of alleged maltreatment, involving 2,447 children, the core sample for the study.

The profile of the families is presented in Table 3.1. Fifty-three percent of the families were two-parent families, either with both biological parents (34%) or with one step-parent/common law partner (19%). Forty-two percent of the families were single parent families, 36% female lead, and 6% male lead. The average age of the investigated children was 7.1. While all age groups were well represented, there were more children in the adolescent age groups than in any other age group. No risk factors were identified for two-thirds of the investigated parents. Thirteen percent of parents had visible problems with alcohol, 7% with drugs (70% of whom were also identified as alcohol abusers), 13 percent appeared to have mental health problems, and spousal physical violence was documented for 17% of parents. The most common form of investigated maltreatment was physical abuse (41%), followed by neglect (30%), and sexual abuse (24%). In 12% of cases there was more than one form of investigated maltreatment. Twenty-eight percent of the investigated cases were substantiated, 31% were suspected, and 41% were unsubstantiated. Seventy-three percent of cases were closed after the initial investigation (28% received post-intake services). Six percent of the children were placed in CAS care, 5% were moved to a non-CAS placement (e.g. relative), and 5% were at risk of placement.

---

* In large agencies a subsample of cases (approximately 25%) was selected. In some instances selection was random, in others, selection was done by having district offices complete forms on a rotating basis.

Table 3-1: Profile of OIS Sample (N=2,447)

Variable	% of investigated children
Sample size	
# of investigated children	2,447
# of investigated children	1,898
Children	
age**	7.1
male	49%
Family Structure	
Two biological parents	34%
Biological parent & step-parent	19%
Single-mother	36%
Single-father	6%
Separated/divorced	46%
Parent age	
Teen parent at time of first birth	6%
Parent<25	
Parent race	
White	77%
Black	5%
Native	5%
Hispanic	2%
East & South East Asian	3%
South & West Asian, & North African	2%
Income	
Social assistance*	38%
Housing	
Moved last 6 months	18%
Public	18%
Rural	16%
Unsafe/Inadequate	5%
Parent risk factors	
Alcohol abuse	13%
Drug abuse	7%
Mental health	13%
Spousal physical violence	17%

Investigated maltreatment	
Physical abuse	41%
Sexual abuse by parent	11%
Sexual abuse by other	13%
Neglect	30%
Emotional maltreatment	10%
Multiple forms of maltreatment	12%
Re-opened case	46%
Substantiation	
Substantiated	28%
Suspected	31%
Unsubstantiated	41%
Post-intake services planned	27%
Placement	
CAS care	6%
Informal non-CAS placement	5%
Risk of placement	5%
Court	
Child welfare court application	8%
Risk of child welfare court	4%
Police investigation	23%
Criminal charges laid	6%

* 25% missing data for source of income, if missing data are excluded, the proportion of children dependent on social assistance is 50%.
** the value is the average or mean age.

Data collection

Data were collected directly from the primary investigating worker using a two-page checklist describing child and family background, source and reason for referral, case disposition (substantiation, placement, child welfare court and criminal court), nature and severity of maltreatment, and identity of perpetrator. The OIS form was completed simultaneously with the written assessments that child welfare agencies are required to provide within 21 days of the initial complaint. The first page of the form was completed for every investigated family, and the second page, which provides details about the investigated maltreatment, was completed for every investigated child. Additional maltreatment forms (second page) were completed in families where there was more than one investigated child. The form was designed on the basis of the questionnaires used for the two U.S. National Incidence Studies (U.S.D.H.H.S.,

1983, 1986). The Ontario version of the form was pilot tested in two agencies, and on-site training was provided to all participating workers (see Trocmé et al., 1994).

Substantiation

Case substantiation is the outcome variable used in the present analysis. A three point scale was used to rate the level of substantiation for all investigated children. A case was considered substantiated if it was the worker's professional opinion that there was sufficient evidence that abuse or neglect probably had occurred (i.e. the worker would be prepared to testify in court to that effect as an expert witness, even though the worker may be uncertain whether the evidence met all legal evidential requirements). A case was considered suspected if there was not enough evidence to substantiate maltreatment, but neither was there enough evidence to rule out the possibility of maltreatment. A case was unfounded if there was sufficient evidence to conclude the child had not been maltreated.

Independent variables

The framework developed by Groenveld and Giovannoni (1977) was used to organize the independent variables into three main groupings: variables describing the maltreatment incident, variables describing the family background, and agency or case processing variables. Maltreatment related variables include severity of harm, form of maltreatment, alleged perpetrator, child age, and gender. Severity of harm is a composite variable created by combining ratings on a nature of harm scale (physical injury, health condition, emotional harm) with ratings on a severity of harm scale (no harm, risk, probable, moderate, serious, fatal).* The nature and severity of harm ratings are combined for this analysis into five mutually exclusive categories: no harm, physical harm (moderate to fatal physical harm), risk of physical harm (including risk and probable harm), emotional harm (moderate to serious), risk of emotional harm (risk and probable). The OIS form includes seventeen different subtypes of maltreatment, and allows for coding up to four different types per child. These are collapsed into six categories: sexual abuse by a parent, sexual abuse by a non-parent, physical abuse, neglect, emotional maltreatment, and multiple forms of maltreatment. All cases involving more than one form of maltreatment are included under the latter category. Seven alleged perpetrator codes are used: mother alone, father alone, step-father/common-law partner alone, both parents, other relative, acquaintance, and other. Child age is coded as a categorical variable because of the non-linear relationship with the outcome variables. Six age groups are used. Child gender is coded as male or not male.

Family background variables include a parent risk factor checklist (alcohol abuse, drug abuse, parent mental health, and physical violence between parents), and an environmental risk factor checklist (public housing complex,

* The severity of harm rating refers to any injury or condition observed, whether or not it is attributed to child maltreatment. Serious harm includes situations where there are observable injuries or conditions requiring professional intervention. A moderate harm rating signifies that the injuries or conditions are observable for at least 48 hours after the incident. Probable harm refers to situations where there is no observable harm, but the nature of the circumstances indicate that harm is likely. Risk of harm is any situation where harm has not yet occurred but is likely if circumstances do not change.

moved in last six months, unsafe or inadequate housing, and receiving social assistance.* These variables reflect global worker judgment. Cases that had been referred because of child behaviour problems are added to the risk factor variables. Because this particular variable is part of a different section of the OIS form (reason for referral) it is likely that it underestimates the actual number of cases involving child behaviour problems. Family structure data are collapsed into five main categories (single-mother, single-father, two biological parents, biological parent and step-parent, other), and a separate divorce or separation variable is included in the analysis as well. Nine possible parent race categories are collapsed into six categories on the basis of substantiation rates: White; Black; Native, East and South-East Asian (e.g. Chinese, Japanese, Korean, Vietnamese, Filipino, Indonesian); South Asian, West Asian, and North African (e.g. Indian, Pakistani, Sri Lanka, Arab, Turkish, Armenian); and Hispanic.

Agency variables include source of referral, geographic region (North, South Central, South East, and South West Ontario),** and agency size. Two variables from a parallel study of 60 percent of the workers involved in the OIS study are also included in the analysis: whether or not a worker had an MSW, and whether a worker had more or less than ten years of child welfare experience. Findings using worker data should be viewed as exploratory because data was missing for 40% of the cases.

Analysis

The analysis was conducted in two stages. Substantiation rates were first calculated for the maltreatment, family background, and agency variables for the full sample of 2,447 investigations. Nineteen categorical independent variables were selected for this analysis. Non-dichotomous variables were converted to dichotomous or dummy variables, yielding a total of 77 dichotomous variables. Crude odds ratios were calculated for each dichotomous variable to estimate the relative odds of substantiation (versus a case being suspected or unfounded) in the presence of each individual variable compared with the absence of that variable. Ninety-five percent confidence intervals were calculated for each odds ratio, and all statistically significant variables were then selected to be entered in a series of regression models.

The second stage of the analysis used logistic regression to calculate the relative association of each variable with substantiation with control for confounding. Logistic regression was selected because it allows comparison of different models and can factor in the relative contribution of a large number of independent variables. Substantiation was dichotomized for the analysis by comparing the unsubstantiated cases with the substantiated cases. Suspected cases (N=831), and cases with missing information (N=143), were not included in the regression analysis, yielding a subsample of 1,473 cases. Variables with significant odds ratios were entered in the analysis. Models with different combinations of maltreatment, family, and agency variables were compared in

---

* Income data were collected but were not complete enough to be included in this study. There also was 25% missing data on the social assistance question, but this was not felt to be high enough to warrant exclusion. Cases with missing social assistance data were included in the analysis.

** To maintain agency confidentiality these are recoded in random order as regions A, B, C and D.

order to determine the contribution of each set of variables to substantiation. An analog of the total variance explained by the model (R^2)was estimated by using the procedure suggested by Agresti (1990, p. 110).*

Findings

Bivariate analyses

Table 3.2 presents the substantiation rates for the maltreatment, family background, and agency variables. The bivariate analysis shows that all three sets of variables are significantly related to variations in substantiation rates, and that, as hypothesized, the maltreatment variables are most strongly associated with substantiation. Sixty percent of cases involving physical injuries and 70% of cases involving observable emotional harm are substantiated, whereas only 19% of cases involving no evidence of harm or risk of harm are substantiated (odds ratio = 0.19). Sixty-three percent of cases where there was evidence of risk of physical harm or probable physical harm, and 60% of cases involving risk of emotional harm or probable emotional harm are substantiated. Cases involving observable emotional harm are more likely to be substantiated than are cases involving physical harm. The rate of unfounded cases for physical injuries was 16%, whereas it was only 1% for cases involving emotional harm. The difference is most likely explained by situations where children with moderate to serious physical injuries are referred for suspected physical abuse, which after investigation are found to be non-abusive accidental injuries. Rates of suspected maltreatment are associated with the presence of observable evidence. Twenty-six percent of cases involving observable physical harm, and 28% of cases involving observable emotional harm are classified as suspected, whereas 31% of cases involving risk of physical harm and 40% of cases involving risk of emotional harm are classified as suspected.

Duration of maltreatment, and form of maltreatment are also strongly associated with level of substantiation. The chance of substantiation increases as a direct function of duration (Kendall's Tau b=0.48). Situations involving chronic alleged maltreatment (more than six months), are four and a half times more likely to be substantiated than are all other situations (odds ratio = 4.58). Substantiation rates for forms of alleged maltreatment vary in an interesting fashion. The cases that are least likely to be substantiated are cases involving suspected emotional maltreatment (odds ratio = 0.45), physical abuse (odds ratio = 0.69), and parental sexual abuse (odds ratio =.69, not significant at p). The difficulty in substantiating emotional maltreatment is to be expected given that this is not a well established investigatory category. Ontario's child welfare legislation does not include emotional maltreatment as grounds for court ordered intervention (Trocmé et al., 1994). However, this form of maltreatment has the largest proportion of suspected cases (52%), and the second lowest proportion of unfounded cases (33%), indicating that while it may be more difficult to substantiate emotional maltreatment, it nevertheless is considered to be a serious form of maltreatment. The lower substantiation rate for physical abuse cases is to be expected given that some of these cases involve misdiagnosed accidental injuries, while others may involve inappropriate

---

* (Maximized Log Likelihood constant - Maximized Log Likelihood model)/Maximized Log Likelihood constant.

Table 3-2: Substantiation Rates

Variable	Unfounded	Suspected	Substantiated	Odds Ratio: Substantiated vs. suspected or unfounded *
Overall rate	43%	30%	27%	
Maltreatment variables				
Injury				
No injury	51%	31%	19%	0.14
Observable physical harm	16%	26%	59%	4.24
Risk of physical harm	6%	31%	63%	4.85
Observable emotional harm	1%	28%	70%	6.65
Risk of emotional harm	1%	40%	60%	4.37
Duration of maltreatment				
No maltreatment	70%	29%	-	-
Single incident	34%	28%	38%	1.89
Less than six months	14%	42%	44%	2.27
More than six months	7%	38%	56%	4.58
Alleged maltreatment				
Sexual abuse by parent	51%	26%	23%	ns
Sexual abuse by other	40%	28%	33%	1.32
Physical abuse only	51%	26%	23%	0.69
Neglect	36%	33%	31%	1.24
Emotional maltreatment only	33%	52%	15%	0.45
Multiple forms of maltreatment	26%	37%	36%	1.58
Perpetrator				
Mother	44%	31%	25%	0.81
Father	45%	32%	23%	0.70
Step-father	37%	31%	32%	ns
Both parents	27%	36%	37%	1.6
Relative	31%	28%	41%	2.00
Acquaintance	39%	28%	33%	ns
Unknown	59%	28%	12%	0.42

Child age				
under 1	41%	30%	29%	ns
1 to 3	45%	36%	20%	0.59
4 to 6	45%	33%	23%	0.73
7 to 9	44%	30%	25%	ns
10 to12	41%	27%	32%	ns
13 to 15	34%	28%	38%	1.85
Child male	39%	34%	27%	ns
Family & environment				
Alcohol abuse	25%	36%	39%	1.84
Drug abuse	29%	39%	32%	ns
Mental health	31%	35%	34%	1.40
Spousal violence	35%	40%	26%	ns
Child behaviour problem	35%	32%	32%	ns
Moved in last six months	35%	38%	28%	ns
Public housing complex	37%	33%	30%	ns
Unsafe/inappropriate housing	20%	29%	51%	2.90
*Social assistance***	41%	34%	25%	0.82
Family Structure				
Single-mother	44%	31%	25%	0.79
Single-father	44%	24%	32%	ns
Two biological parents	40%	31%	29%	ns
Step-parent	36%	31%	33%	1.36
Other	47%	33%	20%	0.63
Separated/divorced	44%	31%	25%	0.78
Adolescent parent at first birth	41%	34%	25%	ns
Parent <25	38%	37%	25%	ns
Parent race				
White	43%	30%	26%	0.82
Black	34%	35%	32%	ns
Native	28%	31%	42%	1.90
East & South East Asian	36%	24%	40%	1.90

South & West Asian & North African	39%	26%	35%	ns
Hispanic	39%	43%	19%	0.58
Agency variables				
Previous referral				
No previous referral	44%	29%	26%	ns
Child previously maltreated	44%	27%	29%	ns
Perpetrator previously reported	31%	40%	29%	ns
Case previously opened	37%	34%	29%	ns
Referral source				
Parent	35%	31%	34%	1.40
Non-custodial parent	61%	27%	12%	0.37
Child	36%	33%	31%	ns
Relative/Neighbour	44%	32%	24%	ns
School/Daycare	44%	27%	29%	ns
Police	34%	28%	38%	1.60
Health professional	33%	37%	29%	ns
Anonymous	65%	21%	14%	0.40
Region				
A	42%	30%	28%	ns
B	39%	28%	34%	1.40
C	46%	35%	19%	0.52
D	37%	32%	32%	ns
Rural community	35%	32%	33%	1.32
Agency Size				
Small	36%	31%	32%	ns
Midsize	48%	29%	23%	0.71
Large	40%	32%	29%	ns
*MSW****	36%	31%	33%	1.30
*10 + years experience****	48%	31%	65%	0.21

* Odds ratios significant at p .05
** 25 percent missing data
*** 40 percent missing data

physical discipline; 77% of all abuse allegations are related to discipline problems.

Relationship with the alleged perpetrator is also significantly associated with case substantiation. One of the biological parents is the alleged perpetrator in 54% of investigations (33% mothers, 21% fathers), and these cases are generally less likely to be substantiated. In contrast, cases where the alleged perpetrator is another relative, or both parents, are more likely to be substantiated (odds ratios 1.60 and 2.00, respectively). Excluding infants, case substantiation rates are positively associated with age (Kendall's Tau-b=.13, p.001) with higher substantiation rates for cases involving adolescents. Substantiation rates do not vary significantly in terms of child gender.

Two items in the parent risk checklist proved to be strongly associated with substantiation: alcohol abuse (odds ratio = 1.84) and parent mental health problems (odds ratio = 1.40). While substantiation rates for cases involving suspected drug abuse or spousal physical violence are not higher than for other cases, the rates of suspected maltreatment are 39% (odds ratio = 1.48) and 40% (odds ratio = 1.58). Cases involving families living in unsafe or inadequate housing are at three times the risk of being substantiated (odds ratio = 2.90), but cases involving families receiving social assistance are less likely to be substantiated (odds ratio = 0.82). Analysis of the incomplete income data that were collected indicate that low-income families are generally less likely to be substantiated than are middle and upper income families. One possible explanation is that low-income families, and in particular families receiving social assistance, are more likely to be subjects of an inappropriate report. The low rate of substantiation for single-mother families may also reflect similar reporting bias which is not born out by investigation (odds ratio, 0.79). Step-fathers generally emerge from this study as being a very high-risk group. Nineteen percent of all investigated families include a step-father, and investigations in these families are more likely to be substantiated than in all other types of families (odds ratio = 1.36). Parent age is not associated with variations in substantiation rates. In contrast, substantiation rates vary on the basis of parent race, with lower substantiation rates for White (odds ratio = 0.82) and Hispanic (odds ratio =.50) families, and double the likelihood of substantiation for Native (odds ratio = 1.90) and for East and South East Asian families (odds ratio = 1.90).

Substantiation rates also vary significantly for most agency variables. Previous case opening are not related to higher substantiation rates; however, cases where the perpetrator was previously known are more likely to be classified as suspected (odds ratio = 1.44), although not more likely to be substantiated. Substantiation rates vary significantly by referral source; cases referred by parents (odds ratio = 1.40) and the police (odds ratio = 1.60) are more likely to be substantiated, and referrals received by anonymous sources (odds ratio = 0.40) or non-custodial parents (odds ratio = 0.37) are less likely to be substantiated. There also appears to be considerable variation on the basis of geographic location, with region B having higher than average substantiation rates (odds ratio = 1.40), and region C having considerably lower substantiation rates (odds ratio = 0.52). Similar variations are noted on the basis of agency size, with midsize agencies having lower substantiation rates (odds ratio = 0.71). Worker experience and training have inverse effects on substantiation rates: workers with more than ten years of child welfare experience are

Table 3-3. Goodness of Fit Statistics for Various Logistic Regression Models Predicting Maltreatment Substantiation, 1993 (N=1473)

Model	L2 1	*d.f.*	*p*	BIC*2	Overall % of Accurate Prediction	*R2 3*
(1): Baseline	1991.12				59.9%	
(2): (1) + agency variables 4	108.6	16	0	-8.12	62.5%	0.05
(3): (1) + maltreatment variables 5	594.13	16	0	477.41	76.5%	0.30
(4): (1) + agency variables + maltreatment variables	665.46	32	0	432.02	79.2%	0.33
(5): (1) + agency variables + maltreatment variables + family background variables 6	720.38	45	0	392.12	80.6%	0.36
(6): reduced model (5) 7	700.67	32	0	467.23	80.6%	0.35

(1) For the baseline model, this is -2 log likelihood; for the remaining models it is the "model chi square" - the difference between -2 log likelihood for the baseline model and the model being evaluated.
(2) BIC* is defined as BIC*=Model Chi Square -(model d.f.) [in(N)]. The larger the BIC*, the greater the probability that the model is true given the observed data. See Treiman & Yamaguchi (1993) for further discussion.
(3) The R2 Measures denotes the difference between -2 log likelihood for the baseline model and the model being evaluated, over the -2 log likelihood of the baseline model, i.e. L2/Base L2 from the table. See Agresti (1990), p.110.
(4) The agency variables includes sources of referral, region of agency location, rural community, agency size, the worker with MSW degree, and the worker with 10 or more years experience in child protection services.
(5) The maltreatment variables includes injury, major form of maltreatments, perpetrator variable, and whether the child is teenager.
(6) The family background variables includes risk of parental alcohol abuse, parental mental health problem, parental divorce/separation, inadequate housing, family structure, race of parent, and receiving social assistance.
(7) The reduced model (5) includes agency variables-source of referral, region of agency location, size of agency; maltreatment variables-injury, major form of maltreatments, perpetrator variable, whether the child is a teenager; and family background variables-risk of parental alcohol abuse, parental divorce/separation, inadequate housing condition.

much less likely to substantiate cases, whereas workers with MSW are more likely to substantiate cases.

The picture that emerges from the bivariate analyses is that a broad array of factors are associated with decisions to substantiate. Severity of maltreatment is reflected in substantiation rates, but variation in substantiation rates are also associated with family background, as well as agency related factors. The regression analysis that follows was used to examine the contribution of the agency variables relative to the maltreatment variables.

Regression Analysis

Variables from Table 3.2 with significant odd ratios were employed for the regression analysis.* The variables were grouped into the three sets of independent variables: maltreatment, family background, and agency variables. The three sets of variables were entered consecutively to determine the relative contribution of each set to the prediction of substantiation. Table 3.3 shows

* Duration was not included in the regression analysis, since unsubstantiated did not receive a duration code. Duration was kept in the bivariate analysis because suspected cases had duration ratings.

Table 3-4. Classification Table for the Reduced Model for Maltreatment Substantiation (N=1473)

Observed	Predicted			
	Substantiated	*Unsubstantiated*		
Unsubstantiated	799	74	Specificity:	92%
			Sensitivity:	65%
			Overall correctly classified:	81%
Substantiated	212	388		
			Kappa:	0.58

the comparison of the goodness of fit* of the logistic regression models. Comparison of model 2 (agency variables) with the baseline model (model 1) indicates that, on their own, the agency variables provide limited improvement in predicting substantiation. In contrast, model 3 (maltreatment variables) improve the overall prediction from 59.9% to 76.5%, and explains 30% of the variance. Models 4 and 5 show that, as agency and family background variables are added to the maltreatment variables, the overall prediction rate increases slightly. Thus, all three sets of variables contribute to predicting substantiation, although the maltreatment variables provide the greatest explanatory power.

While the complete model (model 5) has the highest overall prediction rate, it is not the most parsimonious model. The measure of goodness of fit—BIC (Rastery, 1985)—for the complete model is lower than the BIC of models 3 and 4. This is probably due to the spurious effects of some variables that contribute less to the model as other mediating variables are entered in the analyses. A reduced model (model 6) of model 5 was developed by selecting the most significant variables from the three sets of variables. Model 6 fits the data well (BIC = 467) and has the highest rate of accurate prediction. The classification table for Model (6) is presented in Table 3.4. Sixty-five percent of substantiated cases are correctly predicted, and 92% of unsubstantiated cases are correctly predicted. The overall correct classification rate is 81%, correcting for chance, the Cohen's Kappa for model 6 is 0.58.

The parameters for model 6 are presented in Table 3.4 to compare the relative contribution of the independent variables. In table 3.4, "b" is the log odds of maltreatment substantiation from each independent variables. The anti log of b (Exp. (b)) gives the adjusted odds ratio of maltreatment substantiation for each independent variable, controlling for the effects of other independent variables. Thus for example, the odds of substantiation for cases referred by

* Since the differences in the likelihood ratios (L^2) between the baseline model and other models are distributed as X^2, with degrees of freedom equal to the number of independent variables in the model, the goodness of fit of various model can be compared. Here we use BIC* to compare the goodness of fit from different models. BIC* is a measure of the likelihood that a model is true given the data. BIC refers to Bayesian Information Coefficient, introduced by Raftery (1985) as an alternative to X^2 for assessing the goodness of fit of various log linear models. Treiman and Yamaguchi (1992) presented BIC* a modification of BIC for comparing logistic regression models. BIC* is defined as:
BIC*= Model X^2 - (modeld.f.)*In(N)
where N is the number of cases in the analysis. The largest positive coefficient identifies the model most likely to be true given the data.

Table 3.5: Parameters of the Reduced Model for Maltreatment Substantiation Ontario Incidence Study, 1993 (N=1473)

Variable	Omitted Category	b*	Standard Error	Wald Statistics	df	*p*	*R*	Exp(b)
Maltreatment variables								
Injury 1				187.4467	4	0.0000	0.3002	
	No Injury	(-3.3922)						(0.0336)
	Observable physical harm	-0.4396	0.3770	1.3595	1	0.2436	0.0000	0.6443
	Risk of physical harm	0.2325	0.5278	0.1940	1	0.6596	0.0000	1.2617
	Observable emotional harm	1.5723	0.8536	3.3930	1	0.0655	0.0264	4.8179
	Risk of emotional harm	2.0270	0.8376	5.8564	1	0.0155	0.0440	7.5914
Alleged maltreatment 2				25.3482	5	0.0001	0.0878	
	Mixed Maltreatment	(0.4096)						(1.5062)
	Sexual abuse by parent	-0.1523	0.2713	0.3150	1	0.5746	0.0000	0.8588
	Sexual abuse by other	0.2641	0.2523	1.0950	1	0.2954	0.0000	1.3022
	Physical abuse only	-0.3227	0.1647	3.8401	1	0.0500	-0.0304	0.7242
	Neglect only	0.6098	0.1739	12.2923	1	0.0005	0.0719	1.8401
	Emotional maltreatment only	-0.8085	0.4693	2.9686	1	0.0849	-0.0221	0.4455
Perpetrator 3				34.9244	6	0.0000	0.1073	
	Unknown	(-1.2877)						(0.2759)
	Mother	0.0461	0.1561	0.0871	1	0.7679	0.0000	1.0472
	Father	-0.2797	0.1819	2.3642	1	0.1241	-0.0135	0.7560
	Step-father	0.6358	0.2587	6.0421	1	0.0140	0.0451	1.8885
	Both parents	0.2267	0.2202	1.0591	1	0.3034	0.0000	1.2544
	Relative	0.5939	0.2104	7.9668	1	0.0048	0.0547	1.8111
	Acquaintance	0.0599	0.2484	0.0582	1	0.8094	0.0000	1.0617
Teenage Child		0.6099	0.1690	13.0243	1	0.0003	0.0744	1.8403
Family & environment								
Alcohol abuse		0.7415	0.2147	11.9224	1	0.0006	0.0706	2.0991
Drug abuse		-0.5383	0.1539	12.2386	1	0.0005	-0.0717	0.5838
Unsafe/inapp. housing		1.4630	0.3477	17.7030	1	0.0000	0.0888	4.3188
Agency variables								
Referral source 4				38.1463	8	0.0000	0.1055	
	Parent	(0.8123)						(2.253)
	Non-custodial parent	-0.9640	0.4028	5.7275	1	0.0167	-0.0433	0.3814

Child	0.2814	0.3375	0.6954	1	0.4043	0.0000	1.3250
Relative/Neighbour	0.0187	0.1679	0.0124	1	0.9113	0.0000	1.0189
School/daycare	-0.0711	0.1620	0.1928	1	0.6606	0.0000	0.9314
Police	0.6831	0.2128	10.3000	1	0.0013	0.0646	1.9800
Health professional	0.5529	0.1953	8.0141	1	0.0046	0.0550	1.7384
Other	-0.2342	0.2508	0.8723	1	0.3503	0.0000	0.7912
Anonymous	-1.0791	0.4276	6.3693	1	0.0116	-0.0468	0.3399
Region 5			15.9502	3	0.0012	0.0707	
A	(-0.0817)						(0.9216)
B	0.3630	0.1221	8.8321	1	0.0030	0.0586	1.4376
C	-0.4400	0.1345	10.6940	1	0.0011	-0.0661	0.6441
D	0.1587	0.1393	1.2981	1	0.2546	0.0000	1.1720
Agency Size 6			9.3300	2	0.0094	0.0517	
Small	(0.1106)						(1.1169)
Midsize	-0.3190	0.1261	6.3959	1	0.0114	-0.0470	0.7269
Large	0.2084	0.1065	3.8297	1	0.0504	0.0303	1.2317
Constant	1.9414	0.3423	32.1641	1	0.0000		

*The b for the omitted category for the categorical variables are in parentheses.
It denotes the effect of the omitted category compared to the average effect over all categories.
(1) "No Injury" is the omitted category for Injury.
(2) "Mixed Maltreatment" is the omitted category for the major form of maltreatment.
(4) "Parent" is the omitted category for source of referral.
(5) "Region A" is the omitted category.
(6) "Small" is the omitted category for size of agency

the police is 1.98 times greater than for those referred by parents, holding constant all other agency, maltreatment, and family background variables. Cases reported by health professionals are also more likely to be substantiated (odds ratio =1.74). In contrast, referrals from non-custodial parents and anonymous sources are less likely to be substantiated (odds ratio =0.38 and 0.34 respectively). Among the agency variables, region B shows a higher odds of substantiation (odds ratio =1.44) while region C shows a lower chance of substantiation (odds ratio =0.64), compared to region A. Large agencies tend to have a higher chance of maltreatment substantiation (odds ratio =1.23) compared to small agencies. The opposite is true for midsize agencies (odds ratio =0.73).

For the maltreatment variables, risk of emotional harm and observable emotional harm have higher odds of substantiation (7.59 and 4.82 respectively) compared to no injury. The lower chances of maltreatment substantiation for cases involving observable physical harm (odds ratio =0.64) may be due to some physical injuries being caused be domestic accidents, or non-abusive corporal punishment. Comparison of the form of maltreatment variables shows that emotional abuse only, physical abuse only, and sexual abuse by parents show comparatively lower odds of substantiation than sexual abuse by others and neglect only. For the perpetrator variables, allegations involving step-fathers and relatives were more likely to be substantiated (odds ratio =1.89 and 1.81 respectively), while allegations involving fathers had the lowest odds (odds ration = 0.76) of substantiation. Maltreatment reports concerning teenage children had higher chances of substantiation. Cases involving parent alcohol abuse or unsafe or inadequate housing conditions, were considerably more likely to be substantiated (odds ratio =2.10 and 4.32 respectively). However, in cases involving parent drug abuse, the chance of maltreatment substantiation was lower (odds ratio = 0.58).

Comparison of the partial correlation coefficients (*R*) in Table 3.4 shows that injury continues to play a central role in determining substantiation. Injury contributes most to predicting substantiation (*R*=0.30). Second most important predictors are source of referral (*R*=0.11) and the perpetrator variables (*R*=0.11). All other independent variables in the final reduced model [model 6] have a partial correlation coefficients between 0.07 to 0.08.

Discussion

This analysis of 2,447 child maltreatment investigations conducted in Ontario identified a broad array of factors that correlated with case substantiation decisions, including severity of harm, form of maltreatment, relationship of perpetrator, age of child, parent alcohol abuse, inadequate housing, referral source, agency size and agency location. Severity of harm proved to be the strongest predictor of case substantiation, confirming the results from other studies of child welfare dispositions using similar measures of severity (Seaberg & Tolley, 1986; Zuravin et al., 1987; Seaberg, 1988; Giovannoni, 1989; Tjaden & Thoennes, 1992; Winefield & Bradley, 1992).

This finding may not come as a surprise to child welfare professionals but research using other measures of severity of maltreatment has generally failed to find significant relationships between substantiation and severity of harm (Groenveld & Giovannoni, 1977; Runyan et al. 1981; Miller et al., 1982; Katz et al., 1986). One possible explanation for this difference lies in the inclusion of emotional harm and risk of harm in the OIS definition. The presence of any form of harm or risk of harm was associated with increased likelihood of substantiation, and cases involving emotional harm or risk of harm were more likely to be substantiated than were cases involving physical harm. The importance given to emotional harm is consistent with the growing body of research indicating that it is the emotional dimensions of maltreatment that put children at highest risk (Brassard, Germain & Hart, 1987; Erickson, Egeland & Pianta, 1989). In contrast, controlling for all other variables, physical harm was associated with decreased likelihood of substantiation. This finding is consistent with studies that rely on physical injuries (Katz et al., 1986) or hospital admissions (Groenveld & Giovannoni, 1977) as proxy measures of severity of harm. Cases involving physical injuries include an array of possible situations, ranging from accidental injuries, to an isolated incident associated with inappropriate disciplining, to injuries caused by repeated physical abuse. Clearly, the presence of an injury alone should not necessarily lead to substantiation. In addition, maltreatment involving risk of physical harm can in many instances be more serious than situations involving actual harm. For instance, a young child repeatedly found wandering the streets alone at night is in a far more precarious situation than a child injured by a parent's belt.

Substantiation rates vary by form of maltreatment. Cases involving physical abuse were less likely to be substantiated than were cases involving neglect or multiple forms of maltreatment. It is not surprising that studies that have used physical abuse as a proxy measure of severity of maltreatment have failed to find that physical abuse was associated with case disposition (Segal & Schwartz, 1985; Lindsey, 1991b). The findings from the present study clearly indicate that future studies of child welfare case disposition should include measures of both severity of injury and form of maltreatment.

The family background variables also proved to be related to case substantiation, even after controlling for the effects of other correlates. Consistent with studies of parent risk factors, both alcohol abuse (Famularo, Stone, Barnum & Wharton, 1986) and inadequate housing (Zuravin, 1986) contributed significantly to decisions to substantiate. The lower substantiation rate for parents with drug abuse problems is difficult to explain. It is possible that these cases fall into a general prevention category, where there is no evidence of a specific form of maltreatment, but where the overall environment is considered nevertheless to be high-risk. Recent studies indicate that the association between drug use and child maltreatment may not be as clear as has been thought, and that alcohol rather than drug abuse appears to be the most salient risk factor (Murphy, Jellinek, Quinn, et al., 1991; Myers, & Kaltenbach, 1992). Many family background variables were not considered. For instance, Johnson and L'Esperance (1984) found that parent cooperation and willingness to accept services was a central consideration in workers' assessments of risk. Future research on child welfare case dispositions needs to consider the importance of family background in assessing maltreatment.

Agency variables—referral source, agency size, and agency location—were also found to be significantly associated with substantiation rates. The strength of this association is mediated by severity of maltreatment, but agency factors appear to have an additional influence on substantiation rates. Several possible explanations can account for this finding. With respect to the strongest predictor, source of referral, one could speculate that the measure of severity of maltreatment used was not sensitive enough to account for differences in cases referred by the police or medical personnel, compared to cases referred by schools. It is possible that other key variables that are not measured in this study, such as parent cooperation, may explain some of these variations. However, it also is likely that source of referral does indeed have an independent effect, given that credibility of the source of referral, and the amount of information provided with the referral should be factored into the investigation. This probably explains the low rate of substantiation for anonymous referrals and for referrals from non-custodial parents. Groenveld and Giovannoni (1977) argue that the effect of source of referral is related to the level of social control exercised by the person making the referral. While this is consistent with the finding that police and medical referrals are more likely to be substantiated, it is not confirmed by the fact that referrals from parents are also more likely to be substantiated, while referrals from teachers are less likely to be substantiated.

The agency size and agency location variations are more difficult to explain. The effect of geographic variables has been established in several previous studies. For instance, Runyan and colleagues (1981) found that geographic area was one of the strongest predictors of child placement. Wolock (1982) found that workers exposed to larger volumes of serious cases in inner city neighbourhoods had higher substantiation thresholds than did workers from suburban neighbourhoods. However, it is unlikely that a similar explanation could account for differences in substantiation rates in Eastern Ontario compared to Western Ontario. Census data for the four regions were compared, but there appears to be no correlation between these population characteristics and substantiation rates. It appears that different standards are applied depending both on geographic location and size of agency.

The best fit regression model developed in this study lead to an overall correct classification of 80% of cases (Kappa=0.58), and was able to account for 36% of the variance in case substantiation decisions. This accuracy of prediction is an improvement over most previous studies. For example, Runyan and colleagues (1981) developed a model of placement decisions based on 250 variables, but were only able to account for 17% of the variance, with 73% of cases correctly classified (Kappa = 0.28). Miller and colleagues (1983) were able to account for only 18% of the variance in predicting emergency placement decisions. In comparing voluntary to court ordered services, Tjaden and Thoennes (1992) were able to predict 76% of decisions to file court petitions (Kappa = 0.56). Giovannoni's (1989) study of child maltreatment investigations was able to account for up to 39% of the variance in decisions to substantiate.

Yet, a substantial proportion of the variance remains unexplained by the study variables. This can be accounted for by several factors. First, the measurement of variables was crude, and does not reflect the finer distinctions made by investigating workers. Second, many important variables, such as credibility of the reporter, child and parents, or general family functioning, were not included in the study. Third, the analysis does not fully account for the complexity of intervention decisions. Future analysis will examine decisions to substantiate maltreatment broken down by age groups and by forms of maltreatment. Finally, no matter how complex the analysis used, and no matter how many variables are considered, the complexity of each individual situation cannot be reduced to a statistical model.

There is no doubt that the deployment of scarce child welfare resources needs to be carefully re-examined. But the growing emphasis on curtailing the perceived arbitrariness of intervention decisions by developing more structured decision-making procedures may not prove to be as fruitful an avenue as some may hope. The concern over the arbitrariness of child welfare decisions may have more to do with methodological limitations in earlier studies of decision-making than any firm evidence that this is a serious problem. The findings from this study indicate that substantiation decisions appear to be consistent with indicators of severity of maltreatment and family functioning.

Funding for this study was provided by the Institute for the Prevention of Child Abuse. Additional funding for the preparation of this paper was provided through the University of Toronto, Connaught Start-Up Grants.

References

Agresti, A. (1990). *Categorical data analysis*, New York: John Wiley & Sons.

Ards, S., & Harrell, A. (1993). Reporting of child maltreatment: A secondary analysis of the national incidence surveys. *Child Abuse and Neglect.* 17, 337–344.

Berry, M. (1991). The assessment of imminence of risk of placement: Lessons from a family preservation program. *Children and Youth Services Review.*13, 239–259.

Besharov, D.J., (1990). *Recognizing child abuse.*New York, NY: The Free Press.

Brassard, M., Germain, R., Hart, S. (1987). *Psychological maltreatment of children and youth.* New York: Pergamon Press.

Eckenrode, J., Powers, J., Doris, J., Munsch, J., & Bolger, N. (1988). Substantiation of child abuse and neglect reports. *Journal-of-Consulting-and-Clinical-Psychology,* 56(1), 9–16.

Erickson, M.F., Egeland, B., & Pianta, R. (1989). Effects of maltreatment on the development of young children. In D. Cicchetti & V. Carlson (Eds.), *Child maltreatment: Theory & research on the causes & consequences of child abuse and neglect.* Cambridge: Cambridge University Press.

Famularo, R., Stone, K., Barnum, R., Wharton, R. (1986). Alcoholism and severe child maltreatment. *American Journal of Orthopsychiatry,* 56(3) 481–485.

Giovannoni, J.M. & Becerra, R.M. (1979). *Defining child abuse.* New York: Free Press.

Giovannoni, J.M. (1989b). Substantiated and unsubstantiated reports of child maltreatment. *Children and Youth Services Review,* 11, 299–318.

Groenveld, L.P. & Giovannoni, J.M. (1977). Disposition of child abuse and neglect cases. *Social Work Research & Abstract,* 13, 24–30.

Hampton, R.L. & Newberger, E.H. (1985). Child abuse incidence and reporting by hospitals: Significance of severity, class and race. *American Journal of Public Health,* 75(1), 56–60.

Hampton, R.L. (1987). Race, class and child maltreatment. *Journal of Comparative Family Studies,* 18(1), 113–126.

Hutchinson, E.D. (1990). Child maltreatment: Can it be defined?. *Social Service Review,* 64(1), 60–78.

Hutchinson, E.D. (1989). Child protective screening decisions: An analysis of predictive factors. *Social Work Research and Abstracts,* 25(3), 9–16.

Johnson, W. & L'Esperance, J. (1984). Predicting the recurrence of child abuse. *Social Work Research & Abstracts,* 20(2), 21–26.

Kammerman, S.B. & Kahn, A.J. (1990). Social services for children, youth, and families in the United States. *Children and Youth Services Review,* 12(2), 1–179.

Katz, M.H., Hampton, R.L., Newberger, E.H., Bowles R., & Snyder, J.C. (1986). Returning children home: Clinical decision making in cases of child abuse and neglect. *American Journal of Orthopsychiatry,* 56(2), 253–262.

Knapp, M., Baines, B., Bryson, D., & Lewis, J. (1987). Modelling the initial placement decision for children received into care. *Children and Youth Services Review,* 9(1), 1–15.

Lindsey, D. (1991). Factors affecting the foster care placement decision: An analysis of national survey data. *American Journal of Orthopsychiatry,* 61(2), 272–281.

Lindsey, D. (1991). Reliability of the foster care placement decision: A review. *Research on Social Work Practice,* 2(1), 65–80.

Lindesy, D. (1994). *The welfare of children.* New York: Oxford University Press

Miller, B., Shireman, J., Burke, P. & Brown, F. (1982). System responses to initial reports of child abuse and neglect cases. *Journal of Social Service Research,* 5(3/4), 95–111.

Murphy, J.M., Jellinek, M., Quinn, D., Smith, G., Poitrast, F., & Goshko, M. (1991). Substance abuse and serious child mistreatment: Prevalence, risk and outcome in a court sample. *Child Abuse and Neglect,* 15(3), 197–221.

Myers, B.J., & Kaltenbach, K. (1992). Cocaine-exposed infants: Myths and misunderstandings. *Zero to Three,* 13(1), 1–5.

Runyan, D.K., Gould, C.L., Trost D.C. & Lada, F.A. (1981). Determinants of foster care placement for the maltreated child. *American Journal of Public Health,* 71(7), 706–710.

Schwab, A.J., Bruce, M.E. & McRoy, R.G. (1986). Using computer technology in child placement decisions. *Social Casework,* 67(6), 359–368.

Segal, U.A., & Schwartz, S. (1985). Factors affecting placement decisions of children following short-term emergency care. *Child Abuse & Neglect,* 9, 543–548.

Seaberg, J.R., & Tolley, E.S., (1986). Predictors of the length of stay in foster care. *Social Work Research & Abstracts,* 22(3), 11–17.

Seaberg, J.R. (1988). Placement in permanency planning: Own home versus foster care. *Social work Research & Abstracts*, 24(4), 4–7.

Schwab, A.J., Bruce, M.E. & McRoy, R.G. (1986). Using computer technology in child placement decisions. *Social Casework*, 67(6), 359–368.

Treiman, D. J., & Yamaguchi, K. (1993). Trends in educational attainment in Japan. In Yossi Shavit, & Hans-Peter Blossfeld (ed.), *Persisting barriers: a Comparative Study of Education Inequality in 13 Countries*. Boulder, Colorado: Westview Press.

Tjaden, P. G., & Thoennes, N. (1992). Predictors of legal intervention in child maltreatment cases. *Child Abuse and Neglect*, 16, 807–821.

Trocmé, N, McPhee, D., Tam, K.K., & Hay, T. (1994). *Ontario incidence study of reported child abuse and neglect*. Toronto: Institute for the Prevention of Child Abuse.

U.S. Department of Health & Human Services. (1981). *Study findings: Study of national incidence and prevalence of child abuse and neglect*. Washington: Author.

U.S. Department of Health & Human Services. (1988). *Study findings: Study of national incidence and prevalence of child abuse and neglect*. Washington: Author.

Wharf, B., (ed.) (1993) *Rethinking child welfare in Canada*. Toronto: McClelland & Stewart.

Winefield, H.R., & Bradley, P. W. (1992). Substantiation of reported child abuse or neglect: Predictors and implications. *Child Abuse and Neglect*, 16, 661–671.

Wolock, I. (1982). Community characteristics and staff judgments in child abuse and neglect cases. *Social Work Research & Abstracts*, 18(2), 9–15.

Zuravin, S.J. (1986). Residential density and urban child maltreatment. *Journal of Family Violence*, 1(4), 307–322.

Zuravin, S.J., (1987). Anonymous reports of child physical abuse: Are they as serious as reports from other sources? *Child Abuse and Neglect*.11, 521–529.

4

Aboriginal Government of Child Welfare Services: Hobson's Choice? *

Douglas Durst, Josephine McDonald and Cecilia Rich

Aboriginal self-government is frequently promoted as a panacea for the host of social problems affecting Native communities. Canadian Aboriginal leaders have consistently sought control over the development and delivery of services directed towards their elders and their children (Stalwick, 1986). Communities in every region of Canada have sought and gained varying degrees of community control of child welfare services (Armitage, 1993; Hodgson, 1993; Howse & Stalwick, 1990; Hudson & Taylor-Henley, 1987; McKenzie & Morrissette, 1993; Ricks et al., 1990; Taylor-Henley & Hill, 1990; Wharf, 1992). This chapter reports on the findings of a two year study examining Aboriginal self-government of child welfare services in two First Nation communities—the Miawpukek Mi'kamawey Mawi'omi (Council of Conne River Micmacs) located on the south coast of Newfoundland, and the Sheshatshit Innu Band located in Nitassinan/Labrador.

A Ladder of Self-Government

The topics of self-determination and self-government conjure strong feelings and deep aspirations among different cultural groups in Canada. Native leaders see the survival of their language and culture as dependent upon the maintenance and continued development of their distinct society. However, there is the mistaken tendency to use the concepts self-government and self-determination interchangeably. Self-determination refers to the right and the ability of a people or a group of peoples to determine their own destiny. Self-determination is both a principle and a practice. First, there must be the legal, political or structural framework necessary to be sovereign and to operate as a supreme authority within a defined geographic area. Second, the self-determining body must have sufficient financial resources, and third, the body must have an adequate social infrastructure—the knowledge, skills and values (competencies) required to make self-determination happen. Self-government, in turn, refers to the decision-making directly affecting a people, spanning political, cultural, economic, and social affairs. Therefore, people can exercise

* In the seventeenth century, a man named Thomas Hobson owned and operated a livery stable in Cambridge, England. When customers came to rent horses, Hobson released the horses in strict order according to their position near the door. As a result, the customer was given no real choice and was forced to accept what was offered or nothing at all.

self-government in making decisions regarding the welfare of its people without being self-determined.

Aboriginal people in the Americas lived as sovereign nations for tens of thousands of years. The right to self-determination has never been formally conceded to the Europeans, nor has the right to control child welfare (First Nations Child and Family Task force, 1993, p. 47). However, absolute self-determination does not exist. No government, Aboriginal or non-Aboriginal, can act in isolation from the larger society. In Canada, power is divided among various levels of government. Federalism is the outcome of the division of powers enacted through the British North America Act (BNA) and lives on in the Constitution Act of 1982. The BNA defines the powers of the respective levels of government (provincial, and federal). Hence, each Canadian municipality and province has the right to self-determination in some affairs and not in others.

Cassidy (1991, p. 7) pointed out that "self-government may be seen as a reflection of sovereignty and self-determination, but it is important to understand that many First Nations also believe ... that some forms of self-government can be a denial of sovereignty." A central component can be some form of power-sharing comparable to a municipal type of structure, and this is the form of Native self-government emerging in some regions of Canada. This situation raises serious concerns for some Aboriginal leaders. "If self-government is going to reflect sovereignty and lead to greater self-determination, the sources of First Nation's powers and the sharing of powers between First Nations and Canadian governments must be expressed in practical arrangements that grow out of nation-to-nation relationships" (Cassidy, 1991, p. 8). Cassidy's point is a challenge to provincial and federal bureaucrats who constructed and managed a social welfare structure, including the child welfare system, that has systematically undermined the sovereignty of Native people (Durst, 1992, p. 191). In addition, the challenge is compounded by Canadian society which views the pursuit of self-determination as "a threat rather than an inextinguishable entitlement" (Cassidy, 1991, p. 9).

There is also an emerging concern among First Nation women that self-government may not promote gender equality. Many Native women have rejected the position of the federal government to only negotiate with Band Councils, demanding that the *Charter of Rights and Freedoms* be applied to all Aboriginal governments. Their arguments are based on the recognition of abuses from past treaties, legislation, and male-dominated leadership of many non-Aboriginal governments.

The goals of self-government, which include child welfare programs, are: 1) to increase local control and decision making; 2) to recognize the diverse needs and cultures of Aboriginal peoples in Canada; and 3) to provide accountability to locally-elected persons (Frideres, 1993, p. 437). These goals can be accomplished to varying degrees depending upon the level of self-government. Figure 4.1 presents a ladder of self-government that has been expanded and adapted from Boisvert (1986), Johnson (1991), and Hudson and Taylor-Henley (1987). There are five levels of self-government with varying degrees of self-determination: federalist autonomy, co-jurisdiction, co-management/delegated, integrated, and benevolent colonialism.

Figure 4.1: A Ladder of Self-Government

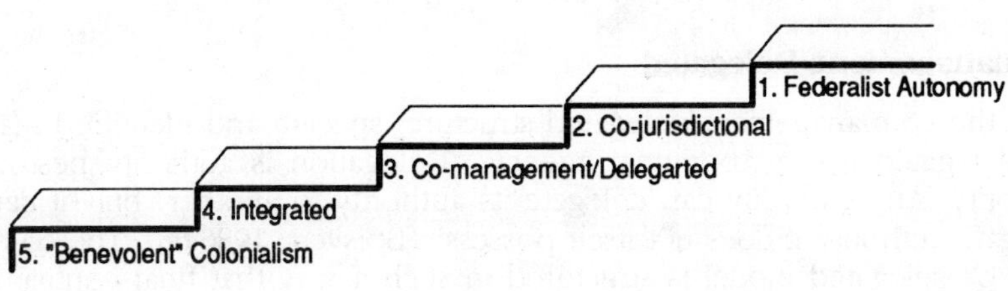

Federalist Autonomy

Most Canadians have an identity that is comprised of more than one cultural or ethnic group, as well as provincial and national identities. How they identify themselves depends upon circumstances. A recent poll found that Newfoundlanders (57%) surpass even Québécois (49%) as identifying with their own province before the country as a whole, with the national average at 22% (Maclean's, 1994). In some jurisdictions, the respective government has exclusive and absolute control. No higher or lower government can interfere, at least directly. Therefore, the establishment of Native government with complete and absolute control over child welfare is congruent with the federal system and a part of the federal structure. The Federation of Saskatchewan Indian Nations is pursuing this model in its plans for child welfare. This approach is not as new or radical a concept as might be thought, since it can be accomplished under amended Canadian federalism.

Co-jurisdiction

It is possible and feasible within the Canadian system to negotiate and implement a co-jurisdictional structure over an identified area. This structure could be a joint and equal partnership or a partnership that recognizes that one party holds exclusive jurisdiction while delegating the responsibilities to another party. An example of this arrangement is the Canadian health care system. The provision of health care is a provincial responsibility but the federal government provides programs and policies effecting the entire country. The Canadian pension program and the unemployment insurance program are national in their delivery but are provincial responsibilities. Yet, the provincial government in Québec has opted out of the federal pension program and sought direct transfer of funds to establish its own program. These co-jurisdictional arrangements require formalized linkages and support systems between the partners.

In 1980, the Spalumcheen Band Council in British Columbia established a unique child welfare agreement. The council passed a bylaw asserting control over all band children including those living off-reserve (Armitage, 1993, p. 160). Although the action appears to exceed the legal mandate of the band, the federal government agreed to fund their efforts and the provincial government respected their authority permitting a co-jurisdictional arrangement. An example of a limited co-jurisdictional agreement regarding Native child welfare can be found in Manitoba where the Hollow Water Council has arranged some control over the legislative and administrative aspects of child welfare services (McKenzie & Morrisette, 1993; Taylor-Henley & Hill, 1990).

Co-management/Delegated

In the co-management/delegated structure, specific and identified matters are delegated to an Aboriginal agency. "Delegation is authority bestowing authority. Any authority can delegate its authority to another" but "it cannot delegate authority it does not itself possess" (Boisvert, 1986:68). The co-managed or delegated model is structured in such a way that final control rests with the senior governing party. Power or responsibility is delegated from one party to another and is not therefore based on an equal partnership. If the parties are in agreement, this arrangement can be established with minimal bureaucratic difficulties and can operate effectively in certain circumstances.

The child welfare tripartite agreements between Native agencies and the provincial and federal governments utilize this structural model. These agreements have the federal government as funder, the provincial government as legislator and authority, and the Indian government as service provider (Hudson & Taylor-Henley, 1987). The final liabilities and responsibilities remain with the province but are co-managed and delegated to the local level, permitting greater local control and decision-making. The current federal policy of the Department of Indian and Inuit Affairs regarding the establishment of Indian Child Welfare Agencies requires the Native organization (band or tribal council) to accept the respective provincial child welfare legislations. Furthermore, as a general rule, the federal government restricts the funding agreement to bands where there are at least 1000 on-reserve children (0–18 years). It is a take-it-or-leave-it policy that not all Native organizations accept. The leaders of the Federation of Saskatchewan Indian Nations have not accepted this position, arguing that their right to protect and care for their children has never been relinquished and the province can not delegate power it does not possess. In Saskatchewan, progress towards the establishment of Native child welfare agencies has been stalled. However, a number of Manitoba Native organizations have agreed to accept provincial legislation and now have the most comprehensive Native child welfare structures in Canada. Studies by McKenzie and Morrisette (1993) and Hudson and Taylor-Henley (1987) provide a comprehensive evaluation of the tripartite agreements in Manitoba.

The Integrated Model

The integrated model incorporates Native input into the existing structures. In child welfare, utilizing Native foster homes, hiring child welfare workers with Native ancestry, and establishing community child welfare advisory committees are examples of how Native input is incorporated. It does not mean significant change to the structures, programs or policies of the mandated government. The Department of Social Services in the Northwest Territories has successfully applied this model to all of its social service programs, incorporating Native advice and direction under provincial-like programs. In the early seventies, territorial authorities in the Department of Social Development actively sought the input of Native organizations and actively employed and trained local Aboriginal community workers to deliver social service programs. Hodgson (1993) describes similar child welfare innovations in the Yukon Territory where a First Nation Justice Council developed intervention plans for department social workers using consensus decision-making. Wharf (1992) provides an example of Aboriginal input in an urban setting through the creation of a Native Child Welfare Unit in Vancouver. The Unit was designed to be active in the developing child welfare policy and procedures and not just limited to the provision of services.

Benevolent Colonialism

Benevolent colonialism fits with the typology although it is not self-government. In the past, programs were imposed by an outside structure with no adaptation or consultation with the consumers of the services. There has been an abundance of literature supporting the argument that child welfare programs were instruments of deliberate and systematic assimilation (Armitage, 1993, p. 134). Moving from the extreme to the more subtle forms of benevolent colonialism in child welfare would include such acts as presenting cultural awareness workshops for white child welfare workers or establishing receiving homes in northern Native communities for children deemed to be in need of protection. Alternatives such as these are improvements over no training for child welfare workers or the dislocation of children to institutions in the southern larger centres but they do represent subtle and possibly insidious forms of colonialism. The fact that they may have been well-meaning makes them no less oppressive.

An examination of the ladder of self-government demonstrates that self-government may not be self-determination. In fact, as some Native leaders argue, some levels of self-government may actually be detrimental to the goals and aspirations of self-determination if they serve to entrap the Aboriginal community into providing services and programs that are dictated by non-Aboriginals. The Native communities of Conne River and Sheshatshit are examined in light of their efforts to gain self-determination, not just self-government, of local affairs.

The Communities

The distinctive nature of the two communities offers a unique opportunity to compare two significantly different Aboriginal communities as they progress towards the common goal of self-determination in respect to governing their child welfare services. The communities represent different cultural groups, possess different histories, and have experienced different types of contacts and relationships with European colonialists, both francophone and anglophone. The legal status and political structures of the bands differ. The Miawpukek Mi'kamawey Mawi'omi (Conne River Band) possess reserve status and their relationship with the federal government is determined by the federal Indian Act (1951, 1985). Until recently the Sheshatshit band of Innu did not have a direct relationship with the federal government and were considered residents of Newfoundland and Labrador according to the Canada/Newfoundland Terms of Agreement of 1949. The latter's political relationships have been shaped by this agreement. Recent arrangements with the federal government have by-passed the province, enabling access to federal support and resources. Culturally and geographically the communities differ. The Conne River Band (population 620) is of Micmac ancestry and is located on the south shore of the island of Newfoundland. Pastore (1978) records the history of this Micmac community, from a white perspective. The Innu of Sheshatshit are Native Indians of the Algonkian linguistic group and their settlement (population 960) is located in the interior of Labrador about 50 kilometers from the community of Happy Valley/Goose Bay.

These communities have adopted different strategies to reach the goal of self-determination. The people of Conne River have been seeking control through co-operation and negotiation, climbing the ladder of self-government one step at a time, moving forward in increments. The Innu strategy has been to gain control through direct confrontation and political pressure—leap-frogging from benevolent colonialism to federalist autonomy. These very different communities afford a unique opportunity to learn about the issues of self-government from two diverse perspectives.

Research Methods

This exploratory study is based on the principles of participatory research. A collaborative process began with the development of the research proposal and continued through to the completion of the project in March 1994 (Durst et al., 1994). Control of the study rested with each Band which hired local researchers to conduct the study in their respective communities. The community researchers began by examining the historical developments of child welfare services in their communities. The findings are based on data from historical records as well as the perceptions of respected elders and community members regarding child welfare and the child rearing practices in each community. Researchers employed focus groups and community meetings to collect data from the community-at-large and to ensure broad participation.

The Findings

The findings indicate that each community has developed its own individualized model for self-government of child welfare programs. The Innu of Sheshatshit do not have status under the Indian Act and are in the pre-negotiation stages of the land claims process. In recent years, the community has been engulfed in a political struggle over recognition of its Aboriginal rights. This conflict has consumed the over-taxed and stressed leadership as well as the community's financial resources. The community has limited choice to determine the extent of community control of child welfare services in light of the serious social and economic problems it faces.

In 1985, the community engaged in its first major conflict with the Department when four Department staff resigned in protest over rigid social assistance policies (Lundy & Gauthier, 1989). The three non-Native professional workers left the community to assume other career options while leaving the Native para-professional unemployed in a community with few employment prospects. Recent conflicts have arisen over the Department's rigid policy regarding the re-unification of adopted children to their parents. Several women who had lost their children to the adoption process years ago are seeking information regarding the whereabouts of their now adult children. The Department maintains its right to withhold information. The anger and frustration of these families permeates the entire community. A "them-us" polarization of emotions remains in the community; the Department is not viewed as a public institution designed to serve the interests of the Innu.

Currently child welfare programs are delivered in Sheshatshit by the provincial Department of Social Services from offices in the community. The offices are conveniently situated in the centre of the community but are located in a cramped renovated house. Social programs such as social assistance, youth corrections, and child and family services have mainly been provided by a non-Native social worker and a Native local homecare worker. The social worker provided the professional aspect of child welfare service and was heavily dependent on the homecare worker for the community and cultural context. In 1993, the Department up-graded and reclassified the homecare worker position to community service worker, recognizing the important contribution this individual made. At various times, the Department encouraged community input and participation through consultation and advisory committees. These efforts have had limited success and represent an effort by the provincial Department to assume an integrated and incremental strategy to self-government.

Only one social worker and one community service worker coordinate all child protection assessment services, child and family preventive and support services, adoption and foster care, services to the disabled and handicapped, and supports to single mothers. These two staff have limited time and the crisis orientation and immediacy of child protection services consistently dominates their workload undermining any effort to expand services into the prevention and support area. The Innu operate an eight-bed group home for young offenders under a contract with the Department. Most of the youth are from Davis Inlet, a neighbouring Innu community, and the home struggles at incorporating Innu culture into its program. Residents in the community complain about the lack of organization and programming for the youth; however, they acknowledge that it does represent an effort towards self-government, albeit at an integrative level.

The Micmac people of Conne River present a contrast. After a long period of community generated political action to gain recognition by the governments of Canada and Newfoundland as Indian people, Conne River was included in 1973 as a native community under a cost shared federal/provincial agreement. A 1984 federal Order in Council registered the Conne River Micmac under The Indian Act. In 1987, the Samiajij Miawpukek Indian reserve, an enlargement of the colonial reserve of 1860, was created.

The Miawpukek Band has always maintained that the Government of Newfoundland and Labrador, and the Government of Canada, must recognize the inherent right of the Miawpukek Band to self government. This includes the inherent responsibility for child welfare services. In the early 1980s, the Miawpukek Band established a small medical clinic to provide for the health needs of the community. Today that "clinic" has grown into Conne River Health and Social Services, an integrated service delivery agency, that employs over twenty-six people in the areas of nursing, social work, addictions, nutrition, homecare, family violence, child and family services, dental, emergency health, computer services, non-insured health benefits and clerical support.

In 1990 the Band decided, given the slow pace at which the recognition of the inherent right to self government was proceeding, to pursue a delegation of authority for child welfare services. In 1991, the Band entered bi-lateral negotiations with the Province for an initial agreement on shared jurisdiction of child welfare services and with the Government of Canada for funding to create the Miawpukek Child and Family Services Program. The agreement with the Department (1993) has the Miawpukek Band assuming responsibility for prevention and treatment services, while the Department maintains jurisdiction over assessment and protection, albeit in consultation with the Band. This Agreement also sees the placement of a provincially employed child protection social worker, jointly recruited by the Band and the Department and paid for by the Band, on reserve with the Miawpukek Child and Family Services Program. The Miawpukek Band and the Department are currently in the process of opening negotiations for the eventual graduated transfer of child protection services to the Band.

The Agreement with the Government of Canada (1993) saw the funding of the Miawpukek Child and Family Services Program and the recruitment of two Band members as family care workers. Services are provided to families in a team approach by these workers, the child protection social worker, the Band social worker, the family violence worker, the addictions counsellors and nursing staff.

The Miawpukek Band has a policy of only recruiting non-band members for those positions where band members do not yet possess the necessary skills or training. It is required, however, that all non-native employees participate in the development and training of a Band member who will eventually assume the full duties and responsibilities of these positions.

Both Sheshashit and Conne River are dependent on the Newfoundland government to provide child assessment and protection services. In Conne River, the Departmental social worker delivers services from Milltown which is a short distance across the inlet but about a 40 minute drive around the bay, providing the roads are in good condition. In Sheshatshit, services are provided in the Department office located in the village. The Council has just negotiated shared control of protection and assessment services, making these services more sensitive and culturally relevant to the community. In Sheshatshit, the community members reported that the department guidelines for assessing the need for child protection are inappropriate. As well, there is a serious lack of communication between the parents and child welfare officials, in spite of the presence of Innu workers employed by the Department. It is believed that court reports written by the child welfare officers are prepared with little or no community input or consultation. The way in which apprehensions are completed is a concern for many parents. The heavy hand of a police escort, for example, intimidates the residents.

Child care is provided in both communities through extended family including grandparents and other relatives. With the lack of housing, single parents frequently live with their parents and their parents become active in the child's rearing. In Conne River, a temporary Day Care Centre (free of charge) was opened during the summer months of 1991 but few people took advantage of this offer. In 1992, day care was again offered with even less of a response than the previous year. It was concluded that formal day care was not needed even though more women were in the work force. Some women, however, reported that there was a need for specialized or therapeutic day care for children with special needs.

Respondents in Sheshatshit identified child care as a source of community irritation. The financial aid provided to approved foster parents is substantially greater than the aid provided for informal child support (regular social assistance). Social assistance is grossly inadequate and does not provide sufficient money for the proper food, clothing, and shelter which these children deserve. If the child is in formal care, however, and is considered a ward of the province, abundant resources are made available to the foster parents. This situation penalizes the natural community support network and reinforces formal foster care. This complaint could be addressed if the special needs allowance under social assistance was increased but the community has no control over the social assistance program. Thirty-one Innu parents in Sheshatshit provide child care for other parents' children. These care-giving parents consistently reported that the social workers do not make regular visits with these families and assess the progress of the children. The social workers do not know the child's history, the family background, or the family providing the care. Regular and frequent home visits are needed. Interestingly, these care givers asked for more involvement from department social workers. The present practice leads to a bizarre situation. To get adequate benefits, the community must abandon its traditional support system and abide by the department's regulations, which often are in conflict with the community's goals of self-determination.

There were no specific services or facilities that address violence against women and children in either community. However, in Conne River the Northern Native Alcohol and Drug Program (NNADAP) workers and medical center social workers were on-call to assist with advice, offer support, or to locate emergency accommodations. In Conne River, the Band initiated a family violence needs assessment that was completed in the winter of 1993 (Conne River, 1993). The people interviewed were forthright and candid about the kinds of abuse that were occurring within the community. Community people have always been aware of abuse but avoided the potential conflict that would be generated by addressing the problem. The assessment found that women did not want a facility where only emergency services were provided for victims of abuse such as a crisis centre or a temporary safe house. The women sought a facility where a variety of services, supports, and resources were available to all women in the community. They would like to see a community Women's Centre where both emergency services and ongoing support could be accessed. No similar research has been undertaken in Sheshatshit, but its residents reported that all forms of family violence including physical and sexual assaults against women and children have been occurring. Generally, it has been men who are the perpetrators and more offences have been reported in recent years. In the past these crimes occurred but were not reported because of shame, guilt, fear of further reprisals, or a wish to avoid community conflict. There is a serious lack of services for both the victims and offenders of family violence (Durst, 1991). The lack of support services and counselling was reported as a major concern for the community. One suggestion was a crisis line where people could call for help and the listener would be able to speak the Innu language and understand the community context.

Conclusions

Each community researcher compiled concluding statements that reflect the beliefs and concerns of the respective communities.

Statement from the Innu People of Sheshatshit

There exists a general frustration with the officials of the Department of Social Services. There is a lack of understanding of Innu way of life, values, customs, and language. The people want a greater appreciation for their Aboriginal community and Innu history from the staff of the Department. The community is determined to gain control over the programs and policies affecting their lives. The Innu of Sheshatshit want to make their own decisions, to assume greater responsibilities, and to take control of the provision of social services. This goal of self-government of social services is based on an long list of criticisms of how the Department has delivered its programs in the past. In addition, the Innu do not understand the Department's policies and procedures and find them confusing and contradictory. The Innu also believe that the department staff do not understand the Innu. Both the social workers and the people feel the tension and frustration. These specific recommendations were made. The Innu people:

- Want improved social assistance benefits for those needing assistance.
- Want job creation rather than being dependent on social assistance.
- Want more recreational activities for their children and youth.
- Want more and improved housing units.
- Want more control in the decision-making affecting community life.
- Want to develop their own policies.
- Want improved financial support for child welfare allowances.
- Believe that the family providing child care should receive support payments regardless of whether or not the child is a member of the extended family.
- Believe that social assistance is an entitlement while waiting for U.I.C. benefits, Old Age Pension, and Widow's Benefits.
- Believe that Traditional adoption should replace departmental adoptions for Innu children.
- Want improved social assistance benefits for single parents.

Statement from the Micmac People of Conne River

Self-government starts from the grass roots—people, elders, talking with the community on where you want to go—not from the government down. Education should focus on who we are and fully understand and appreciate what we have. We have to start to realize how important our ancestors are and know and understand our treaties, customs, and culture. We have to understand what it means when we say "Miawpukek Mi'Kamawey"—"I'm a Micmac and my nation's government is Mi'Kamawey, Grand Council." We have to come to consensus in the community on what self-government is and should contain. Every nation is different and should pick the route that gives them the easiest access. There is no set model, except the basic ground rule—know who you are. You have to have trained people in the community so you don't have to bring anyone from the outside to do the work. Train the people within the community to do the job to prepare for self-government and controlling programs. We have climbed the hill, but in the process we have left behind some vital elements such as a visible Indian Community, and understanding about ourselves and what it means. Everybody has to get involved in order for self-government to work.

Self-government is an inherent, national right that all Indian people have to control their own affairs. The government has to recognize that the Indian people have this right to self-government. Until the Indian people themselves assert this powerful right, nothing will be accomplished. Self-government means having the resources to enable the community to get money to implement, decide and run our own programs. It is our right to hunt and fish anywhere on the Island of Newfoundland. It means being able to do all these things without going outside to ask for any help from any governments. We have the right to be self-governed, we have been saying this for the last 20 years. But, why are we not doing it? We do not have the resources. Why is Conne River so far along in regards to being self-governed? It was because we have a lot of people who are willing to fight for what is theirs. When we went to the government, we were well prepared; research was done before anything happened. People worked hard at getting these things and did not give up when the government said no. They opened the doors themselves and made contacts. For any First Nation seeking self-government, know exactly what you're looking for, be prepared, get the facts, obtain the money, and train people to be able to carry out programs.

Concluding Comments

The communities are at different levels and stages on their independent paths to self-determination. The people of Sheshatshit are at a stage when they have begun to identify problems. They consistently report the inadequacies of the existing social service system and most of their complaints focus on the lack of sufficient resources. They want more money for social assistance, child care services, and housing. More resources are demanded with little discussion about how existing resources could be used more efficiently. There is at present little concern for local control. A general impression exists that the community is economically dependent on the provincial government. Few contacts have been developed with the federal government, with the major orientation long established towards St. John's, Newfoundland. The residents complained bitterly about the Department but many community members were requesting greater Department involvement. When asked about taking control of their programs, many residents were silent, having never considered such possibilities.

The situation in Conne River is considerably different. The community takes pride in boasting about its progress towards self-determination. They contend that they already have self-government. They are seeking ways to work towards self-determination. They are embroiled in consultation and negotiation of further control of child welfare programs. The Micmac people of Conne River believe they have made considerable progress and want to continue the expansion of services under the Band administration. The Micmac people are striving for less provincial interference and greater Band control. The path to self-determination is not the same for all Native groups and it must be kept in mind that all communities are not at the same stage. Diversity must be expected.

Hobson's choice? How much real control has each community in seeking its goal of self-government of child welfare services? To a large extent, it is no real choice at all. There is a limit to the amount of self-government permitted by the funding source. The Band must accept provincial legislation in order to receive federal funds to implement child welfare programs. Hence self-government is restricted to a co-managed/delegated model. The path to self-government is also predetermined by a series of related circumstances or conditions. One of the most obvious conditions is the availability of leadership. The community needs competent and dedicated individuals who are committed to completing the arduous process of gaining greater control of child welfare services. Each community does have its competent leaders but each community is limited both by the number of individuals and the demands placed upon them. The same individuals are consistently called upon to assume leadership responsibilities and these leaders are over-taxed, leading often to burn-out. Leader burn-out impedes the process to self-government.

The process of self-government that leads to greater control requires the collaboration of equal partners among the political stakeholders. Collaboration, negotiation, and consultation are necessary to generate the tripartite agreements between the three stakeholders (the Band, the federal, and the provincial governments) and a key element to this process is a sense of mutual respect. A process of political efficacy must occur within the community to achieve this state of collaboration. The community must achieve a level of empowerment that is recognized, acknowledged, and assumed within the community and, just as importantly, beyond the community by both the federal and provincial authorities. The community has to assume control first and that control has to be accepted by the respective governments and in both communities. The struggle for status and the achievement of land entitlement has empowered the people of Conne River and revived a Micmac spirit in the community. In Sheshatshit, the struggle for land claims and a long standing conflict against low-level military flying over Innu land has solidified the community and facilitated the development of community leaders. The process of protesting and the nature of the struggle itself has had a positive residual effect in developing a sense of empowerment both in the leaders and the community as a whole.

There is a danger, however, that a community will encounter roadblocks and revert to the strategy of conflict which undermines and ultimately destroys the collaborative process based on the mutual respect and equality of the three governments. This would be a move backwards in the path to self-government. The Innu of Sheshatshit seem to be stalled at an integrated level of self-government because of the continuing conflict in negotiations and the lack of a sense of equality among players. In Conne River, on the other hand, the Band leadership has led the community to a delegated model of child welfare services with a vision of greater future control.

The level of self government that a community seeks depends on a number of factors. First, a community that is moving forward requires a sense of political efficacy. The leadership must have the personal strength and mental health to gain the respect and support of the community members which may involve the leaders themselves in a personal healing process. But, before the process can begin, the community must have resolved the political struggle with the external system and begun the process of negotiation as equal stakeholders. This process requires that the provincial and federal officials view the community leaders as partners, hence changing their approach to negotiation from a colonial orientation to a relationship of equals. The community leaders must be able to shift their orientation from the political struggle to the social needs of the community. There is a shift in community direction from political advocacy to social service as the need to address social concerns increases as a community objective. Finally, the entire process is currently capped at a co-management/delegated level of self-government by the federal government's position of insisting on provincial legislation being the final authority. Currently, the path to self-government is very much a Hobson's choice—not much choice at all.

References

Armitage, A. (1993). Family and child welfare in First Nation communities. In B. Wharf (Ed.). *Rethinking child welfare in Canada* (pp. 131–171). Toronto: McClelland and Stewart, Inc.

Boisvert, D. A. (1986). *Forms of Aboriginal self-government.* Kingston, Ontario: Institute of Intergovernmental Relations.

Cassidy, F. (1991). *Aboriginal self-determination.* Halifax, Nova Scotia: The Institute for Research on Public Policy.

Conne River Health and Social Services. (1993). Finding our way: Supporting families in crisis. Conne River, Newfoundland: Conne River Health and Social Services.

Durst, D. (1991). Conjugal violence: Changing attitudes in two northern Native communities. *Community Mental Health Journal, 27*(5), 359–373.

Durst, D. (1992). The road to poverty is paved with good intentions: Social interventions and indigenous peoples. *International Social Work, 32*(2), 191–202.

Durst, D., McDonald, J., & Rich, C. (1994). Aboriginal self-government and social services: Finding the path to empowerment. Conne River Reserve, Newfoundland: Council of the Conne River Micmacs.

First Nations Child and Family Task Force (1993). Children first, our responsibility. Winnipeg, Manitoba, Report of the First Nation's Child and Family Task Force.

Frideres, J. S. (1993). *Native peoples in Canada.* Scarborough, Ontario: Prentice Hall Canada Inc.

Hodgson, M. (1993). Rural Yukon: Innovations in child welfare. *The Social Worker, 61*(4), 155–156.

Howse, Y., & Stalwick, H. (1990). Social work and the First Nation movement: Our children, our culture. In B. Wharf (Ed.), *Social work and social change in Canada* (pp. 79–113). Toronto: McClelland and Stewart Inc.

Hudson, P. , & Taylor-Henley, S. (1987). *Indian provincial relationships in social welfare: Northern issues and future options.* Winnipeg: Faculty of Social Work, University of Manitoba.

Innu Nation & Mushuau Innu Band Council. (1992). Gathering voices: Finding strength to help our children. Utshimasits, Nitassinan (Davis Inlet, Labrador): Innu Nation.

Johnson, I. V. B. (1991). Sharing power: How can First Nations work? In F. Cassidy (Ed.), *Aboriginal self-determination* (pp. 78–80). Halifax, Nova Scotia: The Institute for Research on Public Policy and Oolichan Books, Vancouver.

Lajeunesse, T. (1993). *Community holistic circle healing, Hollow Water First Nations.* Ottawa: Solicitor General Canada.

Lundy, C., & Gauthier, L. (1989). Social work practice and the master-servant relationship. *Le Travailleur/The Social Worker, 57,* 190–194.

MacLean's (1994). How we differ. January 3, p. 11.

McKenzie, B., & Hudson, P. (1985). Native children, child welfare, and the colonization of Native people. In K. L. Levitt & B. Wharf (Eds.), *The Challenge of Child Welfare* (pp. 125–141). Vancouver, British Columbia: University of British Columbia Press.

McKenzie, B. (1991). Decentralization in Winnipeg: Assessing the effects of community-based child welfare services. *Canadian Review of Social Policy/Revue canadienne de politique sociale, 27,* 57–66.

McKenzie, B., & Morrisette, V. (1993). Aboriginal child and family services in Manitoba: Implementation issues and the development of culturally appropriate Services. Paper presented to 6th Conference on Social Welfare Policy. St. John's, Newfoundland.

Pastore, R. T. (1978). *Newfoundland Micmacs: A history of their traditional life.* St. John's, NF: Newfoundland Historical Society.

Ricks, F., Wharf, B., & Armitage, A. (1990). Evaluation of Indian child welfare: A different reality. *Canadian Review of Social Policy/Revue canadienne de politique sociale.* 25, 41–46.

Stalwick, H. (1986). Demonstration of strategies for change: A review of Indian and Native social work education in Canada. Regina, Saskatchewan: Taking Control Project. University of Regina, Social Administration Research Unit, Faculty of Social Work.

Taylor-Henley, S., & Hill, E. (1990). Treatment and healing: An evaluation of community holistic circle healing. Hollow Water first Nations, Manitoba.

Wharf, B. First Nation control of child welfare services. In B. Wharf (Ed.) *Communities and social policy in Canada* (pp. 95–123). Toronto: McClelland and Stewart, Inc.

Zapf, M. K. (1993). Contracts and covenants in social work education: Considerations for Native outreach programs. *LeTravailleur/The Social Worker, 61*(4), 150–154.

5

Child Welfare Standards in First Nations: A Community-Based Study

Brad McKenzie, Esther Seidl and Norman Bone

First Nations' control of the delivery of child welfare services has evolved since the early 1980s as a response to growing concerns over loss of Aboriginal children to the conventional child welfare system and to non-Aboriginal caregivers (Johnston, 1983), widespread awareness of the role of the dominant child welfare system in the colonization of Aboriginal people (McKenzie & Hudson, 1985), and the importance of Aboriginal control of services as an aspect of self-government (Ponting, 1986). By 1991 a delegated model of authority had been adopted by more than 200 First Nations Bands across the country (Armitage, 1993, p. 155), and fully mandated First Nations child and family services agencies have been in place throughout Manitoba since the early 1980s. Within these regional agencies, generally organized under Tribal Council authorities, a decentralized, community-based model of service is common. Governance structures include an agency board, often composed of Chiefs from participating communities, and child and family service committees that provide advice and assistance to agency staff within each community. Services are generally provided by a combination of community-based staff, who provide a broad range of generic services, and regionally-based supervisory and specialist staff.

The tripartite model adopted in Manitoba involves federal funding, provincial responsibility for standards in accordance with provincial legislation, and First Nations administration and delivery of services. Provincial jurisdiction over legislation and standards, and related requirements for accountability, have been contentious issues. Indeed, the initial acceptance of these arrangements by First Nations has always been regarded as an interim measure, and the longer term goal of distinct standards and legislation for First Nations has remained an important priority for many. Existing programs have received favourable reviews (Hudson & McKenzie, 1984; Coopers & Lybrand Consulting Group, 1987; Hudson & Taylor-Henley, 1987) but more recent attention has been directed to service delivery problems (Teichroeb, 1992, September 5; Giesbrecht, 1992). Three general problems are the high number of First Nations children in care, concerns about service quality, and alleged political interference by First Nations governments.

The over-representation of Aboriginal children in care has been attributed to the interventionist role of conventional child welfare authorities. Although children are now in more community-based and culturally-appropriate placements, the evolution of First Nations control over such services has not resulted in a reduction of children coming into care. For example, between 1987 and 1990, a 30% increase in children in care was reported by First Nations agencies in Manitoba (BDO Ward Mallette, 1991, p. 28). This trend should not be surprising. The lack of child welfare services on reserves prior to the 1980s, widespread recognition of physical and sexual abuse within First Nations communities, poor economic and social conditions, the limited funding available for prevention, the lack of complementary social services, and the relatively recent adoption of a community-based service model are likely to contribute to higher case findings.

Service quality concerns and the impact of political interference are two closely related concerns. Urban-based Aboriginal women's groups were the first to publicly express concerns about the impact of political interference on services provided to women and children by First Nations politicians. Allegations of abuse cover-ups and the protection of relatives were highlighted in the highly publicized inquest into the suicide of an adolescent in the care of one agency (Giesbrecht, 1992). Subsequently, First Nations agencies established a working group which developed conflict of interest guidelines and procedures. Concerns about political interference within some communities remain a contentious issue but the report of First Nations' Child and Family Task Force (1993) paid little attention to this issue in recommending a more autonomous and localized service model.

Within specific communities, innovative service approaches have been adopted (Taylor-Henley & Hill, 1990) and a quality assurance review of one First Nations agency provides evidence of high quality services (McKenzie, 1994). However, most service approaches reflect an adherence to conventional models, which are reinforced by existing legislation, standards, and funding arrangements. The development of new, more culturally appropriate standards and models of practice requires time, resources, and knowledge. In First Nations communities this process is complicated by the high demand for crisis services, recognition that many traditional cultural practices have been lost by exposure to residential schools and other assimilative instruments of the dominant society, and limited financial resources.

This chapter describes a community-based approach to the development of Aboriginal child welfare standards in the nine First Nations communities served by West Region Child and Family Services. The participatory research process, launched in June, 1993, by the Board of the agency, is designed to identify standards of child welfare practice which incorporate the community values and customs of First Nations. Results provide guidance both for the provision of services under existing legislation and for the development of policies and standards which may involve substantial departures from provincial policy.

The issue of standards is particularly important in child welfare. The nature of practice involves the intervention of the state, or an alternate authority, in mediating the rights between children and their parents or in intervening to protect the rights and interests of children who may be at risk. Such intervention cannot be arbitrary if the legitimacy of such action is to be recognized, and standards provide criteria for determining this. Standards also provide a basis for examining and measuring practice which in turn can stimulate service improvement, a tool for planning, organizing and administering services, content for teaching and training, and a means of promoting how services may more effectively meet the needs of children (Child Welfare League of America, 1989).

Conceptual Issues

Three issues were considered in planning this study. The first was the theoretical basis for the development of a distinct set of standards to guide child and family service practice in First Nations communities. A second was the relationship of standards to historical and contemporary service issues and experiences. Finally, a research strategy which would engage community members in a longer term change initiative was required.

Arguments for distinct Aboriginal standards of child welfare practice are both political and cultural. Political arguments are based on historical experiences with institutions of the dominant society, including the child welfare system, as mechanisms which oppressed and attempted to assimilate Aboriginal people. These arguments conclude that to achieve liberation it is necessary to achieve self government, including full control over institutions providing services to Aboriginal people and the standards by which those services are to operate. Cultural arguments are based on a recognition of distinct and shared Aboriginal values and practices and the need for culturally appropriate services. There is now general acceptance that early First Nations societies embraced a more holistic, interdependent lifestyle, a social and political structure based on extended families and the clan system, and a decision-making process based on sharing and the building of consensus (Clarkson, Morrissette & Regallet, 1992). However, it is less clear whether such differences are retained today, particularly in First Nations communities located in close proximity to non-Aboriginal communities. The difficulty involves defining traditional Aboriginal cultural values as they are practised today following almost four centuries of contact. While Aboriginal people do not embrace a single philosophy, fundamental differences in the world views of dominant Anglo-European and Aboriginal cultures have been documented (Hamilton & Sinclair, 1991). Specific differences include a greater emphasis on group welfare, group and family reciprocity, harmony with situational circumstances and other persons, teaching through modelling, and pragmatic action among First Nations peoples (Nofz, 1988; DuBray, 1985; Brant, 1990). Beliefs and customs influence behavior and the significance of spirituality, ceremonies, rituals and the use of Elders and extended family have been well-documented (Red Horse, 1980a; Cross, 1986; Edwards & Edwards, 1980). This has contributed to increased use of traditional practices in intervention, including the use of healing circles, sweat lodges, pipe ceremonies, and the medicine wheel (Timpson et al., 1988; Longclaws, 1994).

Traditional values and practices can be used to inform the development of child and family service standards even when communities identify differentially with traditional aspects of culture. Red Horse (1980b) distinguished between traditional, non-traditional, and pan-traditional family lifestyle patterns although he noted that Indian core values may be retained regardless of lifestyle. Morrissette, McKenzie and Morrissette (1993) outlined a similar model in identifying individuals who express values and customs which can be described as traditional, others who may be described as neo-traditional because they express a blend of traditional and non-traditional values, and those who are non-traditional either because they have adopted dominant society values or have become alienated from both mainstream and traditional Aboriginal societies. This model recognizes the different and often conflicting influences emerging in communities between those who adhere to Judeo-Christian values and those who advocate a return to more traditional Aboriginal values and customs. A related issue is Popkewitz's (1988) observation that, in a minority-majority context, it is seldom clear which elements of culture belong to the dispossessed as original aspects of their lifestyle and which have been formed in response to dominant cultures and power relations. These realities suggest that the values, beliefs, and standards of action which shape contemporary Aboriginal lifestyle must be understood within a dynamic context, recognizing both differences among individuals and communities, and the fact that these may evolve or change more quickly than those associated with the dominant society. This requires an approach to standards development as a continuing process, and one that needs to include extensive community input and involvement.

The relationship between standards and service delivery is both subtle and highly complex. In the Indian Child and Family Services Standards Project in British Columbia (First Nations Congress, 1992), researchers found the need to incorporate discussions about service delivery issues because child rearing, family roles, and parenting are shaped by both historical and current relations between First Nations and governments, religious organizations, and social agencies. In designing this study the interplay between service and standards issues was recognized in developing an interview guide which included questions addressing both topics. In addition, a separate questionnaire, dealing exclusively with agency performance and service issues, was designed and administered at an agency workshop involving representatives from each participating community. Finally, the development of standards as an ongoing, evolutionary process required a research design that stressed community education and involvement, and not simply community input.

Method

The research strategy was primarily qualitative (Patton, 1990) and participatory (Cassara, 1985) in engaging communities in a process designed to shape their own distinct standards of child welfare practice. The participatory components of this design included extensive focus group interviews in each community during two rounds of data collection. Stewart and Shamdasani (1990, p. 16) outline several advantages to the use of focus groups. Advantages important to this project were the open response format which provided an opportunity to obtain large amounts of data in the respondent's own words, (allowing for deeper levels of meaning and important connections), the opportunity for respondents to react to and build upon the responses of others, and the ability to obtain extensive information at less cost than individual interviews. An interview guide was constructed to elicit responses related to such topics as the definition of a family, signs of abuse and neglect, out of home placement preferences, and the role of culture in the provision of child and family services. The interview guide was then pretested with a steering committee representative of the groups to be interviewed and revised to include thirteen general topic areas. Focus group interviews were organized in eight of the nine communities served by the agency. Relatively homogenous groups were organized in seven communities. Separate interviews were conducted with Elders, Chief and Council members; local child and family service committee members and community staff; foster parents, natural parents and homemakers; and youth (age 13 to 18). In the final community a combined focus group was conducted due to the small size of this community. Twenty-seven group interviews were conducted, each one lasting between two and three hours. Each focus group included between 8 and 16 individuals, and more than 200 individuals participated in the study.

Each interview was audio-taped and transcribed for analysis. Data analysis involved a series of steps to categorize open-ended responses; these procedures reflect steps generally recommended in the classification and organization of qualitative data (Patton, 1990; Miles & Huberman, 1984; Krippendorf, 1980). Initially, interviews were read by the project staff and descriptive codes were created to capture the range of responses to questions. This was an incremental process and led to the development of more than 300 descriptive variables which could be used to categorize responses to questions. For example, respondents were asked the following question: "How would you define the term family?" Responses which emerged allowed data to be coded and categorized as a) nuclear family, b) extended family, and c) the whole community is like a family. All interviews were then coded and tests for inter-rater reliability were completed on every fifth interview. Adjustments in the approach to coding were made as required and acceptable rates of reliability were achieved. The approach to analysis was inductive in allowing patterns and themes to emerge from the data. As coding was completed, passages were highlighted to illustrate both the range of responses and common responses as directly expressed by participants. Data reduction involved the transfer of important participant responses and researcher comments to a word processor allowing data to be sorted and organized relative to questions and respondent groups. Coded responses were also recorded as nominal data and summarized for each group and community. This enabled the identification of common themes and responses for groups (N=27), communities and the full sample of respondents.

Following analysis and completion of a summary of results, a second round of community consultation occurred. In these interviews, feedback on findings occurred, and further input and direction were received. Specific service standards were developed, and the process followed in the study is likely to lead to ongoing community involvement in the implementation of service improvements and policy change.

Results

Service Concepts in Child Protection

The service concepts that emerged from this research are summarized in Table 5.1. When asked to define their family, 25 of 26 groups that responded stated that relatives such as aunts, uncles, cousins and grandparents were "their family." However, the definition of a family can overlap, and 12 groups identified a nuclear family constellation. Of particular interest was the fact that 10 groups identified the whole community as a kind of family. Custom adoption, defined as the informal placement of children with family or friends, was identified as a familiar practice. As noted by one participant, "people who lived or were raised up with us are adopted into the family."

Table 5.1: Service Concepts in Child Protection

Concept	Most Common Responses
1. Defining Family (N=26)	Includes extended family (non-relatives included as family) Nuclear or immediate family members Community is family
2. Defining the Best Interests of the Child (N=25)	Involves providing good physical care Involves providing good emotional care Involves providing guidance Involves providing safety and protection
3. Defining Neglect (N=25)	Absence of adequate physical care Absence of guidance (supervision and discipline) Absence of emotional care (bonding and nurturing)
4. Indicators of Physical Abuse (N=21)	Unusual marks or brusises Child is often afraid or angry Acting out behabior
5. Indicators of sexual Abuse (N=19)	Child is often afraid or angry Inappropriate sexual behavior

Notes:
(1) For each concept the number of groups who participated in discussing the concept is noted in parenthesis.
(2) Responses are limited to those most frequently reported and these are listed in order, beginning with the most popular item.

Respondents gave generally equal weight to the provision of emotional care, physical care, and guidance in describing the best interests of children. These three general criteria are not markedly different than those identified in present legislation and standards but the teaching of language and traditional values and customs were defined as a critical component of appropriate guidance. Traditional values of respect, sharing, caring, trust and mutual assistance were also repeatedly mentioned as examples of preferred standards of emotional care.

Inadequate physical care and guidance, followed closely by a lack of quality emotional care, were most likely to be associated with child neglect. In-home support services were the preferred measure of intervention in circumstances involving neglect. However, out-of-home placement was advocated if parents do not respond to support services, if they have been warned and fail to respond, or if the level of neglect is too severe. Commonly recognized indicators of physical abuse included abnormal marks or bruises and symptomatic responses like anger, fear, or acting-out behavior. The use of moderate physical discipline, such as spanking on the hands or buttocks, was supported by most groups, and many felt that current policies on child abuse undermined the ability of parents to use reasonable methods of discipline. However, some were opposed to physical discipline, and respondents were divided on whether physical discipline was a traditional Ojibway practice.

Indicators of sexual abuse identified by community respondents included unusual expressions of fear or anger by children and the expression of inappropriate sexual behavior toward others. Most respondents expressed the view that services for sexual abuse needed to be more highly specialized than those available for other forms of abuse, and that it was a particularly difficult issue to deal with in their communities. A high priority was attached to services for sexual abuse because it was a problem that affected so many people. As one respondent stated "sexual abuse has been learned over time and we need time to heal ... In some way it has touched each one of us." Although genuine concern was expressed for the offender, and the need for more offender-focused services was identified, there were different views on where such services should be provided. As noted by one respondent, "in our traditional circles ... nobody should be outside the circle." However, others expressed the concern that the needs of the victim may be neglected if both are treated within the same community. In circumstances involving incest, the offender, not the victim, should be removed from the home. If this was not possible, the victim should be taken into care. Respondents were more likely to advocate placement in cases of abuse than neglect.

A wide range of support services were advocated in situations involving abuse and neglect, and it was the general consensus that these should be provided before placement becomes necessary. The importance of support services was recognized even when the child was removed. The range of services identified included individual counselling, parent education, sharing and healing circles, cultural programming, youth and day care services, and specialized services for the prevention and treatment of sexual abuse.

Placement Resources

In the early 1980s, Manitoba First Nations outlined preferred placement options for out of home care. Priorities, in order of preference, were the extended family, families within the child's community of origin, families within other First Nations communities in the Tribal Council area, First Nations families elsewhere, and non-First Nations caregivers as a last resort. This policy was widely adopted, and was later incorporated as a provincial standard for the placement of all Aboriginal children. Interview questions were designed to obtain feedback on this policy, and the need for further refinement or changes. These findings are summarized in Table 5.2.

Extended family placements within the community were ranked first by all adult groups. Extended family placements outside the community and First Nations foster home placements within the community were given relatively equal weight by adults. First Nations foster homes outside the community were ranked fourth, and non-First Nations homes were ranked as the least preferred option. Youth groups gave relatively equal weighting to extended family placements outside the community and First Nations foster homes in the community. Extended family placements in the community were ranked third by youths and they expressed about equal preference for non-relative First Nations homes outside the community and non-First Nations homes. It is of interest to note that youth were less opposed than adults to non-First Nations homes. Two explanations may account for this difference. First, adult groups were somewhat more likely to support community connections, along with family and culture, as a necessary component of bonding. Second, adults were more conscious of the loss of children from their communities in the 1960s and 1970s, and the fact that many of these children experienced difficulties both in outside placements and in attempting to reintegrate within their communities of origin. For example, one adult respondent observed that children who returned from the United States had "lost their identity ... the community

Table 5.2: Placements Protocols and Planning

Concept	Most Common Responses
1. Placement Preferences (N=25)	Extended family in community Extended family outside the community First Nations foster home in the community First Nations foster home outside the community Non-First Nations foster home
2. Placement Planning (N=18)	Birth family to be involved Extended family to be involved Child to be involved
3. Required Foster Parent Qualities (N=25)	Ability to provide good emotional care (respect, love) Stability (no alcohol or marital problems) Good parenting skills Treat all children equally Good communication skills

Notes:
(1) For each concept the number of groups who participated in discussing the concept is noted in parenthesis.
(2) Responses are limited to those most frequently reported, and these are listed in order, beginning with the most popular response.

laughed at them," while another observed that "rejection is worse when they come back to the community."

There was some acknowledgement that placements outside the community and culture may be required for children with special needs, particularly for short periods of time. However, serious reservations were expressed about placing children in non-Aboriginal resources or communities, and there was a general feeling of loss of control and influence in such situations. One respondent observed that "when you send a child away they turn different," while another said "they lose their traditional ways and are lost when they come back." One respondent summed up the group's feeling in noting "displacement of children happened a lot. We are now getting our children back and have more problems." In general, residential care outside the community was not supported. A typical response was "Those places offer very negative influences such as sniffing and drug awareness ... They offer only a street life and destroy our teachings here in the community." Although clear placement preferences were expressed, it was also recognized that the individual merit of a resource and the needs of the child had to be considered. For example, it was observed that placement in an extended family resource should not be used if the extended family was "part of the problem and could not protect the child."

Questions were also asked about who should be involved in placement planning. A high value was placed on birth and extended family participation, with 12 of 18 groups supporting such involvement in planning. Although respondents stressed the importance of family involvement, they indicated that this should be dependent on the nature of the family's problems. For example, one participant stated that "if there was sexual or physical abuse, parents should not be involved until they get counselling." The child's input was also highly valued, although it was noted that this would be dependent on the child's age. Bonding and attachment was an important consideration with 14 of 16 groups noting this as either important or very important in placement planning.

Respondents were also asked to specify qualities to be considered in the selection of foster parents. All identified qualities reflected emotional rather than material criteria. For example, the ability to provide a good level of emotional care, including love, respect and kindness, and the presence of stability in the home were the most frequently mentioned responses. Good communication skills, good parenting skills, and the equal treatment of both foster and natural children were qualities identified by slightly less than half of the groups. Past involvement with family violence, or alcohol and drug abuse were not regarded as a reason to eliminate potential foster parents. However, more than half of the groups stated that the nature and severity of past problems, as well as the recency of those problems, should be carefully considered when assessing and licensing foster parents. Not surprisingly, some groups were particularly concerned about past problems involving abuse, and this would generally prohibit foster home approval.

Culture and Community

Questions about the importance of culture in child and family services were asked of all adult participants; and findings are summarized in Table 5.3. Almost all groups stressed the importance of culture, and identified language, teachings and ceremonies as important aspects of culture. Respect for others and for their customs was also a highly valued attribute. The incorporation of cultural practices within child welfare was stressed, and many felt the agency had a role in providing cultural training in communities as a way of offering people a different way of life. Groups were asked to define an Elder and the role carried by such a person. Wisdom was the most common characteristic associated with Elders, and the most common role was that of advising and teaching. A response from one group reflects this role, "they help me to solve problems I cannot handle on my own. I go to Elders for guidance and advice. They have experienced life." There was considerable support for the use of Elders as advisors in agency activities, although it was cautioned that such individuals must be credible and well respected in the community. Many respondents expressed concern about the loss of culture, specifically the loss of language, and residential schools were identified as a major cause of loss of culture. As one person explained, "A lot of us went to residential school and we were not allowed to go home or practice our culture." While efforts to regain culture were recognized, there was a feeling that this process would take a long time "because it took a long time to lose."

Interview questions also obtained community feedback on the role of community structures, including Chief and Council and child and family service committees. The preferred role of the local committee was to work with families in resolving problems, provide advice to agency staff, and monitor the implementation of case plans at the community level. There was more disagreement about the preferred role for Chief and Council. Groups were evenly divided about whether such bodies should be directly involved in decision-making on child welfare matters. While there was agreement that Chief and Council should be informed of agency decisions, they also noted the need for local government to avoid interfering with committees and staff in carrying out their responsibilities to protect children at risk. The difficulty of responding to specific complaints from community members was recognized, and many felt that the development of a formal mediation and appeal mechanism might help to deal with this concern.

Table 5.3: Culture and Community

Concept	Most Common Responses
1. Importance of Culture (N=19)	Very important to support Language is critical Ceremonies are key aspects of culture
2. Incorporating Culture in Agency Practices and Programs (N=12)	Important to incorporate Culture should be taught in communities Elders have an important role to play
3. Role of Chief and Council in Child Welfare Decisions (N=16)	Chief and Council should not interfere in Committee decisions Chief and Council should be involved with the Committee in planning

Notes: (1.) For each concept the number of groups who participated in discussing the concept is noted in parenthesis. (2.) Responses are limited to those most frequently reported, and these are listed in order, beginning with the most popular response.

Youth groups interviewed often expressed the view that life in their community was boring, and that there was little to do. They identified a need for organized activities, recreational facilities, and cultural education. Many of these young people had received some form of child welfare services. While they expressed a preference for counsellors who understood their values, beliefs and customs, they were evenly divided on whether they would prefer to talk to someone from inside or outside the community. Some appeared to feel that they would feel less vulnerable with a counsellor from outside their community as "I would feel safer."

Conclusion and Implications

The research process used in this study has been successful in promoting community interest and involvement in child and family service issues. Group participants invested a great deal of time in both data collection phases, and appear committed to further investment in the improvement of services in their communities. Several issues need to be addressed. For example, youth groups raised serious concerns about the lack of community activities, and the need for adult modelling and support. The placement standard articulated by community members when out of home care is required must be examined in relation to the number of special needs children requiring specialized placement resources, and the limited availability of such resources within these communities.

There are implications for the development of culturally appropriate standards in First Nations communities. Many of the views about standards of practice in child welfare are not dissimilar to those identified in conventional standards of good child welfare practice. For example, the best interests of the child is defined, first and foremost, in terms of emotional care, guidance, and physical care. As well, the qualities of good substitute caregivers reflect criteria which are likely to be generally acceptable in most communities. But there are important differences in standards that reflect cultural traditions, and the historical nature of relations between First Nations and the dominant society. Even in these communities, which are less isolated from dominant society than many, traditional values like respect, the importance of the extended family, the custom adoption of non-relatives as family members, and a collective concern for the well-being of the community emerge as important. These findings support theoretical literature which identifies cultural differences, and the importance of modifying child welfare policy and practice to reflect the Aboriginal context.

The issue of bonding and attachment is of special interest. Despite strong concerns for the family, values expressed by participants in this study also reflect a central commitment to the well-being of the child. Concerns were expressed about the need to ensure the health and safety of children at risk, and the high value placed on "a strong positive attachment to parents and caregivers." But the concept of bonding expressed by respondents extends well beyond an attachment to parent or caregiver, and includes an attachment to extended family, community, and culture. These values were expressed directly and are also reflected in preferences identified for children requiring out of home care. Placements outside Aboriginal culture are viewed as a last resort by most, and community attachment was almost as important as extended family attachment in determining the most appropriate placement resource for a child in care.

An important implication concerns the role of child and family services in First Nations communities. Child welfare legislation in Canada requires the provision of protective services to children at risk, and only enables the provision of prevention and family support services. Prevention and family support services are not mandated requirements, and they are seriously restricted because of limited funding. A wide range of family support and prevention services were identified as essential services in these First Nations communities; moreover, child and family services needed to be concerned about all children in the community and about the health and well-being of adults. This was explained by one respondent as, "We need to support the natural parents and work with the family. Our people abuse. I know because I was abused; I am lucky that I received help, so I can help others. We (as a community) have to start dealing with the roots of abuse."

The growing interest in cultural teachings, language, and the importance of Elders is particularly important. There is also the realization that many traditions have been lost and that these have had a significant impact on parenting and the quality of child care provided within First Nations communities over the years. The legacy of residential schools has a continuing impact, a view expressed poignantly by one respondent in discussing the subject of physical discipline:

> It came from the ... schools ... That is not the way of the Indian culture. That is their way. That system will be here for a hell of a long time, that residential school system. You don't know this but you are handing that system out to your own child. I believe that. When I was growing up my father could not show any affection. Now I have trouble showing emotions to my children. I'm passing it on to my children from my parents who were in residential school.

References

Armitage, A. (1993). Family and child welfare in First Nation communities. In B. Wharf (Ed.) *Rethinking child welfare in Canada* (pp. 131–171). Toronto: McClelland & Stewart

BDO Ward Mallette. (1991). *Critique of a proposed federal funding formula for child and family services.* Winnipeg: Author.

Brant, C. C. (1990). Native ethics and rules of behavior. *Canadian Journal of Psychiatry, 35*(6), 534–539.

Cassara, B. (1987). The how and why of preparing graduate students to carry out participatory research. *Educational Considerations, 14*(2,3), 39–42

Child Welfare League of America. (1989). *Standards for service for abused or neglected children and their families.* Washington: Author.

Clarkson, L., Morrissette, V., & Regallet, G. (1992). *Our responsibility to the seventh generation: Indigenous people and sustainable development* (Report to the International Institute of Sustainable Development). Winnipeg: International Institute of Sustainable Development.

Coopers & Lybrand Consulting Group. (1987). *An assessment of services delivered under the Canada-Manitoba-Indian Child Welfare Agreement.* Winnipeg: Author

Cross, T. L. (1986). Drawing on cultural tradition in Indian child welfare practice. *Social Casework,* 67, 283–289.

DuBray, W. (1985). American Indian values: Critical factor in casework. *Social Casework,* 66, 30–37.

Edwards, E., & Edwards, M. (1980). American Indians: Working with the individual and groups. *Social Casework, 61,* 494–497

First Nations' Child and Family Task Force. (1993). *Children first: Our responsibility* (Report). Winnipeg: Author

First Nations Congress. (1992). *Indian Child and Family Services standards project* (Final Report). Vancouver: Author.

Giesbrecht, B. D. (1992). *Report of the fatality inquiries act respecting the death of Lester Norman Desjarlais.* Winnipeg: Queen's Printer.

Hamilton, A. C., & Sinclair, C. M. (1991). *Volume I: The justice system and Aboriginal people* (Report on the Aboriginal Justice Inquiry of Manitoba). Winnipeg: Queen's Printer.

Hudson, P. , & McKenzie, B. (1984). *Evaluation of Dakota Ojibway Child and Family Services* (Final Report). Ottawa: Indian and Northern Affairs Canada.

Hudson, P. , & Taylor-Henley, S. (1987). *Agreement and disagreement: An evaluation of the Canada-Manitoba-Northern Indian Child Welfare Agreement.* Winnipeg: School of Social Work, University of Manitoba.

Johnston, P. (1983). *Native children and the child welfare system.* Toronto: Canadian Council on Social Development.

Krippendorf, K. (1980). *Content analysis.* Beverly Hills, California: Sage.

Longclaws, L. (1994). Social work and the medicine wheel framework. In B. R. Compton & B. Galaway (Eds.), *Social work processes* (5th ed.) (24–33). Pacific Grove, CA: Brooks/Cole.

McKenzie, B. (1994). *Evaluation of the pilot project on block funding for child maintenance: West Region Child and Family Services* (Final Report). Winnipeg: Faculty of Social Work, University of Manitoba.

McKenzie, B., & Hudson, P. (1985). Native children, child welfare and the colonization of Native people. In K. L. Levitt & B. Wharf (Eds.), *The Challenge of Child Welfare* (pp. 125–141). Vancouver: University of British Columbia Press.

Miles, M., & Huberman, A. (1984). *Qualitative data analysis.* Beverly Hills, California: Sage.

Morrissette, V., McKenzie, B., & Morrissette, L. (1993). Towards an Aboriginal model of social work practice. *Canadian Social Work Review, 10*(1), 91–108.

Nofz, M. (1988). Alcohol abuse and culturally marginal American Indians. *Social Casework, 59,* 67–73.

Patton, M. (1990). *Qualitative evaluation and research methods* (2nd ed.). Newbury Park, California: Sage.

Ponting, J. R. (1986). Institution building in an Indian community: A case study of Kahnawake (Caughnawaga). In J. R. Ponting (Ed.), *Arduous journey: Canadian Indians and decolonization* (pp. 151–178). Toronto: McClelland & Stewart.

Popkewitz, T. (1988). Culture, pedagogy, and power: Issues in the production of values and colonialization. *Journal of Education, 170*(2), 77–90.

Red Horse, J. (1980a). American Indian elders: Unifiers of Indian families. *Social Casework, 61,* 490–493.

Red Horse, J. (1980b). Family structure and value orientation in American Indians. *Social Casework, 61,* 462–467.

Stewart, D., & Shamdasani, P. (1990). *Focus groups: Theory and practice.* Newbury Park, California: Sage.

Taylor-Henley, S., & Hill, E. (1990). *Treatment and healing—an evaluation: Community holistic circle healing.* Winnipeg: Faculty of Social Work, University of Manitoba.

Teichroeb, R. (1992, September 5). Native women, Glover feel vindicated. *Winnipeg Free Press,* A10.

Timpson, J., McKay, S., Kakegamic, S., Roundhead, D., Cohen, C., & Matewapit, G. (1988). Depression in a Native Canadian in Northwestern Ontario: Sadness, grief or spiritual illness? *Canada's Mental Health, 36*(2/3), 5–8.

6

The Nature and Effectiveness of Parent Mutual Aid Organizations in Child Welfare

Gary Cameron

This chapter describes the development challenges and reports the outcomes of the Parent Mutual Aid Organizations in Child Welfare Demonstration Project (PMAO), a social support intervention with the primary goal of preventing out-of-home placements of children at risk of neglect or abuse. Underlying the PMAO program model is an assumption that informal ways of helping are relevant and can be made accessible to families using child welfare services. Also, the claim is that partnerships between parents and professionals are possible and that child welfare organizations can realistically create mutual aid networks for their clientele. The model also presumes that many child welfare clients are motivated and able to participate meaningfully in a membership organization. The premise is that Parent Mutual Aid Organizations are capable of preventing out-of-home placements, fostering independence from professional services, and improving individual and family functioning in a relatively low-cost fashion. The PMAO study endeavoured to examine how well these expectations matched the actual performance of Parent Mutual Aid Organizations created in partnership with three child welfare agencies. The study also documented the processes of creating the PMAO and their relationships to the host child welfare agencies.

Conceptual Foundations

The multiple challenges faced by neglectful and abusive families is well-documented (Rothery & Cameron, 1985). Bagley and Thurston (1989) argue that the most rational way of intervening with multi-challenged populations is to design programs that remove as many stressors as possible and provide for early intervention. Schorr (1988) and Rothery and Cameron (1985) concur, finding that multiple services and programs have stronger impacts on these families than single interventions, with the more powerful program models typically building packages that incorporate numerous elements. In addition, they report that high levels of direct contact with families are characteristic of the most effective programs. Further, the child welfare literature repeatedly identifies social isolation as a correlate of child maltreatment and child placement (Garbarino & Stocking,1980), and associates strong and active social networks with reductions in domestic violence (Strauss, 1980) and abusive child rearing behaviours (Hunter & Kilstrom, 1979). More generally, comprehensive reviews of the research literature report an array of evidence demonstrating the physical and mental health as well as community integration benefits of access to informal social support (Cameron, 1990; Cohen & Syme, 1985; Cohen & Wills, 1985; Gottlieb, 1981, 1983; Vaux, 1988; Whittaker & Garbarino, 1983).

Two competing explanations for the helping mechanisms at work have been advanced (Cohen & Wills, 1985; Kessler & McLeod, 1985; Vaux, 1988). According to the buffering hypothesis, concrete, educational and emotional supports provide the individual in high stress situations with benefits that are relevant to managing problems (Thoits, 1982). In contrast, the direct effect hypothesis highlights the benefits of social integration, independent of the problems or levels of stress confronting the person. People are more likely to benefit from a positive social identity, a stronger sense of self-worth, greater life satisfaction, and psychological well-being when they are embedded in a social network that provides involvement in one or more stable, multi-dimensional, reciprocal relationships and when the individual occupies one or more valued social roles (Cohen & Wills, 1985). The PMAO program model presumes that both hypotheses have useful explanatory value. Thus, the model incorporates elements that help to integrate participants in positive social networks as well as to provide relevant problem-solving assistance.

Many professionals acknowledge these rationales for social support but query how they can be expected to create social networks, friendships, or valued social roles for clients who have serious social integration deficiencies, some of whom may lack the social skills needed to sustain such relationships. Froland (1981) suggests that created rather than embedded relationships may be more practical ways for professionals to exploit the potential of informal helping. Mutual aid organizations have been created to provide socially supportive relationships to a range of high-risk populations (Todres, 1982). When individuals are perceived or perceive themselves as deviant or stigmatized, a self-help organization can provide a safe place to go, a place where one can feel at home (Levy, 1976; Weiss, 1973). Many individuals join mutual aid groups to compensate for inadequacies in their personal networks, with the group becoming a surrogate for supportive family and friendship networks (Barkoff, 1979; Gartner & Riessman, 1984; Levy, 1976; Knight et al., 1980; Powell, 1979). People may also turn to a mutual aid group when they are in crisis or in a period of great personal difficulty (Romeder, 1990). While the effectiveness of mutual aid groups has not been extensively assessed (Lieberman & Borman, 1976), Cameron (1990) hypothesizes that mutual aid organizations may be an especially promising and practical way of actualizing some of the benefits of informal social support for child welfare clients.

Method

Procedure

A combination of qualitative and quantitative data was collected between 1988 and 1991 at three child welfare agencies in southwestern Ontario where PMAO were created. Individual interviews were conducted with members of each PMAO as well as a comparison group of child welfare clients receiving regular child protection services at the three host agencies. Time 1 interviews occurred approximately one year after the PMAO were initiated, January through May, 1990. Time 2 interviews occurred from October through December, 1990, and, Time 3 interviews occurred from March through May, 1991. Focus groups were also conducted with the PMAO members to discuss their experiences in the mutual aid organizations during the first and third years of the Demonstration Project, as were interviews with the program staff associated with each PMAO. Also, during individual interviews, PMAO members were asked open-ended questions about their experiences in the mutual aid organizations. Program development workers and the principal investigator kept ongoing program development journals. Program attendance data for the PMAO members was recorded.

Participants

The PMAO sample consisted of all individuals who joined a PMAO at any point during the Demonstration Project. Thus, the PMAO sample size increased throughout the data collection period as new members joined the groups. The Time 1 sample size was 53; the Time 2 sample was 81; and, the Time 3 sample was 97. All PMAO members were recruited from the open protection caseloads of each host agency. Comparison cases were selected randomly from the open protection caseloads of the three agencies. Members chose whether to join a PMAO or not; thus, there may be a self-selection bias differentiating PMAO members from other child welfare clientele. Statistical procedures were used to verify the comparability of the PMAO and comparison group samples. At Time 1, 56 comparison group members were interviewed; at Time 2, 60 were interviewed; and, at Time 3, 58 were interviewed. The comparison sample cannot be assumed to be representative of the broader population of child welfare clients due to differences in research participation rates across different workers and work units. However, the problems and concerns profiles and the demographic characteristics of both the PMAO and comparison samples were very similar to earlier descriptions of Ontario child welfare protection caseloads (Cameron & Rothery, 1985). The interview participation rates were good for the PMAO and comparison samples. For the PMAO members, 94% who were interviewed at Time 1 were also interviewed at Time 2, and 93% who were interviewed at Time 2 were interviewed again at Time 3. For the comparison sample, 86% who were interviewed at Time 1 were interviewed at Time 2, and 93% who were interviewed at Time 2 were interviewed again at Time 3. This high rate of participation at all three time periods increases confidence that the observed changes were typical of the PMAO and comparison group members included in the study.

Intervention

A PMAO was created at each of the three host child welfare agencies. These PMAO were voluntary, membership organizations, providing self-help opportunities to the child welfare families served by that agency. Each PMAO was staffed by a program development worker; parent members were actively involved in managing the organization. The model for the PMAO was a hybrid, combining the diversity and intensity of formal family support programs with the informal helping available in mutual aid groups. Participants were involved in four main types of activities:

1. *Social integration* by helping the family to develop or maintain positive ongoing contacts with social networks, thereby providing opportunities for social participation and providing access to new social roles with the mutual aid organization.
2. *Emotional support* by providing access to genuine intimate relationships which could serve members' needs for understanding and compassion.
3. *Education* by providing knowledge and skills required so that the members could cope more effectively.
4. *Concrete support* by providing some form of material aid such as money, clothing, furniture, babysitting.

Each of the three PMAO took on a life and direction of its own but they were guided by a common set of organizing principles. These are listed from those believed to be the most accessible to those viewed as the most difficult to operationalize within the mutual aid organizations:

1. To allow participants access to high levels of direct contact per week—2 to 5 times in scheduled activities and between meeting contacts among members (Rothery & Cameron, 1985; Schorr, 1988).
2. To provide access to a variety of helping strategies and activities, for example, parent relief, information, personal development courses, emotional support, and concrete resources (Bagley & Thurston, 1989; Barkoff, 1979; Borman & Lieber, 1984; Borman, 1992; Cohen & Wills, 1985; Gottlieb, 1982; Lavoie, 1990; Lieberman & Bond, 1979; Rothery & Cameron, 1985; Romeder, 1990; Silverman, 1980; Whittaker, 1983).
3. To provide a safe place to be and to facilitate access to a positive network of peers (Barkoff, 1979; Borman, 1992; Gartner & Riessman, 1984; Knight et al., 1980; Levy, 1976; Powell, 1979; Weiss, 1973).
4. To help members become friends with each other and to contact each other outside of scheduled meeting times (Borman, 1992; Gottlieb, 1982; Knight et al., 1980; Levy, 1976; Silverman, 1980).
5. To facilitate members becoming helpers as well as receivers of assistance (Borkman, 1990; Borman, 1992, Dunst & Trivette, 1987; Gartner & Riessman, 1984; Riessman, 1965).
6. To facilitate members assuming responsibility for running and maintaining their own organization (Borman, 1992; Dunst & Trivette, 1987; Madara, 1986; Powell, 1987; Silverman, 1980).
7. To encourage members to take part in a broader range of social involvements and to support them in new successful social roles, for example, group leader, student, employee, volunteer (Bronfenbrenner, 1979; Brown, 1986; Dunst & Trivette, 1987; Maton, 1988; McCall & Simmons, 1966; Powell, 1987; Rappoport, 1977; Rothery & Cameron, 1985; Silverman, 1980; Thoits, 1983).

Each PMAO offered an array of program activities and experiences to its members. Recreational activities predominated in the early stages of development, later activities included an increased focus on members' personal growth and on their program development responsibilities. The importance of having fun and celebrating events and accomplishments was highlighted throughout the project. Many of the social activities incorporated elements of skill building and health improvement such as cooking, fitness, and sewing. Diverse educational opportunities were offered ranging from cosmetics demonstrations to information on sexual abuse. Topics receiving greatest emphasis stressed parenting skills, academic and employment skills, and building members' abilities to manage their own organization. Another regular feature was check-in where members informally talked with one another about issues of personal importance. In addition, participants had frequent contact with one another outside of scheduled program activities, calling each other on the phone, visiting each other and organizing outings together.

Results

Participation

Many professional practitioners were doubtful that child protection clients would participate in a PMAO. They argued that the clients they served had too many difficulties in their lives and were too unmotivated or irresponsible to become involved. Thus, it was important for the study to determine if child welfare families would join a PMAO and if those who did were similar to other families typically served by child welfare agencies.

The PMAO and comparison group samples were compared on a broad range of descriptive variables. Two general patterns are evident in this data. First, both groups of respondents were coping with numerous difficulties in their lives. Second, in the initial evaluation time period, the PMAO sample reported higher levels of unemployment, greater difficulty meeting daily living expenses, less satisfaction with neighbourhood resources for children, more social isolation and loneliness, more problems with parenting and home management responsibilities, more dependence on professionals for help with family responsibilities, more frequent health problems, and higher levels of conflict and physical violence between partners. These variables have been associated with increased difficulty in maintaining family well-being and with higher levels of child abuse and neglect. At the beginning of the outcome evaluation period, the PMAO sample demonstrated more difficulties on measures of social support (see Table 6.4) as well as on measures of self-esteem and perceived ability to cope with stress (see Table 6.5). The PMAO sample not only had difficulties typical of child welfare populations, but they may have been experiencing higher levels of stress than the comparison group of families. Thus, it would have been reasonable to expect poorer results for the PMAO sample over the duration of the study.

Second, approximately 50% of members who were referred to a PMAO became actively involved. One to three times a week were typical levels of involvement for active members and most remained active between four and twelve months. In addition, the sites typically operated with core groups of active members numbering between 10 and 20 families at any point in time. However, those sites with lower success in involving new referrals had to process larger numbers of referrals in order to obtain the participation levels eventually achieved.

Out-of-Home Child Placement

A principle objective of the PMAO model was to reduce the amount of out-of-home placement of children in need of protection. The PMAO members consistently used care about one-half to one-third as frequently as the

Table 6.1: Children Being Placed in Care within the Last Year at Times One, Two and Three, at Times Two and Three, and at Time Three

	Time 1	Time 2	Time 3
PMAO	15.4% (8)	17.8% (8)	12.5% (6)
Comparison Group	30.4% (18)*[1]	29.8% (14)[2]	33.3% (15)**

	Time 2	Time 3
PMAO	13.9% (11)	11.0% (8)
Comparison Group	30.0% (18)**	28.0% (16)***

	Time 3
PMAO	14.8% (14)
Comparison Group	29.0% (17)*

* X^2 value probability ≤ .10
** X^2 value probability ≤ .05
*** X^2 value probability ≤ .01

(1) Comparison is between PMAO and comparison group samples during this time period.
(2) 60% of the PMAO placements at this time period were at one site experiencing persistent difficulties.

comparison sample. For the sample available at Time 1, the percent of cases using care in the year prior to Times 1, 2, or 3 was 39% for the comparison group and 19% for the PMAO members; for the sample that became available at Time 2, it was 38% for the comparison group and 14% for the PMAO members. These are ratios of 2:1 and 3:1 in favour of the PMAO sample, despite the fact that they reported higher levels of stress at the beginning of the assessment period. Further, Table 6.1 displays the results of comparing PMAO and comparison group families' child placement rates within the previous year at multiple time periods. Participants present at the initial evaluation time period were assessed at data-gathering Times 1, 2 and 3. Those who joined the PMAO at Time 2 were assessed at Times 2 and 3. Finally those who joined after Time 2 were compared at Time 3 only. For five of the six time periods assessed, PMAO members made statistically significant lower use of child placements than did the comparison group.

Professional Support

An anticipated consequence of the high levels of program involvement and informal contact among PMAO members was that they would need less ongoing support from formal service providers. The data reveal a pattern of greater independence from formal service providers for PMAO members at Sites 1 and 3, but not at Site 2. The counter-intuitive Site 2 findings seemed to be attributable to local agency procedures that required PMAO members to

Table 6.2: Use of Children's Aid Society Services At Times One, Two and Three - Site One and Site Three Samples Combined

	Face-to-Face Contact with Child Protection Worker within Last Month	Face-to-Face Contact with Child Protection Worker within Last 3 Months	Presently Involved in Other CAS Programs
TIME ONE			
PMAO Sample (30)	53%(16)***[1]	82% (22)**	23% (7)
Comparison Sample (39)	92% (36)	100% (39)	42% (16)
TIME TWO			
PMAO Sample (26)	42% (11)*	58% (14)*	15% (4)
Comparison Sample (32)	69% (22)	84% (26)	19% (6)
TIME THREE			
PMAO Sample (28)	14% (4)**	21% (6)***	18% (5)
Comparison Sample (31)	48% (15)	77% (24)	7% (2)

X^2 value probability ≤ .10
** X^2 value probability ≤ .05
*** X^2 value probability ≤ .01

(1) Comparison is between PMAO and comparison group samples during this time period.

maintain contact with a child protection worker and encouraged involvement in other programs at the agency. Table 6.2 compares the frequency of use of child welfare services for the PMAO and comparison samples at Sites 1 and 3, who were followed over the three assessment time periods. These data reveal that the PMAO members showed a far greater percentage of decline in the levels of contact with child protection workers over the evaluation time periods. For example, for PMAO members there was a 61% reduction in having had contact with the child protection worker within the last three months, compared to a 23% decline for the comparison group from Time 1 to Time 3. The PMAO members had statistically significant lower levels of involvement with child protection workers than did the comparison sample. A similar pattern was revealed for the samples followed over Times 2 and 3 and at Time 3.

Structural Integration

An expectation of the demonstration project was that families joining a PMAO would have substantial access to positive social connections that would otherwise not be present in their lives. Table 6.3 compares the PMAO and comparison group members' participation in various types of structured community involvements and their contacts with close friends. Several important patterns are evident. First, PMAO members participated in organized social

Table 6.3: Structural Social Integration For Active Members Through the Parent Mutual Aid Organizations at Times One, Two and Three

	PMAO Sample[1]			Comparison Sample			x^2 (P)		
	Time 1	Time 2	Time 3	Time 1	Time 2	Time 3	Time 1	Time 2	Time 3
Take part at least once a week in organized social or recreational activities	84.3% (43)	88.6% (39)	93.9% (46)	10.2% (6)	23.3% (14)	15.3% (9)	57.9[3] (.0000)	32.9 (.0000)	63.6 (.0000)
* Through PMAO * Outside PMAO	97.7%(42)[3] 9.3% (4)	100% (39) 25.0% (8)	97.8% (45) 13.0% (6)						
Volunteer my time in community at least once a week	31.4% (16)	61.4% (27)	75.5% (37)	3.4% (2)	11.7% (7)	8.5% (5)	13.7 (.0002)	21.4 (.0000)	47.2 (.0000)
* Through PMAO * Outside PMAO	87.6% (14) 31.3% (5)	70.4% (19) 40.7% (11)	86.5% (32) 32.4% (12)						
Belong to a church or community group and attend at least once a week	88.2% (45)	90.9% (40)	79.6% (39)	18.6% (11)	8.3%	15.3% (9)	50.3 (.0000)	58.0 (.0000)	41.2 (.0000)
* Through PMAO * Outside PMAO	95.6% (43) 13.3% (6)	95.0% (38) 27.5% (11)	94.9% (37) 25.6% (10)						
Have one close friend and get together one or more times a week	58.8% (30)	81.8% (36)	71.4% (35)	74.6% (44)	80.0% (48)	67.8% (40)	n.s.	n.s.	n.s.
* Through PMAO * Outside PMAO	58.1% (18) 64.6% (20)	50.0% (18) 69.4% (25)	48.6% (17) 77.1% (27)						

(1) includes only PMAO members who have been inactive less than 5 weeks.
(2) comparison is between PMAO and comparison group samples during this time period.
(3) numbers exceed 100% because respondents could answer yes to both through and outside PMAO.

and recreational activities, volunteered their time and belonged to a church or community group at levels far in excess of those reported by the comparison group members, for whom these types of social involvements were almost non-existent. For example, at Time 3, 94% of PMAO members compared to 15% of the comparison group sample were involved regularly in social and recreational activity; 76% of the PMAO members volunteered regularly compared to 9% of the comparison group; and, 80% of PMAO members regularly participated in church or community activities compared to 15% of the comparison group. Second, PMAO members participated in these kinds of social involvements almost exclusively through their participation in the mutual aid organizations. For example, at Time 3, 98% of PMAO members' participation in social and recreational activities, 87% of their volunteer involvement and 95% of their church or community group participation occurred through the PMAO. Finally, PMAO and comparison group members reported similar levels of contact with a close friend—once a week or more. However, about 50% of the friendly contact for PMAO members was with people that they had met through the PMAO.

PMAO became the center of many members' social lives, but there was attenuation on these measures when PMAO involvement stopped. For example, data for PMAO members, who at the third assessment time period had been inactive for two months or more, reveal that while the relative advantage of PMAO members over comparison group members continued, the differences were much smaller. At Time 3, while 94% of active PMAO members regularly participated in social and recreational activities, this dropped to 35% for inactive members. Similarly, at Time 3, while 76% of active members volunteered their time and 80% regularly attended a church or community group, this dropped to 28% and 20% respectively for inactive members.

Perceived Social Support

The advantage revealed for active PMAO members over the comparison group sample on the structural integration variables was also in evidence on the perceived social support measures. Sixty-four percent of the respondents from the PMAO and 52% of those from the comparison group showed positive change on the Interpersonal Support Evaluation List (ISEL) (Cohen, Mermelstein, Kamarck, & Hoberman, 1985) measure between evaluation time periods one and two. About 35% of the PMAO and 48% of the comparison group members had no change or had negative changes between times one and two. Thirty-five percent of the PMAO respondents were in the higher categories of positive change on ISEL (+11 to +45), while only 20% of the comparison group showed this magnitude of improvement. Similarly, 9% of the comparison group had total social scores that deteriorated by 16 to 50 points over this time period while none of the PMAO declined this much. Table 6.4 compares changes within the PMAO and comparison groups on the ISEL scale and each of its three support subscales, between Times 1 and 2 and between Times 1 and 3. The PMAO sample scored lower than the comparison group members on three of the four social support measures at the initial evaluation time period. The most striking pattern was the improvements revealed on the overall social support measure and on all three subscales between Times 1 and 2 as well as on the overall support scale and on two subscales between Times 1 and 3. In contrast, the comparison group showed no improvement on any of these measures between any of these time periods.

Self-Esteem and Perceived Stress

Data reporting changes in self-esteem and in perceived ability to cope with daily living responsibilities also reveal advantages for PMAO members over the comparison sample. More members of the PMAO sample demonstrated improvement on the Coopersmith Self-Esteem Inventory (Coopersmith, 1987) between times one and two than comparison group members (55% to 39%). Fewer PMAO members showed negative changes in their self-esteem scores (26% to 44%) over the same time period. In addition, the PMAO sample had more people in the highest (6–12) positive change categories (26% to 11%) and fewer in the larger (4–9) negative change categories (8% to 20%) on the self-esteem measure. Greater proportions of PMAO members reported positive change on the Perceived Stress Scale (Cohen, Kamarck & Mermelstein, 1983) than members of the comparison group between times one and two (50% to 38%). The perceived stress scale is a measure of confidence in the ability to cope with stressors in life. Substantially fewer PMAO members reported negative change (24% to 43%)—particularly in the larger (3–10) negative change categories (2% to 17%). Table 6.5 reports changes in self-esteem and

Table 6.4: Changes in Perceived Access to Social Support (ISEL) Scores Across Time Periods One, Two and Three

PMAO Sample (N = 46)

	Time 1	Time 2	Time 3
Appraisal Support	16.9 (5.2)***[1]	18.9 (4.8)	18.4 (3.9)
Belonging Support	15.2 (6.6)**	17.0 (5.9)	17.5 (5.6)**[2]
Tangible Support	15.2 (6.2)***	17.8 (6.4)	17.7 (5.6)***
Total Support (ISEL)	47.6 (16.3)***	54.0 (14.0)	54.0 (13.3)**

Comparison Sample (N = 47)

	Time 1	Time 2	Time 3
Appraisal Support	17.0 (6.4)	17.0 (5.8)	16.6 (5.6)
Belonging Support	16.2 (5.6)	17.0 (5.4)	16.1 (5.7)
Tangible Support	16.5 (6.0)	17.4 (6.0)	17.3 (5.0)
Total Support (ISEL)	49.6 (16.0)	51.0 (15.0)	49.5 (13.0)

* T value probability ≤ .10
** T value probability ≤ .05
*** T value probability ≤ .01
(1) Statistical significance of differences between T_1 and T_2 scores for PMAO sample
(2) Statistical significance of differences between T_1 and T_3 scores for PMAO sample

perceived stress within the PMAO and comparison groups for members present at the first assessment time period, between Times 1 and 2 and between Times 1 and 3. The PMAO sample reported lower self-esteem and higher perceived stress scores than the comparison group at the initial time period. However, by Time 2, the PMAO members showed more positive scores on both of these measures and these positive changes continued at Time 3. These changes were statistically significant for the PMAO sample. In contrast, there were no statistically significant positive changes for the comparison group on either the self-esteem or perceived stress indicators.

Cost Analysis

The PMAO model must be affordable for child welfare agencies to view it as a feasible service option. A cost-effectiveness analysis was not part of the demonstration project research but it was possible to complete cost analyses that revealed advantages for the PMAO model. Data about average agency caseloads, typical numbers of families in a PMAO network, total number of families served in one year, average salaries, child care costs for the PMAO, administrative overhead charges, and child placement costs were used to make a number of estimates of actual child protection and PMAO service parameters. The PMAO model showed annual cost advantages per case between $420 and $869 or a total annual saving to an agency between $16,800 and $34,760—depending on the time in care estimates used in the calculations. It was estimated

Table 6.5: Changes in Self-Esteem and Perceived Stress Scores Across Time Periods One, Two and Three

PMAO SAMPLE (N = 46)

	Time 1	Time 2	Time 3
Self-Esteem (Coopersmith)	13.4 (5.2)**[1]	14.9 (5.6)	15.4 (5.9)**[2]
Perceived Stress (Cohen)	11.2 (3.1)***	10.0 (2.7)	10.0 (3.0)*

COMPARISON SAMPLE (N = 47)

	Time 1	Time 2	Time 3
Self-Esteem (Coopersmith)	14.4 (5.0)	14.0 (5.5)	14.5 (5.7)
Perceived Stress (Cohen)	10.2 (2.6)	10.5 (2.8)	10.6 (2.8)

* T value probability ≤ .10
** T value probability ≤ .05
*** T value probability ≤ .01
(1) Statistical significance of differences between T1 and T2 scores for PMAO sample
(2) Statistical significance of differences between T1 and T3 scores for PMAO sample

that one child protection worker would serve 30 families in one year with program costs and child placement costs of between $64,816 and $78,256. The PMAO was estimated to serve 40 families in one year with total program costs and child placement costs of $69,956. The child protection service cost per case served in one year was between $2,160 and $2,609. The PMAO cost per case served in one year was $1,740.

Program Development Challenges: Lessons Learned

The Parent Mutual Aid Organizations combined the program development requirements of a complicated formal family support program with those of fostering informal helping and mutual aid between parents and those of a democratic membership organization. Creating all the elements required and putting them together in order to build a healthy mutual aid organization can seem like a daunting challenge. Nonetheless, all three PMAOs in the Demonstration Project overcame these obstacles, despite limited access to resources. The program development lessons learned from the Demonstration Project should enable others to shorten the timeframe and lessen the strain of developing a viable PMAO. The program development challenges are too complex to examine in depth here,* but can be highlighted as:

1. Developing a stable, multi-faceted organization is a long-term process that can take from three to five years of effort. The early phases can be especially discouraging.

* An extended discussion of these program development challenges is presented in Cameron, G. (1992). ***Mutual Aid and Child Welfare: The Parent Mutual Aid Organizations in Child Welfare Demonstration Project,*** Waterloo, Ontario: Centre for Social Welfare Studies, Wilfrid Laurier University.

2. As in most other human service interventions, there is a constant struggle to maintain a balance between the accomplishment of operational tasks and the need to create group processes that encourage self-responsibility. Our experience leads us to conclude that an emphasis on the empowerment of group members should be the priority .
3. It is essential to create norms of caring, responsible behaviour and member ownership of group well-being from the very beginning of the PMAO development process. Bad group habits are painful to change; good habits require a good deal of time and practice before they become part of members' customary behaviour.
4. There were two important transition points in the development of these PMAOs. The first was called the "initial development take-off point." This watershed occurred when most of the basic program elements were in place. The second transition point, the creation of stable core program elements, marked the point when the organization had achieved sufficient stability to enable it to consider richer and more diverse program experiences for its members.
5. Member participation, leadership and governance evolve as the PMAO matures and grows. In the early stages, the PMAO only required simple decision making structures that relied on a collective style of leadership. Later, however, as the number of members increased, as program activities expanded, and as members sought out growth opportunities for themselves, these structures became more complex.
6. The character traits of members and the mix of people involved in a PMAO can have a powerful positive or negative impact on program development. Each member of the PMAO had to confront the problems created by other powerful member or members with persistent, dysfunctional ways of relating to other group members. Policies and procedures for managing these difficulties were essential to have.
7. Access to adequate levels of resources such as appropriate space, child care and transportation are critical to PMAO success. Scrimping on support resources will result in less positive program experiences for members and produce a much poorer return on the original investment in the program.
8. The mechanisms linking the PMAO to the organizational structure of the host agency are of crucial importance. The PMAO needs to be connected to the agency through an appropriate administrative unit. In addition, key agency administrators are needed to explain the program model to others and to build support for it within the agency.
9. Central to the successful implementation of a PMAO is the role of the program development worker. This job is very demanding both because of the volume of work entailed and because of its open-ended character. Drawing on knowledge and skills in clinical practice and community development, the position calls for a range of aptitudes not easily found in a single person.

Discussion

The Parent Mutual Aid Organizations were successful in involving members in a diversity of experiences that were not available in other ways through the sponsoring child welfare agencies. Many PMAO members participated several times a week over an extended period of time and over half of the regularly attending PMAO participants contacted other members between scheduled group activities. The PMAO provided many members with high levels of support, with rich and varied experiences, and with a social connectedness that otherwise would have been missing from their lives. Members expressed pride, a sense of ownership, protectiveness, and enthusiasm about their involvement in the PMAO that would be hard to match in programs designed and delivered by professionals. The PMAO became an active hub in the social and interpersonal lives of many members. The outcomes from the evaluation of the PMAO were very encouraging and compare well with those from other intensive family support program models in child welfare.

There were differences across the three demonstration sites with respect to client participation but about half of the parents referred to a PMAO, had patterns of involvement comparable to those desired for mutual aid organizations. These levels of participation suggest that a substantial number of families at risk of abuse or neglect are prepared to join and become actively engaged in mutual aid organizations affiliated with child welfare agencies. However, mutual aid organizations have limited attraction for another group of child welfare clients. There is merit in expanding the availability of mutual aid opportunities for child welfare clients but this mode of intervention is not suitable for all.

High intensity and diversity are key factors in programs that help multiple problem families to cope more effectively and survive as a unit. In a PMAO high intensity and diversity can be achieved with less ongoing support from formal service providers. Participation in a PMAO results in significantly reduced need for out-of-home placement of children. The mutual aid organizations represented the centre of most members' social and recreational lives outside of the home and were also places to find friends. Members would not have benefited from these types of social involvements without participating in the PMAO. These findings suggest that the PMAO intervention model may be able to respond in a substantial way to the problems of isolation and loneliness experienced by many families coming to child welfare agencies for help. PMAO members' social and community participation levels declined once they were no longer active in a PMAO; thus, more attention should be given to developing procedures that explicitly tie members into other positive community and social involvements.

The demonstration project revealed that the PMAO model can make important contributions to the positive social connectedness of many members—allowing more regular contact with other adults, increased involvement in social activities, providing greater opportunities to assume new responsibilities and roles, stimulating more access to informal problem-solving resources such as advice and emotional support when confronting difficult times, and facilitating meeting new friends. This improved social integration should make a positive contribution to members' sense of well-being and to their ability to cope with their daily living challenges. Evidence collected during the demonstration project revealed that PMAO members in fact did show improvement on a number of measures of personal and social functioning. These data indicate that participation in a PMAO substantially increases the likelihood that members will experience gains in self-esteem and have greater confidence in their abilities to cope with their daily living circumstances. All of these benefits are consistent with the rationale for the mutual aid program model in child welfare.

On the other side of the ledger, because of the complexities of supporting informal helping and fostering member responsibilities within mutual aid organizations, the program development requirements of the PMAO model were found to be quite formidable. They were considered to be potentially the Achilles heel of the approach, presenting challenges that, while they were manageable, could lead to major deviations from original intentions. Supporting the program development worker, having access to adequate resources for physical space, child care and transportation, coordination/integration/partnership with the host child welfare agency, member development and the management of interpersonal relations were all complicated program development responsibilities during the Demonstration Project. Objectively, the benefits to participating families and to the sponsoring child welfare indicate the value of continued expansion of mutual aid methods in child welfare. Nonetheless, there is a need to approach this undertaking with respect for the effort and the commitment that will be required to succeed.

One of the PMAO program development worker's expression of her feelings about building a PMAO can serve as a realistic and positive summary of the experiences: "I'm very proud of (the members' accomplishments) and I'm very proud of them. It's been a lot of work and it hasn't been easy, but as far as I'm concerned it's paid off in gold." It is both positive and practical to create mutual aid organizations with families coming to child welfare agencies for help. It is time for this powerful vehicle for helping to be taken seriously and for mutual aid to become a common and respected part of what we do to protect children and to support families.

The National Welfare Grants Division of Human Resources Canada (contract: 4555-1-126) and the Laidlaw Foundation in Toronto, Ontario provided financial support for this demonstration project.

References

Bagley, C., & Thurston, W. (1989). *Family poverty and children's behavioural and learning problems: A review of the evidence* (Monograph No. 7). Waterloo: Wilfrid Laurier University, Centre for Social Welfare Studies.

Barkoff, E. A. (1979). Widow groups as an alternative to informal social support. In M. Lieberman & L. Borman (Eds.), *Self-help groups for coping with crisis.* San Francisco: Jossey-Bass.

Borkman, T. J. (1990). Experiential, professional and lay frames of reference. In T. J. Powell (Ed.), *Working with Self-Help.* Silver Springs, MD: National Association of Social Workers Press.

Borman, L. (1992). Introduction: Self-help/mutual aid groups in strategies for health. In A.H. Katz, H.L. Hedrick, D.H. Isenberg, L.M. Thompson, T. Goodrich, & A.H. Kutscher (Eds.), *Self-Help: Concepts and Applications.* Philadelphia, PA: Charles Press.

Borman, L. D. & Lieber, L. L. (1984). *Self-help and the treatment of child abuse.* New York: National Committee for the Prevention of Child Abuse.

Bronfenbrenner, U. (1979). *The ecology of human development.* Cambridge, Mass: Harvard University Press.

Brown, R. (1986). *Social Psychology: The second edition.* New York: Free Press.

Cameron, G. (1990). The potential of informal social support strategies in child welfare. In M. Rothery & G. Cameron (Eds.), *Child maltreatment: Expanding our concept of helping.* New York: Lawrence Erlbaum. 145–168.

Cameron, G., & Birnie-Lefcovitch, S. J. (in process). Parent mutual aid organizations in child welfare demonstration project: The model and its implementation.

Cameron, G., & Rothery, M. (1985). *The use of family support in children's aid societies: An exploratory study.* Toronto: Ontario Ministry of Community and Social Services.

Cohen, S., Kamarck,. T., & Mermelstein, R. (1983). A global measure of perceived stress. *Journal of Health and Social Behavior, 24,* 385–396.

Cohen, S., Mermelstein, R., Kamarck, T., & Hoberman, H. M. (1985). Measuring the functional components of social support. In I. G. Sarason & B. R. Sarason (Eds.), *Social support: Theory, research and applications.* Dordrecht: Martinus Nijhoff. 73–94.

Cohen, S., & Syme, L. (1985). *Social support and health.* New York: Academic Press.

Cohen, S., & Wills, T. A. (1985). Stress, social support and the buffering hypothesis." *Psychological Bulletin, 98*(2), 310–357.

Coopersmith, S. (1987). *Self-esteem inventories.* Palo Alto: Consulting Psychologists Press.

Dunst, C. J., & Trivette, C. M. (1987). Enabling and empowering families: Conceptual and intervention issues. *Social Psychology, 4,* 443–456.

Froland, C., Pancoast, D., Chapman, N., & Kimboko, P. (1981). *Helping networks and human services.* Beverly Hills: Sage.

Garbarino, J., & Stocking, S. H. (Eds.). (1980). *Protecting children from abuse and neglect: Developing and maintaining effective support systems for families.* San Francisco: Jossey-Bass.

Gartner, A., & Riessman, F. (1984). *The self-help revolution.* New York: Human Sciences Press.

Gottlieb, B. H. (1981). *Social networks and social support.* Beverly Hills: Sage.

Gottlieb, B. H. (1982). Mutual-help groups: Members' views of their benefits and roles for professionals. In L. D. Borman, L. E. Brock, R. Heiss, & F. Pasquale (Eds.), *Helping People to Help Themselves: Self-Help and Prevention.* New York: Haworth Press.

Gottlieb, B. H. (1983). *Social support strategies.* Beverly Hills: Sage.

Hudson, W. W. (1982). *The clinical assessment package: A field manual.* Chicago: Dorsey Press.

Hunter, R. S., & Kilstrom, N. (1979). Breaking the cycle in abusive families. *American Journal of Psychiatry, 136,* 1320–1322.

Knight, B., Wollert, R. W., Levy, L. H., Frame, C. L. & Padgett, V. P. (1980). Self-help groups: The members' perspectives. *American Journal of Community Psychology, 8*(1), 53–65.

Lavoie, F. (1990). Evaluating self-help groups. In J. M. Romeder, *The Self-Help Way: Mutual Aid and Health.* Ottawa: Canadian Council on Social Development.

Levy, L. H. (1976). Self-help groups: Types and psychological processes. *The Journal of Applied Behavioral Science, 12*(3).

Lieberman, M., & Bond, G. (1979). Women's consciousness raising as an alternative to psychotherapy. In M. Lieberman & L. Borman (Eds.), *Self-Help Groups for Coping with Crisis.* San Francisco: Jossey-Bass.

Lieberman, M., & Borman, L. (1979). *Self-help groups for coping with crisis.* San Francisco: Jossey-Bass.

Madara, E. J. (1986). How-to ideas for developing groups. In E. J. Madara & A. Meese (Eds)., *The Self-Help Sourcebook.* Denville, New Jersey: St. Clares/Riverside Medical Center.

Maton, K. I. (1988). Social support, organizational characteristics psychological well-being and group appraisal in three self-help group populations. *American Journal of Community Psychology, 16,* 53–77.

McCall, G. J., & Simmons, J. L. (1966). *Identities and Interactions.* New York: Free Press.

Moos, R. H. (1976). *Evaluating treatment environments: A social ecological approach.* New York: John Wiley.

Powell, T. J. (1979). Comparisons between self-help groups and professional services. *Social Casework, 60*(9), 561–565.

Powell, T. J. (1987). *Self-help organizations and professional practice.* Silver Spring, MD: National Association of Social Workers.

Rappoport, J. (1977). *Community Psychology: Values, research and action.* New York: Holt, Rinehart and Winston.

Riessman, F. (1965). The 'helper' therapy principle. *Social Work, 10,* 27–32.

Romeder, J. M. (1990). *The self-help way: Mutual aid and health.* Ottawa: Canadian Council on Social Development.

Rothery, M., & Cameron, G. (1985). *Understanding Family Support in Child Welfare: A Summery Report.* Toronto: Ontario Ministry of Community and Social Services.

Rothery, M., & Cameron, G. (Eds.). (1990). *Child Maltreatment: Expanding our Concept of Helping.* New York: Lawrence Erlbaum.

Schorr, L. B. (1988). *Within our reach: Breaking the cycle of disadvantage.* New York: Anchor Press.

Silverman, P. R. (1980). *Mutual aid groups: Organization and development.* Beverly Hills, CA: Sage.

Straus, M. (1980). Stress and child abuse. In R. E. Helfer & C. H. Kempe (Eds.), *The battered child.* Chicago: University of Chicago Press.

Thoits, P. A. (1982). Conceptual, methodological, and theoretical problems in studying social support as a buffer against life stress. *Journal of Health and Social Behavior,* 145–159.

Thoits, P. A. (1983). Multiple identities and psychological well-being: A reformulation and test of the social isolation hypothesis. *American Sociological Review, 48,* 174–187.

Todres, R. (1982). *Self-help groups: An annotated bibliography.* New York: National Self-Help Clearinghouse.

Vaux, A. (1988). *Social Support: Theory, Research and Intervention.* New York: Praeger.

Weiss, R. (1973). The contributions of an organization of single parents to the well-being of its members. *The Family Coordinator, 22,* 321–326.

Whittaker, J. K. (1983). Social support networks in child welfare. In J. Whittaker & J. Garbarino (Eds.), *Social Support Strategies: Informal Helping in the Human Services.* New York: Aldine.

7

Interorganizational Policy Development and Implementation: An Examination of The School-Human Services Redesign Initiative in Hennepin County, Minnesota

Laura Bloomberg

The current system for providing human and educational services to individuals at the highest risk for social and economic failure is inadequate. Juvenile crime rates, drugs, insufficient support for families, and budget concerns make clear that "business as usual" in the human service and education arena is no longer acceptable. Identifying the array of problems is not difficult. The challenge lies in identifying and agreeing upon the policies and implementation practices that will have a positive impact on service outcomes for individuals and communities. Crowson and Boyd (1993) speak of the "Noah principle"—no more prizes for predicting rain, prizes only for building arks. Policymakers and service providers alike are faced with the challenge of building arks for the current deluge. The challenge to policymakers is to develop the infrastructure and macro-level policy systems that will support and sustain, but not stifle, restructuring efforts. The challenge to community-level service providers is to develop and implement innovative systems that meet the human needs that seem to overwhelm today's fragmented systems. The most significant restructuring efforts underway are based on an interorganizational design, where multiple agencies, levels of government, or funding streams are brought together to streamline and coordinate the provision of services. Such interorganizational models have a significant impact on the ways in which policymakers develop policy and service providers implement those policies.

Perspectives on Interorganizational Policy Implementation

The development of policy to impact social welfare has been studied from a number of perspectives. McDonnell and Elmore (1987) suggest a focus on the instruments and tools policymakers use to make decisions, and on the conditions under which certain policy instruments are likely to yield optimal results. Policy instruments can be viewed as the mechanisms used to translate substantive policy goals (e.g. increased learning readiness of high-risk students) into concrete actions (e.g. school-based family counselling) (McConnell & Elmore, 1987; Odden, 1991). The instruments used to achieve anticipated results can range from those that are very prescriptive to those that allow for a great deal of discretion on the part of implementers.

McDonnell and Elmore (1987) identified four broad areas of policy instruments—mandates, inducements, capacity-building, and system-change. Mandates are promulgated rules that govern the actions of individuals and agencies. They are expected to produce a level of compliance, and agencies or organizations impacted by mandates often follow them simply to avoid being cited for noncompliance. Typically, funding does not accompany mandated rules and regulation.

Inducements involve the transfer of money to individuals or agencies in return for certain actions. Inducements are expected to lead to the production of valued goods or services. Since the transfer of funds is intended for a specified purpose, inducements are often accompanied by a set of formal regulations designed to assure that money is used consistent with policymakers' intentions.

Capacity-building is the transfer of money for the purpose of investment in material, intellectual, or human resources. Like inducements, capacity-building involves fund transfers; the distinction lies in the anticipated outcome of the policy. Capacity-building is an investment in future benefits that are not clearly defined at the outset. Capacity-building strategies are expected to result in skill enhancement and competence. Results may often take longer to achieve; but the return on investment is longer-term than with the use of inducements.

System-changing transfers official authority among individuals and agencies in order to alter the system by which public goods and services are delivered. The expected effect of this strategy is a fundamental change in institutional structures. It is often accompanied by a change in the incentives which determine the nature and effects of those goods and services. Systems-changing is the policy strategy that has the most significant impact on the ways in which providers of services do business; it entails a complete paradigm shift in the way an organization conceptualizes its mission and the strategies it uses to realize the mission. Because such changes impact the very infrastructure of an organization they do not occur all at once, but evolve over time.

Under what conditions are different policy instruments most likely to produce their intended effects? At issue is the range of options available, the objectives (or need) the policy is designed to address, and the fit between policy development options and desired implementation strategies. The issue of what policy instrument is best utilized to achieve a particular result becomes complex when addressing interorganizational models of system redesign. Policymakers may see a history of system fragmentation and believe that service integration is absolutely necessary; policy implementers (i.e. service providers) may see a need to first and foremost bolster the funding for already overextended programs. Thus, while policymakers desire systems-change, service providers may be looking for inducements or capacity-building policies to be promulgated, where additional funding will become available. The unfortunate result may be that policymakers, in an effort to avoid "throwing good money after bad" through inducements, and out of skepticism that true systems change will occur without prompting, opt for mandates to influence service delivery. Under such circumstances, the result is rarely what was intended (Coe, 1988).

All of the factors impacting the development of policy instruments naturally impact the resulting implementation plans. This interaction becomes particularly vivid when the implementation plan includes interorganizational, or collaborative, efforts. White and Wehlage (1994), in examining the structures surrounding collaboration, ask "If [community collaboration] is such a good idea, why is it so hard to do?" Three perspectives on the challenges inherent in integrated service implementation and collaboration assist in answering this question.

Process-related pitfalls

McLaughlin and Covert (1986) identify 14 potential barriers to effective interorganizational policy implementation: competitiveness, lack of compelling mutual interest, parochial interests, lack of skill in coordinating, difficulty in communicating across disciplines, preoccupation with administrative rather than functional structures, concerns about client confidentiality, resistance to change, external pressures, lack of accountability, lack of monitoring and evaluation procedures, inadequate knowledge of other agencies, negative attitudes, and little consideration of political bases. These barriers address an array of policy implementation considerations (i.e. resources, climate, leadership, etc.) and all have a process component in common. When process is defined as the way in which actions are taken, communications are handled, and conflicts are resolved, each of these fourteen barriers can be reduced or eliminated through an examination of the processes the collaborator uses to carry out business.

Capacity and Will

McLaughlin (1987) suggests that the two most critical factors in determining the success of community-level policy implementation, capacity and will, go beyond the prescription of policymakers. Capacity, or the tools that implementers have available to them, including such intangibles as training and expertise, can be bolstered by policy (e.g. policymakers' use of capacity-building policy instruments), but cannot be created outside of the immediate environment. Each community exhibits differing capacity levels in different arenas; thus, policy implementation may look vastly different based on an individual community's capacity and resources. Staff and administrators throughout organizations participating in a collaboration can exhibit very different capacity levels in terms of training and expertise. The result is that caseworkers might have one perspective on a problem, and how to address it; county administrators may have another, and educators may have an altogether different view of the issue.

Will, or the attitudes and motivation that underlie individuals' responses to policies, is also a crucial factor in the developmental course of policy implementation. In addition to relying on training and professional judgment, implementers will quite naturally judge policies in terms of their personal belief systems, and make their own determinations regarding the appropriateness of the strategy to meet the identified need (McLaughlin, 1987; Odden, 1991). When the best professional judgment and value systems of service providers conflict with that of policymakers, the discrepancies can result in poorly implemented policy, or, in some cases, a completely different path of implementation than that intended by policymakers.

Systems-Oriented Versus Service-Oriented Efforts

The U.S. General Accounting Office (1992) identified distinctions between system-oriented and service-oriented service integration efforts. System-oriented integration efforts strive to create new service-delivery structures and approaches, offer new services, and eliminate conflicting program requirements. Service-oriented efforts link clients and services through co-location and case management. Service-oriented efforts tended to be more successful in terms of increasing communication and getting all collaborating parties to participate actively, especially at the service delivery level. System-oriented efforts were limited in their success because of lack of consensus among the various players, agencies' reluctance to merge and lose their identities and resources, and lack of political support. Service-oriented efforts were easier to achieve because they did not attempt to change state and local organizational structures.

A significant component of this finding is the role of direct line staff workers in service integration. Professionals who work directly with children and families, either from an educational or human service perspective, are trained to have a positive impact on individuals and an impact on systems only to the extent that it serves a direct purpose. Yet, a school-linked services initiative that does not have the positive support of direct service employees may be seriously compromised. Involving individuals at all levels of an organization has implications for which people engage in decision-making, who provides overall leadership to the collaboration, and who interprets policy before translating it into action (Gardner, 1992).

The "Catch 22" between policy development strategies and policy implementation appears clear. Systemic change policies are best developed with wide latitude for implementors but it must often seem to policymakers that very prescriptive mandates are necessary to force system-level reforms on a service-focused delivery system. These potential pitfalls and potholes to collaboration and service integration become clear when viewed from the perspective of actual service delivery reform efforts. One such effort, the School-Human Services Redesign Initiative has been under way in Hennepin County, Minnesota for the past three years.

The Hennepin County School-Human Services Redesign Initiative (SHSRI)

This Initiative is a school-linked approach to reforming the delivery of services to children and families in Hennepin County, Minnesota. The mission is to develop an integrated, comprehensive service delivery system that incorporates schools, public and private social service agencies, neighbourhoods, and communities to meet families' multiple needs. To date, the SHSRI has undergone both a pilot project and planning stage, and is beginning to field test recommended strategies in selected prototype sites across the county.

Pilot Project Development

In 1991, Hennepin County and the United Way of Minneapolis generated discretionary funding to support an array of pilot projects to demonstrate models of collaboration between schools and human service agencies. The overall goal of this capacity-building approach was to provide insights into the strategies that do and do not work when bringing schools and human service agencies together around a common agenda. Specific planning objectives for the pilot projects were:

1. To improve school success for children and youth;
2. To improve and sustain collaborations between schools and human services;
3. To reduce the time school personnel must spend meeting students' social and mental health needs; and
4. To improve accessibility and ease of use of existing services for children, youth, and their extended families (Hennepin County Office of Planning and Development, 1992).

Eleven Learning Readiness Pilot Projects were selected to receive funding from September 1992 through the end of June 1994. With few exceptions the funded projects proposed a model of collaboration where liaisons or family support workers would work with a targeted population of students identified by the school. The services provided by the projects range from peer mediation training and Native American Cultural Pride groups to home visits and informal family counselling.

Each Learning Readiness Project has been asked to collect outcome data on three measures: change in student school attendance, change in parent participation in the school as measured through attendance at parent conferences, and changes in student behavior as measured through a standardized student behavior checklist. This data is still to be aggregated and summarized but it is clear that a consistent, minimal data set used to measure impact across eleven very different projects reveals little about the uniqueness or hidden benefits inherent in each program. External evaluators conducted structured interviews and focus groups with over 120 parents, students, educators, case managers, and administrators across all projects to capture key insights into both the process and outcomes of these projects. Preliminary findings from these interviews indicate that the projects have generally done an impressive job of addressing the goals identified by the policymakers at the outset. Students and teachers impacted by the projects report improved school achievement and reduced class time spent meeting non-academic needs; parents and guardians report easier access to necessary services; schools and agencies report good working relationships (Bloomberg & Hirsch, 1994).

Simply reviewing the extent to which projects have met stated goals overlooks a critical component of the analysis, however. Hennepin County and the United Way initiated the project to identify strategies that could be brought to scale when a full restructuring of the service delivery system was implemented. What has resulted bears a strong resemblance to a project-mentality. The pilot projects are meeting the outcome goals, but only with an additional funding source and extra direct service workers; both will be terminated in a few months. In this situation, the policymakers used a capacity-building approach to policy development, complete with add-on funding for existing agencies and school systems, but they expected a systems-change level of implementation. The current situation is predictable. Project implementers are left wondering why there is no more funding made available to projects that are demonstrating success; the County and the United Way are wondering why schools and agencies did not spend the past two years figuring out how to incorporate these successful models into the ongoing funding streams and operational plans of the organizations.

Planning

A planning process was initiated to examine strategies for ongoing system restructuring while the pilot projects were being implemented. A Redesign Council included policymakers representing Hennepin County, the cities of Minneapolis, Robbinsdale, and Hopkins, and area school districts. This group was responsible for generating broad strategies for interagency cooperation and assuring adequate involvement of all political bases. A lead staff group, comprised of administrative-level policy implementers from the county and each of the cities and schools districts, took direction from the Redesign Council, and was responsible for coordinating all planning efforts and keeping policymakers apprised of the process. The planning goal was to create a proposed restructuring model that would meet the criteria for a streamlined and comprehensive service delivery system. Not surprisingly, the organizations and sectors of the community represented in planning efforts found that working to arrive at consensus about such issues as financing plans and decision-making structures was difficult and time consuming.

In July, 1993, the lead staff planning group, feeling the need for assistance in moving beyond interpersonal issues that seemed to be sabotaging their efforts, asked for an outside evaluator to interview each of the group's members to determine the key process issues that needed to be addressed in order to move on to the real issue of school-human services redesign. Seventeen individuals from the lead planning team were interviewed about the mission of the Initiative, the processes implemented, and the outcomes anticipated. The interim planning report (Rounds & Bloomberg, 1993) identified six primary barriers to the success of the collaborative effort:

1. Lack of trust between organizations;
2. Lack of trust within bargaining units that represent staff of organizations;
3. Power differences among organizations;
4. Turf issues;
5. Doubt about the motives of the partners; and
6. The amount of time spent on the collaborative process.

The planning outcomes were seen by participants as generally positive despite the difficulties identified by key players in this stage. The process was very messy, but the product was met with approval. Specifically, the findings of the Redesign Council and the lead staff team resulted in joint resolutions passed by the Minneapolis and Robbinsdale School Boards, the Hennepin County Board of Commissioners, and the Minneapolis City Council to work together to ensure a comprehensive redesign of services. All recommendations were compiled (School-Human Services Redesign Initiative, 1993) and formed the framework for the next stage.

Development of Prototype Sites

Six prototype sites across three school districts were selected to field test the redesign plans. Each prototype site is a geographic community with a school that primarily serves the community. Prototype collaboratives will eventually include the school, public and private social service and health agencies, and the community itself. A vague framework for service delivery is prescribed in the recommendations, including the delivery of holistic and family-centred services across providers, one lead staff advocate per family, and formal written agreements between providers to clarify roles and responsibilities. Specific implementation plans are left to the discretion of local collaboration councils and barrier-busting committees (School-Human Service Redesign Initiative, 1993). This approach to policy development is in stark contrast to the policy that initiated the original pilot projects. The comparison illustrates the interplay between policy and implementation. The pilot projects had well-planned proposals to develop a model of collaborative services based on a capacity-building request-for-proposals process. The prototype sites, in contrast, are faced with a loosely developed systems-change request with no specific implementation guidelines and no direct funding, only suggestions for re-routing existing funding streams. In theory, the latter will eventually result in the greatest systemic reforms, but the former is meeting the greatest current need.

Establishment of Outcome Measures

Comprehensive outcome measures for each of the initiative's goals are required. A community consensus-building approach to identifying appropriate and valued indicators for outcome measures is currently under way. Over fifty parents, educators, social service providers, and policymakers have participated in a series of consensus-building meetings to identify and prioritize indicators that are both relevant to the stated goals and valued by the community. Five priority indicators have been identified for each of the four outcomes that parallel the initiative's stated goals. The fifth outcome, elimination of gaps between low-income children of colour and middle-income children, will be measured across all other outcomes and indicators.

Outcome 1: Increased School Readiness

A. Percent of children with developmental delays who receive early intervention services

B. Percent of 5-year-old children with basic kindergarten readiness skills

C. Percent of children living in safe and adequate housing

D. Percent of children adequately immunized

E. Percent of low birth weight babies

Outcome 2: Improved School Achievement

A. School attendance rate for students

B. Graduation rate

C. Percent of students' academic time spent on-task

D. Percent of children enroled at the end of the school year who were enroled in same school at the beginning of the year (stability rate)

E. Academic assessment scores

Outcome 3: Enhanced ability of caregivers to support their children's development

A. Percent of families with adequate social and economic resources to parent children
B. Caregiver literacy
C. Percent of caregivers participating in their children's development (vigilance, responsibility)
D. Percent of children living with their own family
E. Percent of children experiencing substantiated abuse or neglect

Outcome 4: A more coordinated, collaborative system of educational and social services for families

A. Percent of caregivers satisfied with school and social services accessibility, quality, and personnel
B. Percent of families with a single access point for services
C. Percent of service providers providing culturally relevant services
D. Percent of cases that use common case plans and single case managers.

The next steps in developing a community-wide outcome measurement plan will be to complete the consensus process by soliciting final approval of the indicators and identifying reliable and socially valid data collection strategies for each one. The challenge is to implement an outcome measurement plan in the most efficient way possible by capitalizing on the strengths and capacities of all the participants in this interorganizational endeavour.

Conclusion

A number of questions remain about the policies and implementation practices that will result in interorganizational systemic change. The war on system fragmentation has had little long term impact, partly because the combat tools have been inadequate, and partly because the war has been fought one small battle at a time. Analyses of interorganizational efforts to restructure systems must take into account the complex interplay among policy development strategies, systems, communities, governments, and individual people. Continued analysis of integrated service efforts must consider the specific dynamics of leadership and authority in interorganizational initiatives, the strategies employed to assess the process, and the impact of such initiatives. Sights must be set on a system that, ten years from now, will look more like today's vision than today's reality.

References

Bloomberg, L. L., & Hirsch, J. (1994). Learning readiness programs: An analysis of process and outcomes. Minneapolis, Minnesota: Institute on Community Integration.

Coe, B. (1988). Open focus: Implementing projects in multi-organizational settings. *International Journal of Public Administration, 11*(4), 503–526.

Crowson, R. L., & Boyd, W. L. (1993). Coordinated services for children: Designing arks for storms and seas unknown. *American Journal of Education, 101*, 140–179.

Gardner, S. L. (1992). Key issues in developing school-linked, integrated services. In R. E. Behrman (Ed.) *The future of children: School-linked services.* Los Altos, CA: David and Lucille Packard Foundation.

Hennepin County Office of Planning and Development. (1992). *When kids and systems collide: A systemic perspective on learning readiness issues in Hennepin County.* Minneapolis, MN: Hennepin County Printing Office.

McDonnell, L. M., & Elmore, R. F. (1987). Getting the job done: Alternative policy instruments. *Educational Evaluation and Policy Analysis, 9*(2), 133–152.

McLaughlin, J. A., & Covert, R. C. (1986). *Evaluating interagency collaboration.* Chapel Hill: University of North Carolina.

McLaughlin, M. W. (1987). Learning from experience: Lessons from policy implementation. *Educational Evaluation and Policy Implementation, 9*(2), 171–178.

Odden, A. R. (1991). The evolution of education policy implementation. In A. R. Odden (Ed.), *Education policy implementation* (pp. 1–12). New York: SUNY Educational Leadership Series.

Rounds, T., & Bloomberg, L. L (1993). *School-human services redesign initiative: Perspectives from lead staff.* Minneapolis, Minnesota: Institute on Community Integration.

School-Human Service Redesign Initiative. (1993). *Proposed Next Steps.* Minneapolis, MN: Hennepin County Printing Office.

U. S. General Accounting Office. (1992). *Integrating human service: Linking at-risk families with services more successful than system reform efforts* (A report to the chairman, Subcommittee on Children and Family, Drugs, and Alcoholism, Committee on Labor and Human Resources, U.S. Senate). Washington DC: Government Printing Office.

White, J. A., & Wehlage, G. (1994). *Community collaboration: If it is such a good idea, Why is it so hard to do?* Madison, WI: Center on Organization and Restructuring of Schools.

8

Improving the Organization and Delivery of Child Welfare Services: Themes, Policy Implications, and Research Agenda

Madeline L. Lovell and A. H. Thompson

Contemporary research suggests that the child welfare system is no longer adequate to meet the needs of Canadian children and families. Today's child welfare mandate has been narrowed to a limited, residual definition of protection. Child welfare agencies are under siege from the escalating numbers of reports of maltreatment, have been forced to allocate an ever larger proportion of available resources to investigations of abuse and neglect, and have few resources to fund services to families (Trocmé & Tam, 1995). Unfortunately, this emphasis fails to address the underlying social problems contributing to the rising complaint rate. Innovative practice strategies directed at developing families' competencies are commonly seen as peripheral to the investigation of maltreatment reports. Re-examining child welfare to determine how to better serve the needs of children, their families, and the communities in which they live is a central task for researchers and policy makers. Care for children's well-being involves the willingness to create and support a broad spectrum of family and child-centred services. Research into the organization and delivery of child welfare services suggests that new paradigms are possible. Programmes that can both strengthen families and address protection concerns appear to be feasible alternatives for at least some parents.

Attention to promising work enriching the social networks of high-risk parents (Cameron, 1995; Fuchs, 1995), empowering parents to act on their own behalf (Wharf, 1995), and developing models of community responsibility and cultural sensitivity (Durst, 1995; McKenzie et al., 1995) can assure that efforts to reform service delivery incorporate an ecological perspective on child maltreatment (Garbarino & Gillian, 1980). Research into the functioning of bureaucratic institutions and the policy development process point to ways of making such services more central on the continuum of child welfare interventions.

Themes

Any assessment of the applicability of research findings must rest on a clear understanding of the purpose of child welfare interventions. Attempts to differentiate between protection and prevention functions mask the fact that any society that values its children must do both. The best way to protect children is to enhance the functioning of families and communities in order that they can then better nurture their young. A continuum of services is necessary for both protection and prevention. Child welfare services can and should be reconceptualized so that workers will no longer be placed in the simultaneous and conflicting roles of "social cop" and counsellor. It is little wonder that contacts often fail to address needs for support and caring when the child welfare worker's primary response to families in trouble must be "What can I do to build a case against you?"

These researchers suggest several fundamental limitations in the approach to delivering services. First, as Brian Wharf points out, child welfare represents a poor woman's social service system and yet our policies and practices are blind to this fact (Wharf, 1995, p.2). The clients of child welfare agencies are poor, live in substandard living conditions in unsafe neighbourhoods, and lack a sense of control in their lives. Such environmental factors immeasurably increase the difficulty of providing the type of parenting deemed adequate by society. Wharf notes the importance of examining the relationship between parenting and the context of families' lives. The strengths of these women are frequently overlooked (Gorlick, 1995). Ironically, the ability of parents to contain their own anxiety and to guard the child from environmental stresses has been found to be among the most critical factors for raising resilient children in the face of unsafe and inadequate living situations (Garbarino, 1992). Policies rarely give priority to empowering parents to take greater control over the conditions affecting their lives. Planning fails to begin with clients' most fundamental needs.

A second organizational deficit has been the lack of cultural sensitivity in the delivery of services to the mosaic of ethnic and racial groups residing in Canada. In recent years, attention has rightly been given to the mistreatment of colonized aboriginal and First Nations communities at the hands of the child welfare system (McKenzie & Hudson, 1985; Johnston, 1983). Assisting aboriginal people to regain control over their families will demand a range of organizational structures to provide the flexibility necessary to respect differences among communities. Appropriate models for such services are only now being developed (Durst, 1995; McKenzie et al., 1995). Mainstream institutions must also incorporate culturally-appropriate intervention strategies in their work. Not only will such agencies continue to serve aboriginal peoples, but they will also serve a growing proportion of non-mainstream children as immigration to Canada continues. School districts in large cities report increasing numbers of children who have English as their second language.

Other often-reported failings of child welfare systems are their fragmentation and slowness in answering changing social needs (Fein & Maluccio, 1992). Contact with numerous social service agencies is a common experience for child welfare clients. The CELDIC report (1970) issued the first of many calls for improved service integration in Canada. Greater centralization has been viewed as a way to reduce the confusion experienced by both clients and service providers. However, little is known about the impact of centralization on the people the system is attempting to serve (Wharf, 1995). Interestingly, little research evidence actually documents the impact of coordinated services on client outcomes.

Finally, the bureaucratic nature of institutions appears to obstruct innovation and responsiveness. Workers report that job frustrations most frequently devolve from organizational pressures rather than the demands of direct practice with often challenging clients and situations (Wharf, 1995). Large bureaucracies frequently seem insensitive to the needs of both clients and staff. The complexity of the tasks at hand fosters a process of goal-displacement by which agencies lose sight of clients in the process of delivering service. Efforts at organizational reform frequently cede greater significance to the evaluation of organizational process than to client outcomes. The impact of reorganization on clients is rarely examined.

Research does, however, provide examples of promising directions for improving child welfare services. New services have been created that reinforce support, empowerment, and skill mastery. For example, the Empowering Women project (Wharf, 1995) starts with the premise that most child welfare clients are poor single parents who are erroneously viewed as inadequate and dysfunctional by existing services. The project reframes the women's problems as survival-related strengths by correctly naming conditions like poverty that contribute to client difficulties. Clients are seen as partners able to share power. Blaming the victim is avoided. Clients become active participants in any planning affecting their lives as well as contributors to social and policy change.

Gary Cameron describes another attempt to create a programme respectful of client abilities. Parent Mutual Aid Organizations (PMAOs) were established within existing child welfare agencies based on the extensive literature suggesting that isolation is a contributing factor to incidents of maltreatment (Polansky et al., 1985; Whittaker & Garbarino, 1983) and that a many-pronged approach is generally more helpful when working with families facing multiple difficulties (Schorr, 1988). The PMAO model represents an integrated intervention to at-risk families. Participants were involved in social integration through building supportive social networks, emotional support, education about skills for more effective coping, and concrete support forms such as money, clothing, and baby-sitting (Cameron, 1995). Useful lessons can be drawn from this approach. Control group parents who were not offered the PMAO option showed two to three times the rate of out-of-home care. PMAO members showed a much greater decline in the use of child welfare services, a higher rate of participation in social and community activities, an increase in self-esteem, and a decrease in reported stress levels at a substantial cost-savings per case.

Research is being conducted in partnership with aboriginal and First Nations communities to determine effective organizational and practice guidelines. First Nations agencies, in the process of assuming responsibility for child welfare services, have at times resorted to adapting procedures from mainstream agencies due to the lack of more relevant models. Brad McKenzie and his colleagues (1995) have undertaken action research with First Nations communities to help them develop their own standards of practice. Such efforts will speed the incorporation of cultural and community values into the organization and delivery of services. Similarly, Douglas Durst's (1995) model of five levels of self-government ranging from benevolent colonialism to complete federalist autonomy indicate that various organizational structures will likely correspond to differing stages of the self-governance process.

In summary, flexibility and responsiveness in meeting individual, family, and community needs appear to be critical variables in reorganizing child welfare. Creative programming exists. The difficulty policy-makers must address is less how to foster new interventions than how to make such programmes an integral part of agency services given the crisis orientation in child welfare (Lovell & Richey, 1991). Innovative and creative services often appear to be marginalized, pushed aside by investigational demands. It is critical to examine organizational factors that contribute to the failure to substantively revamp services in the light of present alternatives. John Lafrance's (1995) work on the managerial styles of social service administrators provides a useful example. He found that bureaucracies may punish visionary risk takers who intuitively lean towards innovations. Perhaps as a result, many managers are more focused on the practical strategies that enhance organizational and personal survival (Lafrance, 1995). Organizational dynamics are not the only obfuscating factors. Policy implementation is itself an extremely complex process. Laura Bloomberg (1995) notes that policymakers have little control over the two most critical components for success, the capacity and will of those who must carry out the changes. Capacity (including training and expertise) can be bolstered but not created. Will, or the attitude toward the change, can be problematic if the values and goals of implementers differ from those of policy-makers. Attention to the process of collaboration and negotiation of differences as well as the correct matching of the desired level of change with appropriate policy instruments is vital.

Implications for Canadian Public Policy

This is a critical period for child welfare reform in Canada. Research can contribute to the change effort by identifying critical issues for reflection and by evaluating possible service options. The research reported here has three major implications for policy-makers. First, policy must assure that innovative programming that addresses a wide variety of needs becomes a vital part of the continuum of child welfare services. Helpful services have the capacity to start where the client is. Second, more attention must be paid to the development of culturally appropriate policies and service delivery systems. Third, findings from research on organizational behavior must be applied to the policy process to maximize the chance of achieving desired results.

Examples of alternative programming exist and offer potential for both protecting children and strengthening families. Components that appear most useful include focusing on client strength rather than dysfunction, empowerment of clients to assume responsible roles at the levels of both individual and community change, and the development of supportive interpersonal networks. Policy directives should require that such services be included within the definition and scope of child welfare services. Service organization and delivery must be informed by an ecological approach to child maltreatment that accounts for the complexity of factors that influence a family's and the surrounding community's ability to care for children (Garbarino, 1986; Bronfenbrenner, 1979). Child maltreatment is best understood by outlining both the stresses external to the family over which it may have little or no control, in addition to parental factors such as knowledge and skills gap (Lovell, 1988;

Kadushin & Martin, 1981). The problems engendered by poverty—poor housing, scarcity of resources, limited respite care, and community violence—must be considered in any attempt to improve parenting. Programmes that address the complexity of family concerns should be encouraged.

Second, policy makers must involve members of different cultural groups to determine child welfare policies and standards that will convey respect for their heritage. Existing policies and procedures must be examined for appropriateness. This process, begun in First Nations and aboriginal communities, should be expanded to other cultural groups. It will be useful to consider a range of structural arrangements and intervention approaches given cultural determinants and varying levels of community autonomy. Policy instruments should encourage the development of culturally appropriate helping technologies by providing specific expectations and guidelines as well as sufficient resources to guide managers.

Third, policy-makers must approach policy development systemically. Nico Trocmé and Kwok Kwan Tam (1995) suggest that efforts to streamline the child welfare system by achieving a more structured decision-making procedure may be ineffective. They found that workers are already making sound decisions in the investigation process and call for a more radical transformation of services. The impact of the interplay between systems—government, communities, families, and individuals—on the formulation of effective strategies deserves careful attention. Child welfare is a provincial matter, thus any analysis of factors that will facilitate change must be done on a province-by-province basis. However, key domains of study will crosscut jurisdictions. For example, the relationship between specific policies and the legislative mandate will require close examination in each province as the legislative framework shapes possibilities for action. It may be necessary to advocate legislative change to support a more diversified response to the risk of child maltreatment. Pitfalls to successful policy implementation such as competitiveness, lack of skill in coordinating, communication problems, lack of accountability, and insufficient evaluation procedure must be avoided (Bloomberg, 1995; McLaughlin & Covert, 1986). A collaborative approach to the twin processes of policy development and implementation would help to ensure that policy creators and service delivery staff share common goals and attitudes. Lafrance's research (1995) suggests that compliance with novel policy is enhanced when managers are given specific instructions to follow that minimize risk. Backward mapping, basing the development of policy on consultations with clients about actual needs, would greatly increase utility and relevance.

New organizational frameworks are worthy of consideration given the inherent dilemma entailed in the dual functions—to support and to protect simultaneously—expected of the child welfare system. For example, the protection and support functions could be separated. Investigation could then be undertaken by the judicial arm of government. Child welfare agencies would be freed to devote their time to strengthening families. Such a proposal remains highly controversial. Many believe that a more unified service to families can be achieved by locating both functions under the same roof, if not within the same worker. In the latter approach, efficiency would be increased by enhanced risk assessment and improved matching of need to intervention.

Research Agenda

Research must be directed towards linking organizational structures with improved client outcomes. All too often the salience of client outcomes as a guide for institutional improvements have been ignored. One method to achieve this end is to fashion demonstration projects in which client outcomes can be examined in the light of the intervention process. Such projects would assist in identifying which elements in the delivery of the programme contribute to goal achievement. It is necessary to do more than simply describe the given intervention. Detailing the clientele and/or the situations for whom the intervention seems most useful, as well as likely implementation difficulties, would be of benefit to administrators contemplating replication. Cameron (1995) models such an analysis by highlighting process components of the PMAO model that potentially could affect successful replication.

Another approach is to create demonstration organizations in which the organizational structure (range of services provided, staffing, flexibility of response) is experimental in nature. Feminist or community-based frameworks are potential guides. Replication of auspicious demonstration projects would pinpoint key contextual variables. Extensive analyses of existing approaches such as privatization or the experience of integrated service delivery now under way in Prince Edward Island could prove highly instructive. Researchers and policy makers will be wise to avoid simplistic, unidimensional solutions given the intricacy of variables influencing child abuse and neglect.

Research can be used to better delineate the components of culturally-appropriate child welfare interventions and services. The work begun in aboriginal and First Nations communities must not only continue but also be extended to members of other cultural groups. Barriers to service will differ across communities as will the help-seeking process. Knowledge of the issues considered to be problems by group members, of the helpers deemed appropriate given the nature of the problem, and of appropriate ways of helping will inform the creation of more responsive organizations.

At the same time, researchers must pay attention to the challenges involved in doing research in communities suffering a history of oppression. Researchers may be viewed with distrust. Consequently, they must be prepared to work with members to develop research goals and methodologies useful to the community as a whole. Models of participatory action research emphasizing collaborative, experiential, and action-oriented strategies offer a means to build knowledge while fostering community responsibility.

Finally, research is needed on means to improve organizational functioning. Relevant questions abound. How can organizations guide and support staff to engage consumers, informal support systems, and communities? What organizational inducements would motivate staff to participate fully in implementing new policy directives? How can the organization minimize the risks entailed for staff who engage in these activities? Answers to such queries will be critical to changing the internal operation of child welfare organizations.

Optimal ways must be found to create research partnerships between policy-makers and academic researchers. Collaboration offers tremendous potential to reshape the child welfare system. However, communication between the two groups can be strained by conflicting perspectives on the gathering of knowledge. Researchers generally focus on what is yet to be discovered, qualifying their conclusions to accord with the limits of the scientific method. Policy-makers, on the other hand, seek unequivocal information about what is already known. Bringing the research process to bear on creative solutions to policy and service delivery dilemmas presents a method to bridge this gap.

One mode of facilitating an ongoing discourse between policy-makers and researchers would be through creation of a national child welfare institute co-sponsored by government and academia. Such a research centre would provide a forum for coordinated action and could establish and oversee demonstration organizations for which present rules and regulations might be waived. A focus on process research would allow examination of the impact of system transformation on client outcomes. Standards and ethics for research practices might be developed in conjunction with concerned community members. Study of incentives and disincentives to partnership would inform dissemination efforts so that policy-makers and administrators remain informed of the viability of new approaches. One possible avenue of communication would be literature reviews on such relevant topics as the prevention models proven to be of benefit in work with high-risk families or the effectiveness of family preservation programmes. Similarly, a synthesis of interdisciplinary perspectives on the diffusion of innovation could profitably inform efforts to effect system-level change. These represent only a few of the possibilities that could result from a dynamic merging of the research and policy processes.

References

Bloomberg, L. (1995). Interorganizational policy development and implementation: An examination of the school-human services redesign initiative in Hennepin County, Minnesota. In J. Hudson & B. Galaway (Eds.), *Child Welfare in Canada: Research and Policy Implications.* Toronto: Thompson Educational Publishing.

Bronfenbrenner, U. (1979). *The ecology of human development.* Cambridge, Massachusetts: Harvard University Press.

Cameron, G. (1995). The nature and effectiveness of parent mutual aid organizations in child welfare. In J. Hudson & B. Galaway (Eds.), *Child Welfare in Canada: Research and Policy Implications.* Toronto: Thompson Educational Publishing.

Commission on Emotional and Learning Disorders in Children (CELDIC) (1970). *One million children.* Toronto: Leonard Crainford.

Durst, D. (1995). Aboriginal government of child welfare services: Hobson's choice? In J. Hudson & B. Galaway (Eds.), *Child Welfare in Canada: Research and Policy Implications.* Toronto: Thompson Educational Publishing.

Fein, E., & Maluccio, A. (1992). Permanency planning: Another remedy in jeopardy? *Social Service Review, 66,* 335–347.

Fuchs, D. (1995). Preserving and strengthening families: Social network intervention of a balanced approach to the prevention of child maltreatment. In J. Hudson & B. Galaway (Eds.), *Child Welfare in Canada: Research and Policy Implications.* Toronto: Thompson Educational Publishing.

Garbarino, J. (1992). *Children in danger: Coping with the consequences of community violence.* San Francisco: Jossey-Bass.

Garbarino, J. (1986). Can we measure success in preventing child abuse? Issues in policy, programming and research. *Child Abuse and Neglect, 10,* 143–156.

Garbarino, J. M., & Gillian, G. (1980). *Understanding abusive families.* Lexington, Massachusetts: Lexington Books.

Gorlick, C. (1995). Listening to low-income children and single mothers: Policy implications related to child welfare. In J. Hudson & B. Galaway (Eds.), *Child Welfare in Canada: Research and Policy Implications.* Toronto: Thompson Educational Publishing.

Johnston, P. (1983). *Native children and the child welfare system.* Toronto: Canadian Council on Social Development.

Kadushin, A., & Martin, J. (1981). *Child abuse: An interactional event.* New York: Columbia University Press.

Lafrance, J. (1995). Bridging the gap: An exploration of social service administrators' perspectives on citizen involvement in social welfare programmes. In J. Hudson & B. Galaway (Eds.), *Child Welfare in Canada: Research and Policy Implications.* Toronto: Thompson Educational Publishing.

Lovell, M., & Richey, C. A. (1991). Implementing agency-based social support skill training with at-risk parents. *Families in Society: The Journal of Contemporary Human Services, 72,* November, 563–572.

Lovell, M. (1988). A review of research evaluating the effectiveness of clinical interventions with abusive parents. *Canadian Social Work Review, 5,* 266–283.

McKenzie, B., Seidl, E., & Bone, N. (1995). Child welfare standards in First Nations: A community-based study. In J. Hudson & B. Galaway (Eds.), *Child Welfare in Canada: Research and Policy Implications.* Toronto: Thompson Educational Publishing.

McKenzie, B., & Hudson, P. (1985). Native children, child welfare and the colonization of Native people. In K. Levitt & B. Wharf, *The challenge of child welfare* (pp. 125–141). Vancouver: University of British Columbia Press.

McLaughlin, J., & Covert, R. (1986). *Evaluating interagency collaboration.* Chapel Hill: University of North Carolina.

Polansky, N., Ammons, P. , & Gaudin, J. (1985). Loneliness and isolation in child neglect. *Social Casework, 66,* 38–47.

Schorr, L. (1988). *Within our reach: Breaking the cycle of disadvantage.* New York: Anchor Press.

Trocmé, N., & Tam, K. K. (1995). Correlates of substantiation of maltreatment in child welfare investigations. In J. Hudson & B. Galaway (Eds.), *Child Welfare in Canada: Research and Policy Implications.* Toronto: Thompson Educational Publishing.

Wharf, B. (1995). Research on organizing and delivering child welfare services. In J. Hudson & B. Galaway (Eds.), *Child Welfare in Canada: Research and Policy Implications.* Toronto: Thompson Educational Publishing.

Whittaker, J., & Garbarino, J. (1983). *Social support networks: Informal helping in the human services.* New York: Aldine.

2

SUPPORT AND PREVENTION PROGRAMMING

9

Assessing the Impact of Family-Based Services

Peter J. Pecora

A variety of social services that focus on strengthening families to prevent out-of-home placement of children have emerged in the fields of child welfare, mental health, and juvenile justice. Forerunners of these services were developed in the 1950s and 1960s as programs to treat the multi-problem family (Geismar & Ayers, 1958; Levine, 1964). Since that time, these placement prevention and family-strengthening services have been described as family-based services, home-based services, services to children in their own homes, and family preservation services. Program design and specific interventions differ, but most of the programs fitting the broader name of family-based services (FBS) share some or all of the following characteristics (Bryce & Lloyd, 1981):

- A primary worker or case manager establishes and maintains a supportive, nurturing relationship with the family.
- A wide variety of helping options are used (e.g., concrete forms of supportive services such as food and transportation may be provided along with clinical services).
- Caseloads of two to twelve families are maintained.
- One or more associates serve as team members or provide back-up with the primary worker.
- Workers (or their back-up person) are available 24 hours a day for crisis calls or emergencies.
- The home is the primary service setting, and maximum utilization is made of natural helping resources, including the family, the extended family, the neighbourhood, and the community.
- The parents remain in charge of and responsible for their family as the primary caregivers, nurturers, and educators.
- Society is willing to invest necessary and sufficient resources in a child's own family to prevent placement as for out-of-home care for that child.
- Services are time-limited, usually 1–4 months.

Family Based Services Program Models

There is wide variation across Canada and the United States in the kind of interventions, duration of services, size of caseloads, and components of service that characterize family-based services (FBS). This is one reason why research findings on FBS programs have been confusing. It is not clear what these services are and who benefits from them. The term "family support" has been used as an umbrella under which to cluster a broad range of family-strengthening programs (Pecora, Haapala & Fraser, 1991). Family-based and family preservation services have both been cited as family support programs although these programs are distinct from the more primary prevention and child development oriented family support programs. These include prenatal care, home-visiting, early childhood education, parent education, home-school-community linkage, child care, and other family-focused services that tend to provide one type of service (e.g., education, housing, financial assistance, or counseling); work with clients exclusively in an office or classroom; treatment provided over a long period of time (one year or more); or planning and monitoring client services delivered by other agencies (Gomby et al., 1993; Kagan, Powell, Weissbourd, & Zigler, 1987; Weiss & Jacobs, 1988). The family, in FBS, is not seen as deficient but as having many strengths and resources (Kagen et al., 1987).

Recently, the Child Welfare League of America proposed a three-tiered typology of family-centred programs:

1. *Family resource, support, and education services.* Community-based services that assist and support adults in their roles as parents. These services are equally available to all families with children and do not impose criteria for participation that might separate or stigmatize certain parents (Child Welfare League of America, 1989, p. 13). These are usually referred to as Family Support Services. Some examples of this type of service are public health nurse visits to parents of newborn infants and the school- or community-based family resource centres being implemented in states such as Connecticut, Maryland, Kentucky, Minnesota and Missouri (Farrow, 1991).
2. *Family-centred services (i.e. FBS).* These services encompass a range of activities such as case management, counseling and therapy, education, skill-building, advocacy, and/or provision of concrete services for families with problems that threaten their stability. The philosophy of these programs contrasts with the more traditional child welfare services in the role of parents, use of concrete and clinical services, and other areas (Child Welfare League of America, 1989, p. 29.) In some areas FBS programs are referred to as family preservation services. The majority of these programs are currently found in child welfare agencies, although a number of programs have been initiated by mental health centres. FBS program initiatives have recently been started in other service arenas including juvenile justice, developmental disability, adoption, and foster care reunification programs. Hawaii's Healthy Start program, for example, provides a comprehensive array of health care, counseling and concrete services to families judged to be at moderate- to high-risk of child maltreatment (Breakey & Pratt, 1991).
3. *Intensive family-centred crisis services.* These services are designed for families in crisis, at a time when removal of a child is perceived as imminent, or the return of a child from out-of-home care is being considered. Yet the reality is that this service model is also being applied to chronic family situations, involving child neglect or abuse, where the family is not in a state of crisis. These programs often share the same philosophical orientation and characteristics as family-centred services,

> but are delivered with more intensity (including a shorter time frame and smaller caseloads), so they are often referred to as intensive family preservation service or IFPS programs. Caseloads generally vary between two to six families per worker. Families are typically seen between six and ten hours per week, and the time period of intervention is generally between four and twelve weeks. The emphasis of these services is on providing intensive counseling, education, and supportive services to families, with the goal of protecting the child, strengthening and preserving the family, and preventing what would be an unnecessary placement of children (Whittaker, Kinney, Tracy & Booth, 1990). In some cases, however, the primary case goal is to reunite children with their families. (Child Welfare League of America, 1989, pp. 46–47.) In this chapter, these programs are referred to as IFPS—Intensive Family Preservation Services, and include IFPS programs such as HOMEBUILDERS™ in Washington, Intensive Family Services in Maryland, and certain types of Families First programs in various states.

The IFPS service model differs from other FBS service models where few concrete services are provided, therapists see families primarily in an office setting, and longer service periods of six months or more are used. A major challenge for the broader FBS service movement is to determine which service models are most effective for particular types of families and children. The target population for both FBS and IFPS programs is usually families in serious trouble, including families no longer able to cope with problems that threaten family stability, families in which a decision has been made by an authorized public social service agency to place a child outside the home, and families whose children are in temporary out-of-home care and are being reunited. Some programs emphasize a crisis orientation. Yet many families served by these agencies are not in crisis, but have been trying to cope with an abusive or neglectful family member, child mental illness, juvenile delinquency, or other problem for some time. Thus, these services may be appropriate for families seen by the child welfare, juvenile justice, or mental health systems, as well as adoptive or foster families facing potential disruption (Barth, 1991; Dore, 1991; Haapala, McDade, & Johnston, 1988; Hodges, Guterman, Blythe, & Bronson, 1989; Walton et al., 1993, Whittaker & Maluccio, 1988).

Program Limitations Need to be Recognized

A number of critiques of FBS evaluation research have been published recently, many of which are theoretically attractive but overly simplistic, rely on a superficial review of FBS research literature, and/or ignore positive FBS research findings. In contrast, I believe that FBS represent a significant step in the evolution of social services, and some of the initial program results are indeed positive. But FBS programs will not replace other types of child and family services or broader societal and service system reforms (Halpern, 1990). A number of case situations can be addressed by FBS programs alone. Some families, however, will always be in need of one or more other child welfare services such as day treatment, family foster care, residential treatment or adoption; and most will need other preventive or support services such as income support, child care, parent education, substance abuse treatment, or job training (Pecora et al., 1995).

It must be emphasized that studies of FBS and other programs have documented that many families need assistance with housing, food, medical care, employment, and basic financial support. Most of the families served by public systems live in communities with few resources to help parents or support healthy child development. In addition, families experience other problems, such as ineffective communication among family members, poor self-esteem, diagnosed mental illness, lack of social support, and pronounced deficits in parenting or basic social skills. Many of these stem from larger societal problems and/or significant psychological or social impairment (Polansky et al., 1981; Polansky, Gaudin & Kilpatrick, 1992). There is a danger that FBS programs will be oversold as a cure-all for families because of their emphasis upon family strengthening and early reports of cost-effectiveness.

One of the major dangers of this movement is that public assistance, housing, health care, and other services which are essential to child and family well-being might be cut to fund FBS. FBS programs are just one of an array of services that must be available to support families through the life cycle. Families may not be able to maintain the gains made during FBS, and children may be vulnerable to continued abuse or neglect without a broader network of family supports available in the larger society and local community. Furthermore, some families need services on a long-term basis and are not well served by a short period of intensive work (Maluccio, 1991). Other families need a high quality foster care service to help them through a difficult period or until the child reaches adulthood (Fanshel, Finch & Grundy, 1990). It is incumbent upon researchers and program staff to point out the place of FBS programs within the larger network of services, and to emphasize to policy makers that both the short and long-term success of these programs is dependent upon the family's ability to access a range of community services and other societal supports. An evaluator must consider how the availability of these services will affect the success of the program.

Defining Program Effectiveness

What outcome criteria can be used to judge the effectiveness of FBS with various kinds of family situations? Criteria used to evaluate these programs have been placement prevention; number of placement days used; reduction in the restrictiveness of placement location; reports of child maltreatment; changes in child, parent, and family functioning; family reunification; and consumer satisfaction ratings (Pecora & Rzepnicki, 1994). Table 9.1 summarizes evaluation results for each of these criteria. With the exception of placement prevention, the results have been somewhat positive, but mixed. The variability in outcomes is due, in part, to the limitations in the research methods and measures used, few analyses of findings by sub-populations of families, lack of stability in some of the programs, and that FBS may not be effective for certain kinds of family situations.

Placement Prevention

Placement prevention has been the focus of much of the research. There are a number of problems with using placement prevention rates as a primary measure of success:

Table 9.1 Outcome Criteria and Findings From Selected Studies of Family-Based Services

Days in Placement and Case Closure

Children in the IFPS treatment group spent significantly fewer days in placement than comparison group children (AuClaire & Schwartz, 1986, pp. 39–40*; Nelson, 1984+; Yuan et al., 1990, p. v*).

The likelihood of case closing for the FBS cases was 46% greater than for the control group cases (Littell & Fong, 1992 as cited in Rzepnicki, Schuerman, Littell, Chak, & Lopez, 1994, p. 61*).

There is some evidence that FBS may shorten the placement time of those children served by the program. In one study in Connecticut, more than half of the children placed were home within 12 months compared to the state-wide average placement duration of 31 months (Wheeler, Reuter, Struckman-Johnson, & Yuan, 1992, p. 5–10).

Changes in Placement Rate

In Michigan counties where IFPS programs were established using a "staging approach" where some counties that did not yet have the service were used as comparison sites, out-of-home placement rates grew more slowly in the counties with IFPS than those in non-served counties. In those counties where IFPS programs were implemented later, placement rates also appeared to slow as a consequence of the service. Considerable costs were saved by the governmental agencies in those counties as a result of the placement trend decrease (Visser, 1991 as cited in Bath and Haapala, in press).

Restrictiveness of Placement

Treatment group used a larger proportion of shelter care days compared to other forms of placement (Yuan et al., 1990*).

Children in the FBS treatment group used less restrictive placement options (Kinney & Haapala, 1984*; Willems & DeRubeis, 1981, pp. 16–25*).

Further Reports of Child Maltreatment

Treatment group children (n= 52) from chronically neglecting families had fewer subsequent reports of child maltreatment compared to control group children (n=19) (Littell et al., 1992, pp. 8, 16*).

Improving Child, Parent, and Family Functioning

Improvements in child and family functioning were found, with the treatment group being rated as better in several areas compared to the control group (Feldman, 1991a, pp. 30–33*). In some studies the differences in improvement found at about seven months after FBS services began, however, did lessen over time, with few differences reported by parents at a 16 month follow-up (Rzepnicki et al., 1994, pp. 67–68*).

In a quasi-experimental study, ratings by workers and clients indicated improvement in caretaker parenting skills, verbal discipline, knowledge of child care, child's school adjustment, child oppositional or delinquent behavior, and child's oppositional behavior in the home (Spaid, Fraser & Lewis, 1991, pp. 139–156).

In the Los Angeles study of two IFPS programs, there were improvements in the following areas of family functioning: Parent-child interactions, living conditions of the families, financial conditions of the families, supports available to families and developmental stimulation of children (Personal Communication, J. McCroskey & W. Meezan, January 4, 1994*).

Parental use of new skills at six month follow-up was higher in a recent family reunification study using an experimental design (E = 62, C = 58) (Walton, 1991, pp. 113–114; Walton et al., 1993*).

Family Reunification
Stein, Gambrill, and Wiltse (1978*) emphasized behaviorally-specific case planning to achieve more permanent plans for children in family foster care. They found that more experimental group cases were closed (50%) than comparison group cases (29%), and a greater number of experimental group children were returned to their birth families.

Lahti (1982, p. 558*) found that 66% of the treatment group children either returned home or were adopted, as compared to 45% of the comparison group children, when special efforts were made to provide services to birth families.

A recent experimental study of IFPS focused on serving children who were in foster care for more than 30 days and who were randomly assigned to receive a three month IFPS intervention. These children were reunited more quickly, in higher numbers, and remained in the home for a greater number of days during a 12-month follow-up period than the control group youth (Walton et al., 1992*).

Consumer Satisfaction
Primary caretakers have reported relatively high satisfaction levels with most aspects of the FBS service (Hayes & Joseph, 1985; Magura & Moses, 1984, p. 103), including studies that involved comparison of the FBS-served parent ratings with those of parents receiving traditional child welfare services (McCroskey & Meezan, 1993, p. 6; Rzepnicki et al., 1994, p. 77*).

Primary caretakers mentioned as positive the ability of the worker to establish a good rapport with them, as well as the teaching of communication, problem-solving and chore chart/reward systems (Pecora et al. , 1991a).

In a recent family reunification study using an experimental design (E = 62, C = 258) consumer satisfaction ratings in a number of areas were significantly higher for the experimental group families (Walton, 1991, pp. 106–109*); Walton et al., 1993).

Juvenile Delinquency Reduction
In a quasi-experimental study of a home-based service program, based on Alexander's behavioral systems family therapy (Alexander and Parsons, 1982), the FBS treatment group participants were assigned based on the need to prevent placement or reunify, and high likelihood of re-committing a delinquent offence within one year. Recidivism in juvenile delinquency differed between the FBS and comparison groups (11.1% treatment, 66.7% comparison group, $p = .01$). When the recidivism rates were adjusted for different follow-up periods, the differences were maintained (5%, 25%) (Gordon et al., 1988, p. 250*).

A home-based FBS program using the Multi-Systemic Treatment (MST) model was used as the treatment for 43 youth (an additional 41 youth were in the control group) to reduce rates of institutionalizing young juvenile offenders. At 59 weeks post-referral, youth who received MST had statistically significant lower arrest rates, had an average 73 fewer days of incarceration, and had less self-reported delinquency (Henggeler, Melton, & Smith, 1992*).

* $p \leq .05$.
** $p \leq .01$.
*** $p \leq .001$.

*An experimental or case overflow research design was used in these studies.

- Placement prevention is a case event that is an imperfect proxy for the actual outcomes being sought, namely improvements in child, parent and family functioning.
- Early studies did not include comparison or control groups. Forming these groups in a rigorous manner has been difficult because of difficulties in risk assessment, referral patterns, and organizational problems (Feldman 1991b; Rzepnicki, Shuerman, & Littell, 1991; Tracy, 1991; Yuan et al., 1990).
- Intake criteria, client screening methods, treatment models, program stability, client characteristics, and other critical factors may vary. Placement definitions, family monitoring methods, and follow-up periods differ across studies, and have also made comparisons difficult.
- There is a need to distinguish the degree of appropriateness of placements. Some placements may be in the best interest of the child and family. Others may not be. The lack of difference found in some studies might be altered if, upon further examination, the comparison group had a higher number of inappropriate/ undesirable placements compared to the IFPS treatment group.

Reviews of the literature indicate that there are mixed findings with respect to placement prevention rates for IFPS (Bath & Haapala, 1994; Frankel, 1988; Magura, 1981; Pecora et al., 1995; Rossi, 1992; Wells & Biegel, 1991). Differences found in placement rates varied from zero to 40%. Summary statistics reported should be viewed with caution since they provide only a fraction of the research data generated by the studies. Nevertheless, in some of the recent large-scale evaluations, placement prevention rates were not significantly different between the treatment and control groups. Sub-group analyses by child age, type of case or other variable might reveal significant differences. One might also argue that the field needs other measures of placement-related outcome that may be more sensitive to variations in service. Days in placement remains an important supplementary outcome criterion. A number of studies found that children in the IFPS or FBS treatment groups spent significantly fewer days in placement as compared to the comparison group children. Studies of whether delays in child placement are beneficial need to be conducted, along with studies of how children actually fare when FBS programs allow them to remain at home.

Restrictiveness of Placement

Reducing the restrictiveness of the placement is an important but infrequently used outcome measure. The growing literature on kinship care is beginning to describe some of the benefits of children being cared for by relatives as compared to placement in a non-related foster home or group care facility (Child Welfare League of America, 1992). The cost differences can be dramatic. For example, even treatment foster care rates are much lower than the $40–80,000 annual costs of residential treatment. So an IFPS program may be very beneficial if it can safely divert youth from psychiatric hospitalization, juvenile corrections facilities, or residential treatment to relative, foster family, or group home care. The optimal outcomes are some form of permanent care—ideally, return home or adoption. But in certain cases, diversion from residential treatment to family foster care can be cost-effective and the best alternative for the child. Unfortunately, only a few studies have looked at the proportion of shelter care days used as compared to other forms of placement

(Yuan et al., 1990), and use of less restrictive placement options overall (Kinney & Haapala, 1984; Willems & DeRubeis, 1981). And there are serious methodological challenges that remain to be overcome such as developing a credible means of determining that a youth should be (or would have been) placed in a particular setting so that placement diversion can be validly assessed. Yet this is an important outcome to be achieved as exemplified by the continuing success of wraparound placement diversion programs used for a small but costly group of highly disturbed youth, and the efforts of many long-term family foster care programs to maintain youth in a foster family rather than in an institutional setting (Fanshel et al., 1990).

Preventing Further Reports of Child Maltreatment

FBS programs have little value if they are not able to protect children from further serious maltreatment. Only a few experimental or other studies have measured whether some of these programs reduce further reports of child abuse or neglect (Littell, et al., 1992; Theiman & Dail, 1992; Yuan et al., 1990). A number of methodological challenges must be addressed to do this. First, there is often greater surveillance of FBS families compared to comparison group families because of the nature of the service, especially if it is home-based. This is exacerbated by the lack of reporting in many comparison group cases, even by mandated reporters, because of worker overloads and because staff may feel that nothing could be done to help the situation. Second, family-worker rapport may make self-reporting by the parents or children more likely if they have some confidence in the worker's ability to help them with that problem. Third, criteria for substantiation of reports need to be operationally defined and monitored closely to ensure reliable data. This is a critical outcome measure with significant methodological problems to overcome and little current research data. Total elimination of subsequent reports would be unrealistic to expect given relatively high recidivism rates in child neglect, physical abuse, and sexual abuse. And many chronic neglecting families and other serious family situations may need more ancillary and follow-up services than are typically provided by some FBS programs in order to be successful. Nevertheless, when further studies are conducted, compared to other forms of treatment, FBS programs should be expected to effectively reduce further reports for certain types of cases.

Improving Child, Parent, and Family Functioning

Improving child and family functioning is the primary area of focus for assessing program effectiveness for many clinicians, program administrators and researchers. One of the challenges involves matching the program objectives, intervention methods and areas of functioning to be addressed. It is unwise to focus on improvements in child academic functioning if the primary goals of the intervention are improvement of specific parenting skills or increasing the family's use of social supports in their neighbourhood. Developing the social support networks of families has been recognized by a few FBS agencies (e.g., Tracy, 1991).

The preliminary findings of the experimental studies in this area are mixed, while the quasi-experimental and qualitative research is more positive. For example, in the most recent study in New Jersey, improvements in child and family functioning were noted for both the treatment and comparison groups, with the treatment group being rated as better in a few areas (Feldman, 1991a). In another quasi-experimental study, ratings by workers and clients indicated areas where improvement had occurred such as caretaker parenting skills, verbal discipline, knowledge of child care, child's school adjustment, child oppositional or delinquent behavior, and child's oppositional behavior in the home (e.g., Spaid, Fraser & Lewis, 1991, pp. 139–156). In the Los Angeles study of two IFPS programs, there are some preliminary indicators of improvement in these areas, but they vary by agency and type of functioning (W. Meezan & J. McCroskey, Personal Communication, December 10, 1993). For the Los Angeles and other studies, such as the massive effort being undertaken in Illinois, these kinds of family functioning data were analyzed by client sub-groups to better ascertain the differential effectiveness of some of these programs with certain kinds of clients. Differences in the service model across the participating programs, for instance, necessitates a number of special analyses by type of program model.

Family Reunification

The use of FBS for family reunification is receiving more attention but has not been extensively evaluated. Application of FBS to children already in foster care for more than 30 days eliminates the problems of trying to ensure whether or not the referral criterion that the child is at risk of imminent placement has been met. Two previous experimental studies are relevant even though the services were not as intensive. They used staff members with special training in time-limited, goal-oriented case planning with lowered caseloads. Stein, Gambrill, and Wiltse (1978) emphasized behaviourally-specific case planning to achieve more permanent plans for children. They found that more experimental group cases were closed (50%) than comparison group cases (29%), and a greater number of experimental group children were returned to their birth families. In another study, Lahti (1982) found that 66% of the treatment group children either returned home or were adopted, as compared to 45% of the comparison group children. One recent experimental study of IFPS focused on serving children who were in foster care for more than 30 days and who were randomly assigned to receive a three-month IFPS intervention. These children were reunited more quickly, in higher numbers, and remained in the home for a greater number of days using a 12-month follow-up period compared to the control group youth (Walton et al., 1992). Further research remains to be conducted, but this may be one of the program areas where IFPS is most effective.

Consumer Satisfaction

Studies of client satisfaction and client viewpoints about what made the service effective or ineffective are producing intriguing information when a focused set of questions is used. Haapala (1983) asked consumers about critical incidents that helped make a difference in their work with the IFPS therapist. These incidents were later clustered into eight themes and were then correlated with child placement. The provision of concrete services and session interruptions (which may have provided the worker with opportunities to teach or demonstrate problem-solving and other skills) were most strongly associated with placement prevention (Haapala & Fraser, 1987).

In other studies, primary caretakers reported relatively high satisfaction levels (e.g., Hayes & Joseph, 1985; Magura & Moses, 1984). But satisfaction ratings did vary from program to program. In one study, primary caretakers mentioned as positive the ability of the worker to establish a good rapport with them, as well as the teaching of communication, problem-solving, and chore chart/reward systems (Pecora et al., 1991a). These initial results are positive but consumer ratings from treatment and control group studies must be examined to more conclusively determine if these services are truly more effective than traditional or other types of child welfare services. Consumers can be asked about the process of service delivery, as well as what skills they learned and other important outcomes. Finally, consumer ratings are typically positive, so studies must use very specific questions to counteract this tendency, and to pinpoint areas of satisfaction versus dissatisfaction.

Conclusion

The FBS research data, including reports from consumers and practitioners, are beginning to form a growing body of evidence about the effectiveness of this service. The program evaluation results, while promising, are far from conclusive because of a number of problems, including the use of few experimental designs, small samples, program implementation problems, few qualitative studies, and inadequate assessment measures. Legislators, as well as state agency administrators, are rightfully requiring programs to gather some form of evaluation data to provide evidence of their effectiveness relative to more traditional approaches. The evaluation studies need to carefully match measures to treatment objectives and methods. And outcome criteria beyond placement prevention must be incorporated. The field lacks information about which particular types of programs are most effective for different client groups and which program components are most important (e.g., delivery of services in the home, active listening, client goal-setting, concrete services). Various studies are just beginning to look at sub-populations and estimating the value of various intervention components (Bath, Richey & Haapala, 1992; Fraser et al., 1991; Haapala, 1983; Lewis, 1991; Nelson & Landsman, 1992). A number of FBS programs are experimenting with special assessment and intervention methods for engaging substance-abusing families.

Life-course studies of families and youth involved in FBS are needed. What circumstances brought these children to the attention of the child welfare system? What services have been provided and what placements have occurred before, during, and after FBS? Snapshot views need to be supplemented with both quantitative and qualitative research on the family in context of their support networks and community characteristics.

FBS programs are not a panacea. They are just one part of the larger array of family services that must be available to families. Early evidence of the effectiveness of these services from a variety of sources must be considered with the less positive findings from recent experimental studies. This provides cautionary information that must be considered as future programs and evaluation studies are implemented. FBS is in the beginning stages of a longer process of service refinement and evaluation. It is all too easy to hold new program models and under-funded or premature evaluation efforts to high standards and find them not measuring up. The effects of these programs will be better established as FBS programs are refined, follow-up services necessary for some family situations are identified, and additional rigorous quantitative and qualitative studies are conducted.

Special thanks to Mark Fraser, Charles Gershenson, Jacquelyn McCroskey, William Meezan, Kristine Nelson, and Mary Rodwell for suggestions on sections of this paper.

References

Alexander, J. F., & Parsons, B.V. (1982). *Functional family therapy.* Monterey, CA: Brook/Cole Publishing.

AuClaire, P. , & Schwartz, I. M. (1986). *An evaluation of the effectiveness of intensive home-based services as an alternative to placement for adolescents and their families.* Minneapolis: Hennepin County Community Services Department, and the University of Minnesota, Hubert H. Humphrey Institute of Public Affairs.

Barth, R. P. (1991). An experimental evaluation of in-home child abuse prevention. *Child Abuse and Neglect, 15,* 363–375.

Bath, H. I., & Haapala, D. A. (1994). Family preservation services: What does the outcome research really tell us? *Social Services Review,* 68(3), 386-404.

Bath, H. I., Richey, C. A. & Haapala, D. A. (1992). Child age and outcome correlates in intensive family preservation services. *Children and Youth Services Review, 14*(5), 389–406.

Breakey, G., & Pratt, B. (1991). Healthy growth for Hawaii's "healthy start:" Toward a systematic statewide approach to the prevention of child abuse and neglect. *Zero to Three,* (April).

Bryce, M., & Lloyd, J. C. (Eds.). (1981). *Treating families in the home: An alternative to placement.* Springfield, Illinois: Charles C. Thomas Publishers.

Child Welfare League of America. (1992). *Report of CWLA North American Kinship Care Policy and Practice Committee* [Draft]. Washington, DC: Author.

Child Welfare League of America. (1989). *Standards for service to strengthen and preserve families with children.* Washington, DC: Author.

Dore, M. M. (1991). *Family-based mental health services programs and outcomes.* Philadelphia, Pennsylvania: Philadelphia Child Guidance Clinic.

Fanshel, D., Finch, S.J., & Grundy, J. F. (1990). *Foster children in a life-course perspective.* New York: Columbia University Press.

Farrow, F. (1991). Services to families: The view from the states. *Families in Society: The Journal of Contemporary Human Services, 72*(5), 268–275.

Feldman, L. H. (1991a). *Assessing the effectiveness of family preservation services in New Jersey within an ecological context.* Bureau of Research, Evaluation and Quality Assurance. New Jersey Division of Youth and Family Services.

Feldman, L. (1991b). Target population definition. In Y.T. Yuan & M. Rivest (Eds.). *Evaluation resources for family preservation services.* Newbury Park, California: Sage.

Frankel, H. (1988). Family-centred, home-based services in child protection: A review of the research. *Social Services Review, 62,* 137–157.

Fraser, M. W., Pecora, P. J., & Haapala, D. A. (1991). *Families in crisis: The impact of intensive family preservation services.* Hawthorne, New York: Aldine de Gruyter.

Geismar, L., & Ayers, B. (1958). *Families in trouble.* St. Paul, Minnesota: Family-Centred Project.

Gomby, D. S., Larson, C. S., Lewit, E. M., & Behrman, R. E. (1993). Home visiting: Analysis and recommendations. *The Future of Children—Home Visiting, 3*(3), 6–22 (Los Angeles: The David and Lucille Packard Foundation).

Gordon, D. A., Arbuthnot, J., Gustafson, K. E., & McGreen, P. (1988). Home-based behavioral-systems family therapy with disadvantaged juvenile delinquents. *The American Journal of Family Therapy, 16,* 243–255.

Haapala, D. A. (1983). *Perceived helpfulness, attributed critical incident responsibility, and a discrimination of home-based family therapy treatment outcomes: Homebuilders model.* Report prepared for the Department of Health and Human Services, Administration for Children, Youth and Families (Grant #90-CW-626 OHDS). Federal Way, Washington: Behavioral Sciences Institute.

Haapala, D. A., & Fraser, M. W. (1987). Keeping families together: The Homebuilders model revisited. Federal Way, Washington: Behavioral Sciences Institute (mimeograph).

Haapala, D. A., McDade, K., & Johnston, B. (1988). *Preventing the dissolution of special needs adoption families through the use of intensive home-based family preservation services: The Homebuilders Model.* (Clinical Services Final Report from the Homebuilders Adoption Services Continuum Project.) Federal Way, Washington: Behavioral Sciences Institute.

Halpern, R. (1990). Fragile families, fragile solutions: An essay review. *Social Service Review, 64,* 637–648.

Hayes, J. R., & Joseph, J. A. (1985). *Home-based family centered project evaluation.* Columbus, Ohio: Metropolitan Human Services Commission.

Henggeler, S. W., Melton, G. B., & Smith, L. A. (1992). Family preservation using multisystemic therapy: An effective alternative to incarcerating serious juvenile offenders. *Journal of Consulting and Clinical Psychology, 60,* 953–961.

Hodges, V. G., Guterman, N. B., Blythe, B. J., & Bronson, D.E. (1989). Intensive aftercare services for children. *Social Casework, 70*(7), 397–404.

Kagan, J., Powell, D. R., Weissbourd, B., & Zigler, E. (Eds.). (1987). *America's Family Support Programs.* New Haven, Connecticut: Yale University Press.

Kinney, J., & Haapala, D. (1984). First year Homebuilders mental health project report. Federal Way, Washington: Behavioral Sciences Institute (mimeograph).

Lahti, J. (1982). A follow-up study of foster children in permanent placements. *Social Service Review, 56,* 556–571.

Levine, R. A. (1964). Treatment in the home. *Social Work, 9*(1), 19–28.

Lewis, R. E. (1991). What are the characteristics of intensive family preservation services? In M. W. Fraser, P. J. Pecora, & D.A. Haapala (Eds.), *Families in crisis: The impact of intensive family preservation services.* New York: Aldine de-Gruyter.

Littell, J. H., & Fong, E. (1992). Recent findings on selected program outcomes. In J. R. Schuerman, T. L. Rzepnicki, & J. H. Littell (Eds.), *An Interim Report from the Evaluation of the Illinois Family First Placement Prevention Program.* Chicago: Chapin Hall Center for Children at the University of Chicago.

Littell, J. H., Kim, J. L., Fong, E. & Jones, T. (1992). Effects of the Illinois Family First Program on selected outcomes for various kinds of cases. Chicago: The University of Chicago, Chapin Hall Center for Children (mimeograph).

Magura, S. (1981). Are services to prevent foster care effective? *Children and Youth Services Review,* 3(3), 193–212.

Magura, S. & Moses, B. S. (1984). Clients as evaluators in child protective services. *Child Welfare, 63*(2), 99–112.

Maluccio, A. N. (1991). The optimism of policy choices in child welfare. *American Journal of Orthopsychiatry, 61*(4), 606–609.

McCroskey, J. & Meezan, W. (1993). Outcomes of Home-Based Services: Effects on Family, Functioning, Child Behavior and Child Placement. Paper presented at Empowering Families Through Building our Ecology, Fort Lauderdale, Florida.

Nelson, J. P. (1984). *An experimental evaluation of a home-based family-centered program model in a public child protection agency.* Unpublished doctoral thesis. University of Minnesota, School of Social Work.

Nelson, K., & Landsman, M. J. (1992). *Alternative models of family preservation: Family-based services in context. Springfield, Illinois: Charles C. Thomas.*

Pecora, P. J., & Rzepnicki, T. L. (1994). Are family preservation services effective in terms of placement prevention and other outcomes? In E. Gambrill & T.J. Stein (Eds.), Controversial issues in child welfare. Needham Heights, Maryland: Allyn and Bacon.

Pecora, P. J., Bartlomé, J. A., Magana, V. L., & Sperry, C. K. (1991a). How consumers view intensive family preservation services. In M. W. Fraser, P. J. Pecora, & D. A. Haapala (Eds.), *Families in crisis: The impact of intensive family preservation services.* Hawthorne, New York: Aldine de Gruyter, 225–271.

Pecora, P. J., Fraser, M. W., Nelson, K., McCroskey, J., & Meezan, W. (1995). *Evaluating Family-Based Services.* Hawthorne, New York: Aldine de Gruyter.

Pecora, P. J., Haapala, D., & Fraser, M.W. (1991). Comparing intensive family preservation services with other family-based service programs. In E. M. Tracy, D. A. Haapala, J. Kinney, & P. J. Pecora (Eds.), *Intensive family preservation services: An instructional sourcebook* (pp. 117–142). Cleveland, Ohio: Mandel School of Applied Social Sciences, Case Western Reserve University.

Polansky, N. A., Chalmers, M. A., Buttenweiser, E., & Williams, D. P. (1981). *Damaged parents: An anatomy of neglect.* Chicago, Illinois: University of Chicago Press.

Polansky, N. A., Gaudin, J. M., Jr., & Kilpatrick, A. C. (1992). Family radicals. *Children and Youth Services Review, 14*, 19–26.

Rossi, P. H. (1992). Assessing family preservation programs. *Children and Youth Services Review, 14*(1–2), 77–97.

Rzepnicki, T. L., Shuerman, J. R., & Littell, J. H. (1991). Issues in evaluating intensive family preservation services. In E. M. Tracy, D. A. Haapala, J. M. Kinney, & P. J. Pecora (Eds.), *Intensive family preservation services: An instructional sourcebook*. Cleveland, Ohio: Case Western Reserve University, Mandel School of Applied Social Sciences.

Rzepnicki, T. L, Schuerman, J. R., Littell, J. H., Chak, A., & Lopez, M. (1994). An experimental study of family preservation services: early findings from a parent study. In R. Barth, J. Duerr-Berrick, & N. Gilbert (Ed.), *Child Welfare Research Review*, (Volume 1, pp. 60–82). New York: Columbia University Press.

Spaid, W. M., Fraser, M. W., & Lewis, R. E. (1991). Changes in family functioning: Is participation in intensive family preservation services correlated with changes in attitudes or behavior? In M. W. Fraser, P. J. Pecora, & D. A. Haapala, (Eds.), *Families in crisis: Findings from the family-based intensive treatment project* (pp. 131–148). Hawthorne, New York: Aldine de-Gruyter.

Stein, T. J., Gambrill, E. D., & Wiltse, K. T. (1978). *Children in foster homes: Achieving continuity of care*. New York: Praeger.

Szykula, S. A., & Fleischman, M. J. (1985). Reducing out-of-home placements of abused children: Two controlled field studies. *Child Abuse and Neglect, 9*(2), 277–283.

Theiman, A. A., & Dail, P. W. (1992). Iowa's family preservation program: FY 1991 evaluation. *The Prevention Report*, (Fall, 1992), 14–15.

Tracy, E. M. (1991). Defining the target population for intensive family preservation services: Some conceptual issues. In K. Wells & D. E. Beigel (Eds.), *Family preservation services: Research and evaluation*. Newbury Park, California: Sage Publications.

Visser, K. (1991). Original Families First counties versus original non-Families First counties. Lansing: Michigan Department of Social Services. Unpublished memorandum.

Walton, E. (1991). The reunification of children with their families: A test of intensive family treatment following out-of-home placement. Unpublished Ph.D. dissertation, University of Utah, 1991.

Walton, E., Fraser, M. W., Lewis, R. E., Pecora, P. J., & Walton, W.K. (1993). In-home family-focused reunification: An experimental study. *Child Welfare, 72*(5), 473–487.

Weiss, H. B., & Jacobs, F. H. (Ed.). (1988). *Home visiting*. Newbury Park, California: Sage Publications.

Wells, K., & Biegel, D. E. (Eds.). (1991). *Family preservation services: Research and evaluation*. Newbury Park, California: Sage Publications.

Wheeler, C. E., Reuter, G., Struckman-Johnson, D., & Yuan, Y. T. (1992). *Evaluation of state of Connecticut intensive family preservation services: Phase V annual report*. Sacramento, California: Walter R. McDonald & Associates, Inc.

Whittaker, J. K., Kinney, J. M., Tracy, E. M., & Booth, C. (1990). *Reaching high-risk families: Intensive family preservation in the human services*. Hawthorne, New York: Aldine de Gruyter.

Whittaker, J. K., & Maluccio, A. N. (1988). Understanding families in trouble in foster and residential care. In F. Cox, C. Chilman, & E. Nunnally (Eds.) *Families in Trouble* (Vol. 5). Newbury Park, California: Sage Press.

Willems, D. M., & DeRubeis, R. (1981). *The effectiveness of intensive preventive services for families with abused, neglected or disturbed children*. Trenton, New Jersey: Bureau of Research, New Jersey Division of Youth and Family Services.

Yuan, Y. T., McDonald, W. R., Wheeler, C. E., Struckman-Johnson, D., & Rivest, M. (1990). *Evaluation of AB1562 in-home care demonstration projects, Volume 1: Final report*. Sacramento, California: Walter R. McDonald & Associates.

10

Preserving and Strengthening Families and Protecting Children: Social Network Intervention, A Balanced Approach to the Prevention of Child Maltreatment

Don Fuchs

Families with children at risk for out-of-home placement have long been a major concern of the child welfare system. A variety of supportive placement-prevention services designed to strengthen families' coping capacities or to assist in the replacement of children have emerged to respond to the increasing numbers of children coming into care. However, many of the placement-prevention services, such as intensive family preservation programs and home builders programs, are developed on narrow notions of parental support and the informal helping context in which the parents raise their children (Barth, 1991; Frankel, 1994; Kinney, et al., 1991). This makes placement prevention difficult, replacement of children in their own home ineffective, and often puts children at increased risk to further maltreatment. Many children remain at risk because these programs provide only cursory assessments of the nature of stress, support and risk factors which exist in the family and neighbourhood social networks of at-risk families.

This chapter reports experiences of the Neighbourhood Parenting Support Project, a form of social network intervention that attends more directly to the role played by the informal and formal helping contexts in placement-prevention and family preservation. The Neighbourhood Parenting Support Project was an experimental four-year research and demonstration project involving two inner city, high-risk, multi-cultural neighbourhoods in Winnipeg. Research findings on the interrelationship between stress, support, and risk to child maltreatment were used to direct the development of an approach to preventive intervention at the local neighbourhood level. Outcomes of the social network intervention and implications of these findings for directing primary prevention programs are predicted. The Project results offer directions for child welfare services, directions that are aimed at preventing child maltreatment by meshing the local neighbourhood formal and informal helping systems to strengthen the social fabric.

The Project and Neighbourhood Parents

The Neighbourhood Parenting Support Project carried out parenting support network research and demonstration activities from 1988 to 1992 in two neighbourhoods in central Winnipeg. The neighbourhoods had 3 to 4 times the city average of child protection case prevalence. The Project goals were: (1) to study the relationship between stress, social support for parenting, and risk for child maltreatment in parents' personal and neighbourhood networks; (2) to devise, develop, and demonstrate a method to intervene in informal personal and neighbourhood networks to strengthen support for parenting and thus reduce the risk of child maltreatment; and (3) to develop ways to mesh formal services with informal support and helping networks. Neighbourhood A was targeted for the neighbourhood parenting support project intervention; Neighbourhood B was a comparison neighbourhood.

The Project staff entered the focal neighbourhoods by connecting and consulting with key agency services providers, resident participants on various community agency boards, and key informants in the neighbourhood. Child protection and family support cases were mapped on neighbourhood maps in order to determine residential patterns of child protection cases. Project staff carried out two community consultation surveys of parenting support in the two inner city Winnipeg neighbourhoods by interviewing a random sample of resident parents (Warren 1989, 1991). The surveys provided consultation with parents about what it was like to live and be a parent in their particular neighbourhoods, the stresses that parents experienced both in their personal lives and in carrying out their parenting responsibilities, and the supports they received from their personal social networks (i.e. the connections they had with family members and others in their immediate household, friends, relatives and neighbours in their neighbourhood and friends and relatives living outside their neighbourhood). The multicultural nature of the two focal neighbourhoods required Project interviewers to communicate in eleven different languages. Over twenty ethnocultural groups were represented by the parents interviewed.

Findings from the neighbourhood consultation surveys indicated that parental stress was high. Most families were living below the poverty line. Sixteen percent of the families experienced economic distress to the point of missing meals because of lack of money. The majority of families lived on social assistance. Most families experienced life crisis stress at a level of 2 to 3 times that parents experienced in similar studies (Warren, 1991). The level of daily personal and parenting worries and concerns was twice that recorded in similar studies (Warren, 1991; Avison, Turner & Noh, 1986). Psychological distress as measured by The Center for Epidemiological Studies—Depressed Mood Scale (CES-D) (Radloff, 1977) indicated that a majority of parents experienced "daily blues" and longer-lasting depression episodes. Many parents experienced high levels of parenting child care demand stress. Stress from housing and neighbourhood factors was high. Most parents were able to list positive features about their neighbourhoods but a majority of parents said that they would likely move within two years because of high rates of crime, gangs of young children and teenagers vandalizing the neighbourhood, drunken persons

Table 10.1: Summary Comparison of Basic Indices of Parent Stress, Support, Risk By Neighborhood Two

Index	Pre Intervention		Post Intervention	
	Neighborhood (N=69) (N=51) Intervention	Comparison	Neighborhood (N=64) (N=47) Intervention	Comparison
Number of Formal Services Used	2.23	1.98	1.95	1.62
Number of Different People Talked to About Problem	2.00	1.63	3.56	3.04
Life Events	4.07	3.45	3.55	2.85
Recent Concerns	6.26	5.57	6.78	6.15
Maltreatment Risk Score[1]	43.86	44.08	40.7	40.47
Number of Helpers in Network	3.25	2.84	2.67	1.85**
Age of Respondent	30.19	31.78	30.97	33.7

[1] Avison & Turner Child Maltreatment Risk Index Scores

roving through the neighbourhoods, worries about their children going to and from school, and dissatisfaction with recreation and education facilities and programs for their children.

The level of social support parents received to balance off these stresses was often minimal. At the time of the second survey in 1991, parents in the intervention neighbourhood (Neighbourhood A) could name only an average of 2.7 persons out of a maximum of 5 in their social network who gave them social support with parenting concerns, tasks and responsibilities; only 1.85 parenting support persons could be named by parents in the comparison neighbourhood (Neighbourhood B). While over 80% of parents said they had someone with whom to talk over personal concerns, the number and diversity of such persons was small. Furthermore, parents were receiving a minimal amount of support from formal health, education, and social services. Neighbourhood A received an average of 2.0 services and Neighbourhood B, an average of 1.6 services in the past six months. From 1989 to 1991 this number had declined by 10% in Neighbourhood A and 20% in Neighbourhood B. The parents indicated that fewer than 50% were satisfied with the parent support services they received in general and in the neighbourhood as well.

Use of the Avison and Turner child maltreatment risk scale (1986) indicated that risk levels were at least twice that of other communities where the same risk indicator was used (Lugtig & Fuchs, 1992). The neighbourhood survey data were used by the Project research staff to develop a profile of those factors which were associated with child maltreatment risk. Tables 10.1 and 10.2 compare the major stress/support/risk factors by neighbourhood and high and low-risk groupings. The main personal and social stress factors associated with parental risk of maltreatment were daily concerns, worries about living and parenting, depressive symptoms, and extreme thinking (excessive concerns

Table 10.2: Summary Comparison of Basic Indices of Parent Stress, Support, by Abuse Risk Level After Intervention in August 1991

Index	Abuse Risk	
	Low (N =55)	High (n =56)
Number of Formal Services Used	1.80	1.82
Number of Different People Talked to About Problems	3.27	3.41
Life Events	3.11	3.39
Recent Concerns	5.85	7.16
Abuse Risk (Avison & Turner)	36.09	45.04
Depression CES-D Scores	11.56	18.09
High Risk Factors (Avison & Turner)	6.67	7.82
Child Care Demand	26.71	29.21
Number of Helpers in Network	2.49	2.16
Age of Respondent	32.00	32.25

about privacy, control of child, and use of excessive physical force in child management). Table 10.1 shows that parents in both neighbourhoods experienced high levels of stress and risk of child maltreatment. Further in spite of the high stress level, the intervention neighbourhood (A) had a significantly higher level of support both before and after intervention. Table 10.2 identifies recent concerns, depression, and high levels of child care demand as some of the more noteworthy difference between the high and low-risk groupings.

Like Corse, Trickett & Schmid (1990) the Neighbourhood Parenting Support Project found that high-risk mothers seemed to experience less support from outside the family than did mothers from low-risk families (Warren, 1989). These mothers reported having fewer relationships with, and receiving less parenting support from, friends and co-workers. They were less likely to engage in activities such as community events which allowed for outside contacts. Additionally, they reported less satisfaction with the overall help available to them as parents. The survey findings are consistent with other researches (Corse, Schidd & Trickett, 1990; Telleen, 1990; Whittaker, 1986; Whittaker, et al., 1990), in finding that the social environment of the mother in a high-risk family appears to be a precarious one in which there is limited help available to deal with the inevitable frustrations and challenges of child-rearing. Their families of origin were often perceived as nonsupportive and conflicted, while few opportunities existed outside their families to balance these limited inner resources. External contacts were few, and there was little involvement in community activities. Even when contact with helping professionals was made mandatory by child and family service agencies, these relationships were not experienced as supportive. Lack of awareness or trust of potential resources contributed to the mothers' limited social contacts. Parents with negative attitudes and expectations concerning the usefulness of network resources for help in the resolution of problem situations tended to be less trustful of seeking out others in times of need (Lugtig, 1990). High-risk mothers found it difficult to form and sustain relationships with others due to poor social network skills and lack of trust and awareness of available resources. In addition, high crime rates, transience of neighbourhoods, and social indifference mitigated against trusting involvement in community activities and social relationships.

The survey findings are consistent with other research (Corse, Schmid & Trickett, 1990; Susman et al. 1985; Telleen, 1990), in that mothers from high-risk families differed from low-risk mothers on a number of important aspects of parenting. Mothers from high-risk families seemed to take a more rigid and/or authoritarian stance on discipline matters (Belsky, 1984). They were more likely to believe in ruling by anxiety induction or physical punishment and were less likely to endorse rational and reasoning techniques. The research of Corse, Schmid & Trickett, (1990) provided some evidence that contact with people outside the nuclear and extended family, such as peers and professionals, altered the beliefs and practice of parents in ways that family members, by virtue of their shared life experiences and similar parenting attitudes did not. Their findings, as well as the anecdotal evidence of the Neighbourhood Parenting Support Project, seem to indicate that information from friends and helping professionals presented the high-risk mother with new ideas that challenge her own way of thinking, provide her with new models of interaction, and cause her to monitor her behavior more carefully.

The project found that outside of home neighbourhood contacts gave parents and children time away from each other, allowing each a break from continual intensive interaction that could fuel impulsive abusive behavior. Similarly, satisfying relationships with others appeared to lessen the parent's need to look to the child for gratification. The malfunctioning relationships in high-risk families appeared to be maintained when little new input of ideas and energy was allowed into the family system, allowing the cycle of abuse to continue (Telleen, 1990). These findings indicate the importance of understanding the families' ecologies and the nature of the relationship between the ecological context and the risk of child maltreatment.

Mothers from high-risk families experienced difficulties in many aspects of their social networks (Lugtig, 1990; Warren, 1991). Consequently, it was essential to target interventions at multiple levels to bolster available support, particularly when such interventions served to create effects in adjacent levels as well (Belsky, 1984). For instance, identifying social support available to a high-risk family and intervening at the personal social network level, with the high-risk mother, served to improve the social network skills and trust level of the individual parent (Ballew, 1985). It also strengthened the supportive pro-social relationships and fostered a feeling of support, belonging and identification within her network.

The community consultation with key informants and the community surveys contributed to development of the central hypothesis of the Project. The Project hypothesis was that child maltreatment risk could be reduced at both the neighbourhood level and at the parent level if social support for parenting could be strengthened. Indications of social support are formal service use, personal network diversity, parenting support network size, and neighbourhood child care norms (neighbourhood context).

Social Network Intervention

A method of social network intervention was derived from the social network intervention elements (Maguire,1980, Fuchs & Costes, 1992; Fuchs, 1993). The social network of each person was identified and mapped, and plans made and carried out for changing the connections or links in ways that would provide the focal person with more resources and support. Network identification, mapping, and linking was done by consulting, connecting, convening, constructing, and coaching. The social network method was developed for use by a neighbourhood worker to assist parents to make changes for the purpose of increasing support in their networks and thereby reducing their level of risk to child maltreatment in the high-risk neighbourhoods.

A neighbourhood parenting support worker made connections with about 100 parents in neighbourhood A over a two year period. A cohort of 26 parents agreed to participate in the in depth research data collection relating to their social network identification, mapping and linking. In addition, the support worker provided direct social support and coaching in the areas of (1) problem identification and solving, (2) networking skills, (3) parenting skills, (4) support and help-seeking skills, (5) communication skills and (6) support giving skills. It was necessary for the worker to connect with parents in the neighbourhood and with neighbourhood networks. The neighbourhood parenting support worker joined with and supported neighbourhood central figures, natural helpers, and network connectors to develop a referral network and neighbourhood parenting support network structures. The worker activities included work with parents, work with the neighbourhood, and work with other professional workers and agencies.

Social network intervention with parents included activities such as exploring parental concern, examining stresses and supports in the parents social networks through mapping the parent's personal network, and developing a plan which could change the parent's network. Network change activities were directed at weakening ties with stressful persons or agencies; clearing stress from a particular network link by mediation, brokerage or other activities; strengthening ties with persons or agencies who could provide stronger or better support; and connecting the parent with other persons for purposes of network construction.

The following two case examples illustrate the worker's activities with two types of neighbourhood families. Susan, a single parent mother of 4 children, was initially linked to the project worker as an isolate, strongly tied to her dysfunctional family. Her 13-year-old boy was in the care of the child and family service agency because of his acting-out behavior. It was also discovered that the 13-year-old was sexually abused by his grandmother or another member of Susan's family. The younger children (aged 9,6, and 2) were living with Susan.

The networker worked with Susan on increasing her network size and density and on increasing the frequency of contact with other neighbourhood mothers and on appropriate reciprocity in her relationship with other mothers. Finally the networker worked with Susan on improving the flow of social support resources over her local neighbourhood network.

Susan has become less crisis focused and has a more diversified neighbourhood network. She has become less dependent on her family ties and takes an active role in recruiting, maintaining new network ties to assist her with the parental social support that she needs to cope as a parent in her neighbourhood. Susan has greatly improved her parenting of the children in her care and the child and family service agency has replaced her teenage son back with her.

The G. family was comprised of a mother Jane (in her late 20s), father John in his mid 30s oldest son 9, middle son 6, daughter 2 years of age. The couple had been together for 10 years. They had many ups and downs, with a history of physical violence and substance abuse between them. John's and Jane's families of origin were extremely dysfunctional and abusive.

By strengthening the ties with other supportive individuals and clusters of mothers, and increasing the flow of social support from other more functional mothers, the networker increased the amount and the diversity of personal and parenting social support available to Jane at the local neighbourhood level. In addition, by reducing the frequency of contact, and increasing the number of shared activities with other network members, the networker was able to loosen the dysfunctional ties between John and Jane and between Jane and her former drinking family members and friends which represented a threat to her and her children.

The intervention has increased the number of Jane's supportive network ties and has increased the amount of personal and parental support available to Jane which has reduced her perceived sense of social isolation and increased her capacity to parent her children. Further it has increased her capacity to develop, maintain, restore and use her social network ties to assist her with personal and parenting concerns.

The worker's activities in the neighbourhood consisted of (a) constructing a network of neighbourhood parents, (b) identifying and providing consultative support to neighbourhood helpers, (c) participating in the life of the neighbourhood through helping out at the parents' meetings, convening neighbourhood network meetings, and participating on the boards of directors of the neighbourhood support agencies such as the Family Centre and the Day Care Centre, (d) supporting the development of a parents' babysitting co-op, e) assisting a neighbourhood parent to develop a neighbourhood resource booklet, and (f) participating in a parent peer counselling program sponsored by a local health agency.

The worker established contact with over fifty workers and agencies. The multiplicity of agencies involved in the lives of the parents illustrates the degree to which formal systems had become an integral part of the lives of citizens. The worker's role with formal systems was (1) to make sure the parent was steered to the appropriate resource, (2) to coach the parent in the appropriate use of the resource, (3) support the parent in using the resource by attending with her where necessary, and (4) coordinating the resources with the parent where there were a multiplicity of resources involved. Coordination usually involved convening network sessions or assemblies of informal supporters and members of the formal agencies involved for the parent. The worker attempted to strengthen the parent's capacity to deal with formal systems personnel on her own, with the aid of social network coaching assistance, so that the parent's personal social skill and self help capacity would be enhanced.

Table 10.3: Comparisons Between Parents Participating in Network Intervention and Key Subgroups in Terms of Support Ratio and Risk Indicators

	Intervention Network Parents	Cross-Section of all parents in neighborhood	Parents who report recent family violence	Background experience of violence in childhood	Above average recent concerns problem load	CFS Agency case
Parent Support/Stress or Ratios [1]	1.8:1	1.3:1	1.2:1	1.2:1	1.1:1	0.9:1
Avison & Turner risk scores	39.4	40.7	41.7	40.9	41.9	44.1
CES-D Depression Scores	28.7	31.3	34.0	31.7	33.4	34.3
	(N=19)	(N=64)	(N=19)	(N=30)	(N=39)	(N=17)

[1] Ratio represents the average number of parental social supporters available per parental stressor across the various parent groupings.

Results of Social Network Intervention

The Project provided direct parenting support to 100 parents. It assisted in enlarging and diversifying their social support and parenting support networks with an increase in the level of personal and parenting support in the networks. Emotional support, information and advice, and concrete support increased between Time 1 and Time 2, particularly among the high-risk parents. The Project examined in greater depth the stress and support risk factor results for an enhanced intervention cohort of 19 parents, and compared these results with the broader neighbourhood sample of parents at Time 2 (Summer, 1992). Further it compared the intervention neighbourhood (Neighbourhood A) with an adjacent neighbourhood (Neighbourhood B) that was at a similar vulnerability to risk at Time 1 (Summer of 1989) and Time 2 (Summer of 1992).

Table 10.3 provides findings from the project evaluation. The intervention cohort had a lower level of risk at Time 2 than parents in neighbourhood A, higher level of support, lower level of depression, and lower level of family violence than other neighbourhood A parents. However, observations suggested that support gains are fragile in the face of the heavy stressors in this neighbourhood and require a longer term sustaining effort with a great deal of continuity and consistency. The parenting support networks in neighbourhood A at time 2, although decreased in size from time 1 were still higher than neighbourhood B at time 2 and this difference had increased over the two year period. Further, the use of neighbour-friend support had increased in neighbourhood A between time 1 and time 2 by 25% in contrast to an increase in neighbourhood B by 10%. Intervention neighbourhood parents had much higher levels of membership and participation than their comparison neighbourhood counterparts. Finally, the support to stress ratio of the parenting support networks increased slightly in neighbourhood A from time 1 to time 2 but decreased by 13% in Neighbourhood B over the same period.

Social network intervention can assist both low and high-risk parents to alter the size, composition, and supportive content of their parenting support networks and thus increase and enhance the level of social support. Informal network helping can be meshed with formal systems of help through the intermediary of parenting support workers and this can add to the level of the parent's support. The project findings also suggest that social support and social network constructs are valuable in assessing child maltreatment risk levels in family and neighbourhood contexts. Social support and social network constructs can be used to design, implement, and evaluate preventive as well as treatment programs. Services must be developed at the local neighbourhood level to increase the parenting support for individual parents and the neighbourhood as a whole to prevent placement of children or the risk of reabuse on return home. Failure to assess and work with the social support structure of the parent and the neighbourhood places children and families at risk to child maltreatment.

In summary, major findings of the Project are (1) that informal helping and support can be strengthened by social network intervention, (2) the formal systems can be meshed with informal structures, and (3) that risk for child maltreatment in a community can be reduced by social network intervention. The Project's research findings and intervention model provide a promising resource for policy planners, program developers, and practitioners in efforts to blend informal and formal helping structures with respect to family preservation and other forms of placement-prevention interventions. The project has provided a promising model for strengthening community networks to produce safer, healthier social contexts for the return of children to families after being in care. The approach provides a means to assist neighbourhood parents in high-risk areas to acquire the support they need to continue to parent their children in rapidly changing and stressful social ecologies.

This research was funded by the Welfare Grants Division of Health and Welfare Canada.

References

Avison, W. R., Turner, R. J., & Noh, S. (1986). Screening for problem parenting: Preliminary evidence on a promising instrument. Child Abuse & Neglect, *10*, 157–170.

Barth, R. (1991). An experimental evaluation of in-home child abuse prevention services. *Child Abuse & Neglect, 15,* 363–374.

Ballew, J. R. (1985). Role of natural helpers in preventing child abuse and neglect. *Social Work, 30,* 37–41.

Belsky, J. (1984). The determinants of parenting: A competence model. *Child Development,55,* 83–96.

Corse, S., Schmid, K., & Trickett, P. (1990). Social network characteristics of mothers in abusing and nonabusing families and their relationships to parenting beliefs. *Journal of Community Psychology, 18*(1), 44–59.

Frankel, H. (1994). Family-based approaches to placement prevention in child welfare. Unpublished Manuscript. Winnipeg: University of Manitoba.

Fuchs, D., & Lugtig, D. (1989). The prevention of child maltreatment in high-risk multiethnic and multi-cultural neighbourhoods. (Occasional Paper Series #06931). Winnipeg, Manitoba: Child and Family Research Group, Faculty of Social Work.

Fuchs, D., & Costes, T. (1992). Building on the strengths of family and neighbourhood social network ties for the prevention of child maltreatment: A groupwork approach. In D. Fike & B. Rittner, (Eds.), ***Working from strengths: Proceedings of the Miami symposium of the Association of Social Work with Groups.*** Miami, Florida: Centre for Group Work Studies.

Fuchs, D. (1993). Building on the strengths of family and neighbourhood social network ties for the prevention of child maltreatment. In M. Rodway & B. Trute (Eds.). *Ecological Family Practice: One Family, Many Resources.* Lampter, Wales: Edwin Mellen Press.

Kinney, J., Haapla, D., & Booth, C. (1991). *Keeping families together. The homebuilders model.* New York: Aldine De Gruyter.

Lugtig, D. (1990). A report to the Laidlaw Foundation on the development and cross cultural pre-testing of the neighbourhood parent support survey instrument (unpublished monograph). Winnipeg: University of Manitoba.

Lugtig, D., & Fuchs, D. (1992). Building on the strengths of local neighbourhood social network ties for the prevention of child maltreatment (unpublished monograph) Winnipeg: University of Manitoba.

Maguire, L. (1991). *Social support system in practice.* Silver Spring, Maryland: NASW.

Olsen, R. (1986). Integrating formal and informal social care: The utilization of social support networks. *British Journal of Social Work, 16*, 15–22.

Radloff, L. S. (1977). The CES-D scale: A self-report depression scale for research in the general population. *Applied Psychological Measurement, 1*, 385–401.

Susman, E., Trickett, P. , Iannotti, R., & Hollenbeck, B. E. (1985). Child-rearing patterns in depressed, abusive and normal mothers. *American Journal of Orthopsychiatry, 55*(2), 237–251.

Telleen S. (1990). Parental beliefs and help seeking in mothers' use of a community-based family support program. *Journal of Community Psychology, 18*(3), 264–276.

Telleen, S. (1985). *Parenting social support index: reliability and validity.* Chicago: The University of Illinois At Chicago.

Turner, R. J., & Avison, W. R. (1985). Assessing risk factors for problem parenting: The significance of social support. *Journal of Marriage and the Family, 15*(1), 881–892.

Warren, D. I. (1980). Support systems in different types of neighbourhoods. In J. Garbarino & S. Stocking (Eds.), *Protecting children from abuse and neglect.* San Francisco: Jossey-Bass.

Warren, D. I. (1989). Neighbourhood parenting support: Preliminary comprehensive report on findings derived from the community survey, (unpublished monograph). Faculty of Social Work, University of Manitoba, Winnipeg, Manitoba.

Warren, D. I. (1991). Neighbourhood parenting support project: Preliminary comprehensive report on the findings derived from the community surveys. Unpublished Monograph, Faculty of Social Work, University of Manitoba, Winnipeg, Manitoba.

Whittaker, J. K. (1986). Formal and informal helping in child welfare services: Implications for management and practice. *Child Welfare, 65*(1), 17–25.

Whittaker, J., Kinney, J., Tracy, E.M., & Booth, C. (1990). *Reaching high-risk families: Intensive family preservation in human services.* New York: Aldine.

11

Social Prevention: A Study of Projects in an Urban Environment

Nicole Dallaire, Claire Chamberland, Sylvie Cameron and Jacques Hébert

The socioeconomic situation in Canada and other industrialized countries is steadily deteriorating. The increased polarization in our societies coupled with rising violence, unemployment, insecurity, and poverty are very troubling phenomena. This social and economic crisis is not a passing condition but rather a mutation requiring major adjustments in the way social and economic life is organized (Crozier, 1987; Gallo, 1989; Robin, 1993). This context is dimming the future prospects of youths who are victims of macrosocial imbalances and is placing a heavy load on them (Grand'Maison, 1992).

Prevention practitioners often feel powerless in the face of these upheavals, but a realignment of practice models could provide solutions that are better suited to the present context. Interdisciplinary practice and the ecological model provide a more concrete and accurate understanding of macrosocial dimension. This is a far cry from the conventional, disease-oriented, biomedical model that focuses mainly on the deficits identified in youths and their parents, independent of the characteristics of their living environment. The ecological model takes a holistic approach to social problems, considering psychosocial, cultural, political and economic dimensions as well as their interrelation with each other (Chamberland et al., 1993). The study of youth problems by merely looking at how they emerge at the individual or family level is not possible with these new conceptual tools. Individual deficits are also manifestations of social problems and require profound changes in the way intervention is designed. The changes deal mainly with the choice of targets for action and of strategies, including empowerment strategies.

This realignment of practice models has filtered into the political discourse on health and welfare. In 1988, the Department of National Health and Welfare adopted a broadened definition of mental health to take account of the interaction between individuals and their environment. Importance was attached to fundamental values on which society must be built to bring mental health within everyone's reach. These values include equality, justice and equitable sharing and exercising of power. An interactive definition of mental health involves the ability of an individual, group, and environment to interact in a way that will promote well-being, the optimal development and use of mental skills (cognitive, emotional and relational), the attainment of just individual and collective goals, and the creation of fundamental conditions of equality (Government of Canada, 1988, p. 7). Reducing inequalities, increasing prevention, and promoting autonomy were the challenges that had to be taken up to ensure equal access to health.

Québec's youth task force report, Le rapport du groupe de travail pour les jeunes (Gouvernement du Québec, 1991), ranked the war on poverty as the primary objective for public authorities to significantly reduce psychosocial problems having an impact on children and youths. The Conseil des affaires sociales [social affairs council] (1989) had already shown that no progress had been made in the war on poverty for ten years and that 46% of Québec's population lived in areas that were disintegrating economically and socially. These areas presented the same social problems: low levels of education, higher rates of educational maladjustment and delinquency, low incomes, housing in need of major repair, and so forth.

Child poverty is closely tied to economic and social underdevelopment. In 1992, the Québec government presented its new health and welfare policy. Six of the 17 aims were related to the social adjustment of youths and their families: reducing cases of sexual abuse, physical abuse and negligence towards children, lessening serious behaviour disorders and delinquency in young people, and decreasing the number of cases of domestic violence against women. The new policy adopted an integrated approach in which determining health factors could be acted upon through six comprehensive strategies: 1) to promote enhanced human potential, 2) to support living environments and develop safe, healthy environments, 3) to improve living conditions, 4) to take action for and with vulnerable groups, 5) to harmonize public health and welfare policies and actions, 6) to orient the health and social services system towards seeking the most cost-effective solutions (Gouvernement du Québec, 1992, p. 134). The strategy to improve living conditions requires developing action plans that reduce poverty, increase availability of low-cost housing, and promote creating steady jobs and access to the labour market.

Implementing these strategies from an empowerment perspective constitutes an essential choice in pursuing an objective of reducing social inequalities and promoting universal health (Blanchet et al., 1993; Chamberland et al., 1993). Swift and Levin (1987) propose a definition of empowerment:

> [E]mpowerment: 1) refers both to the phenomenological development of a certain state of mind (e.g., feeling powerful, competent, worthy of esteem, etc.) and the modification of structural conditions in order to reallocate power (e.g., modifying the society's opportunity structure)—in other words, empowerment refers both to the subjective experience and the objective reality; and 2) is both a process and a goal (p. 73).

Unequal sharing of power constitutes a major determining factor in the deterioration of home environments and of individuals (Albee, 1988; Mullender & Ward, 1991; Swift & Levin, 1987) as it inhibits individuals from taking an active part in building the social structures that determine their quality of life and living conditions. Mullender and Ward (1991) sum up how this empowerment perspective translates into practice:

> Practice should be based on an understanding that the social structure, the way particular societies are organized and their norms and institutions are the source of much human suffering. Besides this practice needs to flow from group members' own recognition of how social institutions and socially constructed attitudes inhibit their opportunities in life (Mullender & Ward, 1991, p. 126).

Adopting an empowerment perspective in the development of social services is a choice of values (Price, 1990) that favours going beyond the dominant technocratic model that leads users to passive consumer relationships (Bélanger & Lévesque, 1991; Crozier, 1987; Rappaport, 1981). One critique of social protection systems blames state bureaucracy and the nature of practitioner-user relationships (Rappaport, 1981) for transforming users into wards who are dependent on corporate systems that treat them like children (Crozier, 1987, p. 149). Dependent clients will easily become alienated, will not take part in performing services, and cannot be relied upon to take part in their own management (Crozier, 1987, p. 156). Clients should be co-producers of services, active citizens who feel responsible for themselves and for the quality of their environment (Breton, 1994). Intervention should also foster social change (Heller, 1990), build on the strengths of individuals and communities (Breton, 1993; Mullender & Ward, 1991), produce political and economic changes (Blair, 1992; Bouchard, 1983; Elias, 1987; Rappaport, 1992) and therefore challenge the status quo (Chavis & Wandersman, 1990; Price, 1990).

Towards a New Concept Of Social Prevention

Social prevention that is more critical and multidisciplinary and adopts an empowerment agenda can broaden its scope significantly. Social prevention covers all the preventive and promotive practices in which concerted efforts between the various levels (psychosocial, social, political, cultural, economic) focus on resolving or reducing the social problems of a neighbourhood, locality, region or group, and on promoting living environments that foster the development of individual and collective potentials as well as the establishment of resource and power-sharing policies.

The nature and scope of the causes identified when analyzing a social problem determines, in part, the choices made in developing preventive intervention, especially as to objectives, targets, and strategies (Chamberland, 1994; Porter, 1981). It is essential to go beyond identifying risk factors, including socioeconomic ones (poverty, unemployment, insecurity), and to also identify the cultural, political, and economic processes that contribute to perpetuating these conditions. Identifying macrosocial factors as major components in the etiology of social ills reappeared as a research strategy in the early 1980s. Albee (1986) focused on all forms of discrimination and exploitation as well as on research on a just society. Some twenty years earlier, the American war on poverty had directed action towards socioeconomic factors such as jobs, immigration, health, the integration of youths. Initially, maximum citizen involvement and participation was sought, but, in the course of process, this concern was sidetracked by political policy-makers who feared too much disruption (Moynihan, 1969). Little by little this social vision faded away (Klein, 1987; Elias, 1987; Rappaport, 1992).

Preventive intervention has traditionally been aimed at reducing or eliminating risk factors and pathogenic conditions (factors that heighten the chances of a problem emerging) and increasing protection factors, especially those that limit the effects of stress, such as social support, self-esteem, and social skills (Blanchet et al., 1993; Porter, 1981; Lafortune & Kiely, 1989). Pransky (1991) described the similarities in the configurations of factors at the root of various problems affecting youths (suicide, drug addiction, delinquency, and so forth). The aim of intervention is to reduce or eliminate the common factors that

Table 11.1: Selected CLSC Territories in the Montreal Area

Socioeconomic Level		
Upper	**Middle**	**Lower**
Pierrefonds (MI)	Marigot (L)	Centre-Sud (MI)
Samuel de Champlain (M/e)	Olivier-Guimond (MI)	Villeray (MI)
	Plateau Mont-Royal (MI)	St-Henri/Petite-Bourgogne (MI)
	Vieux-Lachine (MI)	Parc-Extension (MI/e)
	Côte-des-Neiges (MI/e)	Longueuil-Ouest (M)
	St-Hubert (M)	

(MI = Montreal Island, L = Ville de Laval, M = Montérégie, e : ethnic component)

contribute to creating each of these problems, by putting into place a set of community related measures that offer support to youths and their families at various stages of their lives, and that also concern the quality of their living environment such as school and the workplace as well as public policies. These measures must be built on a solid base of decent living conditions (jobs, income, education, housing) for all citizens.

The concept of empowerment is reaching an increasingly broader audience. However, this notion is sometimes used in a narrow sense, as if it could be an individual act independent of the action of others (Breton, 1994; Heller, 1990). Several authors (Breton, 1994; Swift & Levin, 1987; Mullender & Ward, 1991) focus on the purpose of empowerment, which is to bring about structural change through collective action. Developing self-esteem, skills, and motivation (Breton, 1994) along with educating users on political issues (Albee, 1988; Breton, 1994; Freire, 1974; Kidder & Fine, 1984; Swift & Levin, 1987) have been used to gain and maintain power. Pursuing an objective of power-sharing between practitioners and citizen-users forces a challenge to the legitimacy of practitioner expertise in developing, distributing, and evaluating services (Groulx, 1994; Guba & Lincoln, 1989; Rappaport, 1981).

The purpose of this research is to increase empirical knowledge of preventive practices and to ascertain how close they come to a broadened and more social view of prevention. The primary objective was to chart the diversity of prevention-promotion practices aimed at reducing social problems affecting youths and their families and, secondly, to assess the presence of factors related to the dimensions of social prevention.

Methods

The sample was 200 primary and secondary prevention and promotion projects in the Montréal area; 79 were in institutions—local community service centres (CLSC), and schools and 121 were from the community sector (youth centres, family centres, women's centres, support groups, and so forth). The institutional projects are being implemented in agencies that come directly under government jurisdiction and are wholly run by the public sector. The community projects fall under community organizations that are operated autonomously and the funding sources of which are diversified. The sample included 200 projects identified in 13 CLSC territories (37 in Montérégie, 17 in Laval, and 146 on Montréal Island) identified in Table 11.1. Territories were selected to be representative of communities with mixed ethnic and economic

Table 11.2: Topics for the Interviews, Number of Possible Replies and the Number of Categories and Subcategories for Each Topic Area

Topics	Number of Possible Replies	Number of Categories	Number of Subcategories
A) Identifying the problematics of the project	2	9	80
B) Identifying targets for action	1	-	-
1 population	1		
2 home environment	1		
3 policy-makers			
C) Types of activities (concrete means used to attain goals)	5	0	17
D) Types of strategies (specific objectives of activities)	10	14	39
E) Nature of the links between agencies	4	-	6
F) Criteria for evaluating the project's success	5	7	27
G) Conditions contributing to the project's success	5	10	65
H) Funding sources	3	-	6

features and having a high ratio of youths. Each of the projects had been in operation for at least two years. Most projects provided preventive actions directly targeted for youths (0–18 years old) and their families. Some projects, however, served the population of the territories as a whole and were included because of their indirect benefits to children (consultation committees, support associations, welcoming services for newcomers, and so forth). Families presented at least 60% of the clientele for these projects.

Five interviewers collected data using a project-identification and interview procedure. Projects were identified by reviewing relevant literature (periodicals, reports, etc.) and using key informants who knew which projects in their territories were viewed as successful. Data collection took place with project supervisors and practitioners through telephone interviews of between 20 to 45 minutes in length. Table 11.2 shows the topics covered in the interviews.*

Subcategories were developed for each topic until the material was exhausted (Deslauriers, 1991; Grawitz, 1993; Mayer & Ouellet, 1991). This process allowed for significant topics to be taken into account in the analysis, though they may be poorly represented numerically, and enabled us to keep within

* A copy of the interview schedule is available from Nicole Dallaire, School of Social Work, Université de Montréal, C. P. 6128, Succursale Centre-Ville, Montréal, Québec, H3C 3J7.

Table 11.3: Identified Client Problems by Type of Agency

Problems	Type of Agency		
	Institutional Projects (n = 79)	Community Projects (n = 121)	Total (n = 200)
Youth adjustment	(48) 49.5%	(29) 18.4%	(77) 30.2%
Material living conditions	(2) 2.1%	(45) 28.5%	(47) 18.4%
Family environment	(12) 12.4%	(26) 16.5%	(38) 14.9%
Social supports (lack of support and resources)	(8) 8.2%	(28) 17.7%	(36) 14.1%
Promoting strengths	(17) 17.5%	(17) 10.8%	(34) 13.3%
Social Values	(3) 3.1%	(10) 6.3%	(13) 5.1%
Perinatal care	(7) 7.2%	(3) 1.9%	(10) 3.9%
Totals	(97*) 100%	(158*) 100%	(255*) 100%

*Totals refer to number of problems identified in each area

the practitioners' frames of reference. Subcategories were generally grouped into larger categories to facilitate the presentation of the findings (see Table 11.2). During the process, some categories were merged and others were subdivided. To ensure objectivity, the coding system was agreed to by an inter-judge panel on one third of the material. The data were examined depending on whether the projects operated in an institutional or community setting and to provide a profile of preventive practices.

Findings

Diversity of Problems

Eighty subcategories of problems were identified and divided into seven general categories. Table 11.3 presents information about the problems. The three general categories of youth's adjustment, family environment, and material living conditions accounted for 64% of the identified problem. Local support deficiencies, perinatal care, and societal values shared 23% of the replies. Some projects targeted no specific problem but couched their intervention in proactive terms, such as promoting the strengths of youths, families, and neighbourhoods; 13% of the problems were identified in this way. Problems that directly affected youths (suicide, delinquency, dropping out of school, etc.) were most frequently reported and accounted for 30% of the total number of replies. They represented 50% of the replies of respondents from the institutional system and only 18% of replies from the community sector. On the other hand, the community sector ranked the material living conditions of families as the greatest concern (29%) whereas this category made up only 2% of problems identified from institutional settings.

Table 11.4: Targets for Action by Type of Agency

Target Populations	Type of agency		
	Institutional Projects (n = 79)	**Community Projects (n = 121)**	**Total (n = 200)**
Population	(77) 97.5%	(119) 98.3%	(196) 98.0%
Parent-child	(23) 29.9%	(37) 31.1%	(60) 30.6%
Youths	(24) 31.1%	(19) 16.0%	(43) 21.9%
Parents	(18) 23.4%	(9) 7.5%	(27) 13.8%
Other	(6) 7.8%	(29) 24.4%	(35) 17.9%
Population within the territory	(6) 7.8%	(25) 21.0%	(31) 15.8%
Living Environment	(17) 22.0%	(39) 32.0%	(56) 28.0%
Economic and political policy-makers	(1) 1.2%	(28) 23.5%	(29) 14.5%

Note: Information refers to number and percent of total agencies that identify each target population; agencies may have several target populations.

Targets for Action

Information about targets for action identified by the project is summarized in Table 11.4. A very high proportion of preventive action targeted individuals and groups (98% of the projects). Most often, projects tried to reach parents and children (31% of the projects). Services that addressed the entire population of a territory were provided in 16% of the projects. These usually benefitted children indirectly, such as workshops on poverty, community economic development agencies, or housing co-operatives. Twenty-eight percent of the projects sought to change living environments so that they could better satisfy the needs of the population. This might involve improving the climate at school by changing the school structure, or offering training to police officers so that their approach could be better suited to the needs of youths. Only 15% of the projects attempted to influence economic and political policy-makers at the various levels of government (municipal, provincial, or federal). Just one of these projects was institutional.

Interventive Activity

Activities are the means used to attain objectives and were listed under 17 categories. Table 11.5 shows that four of the activities—training, group intervention, concrete support to parenting and recreation—made up 58% of all replies. Training and group intervention weighed more heavily in the activity profile of projects in an institutional setting while concrete support to parenting and recreation were more likely to be associated with the community sector.

Table 11.5: Intervention Activity by Type of Agency

Type of Activity	Type of Agency (N = 200) Institutional (n = 79)	Community-based (n = 121)	Total (n = 200)
Structured training or education[1]	(47) 28.1%	(70) 17.9%	(117) 21.0%
Group intervention	(32) 19.1%	(35) 8.9%	(67) 12.0%
Concrete support	(13) 7.8 %	(65) 16.6%	(78) 14.0%
Recreation	(8) 4.8%	(53) 13.6%	(61) 10.9%
Intervention with individuals	(19) 11.4%	(13) 3.3%	(32) 5.7%
Provision of human resources	(8) 4.8%	(18) 4.6%	(26) 4.7%
Access to documentation	(4) 2.4%	(19) 4.9%	(23) 4.1%
Job readiness training	(1).6%	(13) 3.3%	(14) 2.5%
Development of services	(0)	(11) 2.8%	(11) 2.0%
Facilitating access to the resource	(2) 1.2%	(8) 2.0%	(10) 1.8%
Street Work	(1).6%	(5) 1.3%	(6) 1.1%
Other	(13) 7.8%	(14) 3.6%	(27) 4.8%
Support for living conditions[2]	(3) 1.8%	(20) 5.1%	(23) 4.1%
Consultation	(4) 2.4%	(19) 4.9%	(23) 4.1%
Head-start	(6) 3.6%	(5) 1.3%	(11) 2.0%
Social change strategies	(0) 0.0%	(21) 5.4%	(21) 3.8%
Screening	(6) 3.6%	(2) 0.5%	(8) 1.4%
Total	(167) 100%	(391) 100%	(558) 100%

(1) This category covers a broad range of educational activities: courses, language workshops, seminars, lectures, testimonies, structured programs (except head-start programs), thematic get-togethers.
(2) The actions that are involved here targeted individuals directly and were more of a palliative to difficult living conditions: food banks, soup kitchens, house searching, etc.

Strategies

Table 11.6 provides information about the aims of the intervention activities used by the projects. Interviewers first took note of the activities reported and then asked for the aims for each activity. Decoding the data relative to this question posed the greatest challenge, requiring several category readjustments as the information took shape. In some instances, strategies had to be interpreted from a comprehensive knowledge of the project or a broader description of the activities. All questionnaires were revised twice before being

Table 11.6: Strategies of Intervention Activities by Type of Agency

Strategies	Institutional Projects (n = 79)	Community Projects (n = 121)	Total (n = 200)
To support the living environment and develop healthy, safe environments	(86) 49.7%	(189) 50.9%	(275) 50.6%
To support youths	(48) 27.7%	(47) 12.6%	(95) 17.5%
To strengthen parent-child relationships	(29) 16.8%	(37) 10.0%	(66) 12.1%
To support parents as an adult	(8) 4.6%	(81) 21.8%	(89) 16.4%
To support the workplace	(1) 0.6%	(11) 3.0%	(12) 2.2%
To promote multi-ethnic integration	(0) 0.0%	(13) 3.5%	(13) 2.4%
To strengthen human potentials: youths and parents	(70) 40.4%	(78) 21.1%	(148) 27.2%
Preschool education	(3) 1.7%	(4) 1.1%	(7) 1.3%
Parent education	(19) 11.0%	(7) 1.9%	(26) 4.8%
Adult education	(5) 2.9%	(14) 3.8%	(19) 3.5%
Youth education	(43) 24.8%	(53) 14.3%	(96) 17.6%
To develop and harmonize services	(10) 5.8%	(38) 10.2%	(48) 8.8%
To become involved in community life	(6) 3.5	(22) 5.9	(28) 5.1
Adults	(5) 2.9%	(17) 4.6%	(22) 4.0%
Youths	(1) 0.6%	(5) 1.3%	(6) 1.1%
To change social relations	(1) 0.6%	(30) 8.1%	(31) 5.7%
To improve living conditions: jobs, housing, economic development of the neighborhood	(0) 0.0%	(14) 3.8%	(14) 2.6%
Totals	(173) 100%	(371) 100%	(544) 100%
Mean =	2.2	3.1	2.7

submitted to an inter-judge panel for approval. Thirty-nine different strategies were identified and grouped together under six general categories:

1. To support living environments and develop healthy, safe environments. This includes internal support to the parent-child bond, direct support to youths, support to the school setting, support to the workplace, and support to parents outside of the exercise of the parenting role (indebtedness, unemployment, separation, community integration, etc.).
2. To strengthen human potentials (educational approaches with closed groups and a structured curriculum).

Table 11.7: Criteria for Evaluating the Success of Projects

Criteria	Institutional Projects (n = 76)	Community Projects (n = 117)	Total (n = 193)
Participation and satisfaction	(76) 35.8%	(139) 40.4%	(215) 38.7%
Effects on users	(91) 42.9%	(87) 25.3%	(178) 32.0%
Characteristics of the agency[1]	(13) 6.1%	(43) 12.5%	(56) 10.1%
Characteristics of the intervention[2]	(20) 9.4%	(41) 11.9%	(61) 11.0%
Neighbourhood changes	(2) 0.9%	(14) 4.1%	(16) 2.9%
Other	(4) 1.9%	(15) 4.4%	(19) 3.4%
Characteristics of practitioners	(6) 2.8%	(5) 1.5%	(11) 2.0%
TOTALS	(212) 100%	(344) 100%	(556) 100%

(1)For instance: the viability of the resource, increase in budgets, expansion of the resource.
(2)For instance: quality of the intervention, project used as a model for other projects, program that reaches the clientele.

3. To develop and harmonize services.
4. To become involved in community life. This implies that users play an active role in the management, organization and distribution of a resource's or program's services.
5. To change social relations such as correcting inequalities between groups.
6. To improve living conditions through structural changes rectifying unequal access to housing, employment or income, correcting regional inequalities.

Support strategies to individuals and living environments accounted for 51% of all replies. Institutional settings more often offered support strategies for youths and their living environment than did projects in community settings. Projects in community were more likely to offer intensive support to parents for the problems they encountered outside parenting activities, as well as to needs that indirectly affected family welfare. Thus, parents received support to overcome indebtedness, combat isolation, hunt for a job, find suitable housing, save money on food, and so forth. Strengthening human potentials (preschool education, parent education, adult education, general education of youths) represented 27% of the overall strategies but was more likely to be an aim for projects in an institutional setting than those in a community setting. General education of young people represented 18% of all strategies and included ensuring that youths had access to relevant information enabling them to make appropriate choices in the important areas of their lives, developing personal skills, and self-esteem. Aims for structural changes—changing social relations and improving living conditions—were almost nonexistent in the institutional sector but were used occasionally in community projects. Projects in the community sector averaged 3.1 strategies per project compared with 2.2 projects in the institutional sector.

Table 11.8: Conditions Contributing to the Success of Projects

Conditions of Success	Type of Agency Institutional Projects (n = 75)	Community Projects (n = 114)	Total (n = 189)
Features of agencies	(60) 30.8%	(59) 19.7%	(119) 24.1%
Features of practitioners	(48) 24.6%	(68) 22.7%	(116) 23.4%
Features of intervention	(41) 21.0%	(47) 15.7%	(88) 17.8%
Relationships between agencies	(13) 6.7%	(39) 13.0%	(52) 10.5%
Characteristics of users	(9) 4.6%	(23) 7.6%	(32) 6.5%
Characteristics of volunteers	(1) 0.5%	(27) 9.0%	(28) 5.7%
Relationship between practitioners and users	(12) 6.2%	(10) 3.3%	(22) 4.4%
Empowerment	(1) 0.5%	(17) 5.7%	(18) 3.6%
Characteristics of the population	(4) 2.0%	(9) 3.0%	(13) 2.6%
Coordination	(5) 2.6%	(1) 0.3%	(6) 1.2%
Other	(1) 0.5%	(0) 0.0%	(1) 0.2%
Totals	(195) 100%	(300) 100%	(495) 100%

Evaluating a Project's Success

What criteria do projects use to evaluate success? Twenty-seven subcategories were suggested and grouped into seven general categories. This information is presented in Table 11.7. Respondents judged success primarily by the criteria of satisfaction and participation (39%), by the effects on users (32%), changes observed in the structure and organization of the agency (10%), the characteristics of intervention (11%), and changes to the neighbourhood (3%).

Table 11.8 presents information about what respondents believe contributes to the success of the projects. The material collected led to the creation of 65 categories divided into 10 general categories. The conditions related to the features of agencies (funding, permanent staff, support from sponsoring agencies, etc.), of interventions (intervention process, conditions), or of practitioners (commitment, competence, team spirit, etc.) accounted for 76% of the institutional profile and 58% of the community profile. Recognition of volunteer action and empowerment constituted 1% of the conditions of success reported by the institutional sector and 15% of those reported by the community sector.

The community sector granted a greater importance to links between agencies as a condition of success. The projects maintain several types of links with each other. Eighty-six percent exchange information, 68% exchange services, 58% establish partnerships to provide consultation, and 27% mobilize

Table 11.9: Empowerment as a Process: From Support Received to Community Involvement

Aims	Type of Agency Institutional (n = 79)	Community-based (n = 121)	Total (n = 200)
For Parents			
Support for the parent-child bond	(29) 16.8%	(37) 10.0%	(66) 12.1%
Support to parents	(8) 4.6%	(81) 21.0%	(89) 16.4%
Sense of belonging	(3) 1.7%	(23) 6.2%	(26) 4.8%
Involvement in the agency or community	(5) 2.9%	(17) 4.6%	(22) 4.0%
For Youths			
Support to youths	(48) 27.7%	(47) 12.6%	(95) 17.5%
Sense of belonging and positive experiences	(7) 4.0%	(12) 3.2%	(19) 3.5%
Youth involvement in their living environment	(1) 0.6%	(5) 1.3%	(6) 1.1%

The figures in this table were taken from data gathered on strategies that illustrate our thesis.

to exert pressure. Important differences separated the two sectors. In the community sector, 41% of the projects exerted collective pressures compared with 4% of institutional projects. Eighty percent of the projects that emerged from the institutional sector benefitted from ongoing funding compared to 12% of community projects. Conversely, grants allocated for only one year or one grant with no guarantee of renewal, along with other forms of concrete support (volunteer work, loans of material) made up 90% of the types of funding mentioned by the community sector and only 27% of those reported by the institutional sector.

Empowerment: A Process and a Goal

The scope of benefits stemming from membership in a community-based group is closely linked to the level of involvement (Powell, 1985; Chavis & Wandersman, 1990). Being involved in a community agency is an effective means of enabling individuals to develop knowledge, self-perceptions, political representations, and skills needed to actualize a "sense of empowerment" (Prestby et al., 1990). Some resources offer their members support, social activities, and opportunities to become socially involved. This support comes in the form of specific assistance for the problems encountered (consultations, training, support, etc.). Social and cultural activities are opportunities to develop a sense of belonging and togetherness. Taking part in decisions about the agency, involvement in committees, or the chance to play a helping role are the main routes to participation in the life of the agency. Table 11.9 shows the impact of support aims for parents or youths in general. Social involvement,

Table 11.10: Empowerment as a Process: An Exercise in Democracy Projects Involving a Recognition of Power Relationships

Select Parameters	Type of Agency					
	Institutional Projects 1,2,3,5, (n = 79) 4 (n = 75)		Community Projects (n = 114) (n = 121)		Total (n = 200) (n = 189)	
[1]Projects aimed at reducing inequalities caused by exclusion or marginalization						
Yes	(0)	0%	(28)	23.0%	(28)	14.0%
No	(79)	100.0%	(93)	77.0%	(172)	86.0%
[2]Strategies: Changing social relations						
Advocacy	(0)	0.0%	(24)	6.5%	(24)	4.4%
Equity between the sexes	(1)	0.6%	(6)	1.6%	(7)	1.3%
[3]Activities						
Tactics for Social Change	(0)	0.0%	(21)	5.4%	(21)	3.8%
[4]Conditions of Success						
Power sharing or mobilization	(1)	0.5%	(17)	5.7%	(18)	3.6%
[5]Links between Agencies						
Exerting pressure in co-operation with other agencies	(3)	1.9%	(50)	14.3%	(53)	10.4%

Posterior analysis of various key variables likely to provide an operational definition of empowerment.

however, was rather weak, although slightly greater among parents involved in the community sector.

Empowerment involves a recognition that social groups are excluded based on sociodemographic, physical, or emotional characteristics. It also implies a recognition of the unequal distribution of resources, as well as a desire to allow these groups to democratically exercise a greater collective control to restore equity (Breton, 1994). Table 11.10 divides the data into various topics to bring out the presence of social action within the projects. The expression “social action” imparts an idea of conflict to action (Touraine, 1992) that is aimed at individual and collective freedom and defends excluded persons against technocratic justifications of social order and the invasion of economic power. In the broadest sense, social action ultimately seeks to counter various forms of inequalities, discrimination, or exclusion (social and economic). Fourteen percent of the project were pursuing this objective to varying degrees (institutional, 0%; community, 23%). Substantial differences in the discourse of practitioners emerged, depending on whether they worked in the institutional or community sector. Few practitioners in the institutional projects referred to power relationships in their discourse while this reading of social conflict was more developed in community settings.

The process of empowerment must lead to a change in the living conditions of communities. In the institutional setting, only 2.1% of the programs targeted living conditions. Moreover, no intervention strategy involved changing living conditions (contributing to job creation, housing renewal or creation, income improvement, and so forth). On the other hand, living conditions constituted 28.5% of the problems reported by the community sector while only 3.8% of the strategies involved structural changes. But the community setting offered extensive support to parents regarding their difficult living conditions. Palliative support to difficult living conditions may constitute an alternative action that was more popular than social action for structural changes. In short, empowerment, as we have defined it, seems to be practically non-existent in the institutional sector and very poorly developed in the community setting.

Prevention in the Institutional and Community Sectors: Complementary Services?

The findings have highlighted a difference between the institutional and community sectors for each of the topics. The institutional setting differs mainly in that it offers perinatal care, early childhood services, and services for youths. Analysis of the projects' problems and targets for action is more limited. The aims are diversified but not usually directed at political and socioeconomic change or social action. Generally speaking, the community sector is more likely to touch on community factors as a whole (economic conditions, political environment, formal and informal supports, and individual characteristics). The issues of equity and democratization seem to receive a higher degree of recognition and the debate tends to be more politicized. Adults find more support to withstand environmental stress and more opportunities to develop a sense of belonging in community projects. More specifically, the community setting promotes individual access to better living conditions (food, adequate housing, jobs, fighting indebtedness) to a far greater degree than the institutional sector.

Both the institutional and community sectors may deliver complementary services that are needed. The Commission on Health and Social Services (1988, p. 186) indicated that community agencies provide answers to needs that are not filled by the public system and offer the opportunity to deal with and treat the problems from a different perspective. Complementarity may constitute a force insofar as it is explicitly recognized and validated. The Commission went on to explain that explicit recognition of community agencies "would need to take shape under adequate conditions and funding, with respect for the nature, operations, and autonomy of these agencies and by establishing co-operation between the public system and community resources" [our translation] (Bélanger & Lévesque, 1992). Unfortunately, uncertainty and lack of funding still characterized community services, thus limiting their autonomy and capacity to take action. The compromise between community services and those provided by the state is fragile (Bélanger & Lévesque, 1992). The burdensome responsibilities that befall community groups, especially struggling for democratization, reducing inequalities, improving living conditions, and seeking new development models, make them indispensable partners in the construction of a more equitable society for youths and their families. Support for their actions continues to be a priority that cannot be overlooked. Further, although the community sector comes closer to the broadened definition of social prevention, a glance at the socioeconomic reality in Québec shows that these efforts are not enough.

Social prevention requires adequate living conditions for all and meeting basic needs of youths and their families (Pransky, 1991). This foundation is still lacking in Québec. Dropping out of school is still an acute problem. Public education is in a state of crisis and the very chaos that reigns there constitutes a risk factor for youths. The housing situation is still deteriorating (FRAPRU, 1994) while the federal government has just withdrawn its financial support to the provinces in this field. Child poverty marches on despite the federal government's promises to fight this problem (CCDS, 1993). The job crisis remains while the political will to develop a policy of full employment is coming along with great difficulty. Social prevention in Québec seems to be slowly emerging. Society is on a dangerous curve (Bouchard, 1988) with an increasing number of its members foundering in marginalization and exclusion. More and more children will be born into poverty, relegated to the fringes of society. What will the role of practitioners be in this decade of economic growth coupled with unemployment that brings multiple forms of jeopardization and exclusion stemming from a whole set of social and economic processes (Gaullier, 1992)? Until now, safety measures have consisted mainly of offering "defensive driving courses" to groups that are most at-risk, allowing them to better withstand stress and suffering. Intervention sectors have chosen to deal with phenomena of socioeconomic change primarily from the angle of individual characteristics, giving individuals the responsibility to pull themselves through. But, is it not time that decisive steps were taken to straighten out this dangerous curve?

Users and participants will be transformed into active citizens when institutional and community sectors have adopted an outlook of empowerment that will run through all socioeconomic services and interventions. It also enables welfare recipients to retain their dignity:

> Only empowerment can encourage risk-taking, unleash energy, stimulate creativity, instill pride, build commitment, prompt the taking of responsibility, and evoke a sense of investment and ownership (Guba & Lincoln, 1989: 226–227).

Education about social issues constitutes a vital dimension of empowerment and focuses attention on the structural changes to be made. Thus each person could take from and give to his or her community, reach his or her full potential, and participate directly in creating, changing, and harmonizing resources (Breton, 1994). Multidisciplinary practice, democratization of knowledge, adoption of an ethic of solidarity and responsibility, and valuing citizenship education are not costly practices. They can, however, bring about profound changes in the values and attitudes on which citizens predicate their actions, and increase the synergy between the services delivered by the state and community groups.

References

Albee, G. W. (1986). Toward a just society: Lessons from observations on the primary prevention of psychopathology. American Psychologist, *41*(8), 891–898.

Albee, G. W. (1988). *Prevention, powerlessness, and politics: Readings on social change.* Newbury Park, California: Sage Publications.

Blair, A. (1992). The role of primary prevention in mental health services: A review and critique. *Journal of Community & Applied Social Psychology, 2,* 77–94.

Blanchet, L., Laurendeau, M.-C., Paul, D., & Saucier, J.-F. (1993). *La prévention et la promotion en santé mentale: Préparer l'avenir.* Boucherville: Gaëtan Morin Éditeur.

Bélanger, R., & Lévesque, B. (1991). La théorie de la régulation, du rapport salarial au rapport de consommation. Un point de vue sociologique. *Cahiers de recherche sociologique, 17,* 17–51.

Bélanger, R., & Lévesque, B. (1992). Le mouvement populaire et communautaire: de la revendication au partenariat (1963–1992). In G. Daigle & G. Rocher, (Eds.), *Le Québec en jeu.* Montréal: Presses de l'Université de Montréal.

Bouchard, C. (1988). La pauvreté, comme une courbe dangeureuse. *Transition,* 18(3), 9- 11.

Bouchard, C. (1983). Non à la prévention. In J. Arseneau, C. Bouchard, M. Bourgon, G. Goupil, J. Guay, F. Lavoie, & R. Perreault, (Eds.), *Psychothérapies Attention!.* Québec: Québec Science Éditeur.

Breton, M. (1994). Relating Competence—Promotion and Empowerment. *Journal of Progressive Human Services, 5*(1), 27–44.

Chamberland, C. (1994). Réflexions d'inspiration galiléenne: Implication pour la prévention. Sous la direction de Réjean Tessier, *Enfance, Famille et contextes de développement.* Québec: Presses de l'Université Laval.

Chamberland, C., Dallaire, N., Cameron, S., Fréchette, L., Hébert, J., Lindsay., J. (1993). La prévention des problèmes sociaux au Québec: réalité québécoise. *Service social, 42*(3), 55–81.

Chavis, D. M., Wandersman, A. W. (1990). Sense of community in the urban environment: A catalyst for participation and community development. *American Journal of Community Psychology, 18,* 55–81.

Commission d'enquête sur les services de santé et les services sociaux. (1988), *Rapport de la commission d'enquête sur les services de santé et les services sociaux,* Québec City: Les Publications du Québec.

Conseil canadien du développement social (1993). *La pauvreté des enfants au Canada, rapport 1993.* Ottawa: Services des publications CCDS.

Conseil des affaires sociales (1989). *Deux Québec dans un. Rapport sur le développement social et démographique.* Boucherville: Gaëtan Morin Éditeur.

Crozier, M. (1987). *État modeste État moderne.* Paris: Fayard.

Deslauriers, J. P. (1991). *Recherche qualitative.* Montréal: McGraw Hill.

Elias, M. J. (1987). Establishing enduring prevention programs: Advancing the legacy of Swampscott. *American Journal of Community Psychology, 15*(5), 539–553.

Front d'action populaire en réaménagement urbain, (1994). Document de référence sur le logement social, unpublished paper, FRAPRU, Montréal.

Freire, P. (1973). *Education for Critical Consciousness.* New York: Continuum.

Gallo, M. (1989). *Manifeste pour une fin de siècle obscure.* Paris: Éditions Odile Jacob.

Gaullier, X. (1992). La machine à exclure. *Le Débat, 69,* 168–188.

Government of Canada, Department of National Health and Welfare (1988). *La santé mentale des Canadiens: vers un juste équilibre.* Ottawa: Supply and Services, Canada.

Gouvernement du Québec. (1991). *Un Québec fou de ses enfants* (Rapport du Groupe de travail pour les jeunes). Québec City: Ministère de la Santé et des Services sociaux.

Gouvernement du Québec. (1992). *La politique de la santé et du bien-être social.* Québec City: Ministère de la santé et des services sociaux.

Grand'Maison, J. (1992). *Le drame spirituel des adolescents.* Montréal: Fidès.

Grawitz, M. (1993). *Méthodes des sciences sociales.* Paris: Dalloz.

Groulx, L. H. (1994). Participation, pouvoir et services sociaux. In F. Dumont, S. Langlois, & Y. Martin (Eds.), *Traité des problèmes sociaux.* Québec: Institut québécois de recherche sur la culture.

Guba, E. G., & Lincoln, Y. S. (1989). *Fourth generation evaluation.* Newbury Park, California: Sage.

Heller, H. (1990). Social and community intervention. *Annual Review of Psychology, 41,* 141–168.

Kidder, L., & Fine, M. (1986). Making sense of injustice: Social explanations, social action, and the role of the social scientist. In E. S. Seidman & J. Rappaport, (Eds.), *Redefining social problems.* New York: Plenum Press.

Klein, D. C. (1987). The context and times at Swampscott: My story. *American Journal of Community Psychology, 15*(5), 531–553.

Lafortune, D., & Kiely, M. C. (1989). Prévention primaire des psychopathologies: Appellation contrôlée. *Santé mentale au Québec, 14*(1), 54–68.

Mayer, G., & Ouellet, F. (1991). *Méthodologie de recherche pour les intervenants sociaux.* Boucherville: Gaëtan Morin Éditeur.

Moynihan, D. P. (1969). *Maximum feasible misunderstanding: Community action in the war on poverty.* New York: The Free Press.

Mullender, A., & Ward, D. (1991). Empowerment through social action group work: The self-directed approach. *Social Action in Group Work.* New York: Haworth Press.

Porter, R. A. (1981). Conceptual parameters of primary prevention. In M. Nobel (Ed.), *Primary prevention in mental health and social work: A source of curriculum and teaching materials* (pp. 13–36). New York: Council on Social Work Education.

Powell, T. J. (1985). Improving the effectiveness of self-help. *Social Policy, 16*(2), 22–29.

Pransky, J. (1991). *Prevention the critical need.* Springfield, Missouri: Burrel Foundation & Paradigmpress.

Prestby, J. E., Wandersman, A., Florin, P. , Rich, R., & Chavis, D. (1990). Benefits, costs, incentive management and participation in voluntary organizations: A means to understanding and promoting empowerment. *American Journal of Community Psychology, 18,* 117–149.

Price, H. P. (1990). Wither participation and empowerment. *American Journal of Community Psychology, 18,* 163–167.

Rappaport, J. (1981). In praise of paradox: A social policy of empowerment over prevention. *American Journal of Community Psychology, 9,* 1–25.

Rappaport, J. (1992). The dilemma of primary prevention in mental health services:

Rationalize the status quo or bite the hand that feeds you. *Journal of Community & Applied Social Psychology, 2,* 95–99.

Robin, J. (1993). *Quand le travail quitte la société post-industrielle.* Groupe de Réflexion Inter et Transdisciplinaire (GRIT).(ed), Paris: Polyglottes.

Swift, C., & Levin, G. (1987). Empowerment: An emerging mental health technology. *Journal of Primary Prevention, 8*(1 & 2) 71–93.

Touraine, A. (1992). *Critique de la modernité.* Paris: Fayard.

12

Family Group Decision Making: An Innovation in Child and Family Welfare

Gale Burford and Joan Pennell

Canadians are increasingly aware of the prevalence of family violence and its devastating consequences, and they are increasingly frustrated by the inability of government and community programs to stop the abuse. As a consequence, there is a greater openness to search for alternative strategies to promote child and family well-being. One such alternative is the model of family group decision making that is being developed and tested in Newfoundland and Labrador. The model is premised on the philosophy that halting family violence requires a collaborative effort by families, their communities, and public authorities. Social networks within and around the family must be mobilized to plan and provide necessary support and protection.

The Demonstration Project

The Family Group Decision Making Project began accepting referrals of families at three sites in the province of Newfoundland and Labrador in January 1994. This followed nearly two years of work developing a cooperative base provincially and in each host community to assure that the model was adapted with sensitivity to regional and cultural needs and preferences (Pennell & Burford, 1994). The approach is based on the New Zealand experience (Atkin, 1991; Connolly, 1994; Hassall & Maxwell, 1991; Maxwell & Morris, 1993; Paterson & Harvey, 1991) with the family group conference and reflects the resurgence of interest in the inclusion of families evident throughout the practice literature (Burford & Casson, 1989). The philosophy draws on three major contributions to the rethinking of child and family welfare: aboriginal leadership in rebuilding traditions of community-mindedness that sustain caring by the extended family (Hodgson & "Phyllis," 1990, p. 35); feminist teachings that children can only be protected if their female caregivers have a say over their own lives (Callahan, 1993); and a growing recognition in the criminal justice system that holding perpetrators accountable must not generate the alienation which render family and community members unsafe (Braithwaite, 1989; MacLeod, 1990).

The project uses the family group conference as a means of creating a family-community-government partnership to halt family violence. The family group conference is a meeting where members of the immediate family group come together with extended kin and carefully selected members of the family's social support network to develop a plan for stopping the violence. The family is respected for its expertise—no one can know a family the way the family members do—and they can take the initiative in shaping such a plan if offered support and protection throughout the process. The project aims to stimulate mobilization of relationships and resources both within the family and in the formal and informal helping network around the family. The family group is to receive resources and protection from an infrastructure comprised of all government and non-government agencies with a mandate to prevent or intervene into family violence. These helpers are expected to cooperate in the provision of material and non-material resources to assist the family in carrying out their plan. None of the legally mandated authorities, however, are to turn their roles over to the project or the families. Each continues to carry out its role but do so with respect for the family realizing that this is an opportunity for the family members to come up with their own plan of action.

Three sites were selected for the demonstration project. Communities were selected that evidenced readiness to tackle the problem of family violence and were interested in the model itself. The sites taking part in the demonstration include the Inuit community of Nain on the remote northern coast of Labrador; the rural Port au Port Peninsula with inhabitants of French, English, and Micmac ancestry; and St. John's, the largest urban centre in the province.

An advisory committee was formed at each project site to plan how the project could be fitted to local context and cultures. The advisory committees include a broad spectrum of government and non-government representatives. These committees have been actively involved in planning the establishment of the project locally and in the hiring process to select, at each site, a coordinator and a researcher who have knowledge of the community and who share a similar ethnic or experiential background to the families in that community. Community panels, consisting of representatives from local agencies and community organizations, have also been established in St. John's and on the Port au Port Peninsula. These panels provide consultation to the project coordinators on how best to work with specific families and how best to organize the individual family group conferences. In Nain, the same group serves in both the advisory and the consultative roles and, in addition, the Labrador Inuit Health Commission is paid to have one of their staff provide weekly consultation to the coordinator. The project co-directors, with the assistance of the support staff, provide overall management and staff training. The project team, consisting of the site staff and co-directors, determines policies through monthly teleconferences. A provincial committee provides guidance to the entire project. The provincial committee includes senior representatives from government (e.g., child welfare, Correctional Services of Canada, police) and non-government provincial bodies (e.g., Provincial Association Against Family Violence) and is linked with the three project sites.

A collaborative action methodology is being used to evaluate the project's implementation and outcomes. Collaborative, or participatory, action research entails action for positive social change and collaboration among participants from diverse sectors and disciplines (Barnsley & Ellis, 1987; Kirby & McKenna, 1989; Maguire, 1987; Stull & Schensul, 1987; Whyte, 1991). Researchers in the area of victimization have been accused of producing findings that either are irrelevant, or, worse, endanger further the safety of victims and survivors (Dobash & Dobash, 1981; Hoff, 1988; Wardell, Gillespie, & Leffler, 1983). The methodology in this project is meeting such charges by including participating communities directly in formulating the study questions and design, collecting and analyzing the data, and disseminating the findings. Moreover, attention is being directed not only at families and their communities but at the full range of participants including government and university. Advocates of collaborative action research have observed its numerous benefits. Participation of those being studied improves the quality of the research by raising awareness of the local situation and facilitates monitoring of both the ongoing process and the eventual outcomes (Hoff, 1990). Participant input also heightens the validity and quality of the data analysis (Dalton, 1985; Yin, 1984) as university-based and community-based researchers engage in a continuous mutual learning strategy (Whyte, Greenwood, & Lazes, 1991, p. 42). Participants can reshape their actions to better achieve objectives as they reflect together on what they are doing. Learning by doing enhances people's effectiveness and increases their confidence in taking charge of their collective welfare (Friedmann, 1987).

Effecting collaboration, however, is not a straight-forward process when engaging participants who are separated by geography, culture and language, formal education, position of authority, and who enter the project at different times and for different reasons. Collaboration becomes a process of creating a forum that fosters people's capabilities to contribute in a manner that is responsive to their needs and objectives and those of the project. For the co-directors, collaboration means helping to build a system which ensures that they and the other participants hold each other accountable for the conduct of the project. The local advisory committees have been crucial in maintaining a collaborative action approach and adapting the intervention for use in their community or region. They bring knowledge of the community mores and practices and are sensitive to current local developments. They have the capacity to guide the principal investigators in designing and carrying out a study that respects the community's culture, safeguards the evaluation participants, and secures the support and participation of local people in the study.

A Case Example

The family group conference is a relatively unfamiliar approach in Canada. A case example can illustrate the process and show how the evaluation methodology is connected to the intervention. The research design uses both qualitative and quantitative measures to retain data about referral and preparation, holding the conference, and follow-up stages of the family group conference. This case example was compiled from the research instruments and reflective journals submitted by the coordinator and researcher at one project site.

Referral and Preparation

Twenty-two members of three different branches of a family gather at a parish community hall to consider what to do about the long-term sexual abuse of a now adolescent family member by her recently convicted and incarcerated stepfather. The Family Group Conference Coordinator gets things going by introducing the procedures for obtaining consent for the researcher to remain in the room to observe the conference. She makes introductions and reviews housekeeping items and the purpose of the conference. The Coordinator has spent the past 4 weeks speaking individually to those present in the room, preparing them for what to expect, how they might feel, and how they might make others feel. She has consulted on several occasions during that time with her local community panel, and the project administrators, about the family in order to assist her in preparing the family for the conference. Her local advisory committee continues to oversee the development of the project in that area. The research forms have been filled out and the mother found the social network analysis particularly interesting. She had already given her consent to having the researcher come to the conference. The researcher is a local person who is known to several people in the room.

With the consent of the family, the referring agency (Department of Social Services) provides a package of materials on the family to the Coordinator. This information is used to assess the suitability of the family for the Project and to plan the family group conference. The referral package from Children's Protection Services (CPS) is expected, along with descriptive and demographic information, to include the comprehensive risk assessment (New York State Department of Social Services, 1992) which includes the initial safety assessment.

The family group conference coordinator works with the referred family members to fill out a number of recording forms and research instruments. These include a social network map (Tracy & Whittaker, 1990), questions about the availability of a close friend or confidant, and a scale, devised specifically for this project, for assessing the characteristics of the abuse in the family. The social network analysis is used to assist in determining who should be invited to the family group conference and to measure changes in the family's network over time. The close friend scale aims to elicit the participant's subjective assessment of the availability of a close friend or confidant with respect to past and future disclosures of abuse. The abuse scale aids in categorizing the types of violence within the family according to the gender and adult/child status of the perpetrators and victims. Preparations are being made to introduce the Looking After Children Assessment Records (Parker et al., 1991), into the evaluation to monitor how children are developing and determining what steps need to be taken to promote their development.

Holding the Conference

Besides the coordinator, the researcher, and the family members, those present in the room include the worker from the children's protective services division of child welfare who referred the family to the project, a police officer, and a support person selected by the teenage victim. The role of the support person is to stay by the victim and provide emotional support. The project team, including the coordinator and the project administrators, have deliberately broken our own rule by allowing the support person to be a same-age friend of the victim, rather than an adult. The victim and her friend, their mutual foster mother, the child welfare worker and everyone else concerned, have convinced us that the friend is an obvious and suitable choice. To keep the project team happy, a second support person, an adult family member, is identified by the young woman. The young woman has been sceptical about coming to this conference because she thinks everyone in the family, especially her biological father, blame her for the abuse.

Once the introductions are complete, and an opportunity has been given to those present to ask general questions, the coordinator invites the child welfare worker to report to the group on the concerns prompting his referral of this family. He does this factually and respectfully. The young woman wants to move home with her mother despite the fact that child welfare believes this mother has failed to protect her daughter. The mother has already declared both her forgiveness of the perpetrator for what he has done and her intention for him to move back into the family home upon release from prison. As the child welfare worker speaks, the brother of the biological father walks out of the room in an open display of anger. The biological father of the victim has refused to come to the conference, so this brother is attending, along with his brother's wife, the stepmother of the victim. The stepmother is quite supportive and openly cares for the victim but is uneasy about defying her husband. The conference continues. The police officer reports the details of the investigation which prompted the charges. The fact that other adult males from this family have also been convicted of sex related offences against children is not mentioned—but this is known to all present. None of these men are attending the conference. Like the child welfare worker, the constable is factual and compassionate and the family listens intently. Despite the fact that the perpetrator admitted to all charges and was convicted, many of the family members present, who all live in the same community, knew few of the details.

Next, the project coordinator presents the views of the victim and those of an aunt who could not come to the conference. They have each asked her to do this for them. She then reads out the views of the perpetrator from a letter he has written to the conference. After hearing the first line of the letter, a brother of the perpetrator begins to cry and in the words of the coordinator slams out of the room. The coordinator finishes the letter at which point several family members are openly sobbing.

The coordinator then introduces the transition to the family's private deliberation time and she, the child welfare worker, and the police officer leave the room and go to the kitchen to prepare lunch for the family. From there they can see the brother of the perpetrator leaning over the fence behind the church vomiting. Since the constable has to go back to his office anyway, he volunteers to go comfort the man on his way out. In approximately five minutes the brother rejoins the group. A little more than an hour has passed since the conference began.

Back at the conference, the abused young woman and her peer support person are sitting in an adjacent room where they have been, at the young woman's request, from the beginning. From there they can hear the conference, and be heard when questions are directed towards them, but they cannot be seen. The family has heard the young woman crying already at this point in the conference. Two chairs are being kept vacant in the conference room in case the young woman and her friend decide to join the circle.

The only non-family people left in the room are the peer support person for the abused young woman and the research observer. The observer's reflective notes are instructive in describing this part of the conference:

> I was feeling very emotional at this time and felt I needed a break away ... I felt the conference was starting to fall apart as people were scattering everywhere. But once I did break away, I realized a key important thing. All three families were holding the conference by supporting each other. I learned at this time two different family members went to retrieve [the biological father's brother] on a voluntary basis. The family members were sister of offender and grandmother of abused child ... Also at the same time [another] sister of offender was really breaking down outside, again two other family members comforted, hugged and supported her and [another member] ... I also think that if anyone from immediate family went to retrieve paternal uncle none of them would have come back. Meanwhile, back inside the remaining family members of maternal family

> were standing around chatting and laughing with abused child and each other. As group recovered from all information they had just received, all started to focus on main issues. Abused child seemed at ease and together, as did everyone at this time (approximately 15 minute break). Also at this time the circle had formed again excluding paternal uncle [and the two women who had gone to him].

After the circle had reformed, ten minutes passed, during which time several people are sobbing and everyone appears to the observer to be in pain, but no one speaks. Finally, a woman goes to the room where the coordinator and social worker are preparing sandwiches for the family's lunch and declares, "This isn't working." The coordinator encourages her to go back and help work it out. In the meantime, the paternal uncle and the two women who went to him return to the room. After a brief silence, the offender's sister who had been outside with the paternal uncle, started, in the words of the observer, talking about "making him responsible for his actions … She expressed on her whole family's behalf how sorry they were." She blamed the offender and directed the discussion to why they were brought together and named the "abused child." The entire mood of the conference turned to planning. One and a half hours later, of which 30 minutes involved soup and sandwiches for lunch, the family has a written plan which the child welfare worker, and the abused young woman, approve on the spot as an acceptable plan for keeping the young woman safe. One woman representative from each of the three branches of the family have suggested to the young woman that they meet with her regularly to find out her views about what is happening and to support her going to treatment—which is what she wants to do. The young woman wants to live in the home with her mother at least until her stepfather gets out of prison. The family will meet again to decide what needs to be done prior to his release.

Descriptive data are being compiled on the numbers and general characteristics of family members and families proceeding to a group conference, the numbers of families who reach consensus about a plan, the characteristics of their recommendations, and the acceptability of those plans by the authorities. The evaluation notes the extent to which the families received the necessary material, legal, and other support from public authorities and community organizations for their plan. A family group conference evaluation form is used to secure the opinions of all participants as soon as the conference is over. And still another is used to elicit more detailed feedback and evaluation in an interview with sample family members within a day or two after the conference. A decision strategy instrument (Pennell, 1990) has been adapted for use by the coordinator, the researcher, and sample family members to categorize the conference resolution processes. These various instruments have been refined on the basis of feedback from families and site staff.

The families are asked if they will permit an observer (the site researcher) to be present during their family group conference. The observer documents who participates in the sessions, to what extent, and in what ways through the use of a structured instrument. The coordinator and the researcher also keep logs and reflective journals. In particular, the researcher writes a detailed set of reflective notes about the conference immediately afterwards. For example:

> Total cost of the conference to the child welfare department, except for the worker's time: nothing. Total cost to the project, aside from fixed costs: $158.00. This includes phone calls, rental of the parish hall, car travel for the coordinator

and the meal. The counselling service for the young woman is provided through an available health department service.

In the after the conference interviews held with individual family members within the next two days the researcher paraphrases one family member:

> Only concern is [abused child]. Thought this was great for ... [her] ... becoming aware that everyone was there to support her, and that no-one was mad at her or blamed her for anything.

And another:

> Although safety measures have been secured around [abused child], I feel concerns for [other very young child of perpetrator] in the home upon return of [the offender]. I feel disappointed that he did not express [in his letter] condolences to the grandparents and biological father's family as we were all brought together for ongoing support.

The young woman reports, for now, that she is happy with the plan that has been developed. She found it "really neat that 22 people in my family came together for a whole day to talk about me." With her consent, she will be asked about this, and many other relevant questions by this same researcher, at regular intervals for at least the life of the project.

These comments all underscore the potential for the family group conference to serve as a potent stimulus for re-mapping the participants' social networks. The interviewees expected the family group conference to take care of those who had been victimized and to respect and strengthen the integrity of the family group.

Follow Up

The written plan from each family group conference must include a system of monitoring and the scheduling of a review. The site researchers will assist with the review. All families coming to the project are asked to participate in follow-ups on their involvement. Information will be gathered by interviewing family members and various professionals about the family's current situation and whether the abuse continues, has abated, or has changed in some way positively or negatively. The site researchers will collect data from a range of sources, family and professional, in recognition that abuse is difficult to measure and that any one approach has its limitations (Yllö, 1988).

Interviews will cover the family's assessment of their own needs, their history of involvement with child welfare, the way their plans have been implemented, and their current concerns and evaluation of the situation. The children's protection services worker will provide a current evaluation of the family on the comprehensive risk assessment scale. Interviews with professionals, including the Department of Social Services social worker, and with community or extended family members, will cover what has actually been implemented, how the person evaluates the effectiveness of the arrangements, and the current situation of survivors or other members presumed to be at risk. Professionals will be asked to conduct a review of their own files using an events/facts checklist. This will include approaching medical personnel to produce a trauma history (McKay, 1994; Stark & Flitcraft, 1991) and the police and child welfare workers to produce information about their contacts with the family after the family group conference. Instruments used in the initial stages (social network map, close friend scale, abuse scale) will be re-administered at each follow-up.

The Looking After Children assessment records will be administered a second time near the end of the demonstration project. Interviews and focus groups will be conducted at six-month intervals to find out the views of various stakeholders (e.g., project staff, community representatives) on the model and its implementation.

Two comparison groups are being established to assess the impact of the family group conference. The first comparison group consists of families in each of the host communities that are not involved with child protection services. This group will allow comparison between project families and a base-line of "good enough" parenting in that community. The second comparison group is to be made up of families who are involved with Children's Protection Services but who do not come to the Project. In this manner, the project can measure the progress of these families against those going through the project. Local researchers will administer the Looking After Children assessment records and the social network map to both comparison groups.

Progress and Findings

Building a Collaborative Infrastructure

Work was necessary in the host communities during the time the grant proposal was being written and staff were hired. The provincial Department of Social Services, Division of Child Welfare, provided a seed grant for the co-principal investigators to begin that work as part of proposal development; the project would never have got off the ground without it. This model touches on personal, professional, and ideological sensibilities; thus, involvement of regional and local representatives is required to adapt family group decision making for use in a particular community or by a particular group.

Collaboration at the local level must be supported by cooperation among key departments and organizations at the provincial level. Local participants need to know that their involvement will be approved and facilitated by their senior administrators. Senior bureaucrats have provided directives and encouragement to their representatives at the local level to take part in the project. The latter, in turn, have educated the superiors about the requirements for their participation. Funding brings the need for collaboration at the local and provincial levels rapidly to the forefront. Ideological concerns are revealed in discussions about who should underwrite the conference costs and to what extent. The idea that families ought to have a say in what happens to them appeals to many people; but the realization that the family is to be left alone in a room to talk among themselves, without a professional facilitator or therapist present, quickly highlights differences. The idea of paying travel costs for family members to be brought together is a foreign concept to government officials. Virtually everyone involved thinks the idea of government departments' pooling resources with one another around a particular family's plan to be a sound idea, but there are a myriad of obstacles to accomplish this. One senior corrections official observed:

> What you are asking me to do is completely change the way I do business. Instead of just purchasing a block of service from someone, you want me to flexibly contribute to a particular family's plan along with other agencies and government departments involved with that family.

Attuning the Project to Local Cultures

The host communities are ensuring that the project is adapted to respond to their particular contexts. Each of the project sites has constituted an advisory committee and, in the cases of St. John's and the Port au Port Peninsula, a community panel to reflect distinctive cultural alignments. In Nain the advisory committee has representation from the indigenous population as well as from the public authorities. This group asserted from the start that the project should be geared to helping them find solutions to their own problems rather than having solutions imposed from the outside. Moreover, they set forth a plan for ensuring community ownership and project sustainability. The result is that the project is housed within, and receives consultation from, the Labrador Inuit Health Commission. Nain's remote location and distinctive culture have given this site the most latitude to experiment with various interventive strategies.

The advisory committee on the Port au Port Peninsula has representation from significant community bodies, including francophone, Micmac, women's, church, and school organizations. The committee members recognize that they are representing a number of small and isolated communities, each with a strong sense of identity and distinctive social practices. Because of the close relations within these small communities, the advisory committee has formulated additional policies to help to maintain the confidentiality of family group deliberations.

The advisory committee in St. John's has a far greater population to represent. As a consequence, it has not been as closely aligned with local populations but instead with community organizations. The advisory committee and community panel are composed of a large number of professionals representing a wide spectrum of service and advocacy organizations. The presence of the professionals is also more evident in the family group conferences because of their greater availability and a greater expectation of their input.

Broadening the Referral System

Seven conferences have been held, three at one site and two at each of the other, in the first five months of the project. Two of these were reconvened to make modifications in the plan and one was reconvened for a regular review. Referrals were slow in coming from child welfare workers despite a high level of enthusiasm for the model. Initially, some workers were reported to be reluctant to refer dysfunctional families for a conference on the assumption that these families could never be expected to come up with a sound plan. At the same time, the project has stressed getting the family group conference right, especially at the beginning, rather than dealing with high numbers.

A refinement, initiated by managers in the Child Welfare Division, allows referrals to originate with *any* agency, including the police, so long as the family in question has a child involved with Children's Protection Services and the child welfare worker okays the referral. This change occurred after hearing of several instances where the family refused a referral from the child welfare worker. The discovery, at one local advisory committee meeting, that potential referring agents (shelters for women, police, schools, mental health workers, etc.) all tend to know which families are being followed by child welfare anyway appears to hold true in all three host communities. This has opened the doors to more open sharing of information about referrals and is supported by both the mandatory reporting statute in the province and a recently signed agreement between police and child welfare to openly share information about child abuse. Two families, who refused to be referred to the project by a child welfare worker, gave consent when approached by another person.

Extending Support Networks Within and Around Families

The number of family members attending conferences has ranged from eight to twenty-two. A total of 81 family members and friends have attended the seven conferences. Twenty-one formal helpers have attended conferences; the resource people who have been invited by the coordinators to attend have included representatives from child welfare, police, immigration, medicine, counselling, education, and foster care. One family was surprised to learn that they had kin in the community that they did not know about. Concentrated efforts are being made to bring in previously non-involved family members, often from the paternal side, including situations where ex-nuptial children are involved.

Five of the seven families who have had family group conferences could not be depicted as isolated. They come from rather dense, but somewhat negatively charged, social networks. In four of these situations, tensions between the family and Children's Protection Services figured centrally in the referrals; the families were dissatisfied with child welfare workers' efforts to impose solutions. A helpful stance for the child welfare worker was to approach the family at the conference with the attitude that, "What we have been doing is not working." Police and child welfare workers have found some comfort in including the family; they have not felt that everything was on their shoulders and that the family was taking some of the responsibility.

Family members who have participated in second conferences arrived with confidence and clarity about the aims of the meeting. This supports the original hopes that the addition of this model to a community will realign its mechanisms for weaving supportive networks. The project is expected to result in the evolution of a cadre of experienced individuals who will be recognized by both the informal and formal helpers in that community for their expertise.

Ensuring Adequate Preparation

The length of time it has taken to organize the seven conferences ranges from two to four weeks. There is no reason why each coordinator cannot have about three families in the planning stage at one time. The length of the conferences themselves have ranged from four hours to over eight hours. One conference was scheduled for short meetings over a three-day period. Four have involved bringing in family members from outside the community, one of these from outside the country.

Careful preparations are essential in gathering together the right mix of participants, including currently involved family members and others who could make a constructive contribution. The views of family members about who cannot attend the conference need to be secured; and, as evident from the case example, the reading out of their statements at the conferences may have a very powerful impact and may help the family group in their planning. The family and professional members need to be briefed on how the conference works and how they can best participate. Thus, the coordinators spend time helping family members to discuss their fears and to consider strategies that will help them be most comfortable at the sessions. The coordinators have also coached child welfare and other workers on how to make their presentations in a way that informs without dictating what plan the family group should reach.

Monitoring for Safety

Four of the seven families who had conferences were referred for child neglect. One of these also involved physical abuse of the children. Three of the families were not actively involved with family violence at the time of the referral. The current problems in all four of these situations could, however, be traced to previous abuse of either the caretaker or of the children (e.g., a divorce had taken place and the abuse had stopped). Workers may have been reluctant to refer families characterized by active violence.

One family, currently in the preparation stage for a conference, was referred on an undertaking initiated by the police. An adult member of this family had been actively and recently violent toward other members. The police undertaking stipulated that the offender was to report to the coordinator within 24 hours. No commitment to take part in the project was implied in the undertaking. He had only to check-in with the coordinator. In the meantime, the coordinator determined whether or not the other members of the man's family wished to participate in the project. Concerns that this referral may put the abused persons in a position where they are forced to take part in the project have not materialized. This is one of the families that refused to be referred when approached by the child welfare worker, but once the project was explained to the perpetrator and other family members, they willingly consented to participate.

Careful monitoring that referrals of this type may place vulnerable members at risk of further abuse is taking place. The alternatives, however, seem to include doing nothing or pursuing charges without also offering the family support as well as involvement in stopping the abuse themselves. Family group decision making may be a way to reduce the perceived tendency that the justice system re-abuses victims by leaving them out of the process. Family group conferences should not be introduced at a time when they could be perceived as subverting the aims of justice (e.g., be used by the perpetrator to argue for a withdrawal of charges or a stay of proceedings). A perpetrator may introduce, at the time of sentencing, that he has attended a family group conference; this does not presently constitute a threat to vulnerable members of the family but will be watched closely.

Addressing A Full Range of Abuse

There will be an overlap between child welfare and youth corrections involvement in some families. The Division of Youth Corrections has recently asked to refer families and a proposal is being presented to extend the project to test the model with young offenders. Two of the seven families attending conferences have had a young offender involved either as the perpetrator of violence or as one of the neglected young people in the family. Presently, the project only receives referrals directly from the Department of Social Services, or from other agencies that have been endorsed by child welfare, because the referring agency must be willing to underwrite the costs associated with bringing the families together and resourcing outcomes from the families' plans.

The project staff are attempting to negotiate agreements with other agencies because this is an important step toward getting the family to focus on violence against family members other than a child. Families can sidestep addressing this kind of abuse since there is no legal leverage that can be brought to bear along with the offer of support to help. Agencies such as the police and Correctional Services of Canada are involved in providing resources within their respective mandates. These resources can be offered to families referred by child welfare when they overlap with these other services. They, however, have not worked out ways to allocate resources to underwrite referrals of their own when a child might not be involved.

According a Say for Families

The wishes of the families have been consistent with and supportive of the needs and well-being of the children involved. This occurs even when the recommendations have come from family members exhibiting severe problems in their own social functioning. All seven families developed plans and all the plans have been acceptable to the child protection workers involved. Two required a second meeting of the family, or further discussion between the coordinator and the family members individually, to make refinements in the plan, but in no case were out-of-town relatives brought back for the second conference. Instead, a speaker phone was used. One family requested a second meeting to review a plan that was not working.

The families' requests for assistance have been modest, with perhaps the most contentious being for the Department of Social Services to purchase a washer, dryer and bed for a young mother at the recommendation of her aunts and mother. The family members concluded that the children would benefit most if the behaviour management specialist and the housekeeper, both being paid for by Social Services, were removed because the young mother had resisted their involvement over an extended period of time. Family members agreed to supervise the mother's care of the children but thought the four-year-old should have her own bed, so that she could begin making overnight visits from the foster home to her mother without having to sleep in the same bed as her mother. They also asked the Department to put their relative on a list for better housing and to purchase a washer and dryer to facilitate helping the young mother on site with the care of her 10-month old. The worker agreed to supply these items but it took the Department over two months to authorize their purchase, despite the approval of senior management. This is the only example of anyone agreeing to something at a conference that was not quickly followed through on.

Family members have carried out their agreed tasks almost immediately. The young mother in this case voluntarily entered a counselling relationship a month after the conference; something that her worker and some family members had been trying for some time to pressure her into doing. The biological father of the eldest child and his parents attended a review conference for this family. He had never been involved previously with his child although his parents had longed for contact with their granddaughter. The young mother agreed, at this second conference, that the foster mother of three years (an aunt) and the maternal and paternal grandparents all would have contact with the child.

The supports and suggestions of family members are often unique and not typical of the help offered by professionals. Solutions which could only be known, or offered, by family have emerged in each conference. For example, the brothers in one family offered, at the suggestion of an elder, to help their sister in the traditional way by taking a share of fresh meat and fish to her each time they hunted or fished successfully rather than her having to ask for it. At another conference, a sexually abused man came from a great distance to attend the conference to explain to his much younger, teenage step-brother, how he had dealt in his life with the sex abuse towards him by their common abuser, their father. In a different conference, the senior members of the family said that their relative's children should stay with foster carers whom they would not have chosen in the first place. They recognized that the children had adjusted and that their lives should not be disrupted unless their mother quits drinking. They wanted continued access between the mother and the children; something the foster carers themselves promoted.

Implications of Findings

There is no reason why families should not be given an opportunity to have a say of this kind. The experience to date supports the notion that the family group conference can serve as a means of stimulating the rebuilding of connections within families and in mobilizing formal helpers to gear their interventions to mesh with the family's plan. The model is being carried out as an extension of the present system of services in the province. There are some obstacles to organizations other than child welfare underwriting the costs of this model but no radical restructuring of services was necessary to carry out this effort. Both common sense and experience with organizations like the provincial Department of Probation and Correctional Services of Canada suggest that they will be able to contribute to plans in this way, if they make a determined effort to be part of including families. A change in practice has been necessary to include the family in decision making and to demonstrate respect for the worth and ability of the family to pull together when asked to do so.

This project is sponsored by Health Canada, Canada Department of Justice, Solicitor General of Canada, Human Resources Development Canada and is co-sponsored in Nain by the Labrador Inuit Health Commission.

References

Atkin, B. (1991). New Zealand: Let the family decide: The new approach to family problems. *Journal of Family Law, 29*(2), 387–397.

Barnsley, J., & Ellis, D. (1987). *Action research for women's groups.* Vancouver: Women's Research Centre.

Braithwaite, J. (1988). *Crime, stigma and reintegration.* Cambridge: Cambridge University Press.

Burford, G., & Casson, S. (1989). Including families in residential work: Educational and agency tasks. *British Journal of Social Work, 19*(1), 19–37.

Callahan, M. (1993). Feminist approaches: Women recreate child welfare. In B. Wharf (Ed.), *Rethinking child welfare in Canada* (pp. 172–209). Toronto: McClelland & Stewart.

Connolly, M. (1994). An act of empowerment: The children, young persons, and their families act (1989). *British Journal of Social Work, 24,* 87–100.

Dalton, J. H. (1985). Involving community groups as research partners. In A. Wilson (Chair), *Democratic group functioning: Integrating research and community service.* Symposium of the Pennsylvania Sociological Society, University of Pittsburgh, Pittsburgh, Pennsylvania.

Dobash, R. E., & Dobash, R. P. (1981). Social science and social action: The case of wife beating. *Journal of Family Issues, 2*, 439–470.

Friedmann, J. (1987). *Planning in the public domain: From knowledge to action*. Princeton, New Jersey: Princeton University Press.

Hassall, I., & Maxwell, G. (1991, May). *The family group conference: A new statutory way of resolving care, protection and justice matters affecting children*. Paper Presented at Ensuring our Future: The fabric of childhood in Australian Society Conference, Adelaide, Australia.

Hodgson, M., & Client, Phyllis. (1990). In T. A. Laidlaw, C. Malmo, & Associates, *Healing voices: Feminist approaches to therapy with women* (pp. 33–44). San Francisco: Jossey-Bass.

Hoff, L. (1988). Collaborative feminist research and the myth of objectivity. In K. Yllö & M. Bograd (Eds.), *Feminist perspectives on wife abuse* (pp. 269–281). Newbury Park, California: Sage.

Hoff, L. A. (1990). *Battered women as survivors*. London: Routledge.

Kirby, S., & McKenna, K. (1989). *Experience research social change: Methods from the margins*. Toronto: Garamond Press.

MacLeod, L. (1990). *Sharing the responsibility for justice*. A speech presented at the Provincial Symposium on Woman Abuse and the Criminal Justice System, Moncton, New Brunswick.

Maguire, P. (1987). *Doing participatory research: A feminist approach*. Amherst, Massachusetts: Center for International Education, School of Education, University of Massachusetts.

Maxwell, G., & Morris, A. (1993, August). *Family Group Conferences: Key Elements*. Paper presented at the Mission of St. James and St. John, Melbourne, Australia.

McKay, M. M. (1994). The link between domestic violence and child abuse: Assessment and treatment considerations. *Child Welfare, 73*(1), 29–39.

New York State Department of Social Services. (1992). Comprehensive Risk Assessment. Adapted from the New York State Risk Assessment and Service Planning Model. Albany, New York: Division of Administration and Office of Human Resource Development.

Parker, R., Ward, H., Jackson, S., Aldgate, J., & Wedge, P. (1991). *Looking after children: Assessing outcomes in child care*. London, England: HMSO.

Paterson, K., & Harvey, M. (1991). An evaluation of the organization and operation of care and protection family group conferences. Wellington, New Zealand: Department of Social Welfare.

Pennell, J. (1990). Democratic hierarchy in feminist organizations. *Dissertation Abstracts International, 50*/12-A, 4118. (University Microfilms No. AAD90–15034).

Pennell, J., & Burford, G. (1994). Widening the circle: The family group decision making project. *Journal of Child & Youth Care, 9*(1), 1–12.

Stark, E., & Flitcraft, A. H. (1991). Spouse abuse. In M. Rosenberg & M. Fenley (Eds.), *Violence in America: A public health approach* (pp. 123–157). New York, NY: Oxford.

Stull, D. D., & Schensul, J. J. (Eds.). (1987). *Collaborative research and social change: Applied anthropology in action*. Boulder, Colorado: Westview Press.

Tracy, E. M. & Whittaker, J. K. (1990). The social network map: Assessing social support in clinical practice. *Families in Society, 71*(8), 461–470.

Wardell, L., Gillespie, D. L., & Leffler, A. (1983). In D. Finkelhor, R. J. Gelles, G. T. Hotaling, & M. A. Straus (Eds.), *The dark side of families: Current family violence research* (pp. 69–83). Beverly Hills, California: Sage.

Whyte, W. F. (Ed.). (1991). *Participatory action research*. Newbury Park, California: Sage.

Whyte, W. F., Greenwood, D. J., & Lazes, P. (1991). Participatory action research: Through practice to science in social research. In W. F. Whyte (Ed.), *Participatory action research* (pp. 19–55). Newbury Park, California: Sage.

Yin, Robert K. (1984). *Case study research: Design and methods*. Beverly Hills, California: Sage.

Yllö, K. (1988). Political and methodological debates in wife abuse research. In K. Yllö & M. Bograd (Eds.), *Feminist perspectives on wife abuse* (pp. 28–50). Newbury Park: Sage.

13

Taking Risks with Families at Risk: Some Alternative Approaches with Poor Families in Canada

Michèle Kérisit and Nérée St-Amand

This chapter will present findings from a research project begun in 1992. The project, "Poor Families: Alternative Approaches to Working With Low-Income Families," explores community survival and self-help mechanisms for poor and often marginalized families that form the majority of the clientele of child protection (Kérisit & St-Amand, 1993a). A survey was conducted of support systems and community organizations that have adopted and devised ways of doing things that depart from the conventional models of the public system in charge of child protection and welfare. Alternative agencies have been identified throughout Canada and force a rethinking of protection intervention with poor families.

Starting Point

The primary aim of the research was to gain an understanding of the survival strategies used by disadvantaged families and the dynamics within alternative support and community service networks throughout Canada. A beginning premise was that local communities, even very poor ones, and the families living in them have a certain dynamism, a sense of survival, that could disprove the prevailing discourse that depicts them as being dependent, unmotivated, dysfunctional, having multiple problems, and so forth (Kérisit and St-Amand, 1993b). Institutional systems and practitioners usually consider disadvantaged families as problems and adopt intervention measures that are defined in terms of deficits, needs, or handicaps. Thus, they advocate action to satisfy needs the families do not always see as being real (Colin et al., 1992; Liffman, 1978). Solutions adopted by the institutional system do not reach families that are wary of these types of interventions (Pitrou, 1992; Carniol, 1987; Autès, 1980; Donzelot, 1977; Selig, 1976). For example, fear of losing custody of children, or of being deemed unfit to care for them, and the strategies adopted to reclaim children who have already been apprehended are recurrent themes in our interviews with mothers who were using the resources. Even more serious is that some public system interventions have unintended effects that exacerbate the families' problems (Wharf, 1992). The sixties' scoop of Native children is one of the most glaring examples of this (Johnston, 1983).

A great number of agencies and groups have emerged from the social movements of the past few years and are devising and creating new forms of support and self-help focused on individual and collective empowerment of families (Bouchard, 1991, p. 62; Novick & Volpe, 1989). But these resources are not highly valued and their financial position is shaky. They are not considered as belonging fully to the child-welfare intervention system, are viewed as extras—necessary extras, maybe, but not central—to current interventions in this field. Yet, they are very often a last resort, not only for families, but also for agencies in the institutional system that refer clients they no longer know what to do with. These community agencies focus work on the structural dimension of poverty (lack of jobs and training, unreliable housing and food supplies), are often outgrowths of short-term local initiatives, and are characterized by the diversity of their approaches and the originality of their interventions. These agencies also bring about innovations to the extent that their flexibility, culture, and adaptable grassroots organizational structures allow them to devise new approaches and adapt quickly to the community's problems and resources. This does not mean that innovation does not take place in institutional services, but the flexible organizational structures of community organizations and their integration into the communities enable them to meet the needs of the community more directly and to devise on-the-spot, innovative interventions.

Exploratory Research

Families are social actors despite the very limited control they have over the policy making that affects them. The study sought to identify the other side of intervention, the side that stems from the vitality of the families themselves and is often forgotten when dealing with poverty. The research validates local, bottom-up initiatives. It examines how microsocial phenomena (local support groups, the experience of poverty, local organizational cultures) are connected to macrosocial phenomena (unemployment, social movements). A research method and process was adopted that fitted with the aims of the research, keeping in mind both the importance of the tools chosen to explore the sphere of alternative intervention with poor families and the limitations of such an undertaking.

Research Study Process

Directories of community resources are published in all regions of Canada. They were used to make a list of community agencies that focused on the problems of family and poverty in the various provinces. Key sources in the provinces were interviewed; snowballing procedures were used to identify agencies that others brought to our attention. A description of the project was mailed to 679 agencies that met initial criteria defining alternative agencies. Each agency was asked if they met the description, which was based on research on renewing practices in the mental health field (St-Amand & Clavette, 1991; Chaume, 1988; Rhéaume & Sévigny, 1987). The agency needed to meet the following criteria:

- Involve disadvantaged families in its various levels of policy making;
- Propose one or more original programs that clearly differ from conventional or institutional interventions;

- Use an approach based on a social rather than individual diagnosis of a family's problems;
- Have advocacy for poor families as part of their mandate;
- Respect the culture and traditions of the families and their communities as well as take account of their collective history.

Of 679 mailouts, 232 agencies replied; 172 sent complete background material (research papers, annual reports, pamphlets, etc.). One hundred and seventeen were chosen for the study. Agencies were from all 10 provinces, but not from the Northwest Territories and the Yukon. Also, most of the agencies were located in larger urban centres. Printed information was provided by the agencies and was supplemented by 30 telephone interviews and 52 on-site visits. Community workers and parents were interviewed to grasp the extent to which the approaches fitted in with the theoretical grid and how they differed from conventional approaches. Local projects are not always easy to locate; they are fragile and disappear without ever being listed anywhere. Moreover, what may be "alternative" in one context may not necessarily be so in another. Thus, case studies were used to provide detailed data filled with real life situations and showing the complexity of the link between the macrosocial trends (social policies and movements) and everyday practices within local communities (Yin, 1984). This exploratory approach provides a comparison between the initial concept of what the term "alternative" could mean and the data provided by the agencies.

Qualitative Approach

An inductive qualitative approach (Glazer & Strauss, 1967) allows for empirical construction of data. Tentative categories were set up and then recast during data collection. A qualitative study that stresses process will take account of the historical, geographic, and political context that is so important to understanding self-help strategies used by families and their networks. A qualitative study takes account of the concerns of the social actors as they are experienced in everyday life. The emphasis is placed on the whole social setting, i.e., all the places and times where social relations take concrete shape rather than the social structure (Soulet, 1987, p. 14). Qualitative social science places the social actor at the centre of its concerns and seeks meaning for the subject in a situation that is its own through its own action (Soulet, 1987:15). The findings of the study presented in this chapter are the result of analyzing semi-structured individual and group interviews of community workers and parents who were active in alternative resources.

Interactive Research

Qualitative studies based on the grounded theory involve going back and forth between collecting and analyzing data. This allows an interactive dimension and feed-back from alternative agencies. The agencies are kept informed of the analyses through a liaison bulletin, *Alternatives*. An inventory of resources, *This Is Our Place*, has been sent out to the community resources contacted by the project. This publication includes a reflection on what researchers were told during our interviews, descriptions of agencies that are innovative in their work with disadvantaged families and gives agencies the opportunity to provide feed-back. *This Is Our Place* and *Alternatives* provide channels of communication among the agencies. The agencies often work in isolation, lack staff, time and money, and do not always have the means to become aware of experiences that are parallel or similar to their own. The expertise and experience of an advisory committee made up of practitioners working in the field was available from the beginning of the research. The study was action-oriented in that the researchers' concerns were aimed at changing intervention practices. However, the scope of research area was so broad that it was not possible to establish a close dialogue between the majority of the people involved in the alternative resources and the research team. This limitations of the undertaking is linked to the constraints of time and distance.

Four Case Studies

Elm Hill: From Survival to Development

The Elm Hill community is isolated from the urban centres of southern New Brunswick. It had been a thriving community back in the 1800s, mainly because the fruits and vegetables grown there, with the help of river transportation, were destined for the cities and towns along the St. John River. Elm Hill is the province's only black community; its inhabitants came with Loyalists from the United States at the time of the American Revolution. With the advent of roads and railways, Elm Hill became increasingly poorer and cut off from regional economic currents. In 1988, a commission set up to assess the province's housing problems labelled it "New Brunswick's Third World." Houses were dilapidated, roads impassable, and children in need of protection from abuse and neglect. There were no cars and schoolchildren were openly discriminated against; for instance, the children had to sit at the back of the bus to go to school in Gagetown. These were serious problems for a community with a population of around forty.

Premier McKenna was shocked by the media attention this situation received and personally stepped in and asked that the community be taken care of immediately. A professional community worker was directed to handle the case. The situation has since taken an upward turn with the help of Elm Hill residents and a multidisciplinary committee of community workers. Several housing units have been built, residents have renovated the community centre, and undertaken community garden projects under the supervision of community members with the aid of community workers. Families that had been totally excluded from the mainstream are mobilizing, identifying their needs, and the means to satisfy them. The only person to have finished Grade 12 has moved back from Montréal to live in Elm Hill and is demonstrating remarkable leadership qualities.

A meeting with the committee of practitioners and a group of parents clearly showed that a collaborative approach had been used that had left the power in the community's hands, right down to the smallest details. Situations that could be labelled protection had been resolved using the local community, rather than the law or professional practice criteria. The committee of practitioners had always favoured steps built upon the community's resources. Child protection took on a special meaning, based on local rather than universal welfare criteria. Of course, this type of approach implied mutual trust between the professionals and disadvantaged families. Bit by bit the senior community worker was able to mobilize the community by showing complete faith in the families' abilities to take charge of themselves and through a destigmatization process. Mobilizing political power ensured that resources would be allocated to the community.

Regroupement des femmes sans emploi du Nord du Québec: From Isolation to Togetherness

The Regroupement des femmes sans emploi du Nord du Québec [Association of unemployed women of northern Québec] was established in 1983 and welcomes poor women from the Québec City area to promote and protect their rights. In the early '80s, a community worker at a local community service centre noticed that single mothers and single men were the two categories of people who were particularly poor, isolated, and lacking in resources. She set up support and encounter groups for these clients. The men's group did not last long but, for the women, mobilization has developed rapidly over the past ten years. Their approach enables women to undertake advocacy action. This resource is very active in the various facets of social service reform that Québec has been undergoing. The agency does not believe that mandatory back-to-work programs suit the needs of unemployed women or helps them to reintegrate socially. Moreover, Regroupement des femmes sans emploi du Nord du Québec is challenging the requirement to do volunteer work in exchange for welfare benefits. The unemployed women involved in this agency make the policies; the board, made up entirely of participants, mirrors the user population. The two community workers sit in on board meetings but do not have a vote. The group is also proposing a program for preparing women to enter the labour force. The title of the program, which translates as "Able but Not Ready," indicates that the route to a paying job does not merely involve an institutional and bureaucratic definition of job-readiness, which do not suit unemployed women's living conditions. A volunteer female lawyer comes to the centre every month to offer legal information; sessions have been organized to discuss problems of custody, divorce, support payments, social assistance, and so forth. Through collective activities (community meals, coffee klatschs), the participants are establishing bonds of friendship and support that enable them to overcome their isolation, become aware of the political problems with which they have to contend, and to respond to them collectively. Various programs (telephone assistance, clothing counters, help in filling out forms) meet the day-to-day needs of women faced with financial and welfare problems.

The Candora Society: From Self-help to Job Training

Candora is a community agency located in a northeast Edmonton shopping centre. Most of the people at Candora, 75 to 80% of whom live below the poverty line, are single mothers. Candora's structure is non-hierarchical and collective. The board, made up of community volunteers, is charged with adapting the agency to suit the needs that are expressed by participants in community activities. The agency is made up of Native, non-Native, and Latin American women working together to improve living conditions in the neighbourhood. Two permanent employees share one full-time position. The activities and interests of Candora's women include the community garden, collective kitchen, Native craft workshop, writing workshop on participants' life experiences, and involvement in a great number of local and provincial coalitions. The agency also takes in a group of senior women, has a support group for Hispanics, and publishes a community newsletter. Candora offers all its members a participatory education program called *Life Choices*. Free daycare is made available to participants.

A Community Advocacy Project and an Employment Preparation Project make Candora unique. The Community Advocacy Project provides part-time jobs to fourteen women working as community workers for five paid hours a week. This way of getting women involved in improving their living conditions is a departure from the idea that outside experts should be brought in to solve local problems. This project is a breakthrough in access to jobs for many women as it enables them to enhance their self-esteem, broaden their network of relationships, and gradually make changes in their home environment. The Employment Preparation Project offers progressive job training. Program participants begin by working five hours a week and six months later are in a 20-hour-a-week work schedule. *Life Choices* is a preliminary but integral part of the program. The employment preparation portion focuses on job placement, support, planning, and job searching. Gradual entry into the labour force takes account of the constraints that are particular to mothers with responsibility for children, especially during that sometimes difficult transition period from home to the labour market.

At Candora, the activities, carried out under one single roof, are multiple and free-flowing. For instance, while a group of women is discussing what should be done to ensure that the municipality will co-operate to improve neighbourhood safety, others are cooking a meal together while their children are playing in the next room. The conversation passes from the cooking group to the safety group. What might be seen as three programs—collective kitchen, community development, and daycare—are an indivisible whole, re-creating the support that is so often lacking in the everyday living environment and in places that offer specialized services.

Anishinabe R.E.S.P.E.C.T.: From a Sense of Belonging to Training

Anishinabe R.E.S.P.E.C.T. was founded in 1981 as a community-based agency for Natives living in Winnipeg and to prepare victims of chronic unemployment for the work force or school. Anishinabe R.E.S.P.E.C.T. has adopted a holistic approach that takes account of participants' job and training needs and helps them to undertake personal, family, and collective process towards betterment. The agency offers counselling services to victims of sexual abuse along with family counselling services. The presence and involvement of elders in the employment preparation classes and the emphasis on contemporary Native spirituality has Anishinabe R.E.S.P.E.C.T. well rooted in the culture of its participants. This helps to provide a sense of belonging, in a context of being excluded from the mainstream of society and experiencing problems in adjusting to an urban setting. The organization's staff is Native.

Anishinabe R.E.S.P.E.C.T. has made the family the central core around which it has structured its programs. The agency requires that two members of the same family take part in the training program. Classes are made up of pairs linked by family ties in the broad sense of the term (mother-daughter couples, sisters, cousins, spouses, but also friends). This arrangement allows participants to find support within their own living environment and have someone they can depend on to share similar experiences and aspirations. The 26-week program combines eleven weeks of classroom support activities and fifteen weeks of practical training in the workplace. The eleven weeks of courses enable participants to explore their attitudes towards work, to take stock of their family and social lives, and to acquire communication and problem-solving skills. The aim of Anishinabe R.E.S.P.E.C.T. is to provide work experience in novice positions rather than in specialized jobs. Anishinabe R.E.S.P. E.C.T. works in co-operation with a number of community-based agencies, particularly Native agencies, that provide services to families and women in Winnipeg's North End. Part of the training is aimed at integrating participants into the community service networks in their communities.

Some Characteristics of Alternative Resources

None of the four agencies described above focuses directly on the issue of child welfare or on protection, yet each works towards this by taking account of the general betterment of families and communities. The originality of alternative agencies centres on the manner in which the issue of job training (so central to the integration strategies of agencies) is related to the problem of family poverty; the creation of support spaces; the importance of gender, race and culture in developing appropriate action for disadvantaged families; and redefining relationships within agencies in the area of family involvement and empowerment.

Job Training and Family Poverty

Job access is central to the validation and mobilization of families. The welfare of children comes hand-in-hand with the economic welfare of mothers which in turn comes with the socioeconomic development of the community. Many agencies therefore try to break the exclusion from the mainstream of society by putting job access strategies in place and integrating them into other related activities. In order to do that, alternative agencies depend on the possible adjustment between what Melucci calls "inner time" (the subjective periods of inner experiences, affections, emotions and natural cycles) and "social time" as marked by the various social roles individuals play and by the objective division of time marked by the clock (Melucci, 1989, p. 104). Alternative agencies recognize the current break between these two ways of experiencing time and work to reconcile these two different times. For instance, in the job preparation programs, the curriculum responsible for readying participants for the time structure of jobs is punctuated with periods of reconciliation with inner time. This is done either by gradual integration into the labour force (Candora), by introducing family counselling services and finding room for the spiritual and cultural dimensions of adjustment (Anishinabe R.E.S.P.E.C.T.), or by recognizing the need to "leave room to express what one is experiencing" (Regroupement des femmes sans emploi du Nord du Québec). Each of these agencies recognizes the fragmenting of social roles that is characteristic of our society, especially the tensions created by the multiple tasks required of mothers and the lack of support they receive from their surroundings.

Reconciling inner time (often developed in the isolation that is typical of the lives of people living in poverty) and social time comes about through people being there for each other and especially through the circularity of talking. This was the reason for the importance of the talking circles that had been developed out of First Nations traditions in Native agencies, and the discussion groups that sprang from the women's movement dynamic. Activity programming divided into regulated time segments, be they for individuals or groups, rapidly becomes incompatible with the organization's objectives. One community worker explained, when speaking about organizing support groups in conventional family agencies, "They'll have very structured groups and, for the majority of women who come here, groups have meant either school or jail, both not very good experiences, so they are very wary of that." The social bonds that develop, the friendships that are shaped informally and are carried over into the communities, are not very amenable to being programmed.

Creating A Support Space

Isolation and lack of resources often result in families' being excluded from places where informal social bonds are formed. For disadvantaged families, having one's own space where people can get to know each other better, where they can share with others, if only to talk to other parents who are having the same problems, is vital. An open place is preferred where one feels at home and can reweave social bonds that have been broken and destabilized by poverty. Most alternative agencies and networks are simple places, open to all, where activities are not just limited to a specific, predetermined, permanent program such as employment preparation classes. The agency becomes a meeting place, a centre where parents and children come and go without necessarily having to do anything. What these families want is to be with other people. Candora sums this up in one of its documents:

> Much more than specific skills are developed through organized activities. Newly arrived immigrant women learn English and Canadian culture; those who speak English become familiar with other cultures and different ways of doing things. Problems are shared, friendships are born, and the feeling of belonging to a community is built.

This is not a matter of receiving a service geared to a need (training, housing, food, and so forth) that has been defined as a deficiency brought on by one's own incompetence as a parent. Rather, the process is one of creating ties by expressing one's needs around a table, sipping a cup of coffee. This is how awareness-raising spaces are developed. This is also how other needs are identified, the satisfaction of which is sought in other agencies or by expanding the agency in which one finds oneself. One goes from the desire for welfare to the desire for well-being. This search leads parents to become actors in their own life histories, that is, to shape the tools of self-determination and empowerment within a community that, very often, leads agencies to change configurations and modes of operation. This is a risky operation especially when considering the pressures of the political and financial context in which alternative agencies find themselves.

Gender, Race, Culture and Class Mediation

Alternative agencies always come within the sociocultural framework that mediates social ties at the local as well as national level as parents put meaning back into their family and social lives. This is why agencies are so responsive to the impact of gender, race, and culture on family life and the way people identify their needs. Community workers and volunteers well represent the ethnic and racial makeup of the neighbourhood or locality in which agencies are being developed. Employment equity has often been imposed by the leadership in many conventional social agencies. Alternative agencies often have already realized that, if they are to offer support areas to their user families, the staff need to be representative of the families using the agency and be able to relate meaningfully to these families through their surroundings.

Agencies have structured themselves so as to give meaning to the families' situations by taking account of the historical, sociopolitical, and cultural bases of their victimization. Alternative agencies are more deliberately political in their approach and place emphasis, not on meeting needs, but on the process by which the needs are defined and operated in the framework of what Nancy Fraser calls "the politics of need interpretation" (Fraser, 1989:146). The unequal relations of gender, race and class and the symbolic reaffirmation of one's values and actions cannot be ignored. Anishinabe R.E.S.P. E.C.T. demonstrates this grounding by tying employment training to cultural reappropriation with the presence of elders in its courses. Such an approach involves quite a number of risks. Agencies adopting a value-oriented approach (Godbout, 1990: 248) risk undertaking activities and choosing priorities that do not necessarily correspond to the prevailing norms that define child and family welfare in terms of middle-class values. The Elm Hill parents' group, for instance, had decided that renovating the community centre was a priority. The interior paint, rather than structural work to the roof, was determined to be the first priority. The centre had at least seven or eight pails to collect the rain coming in through the roof. The parents knew very well that they would have to attend to the roof sooner or later but, by making the paint the main priority, they chose to enhance the value of the centre immediately by making it more appealing at first glance and by inverting the order in which conventional intervention is often conceived. To paraphrase Jacques Godbout (1992), "first create the ties, then create the goods."

Family Involvement and the Challenges of Professionalism

The focus of empowerment strategies by alternative agencies is the mechanism that allows parents to identify their needs and to satisfy them in a flexible way. Some agencies, such as Regroupement des femmes sans emploi du Nord du Québec, are run by the women themselves. However, it is often difficult for families living in poverty to commit to sitting on a board of directors or executive board. Candora and Anishinabe R.E.S.P. E.C.T. have boards that, though they may be community-based, are not made up exclusively of users. User involvement is often regarded as the culmination of personal and collective efforts undertaken by parents within the agency. Elm Hill has an institutional board of practitioners that is active in the leadership of the community. The initial idea of focusing the definition of "alternative" on the involvement of user families in agency boards, and therefore in the policy making of the agencies, had to be thoroughly reexamined during the study.

Looking only at formal policy-making mechanisms may overlook one of the essential dynamics of alternative agencies and networks. The role of permanent staff is crucial. There is no doubt that some initiatives would never have seen the light of day if it had not been for the interventions of professionals (Regroupement des femmes sans emploi du Nord du Québec and especially Elm Hill) and the required political impetus from influential people within the institutional system. Data collected from community workers as well as from families suggests that it is not feasible to look for alternative forms of intervention in radical opposition to the role of professionals, as can be done in the mental health field. The manner in which policies are determined in alternative resources became clear by redefining staff-family relationships. These relationships, characterized by a very deep trust between staff and parents and by the desire to establish ties on an equal footing, are the basis on which alternative approaches become coherent. Thus, taking risks with families at risk is being able to express and experience mutual trust. It is one of the keys to understanding the dynamics of alternative resources. Mutual trust is shaped by two different strategies.

First, understanding between families and practitioners does not come from intellectual views learned at school or university. It arises from the fact that they have experienced the same problems, hopes and aspirations as poor families. It also stems from cultural, ethnic, and racial representativeness. Often, the mothers who first came to the agency for the activities later became volunteers and were hired as permanent staff, even at the cost of having to earn a specific diploma later on. Continuity in the progression and experience of the people who come to an agency creates remarkable cohesion within alternative resources. It makes trust possible, places relationships on an equal footing, and creates a dynamic solidarity where the leaders (be they part of the staff or the families) share the same experiences or, at least, the same aspirations.

A second situation is one in which permanent staff members already have a university education and do not necessarily share the same life experiences as the user mothers. What characterizes the relationship here is the permanent staff's commitment to a coherent political view of intervention in the broad sense of the term. This is not a symbiosis between practitioners and families, but a coalition and alliance, an alliance that is often shaped through questioning. As one of the community workers told us:

> A voice for the voiceless...is what is needed. Yes, the poor can get organized but only provided that there are intellectuals who accept to enter into in an alliance with them. It also signifies being confronted with one's values and making life choices, because it means not working for the same wages as in the [public system]. You can see our working conditions: we do not know from one year to the next whether we will keep our [salaries].

In both cases, the cohesive relations between permanent staff and families reinforce their policy-making powers relative to a board that is often designed as a third—and only third—party in the policy-making process. Community worker-family relationships are on a completely different plane from that of traditional relationships with professional practitioners. Many people have symbolized this relationship by refusing to consider the family as a client, a term that was often objected to in the interviews. Family involvement in the agencies was not a given. As Godbout has demonstrated (1987), user involvement in agencies is not necessarily the key to new forms of social democracy. On the other hand, what the study seems to show is that there presently exists a redefinition of professionalism that is experimenting differently with traditional social work values such as objectivity and neutrality.

Conclusions: Some of The Issues

Three issues concern the very existence of agencies such as those just described, as well as the direction social policies centred on a renewal of social practices could take. These issues cannot be analyzed if the huge social restructuring undertaken by the various levels of government in Canada is ignored. Lamoureux and Lesemann (1987) have analyzed the interface between government and community agencies in a context of government spending cuts and privatization. Brad McKenzie (1994) brought out the confusion and ambiguity surrounding current efforts to decentralize service delivery. A preliminary identification of tension zones that make or break alternative agencies is possible based on the research.

Culture Clashes: Talk Around a Table versus Programmed Rationality

Tension exists between the logic of sociability that is being developed by alternative resources and the logic of service programming currently being defined in terms of management and rationalization of public health and social services. What is important is the solidarity that is made accessible—physically, psychologically and socially—through an open, free-flowing organization of space and a high responsiveness to individual and collective cycles of the families using the resources. According to one community worker, these families can indeed "get involved slowly, at their own pace" and in a way that is deeply grounded in the local cultures and subcultures.

On the other hand, against a backdrop of government cutbacks and opting out, the public system is currently relying more and more on community resources to solve situations that were formerly within government purview. Many community-based agencies spoke of "Friday night crises": public institutions close for the weekend and send them whole groups of people who are not in enough trouble to benefit from heavy institutional support but who have enough problems to disrupt the everyday operations of an agency. Community agencies are forced to satisfy and prioritize an increasingly greater number of needs for an increasingly needful population. A logic of programming and sectoring aimed mainly at government services results in agencies that are based on developing informal sociability being threatened as they are forced to stretch their capacities to the absolute limit. Agencies find themselves caught up in a system of locks into which each successive overflow from the cumbersome public system is channelled (Lamoureux & Lesemann, 1987, p. 200).

Responsiveness to family cycles is caught in a net that is tightening around demands for protection and crisis intervention. Alternative agencies are no longer alternative in the sense that they provide services that are different, but rather because they have become a means of last resort. More and more they must organize needs into a hierarchy. There is strong pressure for them to conform to institutional practice models, without the benefit of the financial support their partners in the public sector are granted. The tension that threatens the autonomy of alternative agencies is particularly sensitive to the caseloads of the community workers and their relations with the public sector. Community workers find themselves at the junction of two opposing trends. On the one hand, their choice brings them to focus their practices on community-based intervention with poor families. On the other, faced with increased problems resulting from social services being blocked from above, community workers must satisfy complex needs, such as those stemming from problems of incest or sexual abuse, that often require specialized intervention. The agencies are faced with increased sectoring of the public system and the shifting of social management to the local level without restoring the balance of local power that is still in the hands of large institutions. Alternative agencies are viewed as complementary, which is a threat to their autonomy.

This loss of autonomy also involves many other practices affecting the everyday life and dynamism of agencies. An example is the desire to rationalize alternative community services by basing evaluation and funding on objective criteria of efficiency, complementarity to public services, and in terms of priorities and targeting that stem from social policies—that is, from an institutional logic (Lesemann, 1994). In the child welfare field, intervention effectiveness is often grounded in individual child development indicators and the risk of families relapsing, even if the social environment is somewhat taken into account. But the alternative agencies focus primarily on collective development and empowerment. As one community worker told us: "They want to know how many children don't wet the bed any more, while we are just struggling to survive." Another dimension of intervention effectiveness limits the criteria of success to one of the organization's activities, while it is its involvement in a whole array of related and complex activities that makes it effective. Candora's primary mandate, for instance, is employment preparation and, coincidentally, community development. It was not designed to fight violence against women, its grants do not come from that source and it cannot lay claim to these funds. Yet, one of the agency's participants stated—as did a number of others in other agencies—that it was thanks to Candora that she managed to get out of a situation of domestic violence. An evaluation of this agency would overlook this aspect of its work, and yet it constitutes a huge part of the support work carried on there.

The question is to determine on which criteria an evaluation of empowerment is going to be based. Who will define these criteria? The conflict between the need for the government to target populations (e.g., battered women) in a significant way, and a practice of intervention that could be called holistic, has an impact on resource development and funding. Some granting agencies, rather than trusting alternative agencies, determine and run them through their policies of fund allocation or management; others put their full trust in the agencies and are not too demanding about reports, and so forth. The accountability of alternative community agencies was not challenged in the comments collected from community workers. However, the definition of criteria of success and the operationalizing of evaluative research were the targets of comments calling for an honest and thorough debate on the issue. Rules that are too rigid and forms that are too complicated are a huge tax on community resources. Funding on a project-by-project basis, which is currently the only way agencies can survive, requires investing resources in staff time and effort and adapting to the evaluation criteria set by multiple authorities that are often not very aware of what alternative agencies do. This type of funding eats up energy and money that many agencies do not have and requires an understanding of the logic of bureaucratic programming that has not necessarily been acquired by those very people the grant program is supposed to be addressing. As one parent involved in one of the agencies we visited explained: "We don't speak the same lingo!" This is a question of culture clash.

Centrality of Women's Work

The overwhelming majority of people who were active in the groups we studied were women, either consumers of alternative agencies or permanent staff members (the line between the two is not always very clear-cut). These are the people who devise, create or dream up new solutions in the field of community services. With the possible exception of some Native agencies, the absence of men as parents as well as practitioners was striking. There was a silence surrounding this subject that needs to be pointed out. Mothers only rarely mentioned the contribution of their children's father to their lives. When it was mentioned, more often than not, it was to bring up incidents of violence that had led them to seek help. Further, the majority of community workers working in alternative agencies were paid salaries that, more often than not, were below the poverty line. Many agencies could not survive without the support of volunteers or semi-volunteers, the overwhelming majority of whom are women.

Initiatives to privatize and deinstitutionalize have shifted responsibility for care to families in the name of individual and family empowerment. This shift represents an increased burden for women who are traditionally responsible for the labour of love in patriarchal families (Guberman, Maheu, & Maillé, 1993). The restructuring of social and health services that, to a certain extent, strives to give local communities as well as individual and community-based services renewed vigour, brings the issue of women's work to the forefront. Entrusting the front-line work to community agencies without giving them either the recognition or the funds that would enable them to do a proper job means exploiting women's work yet again. What are the costs associated with not making the problems of inequity in the area of gender and women's work the focus of the analyses of social practices and policies aimed at support to families? Child welfare is grounded in great part in the need to reweave the social ties within the grassroots community. What is the role for men, as community workers and as fathers, in an undertaking that is presently being conducted in the main by women?

This project was made possible through a grant from the Welfare Grants Directorate of the Department of Human Resources Development.

References

Autès, M. (1980). *Pauvreté et lutte contre la pauvreté.* Paris: Centre de recherches économiques, sociologiques et de gestion.

Bouchard, C. (1991). *Un Québec fou de ses enfants* (Youth Task Force Report). Québec City: Ministère de la Santé et des Services sociaux.

Carniol, B. (1987). *Case critical: Challenging social work in Canada.* Toronto: Between the Lines.

Chaume, C. (1988). *Les pratiques alternatives en santé mentale au Québec: un portrait de notre différence.* Montréal: Regroupement des resources alternatives en santé mentale au Québec.

Colin, C., Ouellet, G., Boyer, G., & Martin, C. (1992). *Extrême pauvreté, maternité et santé.* Montréal: Éditions St-Martin.

Donzelot, J. (1977). *La police des familles.* Paris: Éditions de Minuit.

Fraser, N. (1989). *Unruly practices: Power, discourse and gender in contemporary social theory.* Minneapolis: University of Minnesota Press.

Glaser, B. G., & Strauss, A. L. (1967). *The discovery of grounded theory.* Chicago: Aldine.

Godbout, J. (1987). *La démocratie des usagers.* Montréal: Boréal Express.

Godbout, J. T. (1990). Le communautaire et l'appareil. In M.-M. Brault & L. Saint-Jean (Eds.), *Entraide et associations* (pp. 339–361). Québec City: Institut québécois de recherche sur la culture.

Godbout, J. T. (1992). *L'esprit du don.* Montréal: Boréal.

Guberman, N., Maheu, P. & Maillé, C. (1993). *Et si l'amour ne suffisait pas ... Femmes, familles et adultes dépendants.* Montréal: Éditions du remue-ménage.

Johnston, P. (1983). *Native children and the child welfare system.* Ottawa: Canadian Council on Social Development.

Kérisit, M. & St-Amand, N. (1993a). Pauvreté et pratiques alternatives: conséquences pour les politiques sociales. Paper presented at the 6th Congress on Social Policies, St. John's, Newfoundland.

Kérisit, M., & St-Amand, N. (1993b). *Familles-problèmes ou familles-ressources? Approches alternatives aux interventions actuelles auprès des familles pauvres.* Deuxième symposium québécois de recherche sur la famille [second Québec symposium on family research]. Trois-Rivières, Québec.

Lamoureux, J., & Lesemann F. (1987). *Les filières d'action sociale. Les rapports entre les services sociaux publics et les pratiques communautaires. Rapport présenté à la Commission d'enquête sur les services de santé et les services sociaux.* Québec City: les Publications du Québec.

Lesemann, F. (1994). La pauvreté: aspects sociaux. In F. Dumont, S. Langlois & Y. Martin (Eds.), *Traité des problèmes sociaux* (pp. 581–604). Québec City: Institut québécois de recherche sur la culture.

Liffman, M. (1978). *Power for the poor, The family centre project: An experiment in self-help.* Sidney: George Allen & Unwin.

McKenzie, B. (1994). Decentralized social services: A critique of models of service delivery. In A. F. Johnson, M. Stephen, & P. J. Smith (eds.), *Continuities and discontinuities: The political economy of social welfare and labour market policy in Canada* (pp. 97–110). Toronto: University of Toronto Press.

Melucci, A. (1989). *Nomads of the present: Social movements and individual needs in contemporary society.* London: Brookmount House.

Novick, M., & Volpe, R. (1990). *Children at risk: A review prepared for the children at risk subcommittee of the Laidlaw Foundation.* Toronto: The Laidlaw Foundation.

Pitrou, A. (1992). *Les solidarités familiales. Vivre sans famille?* (2nd ed.). Toulouse: Éditions Privat.

Rhéaume, J., & Sévigny, R. (1987). Les enjeux sociaux de la pratique dite alternative. *Revue canadienne de santé mentale communautaire, 6*(2), 133–147.

Selig, A. L. (1976). The myth of the multi-problem family. *American Journal of Orthopsychiatry, 46*(3), 526–532.

Soulet, M. H. (1987). La recherche qualitative ou la fin des certitudes. In J. P. Deslauriers (Ed.), *Les méthodes de la recherche qualitative* (pp. 9–22). Sillery: Presses de l'Université du Québec.

St-Amand, N., & Clavette, H. (1991). *Entraide et débrouillardise sociale. Au-delà de la psychiatrie.* Ottawa and Montréal: Canadian Council on Social Development.

Wharf, B. (1992). *Communities and social policy in Canada.* Toronto: McClelland & Stewart Inc.

Yin, R. K. (1984). *Case study research: Design and method.* Beverly Hills: Sage Publications.

14

Deciding About Justice for Young People in New Zealand: The Involvement of Families, Victims and Culture

Gabrielle M. Maxwell and Allison Morris

How should young offenders be dealt with? At other times in history, the aim was to bring the young person back into the social group. This was particularly so in some indigenous systems of justice. Such systems are usually based on agreements involving the whole community; the desired outcomes are a reconciliation between offenders and their families and victims and their families, and the restoration of harmony within the community. These methods were among those used by Maori for resolving disputes prior to European colonization. Western youth justice philosophies have been rather different. At different times they have emphasized different mixtures of a welfare and a just deserts or a crime control approach to offending. Western models have been heavily criticized in New Zealand, as elsewhere, as doing little to change the attitudes or the behaviour of young offenders. Criticism has also come from proponents of models of restorative justice who have emphasized the importance of victims and of the achievement of social balance through the processes that are used to resolve the issues. The approach which has been in place in New Zealand since 1989 brings together a number of different ideas about how to deal with a young person who offends. Some parts reflect a justice approach with an emphasis on accountability, protecting rights, and diversion. Some parts are distinctive to New Zealand, in particular, the emphasis on the involvement of families and victims in decision making and the emphasis on culture.

The central and most novel feature of the New Zealand approach is the use of the family group conference (FGC), a forum for group decision-making that involves police, young people and victims together with their family, family group, whanau (descendants of a common ancestor), hapu (the clan) and iwi (the tribe) in determining what will happen and thereby obtaining the support of all parties for the outcomes. The process is expected to be sufficiently flexible so that issues can be dealt with in a culturally appropriate manner. The Act also emphasizes that criminal proceedings should not be used if there is an alternative means of dealing with the offending or for welfare purposes, juveniles should be kept in the community, age should be regarded as a mitigating factor, sanctions should be the least restrictive possible, juvenile offenders should be held accountable for their acts, and due regard should be

Exhibit 14.1 The objects and principles of youth justice in New Zealand

Achieving justice

accountability—emphasizing the importance of young people paying an appropriate penalty for their crime and making good the wrong they have done to others

reducing time frames—making decisions and arranging penalties as soon as possible so that what happens makes sense to the child or young person

protecting rights—emphasising the protection of young people's rights

diversion—keeping young people out of courts and preventing the use of labels that make it difficult for young people to put early offending behind them

Responding to needs

enhancing wellbeing and strengthening families—making available services that will assist the young person and their family

Providing for participation

family involvement—involving families and young people in making the decisions for themselves and taking charge of their lives

victim involvement—involving victims in the decisions about what will happen

consensus decision making—arriving at decisions which are agreed to by the family, the young person, the police and victims

Being culturally appropriate

culturally appropriate ways of resolving matters—allowing families to choose their own procedures and the time and place of meetings

culturally appropriate ways of providing services—developing and funding a range of services that suit different cultural needs and wishes and are operated by people sensitive to that culture

culturally appropriate penalties—encouraging the creation of penalties which reflect different cultural responses

given to the interests of the victim. The main objects and principles of the New Zealand approach are set out in Exhibit 14.1.

Pathways Through the New Zealand Justice System

The youth justice system deals only with children and young people who are at least 10 years and who are under 17 years of age at the time that they offend. Those under the age of 10 years are not regarded as being responsible for their offences. After the age of 10 years anyone, young or adult, who commits murder or manslaughter goes before the High Court. However, all other offences committed by young people are dealt with, at least initially, in the youth justice system. This includes very serious offences such as rape, robbery, and assault. Those aged 10 and under 14, except if the offence involves murder and manslaughter, cannot be charged in court. However, when the number, nature or magnitude of the offence is such as to give serious concern for the well-being of the child, he or she may be referred for a family group conference (FGC). Once young people have reached the age of 17 they are treated as adults; when they offend they are usually arrested and appear in the

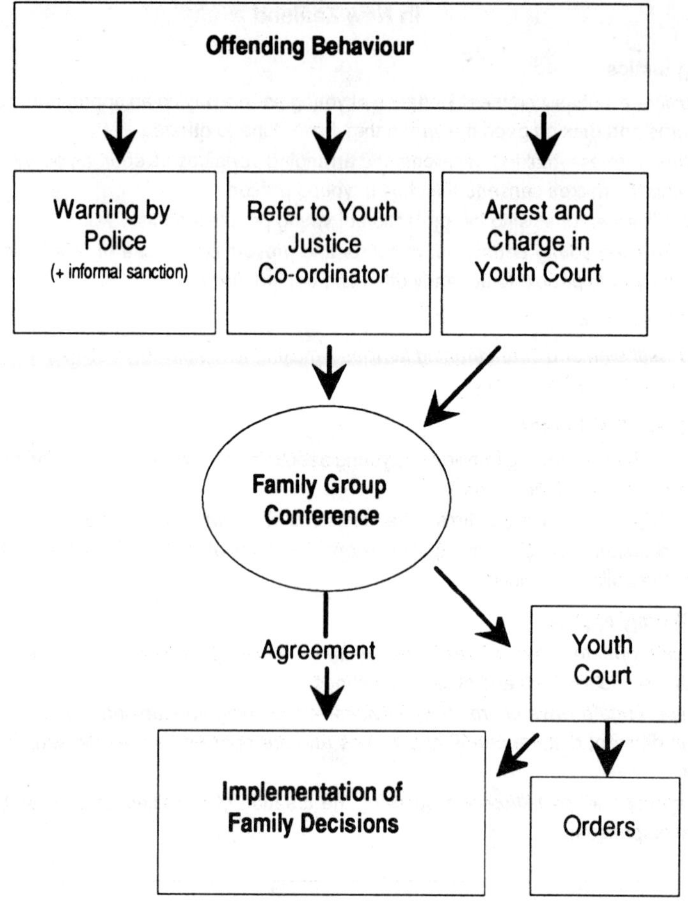

District or High Court depending on the seriousness of the offences. The Act describes those aged 14 and under 17 as young persons and those under 14 as children but here, for the sake of simplicity, all those aged over 10 and under 17 are referred to as young people. Exhibit 14.2 provides a description of the possible pathways through the new system.

The police have three main options when juvenile offenders are detected: they may warn the juvenile and/ or arrange informal sanctions, they may refer the juvenile for an FGC, or they may arrest the juvenile. Minor and first offenders are expected to be diverted from prosecution by means of an immediate (street) warning. Where further action is thought necessary, the police may refer juveniles to the police Youth Aid Section (a specialist unit dealing only with juveniles) for follow-up such as a warning in the presence of the parents. The Youth Aid Section may also require an apology to the victim and give the child or young person an additional sanction, for example, some community work. The intention underlying the 1989 Act is to encourage the police to adopt low key responses to offending by young people except where the nature and circumstances of the offending mean that stronger measures are required to protect the safety of the public. In 1990, approximately 60% of all young people found offending by the police were dealt with by police warning or informal sanctions. The juvenile is referred to a youth justice coordinator (YJC) for consideration for an FGC where Youth Aid Sections feel that action beyond those they normally arrange themselves is required. Approximately 30% of all cases dealt with by the police were referred for an FGC in 1990.

Only a minority of juvenile offenders (about 10% in 1990) are being arrested in New Zealand; this compares with approximately a third in 1984. Almost all juveniles who are arrested are referred to the Youth Court. But these youth must be referred by the court to an FGC which then considers how to deal with the case. The Youth Court cannot dispose of a case without considering the recommendations of the FGC. Some offenders, at a later stage, may be referred from the Youth Court to the District Court or to the High Court depending on the seriousness of the offence and the previous offence history of the offender. But such transfers are rare and the vast majority of juvenile offenders are now dealt with in the youth justice system.

The youth justice coordinator (YJC) is employed within a special section in the Department of Social Welfare (DSW), called the New Zealand Children and Young Persons Service (CYPS). This section works with children, young people and their families when there are problems over who will care for the children, when they need protection from harm, or when there has been offending. In the latter case, the person who has overall responsibility is the YJC. Briefly, the YJC receives a referral for an FGC from the police, contacts the family and arranges the FGC. If the YJC thinks that the offence is not very serious or if there has not been any previous offending, the YJC will negotiate with the police to encourage them to arrange for warnings or informal sanctions. The YJC also arranges FGCs that result from a referral by the Youth Court after there has been an arrest and charge in court. The YJC is assisted by a team of social workers.

The family group conferences lie at the heart of the new procedures and are a means of avoiding court processes and court sanctions as well as a means of determining how to deal with juveniles who commit offences. FGCs involve a meeting of the young person, his or her advocate (a barrister, solicitor or lay advocate) if one has been arranged, members of the family, whanau or family group and whoever they invite, the victim or their representative, the police, the YJC, and a DSW social worker in cases where the DSW has had a statutory role in relationship to the custody, guardianship or supervision of the young person. Other support people can also attend FGCs—for example, brothers and sisters, family friends, teachers, youth club organizers, and the like. The involvement of victims is of particular importance and has potential advantages both for the young person, who is helped to understand the effect of his or her offences on another person, and for the victim who is given an opportunity to express his or her feelings, to understand more about what happened, and to have a say in the decisions.

The FGC only considers cases where the young person has not denied the alleged offences or has already been found guilty. The intended focus of the FGC is the young person's offending and matters related directly to the circumstances of that offending. The Act specifically states that criminal proceedings are not to be used solely to intervene in the life of the young person on welfare grounds. This has been interpreted to imply that FGCs should focus primarily on issues of accountability rather than welfare. Thus the purpose of the meeting is to confront the young person with his or her offending and to decide on the most effective response to it. After accountability has been dealt with, the FGC can approve plans that enhance the wellbeing of the young person and support the family. If it becomes clear that there are serious matters relating to the care or protection of the young person, the YJC should refer the case to a care and protection coordinator, who operates under separate statutory provisions.

The participants at the FGC formulate a plan for the young person and make recommendations about what should happen in order to make the young person accountable for his or her offences. The range of possibilities include work in the community, work for the victim, reparation or an apology, donations to a charity, restrictions on the liberty of the young person for a specified time (such as grounding, curfew, not driving a car etc.), and are limited only by the imagination of the parties. The FGC may recommend prosecution in the court and request specific court orders if it thinks these are appropriate. In addition, the FGC may agree to plans and recommendations designed to enhance the young person's wellbeing and to support the family. The plans and decisions are binding when they have been agreed to by all those present at an FGC (and, where relevant, accepted by the court). Ideally the process moves the young person through shame, to remorse, to reparation, and to reacceptance while the victim expresses anger and hurt, is acknowledged, receives redress, and is healed.

A court process is now used for only a small proportion of young offenders. The Youth Court has been created as a branch of the District Court to deal with youth justice cases only. The establishment of the Youth Court underlines the principle that the offending of young people should be based on principles of criminal justice, not welfare; that is, not on reforming or helping the offender but on notions of accountability and responsibility for actions, due process, legal representation, requiring judges to give reasons for certain decisions, and imposing sanctions which are in proportion to the gravity of the offence. Before making a decision about the appropriate outcome, the Youth Court must have regard to the plans and recommendations of the FGC.

In summary, the system developed in New Zealand is based on achieving justice through accountability, protection of rights, and definite time frames. At the same time, there is a concern for minimizing the damage to those young people who come in contact with the criminal justice system. This is done by avoiding court proceedings wherever possible and by providing access to culturally appropriate programmes and to services that may enhance the wellbeing of young people and strengthen their families. The goal is to help to reduce social disadvantage without removing young people from their families and communities. The most unique aims centre on the notion of participation. Families and young people can participate in decisions; victims can become involved; decisions are to be made by an agreement of all the interested parties; and the manner in which decisions are taken should, as far as possible, be responsive to the culture of the young person and his or her family. Procedures within the police, within CYPS, and within the court system have all been modified in order to accommodate these notions. This then is the system in theory—what of the system in practice?

Research

From August 1990 to May 1991, the authors and a team of 10 researchers followed what happened to nearly 700 young people who came to attention for offending in one of five different areas of the country (Maxwell & Morris, 1993). Researchers attended the FGCs that were arranged for just over 200 young people and interviewed them, their families, the victims and the professionals who were involved with them. When cases resulted from an arrest (there were 70 of these), researchers interviewed the arresting officer and followed through what had happened in the Youth Court. Researchers followed up what happened subsequently for most of these young people, by interviewing families and checking files three to six months after the first contact. Researchers also collected relevant statistics from national data bases and compiled them from the files kept by police, welfare services, and the courts. The research was bicultural. Maori advised in the planning stages, helped with the design of questions, interviewed Maori young people and families, advised on the analysis of the data, and wrote or advised on the sections relating to Maori. A Samoan researcher also participated in the interviews of Pacific Island families and commented on the report. The goals of the research were to describe how the Act was working in practice and to evaluate the extent to which it was meeting its aims.

Achieving Justice

Central to the idea of accountability is that offenders are responsible for their offences and that the focus in making decisions is on the offence and not the offenders. The penalty is not chosen because it is thought that it might reform the particular offender or because it might stop others from offending. Rather it is related to the offence, so that the more serious the offence the more severe the penalty, and the more minor the offence the less severe the penalty. Penalties have fixed limits and once a decision has been made, the offender knows exactly what he or she has to do to clean the slate.

The results of the research show that, in practice, a larger number of young people were being made accountable than had previously been the case. More than eight out of ten of those who had FGCs, including those who went to the Youth Court, received active penalties; that is, they made reparation, paid donations, carried out work in the community or for the victims, and/or had restrictions placed on their liberty. The figure reached 95% when apologies were added. Thus doing nothing is rare. More importantly, during the research, 87% of the tasks agreed to by the young person were completed either fully or substantially. These findings contrast with the earlier system. A similar proportion of young offenders appeared before the court as now have an FGC, but only 60% of them received a penalty which made them accountable and apologies to victims were rare.

Children and young people live in a world where time seems different than for adults; a few days can seem a very long time. Penalties are likely to be less effective when they occur long after the offence and its discovery. Hence dealing with young people as quickly as possible is a priority in the new system. Although many FGCs did not meet the tight time limits set down in the Act (14 days for court ordered FGCs and 21 days for others), most were held and resolved within time frames that made the process relatively meaningful to the young person. Reaching decisions in the Youth Court, on the other hand, was often slow, especially where charges were denied.

Young people generally do not know as much about their rights as adults and are more vulnerable than adults. They are particularly vulnerable to pressure from adults. For example, they can easily be confused by complicated questions and may agree to what someone else suggests just because they are tired and frightened. Increasingly, methods of policing used for adults were recognized as having harmful effects on young people. For example, there is some evidence that young people begin seeing themselves negatively as a result of their experience of being arrested, questioned, and detained by the police. There has also been increased recognition of the vulnerability of young people held and questioned in police stations. Such concerns resulted in pressure to clearly set out procedures that would protect the rights of young people by having their rights explained, by having a parent or other adult present when they are being questioned by the police, and by having legal advice and representation.

There has been much comment and debate about the sections of the Act dealing with rights. Two main issues emerge: informing young people of their rights and ensuring that young people can consult a parent or other adult and have that person present during questioning. The police have complained that telling young people about their rights results in young people refusing to accompany them for questioning. This in turn, according to the police, makes police seem weak, encourages young offenders to treat them with derision, and creates a class of hardened young criminals. The police also complain that the current provisions make it difficult for them to obtain a confession. Some officers maintain that if they inform young people of their right to remain silent, they will be unable to solve the case by questioning the alleged offender. This criticism is directed not merely at the Act but at a right which has traditionally been regarded as the core right of common law systems. The provisions of the Children, Young Persons and Their Families Act, 1989, do, however, go further than in the case of adults. In particular, the Act emphasizes the vulnerability of young people and their rights to special protection during any investigation relating to the commission or possible commission of an offence.

There is little support from the research for police complaints about difficulties stemming from the new provisions although, despite this, some legislative changes are pending. For instance, there were no examples of young people walking away from the police with impunity. All the young people in the sample either collaborated with the police officer or were arrested. And most police officers in the sample appeared to be able to operate successfully within the framework of the Act (even though many of them did not fully understand and follow all of its provisions). It is hard to appreciate the vulnerability of the young when faced with a rebellious young person. However, except in one or two very exceptional cases, the researchers did not find that the young people interviewed were hardened criminals, well informed about their rights, and determined to make a mockery of the law. The findings agree with the views of those who drafted the legislation; young people are generally unaware of their rights and very vulnerable to pressure from authority.

In general, the police attempted to notify the families of the young people who were taken to the police station but sometimes there was a considerable delay before this occurred and questioning proceeded meanwhile. Some police officers appeared to hold the view that it was only necessary to notify families and ensure the presence of an adult when a statement was to be taken for use in evidence and that it was not necessary, therefore, during general preliminary questioning about the young person's involvement in the offence. This view is clearly at variance with the wording of the Act. Complaints were frequently made by police officers about the time wasted in attending to these requirements and the difficulty of obtaining an adult's presence. Nevertheless, most officers who attempted to do so were able to obtain a suitable adult within a reasonable time. On the other hand, there were no cases in the sample in which either the arresting officer or the young person informed us that a barrister or solicitor had been present during the interview. A few young people said that they had asked for a lawyer to be present and this was treated dismissively. This again raises the question of the extent to which young people are being systematically informed of their rights.

Young people's rights are also protected through the provision of legal representation. However, most young people in the sample were dealt with without legal advice or representation (because they were dealt with by police warning or by direct referral to FGCs). Discretionary decision-making does take place at these points, but these young people miss out on appropriate advice or representation. There were no examples of youth advocates becoming involved in non-court cases. Thus there was no opportunity for young people attending non-court FGCs to have legal advice about whether or not they should admit the offence or the consequences of any admission. Nor did the young people have legal advice in the FGC when they wished to question details in the summary of facts. The Government has agreed to extend the role of youth advocates to meet such situations although there is evidence that this is not happening in all areas. Even in those cases where the court ordered the FGC, only 59% of FGCs were attended by youth advocates although in all cases where charges were laid in court a youth advocate was appointed. Many of the youth advocates served their clients' interests well. In other cases, however, clients received a token service with little effective consultation and representation. Some youth advocates were not well-versed in the Act. Others appeared unaware of the details and background of the case. Others still appeared to be arguing in the interests of justice in general or on behalf of the victim rather than on behalf of their client.

Diversion

Almost all young people, at one time or another during their teens, do something which can land them in trouble. Most are never caught and grow up to be respectable citizens. Even when they are caught, most are dealt with informally by the police, often in conjunction with their parents, and without the need for a court appearance. But some young people are dealt with formally, with harmful effects, by the courts and institutions. It is important, therefore, to keep young people out of courts and institutions whenever possible, to divert them, and to find other ways to deal with them, which in the long term.may help both they and their families and the communities to which they belong. Such an approach is in keeping with attempts to avoid penalties that are heavier than are warranted by the offending. This emphasis on the offence and on choosing the lowest possible penalty consistent with the harm caused by the offence means that young people pay their penalty and then get on with their life as part of the community. To a very large extent, the Act has been successful in diverting young people from both courts and institutions. The proportion of young people arrested has gone down from approximately a third in 1984 to only about 10% of those coming to police attention. Only 16 per 1000 young people appeared in the Youth Court in 1990 compared with an average of 63 per 1000 in the three calendar years immediately preceding the Act.

Furthermore only half of the young people in the sample appearing in the Youth Courts were made the subject of a court order and less than 2% of those orders resulted in some type of custodial detention. Those who are placed in custody had generally either committed very serious offenses (for example, aggravated robbery, rape or arson causing major destruction), had committed a large number of offences (one youth in our sample was finally sentenced on 117 charges), or had an extensive history of previous offences. But less than half the number of young people received custodial penalties (including prison sentences) than in the recent past. While there were 200 places in residences for young offenders prior to the Act, there are now only 76. The reduction in residential places comes about because fewer young people receive sentences of supervision with residence, the sentences are generally shorter, and there are fewer young people being remanded in custody. There have been complaints about the reluctance of DSW to place young people remanded in custody in residences, but there is no evidence in our research of serious adverse consequences from remanding young people to their families or to other community placements. New Zealand has been extraordinarily successful in reducing the number of young people dealt with in courts and placed in custody.

A common concern about systems introduced to divert young people from courts is that, paradoxically, if more young people are drawn further into the youth justice system than previously, the net is widened. The study attempted to determine whether those referred to an FGC were comparable with those who would previously have gone to court or whether FGCs were being used for those who would simply have been warned in the past. The total number of young people being referred to FGCs is very similar to the number who, in the past, could have been expected to appear in the court. Thus, there was no evidence that more young people were being drawn into the youth justice system than in the past. On the other hand, more young people are being made accountable now than previously. Whether this is good or bad can be debated. Some would say that to increase the severity of sanctions is also to widen the net. However, the imposition of recognized sanctions in a larger number of cases needs to be offset against the unacknowledged penalties experienced by the many families and young people who went through the court processes (for example being bailed, being charged in court, and having to appear in court) even if no formal penalty was ever put in place. In the old system, a large number of young people were processed through a court system which stigmatized them and introduced young offenders to one another.

Responding to Needs

The New Zealand system emphasizes the importance both of ensuring that young people are held accountable for their actions through the use of appropriate penalties and of enhancing the wellbeing of young people and strengthening their families. There are two possible ways of doing this. First, cases of suspected abuse or neglect can be referred to the distinct care and protection system that is intended to focus on welfare needs. Second, the option remains in cases where care and protection issues are not central for the youth justice system to help the child and family by referring them to services available in the community and providing funds for this if necessary. Difficulties arise with both of these solutions.

The main focus of a youth justice FGC is on accountability; the other needs of the young person and his or her family may not be discussed at all. Also, there are difficulties in focusing on the problems faced by the young person and his or her family in a meeting with the victim present—either because dealing with the offending is a difficult task or because the provision of services to the offender and his or her family seems inappropriate in cases where the victim's needs are also great and cannot easily be met. For instance, in one case in the study, the young victim had his car, which was his most precious possession, stolen, was without a job, and had just lost the training allowance that had enabled him to be independent from his parents. There seemed little natural justice in arranging for the young offender to attend a training course and receive an allowance in this situation, especially as the young person and his family were unable to offer to pay for the replacement cost of the uninsured car.

Referral for a care and protection FGC is also not necessarily a solution. Many of the cases referred there from the youth justice system during the course of the research were not dealt with, partly because of staff workload and partly because care and protection coordinators maintained that the issues should have been dealt with by the YJCs. One example of such a case was a group of four young people from two nearby families who became involved in regular offending. All four had previously been under the supervision of DSW, but were no longer considered the responsibility of the care and protection social workers because they were older and had offended. Their parents, however, provided little supervision and the local schools had been unable to manage them. Despite referrals to the care and protection co-ordinator, no help was provided during the period of the research. Furthermore, the tasks agreed on at the youth justice FGC were not completed and the young people were involved in further vandalism and petty theft in the local area.

Some parents reported seeking the help of DSW when they began to have difficulty managing their children and before any offending had occurred. However, they reported that DSW had said that it was unable to help them. It seems a sad irony that the services cannot be made available to families who seek help to prevent offending before it has occurred. Even those families who have FGCs find that the necessary services are not always able to be provided. Sometimes the necessary programmes were simply not available. Some families asked for support and training in parenting but many who had been unable to control rebellious teenagers in the past found that life after the FGC was unchanged. Some young people were referred to an overloaded counselling service which had a waiting list of several months. Others had long waits for vocational and anger management programmes. Job training programmes were cut during the course of our study with the result that the few remaining schemes were asked to take several young offenders at once, potentially recreating the conditions for a school for crime. The Act makes provision for providing services and support for families and young people through iwi and cultural authorities, but no such authorities have been set up with funds. Several marae did offer services for Maori families and young people, but they did so without adequate funding.

Providing for Participation

Society often blames the family for their child's offences and holds the parents responsible for them in very negative and punitive ways. At the same time, parents and the wider family have been excluded from any direct involvement in most juvenile justice systems. Decisions are made for and about them. The New Zealand idea of a partnership between the state and families to resolve the issues which affect children is a novel one. The underlying intention of the New Zealand system is to involve families, to give families themselves responsibility to deal constructively with their children's offending, and to restrict the power of professionals, in particular the power of social welfare professionals. To speak of the involvement of offenders in conventional criminal justice systems is a contradiction in terms. Offenders do not participate much in court proceedings; rather they watch passively and remain uninvolved. And they rarely have any direct contact with victims (after the offence has been committed). It is now increasingly accepted that young offenders should be involved in determining what should happen to them as a result of their offending, and that they should participate in the decision. Young people who offend must feel a part of (rather than apart from) what happens to them so that they can better understand the consequences of their actions from the perspective of the victim, accept responsibility, and make a commitment to making good the harm. In particular, families and young people are expected to play a full part in making the decisions about the offending through the mechanism of family group conferences (FGCs).

The research showed that a major area of failure in fulfilling the intentions of the Act was in the lack of involvement of young people. Only a third of the young people in the sample felt involved (although a few more said that they had felt partly involved) and less than a fifth felt that they had been a party to the decision. Involvement was even less in the Youth Court. In part, this is undoubtedly because nobody seems to expect the young people to actually speak on their own behalf or to express opinions, neither the professionals, the parents, nor the young people themselves. The consequences of a situation wherein young people seem to be playing the role of a puppet in a drama where, though they are the centrepiece, they never have a speaking part, are almost certainly that they are likely to be distanced from the decisions. The young person is likely to feel uncommitted to decisions made by others. Nevertheless, the FGC did involve a substantial group of young people in the procedure in contrast to other jurisdictions.

In contrast to the young people, two-thirds of the parents said they felt involved and 62% said they had been one of those making the decision. The FGC has provided a way of giving parents a real part in decisions both about repairing the damage caused by their child and about the future of their child and their family. Fears about the process not working because so many of the families are dysfunctional, or would not attend, or would not play an effective part were not realized. In practice, families almost invariably attended and were able to participate. It was usually possible to find relatives, friends, or neighbours who could provide some support when problems were experienced in the family. Positive outcomes were observed in families that could readily have been dismissed as dysfunctional on a superficial analysis.

The Youth Court was less successful in involving families and many families remained puzzled by its procedures. In part, the problems lie in the unfamiliar rituals and procedures, in part, in the failure of court personnel to explain fully what will happen and, in part, in the frequent remands and long delays. There was a failure by the Youth Court to develop new methods of providing an opportunity for parents to participate and for there to be a system by which parents (and young people) could be helped to prepare what they would like to say to the judge. The first step towards effective participation is better information and understanding so that families and young people will know what to expect. The second essential is that the FGC and court processes are managed in such a way that both families and young people are expected to contribute and that they are prepared for this.

There has been a growing focus on the needs and wishes of victims. In New Zealand the Victim of Offences Act 1987 provides for the police to take victim impact statements which are used in evidence in court proceedings; victims' views influence the way police handle an offence; victim support services are being developed; courts are sometimes prepared to hear submissions from victims on sentencing; and reparation (payment of the cost of damage and/or stolen property) is now used as a sentence. There have been moves in most Western countries towards reconciliation meetings between victims and offenders or finding ways in which victims could participate in the sentencing process, or at least have their views taken into account. Few jurisdictions have gone as far in involving victims as the new system of youth justice in New Zealand. One of its key principles is that any measures for dealing with offending by young persons should have due regard to the interests of any victims of that offending. Victims can attend FGCs.

In practice the data showed that victims attended about half the FGCs where a victim could be identified and this represents a dramatic change. However, with better planning, more victims would have attended. Very few victims failed to attend because they were reluctant to meet the young person or were afraid of further retribution. Many victims said that the results of FGCs were positive; they received apologies, they received reparation or had work done for them, and they felt better about the whole affair as a result of participating in the FGC. Others (about a quarter) said that they felt worse as a result of attending the FGC. There were a variety of reasons for this; perhaps the most frequent and important was that the victim did not feel that the young person and his or her family was truly sorry. Other less common reasons included the inability of the family and young person to make reparation, the victim's inability to express themselves adequately, the feeling that the punishment was not harsh enough, and the impression that nothing had been done so that reoffending by the young person would be less likely. One case, involving a young person who had admitted a serious injury, was dealt with in a large marae-based FGC in which most of the proceedings were conducted in Maori. The Pakeha (New Zealanders of European origin) relatives of the seriously injured victim felt very alienated and hurt by the process which seemed to exclude them. They were also distressed to find that most of the time was spent considering the young person and his family rather than their needs.

Only half the victims were satisfied with the outcomes. Sometimes this was because of a disagreement with the decision of the FGC as too soft or too harsh, but sometimes it was because the promised arrangements fell down afterwards. The responsibility for this lay as often with the professionals as the young person and his or her family. Other victims were simply never told the eventual outcome. Also, instances were observed where the victims had unrealistic expectations about what might happen, especially with respect to reparation. This increased their dissatisfaction.

Ensuring that victims are well informed and well supported could undoubtedly lead to improvements. Victims' involvement in FGCs need to be approached with considerable care. They require time to think about meeting the offender and his or her family and, in serious cases (such as rape, serious physical injury and arson), they need time to explore (with the help of the YJC or a youth justice social worker) the best way they can contribute to the process and what type of contribution they might wish to make. Some victims prefer not to be part of the decision-making but are prepared to explain to the offender the impact the offence has had on their life (although their views can change during a meeting). Others prefer not to meet the offender but would still like to have their views represented. The police or a social worker often undertake this responsibility. Sometimes a representative of the victim attended and in other instances the victim was accompanied by supporters, usually family or friends who saw their role as principally to stand by the victim rather than making demands on behalf of the victim. In some areas, victim support groups have been set up and they perform a valuable role in providing victims with information, support, and advice. Cases were observed where a victims' representative attended the FGC with the goal of ensuring that the victim's rights were recognized and that reparation was made.

But there are other issues. Victims' satisfaction with the FGC process depends on more than just what happens in the FGC and how it has been arranged. Many victims feel that they get a rough deal. In part, this is because there are only limited systems of compensating victims for the effects of crime, victims are often not well informed about what to expect or what usually happens when an offender is charged in court, support services exist in only a few communities, and necessary follow-up services, such as counselling for those who have been harmed, are not always publicly funded. The current wave of indignation in the media over the injustices suffered by victims readily fans demands for retribution. Harsher punishment is not the answer. Other responses to the whole range of needs of victims can be considered.

The notion of reaching a consensus or an agreement between the family, the young person, and the victim has been given a central place in the new system. Meetings between victims, offenders, and their families are seen as increasing participation, sharing information, and achieving reconciliation. One aim, as in the traditional Maori model, is to achieve social balance by reintegrating the young person in their family and determining an appropriate means of redress for the victim. Another aim is to move away from an emphasis on court judgements towards outcomes shaped by the families themselves and agreed to by all the participants, including the victims. Almost all the FGCs were able to agree on recommendations and plans: 95% in 1990. Thus one might expect all the participants to be satisfied with what occurred and indeed this was the case for most of the police, YJCs, parents, and young people. However, only about half of the victims were satisfied. This raises the issue of whether or not there was a true consensus at all the FGCs. Instances were observed where families and young people, as well as victims, felt obliged to agree with decisions that were, in essence, made by the professionals. There is a constant problem with decision-making in groups composed of both professionals and clients. It is easy for those whose job involves them in attending such meetings and who are knowledgeable and experienced to exert undue influence over the other participants. Over time, processes can become formalized so that another type of court is created. It is essential that the principal parties—young people, families and victims—should be satisfied that the decision is one with which they agree.

Being Culturally Appropriate

The New Zealand approach is an attempt to develop a system of justice that allows different ethnic groups to resolve matters in culturally appropriate settings using culturally appropriate procedures and that provides access to culturally appropriate services. Hence the new youth justice system in New Zealand seeks to re-introduce elements of indigenous responses to dealing with offenders. This is partly a recognition of obligations that were set out in the 1840 Treaty of Waitangi, which laid down the conditions of a partnership between Maori and Pakeha within New Zealand; it is also a reflection of the growing acceptance of Maori culture and values. New Zealand's population is made up of different ethnic groups. Numerically, the largest group is Pakeha—nearly 70% of the juvenile population. Those of Maori descent make up around 21% of the juvenile population and Pacific Island Polynesians 8%.

Although Maori and Pacific Island Polynesian make up less than a fifth of the New Zealand population, they are over-represented in indices of social and economic deprivation such as higher infant mortality rates, lower life expectancy, higher unemployment, and lower incomes. Maori are also over-represented in the population of known offenders, including juvenile offenders. According to 1992 police statistics, among the known juvenile offender population, 45% are described as Maori. The new procedures recognize the over-representation of Maori among juvenile offenders and respond by using aspects of traditional, extended family (whanau) decision-making methods for the resolution of conflict.

The role of whanau is important in both Maori and Pacific Island Polynesian child-rearing and decision-making. Maori children often live from time to time with different relatives within their whanau. This occurs in part because the child is considered not simply the child of the birth parents but also of the whanau, hapu, and iwi. Bringing up children and dealing with their delinquencies is a communal responsibility. In pre-colonial times most decisions, whatever their nature, were customarily made by the whanau, hapu, or iwi depending on the importance and nature of the decision. The involvement of whanau, hapu, and iwi is mentioned in the new legislation as being important in both discussions and decisions about appropriate solutions to juvenile offending.

To recognize and acknowledge the validity of Maori cultural and social traditions is a significant step. But it is not only the practical aspects of the cultural responsiveness of the legislation that is important. The social welfare and criminal justice systems have been based in the past on English traditions, and Pakeha have, for the most part, occupied the most influential positions. Thus, decisions affecting Maori people have been made by Pakeha and traditional Maori structures have become weakened. The new system seeks to empower Maoridom. It seeks to involve Maori directly in decisions about their young people and to acknowledge their identity as tangata whenua (the people of the land). Such an emphasis also has implications for other cultural groups in New Zealand and may lead to the recognition of a variety of cultural practices within the justice system.

But to what extent can Western systems of criminal justice accommodate elements of an indigenous approach? To be truly responsive to the needs of different cultures requires a different way of reaching decisions, a different type of spirit and underlying philosophy, and different outcomes from those traditionally available in criminal justice contexts. In each of these respects, the practice of youth justice in New Zealand shows both limitations and successes. The FGC is an attempt to give a prominent place to how decisions are reached but the FGCs often failed to respond to the spirit of Maori or to enable outcomes to be reached which are in accordance with Maori philosophies and values. At times, FGCs could and did transcend tokenism and embody a Maori kaupapa (process), but not often. To do so involves seeking out the right people to advise and handing over the management of the process to whanau, hapu, and iwi. Also, money for iwi services and iwi authorities has not yet been allocated in sufficient amounts for a truly cultural approach to be taken.

Courtroom rituals that are likely to have the most impact will be those that are meaningful in terms of the cultural background of the offender. For Maori families, court procedures which blend Maori and Western traditions are consistent with the objectives of the Act and are more likely to be effective in reinforcing the message of the court than a traditional Western approach. This is especially true given the existence of a Maori protocol, widely understood within Maoridom, for dealing with disputes. The protocol involves the expression of remorse, encompasses reparation, allows decisions to be reached that settle the dispute, and includes the participation of the principal parties to the dispute in the proceedings. It implies that whanau should attend the court to speak on behalf of their young people. Allowing whanau to have their say is important and is not just special treatment. The costs to the court are greater in terms of the time taken but both the process and the outcomes are likely to be better as a result.

There has been only limited acceptance of the idea that outcomes should involve bringing the offender back into the family group which then, as a group, makes good the damage to the victim. There has been no discussion at all of how paying one's penalty might be given a cultural meaning and significance. On the other hand, there are difficulties in knowing what this might mean. Traditional Maori methods of justice were not always benign; they could involve death, slavery, or exile. And, even today, there are varied views on what it means to talk about justice in the Maori way. The process (and hence its spirit and outcomes) of the new system remains largely Pakeha and unresponsive to cultural differences. For many of the Maori and Pacific Island participants, however, there is at least the potential for FGCs to be more able to cope with cultural diversity than other types of tribunals.

Inherent Contradictions

There is a problem in providing for the needs of young people and strengthening families in an FGC which is designed to focus on accountability. The difficulty of facing up to the offending itself and finding a solution that meets the needs of victims are considerable; solutions that provide for the needs of the young person and the family can seem unjust when the victims' needs cannot be met. In addition, there is the irony that services are sometimes only provided for young people and families after offending occurs. Retaining a primary focus on accountability is essential in a youth justice system. The answer to these conflicts, therefore, may lie in separating even further the systems which deliver justice from those which deliver welfare. The best solution to the needs identified in FGCs lies in more general areas of social policy; suitable services and programmes should be readily available throughout the community to all young people and their families.

Participation by families, young people and victims should ensure that the outcome is fair to all. Involvement in a process of consensus decision-making is, however, likely to result in very different outcomes for each young person; different victims have different views on what should happen and so too do different families. It is, therefore, difficult to achieve penalties that are in proportion to the offence, equal for all those who commit similar offences, and no greater than is necessary given the nature of the offence. In practice, the importance of similar penalties for similar offenders has to be balanced against achieving solutions that are seen to be fair by all those who take part in a particular FGC. One possible safeguard against inconsistent penalties is to ensure that everyone is informed about the penalties which courts tend to use for a particular type of offence. Although the YJC has the power to withhold agreement when the proposed sanctions seem unreasonable, to do so is to retain control in the hands of the professionals. Alternatively, inconsistency could be accepted provided that the decisions was truly agreed to by the young person, his or her family, and the victim. In such circumstances, the advantages of participatory decision-making are greater than the importance of maintaining exactly similar penalties in all cases.

The focus in the FGC is inevitably very much on the young person and his or her family. It is they who are consulted about who will be present, where the FGC will be held, and what procedures will be used. The discussion centres on what the young person has done and what should happen to the young person in future. Some commentators (including the Principal Youth Court Judge), on the other hand, see the FGC as ideally centred on the victim and the needs of the victim. In practice, many victims feel that they are peripheral to what happened. Requirements to consult victims about the venues, timing, and procedures at FGCs, and allowing them to have supporters present with them at FGCs are currently the focus of amendments to the Children, Young Persons and Their Families Act. Such changes are symbolic of a shift in focus in the FGC away from the offender and his or her family and towards the victim. This could defeat some of the other goals of the Act. These changes could also increase the tensions in the FGC and make it less likely that the family and the young person would be heard, their needs would be met, and they would be truly party to the decisions. There is also the fact that, although most victims do not demand savage penalties, there is considerable variation in what different victims feel is fair. Increasing their voice could lead to more variations in sanctions and may undermine other goals in the Act.

Making processes more culturally appropriate may work well when both victim and the offender are from the same culture, but, otherwise, it may increase tensions, as in the example where Pakeha victims were unable to understand or effectively participate in marae processes. Responding more flexibly in the type of meetings is an option; for instance, preliminary meetings between victims and family members may enable a Pakeha victim to feel supported and participate on the marae. Alternatively, a sequence of meetings in different locations could be arranged to hear and respond to the victim and to hear and respond to the young person. However, in many cases there will be no simple method of increasing the cultural appropriateness of processes and, at the same time, meeting victims' needs.

Another problem that arises in attempting to meet the needs of the victim in the FGC is that families and young people differ in their ability to make repayment to the victim. Some victims receive full compensation while others receive virtually none. And other needs of victims may become apparent at the FGC. Inevitably those needs will, at times, go beyond the ability of the FGC to find solutions. The contrast when victims' needs remain unmet and yet the needs of the young person and his or her family are provided cannot be fair or just.

The state is another important party to the decision-making. It is the professionals who represent the state who actually make the arrangements for FGCs, invite the participants, manage the process, and must agree to the decisions. It is the state's interests which are being served. The FGC is a process for ensuring that young people are made accountable to the state, as part of its responsibility for dealing with offending. It is the state that makes the rules and it is the state that retains control by requiring that the police, the YJC, and, in some cases, the Youth Court endorses decisions of the FGC. Questions can, therefore, be asked about the extent to which families are truly empowered in an FGC. Indeed, the increase in the extent of accountability under this system can be seen as an expansion of the system of social control. The involvement of families in decision-making can be seen, cynically, as an effective way of making them instruments of the state. And the reality of family agreement can be questioned, despite the number of families who reported that they were satisfied, as many families may well feel that the decision chosen was the lesser of alternative evils. On the other hand, it can be argued that, despite the reality of the state's control over the FGC, increasing the voice of families in decision-making has real and important effects. The involvement of families can lead to different solutions than would have been imposed by a court. The participation and agreement of families may also actually change the life of the family because they become more actively involved in taking responsibility for the young person. And the increased support that family members may give one another as a consequence of sharing the problem may offer further benefits to families.

While the emphasis in the Act is on justice, some aspects of the system still represent a crime control approach. For instance, in a justice model, only the nature of the offence is to be taken into account but previous offence history affects the decision-making of professionals at all points in the system. Both in the courtroom and in the FGC, police officers and prosecutors argue for the level of the penalty to reflect the amount of previous offending and arrest; custody and incarceration are often seen as the most appropriate responses to recidivism. In other respects, the attitudes of professionals are still, in practice, often influenced by a crime control philosophy. For instance, a complaint frequently heard was that the system does not work for the hardened offender or the top 5% of young offenders. In part, this statement reflects the fact that some of the young people who appear in the Youth Court reoffend before their earlier offending has been dealt with. In such cases, many months can go by before any penalty is imposed.

From time to time, media stories reflect a moral panic about youth crime—it is getting out of hand, and so on. This is reminiscent of events in England and Wales which preceded the increased use of custody in the 1970s and in Western

Australia, England and Wales more recently where legislation was introduced with the aim of imposing long periods of custody on young joy-riders. The justification for increased severity was that the police (and magistrates or judges) were powerless to deal with juvenile crime and that juvenile offenders were running amok. Neither of these claims was true in either England or Western Australia; nor are many of the claims now being made in New Zealand. However, they may create a climate of public opinion which makes it increasingly difficult to resist pressures for change in a more punitive direction.

Conclusions

Reoffending has often been the yardstick by which commentators have measured the success of changes in criminal justice policies and this Act is no exception. Anecdotal evidence has been used to claim both remarkable successes and devastating failures. Some argue that the Act is failing because of the reoffending of a minority. But the success or failure of particular offenders can never be entirely the result of any legislative change. In fact, it is not even possible to determine the impact of the new system on reoffending because there is not adequate information on the reoffending rates of juveniles before the Act. And, even if there was sufficient information, there would still be problems. Reoffending is not a good indicator of the success or failure of any changes in the criminal or youth justice system. Some young people may offend and yet not be detected; some may be detected committing an offence but are not charged or convicted and so appear not to have reoffended. Furthermore, many other factors which also change over time (for example, population patterns, unemployment, social and economic difficulties, or migration) affect reoffending more than the ways in which the criminal justice system impacts on offenders. Having said all this, it must be accepted that underlying the various goals in the Act is the expectation that, in the longer term, crime and reoffending rates might be affected, especially if there are other changes in social policy. And so any eventual influence on crime and reoffending must depend on first achieving the goals of the Act.

Giving effect to the goals of the Act was initially hampered, in part, by resistances to the new philosophy. Understanding of and commitment to the Act's goals were not always present and, inevitably, some professionals failed to accept the changes; police continued to arrest for relatively minor offences, social workers continued to advise families on what they should do, and youth advocates failed to consult adequately with their clients and assist them to participate in proceedings. YJCs, Youth Aid officers and Youth Court judges all found that they needed to develop new skills, especially in relation to working with victims, communities, and different cultural groups. On occasion, the quality of professional practice and the skills of professionals were not adequate to the tasks asked of them. At times, statutory requirements were not met, particularly with respect to cautioning and questioning by the police, arranging for victims' involvement, meeting time frames by DSW, and in explanations about procedures in the Youth Court. Training for professionals is a necessary precursor to realizing these goals.

Difficulties have, inevitably, arisen in reconciling the sometimes conflicting goals. Resolving welfare issues can conflict with the focus on justice. Meeting victims' needs is not always possible in an FGC. Inevitably, too, there are tensions between the goal of controlling young people and giving families more say, between participatory decision-making and equal and proportionate penalties, and between the involvement of several different cultural groups in the procedures. Nor has there been any resolution of the extent to which the process should be given over to indigenous groups to arrange, modify, determine penalties, and provide programmes. The necessary steps to resource iwi and cultural authorities have not, at the time of writing, been taken and there are still too few suitable services and programmes. More recently, in response to budget overruns, it has been proposed that the service delivery groups responsible for youth justice and care and protection be amalgamated into a single group. Such an amalgamation would make it even more difficult to achieve the distinctive goals of the welfare and justice systems for children and young people. Amalgamation could lead to youth justice becoming secondary to the care and protection system in the allocation of staff and resources.

Nevertheless, there have been major changes positive changes; many of the goals of the Act are being achieved and there has been considerable satisfaction among many of those involved with the outcomes. Diversion was a primary aim and this has been achieved. At the same time, nearly all young people who are involved in offending that is considered sufficiently serious to warrant an FGC are being made accountable for their offences. Families are participating in the processes of decision-making and are taking responsibility for their young people in most instances. Extended families are also becoming involved in the continuing care of their kin and as an alternative to foster care and institutions. Greater acknowledgement is being given to the customs of different cultural groups and, in some instances, traditional processes have been used to reach agreements. Victims are also being involved to a greater extent than they were before and than is customary elsewhere.

References

Maxwell, G. M., & Morris, A. (1993). *Family, victims and culture: youth justice in New Zealand*. Social Policy Agency and Institute of Criminology, Victoria University of Wellington.

15

Support and Prevention Programming: Themes, Policy Implications, and Research Agenda

Suzanne Geoffrion and Sandra Scarth

The system designed to help children and youth and their families is quickly being overtaken by a massive change in society and the economy. Traditional helping strategies no longer relate to today's realities. The problems experienced by individuals and groups need to be addressed within their socio-historical contexts with parameters such as race, culture, gender, employment, and economic wealth being regarded as important. Services must become more inclusive, flexible, and truly responsive to the immediate needs of families and their communities. Prevention and family support programming present promising directions for child welfare.

Research Findings

Nicole Dallaire and her colleagues (1995) propose an ecological model of prevention which focuses on the wholeness of the family and builds on individual and collective strengths to ensure the well-being of the community. Their research assesses how the diverse prevention practices of over two hundred projects in Montréal's institutional and community agencies encompass the dimensions of a holistic and socio-economically oriented definition of prevention. Marked differences appear between the two sectors. Institutional agencies offer specific, time-limited individual and family services aimed at enhancing the parent and child relationship. The community agencies worked on improving the social conditions such as inadequate income, housing, and employment that caused stresses in the daily lives of families. Institutional agencies collaborated on case management concerns while the community agencies engaged in collective social action. Strategies of empowerment were under-utilized in both. Essential services are provided by both groups, and linkages are emerging. True partnership will be based on the recognition and appreciation of the potential role, values, norms, and structures of the community-based sector. Inequities in funding and public support will need to be addressed.

Michele Kérisit and Nérée St-Amand (1995) explore the role of community-based alternative agencies. They are intrigued by the resourcefulness and means of survival of at-risk families and challenge us to go beyond preoccupations with limitations and deficits. Clients are presented as capable activists in their own lives. Their study highlights innovative practices observed in four organizations across Canada that demonstrated a commitment to the empowerment of families. These organizations considered the well-being of the child in the context of the family's economic well-being and access to employment. Simple and open meeting places were provided to encourage parents to come together to define their needs, to network, and to seek common solutions. Relationships between parents, professionals, and volunteers were based on mutual trust and shared objectives. Strategies were in place to deal with class, gender, and racial distinctions; employment equity evolved naturally. The researchers express concern regarding the vulnerability of these alternative resources as governments pursue strategies of service rationalization and integration. Current funding and program evaluation criteria do not easily capture the responsiveness, flexibility, and fluidity of these projects. Tensions may consequently grow between the two systems as competing and conflicting values emerge.

Don Fuchs (1995) reports on the outcomes of a new form of social network intervention which attempts to enable families and communities to share responsibility for protecting children. The relationship between informal and formal helping systems is examined in the area of placement prevention and family preservation. The Neighbourhood Parenting Support Project carried out research and demonstration activities from 1988 to 1992 in two central Winnipeg neighbourhoods that have had three to four times the city average of child protection case prevalence. The project staff entered the focal neighbourhoods through a process which connected with agency service providers, residents, and key informants. Consultations were held with parents about what it was like to live and be a parent in their particular neighbourhoods. Information was gathered on the support received from extended families, friends, and others. Stresses were high; parents were isolated with limited help available to deal with the challenges of child-rearing. Interventions were consequently targeted at multiple levels to increase the size and diversity of personal and parenting support networks. The conclusions of the project are noteworthy. Informal helping and support can be strengthened by social network intervention, formal systems can be meshed with informal structures, and risk for child maltreatment in a community can be reduced by this integrated approach.

Gabrielle Maxwell and Allison Morris (1995) describe the development of the family group conference, a decision-making forum utilized in the New Zealand youth justice system. Traditional Maori practice involved the victim and the offender, first in acknowledging guilt and expressing remorse, and second in finding ways to restore the social balance so that the victim could be compensated by the group and so that the offender could be reintegrated into the group. This philosophy has led to victim involvement becoming an integral part of the justice system. This research followed the experiences of over two hundred youth. Maxwell and Morris found that these youth assumed responsibility for their actions, paid reparation, and/or accepted a penalty outside of the usual court process. Families expressed appreciation of the informality of the family group conferences, the facility for all to express their opinions, the possibility of having the meetings in their own homes, and the opportunity to have family support available. All preferred this method for reaching decisions and involving them in the process. Over 60% of the victims also found participation in the family group conferences positive and rewarding. Offenders, for the most part, remained with their family and in the community. Efforts at ensuring culturally appropriate interventions, however, were not as successful as initially hoped.

The Family Group Decision-Making Project in Newfoundland and Labrador is based on New Zealand's approach and draws on the experience of self-government among aboriginal groups in Canada. Gale Burford and Joan Pennell (1995) state that the model is premised on the philosophy that halting family violence requires a collaborative effort by families, communities, and public authorities. Social networks within and around the family are mobilized to plan and carry out necessary protection and support. Results to date are preliminary as only seven families have participated. However, all have come up with plans that were acceptable to the child protection worker and have carried out their agreed-to tasks.

Peter Pecora (1995) assesses the impact of family-based services, an approach to strengthening families in serious trouble and preventing out-of-home placement. Evaluation results have been generally positive for outcome criteria including number of placement days used, reduction in the restrictiveness of placement location, reports of child maltreatment, changes in child, parent, and family functioning, family reunification, and consumer satisfaction ratings. Pecora emphasizes that these services cannot replace other types of child and family services or broader societal and service system reforms.

Canadian Social Policy Implications

Canadian social and economic policies have not traditionally been aimed at eradicating the problems of poverty, sexism, violence, and racism. A commitment to a social reform agenda and a call for action have yet to be heard. The national review of the social security system provides an opportunity to make the socio-economic well-being of children and families a priority. All policies should be assessed in terms of their impact on the well-being of children. The question of who is responsible for raising children is a concern of all communities and levels of government. Much has already been said, for example, about the need for a national child day care strategy. Policy-makers and child advocates are beginning to cast the importance of support services to children in terms of an investment in children as the work force of tomorrow. But this can be a dangerous approach as we risk losing compassion and simple appreciation of childhood. Governments and the voluntary sector are becoming more interested and involved in the area of prevention. A compendium of the Canadian experience with prevention and family support would enhance the public's understanding and interest in a social reform orientation. Issues of child and family services support become highly politicized as decision-makers seek to fund services that reach those truly in need and demonstrate positive outcomes. Funding criteria in the Canada Assistance Plan present a barrier to the development of preventive services. New funding mechanisms should be explored to provide incentives that will move systems toward preventive, community-based services.

The interface between the formal and informal helping systems presents a number of challenges; imbalances of power and resources between the two may create tension and conflict. Can the informal system be integrated into the formal system without losing its unique responsiveness and relevancy? A recurring theme has been the role of the community in supporting parents in raising healthy children and youth. But is the public ready to accept this responsibility, or will this continue to be a labour of love, primarily done by unpaid women? Can young men be prepared to be adequate providers, husbands, and fathers? Will turning to the community to share the responsibility of raising children influence the balance of legal power among parents, the state, and the child?

Research Agenda

A Canada-wide data base is required to help measure the well-being of children and families who come into contact with a child protection service and families who do not. Comparisons need to be made of communities with high and low rates of child abuse, as well as those with and without adequate family support programs. How do these communities differ? Does prevention and family support programming reduce child abuse and neglect or simply enhance family functioning? The National Longitudinal Survey of children (1994), a recent federal initiative, will provide an account of experiences of Canadian children as they grow from infancy to eleven years of age. This information, along with a commitment to a best-practices approach, may improve ability to respond to the needs of children and families at risk.

Interest in examining what organizational structures, processes, and activities are associated with positive client outcomes is encouraging. Participatory models of inclusion, collaboration, and restoration require further analyses, as does the role of women in the development of alternative solutions. The effectiveness of mediation and other non-adversarial dispute resolution strategies must be explored. Informal helping systems appear to be more responsive to the needs of the Native and multi-cultural community. Can they influence the institutional sector? A thorough study of a community development approach needs to be pursued; the building of social networks, links, and connections is a complex undertaking. How can services be organized collaboratively to have a larger impact on distressed neighbourhoods?

Finally, researchers need to adopt a multi-dimensional and multi-disciplinary approach combining structural analysis with qualitative, quantitative, and longitudinal methodologies. Consumers and communities need to participate in the development and evaluation of the services designed to meet their needs. Findings must be presented in understandable language and available to the public at large.

References

Burford, G., & Pennell, J. (1995). Family group decision making: An innovation in child and family welfare. In J. Hudson & B. Galaway (Eds.), *Child welfare in Canada: Research and policy implications.* Toronto: Thompson Educational Publishing.

Dallaire, N., Chamberland, C., Cameron, S., & Hébert, J. (1995). Social prevention: A study of projects in an urban environment. In J. Hudson & B. Galaway (Eds.), *Child welfare in Canada: Research and policy implications.* Toronto: Thompson Educational Publishing.

Fuchs, D. (1995). Preserving and strengthening families and protecting children: Social network intervention a balanced approach to the prevention of child maltreatment. In J. Hudson & B. Galaway (Eds.), *Child welfare in Canada: Research and policy implications.* Toronto: Thompson Educational Publishing.

Kérisit, M., & St-Amand, N. (1995). Taking risks with families at risk: Some alternative approaches to working with poor families in Canada. In J. Hudson & B. Galaway (Eds.), *Child welfare in Canada: Research and policy implications.* Toronto: Thompson Educational Publishing.

Maxwell, G., & Morris, A. (1995). Deciding about justice for young people in New Zealand: The involvement of families, victims and culture. In J. Hudson & B. Galaway (Eds.), *Child welfare in Canada: Research and policy implications.* Toronto: Thompson Educational Publishing.

National Longitudinal Survey of Children (1994). *Overview of survey instruments* (Catalogue No. 94–02). Ottawa: Human Resources Development Canada, Social Program Information and Analysis Directorate.

Pecora, P. (1995). Assessing the impact of family-based services. In J. Hudson & B. Galaway (Eds.), *Child welfare in Canada: Research and policy implications.* Toronto: Thompson Educational Publishing.

3

FOSTER CARE PROGRAMMING

16

Treatment Foster Care and Reunification with a Family: Children Likely to Experience Family Placement after Treatment Foster Care Services

Barbara Thomlison

This chapter presents the findings of a study of factors associated with children who are likely to experience family reunification following treatment foster care services. Treatment foster care provides children who have serious emotional and behavioral difficulties with intensive and extensive services in normalizing environments such as family, school, and community. The goal of treatment foster care is to promote permanence, stability and family continuity for children through individualized strength-based services (Meadowcroft, Thomlison & Chamberlain, 1994). Programs differ in terms of intensity, structure, type of training, nature of support provided, and amount of payment provided to treatment parents (Chamberlain, 1990; Chamberlain & Reid, 1991). Carefully selected treatment parents work with one child at a time as part of a comprehensive agency team support system. Program staff usually have a small caseload of four to six children. The advantage of these programs is the flexibility to respond to the diverse needs of children, to the range of clinical problems, and the shifting community needs (Meadowcroft et al., 1994). Individual children's needs drive the program design in treatment foster care rather than children being expected to fit into the therapeutic available milieu.

Systematic research addressing the effectiveness of treatment foster care services is limited (Hudson, Nutter, & Galaway, in press; Meadowcroft et al., 1994; Rivera & Kutash, 1994). The most prevalent measure for evaluating effectiveness is placement to a less restrictive living environment. Discharge rates indicate from 62% to 89% of children are successfully placed in less restrictive environments after treatment foster care services. Family reunification is a desired outcome for children in out-of-home care. Reunification services encourage the optimal level of child and family reconnection from complete family re-entry to other forms of contact, affiliation, and visiting with family and relatives as appropriate to each case (Maluccio, Warsh, & Pine, 1993). Studies indicate that between 50 percent and 75 percent of children in care will eventually return to their families at some time (Bullock, Little, & Millham, 1993; Goerge, 1990; Rowe, Hundleby, & Garnet, 1989). Most children return to family and family networks as an unplanned contact or as a last resort when they leave care. Bullock, Little, and Millham (1993) identified key factors of successful return home to include the retention of a role for the child in the family and the presence of a warm and accepting relationship from the mother. Of the children who return home, 33% experience continuing problems which contribute to placement re-entry (Fein & Staff, 1991; Hess, Folaron, & Jefferson, 1992). These findings suggest the need to provide planned, intensive efforts to support children in out-of-home placements toward family reunification.

Treatment foster care programs are compatible with family preservation services. Identifying the families, children, and elements of treatment foster care service that impact on family reunification is important for three reasons. First, families provide a lifelong reference for children regardless of their strengths and resources. Second, the direct and indirect influences of families on children cannot be underestimated in terms of social and clinical outcomes of children. Third, it is essential to prepare children and youth for eventual opportunities to establish or re-establish their biological family network.

Method

The purpose of this exploratory study was to identify variables associated with successful family placements after treatment foster care services. Reunification of children to family placement was viewed as an indirect positive measure of a child's adjustment following treatment foster care services. Family placement included return to biological parents, relatives, and foster families.

Data was collected from 155 children who received treatment foster care services in Alberta, and from 49 treatment parents, who provided the services to the children. Children with child welfare status who were identified as needing a specialized placement due to severe emotional and behavioral problems and who were unable to be maintained in regular foster care settings were referred to a centralized multidisciplinary child welfare placement committee for placement to one of six treatment foster care programs. The treatment parents were derived from the case records of the 155 children. A final population of 49 treatment parents, who provided 100 treatment foster care placements for the children, agreed to participate in the study. No parents refused, but designated treatment parents could not be located by conventional efforts for 27% of the children. Independent variables were grouped as child, family and service variables. Data were obtained using the child behavior checklist (Achenbach, 1991) and two specifically developed instruments. Sources for data collection were the children's case records and the treatment parents. Data from children's case records were collected by three MSW students. Treatment parent data were obtained through group or individual administered questionnaires and interviews by the researcher.

Fifty-six percent of the children were under 12 years of age. Children first experienced treatment foster care placement services at an average of 10 years of age, but programs served children from 2 years to 18 years of age. Two groups of children were in treatment placements: (1) children who had first entered out-of-home care at an early age perhaps as young as at birth, and (2) children who entered care as late as 16 years of age. Children spent a mean of 3 years in various placements before treatment foster care services were

Table 16.1: Summary of Restrictiveness of Living Environments for Children's Post-Placement Status (N = 154)

Rank	Living Environment	Number	Percent
1	Independent living by self	4	2.6
2	Independent living with friend	1	.6
3	Home of natural parents (as an 18+ years old)	0	0
4	Home of natural parents (as a child)	53	34.2
5	School dormitory	0	0
6	Home of a relative	5	3.2
7	Adoptive home	0	0
8	Home of a family friend	3	1.9
9	Supervised independent living	0	0
10	Regular foster care	16	10.3
11	Specialized foster care	9	5.8
12	Individual home-based emergency shelter	0	0
13	Foster family-based treatment home	26	16.8
14	Group home	15	9.7
15	Residential job corps center	0	0
16	Group emergency shelter	0	0
17	Residential treatment center	18	11.6
18	Wilderness camp	0	0
19	In-patient in medical hospital	1	.6
20	Drug/alcohol rehabilitation center	0	0
21	Intensive treatment unit	1	.6
22	Youth correctional center	2	1.3
23	City detention unit	0	0
24	State mental hospital	0	0
25	Jail	0	0
	Totals	154*	99.2*

*Post-Placement data missing for one case

encountered. A mean of 11 reported referring problems were present for children at entry into treatment foster care. Most entered out-of-home care due to neglect and physical abuse. The mean length of treatment exposure was 304 days (median was 163 days). Sixty-one percent were males.

Treatment parents were young and well educated. The mean age of treatment foster parents was 36 years for mothers and 39 years for fathers.

Forty-eight percent of treatment mothers and 69% of treatment fathers had completed university level education. No mothers had less than high school education, and only 5% of fathers were in this category. Ninety-three percent were two-parent families. Forty-eight percent had two biological children at home. Eighty-six percent had one foster child residing in the family at any one time. Little variation in ethnic background was reported.

Placement status data were obtained by using the Restrictiveness of Living Environment Scale (ROLES) as an outcome indicator (Hawkins, Almeida, Fabry, & Reitz, 1992; Martin & Hawkins, 1992; Thomlison & Krysik, 1991). This ratio scale provides a restrictiveness score for each child's placement. Restrictiveness scores were calculated for children's post-placement status as a measure of service effectiveness. A summary of children's (n=155) mean restrictiveness scores for post-placement environments is summarized in Table 16.1.

Results

Treatment foster care services successfully placed children to less restrictive environments; the majority were placed with families. Seventy-two percent (112) of the children returned to families: 34% (53) children returned to the home of biological parents, 2% (3) went to live with family friends, 3% (5) went to relatives, while 16% (25) went to live in foster families. An additional 17% (26) children continued to live in another treatment foster family placement. Three percent (5) moved to independent living arrangements. Before treatment foster care services of all the children were considered as too difficult for family placement. The decreased restrictiveness of these children's placements at exit from treatment foster family care indicates an improvement in functioning.

An increase in placement restrictiveness occurred for 28% (42) children. Table 16.1 shows that 10% (15) children moved to group homes, 12% (18) went to residential treatment centres, 1% (2) were discharged to psychiatric in-patient care hospitals, and 1% (2) moved to youth correctional or youth detention facilities. The increased restrictiveness for these children may indicate the need for more time in intensive treatment settings before progression to family environments.

Multivariate analysis provides a profile of those children likely to have a successful placement to a family-based outcome. Table 16.2 displays results of the key child, family, and service correlates of children likely to experience successful family placement at the time of discharge. Service variables played a strong role in the model followed by child characteristics. Sixteen variables from the factors associated with family placement make up the profile.

Stepwise multiple regression was performed using all 16 independent predictor variables identified as correlates of successful post-placement status. Summary results are presented in Table 16.3; only nine of the sixteen variables were retained in the full prediction model.

Fifty-four percent of the variance in post-placement status is explained by three child, no family, and six service variables. Child considered for return home accounted for 23% of the explained variance at post-placement. Gender of practitioner and problems with drugs added 11% and 8%, respectively, of explained variance to the model. The remaining variables each had a modest effect on the explained variance. Program services appear to have an effect on post-placement status outcome only when all three groups are examined simultaneously.

Table 16.2: Characteristics Associated with Children Likely to Experience Family Placement (N = 155)

Child Characteristics

The child does not have permanent guardianship status

The child does not have a placement history in group emergency shelters

The child does not have other problems at school other than academic problems

The child does not have a history of problems with stealing

The child does not have verbal aggression problems with adults

The child does not have problems of drug abuse

Family Characteristic

Acute medical problems are not present in one of the parents

Service Characteristics

Program Service Characteristics

The child is considered for return home

The gender of the practitioner is female

The treatment objectives are completed

The practitioner has a small caseload of less than 6 treatment families

The practitioner does not have a diploma in social services

Treatment Foster Family Service Characteristics

The child had contact with biological parents

The biological child of treatment parents has a positive relationship with foster child

The treatment parent experiences role satisfaction

The child has a warm and connected relationship to the treatment foster parents

Discussion

Treatment foster care services appear to stabilize children with extensive problems and placement histories. Seventy-two percent of children returned to family-based living and 37% of the children reunited with their biological families or were placed with relatives. A key factor appears to be the need to clearly delineate a case plan for the reunification of children. Children with behaviours such as stealing, abuse of drugs, and verbal aggression toward adults posed a greater challenge than other children to both the practitioner and treatment parents in this study. Treatment parents and practitioners may need special resources and enhanced skills for improved outcomes for these children. Henggeller, Melton and Smith (1992) achieved positive outcomes for both short term and long term efficacy for family preservation using multisystemic approaches with serious and persistent juvenile offenders. These intervention methods need to be reviewed for use in treatment foster care models. Social workers with caseloads of six treatment families or less were more effective than those with more than six families. Treatment parents who were more satisfied in their role, and whose biological children felt satisfied, also

Table 16.3: Results of Stepwise Regression Analysis Predicting Restrictiveness Scores Using Predictor Child, Family, and Service Variables (N = 155)

Step	Variables*	Total R2	R2 Change	t-value	p	Beta
1	Was the child considered for return home?	.23	-	-6.048	<.0000	-.36
2	Female practitioner	.34	.11	-.4.53	<.0000	-.45
3	Did the child have problems with abuse of drugs?	.42	.08	4.64	<.0000	.28
4	Was the child attached to the treatment foster parent?	.45	.03	-2.77	<.0063	-.16
5	Did the child have problems of verbal aggression with adults?	.47	.02	2.58	<.0108	.15
6	Satisfaction in the role of treatment foster parent?	.49	.02	2.99	<.0033	.18
7	Satisfaction between the natural foster children and the foster child?	.51	.02	-2.43	<.0163	-.18
8	Did the child have a history of problems with stealing?	.52	.01	2.45	<.0154	.14
9	Number of treatment foster families on caseload?	.54	.02	-2.03	<.0446	-.20

p < .05 (two tailed test)
* dummy variable with listed category = 1

achieved more successful results with children. Female practitioners were more likely than their male counterparts to effect a family placement. However, these findings must be interpreted with some caution since there were more females than males, and specific practitioners may have been over-represented across the 155 cases. These findings appear to be linked to programs with family reunification orientations. Effective family reunification may be a function of "intensive and goal directed services."

The results of the analysis should be interpreted cautiously for three reasons. First, the findings may not be generalizable beyond the study region. The province of Alberta may be unique in the extensive use of treatment foster care programs. Second, the research design was limited to case record reviews and, while interrater reliability was high, quality of file data varied. Treatment foster parent data may suffer from limitations of recall. Program maturation effects may also be a factor in the treatment foster care services. Third, the strength of statistically significant correlation coefficients observed were considered as moderate predictors of post-placement status. Placement of children is affected by many different child, family, community, and system factors. For some children the immediate post placement setting may not be the child's final outcome. Finally, the use of treatment foster care services appears to be a potentially effective family preservation model as an intervention that most children and youth benefit from. The next research steps need to refine the nature of intensive treatment foster care – interventions to further develop the model.

References

Achenbach, T. M. (1991). *Manual for the child behavior checklist/4–18 and 1991 profile.* Burlington, VT: Department of Psychiatry, University of Vermont.

Bullock, R., Little, M., & Millham, S. (1993). *Going home: The return of children separated from their families.* Dartmouth: Dartington Social Research Unit.

Chamberlain, P. (1990). Comparative evaluation of specialized foster care for seriously delinquent youths: A first step. *Community Alternatives: International Journal of Family Care, 2,* 22–36.

Chamberlain, P. , & Reid, J. (1991). Using a specialized foster care community treatment model for children and adolescents leaving the state mental hospital. *Journal of Community Psychology, 19(3),* 266–276.

Fein, E., & Staff, I. (1991). Implementing reunification services. *Families in Society, 72(6),* 335–343.

Goerge, R. (1990). The reunification process in foster care. *Social Service Review, 64,* 422–456. Washington, DC: Child Welfare League of America.

Hawkins, R., Almeida, C., Fabry, B., & Reitz, A. L. (1992). A scale to measure restrictiveness of living environments for troubled children and youths. *Hospital and Community Psychiatry, 43,* 54–58.

Henggeler, S., Melton, G., & Smith, A. (1992). Family preservation using multisystemic therapy: An effective alternative to incarcerating serious juvenile offenders. *Journal of Consulting and Clinical Psychology, 60,* 953–961.

Hess, P. , Folaron, G., & Jefferson, A (1992). Effectiveness of family reunification services: An innovative evaluative model. *Social Work, 37*(4), 304–311.

Hudson, J., Nutter, R., & Galaway, B. (in press). Evaluation research on treatment foster care programs serving youth: A review and suggested directions. *Social Work Research & Abstracts.*

Maluccio, A., Warsh, R., & Pine, B. (1993). Rethinking family reunification after foster care. *Community Alternatives. International Journal of Family Alternatives, 5,* 1–15.

Martin, C., & Hawkins, R. (1992). The restrictiveness of living environments scale (ROLES): West Virginia replication of a simple device for program evaluation, policy planning, and placement decision-making. *Community Alternatives. International Journal of Family Care, 4,* 71–79.

Meadowcroft, P. , Thomlison, B., & Chamberlain, P. (1994). Treatment foster care services: A research agenda for child welfare. *Child Welfare, LXXIII*(5), 565–581.

Rivera, V., & Kutash, K. (1994). Therapeutic foster care. Components of a system of care. *What does the research say?* (pp. 81–100). Tampa, FL: Research and Training Center for Children's Mental Health, University of South Florida, Florida Mental Health Institute.

Rowe, J., Hundleby, M., & Garnett, L. (1989). Child care now. *A survey of placement patterns.* London: British Agencies for Adoption and Fostering.

Thomlison, B., & Krysik, J. (1991). The development and use of an instrument to measure the restrictiveness of children's living environments. *Research on Social Work Practice, 2*(2), 207–219.

17

Specialist Foster Care Program Standards in Relation to Costs, Client Characteristics, and Outcomes

Richard W. Nutter, Joe Hudson, Burt Galaway, and Malcolm Hill

The change from treating children in institutions to providing treatment in foster family care has been accompanied by an array of different labels in North America. Examples are parent counsellors by Larson, Allison, and Johnston (1978); parent-therapist by Rubenstein, Armentrout, Levin, and Herald (1978); teaching-family by Maloney, Fixsen, and Phillips (1981); professional parenting by Jones and Timbers (1983); family-based treatment by Hawkins and Meadowcroft (1984); foster family-based treatment by Hawkins, Meadowcroft, Trout, and Luster (1985); individual residential treatment (Update, 1986), specialist foster family care by Galaway (1989); specialized foster care by Snodgrass and Bryant (1989); and therapeutic family care, therapeutic foster care, treatment family care, professional foster care, and intensive foster care by Stroul (1989). Proponents of specialist foster care (SFC), by whatever label, believe in the benefits of family-centred, community-based, systematic approaches to the treatment of children with special needs. Virtually all SFC programs involve an integration of child welfare and mental health treatment practices. There is widespread agreement that specialist foster care should include four critical elements: (a) children whose needs or behaviours are such that they would normally be placed in relatively restrictive out-of-home treatment settings; (b) carefully selected foster carers who receive pre-service and in-service training and ongoing support to provide family-centred nurturing environments; (c) individual treatment plans as part of the service agreement; and (d) a clearly articulated program philosophy with strong community linkages (Galaway, 1989, 1990; Hawkins, 1989; Snodgrass, 1989; Stroul, 1989). However, there are significant differences among approaches to SFC. Snodgrass (1989) and Galaway (1989) illustrate some of these differences. Robert Snodgrass (1989) would require foster carers to carry out individually designed treatment interventions that include "... a stated, measurable goal, a written set of procedures for achieving the goal, and a process for regularly assessing the result." These treatment plans are designed by mental health experts who supervise delivery of the interventions by foster carers. Thus a SFC program must have mental health professionals on staff responsible for designing and supervising treatment services. This contrasts with Galaway's (1989) emphasis on normalization and developing social networks. Specialist foster carers need training and support to ensure that challenging children experience family life. Emphasis in the home is on family living rather than on treatment. Networking activities assist youths to develop informal social support systems as well as to access formal services in the community. Mental health, educational, medical, dental, and other types of services are secured in the community rather than provided by the SFC program and foster carers. Galaway (1989) argues that helping young persons to use community resources should increase their ability to use necessary services after they leave SFC.

The programs included in this report claim to meet all six of the following criteria:

1. The program is explicitly identified as a specialist or treatment foster care program with an identifiable name and budget.
2. Payments are made to foster carers at rates above those provided for regular foster care.
3. Training and support services are provided to the specialist foster carers.
4. A formally stated goal or objective of the program is to serve clients who would otherwise be admitted to or retained in a non-family institutional setting.
5. Care is provided in a residence owned or rented by the individual or family providing the treatment services.
6. The specialist foster carers are viewed and dealt with as members of a service or treatment team.

An important refinement to the debate about the essential or defining characteristics of SFC has been the debate about standards for SFC programs. Proposed standards have included amount of pre-service and in-service training required of foster carers, size of caseloads carried by SFC professionals, number of clients permitted in each SFC home, duration of written treatment plans, and inclusion of birth parents into the SFC treatment process. Supporters believe these restrictive standards will increase the quality and effectiveness of SFC. Opponents argue that there is no compelling evidence that SFC programs with smaller caseloads, fewer children per home, more hours of pre-service and in-service training, and so forth, are of higher quality or produce better outcomes than SFC programs that would not meet some or all of the more restrictive standards. Their argument is that, if restrictive standards don't increase quality and outcomes, then all that more restrictive standards will do is increase the cost of SFC.

Our most recent surveys of SFC in Canada, the U.K., and the U.S. contain data about program costs, program standards and program process, client characteristics, and outcomes. These data can be used to address some questions relevant to the standards debate. First, do programs with lower caseloads, lower maximum clients per home, shorter duration treatment plans, more foster carer training, and more frequent foster carer support group meetings produce better outcomes? Second, are these same program characteristics associated with higher costs, either per client month or per client? Third, are the clients' age, sex, ethnic group, major reason for SFC placement, pre-

SFC living situation, and legal relationship to birth parents related to relationships among standards, costs, and outcomes?

Method

The North American survey was the third we have conducted (Nutter, Hudson, & Galaway, 1989; Hudson, Nutter, & Galaway, 1992) and was done in six passes. In early September 1991 brief questionnaires were distributed to over 1200 persons connected with foster care programs in Canada and the U.S. to discover if their programs met the definition of SFC, and to obtain the addresses of additional programs. Reminder letters were sent to those who had not responded by the end of September 1991. From these responses, 808 programs that respondents claimed met our six criteria of SFC were identified. In early November 1991 questionnaires were sent to each of these programs. About two weeks later reminder/thank you cards were sent to these programs. Late in December 1991 letters and questionnaires were sent to the programs that had not yet responded. Late in January 1992 another letter and questionnaire was sent to each program that had not responded by then. By April 1, 1992, usable responses had been received from 434 programs. This report includes data from 15 Canadian and 216 United States SFC programs that claimed to meet all six SFC characteristics and supplied data on recently discharged youth 18 years of age or younger. Discharge data was for 104 Canadian and 1671 American youth.

The United Kingdom survey was the same as the one done in Canada and the U.S. apart from some changes in wording to accommodate U.K. usage. Letters requesting co-operation were sent with questionnaires in February 1992 to 230 children's fostering and adoptions agencies. Three reminder letters were sent. By the end of June 1992, 53 completed questionnaires had been received, along with 10 refusals and 109 no-SFC-scheme responses. No reply was received from 58 agencies in the sample. Of the 53 schemes returning usable questionnaires, 38 claimed to meet all six SFC criteria. Of these 38, 21 from England, Wales, and Northern Ireland and 7 from Scotland supplied data on children 18 years of age or younger who had been recently discharged. Discharge data were supplied for 68 Scottish and 174 other U.K. youth. Some respondents indicated that the low number of SFC schemes in the U.K. may be due to upgrading most foster care. Some local authorities have dismantled their separate specialist foster care schemes and have attempted to raise all foster care to the same high standard.

All respondents were asked (a) the total amount of their current annual budget including all expenditures, such as administration, wages, reimbursements and other payments to foster carers, and so forth, and (b) the amount allocated for compensating foster carers from their current total annual budget. Respondents were also asked to report the lowest and highest monthly amounts paid to foster carers in their SFC program for each client in the home. More respondents reported monthly per client payments to foster carers (242, reporting 1907 clients) than reported annual budgets (192, reporting 1335 clients). Five programs (28 clients) provided budget and client data that resulted in estimated per month costs of $6,897 or more. Because these were more than 25% higher than the next highest estimated per month costs ($5375), these cost data were excluded from the analyses reported later in this paper. Three programs (23 clients) provided budget and client data that resulted in estimated per month foster carer costs of over $4,000 per client These estimates were also excluded because they were more than 50% higher than the next highest estimates. Also excluded were the 24 clients from 19 programs who had been in SFC more than five years (60 months) before they were discharged. All of these exclusions were made to avoid distorting, by a few extreme cases, relationships that may exist among the vast majority of cases.

The Variables

The median start-up year for these SFC programs was 1985; half began between 1981 and 1987. Thus, most of these programs were relatively young at the time of this survey. Only 71 of the clients had been served by private, for-profit SFC. About one quarter (513) were served in SFC operated directly by government and the majority (1421) were served by private, not-for-profit SFC. Median program size was 23 clients placed in SFC homes on the census day of November 1, 1991 in Canada and the U.S. and February 1, 1992 in the U.K.

Program Costs

All program cost data were converted to U.S. dollars; Canadian dollars were multiplied by 0.8 and U.K. pounds were multiplied by 2.0 to approximate U.S. dollars. The following program cost variables were calculated.

1. Budgeted monthly cost per client is one-twelfth the total annual budget divided by the number of clients in placement on the census day. The mean budgeted monthly cost per client was $1946, median=$1688 (n=1308).
2. Budgeted total cost per client is budgeted monthly cost per client multiplied by the number of months the client was in SFC. Budgeted monthly cost per client was not calculated for clients who were in SFC less than one month. Mean budgeted total cost per client is $24,261, median=$17,294 (n=1277).
3. Budgeted monthly foster carer cost per client is one-twelfth the annual budget for paying foster carers divided by the number of clients in placement on census day. The mean budgeted monthly foster carer cost per client was $971, median=$834 (n=1300).
4. Budgeted total foster carer cost per client is budgeted monthly foster carer cost per client multiplied by the number of months the client was in SFC. Budgeted total foster carer cost per client was not calculated for clients in SFC less than one month. The mean budgeted total foster carer cost per client was $12,375, median=$8,427 (n=1266).
5. Foster carer fee was the amount received by foster carers per youth per month. Respondents were asked the lowest and highest amount paid monthly for each client in a home. The mean of these two amounts was used to estimate the fee foster carers received per youth per month in each program. The mean foster carer fee was $885, median=$821 (n=1907).

The clients' mean months of SFC treatment was 13, median=9 months (n=2017). Months in care longer than five years (60 months) were excluded from these analyses.

Program variables

Several program variables were available for this analysis.

1. Maximum caseload. Eighty-six percent of these SFC programs set maximum caseload limits for their social workers or other human service professionals. Most (86%) maximum caseloads were set as numbers of clients with the rest being set as numbers of homes. The caseload maximums for homes were typically about one quarter smaller than maximums for clients. The two standards were combined by multiplying home caseload maximums by 1.25. The resulting composite maximum caseload mean is 11, median=10, minimum=2, and maximum=38 (n=1740).
2. Maximum clients per home. Respondents were asked the maximum number of clients in any one of their SFC homes. The mean maximum clients per home is 3, median=3, and mode=2 (n=1750). Of these 1750 clients, 93% were discharged from SFC programs that had no more than five clients in any of their SFC homes. How many others shared each client's SFC home is unknown. Eighty-five percent of these clients were discharged from programs in which no home had more than four clients.
3. Mean clients per home is the number of clients in placement on census day, divided by the number of homes with at least one client. The mean clients per home is 1.6, median=1.5, and mode=1.
4. Hours pre-service training required. Foster carers were required to take a mean of 22 hours of pre-service training, median=20 (n=1956).
5. Annual in-service training required. The mean annual in-service training requirement was 23 hours, median=20 (n=1943).
6. Support groups. Seventy-three percent of foster carers were required to attend support group meetings. The mean annual frequency of support group meetings was 12, median=10 (n=1937). One in eight foster carers was required to attend support group meetings 25 or more times per year.
7. Written treatment plans. Ninety percent of SFC programs had written treatment plans for each client. The reported duration of these plans ranged from 2 weeks to the duration of placement. The mean treatment plan was for 16 weeks, median=12 weeks (n=1730). Of the fixed duration treatment plans, the longest one-eighth were from 26 to 52 weeks.
8. Legal relationship between the birth parents and client. The legal relationship was intact in 31% of the cases; 10% of parents had temporarily relinquished their legal relationship to their child; courts had temporarily removed parents' legal rights to their children in 29% of the cases. Courts had permanently removed parental rights in 22% of cases, forbade contact between the parents and child in 2%, and parents had permanently relinquished their rights to their child in 6%.
9. Parent with client visits is the number of days parents and children visited during the child's last month in SFC. Forty-six percent of the children did not visit with their parents during their last month in SFC. The mean parent visits was 3, median=1 (n=1867). Seventy-eight percent of these children visited with their parents four or fewer times during their last month in SFC. Only one client in ten visited with their parents on more than eight days during their last month in SFC.

Client Characteristics

Five percent of the clients were four years old or less when discharged from SFC and 33% were from 16 to 18 years old. The mean age when discharged from SFC was 13 years, median=14 years (n=2017). Fifty-six percent of the children were males. The proportion of males to females was about the same at all ages. Clients were grouped into three categories of ethnicity—white, black, and other. Sixty-eight percent of the clients were white, 20% were black, and 12% were other.

Respondents were asked to give the primary reason for SFC placement. Canadian and U.S. respondents were asked to select the major reason the former client was placed in the SFC program from the following list: AIDS, alcohol or drug abuse, criminal or delinquent behaviour, mental disability or incapacity, psychiatric or emotional, physical disability or incapacity, physical health other than AIDS, and other. In the U.K., behaviour not criminal was added to the list of alternatives. Many of the other reasons cited by respondents had to do with the child's environment but revealed little or nothing about the child. Examples of environmental issues include violent death of parents, poor parenting, child abuse, home unsafe, family abuse under investigation, least restrictive environment, need for long-term care, and family issues. Reasons for placement in SFC were reduced to six categories (n = 1965): criminal behaviour, 19%; mental disability, 5%; psychiatric or emotional, 58%; behaviour not criminal, 5%; environmental, 6%; and other, 7%. North American children were more likely than U.K. children to be in SFC for psychiatric or emotional reasons whereas behaviour not criminal was a more frequent reason for SFC placement in the U.K.

Clients' preplacement and post-discharge living situations were placed in one of four categories:

1. Parents' or own home — home of parents, and home alone or with a friend, partner, or spouse.
2. Other family — adoptive home, home of client's friend, home of family friend, home of relative, extended family, long-term foster care, home of social worker, adoption by foster parents, and supervised or supported independent living.
3. Other community — armed services, boarding home, regular family foster care, residential school, Native home, college, emancipation at age 18, adult training center, job training center, job corps, adult foster home, hostel, convent, and hostel for learning disabilities.
4. Institution or treatment — adult or youth correction facility, drug or alcohol rehabilitation centre, emergency shelter or refuge, a different treatment family foster care program, group home, homeless, medical hospital (medical or psychiatric ward), nursing home, psychiatric or mental hospital, residential treatment centre, unknown, developmental centre, ICF/MR, hospital for developmentally delayed, deceased, detention, halfway house, guardianship, runaway, maternity home, refugee camp, department of child services, receiving care, diagnostic centre, outward bound, health related facility, and mental handicap hospital.

Twenty-three percent of the children were living in their parents' or their own homes, 6% were living in other family situations, 19% were living in other community situations, and 52% were living in institutions or treatment immediately before placement in SFC.

Outcomes

Living situations at discharge were defined by the same categories as preplacement living situation; 35% of the clients went to their parents' or their own homes when discharged, 21% went to live in other family situations, 9% were discharged from SFC into other community situations, and 34% were discharged to institutions or continuing treatment. Respondents chose reasons for discharge from SFC from the following list of reasons:

1. Former client died (1%).
2. Administrative—former client ineligible because of age, expiry of legal mandate, end of funding, and so forth (9%).
3. Insufficient progress toward achieving treatment goals—referring agent or agency or SFC program decided to remove former client from SFC home (14%).
4. Placement breakdown—Former client refused to stay in SFC home or AWOL (17%).
5. Placement breakdown—foster carers requested that former client be removed from their home (12%)
6. Treatment goals for the former client were achieved (47%).

For this analysis these six categories have been collapsed into three—administrative including client died (10%); breakdown including lack of progress, client-initiated, and carer-initiated breakdowns (43%); and goals met (47%) (n=1986).

Program Characteristics, Costs, and Outcomes

An initial step in exploring relationships among these variables was a bivariate correlational analysis. For this analysis, 18 variables were considered to be ordinal. The cost variables were budgeted monthly cost per client, budgeted total cost per client, budgeted monthly foster carer cost per client, budgeted total foster carer cost per client, foster carer fee, and months in care. Program characteristics for this analysis were maximum caseload, maximum clients per home, mean clients per home, pre-service training, in-service training, support group meetings, treatment plans, legal relationship between birth parents and client, and parent visits. The only client characteristics included in the bivariate correlational analysis were age of youth and preplacement living situation. Discharge living situation was the only outcome variable included in this analysis.

Table 17.1 presents correlations among cost variables. Budgeted monthly cost per client is weakly (r=.30) correlated with budgeted total cost per client, strongly correlated (r=.67) with budgeted monthly foster carer cost per client, and very weakly correlated (r=.21) with foster carer fee. Budgeted total cost per client is strongly correlated (r=.88) with budgeted total foster carer cost per client and strongly correlated (r=.82) with months in care. Budgeted monthly foster carer cost per client is correlated (r=.36) with budgeted total foster carer cost per client, correlated (r=.37) with foster carer fee, and weakly negatively correlated (r=-.22) to both maximum caseload and maximum clients per home.

Table 17.1: Correlations Among Cost Variables and Between Cost and Other Variables*

Cost & related variables	Cost variables					
	Budgeted monthly cost per client	Budgeted total cost per client	Budgeted monthly foster carer cost per client	Budgeted total foster carer cost per client	Foster carer fee	SFC months in care
Budgeted total cost per client	.30	X				
Budgeted monthly foster carer cost per client	.67		X			
Budgeted total foster carer cost per client		.88	.36	X		
Foster carer fee	.21		.37	.23	X	
SFC months in care		.82		.81		X
Maximum caseload	-.35		-.22			
Maximum clients per home	-.33		-.22			
Inservice training					.25	
Support group meetings					.20	
Legal relationship between birth parents and client						.24

*All the reported correlations are statistically significant (p< .001). Correlations less than.20 were omitted because too weak to be practically important. This does not mean that rs greater than.20 are practically important.

Budgeted total foster carer cost per client is weakly correlated (*r*=.23) with foster carer fee and strongly correlated (*r*=.81) with months in care. These results indicate modest relationships between budgeted total and budgeted monthly per client costs. Budgeted monthly per client costs and budgeted costs of foster carers are also modestly related to the monthly fee to foster carers. Length of stay in SFC is strongly related to budgeted total per client costs, but this is to be expected since months in care is part of the budgeted total cost per client and budgeted total foster carer cost per client calculations.

Results in Table 17.1 indicate that budgeted monthly cost per client (*r*=-.35) and budgeted monthly foster carer cost per client (*r*=-.22) are modestly negatively correlated with maximum caseload. Budgeted monthly cost per client (*r*=-.33) and budgeted monthly foster carer cost per client (*r*=-.22) are also modestly negatively correlated with maximum clients per home. These correlations indicate that as caseload maximums and clients per home maximums decrease, budgeted monthly costs increase. The weak correlations between foster carer fee and in-service training (*r*=.25) and between foster carer fee and support group meetings (*r*=.20) indicate that more highly paid foster carers tend to be required to receive more training and share more support. The correlation (*r*=.24) between months in care and legal relationship between birth parents and client is in line with expectations that families with intact legal relationships may be more quickly reunited and a severed legal relationship may indicate a more complex set of circumstances to be resolved, requiring more time. None of the cost variables was correlated at or above r=.20 with any of the other program or any of the client variables in this analysis. There were many smaller, statistically significant correlations between cost variables and other variables but they were too small to be of practical importance by themselves. Their influence is reflected in the factor analysis.

Table 17.2 presents correlations among program, client, and outcome variables. The two measures of client density—maximum clients per home and mean clients per home—are positively correlated (r=.70). Maximum caseload is positively related to maximum clients per home (r=.37) and negatively correlated with preservice training (r=-.22). Preservice training is only very weakly (r=.14) correlated with in-service training. In-service training is more strongly correlated (r=.31) with support group meetings. Parent visits was negatively correlated with legal relationship between birth parents and client (r=-.37). Most visiting occurred when parents' legal rights to their children were intact. Parents visits with their children were less frequent when their legal rights to their children were permanently relinquished or terminated by the courts; in these cases, more than half the parents did not visit with their children during the child's last month in SFC. Both preplacement living situation and discharge living situation were scaled as ordinal variables with 1 being parents' or clients' own home, 2 other family, 3 other community, and 4 institution or treatment living situations. The negative correlations between parent visits and preplacement living situation and between parent visits and discharge living situation indicate that clients visited with their parents more frequently in their last month in SFC if they had been placed in SFC from more normal living situations and if they were leaving SFC to more normal living situations. Parents legal relationship to their children is also related to the children's preplacement living situation (r=.22) and discharge living situation (r=.25). There is a tendency for children who enter SFC from their parents' homes, or are discharged from SFC to their parents' or their own homes, to have an intact legal relationship with their parents. On the other hand, children living in institutions before or after SFC are less likely to have an intact legal relationship with their parents. This is slightly more true of children discharged from SFC to institutions or further treatment. There is a weak linear relationship between preplacement living situation and discharge living situation (r=.22). The largest group of children in each discharge living situation category were children who had been in that same living situation before SFC—preplacement living situation. Children who were in their parents' or own home before SFC were most likely to be living in their parents' or their own home after SFC. Similarly, children who were in institutions or treatment before SFC were more likely to be discharged to institutional or treatment living situations than to any other category of living situation. Treatment plans and age of youth were included in this correlational analysis but neither correlated above r=.20 with any other variable in the analysis. All 18 variables were included in the factor analysis.

Predictors of Outcome

The results of a factor analysis using principal components extraction and varimax rotation (Norusis, 1993) are presented in Table 17.3. Factor 1 groups months in care with the SFCs' budgeted total cost per client and the total cost budgeted to foster carers and also includes a small loading from legal relationship between birth parents and client. Factor 2 groups monthly

Table 17.2: Correlations Among Program Standard, Client, & Outcome Variables*

Program standard, client, & outcome variables	Program standard, client, & outcome varaibles					
	Maximum clients per home	Preservice training	Inservice training	Parent visits	Pre-placement living situation	Discharge living situation
Mean clients per home	0.70					
Maximum caseload	0.37	–0.22				
Support group meetings			0.31			
Legal relationship between parents and client				–0.37	0.22	0.25
Preplacement living situation				–0.20	1	
Discharge living situation				–0.38	0.22	1

*This is not a symtrical matrix. Some variables were related to only one other variable and appear only in a row or a column, not both.

budgeted payments to foster carers, monthly budgeted costs, and levels of pay to foster carers together with lesser contributions from frequency of required support meetings and social worker maximum caseload size; smaller caseloads being associated with higher costs, pay, and more frequent support group meetings. In-service training also contributes a small loading to Factor 2. Factor 3 is primarily client density—mean number of clients per SFC home and maximum clients in any one home. Small positive loading by maximum caseload and foster carer fee also contribute to Factor 3 along with a negative loading from budgeted monthly cost per client. Factor 4 is defined by parent visits, discharge living situation, legal relationship between birth parents and client, and preplacement living situation. The bivariate correlation analysis, indicated that more visits are associated with living at parents' or own home and an intact legal relationship between parent and child. Factor 5 groups pre-service and in-service training of foster carers with duration of treatment plans; shorter duration treatment plans are associated with more foster carer training. Factor 6 is mostly defined by clients' ages at discharge from SFC. A small loading from preplacement living situation indicates that older clients were more likely to be in out of home placements before SFC placement. An even smaller negative loading from in-service training indicates that SFC foster carers who cared for younger children may receive less in-service training than those who care for older children.

Two indicators of outcome were included among these data, the reason the client was discharged from SFC and the client's living situation after discharge from SFC. Discharge living situation and reason for discharge were strongly related to each other. Specifically, clients discharged because treatment goals were met were most likely to be living in their parents' or their own home after SFC, next most likely to be living with other family, followed by living in other community situations, and least likely to be living in a institutional or treatment setting. On the other hand, discharges due to placement breakdowns were most likely to be followed by institutional or treatment placements and

Table 17.3: Factor Analysis of Ordinal Cost, Program Standard, and Client Variables*

	Factors obtained by principal components extraction and varimax rotation					
Cost, program standard, & client variables	**Factor 1**	**Factor 2**	**Factor 3**	**Factor 4**	**Factor 5**	**Factor 6**
SFC months in care	.96					
Budgeted total cost per client	.94					
Budgeted total foster carer cost per client	.92					
Budgeted monthly foster carer cost per client		.81				
Budgeted monthly cost per client		.71	-.47			
Foster carer fee		.64	.29			
Support group meetings		.54				
Maximum caseload		.48	.43			
Mean clients per home			.87			
Maximum clients per home			.85			
Parent visits				-.79		
Discharge living situation				.74		
Legal relationship between birth parents and client	.33			.62		
Preplacement living situation				.52		.43
Preservice training					.74	
Treatment plans					-.73	
Inservice training		.31			.55	-.36
Age of youth						0.83

*Factor loadings less than.25 have not been included in this table. Listwise exclusion of missing data resulted in n=661 for this analysis. The bivariate correlations upon which this factor analysis is based were very similar to those resulting from pairwise exclusion of missing data displayed in Tables 1 and 2.

relatively unlikely to be followed by the former client living at home, with other family, or in an other community setting.

Discharge living situation has been included in the correlational analyses by ordering specific living situations into four categories that reflect a combination of presumed normality and permanence. How to order reason for discharge was less obvious. Goals met is a positive outcome but is administrative discharge a more positive outcome than breakdown? Therefore, reason for discharge has been treated as a nominal variable. Chi square automatic interaction detection (CHAID) is appropriate for use with nominal and ordered variables (Magidson, 1993). CHAID was used to discover which variables and combinations of variables in this data set best discriminate among the categories of discharge living situation and reason for discharge. Another reason for doing the CHAID analyses is to include the client characters of sex, ethnicity, and reason for placement in the analysis. Finally, CHAID seeks interactions among variables whereas data reduction techniques such as factor analysis tend to obscure interactions among variables.

The most powerful predictor of discharge living situation was parent visits. Three-quarters (78%) of children who had visited with their parents eight or more times in their last month in SFC were discharged to live in their parent's home or their own home, and only 9% were discharged to an institutional or treatment living situation. This contrasts sharply with clients who did not visit with their parents during their last month in SFC. Only 11% of clients who did not visit with their parents during their last month in SFC were discharged to their parents' or their own homes and 45% were discharged to institutional or treatment settings. The likelihood of home placement increased and the likelihood of alternate after discharge placements decreased as contact between clients and parents increased.

Age of youth was the most powerful discriminator of discharge living situation among those clients who did not visit with their parents during their last month in SFC. Two-thirds (65%) of the 179 unvisited children less than 10 years old were placed with other families, 23% in institutions or treatment, 6% in their parents' homes, and 6% in other community settings. Among the 406 unvisited 10 to 15 years old children, over half (59%) went to institutions or treatment, few went home (6%), and about equal proportions went to other family (19%) and other community (16%). In both of these groups of unvisited children less than 16 years old, those whose legal relationship with their parents was intact or only temporarily reduced were less likely to be placed with other families after SFC than those whose parents' legal relationship to them had been permanently severed. Over one third (37%) of the 274 unvisited 16 to 18 years old youths went to institutions or treatment, 29% went to other family, 20% went to their parents' or own home, and 13% were discharged to other community living situations. However, in this group, the budgeted total foster carer cost per client was a powerful additional discriminator. Sixty-eight percent of the 50 unvisited 16 to 18 years old clients who had been served by cheaper programs compared to 30% of the 224 unvisited 16 to 18 years old clients served by more expensive programs were discharged from SFC into institutions or treatment. This post hoc comparison indicates that, at least with this group, more expensive may be better. The division point between cheaper and more expensive programs for this discrimination was $5,250 paid to foster carers per client.

Age of youth was also the most powerful discriminator of discharge living situation among the 345 clients who had visited one or two days with their parents during their last month in SFC. However, for the 376 clients who had visited with their parents three to seven days during their last month in SFC, preplacement living situation was the most powerful discriminator of discharge living situation.

Among the 285 clients who visited with their parents eight or more days during their last month in SFC, months in SFC was the most powerful predictor of discharge living situation. Those in SFC more than 15 months were less likely to be discharged to institutions or treatment and more likely to be discharged to other family situations than clients with less than 15 months in SFC. However, the majority of both of these months in care groups were discharged to their parents' or own homes—77% of those in SFC less than 15 months and 80% of those in SFC more than 15 months.

Although parent visits is the most powerful discriminator of discharge living situation groups, other variables also discriminate among post-SFC living situations. In descending order of their predictive power these other variables are legal relationship between birth parents and client, preplacement living situation, age of youth, months in care, budgeted total foster carer cost per client, budgeted total cost per client, reason for placement, ethnicity of youth, maximum clients per home, support group meetings, budgeted monthly foster carer cost per client, mean number of clients per home, and in-service training. These results indicate that parent visits is the only program variable prominent as a predictor of discharge living situation.

Parent visits is the most powerful predictor of reason for discharge. Among the 283 clients who visited with their parents eight or more times during their last month in SFC, 80% were discharged because their treatment goals were met; 59% of the 366 clients who visited with their parents three to seven days during their last month in SFC were discharged because their treatment goals were met. Only 36% of the 1199 clients whose parents visited with them two or fewer days during their last month in SFC were discharged because treatments goals were met. The proportions of goals met and breakdown are similar among clients who were not visited or visited only once or twice. That proportion is reversed among clients visited three to seven days and the proportion of goals met increases further among clients who visited with their parents eight or more days during their last month in SFC.

Other variables significantly related to reason for discharge, in descending order of predictive power, are age of youth, months in care, preplacement living situation, budgeted total cost per client, reason for placement, budgeted total foster carer cost per client, legal relationship between birth parents and client, foster carer fee, budgeted monthly foster carer cost per client, maximum clients per home, budgeted monthly cost per client, preservice training, mean clients per home, and in-service training. As with discharge living situation, with the exception of parent visits, program variables such as maximum clients per home appear reasonably far down the list of predictors. Since parent visits may be an important mediating variable related to outcomes, it seems reasonable to ask which program and cost variables are most strongly related to parent visits.

The parents' legal relationship to their child was the most powerful predictor of parent visits. Clients and parents visited each other most frequently when parents' legal rights were intact and visited less frequently as they or courts diminished that relationship temporarily. Parent visits were even less frequent where parental rights were permanently relinquished or court terminated. Causality is unclear. Courts may diminish rights because parents fail to visit or parents may decease their visits after their rights have been diminished. The 539 parents whose legal relationship with their child was intact visited with their child a mean of 5.2 days during the last month of SFC. The 182 parents who had temporarily relinquished their legal relationship to their child, and the 591 parents whose legal rights to their child had been temporarily removed by courts, both visited their child a mean of 3.2 days during the child's last month in SFC. The 111 parents who had permanently relinquished their legal relationship to their child visited their child an average of once during the their last month in SFC. The courts had permanently severed the legal relationship between parent and child in 420 cases; these parents visited with their child a mean of.6 times in the month preceding discharge from SFC. The 35 parents forbidden by the courts to see their child visited those children a mean of .2 times during their last month in SFC. Preplacement living situation was also a powerful predictor of parent visits. The 405 children placed in SFC from their own or parents' home were visited by their parents a mean of 5 days during the child's last month in SFC, the 119 children who came to SFC from other families were visited by their parents a mean of 2.7 days during their last month in SFC, the 355 children who came to SFC from other community living situations were visited by their parents a mean of 2.1 days, and the 984 children who came into SFC from institutions or treatment were visited by their parents a mean of 2.5 days during their last month in SFC. Other predictor variables of visits in descending order of strength were legal relationship between birth parents and client, preplacement living situation, months in care, ethnicity of youth, budgeted monthly cost per client, budgeted total foster carer cost per client, budgeted total cost per client, support group meetings, preservice training, budgeted monthly foster carer cost per client, foster carer fee, maximum clients per home, treatment plans, and reason for placement. Again, it is clear that program variables are not the most prominent predictors.

Conclusions

These results do not indicate that program characteristics are strongly related to where a child is placed after SFC or whether the child was discharged because treatment goals were met, the placement broke down, or for administrative reasons. Examined program characteristics included social worker caseload size, maximum numbers of clients in each home, mean number of clients in each home, hours of required pre-service and in-service training, frequency of required support group meetings, duration of treatment plans, and fee to foster carers. Thus, these data do not provide strong support for imposing limits on these variables as restrictive standards for specialist foster care programs. Why impose standards that will increase costs in the absence of convincing demonstrations that programs meeting those standards produce better outcomes than programs not meeting those standards? The problem with this question is that it assumes that restrictive standards will increase costs. These results offer no more convincing support for that assumption than they do for the assumption that restrictive standards will increase the quality of outcomes. Some programs with relatively high maximum numbers of clients per home cost more than other programs with no more than one or two clients per home. Similarly, many programs with no required support group meetings or no required in-service training cost more than many programs with monthly or more frequent support group meetings and 20 or more hours of required annual in-service training. Therefore, these results support neither the argument that adherence to restrictive standards will by themselves improve outcomes nor the argument that those same standards will increase cost.

The CHAID analyses did not give prominence to program costs and the program standard types of variables measured in this survey. There are at least four competing explanations for these results:

1. Poor quality data —The data are so unreliable or unrepresentative that even very strong relationships will be only weakly represented.
2. SFC is ineffective—the relationships believed to exist between the operations of SFC programs and their outcomes are, at best, very weak and, at worst, do not exist.

3. Other factors determine cost—the relationships between program characteristics and cost that seem intuitively obvious and sensible are very weak, so weak as to be unimportant in comparison to other correlates of cost.
4. Wrong variables—the wrong program or client or outcome characteristics were measured.

Undoubtedly some of the data are not accurate, errors do occur. However, these data are very similar in most respects to the results of two previous surveys of SFC (Nutter, et al., 1989; Hudson, et al., 1992). In several instances, when data like budget or cost seemed suspect, the programs were called to confirm. In other cases outliers were eliminated in order to not distort the results of the majority on the basis of a few obviously unusual or wrong cases. Further, the variables in this survey were chosen because they are reasonably straightforward, easy to record, and easy to verify. So the data, although not perfect, are probably reliable enough to yield strong relationships if strong relationships exist.

Representativeness is difficult to judge. Reasonably complete results were received from only about half the population of SFC programs initially identified and not all of the SFC programs supplied discharge data on former clients that could be included in this analysis. However, we have seen no theory predicting that the relationships among our variables would be different in the SFC programs not included in this analysis. In addition, other analyses of the surveys have failed to detect strong differences between early and late responders. This does not prove that this sample is representative of all SFCs, but is consistent with that hypothesis.

The hypothesis that SFC is ineffective would argue that SFC is simply another place where the physical needs of challenging children are met, giving those children an opportunity to grow up and become less challenging or, at least, more self sufficient. Sizes of social workers' caseloads, number of children in the home, hours of pre-service and in-service training, frequency of support group meetings, and so forth are irrelevant. The trick is to find an environment that will meet the child's physical needs long enough for the child to become both less challenging and more self-sufficient. To conceptualize this as treatment that is sensitive to intentional and planful manipulation is nothing more than an elaborate ruse that diverts to professionals and paid foster carers resources that should be going to the child's own parents to support maturation of that child. The present data cannot test this hypothesis. It seems plausible to suppose that if the resources that are budgeted per child were used to support and pay birth parents to care for their child, the child would be as well off in many instances.

The correlation between total budgeted amount per client per month and portion of that budget to pay foster carers in this sample of programs is substantial (r=.67). This indicates that nearly half (45%) of the variance of these two variables is shared, but it also indicates that more than half the variance is attributable to other variables. The amount budgeted to pay foster carers per client month is not nearly as strongly related to what these programs said they actually paid foster carers (r=.37). This correlation accounts for less than 14% of the variability in these two variables. There are also only very weak correlations between other variables and cost variables. These low correlations should not be dismissed on the basis of possible strong non-linear relationships because such relationships were not detected in the CHAID analysis of these data.

Programs may vary in terms of the complexity of treatments offered to or purchased for their clients and in terms of their efficiency. These data do not distinguish between SFC programs that tend to fit Snodgrass's (1989) definition of SFC in which the foster carers and other SFC program professionals provide the treatment and SFC programs more like Galaway's (1989) ideal in which most treatment would be purchased from non-program sources. These data do not contain information about the administration of these SFC programs or the intensity of treatment offered that might reasonably account for the unexplained variability in costs.

Costs may also vary among programs and among SFC clients in relation to the severity of reasons for placement that led to placing the client in SFC. Children whose conditions are more challenging may require more resources for their care and remediation. The survey did not gather severity data but respondents were asked the major reason clients were placed in SFC. There are some relationships between reasons for placement and some cost variables. For example, clients in SFC for criminal behaviour are more likely to be in programs where the monthly per client pay to foster carers is between $750 and $1,000 (the third quartile) than in programs that pay foster carers less or more. Clients placed in SFC for psychiatric or emotional reasons are more likely to be in SFC programs that pay foster carers less than $650 per client month (the first quartile). However, this pattern is not sustained across all cost variables. For example, when total per client budgeted cost was used, clients in SFC because of criminal behaviour are more likely to be below the overall median cost and clients in SFC for psychiatric or emotional issues are more likely to be above the median cost. This difference in total budgeted cost is largely because clients placed in SFC for criminal behaviour are in care a mean of 8.8 months and clients in SFC for psychiatric or emotional issues are in care a mean of 14.5 months. Data was not available to indicate why the foster carers of clients with psychiatric or emotional issues are paid less per month than the foster carers of clients with criminal behaviour issues, nor does the data explain different lengths of stay of different groups of clients. These examples demonstrate some limitations of the current set of data.

Perhaps expected relationships were not found because the wrong cost, program, client, or outcome variables were measured. Program characteristics like caseload, numbers of clients in each home, and amounts of training and support may be necessary, but not sufficient, conditions for quality. For example, it is not possible for a social worker to do a good job unless they have sufficient time for each client. Of course, how much time they require will depend upon what they are expected to do and the complexity of the case. Therefore, lower caseloads may be necessary in some circumstances, but by themselves they will not ensure good work or good results. The same applies to training. The hours of training that would significantly enhance the performance of foster carers would depend on what roles were expected of them and how much education, skill, and experience they brought to the situation. However, simply giving them hours of training would not ensure good performance; the training must be appropriate and the foster carers able and willing. Therefore, the fact that we have not found strong relationships between very crude necessary, but not sufficient, standards and cost or outcomes across a very broad range of programs is not surprising. It does mean that to presume adherence to such standards will necessarily enhance quality or outcomes is naive. Gross quantitative data such as caseload size, hours of training, client density, and so forth, can only be sensibly considered within the context of the program model that specifies how the program is supposed to operate—the program logic and structure model.

It is clear that we have not measured what is important about the clients. We know their age, sex, ethnic group, the label under which they were placed in SFC, and where they were living before SFC. This is not much to know about a child, even if it is accurate. We don't know anything about the nature, including complexity and chronicity, of the difficulties than brought the child to SFC. Clients with environmental issues were the most likely of the reasons for placement groups to be discharged because the treatment goals were met. Better, more meaningful descriptions of clients are necessary to make sense of the relationships between program standards, costs, and outcomes. It is equally clear that the outcome measures in this survey are almost as crude as the program and client description data. The living situation to which clients were discharged is a case event, not a description of the client's condition. We have assumed that, other things being equal, discharge to their parents' or their own home is a better outcome for clients than other discharge living situation categories. However, an unknown proportion of these clients were placed in SFC as a more or less direct result of having experienced toxic homes. There is no indication that clients discharged to their parents' or own homes will experience wholesome family life. Children discharged to other families may be in better environments than those returned to their parents' homes. However, there is no reasonable way to distinguish among these cases in the present data. Perhaps the reason for discharge variable, with its distinction between treatment goals met, breakdown, and administrative, is better. However, there is no indication of what the goals were, and in some cases, a child successfully refusing to stay in a placement may be a better outcome than achieving the program's treatment goals for that child.

It may seem unusual to conclude a paper by arguing that the data were inappropriate to the questions asked. However, the data upon which this paper is based are no worse, and in many ways much better, than much of the research literature in child protection from the U.S. and Canada. The lack of strong relationships among variables in this survey, variables that should be related, is a demonstration of the inadequacy of operational definitions, theories, or both. Most current child welfare literature uses case events as proxy measures for the condition of children. An outstanding example of this is the use of staying in the parental home as opposed to out of home placement as the primary outcome measure in early evaluations of family preservation programs. More recent evaluations have improved on this (Pecora, 1995).

We need detailed studies of SFC programs; studies based on well developed program models (Lipsey, 1993; Nutter, 1992). They must measure program inputs, structure, and process in addition to program outputs and outcomes. Valid measures of children and their families must be used instead of the case events so frequently used in the past. These steps will lay the groundwork for comparisons within well defined and well implemented SFC programs. Work in the U.K. by Colton (1988) and by Parker, Ward, Jackson, Aldgate, and Wedge (1991) are significant steps in the direction of careful measurement. Knowledge about how better to serve children in SFC will be gained by careful thought and detailed study. Large scale studies that measure relatively few case event variables can provide broad descriptions of programming efforts but cannot significantly advance knowledge about how and why SFC works or fails to work.

The research reported in this paper was supported by a grant from the Laidlaw Foundation, Toronto, Ontario, Canada.

References

Colton, M. J. (1988). *Dimensions of substitute child care: A comparative study of foster and residential care practices.* Aldershot, England: Avebury.

Galaway, B. (1990) The place of specialist foster family care in a system of child welfare services. In B. Galaway, D. Maglajlic, J. Hudson, P. Harmon, & J. McLagan (Eds.), *International perspectives on specialist foster family care* (pp. 1–16). St. Paul Minnesota: Human Service Associates.

Galaway, B. (1989). Toward a definition of specialist foster family care. *Community Alternatives: International Journal of Family Care, 1*(2), 82–84.

Hawkins, R.P. (1989). The nature and potential of therapeutic foster family care programs. In R. Hawkins & J. Breiling (Eds.), *Therapeutic foster care: Critical issues* (pp. 5–37). Washington, DC: Child Welfare League of America.

Hawkins, R. P. , Meadowcroft, P. , Trout, B. A., & Luster, W. C. (1985). Foster family-based treatment. *Journal of Clinical Child Psychology, 14,* 220–228.

Hawkins, R. P. , & Meadowcroft, P. (1984). *Practical program evaluation in a family-based treatment program for disturbing and disturbed youngsters.* Unpublished manuscript, Press by Ridge Schools, Pittsburgh, Pennsylvania.

Hudson, J., Nutter, R. W., & Galaway, B. (1992). A survey of North American specialist foster family care programs. *Social Service Review, 66,* 50–63.

Jones, R. J., & Timbers, G. D. (1983). *Professional parenting for juvenile offenders.* Final report of program activities, Bringing It All Back Home Study Center, Morganton, North Carolina.

Larson, G., Allison, J., & Johnston, E. (1978). Alberta parent counsellors: A community treatment program for disturbed youths. *Child Welfare, 57*(1), 47–52.

Lipsey, M. W. (1993). Theory as method: Small theories of treatments. *New Directions For Program Evaluation, 57,* 5–38.

Magidson, J. (1993). *SPSS for Windows: CHAID, release 6.0.* Chicago: SPSS Inc.

Maloney, D. M., Fixsen, D. L., & Phillips, E. L. (1981). The teaching-family model: Research and dissemination in a service program. *Children and Youth Services Review, 3,* 343–355.

Norusis, M. J., (1993). *SPSS for Windows: Professional statistics, release 6.0.* Chicago: SPSS Inc.

Nutter, R. W., Hudson, J., & Galaway, B. (1989). A survey of specialist foster family care in North America. *Community Alternatives: International Journal of Family Care, 1*(1), 51–67.

Nutter, R. W. (1992). Program monitoring: The case of ongoing evaluation systems. In J. Hudson, J. Mayne, & R. Thomlison (Eds.), *Action-oriented evaluation in organizations* (pp. 160–179). Toronto, ON: Wall & Emerson.

Parker, R., Ward, H., Jackson, S., Aldgate, J., & Wedge, P. (1991). *Looking after children: Assessing outcomes in child care.* London: Her Majesty's Stationary Office.

Pecora, P. (1995). Assessing the impact of family-based services. In J. Hudson & B. Galaway (Eds.), *Child welfare in Canada: Research and policy implications.* Toronto: Thompson Educational Publishing.

Rubenstein, J. S., Armentrout, J. A., Levin, S., & Herald, D. (1978). The parent-therapist program: Alternate care for emotionally disturbed children. *American Journal of Orthopsychiatry, 48,* 654–662.

Snodgrass, R. (1989). Treatment foster care: A proposed definition. *Community Alternatives: International Journal of Family Care, 1*(2), 79–82.

Snodgrass, R., & Bryant, B. (1989). Therapeutic foster care: A national program survey. In R. Hawkins & J. Breiling (Eds.), *Therapeutic foster care: Critical issues* (pp. 37–79). Washington, DC: Child Welfare League of America.

Stroul, B. A. (1989). *Community-based services for children and adolescents who are severely emotionally disturbed: Therapeutic foster care.* Washington, DC: CASSP Technical Assistance Center, Georgetown University Child Development Center.

Update. (1989). *Program Update: Therapeutic Foster Care, 2*(1): 8–10.

18

Birth Parent Participation in Treatment Foster Care Programs in North America and the United Kingdom

Gord Richardson, Burt Galaway, Joe Hudson, Richard Nutter and Malcolm Hill

The participation of birth parents in the foster placement of children has been recognized as important and incorporated into treatment foster care standards (Foster Family-Based Treatment Association, 1991; Galaway, 1990). Birth parent involvement is held to be an important way to foster the child's sense of identity (Holman, 1975, 1980; Kufeldt, 1991, 1994). The child's need for a sense of identity is recognized as a right by The United Nations Convention on the Rights of the Child (1989). The rationale that continuity of contact between birth parents and children is necessary for the child to maintain and develop his or her sense of identity is also present in the social work research literature (Engler & Mass, 1959; Weinstien, 1960; Holman, 1966, 1975, 1980; Thorpe, 1974; Fanshel & Shinn, 1978; Maluccio & Whittaker, 1989; Kufeldt, 1994).

Previous research has examined the amount and frequency of birth parent visiting and association between birth parent visiting and other variables. Studies indicate that between 13% and 17% of children in foster care are visited regularly by their birth parents. Thorpe (1974) studied a population of 121 children in the care of a local urban authority in the United Kingdom and found that 27% of the population had contact with their birth parents; contact was every six months for 15% of the population and every three months for 12%. Fanshel (1977) studied a population of 28,758 children in care in New York City; 59% of the children in care were not visited by their birth parents, while 14% saw their birth parents at least once a month. Rowe, Cain, Hundleby, and Keane (1984) studied a population of 145 foster children who had been in care for a minimum of three years. They found that 21% of the children had experienced casual contact with birth parents in the last year. Only 17% of the children were classified as having continued visiting from their birth parents.

Birth parent visiting was found to decline as the child's length of time in care increased (Fanshel, 1975, 1977; Aldgate, 1980; Rowe et al., 1984). Fanshel (1975) studied a population of 624 children in New York city and found that the number of visits by birth parents decreased as children were in care for longer periods of time. Aldgate (1980) and Rowe and colleagues (1984) found that birth parent visiting declined over the time a child is in care; in the Rowe study only 12% of children in care over ten years had any contact with birth parents. Birth parent visiting may also be related to the child's age. Children who enter care when they are older are visited more frequently than children who enter care when they are very young or infants (Fanshel, 1975, 1977; Rowe et al., 1984). The reason a child is placed in care has also been related to the frequency of birth parent visiting. Fanshel (1975) found that children who were placed in care due to mental illness or due to their own behaviour were visited more frequently by birth parents than children who had been placed in care because of a parent's unwillingness to continue care, the physical illness of a parent, the neglect or abuse of the child, the abandonment or desertion of the child by the parents, family problems, or the death of a parent. In 1977, Fanshel supported these findings with further data demonstrating that children who were placed in care due to their own behaviour were visited by birth parents more frequently than children who were placed in care for other reasons.

Birth mothers who were evaluated in a positive manner by social workers visited their children more often than those mothers who were not evaluated positively (Fanshel, 1975). Thorpe (1974) found that birth parent visiting almost always occurred when the social worker, birth parent, and foster parent approved of birth parent visiting. Birth parents visited 68% of the children that social workers planned to return to their birth parents, but only 28% of children were visited by their birth parents in cases without such plans (Fanshel, 1977). Visiting significantly increased (Fanshel, 1977) when birth parent visiting was included in the discharge plan. Howard and Proch (1986) found that 52% of birth parents did not visit at all in the year of data collection, and 39% visited less than once a month for cases where no visiting plan had been developed. This compares to 68% of birth parents who visited more than once a month when there was a plan to do so. Hess (1988) conducted interviews with 15 caseworkers and found that the caseworkers believe the frequency of birth parent visiting is dependent on (a) court orders and the influence of others, (b) agency policy and norms, (c) agency resources, (d) considerations related to the child's placement, (e) the goal of the case, (f) the characteristics and needs of the child, (g) the characteristics and needs of the birth parents, and (h) the relationship between the parent and the child.

Mass and Engler (1959) found that equal portions of visited and unvisited children could be classified as disturbed. Weinstein (1960) studied 61 children in the care of the Chicago Child Care Society and found that children who did not have contact with their birth parents scored lower on a well-being measure. Weinstein also found that birth parent visiting was a prerequisite for children to identify with their birth parents. Children who identified predominantly with their birth parents scored highest in well-being. More recent research, however, has not constantly supported this finding. Thorpe (1974) found that birth parent visiting was positively correlated with better child adjustment, but was statistically significant only for children 11 to 13 years old. Fanshel and Shinn (1978) found that birth parent visiting did not emerge uniformly as a significant predictor of changes in the personal and social adjustment of children. There was some indication that birth parent visiting may have played a role in higher IQ scores, higher responsibility and agreeableness, and lower defiance and hostility, but no general conclusions could be drawn. Rowe et al. (1984) found that the best adjusted children were those who were at least five years old before losing contact with their birth parents, but who were now no longer visited by their birth parents. Findings are not yet reported from a demonstration project in Ontario that will yield outcome data from the systematic implementation of an inclusive care model involving birth parent participation (Kufeldt, 1994). Maas and Engler (1959), Fanshel (1975), and Aldgate (1980) all found the absence of birth parent visiting to be associated with longer term care, and the presence of birth parent visiting to be associated with shorter periods of time in care and quicker discharge. For example, Fanshel found that three-quarters of children who were visited by birth parents in care were discharged, while only one third of children not visited by birth parents were discharged.

These previous findings provide information about what variables have been associated with birth parent visiting. Determining the cause and effect sequence of these associations is problematic because the studies have correlational designs and use retrospective data. The research also suggests that birth parent visiting contributes to the best interests of the child by improving the child's well being and shortening the child's time in foster care. But birth parent visiting is only a part of the broader concept of birth parent participation. This study was undertaken to determine the extent to which treatment foster care, the most advanced form of foster care in North America and the United Kingdom (Galaway, 1990), implements birth parent participation in policy and practice. Data was used from the survey of treatment foster care programs reported in Chapter 17 to address six questions:

1. How pervasive are written policies encouraging birth parent participation in treatment foster care programs?
2. How often do birth parents participate in placements?
3. What is the association between policies that encourage birth parent participation and participation itself?
4. Are there relationships between demographic variables such as the child's age, sex, and ethnic background and birth parent participation?
5. Are there relationships between birth parent participation and variables such as the reason for placement, the legal relationship between child and parent, and the pre-placement living arrangement?
6. Are there relationships between birth parent participation and time in care, reasons for discharge, and post-placement living arrangements?

This analysis examines data from 358 TFC programs and from up to 10 clients most recently admitted and up to 10 former clients who had been most recently discharged from each TFC program immediately prior to November 1, 1991 in Canada and the U.S. and February 1, 1992 in the United Kingdom. A total of 2,631 children were admitted to the TFC programs and 2,159 were discharged.

Birth Parent Participation Policies and Practice

The survey asked if TFC programs had written policies that encouraged (a) consultation of birth parents about the placement of children, (b) meetings between program professionals, care-providers, and birth parents to plan placements, and (c) birth parent visiting of children in care. Table 18.1 shows that 85% of the programs (298) reported written policies that encouraged staff to consult with birth parents. Seventy-nine percent (278) had written policies that encouraged parents to meet with staff and care-providers to plan the placement and treatment of children and 94% (330) reported policies that encouraged birth parent visiting during the placement.

Table 18.1 Specialist Foster Family Care Programs with Written Policies about Birth Parent Participation by Country

Country	Canada (N=25)	United Kingdom (N=37)	United States (N=288)	Total (N=350)
Programs with policies encouraging the consultation of birth parents about the placement of children	(22) 88%	(34) 92%	(242) 84%	(298) 85%
Programs with policies encouraging meetings between birth parents and program professionals and care-providers	(22) 88%	(33) 89%	(223) 77%	(278) 79%
Programs with policies encouraging birth parent visiting	(24) 96%	(32) 87%	(274) 95%	(330) 94%

Table 18.2: Frequency of Birth Parent Participation by Country

Recent Admissions (N=2,631)

	Canada	United Kingdom	United States	Total
Cases where consultation of birth parent occurs	(83) 59%	(237) 83%	(1,120) 53%	(1,440) 56%
Cases where birth parent meets with program staff	(73) 52%	(178) 60%	(919) 43%	(1,170) 46%
Cases where birth parent meets with care-provider	(57) 40%	(162) 55%	(705) 33%	(924) 36%
Cases where visiting is included in the treatment plan	(90) 64%	(197) 67%	(1,265) 59%	(1,552) 61%
Cases where birth parent visiting takes place in the month prior to Nov. 1, 1991	(64) 52%	(166) 73%	(1,019) 50%	(1,249) 52%

Recent Discharges (N=2,159)

	Canada	United Kingdom	United States	Total
Cases where consultation of birth parent occurs	(65) 60%	(188) 80%	(921) 53%	(1,174) 56%
Cases where birth parent meets with program staff	(58) 54%	(144) 60%	(808) 46%	(1,010) 48%
Cases where birth parent meets with care-provider	(55) 51%	(125) 51%	(623) 36%	(803) 38%
Cases where birth parent visiting takes place in month prior to discharge	(50) 52%	(122) 63%	(871) 52%	(1,043) 53%
Cases where birth parent visiting is included in the treatment plan	(71) 66%	(158) 65%	(1,017) 58%	(1,246) 59%

Table 18.3: Frequency of Birth Parent Participation by Specialist Foster Care Program Policies of Birth Parent Participation by Country

	Canada		United Kingdom		United States		TOTAL	
Presence or absence of policy encouraging birth parent participation	No Policy	Policy	No Policy	Policy	No Policy	Policy	No Policy	Policy
Recent Admissions (N=2,631)								
Cases where consultation of birth parent occurs	(4) 20%*	(79) 65%	(8) 57%	(229) 84%	(153) 41%	(967) 55%	(165) 40%	(1,275) 60%
Cases where birth parent meets with program staff	(2) 20%	(71) 54%	(14) 47%	(164) 62%	(114) 24%	(805) 49%	(130) 25%	(1,040) 51%
Cases where birth parent meets with care-provider	(2) 20%	(55) 42%	(14) 47%	(148) 56%	(75) 16%	(630) 38%	(91) 18%	(833) 41%
Cases where visiting is included in the treatment plan	(4) 57%	(86) 64%	(13) 57%	(184) 68%	(49) 51%	(1,216) 60%	(66) 52%	(1,486) 61%
Cases where birth parent visiting takes place in the month prior to Nov. 1, 1991	(4) 67%	(60) 51%	(13) 100%	(153) 72%	(39) 41%	(980) 50%	(56) 49%	(1,193) 52%
Recent Discharges (N=2,159)								
Cases where consultation of birth parent occurs	(7) 35%	(58) 66%	(7) 33%	(181) 84%	(130) 40%	(791) 55%	(144) 40%	(1,030) 60%
Cases where birth parent meets with program staff	(5) 50%	(53) 54%	(11) 37%	(133) 63%	(123) 31%	(685) 51%	(139) 32%	(871) 53%
Cases where birth parent meets with care-provider	(6) 60%	(49) 50%	(5) 17%	(120) 56%	(68) 17%	(555) 41%	(79) 18%	(724) 44%
Cases where visiting is included in the treatment plan	(2) 50%	(69) 66%	(0) 0%	(158) 68%	(42) 55%	(975) 58%	(44) 48%	(1,202) 60%
Cases where birth parent visiting takes place in month prior to discharge	(1) 25%	(49) 53%	(0) 0%	(122) 66%	(40) 52%	(831) 52%	(41) 45%	(1,002) 53%

*Portion of cases in No Policy Category.

Birth parent participation was reported for children recently admitted to care (N=2,631) and children recently discharged from care (N=2,159) from the 358 programs that participated in the study. Information about reported birth parent participation is displayed in Table 18.2. Birth parents were consulted in 56% of cases for both recent admissions and recent discharges. Birth parent consultation was more likely to occur in the United Kingdom than in Canada and the United States. Birth parents met with program staff in 46% to 48% of the cases. Programs in the United States were least likely to conduct such meetings; programs in Canada and the United Kingdom conducted meetings between program staff and birth parents in over half the cases. Meetings between birth parents and care-providers occurred in only 33% to 36% of the total cases. In programs in the United Kingdom, however, birth parents met with care-providers over half the time. About half the children were visited by

Table 18.4: Frequency of Birth Parent Participation by Ethnic Group

Recent Admissions (N=2,631)	Black	White	Other	Mixed
Cases where consultation of birth parent occurs	(300) 48%	(1015) 61%	(102) 39%	(23) 54%
Cases where birth parent meets with program staff	(222) 35%	(838) 50%	(87) 34%	(17) 40%
Cases where birth parent meets with care-provider	(162) 26%	(669) 40%	(75) 29%	(14) 33%
Cases where visiting is included in the treatment plan	(358) 57%	(1035) 62%	(141) 54%	(26) 60%
Cases where birth parent visiting takes place in the month prior to Nov. 1, 1991	(271) 47%	(850) 54%	(115) 46%	(21) 50%
Recent Discharges (N=2,159)				
Cases where consultation of birth parent occurs	(167) 39%	(896) 62%	(100) 47%	(18) 53%
Cases where birth parent meets with program staff	(135) 31%	(779) 53%	(85) 40%	(15) 44%
Cases where visiting is included in the treatment plan	(191) 45%	(925) 63%	(123) 58%	(22) 67%
Cases where birth parent visiting takes place in month prior to discharge	(154) 38%	(778) 57%	(107) 52%	(15) 52%

their birth parents during the month preceding the survey for recent admissions, and the month prior to leaving for recent discharges. This type of birth parent participation was more likely than meetings with program staff and care providers, but was less likely than initial birth parent consultation. The likelihood of visiting was much higher in the United Kingdom than in Canada and the United States, but visiting occurred in at least half of all cases among programs in all three countries.

Do written policies encourage birth parent participation? Table 18.3 shows a comparison of birth parent participation in programs with and without written policies. All types of birth parent participation, in both populations, were more likely in programs with written policies encouraging such participation. For example, consultation with birth parents occurred in 60% of the cases in programs with written policies encouraging consultation compared to 40% of the cases in programs without written policies. Birth parent meetings with program staff were also more frequent in programs with written policies encouraging this type of participation. The frequency of such meetings was 26% higher among recent admissions in programs with written policies and was 21% higher among recent discharges. Written policies were also associated with a marginal improvement in birth parent visiting. Written policies encouraging birth parent participation are associated with higher rates of actual participation but written policies may have a more powerful impact in involving birth parents in planning than in visiting.

Variables Associated with Birth Parent Participation

The children's age, sex, and ethnic backgrounds were examined for their possible relationship to birth parent participation. Age was not associated with the frequency of birth parent participation for either recent discharges or recent admissions. Visiting was more likely among recent discharges for older children

Table 18.5: Frequency of Birth Parent Participation by Reason for Placement

Reason for Placement	Alcohol or Drug Abuse	Criminal or Delinquent Behaviour	Mental Disability or Incapacity	Psychiatric or Emotional	Physical Disability or Incapacity	Physical Health	Sexual Abuse/ Behaviour	Behavioral Disability or disorder	Environ-mental
Recent admissions (N=2,631)									
Cases where consultation of birth parent occurs	(46) 73%	(239) 65%	(106) 68%	(750) 49%	(25) 52%	(32) 74%	(18) 46%	(104) 69%	(95) 65%
Cases where birth parent meets with program staff	(30) 48%	(188) 51%	(93) 60%	(641) 42%	(22) 46%	(27) 63%	(11) 28%	(70) 46%	(70) 48%
Cases where birth parent meets with care-provider	(25) 40%	(139) 38%	(92) 59%	(502) 33%	(16) 33%	(12) 32%	(10) 26%	(67) 44%	(52) 36%
Cases where visiting is included in the treatment plan	(48) 76%	(237) 64%	(95) 61%	(868) 57%	(32) 67%	(35) 81%	(17) 44%	(100) 66%	(104) 72%
Cases where birth parent visiting takes place in the month prior to Nov. 1, 1991	(37) 61%	(191) 57%	(83) 60%	(704) 47%	(31) 66%	(19) 68%	(13) 34%	(93) 69%	(72) 60%
Recent Discharges (N=2,159)									
Cases where consultation of birth parent occurs	(49)	(241) 64%	(80) 73%	(612) 50%	(18) 72%	(13) 54%	(14) 52%	(71) 66%	(75) 56%
Cases where birth parent meets with program staff	(28) 38%	(205) 54%	(75) 68%	(560) 45%	(14) 56%	(12) 50%	(9) 33%	(47) 44%	(64) 48%
Cases where birth parent meets with care-provider	(19) 26%	(151) 40%	(65) 59%	(452) 37%	(10) 40%	(3) 13%	(7) 26%	(46) 43%	(52) 39%
Cases where visiting is included in the treatment plan	(54) 74%	(238) 63%	(73) 66%	(688) 56%	(18) 72%	(13) 52%	(14) 54%	(63) 59%	(94) 71%
Cases where birth parent visiting takes place in month prior to discharge	(44) 67%	(207) 58%	(57) 53%	(581) 49%	(11) 50%	(5) 33%	(13) 52%	(61) 62%	(64) 61%

in care but there was no clear pattern by age for birth parent consultation, meetings with program staff, and meetings with care-providers. Likewise, the child's sex was not associated with the likelihood of birth parent participation. Table 18.4, however, shows a pattern of birth parent participation by the child's ethnic group with birth parents of White children more liable to participate than parents of Black children.

Previous research indicated that children placed due to their own behaviour problems or mental illness are visited more frequently than children who are placed for other reasons (Fanshel, 1975, 1977). Information presented in Table 18.5, however, shows no consistent pattern in the relationship between birth parent participation and reason for placement among children in treatment foster care. The few children (about 39) recently admitted due to sexual abuse and behaviour had the lowest participation frequencies, but this trend was not

Table 18.6: Birth Parent Participation by Parent's Legal Relation to the Child

Recent Admissions (N=2,631)	Rights Intact	Rights Temporarily Relinquished	Rights Permanently Relinquished	Rights Temporarily removed by Courts	Rights Permanently Terminated By Court	Contact Forbidden By Courts
Cases where consultation of birth parent occurs	(533) 82%	(208) 84%	(62) 32%	(525) 58%	(84) 19%	(11) 19%
Cases where birth parent meets with program staff	(449) 69%	(163) 66%	(47) 24%	(429) 47%	(57) 13%	(10) 17%
Cases where birth parent meets with care-provider	(371) 57%	(126) 51%	(36) 18%	(321) 36%	(46) 10%	(4) 7%
Cases where visiting is included in the treatment plan	(526) 81%	(186) 75%	(55) 28%	(679) 75%	(85) 19%	(7) 12%
Cases where birth parent visiting takes place in the month prior to Nov. 1, 1991	(422) 72%	(157) 67%	(42) 23%	(553) 64%	(70) 16%	(4) 7%
Recent discharges (N=2,159)						
Cases where consultation of birth parent occurs	(543) 87%	(140) 71%	(37) 29%	(331) 55%	(83) 18%	(6) 33%
Cases where birth parent meets with program staff	(451) 72%	(122) 62%	(35) 28%	(299) 50%	(68) 15%	(5) 30%
Cases where birth parent meets with care-provider	(375) 60%	(93) 47%	(26) 21%	(230) 38%	(49) 1 1%	(2) 11%
Cases where visiting is included in the treatment plan	(528) 85%	(146) 74%	(33) 26%	(426) 71%	(80) 17%	(3) 17%
Cases where birth parent visiting takes place in month prior to discharge	(455) 79%	(116) 61%	(26) 21%	(365) 66%	(55) 12%	(3) 18%

present among recent discharges. Most of the children in both populations were placed in treatment foster care for psychiatric or emotional reasons but these children had equal or less birth parent participation relative to children placed in treatment foster care for other reasons.

Table 18.7: Frequency of Birth Parent Participation by Pre-placement Living Arrangement

	The Parent's Home	Other Family Home (Other than Parent's home)	Community Placement	Institution or Treatment Centre
Recent Admissions (N=2,631)				
Cases where consultation of birth parent occurs	(435) 86%	(92) 50%	(241) 43%	(672) 50%
Cases where birth parent meets with program staff	(377) 75%	(70) 38%	(178) 31%	(546) 41%
Cases where birth parent meets with care-provider	(314) 62%	(58) 32%	(130) 23%	(426) 32%
Cases where visiting is included in the treatment plan	(422) 84%	(88) 48%	(274) 48%	(774) 58%
Cases where birth parent visiting takes place in the month prior to Nov. 1, 1991	(361) 81%	(76) 43%	(224) 41%	(607) 48%
Recent Discharges (N=2,159)				
Cases where consultation of birth parent occurs	(394) 81%	(67) 52%	(183) 46%	(540) 48%
Cases where birth parent meets with program staff	(339) 70%	(56) 43%	(151) 38%	(470) 42%
Cases where birth parent meets with care-provider	(279) 57%	(46) 35%	(108) 27%	(377) 33%
Cases where visiting is included in the treatment plan	(399) 82%	(63) 49%	(201) 51%	(601) 53%
Cases where birth parent visiting takes place in month prior to discharge	(326) 75%	(58) 47%	(165) 44%	(508) 47%

Table 18.8: Recently Discharged Children's Mean Months in Care by Birth Parent Participation

Type of Birth Parent Participation	Mean Months in Care: Yes	No
1. Birth parent consulted about treatment planning?	12.9 years	15.9 years
2. Birth parent met with TFC staff to discuss treatment?	13.2 years	15.2 years
3. Birth parentmet with care provider?	13.6 years	14.6 years
4. Birth parent visiting included in treatment plan?	13.1 years	16.0 years
5. Birth parent visited in the month prior to discharge?	12.4 years	16.7 years

Table 18.9: Recently Discharged Children's Reason for Discharge by Birth Parent Participation

	Birth Parent Consultation		Birth Parent & Staff meetings		Birth Parent Care-Provider Meetings		Birth Parent Visiting in Treatment Plans		Birth Parent Visiting	
Reason for Discharge	Birth Parent was consulted (N=1,173)	Birth Parent was not consulted (N=947)	Birth Parent met with staff (N=1,008)	Birth Parent did not meet with Staff (N=1,118)	Birth Parent met with Care-Provider (N=809)	Birth Parent did not meet with Care-Provider (N=1,320)	Birth Parent Visiting Included in Treatment Plan (N=1,253)	Birth Parent Visiting Not Included in Treatment Plan (N=874)	Birth Parent visited in the month prior to discharge (N=1,045)	Birth parent did not visit in the month prior to discharge (N=950)
Child died	(10) 1%	(9) 1%	(10) 1%	(9) 1%	(8) 1%	(11) 1%	(9) 1%	(10) 1%	(5) -	(14) 2%
Administrative Reasons	(120) 10%	(91) 10%	(104) 10%	(106) 10%	(75) 9%	(135) 10%	(126) 10%	(85) 10%	(94) 9%	(92) 10%
Lack of Progress toward Treatment Goals	(146) 12%	(161) 17%	(121) 12%	(186) 17%	(93) 12%	(214) 16%	(173) 14%	(135) 15%	(140) 13%	(156) 16%
Child Requested	(168) 14%	(185) 20%	(140) 14%	(217) 19%	(121) 15%	(238) 18%	(188) 15%	(169) 19%	(132) 13%	(190) 20%
Care-giver requested	(112) 10%	(136) 14%	(88) 9%	(161) 14%	(79) 10%	(170) 13%	(107) 9%	(141) 16%	(86) 8%	(155) 16%
Treatment Goals met	(617) 53%	(365) 39%	(545) 54%	(439) 39%	(433) 54%	(552) 42%	(650) 52%	(334) 38%	(588) 56%	(343) 36%

The parent's legal relation to the child was associated with birth parent participation. Table 18.6 shows that birth parent participation was highest in cases where the parent's rights to the child were intact, the parent had temporarily relinquished rights, or the parent's rights were temporarily removed by the courts. Birth parent participation was lowest when the parent had permanently relinquished rights, or the parent's rights were permanently terminated by the courts.

Table 18.7 shows that the pre-placement living arrangements of children were related to birth parent participation. Parents of children who lived at home prior to being placed in treatment foster care participated the most in their children's placements. Among recent admissions, parents of children coming from home were consulted about the placement in 86% of cases. About 81% of the children coming from home were visited by their parents in the month prior to November 1, 1991. Parents of children who lived in an institution or treatment centre prior to placement participated more often than parents of children from other pre-placement living arrangements. This was more evident among recent admissions than recent discharges. Among recent admissions, 58% of children coming to programs from institutions or treatment centres had birth parent visiting in their treatment plan. Children coming from previous placements in the community had the lowest frequencies of birth parent participation. In summary, the ethnic background, the legal relationship of the children to parents, and the pre-placement living arrangements were associated with the birth parent participation.

Table 18.10: Recently Discharged Children's Post-Placement Living Arrangements by Birth Parent Participation

	Birth Parent Consultation		Birth Parent & Staff meetings		Birth Parent Care-Provider Meetings		Birth Parent Visiting in Treatment Plans		Birth Parent Visiting	
Reason for Discharge	Birth Parent was consulted (N=1,185)	Birth Parent was not consulted (N=955)	Birth Parent met with staff (N=1,018)	Birth Parent did not meet with Staff (N=1,128)	Birth Parent met with Care-Provider (N=810)	Birth Parent did not meet with Care-Provider (N=1,339)	Birth Parent Visiting Included in Treatment Plan (N=1,266)	Birth Parent Visiting Not Included in Treatment Plan (N=880)	Birth Parent visited in the month prior to discharge (N=1,059)	Birth parent did not visit in the month prior to discharge (N=954)
Discharged to Parent's Home	(595) 50%	(157) 16%	(521) 51%	(232) 21%	(445) 55%	(308) 23%	(634) 50%	(118) 13%	(587) 55%	(117) 12%
Discharged to Family other than Parent's	(172) 15%	(280) 29%	(147) 14%	(308) 27%	(109) 14%	(346) 26%	(180) 14%	(275) 31%	(126) 12%	(300) 31%
Discharged to a Community Placement	(89) 8%	(110) 11%	(76) 8%	(123) 11%	(54) 7%	(146) 11%	(85) 7%	(116) 13%	(64) 6%	(122) 13%
Discharged to an Institution or Treatment Centre	(329) 28%	(408) 43%	(274) 27%	(465) 41%	(202) 25%	(539) 40%	(367) 29%	(371) 42%	(282) 27%	(415) 44%

Outcome Variables Related to Birth Parent Participation

Previous research indicated that children who are visited by birth parents will generally leave care earlier than the others. The findings from this analysis are consistent with previous research. Table 18.8 shows that the average time in care was less for children who experienced birth parent participation, compared to those whose birth parents did not participate, across all indicators of birth parent participation.

Table 18.9 shows reasons for discharge by birth parent participation. Higher portions of children whose parents participated in the placement were discharged because treatment goals were met. Children without birth parent participation were more likely to be discharged due to a lack of progress toward treatment goals or a breakdown in the placement. This pattern is evident in all forms of birth parent participation from consultation through to visiting. Administrative reasons for discharge such as expiration of legal mandate or eligibility due to age or end of funding was not related to birth parent participation.

Birth parent participation was also positively associated with the child returning home after discharge. Information about post discharge living arrangement by birth parent participation is presented in Table 18.10. Children with birth parent participation were much more likely to be discharged to the home of the birth parent. Children without birth parent participation were more likely to go to another family member's home, a community placement, or an institution or treatment centre.

Cross Country Comparisons

Data for the group of TFC agencies and discharged youth used in this analysis come from the United States, United Kingdom, and Canada. The vast majority of agencies and discharged youth, however, were from the United States. Thus important differences within Canadian or United Kingdom programs might be masked by the overwhelming number of American programs and youth. To check for this possibility, all the bivariate relationships were examined controlling for country—United States, United Kingdom, and Canada. The English/Welsh and Scottish programs were combined for the analysis, even though they operate under different legislation, because the numbers were too small for meaningful analysis if treated separately. Further, both the Canadian and American programs operate under provincial and state legislation that will also vary within these countries.

The results of examining demographic variables and birth parent participation by country were generally consistent with the overall findings.* An exception was participation by black parents in the United Kingdom. The parents of black children in the United Kingdom were just as likely as parents of white children to participate in both recent admissions and recent discharges. No differences were found, across the three countries, when looking at birth parent participation by the age and sex of children.

The data were also examined for possible differences across the three countries for birth parent participation by reason for placement, parents' legal relations to child, and preplacement living arrangement. Generally, findings for each country were similar to those for the overall population with a few exceptions. In Canada, among recent discharges, birth parents whose rights to their children had been permanently relinquished were more likely to participate in treatment foster care placements than birth parents in the United States or the United Kingdom. Also in Canada, the birth parents of children who entered treatment foster care from family homes other than the parents' home were somewhat more likely to participate than birth parents from the United States or the United Kingdom.

Examination of the treatment and outcome variables by birth parent participation for each country mirrored the findings from the general findings with a few exceptions. In the United Kingdom, birth parent consultation and meetings between the birth parents and care-providers were not associated with shorter periods of time in care. This contrasts with the findings in Canada and the United States. Also in the United Kingdom, the association between birth parent participation and the achievement of treatment goals is more tenuous than in Canada and the United States.

These differences across countries are to be treated with some caution, given the relatively small number of Canadian and United Kingdom programs and youth and that the general findings are relatively consistent across the three countries. These variations may, however, suggest an area for future comparative study.

---

* Copies of tables not included in this chapter are available from Burt Galaway, Faculty of Social Work, University of Manitoba, Winnipeg, Manitoba, R3T 2N2, fax no. (204) 261-3283).

Discussion and Conclusions

Treatment foster care programs in North America and the United Kingdom have, for the most part, policies that encourage birth parent participation in the form of birth parent consultations, planning meetings that include the birth parent, program staff, and care-givers, and birth parent visiting. Birth parent consultation about placements and birth parent visiting are the most common forms of birth parent participation. Birth parent meetings with care-givers occurred less frequently. Written policies encouraging birth parent participation are associated with higher frequencies of birth parent participation.

Demographic factors such as the child's age and sex are not strongly related to birth parent participation, while ethnic background was associated with different participation rates. In general, birth parent participation is lowest among blacks and highest among whites. There was no consistent pattern in the relationship between birth parent participation and reason for placement, although children placed in treatment foster care due to sexual abuse or psychiatric or emotional problems had less birth parent participation than those placed for other reasons. Birth parent participation was relatively high in cases where the parent's rights to the child were intact or the parent had temporarily relinquished rights and participation was lowest when the parent's rights were permanently relinquished or terminated. These findings are consistent with Hess' contention that structural factors beyond immediate placement circumstances play a role in determining parent visiting and participation frequency (Hess, 1988). Birth parent participation drops as courts terminate parental rights to children. The parents of children who lived at home prior to placement were more likely to participate in placements, while birth parents of children coming from previous community placements, such as regular foster care, were least likely to participate.

Birth parent participation was also related to duration and outcome of treatment measured by time spent in care, reasons for discharge, and post-placement living arrangements. Children who experienced birth parent participation spent less time in care than those where parents did not participate. Birth parent participation was positively associated with discharge because treatment goals were met. Children were more likely to be discharged due to a lack of progress toward treatment goals or placement breakdown when birth parent participation was absent. When birth parent participation was present, children were more likely to live with their birth parents after discharge while an absence of birth parent participation was associated with discharge to another community placement, institution, or treatment facility.

These conclusions provide policy makers, program directors, and program designers with four important pieces of information that can be used in treatment and regular foster care programming. First, written program policies encouraging birth parent participation are associated with higher frequencies of participation. Second, certain groups of parents at-risk of not participating in the placement process may need to be targeted for additional attention. Such groups include parents from minority ethnic groups, parents with children admitted due to sexual abuse or behaviour, parents of children admitted for psychiatric or emotional reasons, parents whose legal rights to the child have been terminated, and parents of children coming from previous placements in the community. Third, birth parent participation is associated with favourable outcomes. The research examined a large population across three countries, and provides clear associations between birth parent participation and meeting treatment goals and returning children to their homes. Fourth, none of the types of birth parent participation measured in this study were associated with negative indicators. This suggests birth parents should be consulted about placements, allowed to visit their children, and empowered to meet with program staff and care-providers. Efforts to facilitate birth parent participation may help to better achieve treatment goals as well as recognize the rights of children who enter foster care.

References

Aldgate, J. (1980). Identification of factors influencing children's length of stay in care. In John Triseliotis (Ed.), *New developments in foster care & adoption* (pp. 22–40). London: Routledge & Kegan Paul Ltd.

Engler, R. E., Jr., & Maas, H. S. (1959). *Children in need of parents.* New York: Columbia University Press.

Fanshel, David (1975). Parental visiting of children in foster care: key to discharge? *Social Service Review, 49*, 493–514.

Fanshel, D. (1977). Parental visiting of foster children: a computerized study. *Social Work Research & Abstracts, 13*(3), 2–10.

Fanshel, D., & Shinn, E. (1978). *Children in foster care, a longitudinal investigation.* New York: Columbia University Press.

Foster Family-Based Treatment Association (1991). *Program standards for treatment foster care.* New York: Author.

Galaway, B. (1990). The place of specialist foster family care in a system of child welfare services. In B. Galaway, D. Maglaglic, J. Hudson, P. Harmon, & J. McLagan (eds.), *International perspectives on specialist foster family care* (pp. 1–16). St. Paul, Minnesota: Human Service Associates.

Galaway, B., Nutter, R., & Hudson, J. (1994). Birth parent participation in treatment foster family care. In B. McKenzie (ed.), *Current Perspectives on Foster Family Care for Children and Youth.* Toronto: Wall & Emerson.

Hess, Peg (1988). Case and context: Determinants of planned visit frequency in foster family care. *Child Welfare, 67*(4), 311–326.

Holman, R. (1966). The foster child and self knowledge. *Case Conference*, 12(9), 295–299.

Holman, R. (1975). The place of fostering in social work. *British Journal of Social Work*, 5(1), 3–29.

Holman, R. (1980). Exclusive and inclusive concepts in fostering. In John Triseliotis (Ed.) *New developments in foster care and adoption* (pp. 69–84). London: Routledge & Kegan Paul Ltd.

Howard, J. A., & Proch, K. (1986). Parental visiting of children in foster care. *Social Work, 31*(3), 178–181.

Kufeldt, K. (1991). Foster care: A reconceptualization. *Community Alternatives: International Journal of Family Care, 2*(1), 1–7.

Kufeldt, K. (1994). Inclusive foster care: Implementation of the model. In B. McKenzie (ed.), *Current Perspectives on Foster Family Care for Children and Youth.* Toronto: Wall & Emerson.

Meadowcroft, P. (1989). Treating emotionally disturbed children and adolescents in foster homes. In J. Hudson & B. Galaway (eds.) *Specialist foster family care: A normalizing experience* (pp. 23–41). New York: Haworth Press

Nutter, R., Hudson, J. and Galaway, B. (1989). A survey of specialist foster family care in North America. *Community Alternatives: International Journal of Family Care 1*(1), 51–67.

Rowe, J., Cain, H., Hundleby, M., & Keane, A.(1984). Long term foster care. New York: St. Martin's Press.

Snodgrass, R. & Bryant, B. (1989). Therapeutic foster care: A national program survey. In R. Hawkins & J. Breiling (Eds.), *Therapeutic foster care: Critical Issues* (pp. 37–79). Washington, DC: Child Welfare League of America.

Thorpe, R. (1974). Mum and Mrs So and So. *Social Work Today, 4*(22), 691–695.

United Nations General Assembly (1989). Forty-fourth session, Agenda item 108, 44/25. Convention on the rights of the child. 61st plenary meeting, November 20, 1989.

Weinstein, E. A. (1960). *The self-image of the foster child.* New York: Russell Sage

19

Moving In and Out of Foster Care

David Rosenbluth

This study examines patterns of foster care use in Saskatchewan. How long do children stay in foster care, how frequently do they move to different foster homes, and how often do they move in and out of foster care? The study also looks at whether these patterns have changed over time. Saskatchewan has a large Native population and a disproportionately large number of Native children who are in care. Past research on foster children in the province estimated that two-thirds of the children in care are of Native descent, including status Indians, non-status Indians, and Métis children (Saskatchewan Department of Social Services, 1986). Many believe that Native children in Canada are caught in the foster system for a longer time than non-native children. This contention has not been empirically examined and forms a part of this current study.

The period of this study, 1986 to 1993, was one of change in child welfare in Saskatchewan. A new Child and Family Services Act was proclaimed. This Act reflected a change in practice and philosophy regarding the relationship between the state, families, and the care for children. The Act provided the legislative base for the principle of least restrictive intervention and emphasized prevention and supporting families with in-home services rather than placing the child in substitute care. An expected consequence of these changes was that there would be fewer permanent wards, fewer children placed in foster care, and those placed would be for shorter periods. Saskatchewan has developed a variety of in-home support programs to aid families where children are at risk of abuse or neglect and of being placed out of the home. Proponents of family preservation programs argue that the government saves money by preventing children from entering foster care, or at least shortening the length of time that they would have been in care had the programs existed.

When empirical data is lacking, people often use images to describe what they believe are central characteristics of a foster care caseload. It is common to hear of children being in drift. This imagery conveys the notion that once in foster care a child is trapped, moving from one placement to another without any clear objectives or stability in their out-of-home placements. Workers also talk of a revolving door in foster care. This connotes a situation wherein children rapidly exit the system following entry—only to enter again a short time later. This image implies an opposite tendency of the system towards several brief spells in foster care. Both kinds of behaviour are found in a foster care caseload. Trocmé (1991) has suggested that in recent years the revolving-door syndrome is becoming more pronounced in Ontario, with workers absorbing increasing demands for services by decreasing the length of time that a child remains on a caseload.

There are two approaches for constructing samples to estimate the length of time children stay in foster care. Longitudinal methods sample from a cohort entering (or leaving) care at a given time and either follow children over their stay in care or calculate how long they have been in care up to their leaving. Examples of this approach are found in Benedict and White (1991), Benedict, White, and Stallings (1987), Lawder, Poulin and Andrews (1986), and Milner (1987). These studies have typically found that children remain in foster care for short periods—from 3 months (Lawder, Poulin & Andrews, 1986) to 6 months (Benedict & White, 1991). Racial differences among children appear to have little effect on the median length of time that they are in care. An alternative to longitudinal studies is to take a cross-section of children in foster care at a given time. These studies (Jenkins, 1983; Seaburg & Tolley, 1986; McMurtry & Lie, 1992; Murphy, 1968) report average lengths of time in foster care to be 2 years or more. These studies also report significant ethnic or racial differences in the time spent in care.

The longitudinal and cross-sectional approaches produce different results but both correctly describe the caseload. How can there be two answers to the question, "How long do children remain in foster care?" Cross-sectional and longitudinal approaches address different questions about children in foster care. The cross-sectional snapshot is useful for describing characteristics of children currently in care and assessing what types of children use most resources. The longitudinal approach is most useful for investigating patterns and characteristics of children who have ever entered care. It would be a mistake to make inferences about the nature and duration of care for all children entering foster care from a cross-section sample of those currently in the system.

Methodology

In this study, both longitudinal and cross-sectional samples are analyzed. Two cross-sectional samples are used, one drawn from children who were in foster homes during March 1986, and the other from those in foster homes during March 1990. The study only tracks children in foster homes; those who were living at home, with relatives, in group homes, or in young offender institutions were not included in the samples. A social services automated information system was used to trace children back in time to the beginning of the foster care spell, and then followed them forward until March of 1986 or 1990. Social and demographic characteristics were collected on each child at the point of entry into the system. These two cross-sections are used to compare children between the years 1986 to 1990. The analysis considers whether the stability of placement has changed over time, and if this can be attributed to different characteristics of children or changes in social work practices.

A third dataset was created of children entering a foster home for the first time during 1988. These children were followed for 4 years, with monthly observations made as to whether or not each was in foster care. The purpose of this sample is to estimate the total time a child stays in foster care, how many different episodes (or spells) in foster care each child has, and how many different homes are used during the 4 years. Social and demographic information was collected for each child at the start of their first spell in foster care.

Table 19.1: Characteristics of Native and Non-Native Children in the Longitudinal Sample

	Native n=483	Non-Native n=234
Sex:		
male	44.5%	44.9%
female	55.5%	55.1%
Average age (years)	6.1	10.2
Agegroup		
0–5 years	54.2%	25.2%
6–11 years	26.1%	15.4%
12–15 years	16.8%	44.0%
16+ years	2.9%	15.4%
Wardship:		
permanent	15.7%	11.5%
not permanent	84.3%	88.5%
Placement: .		
same background	9.4%	90.0%
dif. background	90.5%	10.0%

All information was collected from the automated client index, Social Services' client registry. This system began in the early 1980s, but data from early periods are considered less reliable than more recent data. Two problems particularly affect this study; the coding of constitutional status (or ethnicity) and the registration of clients who were in care for less than a month. Codes distinguishing status Indians, non-status Indians and Métis people were not consistently used in the system's early years; thus, there are many missing values for the child's constitutional status. Status plays an important part in the analysis; these missing observations have been dropped. In 1986, approximately 23% of the children could not be identified by status, but only 10% were unidentifiable in 1990. A second problem with the information system is that children who were in foster care for only a few days or weeks were not always registered on the system. As a result, this study reports on children who have been in care for at least one month.

References are made to spells of foster care and the number of homes in which a child has lived. A spell was defined as one or more consecutive months in care, followed by at least one month not in care. If, for example, a child enters a foster home for a month, returns home for 10 days, and then re-enters foster care for 3 months, this is considered as one spell of 4 months' duration. If the period at home exceeded 30 days, this would have been treated as two separate spells. Within any given spell a child may move from one foster home to another. This study also measures the number of separate foster homes in which a child has lived.

Table 19.2: Average Number of Months Spent in Foster Homes

	Native	Non-Native
Sex:		
male	11.4	13.7
female	10.7	13.3
Agegroup		
0–5 years	11.7	11.8
6–11 years	12.1	21.1
12–15 years	8.1	13.0
16+ years	8.1	10.1
Wardship:		
permanent	29.9	32.9
not permanent	7.6	11.0
Placement:		
same background	9.7	13.2
dif. background	11.2	13.8
All children:		
mean value	11.1	13.5
median value	4.0	7.0

Who are the Children

The 1988 Longitudinal Sample

This sample selects children who first entered foster care during 1988 and follows them on the client index for 48 months, measuring the duration and frequency with which they entered and left foster care. Social and demographic characteristics of the sample are shown in Table 19.1.Native children are much younger (averaging 6 years) as compared to non-Native children (averaging 10 years) at the time they enter. The overall distribution of ages for children is bi-modal, with 45% of children entering foster care between the ages of 0 and 5 years, and 33% entering at age 12 or older.Native children comprise 82% of the younger group while non-Native children comprise 61% of the older group. Unfortunately the data do not provide explanations for the reasons children enter foster care. Discussions with child care workers, however, suggest that the two groups enter foster care for different reasons. The younger children are most likely to enter care because of neglect, abuse or lack of appropriate supervision—all reasons which are attributed to poor parenting. The older children are more likely to enter foster care because of acting-out behaviour, parent-child conflict, and the parents' complaint that the child is out-of-control. Native children are usually placed with families of a different ethnic or status

Table 19.3: Percent of Native and Non-Native Children with Multiple Spells in Foster Care

	Native	Non-Native
Sex:		
male	37.2	25.6
female	36.2	27.6
Agegroup		
0–5 years	43.9	25.4
6–11 years	28.6	22.2
12–15 years	28.4	35.0
16+ years	21.4	8.3
Wardship:		
permanent	42.1	25.9
not permanent	35.6	26.6
Months in foster care:		
3 or less months	13.8	8.1
4—6 months	50.0	34.1
7—12 months	64.7	31.3
13—24 months	74.1	44.4
25 or more months	37.8	25.5
Placement:	17.2	25.9
same background	17.2	25.9
dif. background	37.9	27.3
All children	36.6	26.5

background. Ninety percent of Native children were placed in families with different backgrounds to their own. Younger children particularly tend to be placed out of their own background. The average age of children placed in a family of a different background was 7 years, compared to 10 years for those who were placed with foster families of the same background.

Table 19.2 presents information on the average time in care. The distribution of time in foster care is highly skewed. Many children were in care for very short periods and relatively few were in care for lengthy periods of time. The median time in foster care was 5 months and the mean was 12 months. Length of stays for non-Native children were longer than for Native children (median time for non-natives was 7 months compared to 4 months for Native children). One-quarter of Native children were in care for less than 2 months, and 75% were in care for less than 12 months. For non-Native children, 75% were in

Table 19.4: Average Number of Different Foster Homes for Native and Non-Native Children in the Longitudinal Sample

	Native	Non-Native
Sex:		
male	2.2	2.4
female	2.3	2.4
Agegroup		
0–5 years	2.3	1.8
6–11 years	2.6	2.7
12–15 years	1.9	2.8
16+ years	1.6	1.9
Wardship:		
permanent	3.9	3.6
not permanent	2.0	2.3
Months in foster care:		
3 or less months	1.4	1.2
4—6 months	2.1	1.9
7—12 months	2.7	2.3
13—24 months	3.8	3.2
25 or more months	3.7	3.9
Placement:		
same background	1.5	2.5
dif. background	2.3	2.2
All children	2.3	2.4

care for 18 months or less. There were no significant gender differences for Native or non-Native children in the time they spent in care.

Seventy-one percent of children who entered care did so only once during the 4 years. Table 19.3 shows the number of children with multiple spells in foster care over the 4 years. Thirty-seven percent of Native children had multiple spells in care compared to 26% of non-Native children. Natives who are younger, are permanent wards, or are placed out of their own background are more likely to have multiple spells in foster homes. No child in the sample had more than four 4 spells in care.

Table 19.4 shows that these children normally experience more than one foster home during their stay in care. Fifty-six percent of both Native and non-Native children have been in two or more different homes. Children with multiple spells (younger children, permanent wards, and those placed out of their background) also had been placed in the most foster homes. It is unusual

Table 19.5: Characteristics of Native and Non-Native Foster Children in Foster Care During March 1986 and March 1990

	Native		Non-Native	
	1986 (n=510)	1990 (n=639)	1986 (n=207)	1990 (n=357)
Sex:				
male	56.5%	54.6%	53.1%	49.9%
female	43.5%	45.4%	46.9%	50.1%
Age at start of foster care:				
0–5 years	58.0%	56.5%	34.3%	30.0%
6–11 years	26.9%	30.4%	27.5%	29.4%
12–15 years	12.9%	11.1%	30.9%	34.2%
16+ years	2.2%	2.0%	7.2%	6.4%
Wardship:				
permanent	72.9%	55.2%	61.4%	43.1%
not permanent	27.1%	44.8%	38.6%	56.9%
Age at March (yrs)	10.4	9.5	13.1	11.7

to be placed in many different homes; only 10% had been in more than four foster homes.

Children in 1986 And 1990

Demographic characteristics of Native and non-Native children in foster homes during 1986 and 1990 are shown in Table 19.5. Children of Native ancestry comprise just over half of the children in foster care in each sample. Sixty-six percent of Native children are status Indians, 24% are non-status Indians and the 10% are Métis. Between 1986 and 1990, children entered foster care at younger ages. During this period, the average age at entry of all children dropped by approximately one year. Native children tend to be younger at entry into foster care than non-Native children. The average age at entry for Native children dropped from 10.5 to 9.5 years, and for non-Natives from 13 to 12 years of age. This trend is counter to the overall demographic situation where the average youth age is increasing rather than decreasing. The proportion of males and females is roughly equal and shows little change from 1986 to 1990. The sex distribution of Native children in foster care does not differ significantly from that of non-native children. Native children are more likely to be permanent wards. The percentage of children who are permanent wards dropped from 1986 to 1990 but there is still a significant difference between Native and non-Native children. In 1990 for example, 55% of the Native children were permanent wards, compared to 43% of non-Native children.

Table 19.6: Average and Median Months Spent in Foster Homes From Beginning of Spell Until March 1986 or March 1990

	Native				Non-Native			
	1986		1990		1986		1990	
	mean	median	mean	median	mean	median	mean	median
Sex:								
male	26.2	11.0	25.9	12.0	23.3	11.0	20.7	8.0
female	20.0	11.0	21.7	11.0	27.4	13.0	17.8	5.0
Age at start of foster care:								
0–5 yrs	29.6	12.0	28.2	12.0	33.6	13.0	30.9	9.0
6–11 yrs	18.0	11.0	21.1	12.0	31.6	20.0	18.2	8.0
12–15 yrs	9.3	8.0	12.8	6.0	13.9	9.0	12.2	5.0
16+ yrs	12.9	11.0	10.6	7.0	9.9	8.0	6.9	1.0
Wardship:								
permanent	28.1	12.0	35.0	23.0	33.6	19.0	33.0	18.5
not perm.	11.0	9.0	10.3	5.0	12.0	8.0	8.8	4.0
All children	23.5	11.0	24.0	11.0	25.2	12.0	19.3	7.0

At the two sampling periods, children had already been in foster care for nearly 2 years (see Table 19.6). The distribution of time in care has a positive skew and consequently median values may give a more realistic measure of average time in care. In 1986 the median time already spent in foster care was 11 months, and in 1990 it was 12 months. In 1986, both Native and non-Native children had been in care for similar periods. By 1990, however, Native children were likely to have been in care for a longer time than non-Native children (11 months as compared to 7 months median). The overall reduction in the time children have spent in foster care has not equally affected Native and non-Native children. Non-Native children in 1990 had been in care for a shorter period than in 1986 (12 months in 1990 as compared to 7 months in 1986). But there has been no significant difference in the time Native children have spent in foster care. Only non-Native children were being affected by any impact that legislation and changes in social work practice may be having on overall lengths of stay.

Table 19.7 shows differences between 1986 and 1990 in the number of different foster homes in which children have been placed. The average number of homes has risen, from 2.3 to 2.6, indicating increased movement within the foster system. Average values mask the variability in children's experiences. Fifty percent of children in the 1986 sample had been in at most two different homes, and 10% had been in five or more homes since the start of their spell. In 1990, while the median value was still two homes, 10% of the children had been in seven or more different foster homes. In both samples there were instances where children had been placed in up to 16 different

Table 19.7: Average Number of Homes for Foster Children During Spell

	Native		Non-Native	
	1986	1990	1986	1990
Sex:				
male	2.4	2.5	2.1	2.4
female	2.5	2.8	2.2	2.7
Age at start of foster care spell				
0–5 yrs	2.5	2.7	2.3	2.5
6–11 yrs	2.5	2.7	2.5	2.3
12–15 yrs	2.4	2.1	2.0	2.8
16+ yrs	1.5	1.7	1.2	2.1
Months spent in care				
0–6 months	2.1	2.8	2.0	2.7
7–12 months	2.1	2.4	1.7	2.5
13–24 months	1.5	1.9	1.8	2.2
25–48 months	1.4	1.8	1.6	2.1
49 or more	1.4	1.6	1.3	1.3
Wardship:				
permanent	2.7	3.0	2.5	2.9
not permanent	1.9	2.2	1.7	2.3
All children	2.4	2.6	2.2	2.5

homes since the beginning of their current spell in foster care. Native children have been through more foster homes than non-Native children. Females are more likely to go through multiple foster homes than are males. Those who have been placed in the most foster homes during their spell in care are permanent wards or children who entered care at an early age. There is an inverse relationship between the time spent in care and the number of foster homes. Children who have been in care the shortest times have been placed in the largest number of homes. This may reflect the period in which the child was placed. If multiple placements have become more common over time, then those children who have come into care most recently will be more likely to experience several different foster homes.

Discussion

At first glance the cross-sectional and longitudinal samples seem to give contradictory results. The cross-sectional samples show that Native children generally have longer stays in care and move more frequently, whereas the longitudinal sample shows that Native children are in foster care for a shorter total time. The two types of samples capture different types of children. The

Figure 19.1a: Months in Foster Care - March 1986

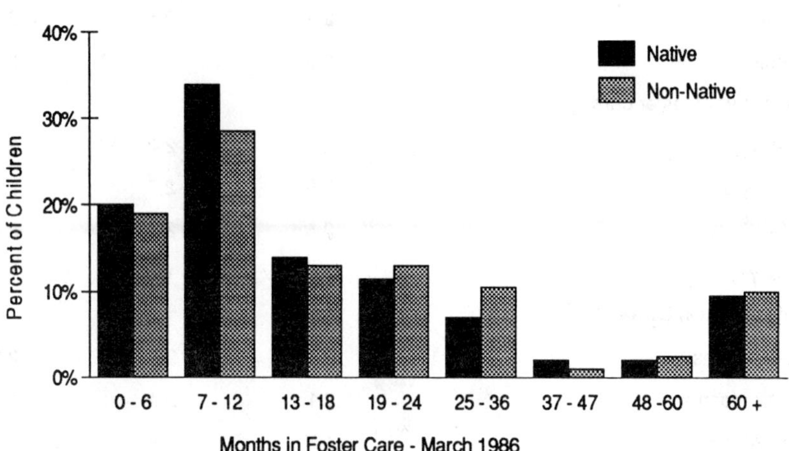

cross-section is over-represented by long term foster children, those who enter and stay on the caseload. They may be a small proportion of those who ever enter foster care but are the majority of those collected through a cross-sectional method. Magura (1979) has suggested that cross-sectional studies which show higher lengths of stay for minority children are really measuring the accumulation of children who have been unable to leave the system. Length of time in care may be mediated by the skills and resources of the family (income, drug and alcohol use, parenting skills, social supports). Native families may have more problems and less ability to overcome the barriers that would result in an early return of the child.

All three samples showed significant age differences between Native and non-Native children. Neglect may be part of the explanation as to why Native children experience foster care at an earlier age than other children. Neglect is generally considered more serious when it involves younger children who have few defensive skills. Older children are better able to fend for themselves when parental supervision is lacking. Many older Native children in care may not be in foster homes but caught in the young offenders system. Young offenders facilities may serve as an out-of-home placement for those who have already gone through foster homes. If young offender facilities disproportionately hold Native youth, then this may partly account for why there are relatively few older Native children entering foster care.

Between 1986 and 1990 there was an overall decrease in the time that children spent in foster homes. One cause may have been the result of changing social work practice, reflected in new provincial child welfare legislation. But changes in practice affected non-Native children more than Native children.

Figure 19.1b: Months in Foster Care - March 1990

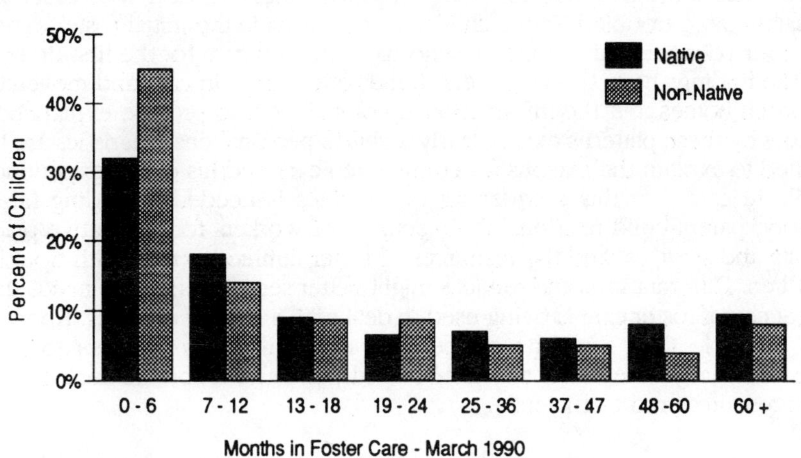

Non-Native children were in care 6 months less than they had been in 1986, whereas there was no difference in the time Native children had been in care. The social and demographic data used in the study can not provide an explanation for this difference. A possible explanation is that the nature of support services (such as parent aides), developed during this period, were not attuned to the needs of Native families and did not serve their purposes well. It may also be that less effort was put into resolving the problems in Native families.

Several research and policy questions arise from the study. An important question concerns how children are channelled into foster care; that is, how is eligibility into care determined and what makes Native children more eligible than non-Native children? To what extent is the child welfare system observing real differences in the risk of abuse or neglect, and to what extent is it measuring cultural differences in the upbringing of children? A related question concerns why the age at which children first enter foster care has decreased. Have economic and social conditions in families become so desperate that children are at serious risk, at ever earlier ages? Have social workers' workloads become so difficult to manage that placement is now used as a first response to dealing with problems? Similarly there may be a variety of explanations for why there is less stability and children are moved more while in foster care. Explanations may have to do with the nature of the home life, the characteristics of the child, the worker's training, or the worker's ability to manage the caseload.

A last issue concerns placing Native children in foster homes with similar or different backgrounds to their own. It is commonly considered preferable to place Native children in homes with a similar background. Native foster families are such a scarce resource that a question arises as to how they should be rationed. Older Native children are more likely to be placed in Native foster homes. Children placed out-of-background, however, are more likely to be in care longer, experience more spells, and be placed in more foster homes. This needs to be looked at more carefully, with deliberate policy decisions made as to what is the best role for Native foster families—to deal with older and possibly more troubled Native children, or to provide the initial foster experience for younger Native children who have entered care for the first time?

The findings have shown general trends of duration in care and movement between homes, but the information is not sufficient to provide explanations as to why these patterns exist. Clearly a child's personal characteristics are too limited to explain the reasons for coming into care and his or her experiences while in care. For this a wider set of variables is needed, including family history, parent-child relations, the resources of workers for alternative placements and services, and the resources of foster families to deal with troubled children. Different in-home services might better serve the family's needs than foster care if foster care is being used to deal with a short-term crisis. Knowing the probable time a child will spend in care will allow workers to more effectively target the family and child's needs, and also ration the department's own resources more efficiently.

Jill Holroyd provided valuable research assistance in helping to prepare and analyze the data used in this project.

References

Benedict, M., & White, R. (1991). Factors associated with foster care length of stay. *Child Welfare, 70*(1), 45–58.

Benedict, M., White, R. B., & Stallings, R. (1987). Race and length of stay in foster care. *Social Work Research and Abstracts, 23*(4), 23–26.

Lawder, E., Poulin, J. & Andrews, R. (1986). A study of 185 foster children 5 years after placement. *Child Welfare, 65*(3), 241–251.

Magura, S. (1979). Trend analysis in foster care. *Social Work Research and Abstracts, 15*(2), 29–36.

McMurtry, S., & Lie, G. Y. (1992). Differential exit rates of minority children in foster care. *Social Work Research and Abstracts, 21*(3), 42–48.

Milner, J. (1987). An ecological perspective on duration of foster care. *Child Welfare, 66*(2), 113–123.

Murphy, H. (1968). Predicting duration of foster care. *Child Welfare, 47*(2), 76–84.

Saskatchewan Department of Social Services. (1986). *Foster Care Review*, Regina: Author.

Seaburg, J., & Tolley, E. (1986). Predictors of the length of stay in foster care. *Social Work Research and Abstracts, 22*(3) 11–17.

Trocmé, N. (1991). Child welfare services. In R. Barnhorst & C. Johnson (Eds.), *The State of the Child in Ontario* (pp. 63–91). Toronto: Oxford University Press.

20

Foster Care Programming: Themes, Policy Implications and Research Agenda

Karen Swift and Lyle Longclaws

The vital importance of stable, continuous and caring bonds between children and their primary caregivers has been recognized. Not only a child's bonds with her or his family of origin, but with the extended family, community, and culture are crucial in promoting a child's sense of identity and well being. These aspects of care have been dramatized by reports of many Native children placed in care outside their culture, often far away from their families of origin and often permanently (Johnston, 1982; Hepworth, 1980). These understandings, grounded in both science and experience, have led to changes in child welfare service directions and priorities, at least in theory. The changes imply some accountability of the state for the quality of alternate care children receive. The trend in North American child welfare has been toward choosing the least restrictive intervention, and the focus has been on maintaining children in their own homes, families, and communities whenever possible, even when serious problems of care exist. A wide range of programs under the general rubric of "family preservation" have been developed to provide support and preventive services to children and their families in order to prevent placement of children in care.

Various efforts aimed at maintaining a child's attachments and/or creating new attachments to parenting figures are generally endorsed when placement cannot be avoided. These include attempts to reduce the number of placements and/or shorten the length of time the child is placed away from home; planning for placement within the child's extended family, community and/or culture; encouraging provision of stable and continuous foster care placement; continued involvement of birth parents with the child while in care; and an effort to provide treatment for some children in care. Recent research in foster care focuses on various aspects of these general directions, questioning (1) the extent to which these directions are actually operative in child welfare service delivery; and (2), the effectiveness of these approaches in sustaining or producing healthy identity development in children who come into care. The four papers included in this section examine one or both of these questions.

Themes

In the past, both foster care drift and revolving-door foster care were frequently standard features of placement. Understandings of attachment, beginning with the work of Bowlby (1969), and extended by clinicians such as Steinauer (1980), have demonstrated the destructiveness of discontinuity of care. Discontinuity may occur through many placements in different foster homes, through long stay in care away from birth parents, and through many brief placements. The least restrictive policy is usually interpreted to mean prevention of placement, if possible, or reducing time in care to facilitate maintenance of the child's bonds with the original caregivers. A corollary is the provision of stable and continuous care while in placement in order to enhance the child's ability to develop and maintain trust in relationships.

David Rosenbluth's (1995) study provides a way of checking to determine whether more stable and shorter placements have resulted from these understandings and policies in a specific jurisdiction. The methodology, which combines a longitudinal examination of the histories of children in care with a cross-sectional examination of children in care at a given time, demonstrates the richness of data and understanding available through a dual approach. For many—especially Native—children, the least restrictive approach has not produced much change in service delivery patterns in the jurisdiction studied. At a time when legislation emphasizing prevention and family preservation had come into effect, average spells in care were shown to have decreased somewhat, but only for non-Native children. But the children surveyed actually experienced an increase in the number of foster home placements, from an average of 2 in 1986 to 3 in 1990. The treatment of Native children remained significantly different from non-Natives. They were found to be over-represented in the care population, to come into care at a much younger age than others, to stay longer, and to be frequently placed outside their own culture.

A second trend in foster care provision is to provide a range of out-of-home services to meet the variety of needs presented by children and their families. Ironically, the need for this approach may have been exacerbated by the least intrusive approach. Efforts to keep children at home longer may mean that they are more troubled and difficult when they do come into care. One approach taken in cases where children are experiencing serious behaviour or emotional problems is known as specialist or treatment foster care. The objectives of programs taking this approach generally involve eventual family reunification, or at least enhancement of the possibility for future placement in non-institutional settings. Richard Nutter and his colleagues (1995) point out that treatment foster care generally includes four elements: (a) it serves children who likely would be placed otherwise in relatively restrictive treatment settings, (b) it makes use of screened and trained foster care providers, (c) it involves individual treatment planning, and (d) it promotes a program philosophy involving strong community linkages. In practice, programs vary substantially, and there is an on-going debate concerning whether more restrictive program standards will increase the quality and effectiveness of treatment foster care. Nutter and colleagues (1995) examine caseloads, training, support, parental participation, costs, client characteristics, and outcomes. Their findings suggest that some of our common sense understandings and beliefs about care, for instance that restrictive standards produce both a higher level of care as well as higher costs, do not necessarily hold up. In fact, it appears that these assumptions have led researchers to the study of relatively less important variables in an effort to evaluate this type of programming. The conclusions of these authors point the way to a research agenda involving what they argue are more important variables, especially those related to the child and the child's experiences before, during, and after care.

In the past, foster care—the provision of an alternate home for children—was seen as a sufficient response for children whose biological parents were unable to care for them. Foster caregivers were viewed as substitute parents, and their task was to provide a warm and nurturing environment for children in their care. Various problems with this approach have been identified. Foster caregivers were not always able to assist children with special emotional needs. White families, however loving, could not necessarily provide non-white children with an appropriate sense of their racial and cultural heritage. A longstanding issue in foster care involves roles and relationships among two sets of caregivers, the birth parents and the foster parents. When foster caregivers are viewed as substitute parents, the role of birth parents often becomes ambiguous and difficult, producing an exclusionary kind of service of which birth parents are not a natural part. An advantage of treatment foster care is that it tends to be more inclusive, with the role of foster caregivers clarified and focused in a more professional direction. This development allows more space for the encouragement of an ongoing relationship between birth parents and their children in care. The survey of treatment foster homes as reported by Gord Richardson *et al.* (1995) examined program policies and experiences in relation to birth parent participation in specialized foster placements. Although most of these programs have policies to encourage such participation, researchers found a gap between policy and practice. Children whose parents remained involved in fact tended to be in care for shorter periods of time, to be discharged home more often, and to have treatment goals met. On the other hand, lower or no participation was associated with discharge to other placements, with lack of progress toward treatment goals, and with placement breakdown. Thus the study supports the view that maintaining contact with birth parents facilitates children's return home and helps to improve their treatment outcomes. The paper also identifies characteristics of parents at risk of not becoming involved, and it makes clear that participation is not only associated with favourable outcomes for children but is not associated with negative outcomes.

Barbara Thomlison's exploratory study of treatment foster care in Alberta further examines child, family and program elements associated with eventual family reunification. Her finding that nearly three-quarters of the children in the study were discharged to family as opposed to institutional settings, although not necessarily generalizable, suggests that the programs have positive effects for children, and are a promising direction for many. All of the children included in the study were considered too difficult for family placement prior to the treatment program; thus, it is significant that one third of them returned home. Twenty-three percent of the post placement variance was explained by one variable, that the child was "considered for return home." This finding suggests that developing a plan for return home, or even making explicit the possibility of return, facilitates this outcome. While the study emphasizes the usefulness of treatment foster care as a model which facilitates family reunification, it should also be noted that most of the children and foster parents in Thomlison's sample were white. This suggests a need for examination of barriers to the inclusion of other ethnic and racial groups in treatment foster care programming, especially given the over-representation of Native and Black children (Hutchinson et al., 1991) in the foster care system.

Policy Implications

Alternate care policies in recent years represent some positive directions. The family preservation direction honours and promotes the child's right to a sense of belonging and connectedness. Knowledge about conditions needed to encourage healthy identity development has produced policies aimed at enhancing continuity and attachments for children. In light of these new directions, practices of shuffling children around in care and of cutting all ties with family, community and culture appear brutal and insensitive. However, the studies in this section also make clear that present policies are not sufficiently comprehensive to improve the chances for many children, nor are they necessarily enforced. Rosenbluth's study demonstrates that practices known to be deleterious to children continue unchecked, especially for Native children. While the findings cannot be generalized across Canada, given jurisdictional differences, this study makes clear the need for regular review to determine whether policy initiatives in fact lead to service changes. The mere passage of new legislation and policy directives does not necessarily alter longstanding patterns of service provision. Nutter and colleagues, Thomlison, and Richardson *et al* describe programs representing new and positive directions developed to provide a healthier alternative for children in care. Yet this sector remains a small, somewhat fragmented, and understudied piece of the overall system of alternative care; many of the children most in need may be denied specialized forms of care.

Policy principles suggested by the research in this section include:

- The deleterious effects on children of discontinuity of care means the state must take more responsibility to ensure continuity of care and must become more accountable for ensuring that current knowledge and policy directives are actually incorporated into practice and service delivery.
- The realization that care and warmth are not a sufficient response for emotionally troubled children points policy makers in the direction of flexibility and diversification of programming efforts to provide specific kinds of help for particular children.
- A more inclusive form of care, inviting and involving birth parents as partners with foster caregivers and child welfare personnel, is a positive policy direction.

Resource Implications

Foster care has provided an extremely low-cost alternate care option. Historically, most of this labour has been carried out by women at rock bottom levels of remuneration, justified by the view that the desire to love and nurture children rather than the desire to be well paid provided the proper motivation to ensure good care. This view has lately come into question. Currently, foster parent groups are advocating not only for better pay but for increased recognition of the skills required for proper caregiving. Training is increasingly being recognized as an important component of good care. Certainly, the treatment programs described in this section rely on better training and remuneration for caregivers than historically has been the case.

The resources required to provide the kinds of care now recognized as necessary are going to increase. Policymakers can expect some new issues to surface in light of this development. One concern is that family preservation will be implemented, not in a manner best suited for children, but as a cost saving option. Another important issue is whether scarce treatment foster care resources will be routed to mainstream children, while Native and other minority children will continue to be subjected to unplanned and discontinuous care. Thomlison's study signals attention to this potential threat.

Implementation Issues

A number of implementation issues can be identified. One is the almost exclusive focus in most legislation and policy on the private family as the sole party held responsible and accountable for the care of children. Once children come into care, accountability for positive outcomes become diffuse and unclear. Child welfare policy and legislation needs to be set in a much broader context, one which identifies care for children as a social responsibility and which further shows how the state and its representatives are to be held accountable for experiences and outcomes of children taken into care. Two of the studies show the importance of written policy and plans in encouraging specific outcomes, a practice that also encourages more accountability by program personnel. Second, policymakers must address the resource issue immediately, because scarcity of resources is likely the most serious potential barrier to the provision of adequate care for children. A third issue involves jurisdictional differences, especially with respect to research and data gathering. A variety of programs are being developed and implemented in Canada, but information and evaluation are difficult to access and use across jurisdictional lines. Finally, diversification of efforts, based on sound research and evaluation efforts, should be a keynote of future policy regarding foster care programming. The era in which a good family could be considered all that a child needs is over. Much more is required to serve children whose connections with birth parents are damaged or severed. A range of programs serving the diverse emotional, cultural, and developmental needs of children in care must be developed.

Research Agenda

Canadian child welfare research has been a poorly coordinated affair, frequently restricted to local program evaluations which are neither theoretically grounded nor widely disseminated. Jurisdictional differences in data gathering categories and practices have exacerbated this problem. An agenda for future research on foster care programming should strive to overcome these serious shortcomings. The directions indicated by research in this section are not comprehensive but rather suggestive of a broad research agenda. Such an agenda would necessarily involve not only a series of questions but specifications of methodology and participants.

Culture remains poorly understood as a concept, and its importance to minority groups is often underrated by members of the dominant culture. There is a need for involvement in research by members of minority groups, and particularly Native people, whose children have been shown time and again to be over-represented in the care system. Rosenbluth's study underlines again that Native children continue to be placed outside of their own culture. A research agenda must include efforts to understand why this practice continues and how culturally appropriate resources might be developed. Action research projects, involving community members in the development and evaluation of culturally appropriate care resources could play a major role in child welfare research.

Knowledge about human development has not necessarily translated into changed practice. Outcomes of specialized and treatment foster care are understudied, and little is known about the experiences of children either in placement or following discharge. There continue to be special issues for Native children, involving reasons why they come into care, their experiences in care, and outcomes for them.

The findings of these four studies also make clear that the capacity to research a diverse range of needs and to evaluate a variety of different kinds of programs is required. Such an approach could work in conjunction with policy approaches, for instance through the development and evaluation of a variety of demonstration projects designed to serve the needs of different populations of children in care. A range of important research questions emerge from current research:

- Most effective types of alternate care for specific children
- Relationship of resources to quality of caregiving
- Variables of caregiving related to outcomes for children
- Effects of placement within vs. outside extended family, community, and culture
- Identification of barriers to stable and continuous placement
- Identification of barriers to non-white children and families participating in some of the more effective programs
- Characteristics of biological families which facilitate or act as barriers to reunification
- Effects of various kinds of interaction between foster caregivers and birth parents.

Research about foster care is of importance for families and children; the following recommendations are made to guide research for Canadian foster care programming:

- A Centre of Excellence should be developed at the federal level to both encourage and disseminate excellence in foster care research. Such a centre could encourage research grounded in sound theory to produce useful knowledge for a wide audience. Such a centre could also facilitate dissemination of local research and evaluation efforts across the country so that programs found to work for particular children could be more widely developed.
- Native children should be the first priority of any research agenda. Native children are over-represented and poorly served in foster care. Research is needed that will lead to the development of culturally appropriate, stable options which enhance children's identity development and sense of belonging. A research agenda should also place other minority groups at the top of its list of priorities.
- Diversification in research approaches, methodology, participation, and questions should be a central tenet of any research agenda. A focus on cost effectiveness is insufficient. Qualitative as well as quantitative methods should be used to ensure that experiential data is captured. Members of minority groups, especially Native people, need to be included as active members of research teams and must have input into the development of

research to ensure relevancy of research questions and directions to the children involved.

References

Bowlby, J. (1969). *Attachment and loss* (Vol. 1 and 2). New York: Basic Books, Inc.

Hepworth, P. (1980). *Foster care and adoption in Canada*. Ottawa: Canadian Council on Social Development

Hutchinson, Y., Nichols, B., Paré, N., & Pépin, M. (April, 1992). Profile of clients in the Anglophone Youth Network: Examining the situation of the black child. Montréal: Ville Marie Social Service Centre and McGill University School of Social Work.

Johnston, P. (1983).*Native children and the child welfare system*. Toronto: Canadian Council on Social Development in association with James Lorimer & Co. Publishers.

Nutter, R., Hudson, J., Galaway, B., & Hill, M. (1995). Specialist foster family care program standards in relation to costs, client characteristics, and outcomes. In J. Hudson & B. Galaway (Eds.), *Child welfare in Canada: Research and policy implications*. Toronto: Thompson Educational Publishing.

Richardson, G., Galaway, B., Hudson, J., & Hill, M. (1995). Birth parent participation in treatment foster care programs in North America and the United Kingdom. In J. Hudson & B. Galaway (Eds.), *Canadian child welfare: Research and policy implications*. Toronto: Thompson Educational Publishing.

Rosenbluth, D. (1995). Foster care in Saskatchewan: Draft or revolving door? In J. Hudson & B. Galaway (Eds.), *Child welfare in Canada: Research and policy implications*. Toronto: Thompson Educational Publishing.

Steinhauer, P. D. (1980). How to succeed in the business of creating psychopaths without even trying. *Training resources in understanding supporting and treating abused children* (Vol. 2 and 4). Toronto: Ministry of Community and Social Services, Children's Services Division: 239–328.

Thomlison, B. (1995). Treatment foster care and family reunification: Factors associated with children likely to experience family placement after treatment foster care services. In J. Hudson & B. Galaway (Eds.), *Child welfare in Canada: Research and policy implications*. Toronto: Thompson Educational Publishing.

4

ADOPTIONS PROGRAMMING

21

Adoption and Mental Health: Studies of Adolescents and Adults

Christopher Bagley

Adoption—the permanent removal of a child from biological parents to new parents, who regard the child legally, socially and psychologically as their own child—is a relatively recent institution. However, custom or traditional adoption in which a couple adopt a child (usually the male child of a relative to carry on the family name, or business) is an ancient practice. The child knows who his or her biological parents are in the traditional form of adoption, and he or she may meet them frequently. In the modern form of adoption the child will usually have no contact at all with biological parents, and neither the child nor his or her adoptive parents will know of the status or whereabouts of the biological parents (Kirk, 1981). This knowledge is usually retained in the sealed records of adoption agencies.

The Psychology of Adoption

The element of complete separation from biological parents at an early age has interested psychologists investigating how the relative roles of heredity and environment influence characteristics such as personality disorder, intellectual achievement, and psychiatric illness. Adoption provides a naturalistic experiment for behavioural scientists, who are able to interview and test the biological parents (either at the time of adoption, or later on), as well as studying the adopting parents (Cadoret, 1990). Data from adoption cohorts have now replaced findings from twin studies as the major source of evidence of genetic factors in the development of intelligence, personality, and adaptation (Locurto, 1990). Several major cohort studies have provided a wealth of publications, and have enriched psychological knowledge on the effects of environment upon human development. In the United States, longitudinal studies of cohorts of adoptees for whom comprehensive information was available on both biological and adoptive parents have been able to estimate the relative contributions of genes, environment, and their interactions in predicting I.Q. scores (Munsinger, 1975; Scarr & Weinberg, 1976; De Vries et al., 1981; Horn, 1983; Berbaum & Moreland, 1985; Labuda et al., 1986; Rice, 1986). These studies show that the relative contributions of genetics and environment on intellectual functioning remain generally stable throughout most of childhood. However, the relative contribution of genetic factors declines in the long run. The best prediction from genetic factors seems to be in the area of verbal intelligence (Cardon et al., 1990). These studies, together with a large cohort study of Danish adoptees (Teasdale & Owen, 1986), indicate that the I.Q.s of adopted children will fall about half way between what would be predicted from the social class of the biological parents (usually, lower blue collar) and the social class of the adoptive parents (usually, white collar). Support for this finding also comes from a study of academic achievements of the 120 adopted children in the British National Child Development Study (NCDS) of some 12,000 children born in one week in 1958 (Bagley, 1993a).

The various follow-up studies of adoption show that a significant amount of the variance in the development of mental illness, alcoholism, criminal behaviour, and personality disorder is attributable to genetic factors (Cadoret, 1990; Bagley, 1993a). The biological parents and relatives of the adopted child have, on average, a higher incidence of mental illnesses and personality disorders of various kinds. These instabilities often contributed to family breakdown or single parenthood which led to infants being available for adoption. The environmental effects of stable family life provided by adoptive homes can greatly diminish the possibility that the child will develop problem behaviours and mental pathology later in life. Nevertheless, adoptees seem to be at somewhat greater risk than the general population for the emergence of these conditions (Cadoret et al., 1976; Cadoret & Gath, 1977; Goodwin et al., 1977; Bohman et al., 1982; Mednick et al., 1984; Parker, 1982).

These issues are put in perspective in Bohman's (1981) Swedish study of 624 unwanted children: one third were adopted, a third grew up in institutions, while the remainder stayed in their families of origin. Those who stayed with a biological parent, in comparison with the adopted children, had profoundly disadvantaged outcomes 23 years later. The likelihood of an individual developing schizophrenia by the age of 23 in the general population comparison group was about 0.5 percent; in adopted children with a biological parent with schizophrenia the risk was about 2 percent, four times the rate expected in an unselected population. In a non-adopted child, who grew up with a schizophrenic parent, the incidence of schizophrenia by age 23 was nearly 10 percent. Thus, although adopted children carrying schizophrenic genes have a greater likelihood of developing schizophrenia, the environment of the adoptive family has in many cases provided a powerful protective factor preventing the emergence of this disease.

Several interacting factors contribute to success or failure of psychological outcomes for adopted children. These factors are usefully gathered together in a model of adjustment in adoption presented in Brodzinsky's (1990) "stress and coping" model. A slightly different model, presented by Bagley (1993a), includes the negative elements of negative heredity; low birth weight and other perinatal problems including a higher incidence of minor birth defects; separation from birth mother; role handicaps of adoptive parents as outlined by Kirk's (1964) account of mental health and adoption; identity problems of adopted adolescents identified by some psychoanalytic writers (Brinich, 1990; Sorosky et al., 1984); and problems of ethnic identity, when adoptive parents belong to a different ethnic group than the children they adopt (Bagley & Young, 1981). However, available research indicates that these negative factors are balanced or outweighed by a number of powerful environmental factors: adoptive parents are carefully screened by social service agencies in terms of good mental health and stability of marriage; adoptive parents provide stability, warmth and love in their parenting styles; they seek the best quality education for their children; and they actively seek high quality medical and supportive services for any problems their adopted child may develop.

The benchmark figure for outcome of ordinary parenting is the 80:10:10 ratio: eighty percent of children will emerge from childhood and adolescence with good mental health and coping skills; ten percent will have some problems, which can be overcome with support or therapy of various kinds; while ten percent will have marked and often enduring problems of adjustment (such as mental illness, criminal behaviour, personality disorder, and alcohol and other addictions). A review of the many outcome studies of adoption (Bagley, 1993a) found that the outcomes of children adopted as infants generally conform to the 80:10:10 ratios observed in the general population; outcomes for children in various risk categories who were not adopted are generally very much worse.

The adjustment of children following adoption across international boundaries provides an interesting case study of human development under changing and potentially adverse social circumstances. The majority of children adopted internationally are adopted by prosperous parents in Europe and North America, and come from Asia and Central and South America. Often such children have undergone early trauma, including abandonment and malnutrition, and are of different ethnic appearance from their adoptive parents. The largest number of children from any one country have come from South Korea, following American involvement in the civil war in that country in the later 1940s and early 1950s. Groups of Korean children adopted in the west have been extensively followed and tested, and the studies are generally in agreement in pointing to an apparently surprising outcome. Following adoption, Korean children have extremely good patterns of adjustment and scholastic achievement, despite early hazards and the need for considerable adjustments in children adopted past infancy (Silverman & Feigelman, 1990; Altstein & Simon, 1991). Bagley (1993a) reviewed the available literature and presented case studies of children adopted in Britain from Hong Kong and Vietnam; he reached a similar conclusion. Vietnamese children were placed for adoption with English parents in 1976 (following the fall of Saigon); many had histories of malnourishment, injury, abandonment in the field of battle, and had lived for months or years in poor quality institutions. Two years after placement, the 22 Vietnamese children had in all but three cases adjusted well, had learned English rapidly, did well in school, and had adjusted favourably in their families and communities. A further follow-up ten years later confirmed this favourable picture; about three-quarters of the Vietnamese adoptees showed good mental health, adjustment, and good scholastic success.

One study in particular illustrates the power of environment to overcome profound, early neglect. Winnick et al. (1975) studied 138 children born in Korea and adopted in the United States at an average age of 18 months. The sample was stratified to include three groups: 41 children who were severely malnourished in the first year of life; 40 children who were moderately malnourished; and 47 children without any history of early malnutrition. The children were all female, full-term, without any apparent handicap at birth. Ten years after placement the well-nourished girls had a mean I.Q. of 112; the moderately-nourished an I.Q. of 106; and the malnourished an I.Q. of 102. Neither schools nor adoptive parents had information on the previous history of malnourishment. The malnourished children had mean heights similar to children in Korea; but those from the other two groups were significantly taller than predicted by the Korean norms. This study suggests that an enriched environment can largely overcome early deprivations. Similar findings have been reported in an adoption study from Jamaica (Grantham-McGregor & Buchanan, 1992) and from the British National Child Development Study (Bagley, 1993a).

Theoretical Assumptions In The Evaluation Of Adjustment In Adoption

Theoretical assumptions for adoption research are grounded in the ego-identity theory of Erik Erikson (1968). This assumes that a child goes through successive identity dilemmas in which, at various stages of development, he or she has to synthesize what has been experienced earlier with new roles and psychological tasks which are demanded at different ages. Particularly important for adoption research is the crucial identity task in adolescence; the adolescent has to resolve the task of integrating previous aspects of identity, and become a young adult capable of making the most of his or her potentials, or self-actualizing as Maslow (1954) and Shostrom (1964) have termed it. These and other accounts of personal development can be synthesized in a theory of identity and global self-esteem in relation to ethnic identity issues (Young & Bagley, 1982). Identity development in the adopted adolescent has the special feature that the child must incorporate into identity structure the knowledge that his or her present parents are not the biological parents, and the knowledge that the original family felt unable to care for him or her. Some writers have argued that this task may make the adopted child particularly likely to develop anxiety and neurosis, with various kinds of identity crisis in early and late adolescence (Sorosky, Baron & Pannor, 1984).

David Kirk (1964; 1981) has argued that the identity problems implicit in the roles of both parents and children in adoptive families can best be solved by openness about the adoption, honesty and enthusiasm about the child's biological origins, and a frank and cheerful acceptance of the idea that being an adopted child is both different and special. Kirk showed that parents demonstrating "acknowledgment of difference" between natural and adoptive parenting laid the foundations for personal stability, ego strength, and good mental health in their adopted children. It is more difficult for parents to deny or minimize the child's natural origins in adopted children whose ethnic origins or physical appearance is different from that of their parents. The acceptance or accentuation of a difference model would seem to be the easiest for the adopting parent to follow in transracial adoption. For inter-country adoptions this would take the form of giving the child a knowledge of, and positive emotional orientation to, both personal ethnicity and country of origin. This approach should produce the best outcomes for identity development. The child cannot usually develop an adequate sense of self, or self-worth, without parental love and the establishment of boundaries within which the child learns and internalizes rules which can successfully guide behaviour in various roles. There is ample research showing the importance of these two antecedents of self-esteem (love, and stability of family structure) in the work of Coopersmith (1981) and others (Bagley et al., 1979).

This framework has an important implication for research on outcomes of adoption. The individual has to draw together, incorporate and make sense of many diverse social and psychological strands in forming his or her identity.

Identity formation is a long-term process; uncertainty and unhappiness at one point in a child or adolescent's development may be a transient phenomenon as the individual copes with problems in the formation of personal identity, at different points in the life cycle. Studies of adjustment of adopted children based on interviews at only one point in time could present a misleading picture. In addition, studies of adjustment before the crucial phase of adolescent identity formation might give an unduly limited, or optimistic picture of outcomes in adoption. Follow-up research on adoption needs to be undertaken at more than one point in development, with a final assessment based on the personal views of the adopted person when he or she is a young adult.

There is a parallel ethical problem in such longitudinal research. Interviewing children and their parents on the subject of adoption may elicit fears, worries, or anxieties which may in the short run be disturbing; but in the long run it may be helpful to face and cope with such problems. Researchers have the ethical obligation to offer help, support and referral where this is needed. But such help may significantly influence the outcome that is being researched. In this action research framework, the act of research can itself influence the outcome positively.

Three Studies Of Adjustment In Adoption

The following studies (Bagley, 1993a & b) illustrate that adoption research should, whenever possible, be longitudinal in nature; should consider a wide range of variables influencing outcome (including whenever possible genetic variables, perinatal factors, and environmental influences); use appropriate comparison groups; use as dependent measures standardized mental health measures of established reliability and validity; and parallel these quantitative approaches, wherever possible, with qualitative evidence based on personal accounts of the adoptees themselves, when they are young adults.

Children in the British National Child Development Survey

The National Child Development Study (NCDS) is based on the follow-up of a cohort of children born in one week in March 1958 in Britain. These children were systematically followed up, with data gathered from parents, schools, medical agencies, and the children themselves in the perinatal period, and at the ages of 7, 11, 16 and 23. The original sample size (some 17,000, of whom 12,500 were retained in the follow-up study at age 16) permitted the identification of a number minority groups, including those with special medical conditions (Bagley, 1986, 1992), ethnic minority groups (Bagley, 1982), and those born to single parents (Bagley, 1977). In this latter group 180 children had been placed with adoptive parents by the time of the first follow-up at age seven. Various comparison and control groups were available from the main cohort. Two comparison groups were generated in the analyses of the NCDS data. First was a random sample of children from the main cohort, who were born in and remained in conventional two-parent family settings. The second comparison group were children from similar social class backgrounds as the biological parents of the adoptees, who had been maternally separated in the first seven years of life, but who had not been placed for adoption; these children remained with relatives, lived in foster or institutional care, or had been returned by social work agencies to their biological mother.

The early follow-ups of the adopted children are described by Seglow and colleagues (1972), Bagley (1977), and Lambert and Streather (1980). When the adopted children were aged 11:

> The only difference to the disadvantage of adopted children was in ease of settling for a few moments. We have a picture of the adopted children as cheerful, co-operative, rather bubbly, and not particularly disturbed in any area. On the Bristol Social Adjustment Guide for Children completed by teachers, adopted children showed some excess of behaviour disorders, but this difference did not reach an acceptable level of significance (Bagley, 1977, p. 47).

The large amount of perinatal data collected indicated that the children who were subsequently adopted often suffered profound disadvantages before, during, and after birth. Their mothers (usually teenaged, single parents) worked long into pregnancy, often smoked during pregnancy, came into birth clinics late in the pregnancy, had children whose mean birthweight was significantly below that of the main cohort, had more abnormal conditions of pregnancy, and gave birth to children who had significantly more minor physical problems at birth. By the age of 16, however, the adopted children were significantly taller and heavier than children in the main cohort, and were achieving in various school subjects at a higher level than the average child (Bagley, 1993a). These differences were a function of the social class of the adoptees. When a class-appropriate control group was examined, the adopted children were merely doing as well as their non-adopted middle class peers in most areas. A positive social environment (provided by advantaged, middle class parents carefully selected through social work screening for good mental health and marital relationships) had resulted in a group of adolescents without major problems of behaviour or adjustment. In contrast, those children who had been separated, permanently or temporarily, from their biological mothers in the first seven years of life, but who were not adopted, had dramatically poorer outcomes than the adoptees in terms of both scholastic achievement and behaviour problems including those observed by teachers, or delinquent behaviour involving police and juvenile court processing. About half of the maternally-separated controls had serious problems of adjustment and behaviour, compared with 11% of the adoptees, and 7% of the non-separated controls matched for social class with the adoptees.

Later stresses could precipitate the psychological illness or type of personality disorder for which the individual is genetically at risk if there is a genetic vulnerability in some of the adoptees. The data available when the adoptees were in mid-adolescence indicates that most of the adoptees have the coping skills and support mechanisms which would buffer them against external stresses. A report of the follow-up when the adoptees were aged 23 is available (Maughan & Pickles, 1990). Interesting sex differences emerged in adjustment; the adopted women at age 23 were doing as well or better than women in the main cohort on indicators of personal and social adjustment and successful employment. The adopted men were slightly disadvantaged on these indicators, compared with the sample from the main cohort. However, both adopted men and women had markedly better adjustment on all indicators than the control group of children born to single mothers, but who were never adopted. For example, 31% of these disadvantaged, non-adopted children became teenaged mothers compared with 11% of the adopted women and 9% of the main cohort sample. Results from British NCDS are very similar to those described by Bohman and Sigvardsson (1990) in their extended follow-up of a cohort of Swedish adoptees. Both the Swedish and the British studies were of adoptions in which the racial background of the adopters and the adoptee's was the same. Transracial and international adoptions present an additional challenge to adopting families, which could, in theory, put the adjustment of the adopted children at greater hazard.

International Adoptions from Hong Kong

A follow-up study was completed of a group of Hong Kong Chinese girls, between 14 and 22 at follow-up, who had been adopted by British parents in the period 1962 to 1964 (Bagley & Young, 1981). All of these girls came from an orphanage in the Territory of Hong Kong. None of the girls had any contact with their biological parents, and the family background was in many cases unknown. All were physically healthy, though some had minor disabilities. At the time of placement the girls were from a few months to 9 years of age. A few of the British adopters were Anglo-Chinese couples, but most were of Caucasian ethnic or racial origin. Contact was made with 76 of the 90 sets of parents in the initial follow-up. These couples had adopted 100 girls (some couples adopted more than one child). The majority of adopters already had biological children when the Chinese girl was placed with them. Sixty seven of the 76 families contacted returned the initial questionnaire enquiring about educational and social progress, and various problems which might have been encountered. Fifty-one of these parents and their 53 adopted children were interviewed, a few more than once. Standardized testing of self-esteem, identity and adjustment was undertaken (Bagley & Young, 1981).

These Chinese girls, between 12 and 18, had become Anglicized to a striking degree. They spoke with regional accents and they shared the interests, pursuits, and values of their adopted brothers and sisters and of their school friends. This was true even of children adopted by Anglo-Chinese couples, or by couples who encouraged a strong interest in Hong Kong and Chinese culture. This cultural interest and awareness was an intellectual rather than an emotional orientation, and was not generally a core part of identity. Parents had varying styles of relating to the adopted children. Some put a strong emphasis on Chinese culture of which they had knowledge and which they admired and respected. Others did not mention these cultural factors, either because they wanted their daughter to be no different from her adopted siblings, or because the child herself resisted any form of cultural education. Children in this latter group were likely to be the youngest children adopted into large families (two-thirds of the adopters already had biological children).

Scholastically the picture was encouraging. The situation in these families was one of material advantage, marital stability, and positive intellectual stimulation and support. All of the children interviewed and tested in the first follow-up were functioning at least at an average level scholastically. About a third of the girls aged 16 or more were undertaking study for advanced level (university admission) examinations. This group of Chinese girls adopted by white, English families (five had Chinese mothers, but all had white, English fathers) had few problems of identity at this first phase of interviewing. Homes were warm and supportive; the only negative features was some degree of anxiety and over-protection in about ten per cent of parents. Scores on a standardized measure of anxiety and self-esteem completed by the adopted girls confirmed the picture of good adjustment; the adopted girls had markedly and significantly better self-esteem than a group of girls of similar age drawn from the general population.

Age at placement was not related to later adjustment; nor was a history of early illness or minor congenital difficulties (e.g. cleft palate, difficulties of hearing or sight), or early fears or tantrums. All of these difficulties seemed to smooth out with the passage of years. Type of family structure (number, age and sex of siblings) was not related to later adjustment; nor was parental death (2 cases) or divorce (1 case). The successful resolution of identity problems and dilemmas earlier in life; the fulfilment in Maslow's terms of various basic needs; strong bonding, and relationships based on love, affection and concerned tolerance; and an authoritative form of parenting based on a firm grounding in moral precepts (often informed by religious belief and practice) created firm ego-strengths in these girls and young women. Five of the fifty families interviewed were experiencing some difficulty in relation to adolescent problems; or the daughters in these families complained that their parents were too protective or too strict. But these problems seemed relatively mild in comparison with some of the acute identity crises which some adolescents experience (Bagley, 1991a).

As many of the Chinese adoptees as could be located were again interviewed nine years after the original follow-up, outlined above. Forty-four of the original 50 young women were located; three of these were interviewed in Hong Kong. We asked these women to reflect on their lives, and on the process of adoption; checked out their current occupational, educational and family careers; and requested them to complete a number of standardized measures of mental health, self-esteem, self-sentiment, and self-development. Control or comparison subjects of similar age and sex were drawn from two community mental health surveys, (Bagley, 1991b). Two random controls (88 in all) were selected for each adoptee. All of the controls were white, and of British, Irish or other European ethnic origin. There was no statistically-significant difference between the adoptees and the controls on the following measures: the Middlesex Hospital Questionnaire (Bagley, 1980) which measures psychoneurosis, anxiety and depression; the revised Coopersmith self-esteem scale for adults (Bagley, 1989a); Shostrom's (1964) measure of personal orientation and self-actualization; and Cattell's measure of self-sentiment (Gorsuch & Cattell, 1977) which is a measure of ego-strength and self-actualization. The educational and occupational achievement of these young women was high in comparison with that of individuals in the general population, a reflection of their middle class background, the quality of the family life they had experienced, their good educational achievements in school, their high achievement motivation, and their good emotional stability. These young women universally identified themselves as English, although some 40 percent maintained a strong emotional or intellectual interest in Chinese culture and institutions. The expressed satisfactions with their adopted families were high, and there were few manifest problems of identity as indicated by a measure designed to establish modes of ethnic identity in minority group individuals (Weinreich, 1979 & 1986).

Adoptions of Native-American Children in Canada

A study of adoption of Native-American children in Canada (Bagley, 1991c) illustrates both the failure of a particular programme of transracial adoptions and the failure of the family circumstances of the adoptive parents to overcome the influence of powerful and pervasive environmental factors, namely prejudice and hostility expressed against Native people in Canada. Random sampling of the adult population in Calgary, Alberta identified parents of European ethnic origins who had adopted an aboriginal child. These surveys (of over 3,000 adults) identified some five percent who had adopted a child. The majority were within-race adoptions (169); 42 of these adoptions served as the comparison group for the 37 adopted Native children with matches for age and sex of the adopted child. In addition, 20 adoptive families were identified in which the child had been adopted from Korea, or Central or South America. A further comparison group identified were 23 children who had been returned from foster care (in Caucasian families) to live with their original extended families on Native Indian reserves in Northern Alberta.

Results of interviews with parents and some of the adolescent adopted children indicated a distinct pattern of adjustment. Fifty-eight percent of the adopted Native children had under gone severe strain, involving profound maladjustment; the comparative figure for the within-race adoptions was 24%; and for the intercountry adoptees, 15%. A fifth of the Native adoptees were living in institutional care compared with 12% of the within-race adoptees, and none of the intercountry adoptees. Native children who had returned to their extended families had relatively good adjustment. Overall, these results were statistically significant. Measures of identity formation (Weinreich, 1986) indicated profound problems relating to ethnic self-consciousness in 49% of the Native children, but in only 3% of the intercountry adoptees. Personal reports from the adoptees themselves indicated that 51% of the Native children compared with 15% of the intercountry adoptees had suffered racial harassment in school despite the fact the many of the intercountry adoptees were oriental in appearance. This suggests that the adoption breakdowns of the Native children may occur because of a pattern of institutional racism. The intercountry adoptees were rarely stigmatized and, like intercountry adoptees in Britain, had rather good adjustment.

Discussion

Adjustment in adoption is a complex issue, presenting challenges to those who attempt to measure influences on human adjustment. Intercountry adoptees have generally good adjustment in Western countries but there are unknown selection biases for this population. Medical screening, for example, may mean that only the healthiest children are placed for adoption; however, such screening could not by itself screen out children carrying genes disposing them to various behavioural and learning problems. Other evidence (Bagley, 1993a) indicates that adoptive parents usually obtain the best possible educational, counselling, and medical services for their children; this could lead to an atypically high rate of detection of problems in the children. There might thus be a bias in adoption studies towards the detection of problems; but, if this is the case, the non-problematic outcomes for most intercountry adopted children become all the more remarkable.

Studies of intercountry adoption in the United States, Norway, Denmark, Germany, The Netherlands, and Israel (Simon & Altstein, 1991; Saetersdal & Dalen, 1991; Rorbech, 1991; Textor, 1991; Hoksbergen, 1991; Jaffe, 1991) indicate that prospective adopters face many hurdles in trying to adopt children from other countries. But outcomes for the intercountry adopted children in these studies appear to be very similar to children adopted in-country, in situations where parent and child are ethnically similar. Children who were older or handicapped at the time of their adoption fared somewhat worse; but the same is true of in-country adoptions, and outcomes for these children are likely to be much more favourable than for children who are not adopted (Altstein & Simon, 1991).

The models of adoption which emerge from these various studies indicate that factors in the background and environment of adopted children interact in complex ways (Brodzinsky, 1990). Adopted children carry the possibility of vulnerabilities derived from genetic heritage and from perinatal stressors (including low birth weight, and trauma before and during birth). They suffer instability in the early weeks or months of life, with separation from parental figures which at some crucial periods may predispose them to depressive illness in later life (Bohman & Sigvardsson, 1990). Adoptive families are particularly prone to a climate of anxiety and overprotection, reflecting anxieties about failures over biological parenting and the role handicaps inherent in adoptive parenting (Kirk, 1981). Adopted children must come to terms with both the cognitive and emotional facts of adoption; this can be traumatic for some if the knowledge of adoption is introduced late in a child's development. Transracially adopted children have to cope with the various racist responses to which ethnic minority children in Western countries are subject. Development phases presenting the child with new identity tasks may be particularly stressful for the adopted child, and such stressors could interact with genetic vulnerability in the development of personality disorder, or psychiatric illness. In addition, many children are now adopted past infancy, and must cope with the legacies of earlier abuse and neglect, as well as various physical and mental handicaps. Where illness of apparent genetic origin emerge, earlier medical records are often difficult to access, because of the policy of secrecy in adoption still practised by many agencies (Bagley, 1993a).

These various challenges to the adjustment of the adopted child seem daunting; what is astonishing is the very good overall adjustment which has been identified in most studies of adopted children. These results lead to the working hypothesis that the environment provided by adoptive parents (who are usually selected on the basis of good mental health, marital stability, and material advantage) has a powerful, protective effect on the adopted child's development. This optimism extends also to intercountry adoption, provided that there are not powerful forces of institutional racism working against adjustment in these adoptions.

References

Altstein, H., & Simon, R. (1991). Summary and concluding remarks. In H. Altstein and R.Simon (Eds). *Intercountry adoption: A multinational perspective* (pp. 183–194). New York: Praeger.

Bagley, C. (1975). Suicidal behaviour and suicidal ideation in adolescents: a problem for counsellors in education. *British Journal of Guidance and Counselling, 3*, 190–208.

Bagley, C. (1977). Adoption and the powerful effects of environment. *Adoption and Fostering, 88*, 45–47.

Bagley, C. (1980). The factorial reliability of the Middlesex Hospital Questionnaire in normal subjects. *British Journal of Medical Psychology, 53*, 53–58.

Bagley, C. (1982). Achievement, behaviour disorder and social circumstances in West Indian children and other ethnic groups. In G. Verma and C. Bagley (Eds.), *Self-concept, achievement and multicultural education* (pp 107–148). London: MacMillan.

Bagley, C. (1986). Social and scholastic adjustment in children with epilepsy and infantile fits: a 16-year follow-up of a national sample. In B. Hermann and S. Whitman (Eds.), *The social dimensions of epilepsy* (pp 85–104). New York: Oxford University Press.

Bagley, C. (1989). Development of a short self-esteem measure for use with adults in community mental health surveys. *Psychological Reports, 65*, 13–14.

Bagley, C. (1991a). Development of an adolescent stress scale for use by school counsellors: Construct validity in terms of depression, self-esteem and suicidal ideation. *School Psychology International, 13*, 31–49.

Bagley, C. (1991b). Child sexual abuse and its long-term outcomes: British and Canadian evidence. *Annals of Sex Research, 4*, 23–48.

Bagley, C. (1991c). Adoption of Native children in Canada: A policy analysis and a research report. In H. Altstein and R. Simon (Eds), *Intercountry adoption: A multinational perspective* (pp 55–82). New York: Praeger.

Bagley, C. (1992). Maternal smoking and deviant behaviour in 16-year-olds: a personality hypothesis. *Personality and Individual Differences, 13*, 377–378.

Bagley, C. (1993a). *Transracial and international adoptions: A mental health perspective.*. Aldershot, U.K.: Avebury.

Bagley, C. (1993b). Chinese adoptees in Britain: A 20-year follow-up of adjustment and social identity. *International Social Work, 36*, 141–155.

Bagley, C. (1993c). Transracial adoption in Britain: A follow-up study, with policy considerations. Child Welfare, 72, 201–212.

Bagley, C., & Evan-Wong, L. (1975). Neuroticism and extraversion in responses to Coopersmith's self-esteem inventory. *Psychological Reports, 36*, 253–254.

Bagley, C., & Young, L. (1981). The long-term adjustment of a sample of inter-country adopted children. *International Social Work, 23*, 16–22.

Bagley, C., Verma, G., Mallick, R., & Young, L. (1979). *Personality, self-esteem and prejudice.*, Aldershot, U.K.: Avebury.

Ben-Porat, A. (1977). Guttman scale test for Maslow need hierarchy. *Journal of Psychology, 97*, 85–92.

Berbaum, M., & Moreland, R. (1985). Intellectual development within transracial adoptive families: Retesting the confluence model. *Child Development, 56*, 207–216.

Bennett, M., & Mostyn, B. (1991). *The intercountry adoption process from the U.K. parent's perspective.* London: International Bar Association.

Bohman, M. (1981). The interaction of heredity and environment: Some adoption studies. Journal of Child Psychology and Psychiatry, 2, 195–200.

Bohman, M., & Sigvardsson, S. (1990). Outcome in adoption: Lessons from longitudinal studies. In D. Brodzinzky & M. Schecter, (Eds.), *The psychology of adoption* (pp 93–106). New York: Oxford University Press.

Bohman, M., Cloninger, R., & Sigvardsson, S. (1982). Predisposition to petty criminality in Swedish adoptees. *Archives of General Psychiatry, 39*, 24–38.

Brinich, M. (1990). Adoption from the inside out: A psychoanalytic perspective. In D. Brodzinzky & M. Schecter (Eds.), *The psychology of adoption* (pp 3–24). New York: Oxford University Press.

Brodzinzky, D. (1990). A stress and coping model of adoption adjustment. In D. Brodzinzky & M. Schlecter (Eds.), *The psychology of adoption* (pp 3–24). New York: Oxford University Press.

Cadoret, R. (1990). Biologic perspectives of adoptee adjustment. In D. Brodzinzky & M. Schechter (Eds.), *The psychology of adoption* (pp 25–41). New York: Oxford University Press.

Cadoret, R., & Gath, A. (1978). Inheritance of alcoholism in adoptees. *British Journal of Psychiatry, 132*, 252–258.

Cadoret, R., Cunningham, L., & Loffus, R. (1976). Studies of adoptees from psychiatrically disturbed biological parents. *American Journal of Psychiatry, 133*, 136–1318.

Cardon, L., DiLalla, L., & Plomin, R. (1990). Genetic correlations between reading performance and IQ in the Colorado Adoption Project. *Intelligence, 14*, 245–257.

Coopersmith, S. (1981). *The Antecedents of Self-Esteem.* Palo Alto, CA: Consulting Psychologists Press.

De Vries, J., Plomin, R., Vandenberg, S., & Kuse, A. (1981). Parent-offspring correlations for cognitive abilities in the Colorado adoption project: Biological, adoptive, and control parents and one-year-old children. *Intelligence, 5*, 245–277.

Erikson, E. (1968). *Identity, Youth and Crisis.* New York: Norton.

Goodwin, D., Schulsinger, F., & Knop, J. (1977). Alcoholism and depression in adopted-out daughters of alcoholics. *Archives of General Psychiatry, 34*, 164–171.

Gorsuch, R., & Cattell, R. (1977). Personality and socio-ethical values: The structure of the self and superego. In R. Cattell & R. Dreger (Eds), *Handbook of modern personality theory*, (pp 675–708). New York: Wiley.

Grantham-McGregor, S., & Buchanan, E. (1982). The development of an adopted child recovering from severe malnutrition. *Human Nutrition, 36*, 251–256.

Hoksbergen, R. (1991). Intercountry adoption coming of age in the Netherlands. In H. Altstein & R. Simon (Eds.), *Intercountry adoption: A multinational perspective* (pp 141–160). New York: Praeger.

Horn, J. (1983). The Texas adoption project: Adopted children and their intellectual resemblance to biological and adoptive parents. *Child Development, 54*, 268–275.

Jaffe, E. (1991). Foreign adoptions in Israel. In H. Altstein & R. Simon (Eds.), *Intercountry Adoption* (pp 161–182). New York: Praeger.

Kirk, D. (1964). *Shared fate: A theory of mental health and adoption.* London: Collier-MacMillan.

Kirk, D. (1981). *Adoptive kinship: A modern institution in need of reform.* Toronto: Butterworth.

Labuda, M., DeVries, J., Plomin, R., & Fulker, D. (1986). Longitudinal stability of cognitive ability from infancy to early childhood: genetic and environmental etiologies. *Child Development, 57*, 1142–1150.

Locurto, C. (1990). The malleability of IQ as judged from adoption studies. *Intelligence, 14*, 275–292.

Maslow, A. (1954). *Motivation and personality.* New York: Harper and Row.

Maughan, B., & Pickles, A. (1990). Adopted and illegitimate children growing up. In L. Robins & M. Rutter (Eds.), *Straight and devious pathways from childhood to adulthood* (pp 36–61). Cambridge: Cambridge University Press.

Mednick, S., Gabriella, W., & Hutchings, B. (1984). Genetic influences in criminal convictions: evidence from an adoption cohort. *Science, 224*, 891–894.

Munsinger, H. (1975). The adopted child's I.Q.: A critical review. *Psychological Bulletin, 85*, 623–659.

Parker, G. (1982). Parental representations and affective symptoms: Examination for an heredity link. *British Journal of Medical Psychology, 55*, 57–61.

Rice, T. (1986). Multivariate path analysis of specific cognitive abilities in the Colorado Adoption Project. *Behavior Genetics, 16*, 107–114.

Rorbech, M. (1991). The conditions of 18 to 25 year-old foreign born adoptees in Denmark. In H. Altstein & R. Simon (Eds.), *Intercountry adoption* (pp 127–140). New York: Praeger.

Saetersdal, B., & Dalen, M. (1991). Norway: Inter-country adoptions in a homogenous country. In H. Altstein & R. Simon (Eds.), *Intercountry adoption* (pp 83–108). New York: Praeger.

Scarr, S., & Weinberg, R. (1976). I.Q. test performance of adopted black children, and biological children. *Intelligence, 1*, 170–191.

Shostrom, E. (1964). A test for the measurement of self-actualization. *Educational and Psychological Measurement, 24*, 207–218.

Silverman, A., & Feigelman, W. (1990). Adjustment in interracial adoptees: An overview. In D. Brodzinzky & M. Schecter (Eds.), *The psychology of adoption* (pp 187–200). New York: Oxford University Press.

Sorosky, A., Baron, A., & Pannor, R. (1984). *The adoption triangle.* New York: Doubleday.

Teasdale, T., & Owen, D. (1986). The influence of paternal social class on intelligence in male adoptees and non-adoptees. *British Journal of Educational Psychology, 36*, 3–12.

Textor, M. (1991). International adoptions in West Germany. In H. Altstein & R. Simon (Eds.), *Intercountry adoption* (109–126). New York: Praeger.

Verma, G., Mallick, K., Neasham, T., Ashworth, B., & Bagley, C. (1988). *Education and ethnicity.* London: MacMillan.

Weinreich, P. (1979). Cross-ethnic identification and self-rejection in a black adolescent. In G. Verma & C. Bagley (Eds.), *Race, education and identity* (pp 157–175). London: MacMillan.

Weinreich, P. (1986). *Manual for identity exploration using personal constructs.* Coventry, U.K.: ESCR Centre for Research in Ethnic Relations, University of Warwick.

Winnick, M., Meyer, K., & Harris, R. (1975). Malnutrition and environmental enrichment in adoption. *Science, 190*, 1173–75.

Young, L., & Bagley, C. (1982). Self-esteem, self-concept and black identity. In G. Verma & C. Bagley (Eds.), *Self-concept, achievement and multicultural education* (41–59). London: MacMillan.

22

Intercountry Adoption in Canada: Predictors Of Well-Being

Anne Westhues and Joyce S. Cohen

Intercountry adoption has become an important social policy issue in Canada. The numbers have grown from less than 10 a year when records were first kept in 1970 (Gravel & Roberge, 1984) to an estimate of more than 2400 a year in 1991 (Sobol & Daly, 1992). Non-relative adoptions in Canada are now as likely to involve children who were born outside of Canada as those born within Canada. Most of the children from out-of-country have a different racial and cultural background from their adoptive parents. The realities of adoption have changed dramatically since the mid-seventies. Once there were more infants available for adoption than homes willing to accept the children; a couple now waits an average of six years for the placement of an infant through a public agency and two years through a private agency (Sobol & Daly, 1992). This reduction in the number of children available for adoption is generally explained by changes in legislation which made abortion legal in Canada, more effective birth control which resulted in fewer births outside of marriage, and an increase in the proportion of single mothers who choose to parent their children instead of relinquishing them for adoption (McDade, 1991). The primary motivation for intercountry adoption today is the desire of an infertile couple to parent a child; prior to the 1980s many adopting internationally were primarily motivated by a desire to improve the child's life-chances.

The increase in the number of children being adopted internationally and the shift in the primary motivation for adoption has surfaced discussion concerning the morality of intercountry adoption (Triseliotis, 1991). Three general positions have emerged—one opposes intercountry adoption, a second sees intercountry adoption as being positive for all involved, and a third recognizes that there are negatives as well as positives which must be considered by both the sending and receiving countries and by the individuals making the decision to relinquish a child for adoption or to adopt cross-nationally.

Opposition to intercountry adoption comes from both developing countries and from those who make class and feminist analyses. They argue that this is one more instance of exploitation of the poor by the rich and that these are children who cannot be cared for within their country of birth because of the inequitable distribution of resources throughout the world (Altstein & Simon, 1991; Ngabonziza, 1991). Critics claim that children adopted cross-nationally may live with a confused sense of ethnic and racial identity (Ryan, 1983; Barrett & Aubin, 1990; McRoy, 1991). Some also argue that the numbers involved in cross-national placements are so small that it doesn't really help poor countries struggling to develop (Ngabonziza, 1991). The final argument in this critique is that international adoption should be avoided because it takes pressure off of governments to effect economic and social changes which would be of particular benefit to women and children (Bartholet, 1988; Barrett & Aubin, 1990).

Advocates of intercountry adoption, who are generally from richer countries, argue that many of the children who have been adopted by parents from Western countries would have died from malnutrition, lack of medical care, or as a consequence of war if they had not been adopted. Thus, it is in the best interest of the individual child to have been adopted. In addition, it meets the need of infertile couples to parent, which seems to be positive all around (Joe, 1978; Bowen, 1992). Intercountry adoption is also a way to help a country deal with the aftermath of disasters like flood, famine, earthquake, or war (Barret & Aubin, 1990; Ryan, 1983).

The third position to evolve finds merit in both sets of arguments. Proponents of this position agree that it is in the best interest of the child to grow up in a sociocultural environment where he or she is not different racially or culturally. Ideally all countries would have the resources to care for their own children when the child's parents are unwilling or not able to do so. Further, there are some children who will grow up experiencing less prejudice in a Western country than in their country of origin (Joe, 1978; Register, 1991). Examples are mixed-race or out-of-wedlock children from some of the Asian countries or children born as a consequence of the sexual assaults associated with so-called "ethnic cleansing" in the former Yugoslavia. Further, it is better for a child to be raised in a family context, with the intimacy and stability that this promises, than in an institution. Children abandoned in China because of their one-child policy, for instance, would be better cared for by a family, even if that family is not Chinese, than within an orphanage.

Research about how children and families involved in intercountry adoption have fared can help with decisions about which of these three positions is most appropriate as a guide to policy development. Research has been completed in almost every Western country which receives children from out-of-country for adoption (United States: Divirglio, 1956; Rathburn, 1965; Simon & Altstein, 1977; 1981; 1987; 1992; Kim, D.S., 1978; Kim, Hong & Kim, 1979; Kim, P. S., 1980; Fiegelman & Silverman, 1983; Wilkinson, 1985; England: Bagley & Young, 1980; Norway: Saetersdal & Dalen, 1991; Germany: Kuhl, 1985; Textor, 1991; Denmark: Pruzan, 1977; Rorbech, 1991; Sweden: Hofvander, Bengtsson, Gunnarby, Cederblad, Kats & Stomholm, 1978; Gardell, 1979; Cederblad, 1982; Finland: Kvist, Viemero & Forsten, 1989; Netherlands: Hoksbergen, 1981; 1984; 1991; Hoksbergen, Juffer, Waardenburg & Klippe, 1987; Verhulst, Althaus, Versluisden Biemen, 1990; Belgium: Wattier & Frydman, 1985; Israel: Jaffe, 1991). Intercountry adoptions have been occurring in significant numbers in Canada for at least fifteen years but there has been only one major study which looked at the outcomes of these adoptions within the country, and that study drew its sample solely from Québec (Gravel & Roberge, 1984). There are no Canadian studies that have focused on the children in adolescence, or have looked at the impact of the adoption on both parents and other siblings in the family as well as upon the intercountry adoptees. The purpose of this study is to fill these knowledge gaps.

The general question posed in this research is how are internationally adopted children and their families faring when the child has reached adolescence or young adulthood? How well-integrated do intercountry adoptees feel within their family at adolescence/young adulthood and how does this compare with their siblings who were born in Canada? What is the level of self-esteem of intercountry adoptees in adolescence/young adulthood and how does this compare with the level of self-esteem of their siblings and the general population? Do intercountry adoptees feel that their parents are satisfied with their school performance? How does this compare with siblings' perception of parent satisfaction with their school performance? How well do intercountry adoptees get along with peers? How do the responses given by intercountry adoptees compare with those given by siblings on these questions? What is the racial and ethnic identification of intercountry adoptees? Are they comfortable with their racial and ethnic background? Finally, are there parent and child variables that predict how well children who have been adopted internationally have done on each of these measures of their well-being?

Method

Sample

The sample was drawn from British Columbia, Ontario, and Québec, and was drawn in three stages. Government records were used to identify families who had adopted a child internationally and who would be at least 12 years of age. In British Columbia, 196 names were identified, in Québec 189, and in Ontario 184. A letter of invitation was mailed to those families where the address could be confirmed as current. This meant that 162 families in British Columbia received the letter, 90 in Québec, and 148 in Ontario for a total of 400 families. Fifty families actually took part in the study from British Columbia, 36 from Québec, and 40 from Ontario, a total of 126 families. The response rate was 31% in British Columbia, 40% in Québec, and 27% in Ontario, with an overall response rate of 32%.

Demographic data was collected about the age of all family members, occupation of mother and father, educational achievement of mother and father, family income, motivation to adopt internationally, family size, gender of siblings, birth order of adopted child and siblings, whether siblings were biological or adopted, how widely-travelled the family was, and the size of community in which they lived. Parents, siblings, and intercountry adoptees were asked to complete a measure of family functioning. Parents were also asked to complete a series of questions which assessed the extent to which they acknowledged the difference between adopting a child and having a birth child.

The mother, father, as many as two intercountry adoptees and as many as two siblings were interviewed in each family. This resulted in interviews with 123 mothers, 113 fathers, 155 intercountry adoptees, and 121 siblings. The interview schedules were kept as similar as possible for the adoptees and siblings, and parallel questions were included in the parent interviews. The instrument was pretested with two families, and revisions made to questions where there was some indication that their meaning was not clear. The interviewers were all child welfare workers, most of whom had worked in adoptions; they were experienced interviewers, familiar with issues in adoption, and familiar with the process of intercountry adoption. The interviews were completed between October 1991 and March 1992. The interview schedule is a mix of fixed response and open-ended questions. Interviews took between one and a half to two hours for the parents and 45 minutes to one hour for the children. Each interview was transcribed to facilitate coding of qualitative data.

Findings

Demographic Characteristics

Parents who participated in the study were well-educated; 51% of mothers and 64% of fathers had a college or university degree. Family income was higher than the median family income in Canada, and parents were more likely to be professionals than in the general population. Many parents were human services professionals such as teachers, social workers, nurses, and doctors. The most common motivation reported for adopting internationally was being drawn to a child in need. Only 18% of families said that infertility was one of their reasons for adopting internationally.

Of the intercountry adoptees, 74% were female and 26% male. They came from Korea (40%) Bangladesh (29%) Vietnam (8%), Haiti (7%), India (4%) and other countries (12%) including Brazil, Columbia, Guatemala, Bolivia, Chile, Mexico, Jamaica, the Philippines, Hong Kong, Cambodia, China, and Zambia. Fifty-four percent were two years or younger when they were adopted. Most came from orphanages, and most were in good health, or with correctable health problems such as malnutrition. The mean age of intercountry adoptees when interviewed was 17 years, with a range from 9 to 37 years.

Proportionally, sex of the siblings were almost the reverse of the intercountry adoptees; 61% were male and 39% were female. The mean age of siblings when the intercountry adoptee came into the family was 5, with a range of not yet born to 16. Seven of the intercountry adoptees were raised as only children. Eighty-seven percent of the siblings were biological children, and 13% were adopted domestically. The mean age of siblings when interviewed was 20, with a range of from 9 to 35 years.

Family Integration

Gill and Jackson's (1983) family integration statements, a series of eight questions about family life, were used to measure the extent to which intercountry adoptees and their siblings felt that they belonged within the family. Responses were given on a four point scale—strongly agree, agree, disagree—and strongly disagree and are presented in Table 22.1. The scores on these eight questions were summarized to obtain an overall score on family functioning. The possible range of scores was from 8 to 32, with a higher score meaning that there was a weaker sense of integration within the family. The actual range for intercountry adoptees was 8 to 29, with a mean of 15.1. For siblings, the range was 8 to 24, with a mean of 13.9. The difference between the two groups was significant ($t = 4.73$, $df = 203.05$, $p < .05$). Thus, the intercountry adoptees scored significantly lower than their siblings on sense of belonging within the family. Compared to their siblings, intercountry adoptees

Table 22. 1: Comparison of Scores on the Family Integration Scale, Intercountry Adoptees and Siblings

Item	Intercountry Adoptees		Siblings	
	M (n=41)	F (n=113)	M (n=73)	F (n=47)
I enjoy family life % Agree	90.3	94.7	95.8	97.8
I would like to leave home as soon as possible when I'm able to % Disagree	43.8	53.5	61.0	77.4 *
Most families are happier than ours % Disagree	89.4	86.8	94.1	91.3 *
People in our family trust one another % Agree	75.6	84.0	92.9	84.8 +
I am treated in the same way as my brother and my sister % Agree	73.2	74.6	87.3	87.2
Most people are closer to their parents than I am % Disagree	78.4	65.5	88.7	74.5 *+
If I am in trouble I know my parents will stick by me % Agree	92.7	93.9	97.1	95.7
My parents know what I am really like as a person	85.3	79.0	91.4	87.0

* significant difference between intercountry adoptees and siblings, using a two-tailed t-test, $p < .05$
\+ significant difference between male and female siblings, using two-tailed t-test, $p < .05$
Note: Agree and strongly agree responses collapsed to agree; disagree and strongly disagree responses collapsed to disagree.

were more likely to agree that they would like to leave home as soon as they were able, that other families were happier than theirs, and that most children were closer to their parents than they. These differences may be explained, at least in part, by the age differences of the intercountry adoptee and sibling groups. Fifty-nine percent of the adoptees were under 18 years of age while 69% of the siblings were 18 or older at the time of data collection. It is not unusual for adolescents under 18 to be eager to leave home and to feel that others have a happier home life than they do in their family. Siblings, who on average were three years older than intercountry adoptees, were also more likely to have left home than adoptees; thus, siblings would be less likely to express a need to leave home and any strained relationships between them and their parents would have been eased by the fact that they were not still living in the family home. It is also worth bearing in mind that while differences in scores on family integration between siblings and intercountry adoptees were significantly different, the difference between an overall mean of 15.1 and 13.9 is small enough that it may have no practical significance.

Table 22.2: Scores on the Rosenberg Self-Concept Scale, for Intercountry Adoptees and Siblings, by Gender

Self-Esteem	Intercountry Adoptees				Siblings			
	Male		Female		Male		Female	
Score	No.	%	No.	%	No.	%	No.	%
Low 0	0	0	4	3.7	0	0	0	0
1	1	2.9	3	2.8	0	0	0	0
2	0	0	6	5.7	2	3.1	0	0
3	2	5.9	9	8.5	5	7.7	4	8.9
4	8	23.5	29	27.4	15	23.1	7	15.6
5	14	41.2	30	28.3	17	26.2	9	20.0
High 6	9	26.4	25	23.6	26	40.0	25	55.5
Total	34	100	106	100	65	100	45	100

* Using a two-tailed t-test, siblings scored significantly higher on self-esteem than intercountry adoptees (t= –3.70, df=248, p < .001). Mean for intercountry adoptees: 4.4; Mean for siblings: 5.0.

Self-Esteem

Self-esteem of the intercountry adoptees, as measured by the Rosenberg Self-Concept Scale (Rosenberg, 1965), is presented in Table 22.2. Self-esteem was found to be higher than in the general population; females reported lower self-esteem than males consistent with the findings for the general population. Sixty-eight percent of the male adoptees and 52% of female adoptees scored high, that is, a five or a six on the scale. For the total sample, 56% of intercountry adoptees scored high compared to 45% in Rosenberg's sample of adolescent Americans. These higher-than-average scores may be explained by the elevated socioeconomic status of the families in the study. Families whose income and education are higher than the general population tend to rear children with higher self-esteem (Rosenberg, 1965). Adoptive families have also been found to be higher functioning than those in the general population (Westhues & Cohen, 1988). Growing up in a well-functioning family may also contribute to the development of positive self-esteem. The self-esteem scores of intercountry adoptees are higher on average than in the general population but the scores of siblings were even higher. Sixty-six percent of male siblings and 76% of female siblings scored in the high range compared to 68% of male adoptees and 52% of female adoptees. The mean for intercountry adoptees was 4.4, and for siblings 5.0, a difference that was significant (t = –3.70, df = 248, p < .001).

Peer Relations

All but three adoptees and two siblings said that they had friends. On the Hudson index of peer relations (Hudson, 1982) almost identical proportions of male intercountry adoptees (11%), female intercountry adoptees (11%) and female siblings (12%) scored above the clinical cutoff, meaning that these proportions were not functioning well with respect to peer relations. An even higher proportion of male siblings (17%) scored above the clinical cutoff, though this difference was not great enough to be significant. There are no norms on this scale for the general population, but estimates of socio-emotional problems within the general adolescent population place the figure at ten percent (Bibby & Posterski, 1992; Brodzinsky, 1990). The higher proportion of male siblings scoring in the problem range on the peer relations index raises the question of whether there are negative consequences of intercountry adoption for male birth children that are not apparent for either intercountry adoptees or for female birth children. An alternate explanation is that families who adopt internationally may be among the most open and nurturing in their culture, or what may be described as more feminine. It may be that male children born into these more nurturing families show an increased probability of difficulty with peer relations whether there are intercountry adopted children in the family or not. They must struggle with the contradictions of the role expectations for them within their families and within the dominant culture that they experience outside the family.

Comfort with Ethnic Background

Loss of identification with one's culture of origin and racial group is a major concern raised by opponents of intercountry adoption. Approximately half of intercountry adoptees in the study thought of themselves as Canadian or Québécois (51% of males; 40% of females). An additional 10% of male adoptees and 5% of female adoptees saw themselves as "hyphenated" Canadians, for example Korean-Canadian. Twenty-three percent of male intercountry adoptees and 38% of female intercountry adoptees thought of themselves ethnically as something other than Canadian. Eight percent of males and 10% of females said that they didn't think of themselves ethnically, and 5% of males and 4% of females said that they didn't know how to think of themselves ethnically. Some will see not thinking of oneself ethnically as a symptom of maladaptation while others will see it as adaptive in a situation where a person is the only one who has a different ethnic background within a family system—a way of fitting in. Those who say that they don't know how to think of themselves ethnically, although a small proportion of the sample, suggest that about five percent of intercountry adoptees are experiencing identity confusion with respect to ethnicity, or don't know what is meant by ethnicity. The figures increase to 13% for males and 14% for females if not thinking about one's ethnicity is regarded as maladaptive. A large majority of males adoptees (83%) and females adoptees (71%) report being either comfortable or very comfortable with their ethnic background. Three percent of male adoptees and 13% of females adoptees report being uncomfortable or very uncomfortable, with the remainder reporting that they are neither comfortable nor uncomfortable with this aspect of their identity. Siblings were more likely than adoptees to say that they were very comfortable with their ethnicity and less likely to say that they were uncomfortable or very uncomfortable than were the intercountry adoptees (chi-square = 37.3, df = 4, $p < .001$).

Comfort with Racial Background

Eleven percent of male adoptees and 17% of female adoptees said that they did not think of themselves racially. Further, 11% of male adoptees and 10%

of female adoptees said that they thought of themselves as white. The countries of origin of these interviewees were Korea, Bangladesh, and Haiti. This suggests that about 10% of adoptees identify with the majority racial group, a finding similar to that in a recent study by Bagley (1993). This may also be a functional adaptation to being a visible minority both in Canadian society and within one's family. Nonetheless, it is of concern because it is unlikely that others, especially those outside the family, will respond to the intercountry adoptees as if they are white. If not thinking about oneself racially is maladaptive, then 21% of males and 26% of females would be regarded as having adjustment problems in the area of identity formation with respect to race.

Similar patterns were found in the responses given to the question about comfort with racial background. Seventy-six percent of male adoptees and 74% of female adoptees said that they were comfortable or very comfortable with their racial background. Ten percent of both intercountry males and intercountry females said that they were uncomfortable or very uncomfortable with their race and the remainder said that they were neither comfortable nor uncomfortable. None of the male siblings and 2% of the female siblings said that they were uncomfortable or very uncomfortable with their racial background. Siblings were significantly more likely than intercountry adoptees to report being very comfortable with racial background (chi-square = 24.1, df = 4, $p < .001$). The finding that 10% of the intercountry adoptees had lost their racial identity to the point of identifying themselves as white suggests that, for some intercountry adoptees, there is the risk of losing a sense of how they present visually to the world. The parent data on this issue are interesting. They suggest that parents feel their children belong to the majority culture to a greater extent than do the children. The communication gap between parents and children on this issue may be the way that parents cope with the fact that they hold a status which they cannot confer on their children.

School Performance

Seventy-one percent of adoptees said that their parents were satisfied or very satisfied with their school achievements. The proportion reported by siblings was 77%. Parents were somewhat more likely to report that siblings were among the most able students (17%) compared to intercountry adoptees (7%) but the difference is not significant. They were no more likely to report that intercountry adoptees (6%) were among the least able, however, than were siblings (7%). A large majority of parents thought that their intercountry adopted children had set realistic career goals or accepted the child's right to choose what he or she wished to become. Nineteen percent expressed some concern about how realistic the goals were, and 2% did not support their choices.

Predictors of Well-Being

A series of stepwise multiple regression analyses were then run to identify which of a number of parent and child variables might be predictors of the child's functioning. The analyses were run in three stages. First, child-related variables were run as predictors of each of the criterion variables; next parent variables were run as predictors of each of the criterion variables; and in the third stage the child and parent variables that had been significant in each of the prior runs were entered together as predictors of each of the criterion variables.

Table 22.3: Predictors of the Well-Being of Intercountry Adoptees

Criterion Variables	Predictor Variables	Step	Beta	Cumulative Adjusted R^2	F	P
Family Integration	Relationship with Mother	1	-.290288	.11	8.97	.004
	Relationship with Siblings	2	-.261202	.17	7.26	.009
	Country of Origin—Haiti	3	.243766	.22	6.70	.011
Self-esteem	Relationship with Siblings	1	-.380470	.10	17.33	.001
	Gender	2	.273001	.15	9.04	.003
	Mother's Score on FAD	3	-.243446	.20	7.25	.009
	Country of Origin—Korea	4	.239650	.25	6.94	.010
Peer Relations	Number of Children in Family	1	.328382	.08	12.49	.001
	Relationship with Father	2	-.232848	.13	6.28	.014
	Country of Origin—Bangladesh	3	-.218825	.17	5.59	.020
Comfort with Ethnic Background	Age at Adoption	1	.202881	.03	4.7	.032
Comfort with Racial Background	Whether Mother Works Outside the Home	1	-.323876	.10	10.2	.002
Parent Perception of School Performance	Country of Origin—Korea	1	-.252531	.05	7.0	.010
Child Perception of School Performance	Score on Ethnic Education Scale	1	-.230611	.04	6.3	.013

The child variables entered in the first stage included gender, number of children in the family, country of birth, age at adoption, relationship with mother, relationship with father, relationship with siblings, and score on the family assessment device, a measure of family functioning (Epstein, Baldwin & Bishop, 1983; Byles, Byrne, Boyle & Offord, 1988). Parent variables entered in the first stage included age, education level, occupation, whether employment was outside the home, ethnic background, score on the family assessment device, and score on a scale assessing the extent to which parents acknowledged the difference between adoption and having a birth child (Kirk, 1964; 1981; 1988). Each of these variables was entered for mother and for father. Also entered were family income, whether preplacement and postplacement services were used, whether one of the motivations for adopting was infertility, a score on whether parents had done things with their children to promote a sense of awareness of their ethnic background, and a score on whether parents had done things with their children to promote a sense of awareness of their racial background. Categorical variables were converted to dichotomous dummy variables.

The results of these analyses are presented in Table 22.3 and show that the predictors of a strong feeling of integration within the family are a close relationship with mother, a close relationship with siblings, and coming from countries other than Haiti. Predictors of positive peer relations were a smaller number of children in the family, a close relationship with father, and coming from Bangladesh. Predictors of self-esteem are having a close relationship with siblings, being male, the mother's assessment that functioning in the family is positive, and coming from Korea originally. The sole predictor of comfort with racial background was that the mother did not work outside the home, and the sole predictor of comfort with ethnic background was age at which the child was adopted—the older the child at adoption, the more comfortable they were with their ethnic background. The only predictor of parent assessment of a child's school performance ability was that the child was originally from Korea, with parents more likely to report that children from Korea were among the most able. Parents having done things with intercountry adoptees like reading about their country of origin, taking them to events where they would learn about their country of origin, or travelling with them to their country of origin meant that they were more likely to think that their parents were satisfied with their performance in school.

Only one variable, relationship with siblings, repeats itself as a predictor of more than one of these measures of well-being. This suggests that the criterion measures used are in fact discrete, and that it is important to think of them as separate indicators of well-being rather than as subscales of a comprehensive measure of well-being. Attachment theory would suggest that a feeling that relationships are close with family members would be a predictor of the well-being of that family member. The findings seem to support this proposition, since relationship with some family member was identified as a predictor of one of the criterion variables in four instances. This finding might also be understood in light of research by Dunn and Plomin (1990) which suggests that siblings who have been the closest to mother are the best adjusted. Having a close relationship with mother and siblings was important to a sense of belonging within the family, a private place, but closeness to father was a predictor of relationships with peers, relationships that are experienced outside the family, or in a public place. The importance of relationships with siblings is reinforced by the finding that closeness with siblings is also a predictor of the intercountry adoptee's feelings of self-esteem, a finding that is also supported by the research of Dunn and Plomin (1990) and Daniels, Dunn, Furstenberg and Plomin (1985).

The findings with respect to country of origin must be regarded as tentative given the small numbers who came from some of the countries. Nonetheless, the findings support the observation of many intercountry adoptive parents and adoption workers that Korean children tend to make particularly good adaptations to life in Canada. The parent assessment that children who were born in Korea are more likely to be among the most able in school is one indication of this positive adaptation. The greater probability of a high score on self-esteem, if one is originally from Korea, may be related to the experience of receiving positive feedback about one's school performance. It may also be that people from Korea experience less discrimination in Canada than those who are darker-skinned, or that Korean children have had fewer deficits, like malnutrition, to counteract than children from poorer countries like Haiti or Bangladesh. The finding that coming from Bangladesh is a predictor of more positive peer relations is difficult to explain. Temperament may be one factor explaining this finding (Thomas & Chess, 1977). In the interviews, parents described children from Bangladesh as relaxed, friendly, outgoing, and wanting to please. These are characteristics which would translate into positive peer relationships. That intercountry adoptees from Haiti are less likely to feel a sense of belonging within the family is also difficult to explain. Particular caution must be taken with this finding, since only 11 of the 155 intercountry adoptees were originally from Haiti. This difference may be explained by the finding that the Haitian children in the sample were significantly younger (mean = 14.7) than the non-Haitians (mean = 18.8) ($t = -7.51$, $df = 21$, $p<.001$). Thus, Haitian children are more likely to be in the middle of their adolescent struggle than are the non-Haitians and, consequently, feeling less like they belong within the family. It may also mean that the more different a child is in skin colour to his adoptive family, the more difficult it will be for the child to blend into the family and develop a sense of belonging.

An unexpected finding with respect to peer relations is that higher scores on the Hudson index of peer relations are associated with a higher number of siblings. That is, peer relations are poorer the larger the family size. The mean family size in our study was four children, with a range from one to fourteen children. The conventional wisdom is that growing up in a large family teaches one good peer relations, since you are constantly interacting with siblings who are more or less your own age. This finding suggests that at some point the experience is not beneficial in terms of peer relations. Perhaps this is because the parents are not able to spend the time that a child needs in working out how to interact positively with peers when the family is too large, and siblings must develop more aggressive styles of behaviour to gain one-to-one parent time. This may be a particular disadvantage when the child has a special need, like belonging to a visible minority group.

The finding that being male is associated with higher scores on self-esteem is well-supported in the literature (Rosenberg, 1965; Bibby & Posterski, 1992). The mothers and intercountry adoptees are less likely to assess family functioning as non-problematic than are fathers or siblings, but it is the mothers' assessment of family functioning that is a predictor of self-esteem. This may mean that self-esteem of intercountry adoptees is more likely to be influenced by the nature of the relationship between mother and child than between the intercountry adoptee and any other family members.

Children of mothers who were not working outside the home were more likely to be comfortable with their racial background than those who were working outside the home. Mothers who are not working outside the home may be more likely to have time to talk with children about things that concern them. The finding that the older the child was at adoption the more likely they are to be comfortable with their ethnic background makes intuitive sense. The older the child, the more fully they would understand their culture of origin, and the more readily they could incorporate that as a part of their identity. The final finding is that parents having engaged in activities which help a child learn about their ethnic background is a predictor of the child's assessment of how well they are doing at school. Enhanced perception of competence at school may be partially due to the fact that these parents taught their children how to deal with discrimination in their early school years. Most adoptees did experience discrimination, and it occurred most commonly at school in the lower grades.

Implications For Child Welfare Policy and Program Development

Should Canada continue to be involved in intercountry adoption? There are at least four different stakeholders' perspectives: the children themselves, the families that adopt them, the child's country of origin, and the child's receiving country. The focus of this research has been on the perspectives of the children and their families of adoption. The intercountry adoptees in this study appear to be well-integrated into their families, have high self-esteem, and have friends and positive peer relations. Further, parents are almost as likely to be satisfied with the school performance of intercountry adoptees as they are with that of other children in the family. Not all the children are free of problems in these areas, but they seem to be no less well-adjusted than would be expected in a representative sample of Canadian adolescents. The only area where concern may be warranted regarding adjustment is with respect to ethnic and racial identity, especially racial identity. Keeping in mind the probable bias in the sample toward families where the adoption experience has been reasonably positive, these data lead us to conclude that Canada should continue to be involved in intercountry adoption.

Research dealing with complex issues raises as many questions as it answers. Are there differences in the well-being of internationally adopted children by country of origin? A further question might be how a child comes to feel that they are a part of a family, particularly when they have been adopted at an older age. The question of whether there is a gender difference in the impact of intercountry adoption on siblings needs to be explored further. Is there a negative impact on self-esteem and peer relations for male siblings in a family which has adopted internationally?

Acknowledgement of difference has been central in the adoption literature for the past thirty years, yet this was not a predictor of well-being for these internationally adopted children. Does the way parents who have adopted internationally think about adoption make a difference to the child's well-being? There has been a significant increase in the number of families adopting internationally primarily for reasons of infertility. This usually means that there are no older birth siblings within the family, as there were in most of the families in this study. These birth siblings may have played an important role in socializing the intercountry adoptees in how to behave with peers, and in that way made it easier for them to be integrated in to Canadian society. Further research is needed to determine whether intercountry adoptees do as well in families where there are no siblings to help teach these roles. Research is also needed which compares the adjustment of internationally adopted children with those adopted domestically, particularly around issues of identity.

Finally, more study is needed to understand what it is that makes children who have been adopted internationally feel comfortable with their ethnic and racial backgrounds. An understanding of what parents or others might have done to produce a feeling of acceptance with this aspect of the child's identity would provide invaluable guidelines to those who will adopt internationally in the future.

This research was supported by a grant from National Welfare Grants, Human Resources Development Canada.

References

Altstein, H., & Simon, R. J. (Eds). (1991). *Intercountry adoption: A multinational perspective.* New York: Praeger.

Bagley, C., & Young, L. (1980). The long-term adjustment and identity of a sample of inter-country adopted children. *International Social Work, 23*(3), 16–22.

Bagley, C. (1993). Transracial adoption in Britain: A follow-up study, with policy considerations. *Child Welfare, 72*(3), 285–299.

Barrett, S. E., & Aubin, C. M. (1990). Feminist considerations of intercountry adoption. *Women and Therapy, 10*(1–2), 127–138.

Bartholet, B. (1988). International adoption. In *Adoption law and practice.* New York: Matthew Bender.

Bibby, R. W., & Posterski, D. C. (1992). *Teen trends: A nation in motion.* Toronto: Stoddart.

Bowen, J. (1992). *A Canadian guide to international adoptions: How to find, adopt, and bring home your child.* Vancouver, British Columbia: Self-Counsel Press.

Brodzinsky, D. M. (1990). *The psychology of adoption.* New York: Oxford University Press.

Byles, J., Byrne, C., Boyle, M., & Offord, D. (1988). Ontario child health study: Reliability and validity of the general functioning subscale of the McMaster Family Assessment Device. *Family Process, 27*(1), 97–104.

Cederblad, M. (1982). *Children adopted from abroad and coming to Sweden after age three.* Stockholm: The Swedish National Board for Intercountry Adoptions.

Daly, K. J., & Sobol, M. (1992). *Adoption as an alternative for infertile couples: Prospects and trends.* Paper prepared for the Royal Commission on New Reproductive Technologies. Ottawa.

Daniels, D., Dunn, J., Furtenberg, F. F., & Plomin, R. (1985). Environmental differences within the family and adjustment differences within pairs of adolescent siblings. *Child Development, 56*(3), 764–774.

Divirglio, L. (1956). Adjustment of foreign children in their homes. *Child Welfare, 39*(9), 15- 21.

Dunn, J., & Plomin, R. (1990). *Separate lives: Why siblings are so different.* New York: Basic Books.

Epstein, N. B., Baldwin, L. M., & Bishop, D. S. (1983). The McMaster family assessment device. *Journal of Marital and Family Therapy, 9*(2), 171–180.

Feigelman, W., & Silverman, A. R. (1983). *Chosen children: New patterns of adoptive relationships.* New York: Praeger.

Gardell, I. (1979). *A Swedish study on intercountry adoptions.* Stockholm: The Swedish Council for Intercountry Adoptions at the National Board of Health and Welfare.

Gill, O., & Jackson, B. (1983). *Adoption and race: Asian and mixed race children in white families.* New York: St. Martin's Press.

Gravel, R., & Roberge, P. (1984). *Le véçu en adoption internationale au Québec.* Québec City: Ministère des Affaires Sociales.

Hofvander, Y., Bengtsson, E., Gunnarby, A., Cederblad, M., Kats, M., & Stromholm, S. (1978). U-landsadotivbarn—halsa och anpassning. *Lakartidningen, 75*, 4673–4680.

Hoksbergen, R. A. C. (1981). Adoption of foreign children in the Netherlands. *International Child Welfare Review, 49*(3), 28–37.

Hoksbergen, R. A. C. (1984). Some main problems in adopting a child. *Report of the seminar on inter-country adoption: International Council on Social Welfare.* Montréal: International Council on Social Welfare.

Hoksbergen, R. A. C. (1987). *Adopted children at home and at school: The integration after eight years of 116 Thai children in the Dutch society.* Lisse: Swets & Zeitlinger B.V.

Hoksbergen, R. A. C. (1991). Intercountry adoption coming of age in the Netherlands: Basic issues, trends and developments. In H. Altstein & R. J. Simon, (Eds.), *Intercountry adoption: A multinational perspective* (pp. 141–160). New York: Praeger.

Hudson, W. (1982). *The clinical measurement package: A field manual.* Homewood, Illinois: Dorsey Press.

Jaffee, E. D. (1991). Foreign adoptions in Israel: Private paths to parenthood. In H. Altstein & R. J. Simon, (Eds), *Intercountry adoption: A multinational perspective* (pp. 161–182). New York: Praeger.

Joe, B. (1978). In defense of intercountry adoption. *Social Service Review, 53*(1), 1–20.

Kim, D. S. (1978). Issues in transracial and transcultural adoption. *Social Casework, 60*(10), 477–486.

Kim, H. T., & Reid, E. (1970). After a long journey. Unpublished Master's Thesis, University of Minnesota.

Kim, P. S., Hong, S., & Kim. B. S. (1979). Adoption of Korean children by New York area couples: A preliminary study. Child Welfare, *58*, 419–427.

Kim, P. S. (1980). Behaviour symptoms in three transracially adopted Asian children: Diagnosis dilemma. *Child Welfare, 59*, 213–224.

Kirk, H. D. (1964). *Shared fate: A theory of adoption and mental health.* New York: The Free Press.

Kirk, H. D. (1981). *Adoptive kinship: A modern institution in need of reform.* Toronto: Butterworths.

Kirk, H. D. (1988). *Exploring adoptive family life: The collected adoption papers of H. David Kirk.* Brentwood Bay, British Columbia: Ben-Simon Publications.

Kuhl, W. (1985). *When adopted children of foreign origin grow up.* Osnabruck: Terre des Hommes.

Kvist, B., Viermo, V., & Forsten, N. (1989). Barn adopterade till Finland fran utomeuropeiska lander. *Nordisk Psykologi, 41*(2), 97–108.

McDade, K. (1991). International adoption in Canada: Public policy issues. (Discussion paper 91.B.1). Ottawa: Institute for Research on Public Policy.

McRoy, R. G. (1991). Significance of ethnic and racial identity in intercountry adoption within the United States. *Adoption and Fostering, 15*(4), 53–61.

Ngabonziza, D. (1991). Moral and political issues facing relinquishing countries. *Adoption and Fostering, 15*(4), 75–80.

Pruzan, V. (1977). Born in a foreign country—adopted in Denmark. *International Child Welfare Review, 36*(2), 41–47.

Rathburn, C. (1965). Later adjustment of children following radical separation from family and culture. *American Journal of Orthopsychiatry, 35*(4), 604–609.

Raynor, L. (1970). *Adoption of non-white children: The experience of a British adoption project.* London: George Allen and Unwin.

Register, C. (1991). *Are those kids yours? American families with children adopted from other countries.* Toronto: Collier Macmillan.

Rorbech, M. (1991). The conditions of 18-to-25-year-old foreign born adoptees in Denmark. In H. Altstein & R. J. Simon (Eds.). *Intercountry adoption: A multinational perspective* (pp. 127–140). New York: Praeger.

Rosenberg, M. (1965). *Society and the adolescent self-image.* Princeton, New Jersey: Princeton University Press.

Rosenberg, M. (1989). *Society and the adolescent self-image* (Revised edition). Middletown, Connecticut: Wesleyan University Press.

Ryan, A. S. (1983). Intercountry adoption and policy issues. *Journal of Children in Contemporary Society, 15*(3), 49–60.

Saetersdal, B., & Dalen, M. (1991). Norway: Intercountry adoptions in a homogeneous country. In H. Altstein & R. J. Simon (Eds.), *Intercountry adoption: A multinational perspective* (pp. 83–108). New York: Praeger.

Simon, R. J., & Altstein, H. (1977). *Transracial adoption.* New York: John Wiley and Sons.

Simon, R. J., & Altstein, H. (1981). *Transracial adoption: A followup.* Lexington, Mass.: Lexington Books.

Simon, R. J., & Altstein, H. (1987). *Transracial adoptees and their families: A study of identity and commitment.* New York: Praeger.

Simon, R. J., & Altstein, H. (1992). *Adoption, race, and identity: From infancy through adolescence.* New York: Praeger.

Sobol, M., & Daly, K. (1992). *Adoption as an alternative for infertile couples: Prospects and trends.* Ottawa: Royal Commission on Reproductive Technologies.

Textor, M. R. (1991). International adoption in West Germany: A private affair. In H. Altstein & R. J. Simon (Eds.), *Intercountry adoption: A multinational perspective* (pp. 109–126). New York: Praeger.

Thomas, S., & Chess, A. (1977). *Temperament and development.* New York: Brunner/Mazel.

Triseliotis, J. (1991). Intercountry adoption: A brief overview of the research evidence. *Adoption and Fostering, 15*(4), 46–52.

Verhulst, F. C., Althus, M. & Versluis-den Bieman, H. J. M. (1990). Problem behaviour in international adoptees:1. An epidemiological study. *Journal of the American Academy of Child and Adolescent Psychiatry, 29,* 94–103; 104–111.

Wattier, P. , & Frydman, M. (1985). L'adoption internationale: Étude clinique d'un groupe d'enfants d'origine asiatique. *Enfance, 1,* 59–76.

Westhues, A. & Cohen, J. S. (1988). *How to reduce the risk: Healthy functioning families for foster and adoptive children* (Volume 2. Research Report). Toronto: Faculty of Social Work, University of Toronto.

Wilkinson, H. S. P. (1985). Birth is more than once: *The inner* world of adopted Korean children. Bloomfield Hills, Michigan: Sunrise Ventures.

23

Adoptions: Themes, Policy Implications and Research Agenda

Christopher Bagley and Peter Gabor

The papers by Anne Westhues and Joyce Cohen (1995) and by Christopher Bagley (1995) have covered the topics of inter-country adoptions in Canada, transracial adoptions of Aboriginal children in Canada and the potentially powerful effects of adoption on children who might otherwise grow up in unstable care situations. These two papers did not aim to provide a comprehensive overview of adoption in Canada. Studies have been carried out on various aspects of adoption in Canada (Sachdev 1984, 1991; Bagley, 1983; Vanier Institute, 1994) but research is still needed in several crucial areas.

Some Implications for Canadian Public Policy

Existing research as well as the following research agenda pose interesting dilemmas in public policy:

- To what extent should the state assist childless couples seeking to adopt an infant, or a child with special needs in Canada? How can the state ensure that the needs of the child in the adoption process (needs which should be paramount) are served in ways which are compatible with the often powerful motivations of childless couples to adopt?
- Should the state monitor the standards and practices of intercountry adoptions, and be concerned with child welfare services in developing countries (through specific development projects such as those offered through Canadian International Development Agency)?
- To what extent should the state support adoption agencies, both public and private, in engaging in an open process of adoption placement?
- How can the state ensure that adopted children of First Nations are not alienated from their cultural heritage, or denied traditional or custom adoption placements?
- To what extent should the state be involved in ensuring that the needs and wishes of adoptees seeking birth parents are met? Are the needs of the adopted child (as a young adult) still of paramount importance?

A highly problematic factor in addressing these policy questions is the nature of the state in the Canadian polity. The Canadian state must be considered at three levels: the national or federal state; the minor states established in each province and territory; and the pre-existing nations of the Aboriginal people of Canada.* The matrix of policy formation implied by the interactions of these three types of government is very complex, and is a major challenge for child welfare policy makers.

A Research Agenda

New research, policy and practice initiatives are urgently required in five key areas. First, what is the nature and effect of open adoption practice in which the birth mother (and perhaps the birth father) and potential adopters have some contact before the child is adopted, and sometimes during the course of the child's development? Open adoption is often advocated by the growing number of private agencies in Canada but measures of outcome and process are lacking.

Second, what are the effects of unsealing birth records as an aid to adoptees seeking the identity of, and possibly contact with, a birth parent? Access to such knowledge remains restricted in most Canadian provinces. Research on this matter carried out in the United Kingdom may provide a good exemplar for Canadian research and policy formation.

Third, the adoptions of children with special needs now constitute about half of all adoptions in Canada. This is an important matter for research and policy development but has been largely neglected by Canadian researchers (Scully, 1993). The category of special needs children can include those with serious mental or physical disabilities; older children, including those with multiple care placements and the existence of emotional or behavioural disorders; mixed-race, older children; and children in sibling groups. Among the issues for research and policy development are the kinds of adoptive placements and post-adoption support which such children and their families need; the role of adoptive siblings in the adjustments of special-needs children; mutual support of adoptive parents of special needs children; support of adoptive parents and their children through potentially disruptive crises; social work practice in the placement of special-needs children, including giving the adoptive parent adequate information about the child's medical and development needs; the role of long term foster parents in the care and adoption of special-needs children; and the role of subsidized adoption in this process of adoption of children with special-needs. Demonstration projects and research evaluation of medium and long-term outcomes could provide valuable information for policy and practice.

Fourth, adoption of Aboriginal children by Canadians of European origin has been a frequent practice. Case history and statistical evidence suggest that such adoptions are often subject to disruption. Further research is needed in these areas. First, what social work practices will place major decision-making with Bands and support the traditional practices of custom adoption, including the use of extended families for child care placement? Second, how can Aboriginal children with mental or physical disabilities (including those asso-

---

* In contemplating this complex conundrum we are reminded of the bitter disputes which have surrounded adoption law in India. Muslims (whose religious law forbids the practice of adoption) have successfully blocked efforts by the federal government of India to establish a secular Adoption Act. One result of this conundrum is that some 25 million babies and young children, presently languishing in orphanages in India, cannot be adopted, either at home or overseas. The only exceptions are children housed in a small number of Roman Catholic orphanages (Bagley, 1993, chapter 10).

Figure 23-1: Model of Stakeholders in the Adoption Process

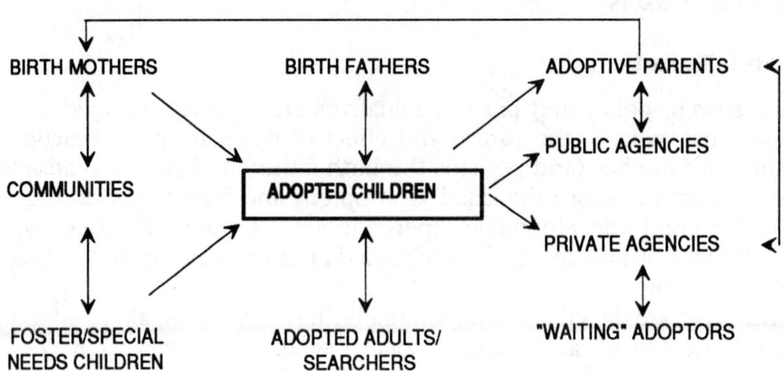

ciated with fetal alcohol syndrome) be supported in their care and development when placed with their extended family? Third, further research is needed into why some adoptions of Aboriginal children by European-Canadian families succeed, and why some Aboriginal children appear to be relatively invulnerable to the stresses of out-of-culture placements.

Finally, there is a need to develop an interactive model to account for the relative roles, role conflicts, values, norms and behaviour of the role-holders, and the mutual obligations, rights and duties of the various stake-holders in the process of adoption. Such a model could draw on the work of David Kirk (1981) and may be similar to the model presented in Figure 23.1. This model identifies ten distinct types of individual, agency or community and is more complex than the "adoption triad of adoptees, birth mothers and adoptive parents" identified by Sorosky, Baran & Pannor (1984). A fundamental assumption in the model is that the needs, interests, and rights of the adopted child must be paramount.

Three types of action and enquiry, including quantitative and qualitative research, are needed to respond to the five priority areas. First, descriptive questions require answers. For example, how does adoption policy and practice differ between agencies and between provinces? How do different role-holders in the model view one another, and their respective rights, roles and duties? What kind of couples adopt (or are willing to adopt) special-needs children? What is the extent and nature of custom adoption in Aboriginal and other ethnic communities in Canada? Second, when valid and reliable data-gathering techniques have been established, and a range of descriptive questions are addressed, longitudinal and cross-sectional analyses can begin to answer some cause-and-effect questions, such as the antecedents of identity development in different types of adoptees, from childhood through adolescence to young adulthood. Another example of long-term research would involve follow-up studies of the effects of contacts between young adopted adults with both parents. Third, research is needed to guide policy and practice conclusions which can be made about particular kinds of placements that reduce the possibility of disruption for special-needs children.

References

Bagley, C. (1995). Adoption and mental health: Studies of adolescents and adults. In J.

Hudson & B. Galaway (Eds.), *Child welfare in Canada: Research and policy implications*. Toronto: Thompson Educational Publishing.

Bagley, C., Young, L., & Scully, A. (1993). *International and transracial adoptions: A mental health perspective*. Aldershot, U.K.: Avebury.

Kirk, D. (1981). *Adoptive kinship: A modern institution in need of reform*. Toronto: Butterworths.

Sachdev, P. (1984). *Adoption: Current issues and trends*. Toronto: Butterworths.

Sachdev, P. (1991). Achieving openness in adoption: Some critical issues in policy formation. *American Journal of Orthopyschiatry*, *61*, 241–249.

Scully, A. (1993). Social work practice and the adoption of special-needs children: A Canadian case study. In C. Bagley (Ed.), *International and transracial adoptions* (pp. 121–134). Aldershot, U.K.: Avebury.

Sorosky, A., Baran, A., & Pannor, R. (1984). *The adoption triangle*. New York: Doubleday. Vanier Institute (1984). *Profiling Canada's Families*. Ottawa: Vanier Institute of the Family.

Westhues, A., & Cohen, J. (1995). Intercountry adoption in Canada: Predictors of well-being. In J. Hudson & B. Galaway (Eds.), *Child welfare in Canada: Research and policy implications*. Toronto: Thompson Educational Publishing.

5

CHILD WELFARE SERVICE EXPERIENCES AND OUTCOMES

24

Listening to Low-Income Children and Single Mothers: Policy Implications Related to Child Welfare

Carolyne A. Gorlick

Children and parents are not passive recipients but play an active role in resisting, complying, interpreting and responding to child welfare activities. The perceived experiences and concerns of children combine to form a missing piece in the discussion about child welfare policy. Through listening to the voices of children we are afforded an opportunity to view their social world, thereby identifying strengths as well as disadvantages from which policy efforts might build. Children interact with others, are sometimes misunderstood, are expected to follow rules they are unable to change and lack power in relation to adults. By also listening to parents, another dimension of the child's social world is offered. The focus of this chapter is single mothers and children on social assistance. The discussion is not an evaluation of a particular child welfare program or policy, but is an attempt to offer a self portrait of low-income single mothers and children. From this picture particular themes of voice and response emerge.

Methodology

A longitudinal research study of 150 single mothers on social assistance in Ontario included three interview sets between 1987 and 1994 at 2 to 2.5 year intervals. The sample retention rate was 84 % (N=125) after the second round of interviews and 72% (N=108) after the final set of interviews. Information reported in this chapter is primarily from the last round of single mother interviews as well as interviews (N=85) with 72 of their children. The children's survey included 62% females and 38% males from 8 to 18 years of age; 39% of children were in the 8—11 year age group, 31% were 12—14 years and 31% were 15—18 years old. Normally one child per family was chosen but both siblings were included when there was a brother and sister. The one and a half to two hour taped mother and child interview schedules contained both quantitative and qualitative questions. The child's interview schedule was also pre-tested for gender and age sensitivity. Preliminary discussion with mothers eliminated sensitive questions such as social assistance affiliation. Mothers indicated that many of the children, particularly younger ones, did not know the family was receiving social assistance.

Themes Of Voice And Response

The Children

The interconnections between school, peers and family articulate and redefine the social world of children. Children living in poverty are frequently characterized as failures or products of inadequate parenting or victims of systemic discrimination. One setting in which these characterizations may be reaffirmed is the child welfare setting, another may be the school. Sixty-five percent of children were in elementary school, 14% in technical and 18% in academic streams in secondary school, and 3% had left school. For 88% of the children, their past school experiences were positive, noting that it was because they did well academically (41%) or had good friends at school (35%). The majority of children (86%) rated current school experiences high but in this instance peer support scored higher than academic achievement. Most children were doing very well academically, with 35% obtaining an A average, 45% a B, and 20% a C; 71% indicating that this was a consistent grade for them. The academic successes were, however, correlated more frequently with elementary as opposed to secondary educational levels. It appears that the children perceive and receive educational supports in their earlier school career. As children proceed to higher school levels these supports are altered within the setting and challenged by external societal and institutional messages that reinforce the negative perceptions of low-income children of themselves and by others.

School experiences and peer interaction are only part of the social world understood by children. Some have witnessed and been a victim of abusive relationships, from a single incident to on-going pressures, either experiencing abuse themselves or witnessing siblings being abused. Some have seen their mothers placed in psychiatric institutions for short periods. Very few children had engaged in criminal activity but some of their brothers had and were removed from the home. Mothers noted that 21% of their children (primarily males) had been or are in foster care. Some children have or were receiving anti-depressants or Ritalin, and a few had been diagnosed with learning disabilities. The family also experienced downward income mobility leading to application for social assistance. About 75% of single mothers at interview time 1 noted a decreased monthly income as a result of marital status change. This was primarily a result of little to no financial assistance from fathers (Gorlick and Pomfret 1991). For many children interaction with fathers had been infrequent and periodic, although 63% of the children had some contact with fathers. Seventy-three percent were 4 years of age or younger when their parents separated, with 10% born to never-married mothers. Thus in identifying key individuals occupying their social world the children viewed their mother as the most important and consistent adult in their lives.

It is misleading to view low-income children as a dispirited group that have given up on themselves and others. Children had positive perceptions of themselves and their abilities as measured by the Child Depression Inventory (Kovacs 1983). Frequency data, however, yielded some gender and age differences. Young females (8–11 yrs) were less sure than older females and males of all ages that things would work out for them, more likely to worry that bad things would happen to them, to say that they think about killing themselves but would not try, had more difficulty making up their minds about

Table 24.1: Relationships Between Selected Variables for the Children

	Age*	Gender*	Perceived Maternal Support*	Child's Self-Perception*
Child's Self-Perception	.16	.15	.74	
Perceived Maternal Support	.08	-.28		
Perceived Poverty			.48	.60

* Gamma is used as the measure of correlation.

things and were unhappy about their physical appearance. On the other hand, young females were more likely to indicate positive responses to school-related achievements. Older females were more likely to respond that they felt like crying many days, were bothered and had trouble sleeping many nights. Younger males consistently indicated problems with school work (such as pushing themselves all the time to do homework) and not doing what they were told. Males ranked consistently high on self perception and were more likely to act out any frustrations at home and school. These gender and age differences in self perceptions and accompanying behaviour are further affected by parental response. If mother-child communication to negative behaviour is not effective, the next response by mothers was to seek outside assistance; in more severe cases, sons were placed in foster care or left home. Thus, during family conflict resolution, sons and daughters experienced differing resolution responses with differing outcomes. For sons the outcome appeared programmatic and/or institutional, for daughters it was individualized within the family.

Table 24.1 shows correlations (gamma) among child's self perception, perceived maternal support, perceived poverty, age and gender. The more perceived support from the mother, the higher the child's perceptions of themselves. There seems to be a level, however, at which more perceived maternal support does not necessarily lead to heightened child self perceptions. This reaffirms the complexity of mother-child interaction and significance of the mother's caring role from the child's perspective.

Families have adapted a variety of strategies to cope. Some of these coping strategies were expressed by older children remembering the transition to a single parent family. Deryk and Jody offer typical responses to the question, "What do you think you have lost and gained from being in a single parent family?":

> I probably missed male guidance. Three females is a lot to handle. I am always being sent out of the room when they talk about stuff or get undressed. On the other hand, it's really helpful in terms of getting to know what your girlfriend is thinking. I probably understand more about women than most guys do. If my father had stayed we would probably be divided up, with my sisters going with mom and me with dad. But my sisters have always talked to me and helped me when I need it. And so does my mom. That's about as good as it gets (Deryk, 16 years old).

> Sometimes I think what it would be like money wise with two incomes instead of one. But I don't even know if I would want to live with both parents now ... because you get (in a single parent family) one on one attention, you get your mother's attention a lot more. You do things more together. I mean two parent families do things together but the decisions are made between the mum and dad. Whereas with mum, a lot of the time she asks for our opinion (Jody, 17 years).

In describing their mothers, children have very positive perceptions as measured by the Parent Perception Inventory (Hazzard et al. 1983). Frequency data yielded age and gender differences. The young female group (8–11 yrs) was more likely to perceive that their mother comforts them, expresses nonverbal affection (hugs, kissing, tickling) plays with them, spend time together and keep after them to do things. Older females (15–18 yrs) were more likely to indicate that mothers involved them in decision-making by letting them decide what to do and engaging in problem solving. Older males (15–18 yrs) more frequently noted mothers would sometimes get mad and warn them about getting into trouble and were generally seen as more critical. Among the 12–14 year age group, regardless of gender, mothers were seen as offering their children significant positive evaluation through compliments and telling them they were good people, as well as helping them with homework or some other difficult activity. Also this group frequently perceived mothers as giving positive reinforcement by thanking them for doing things, and telling them when she liked something they did. Table 24.1 shows that females were slightly more likely than males to perceive maternal support. Overall, 65% of children said mothers were loving and they get along together, 28% said mothers were friends or "pals" and 7% said they did not get along or like their mothers.

The Mothers

Some myths surrounding single mothers receiving social assistance have been: their low educational levels, long term welfare dependency, lack of job motivation, poor self esteem, and the presence of many children (Gorlick 1994). Findings from this study challenge some of these myths. Many single mothers had strong educational backgrounds. Although 27% of single mothers had not graduated from secondary school, 28% had a secondary school certificate, 7% a college diploma, 11% a university degree, 6% nursing or teaching qualifications, 7% clerical or word processing qualifications and 14% other (usually foreign qualifications). Currently for those enrolled in academic and technical courses, 65% are in courses leading to community college entrance and 9.5% in a program culminating in a university degree.

Total time on social assistance (Ontario Family Benefits) included 60.2% for 5 years or less, 25% from 6 to 10 years, 12% from 11 to 16 years and 3% from 18 to 23 years. Seventy percent of mothers said they were still on some form of social assistance during the final interview period. Sixty-seven percent of those no longer receiving social assistance were employed. Gorlick and Pomfret (1993) found that 81.6% of the single mothers were engaged in some form of welfare exit strategy (educational enrolment, program completion and employment) between interviews at time 1 and time 2. The third round of interviews indicated that 49% of the mothers hoped that their income next year would come from employment; 41% said they were currently looking for work. Fifty-two percent said they were hoping to take courses/programs to upgrade, 22% already were and 27% were not planning to take any upgrading courses because some had been completed. Of those hoping to retrain and upgrade their qualifications, 27% wanted programs related to the helping profession (social work and nursing), 19% business, 14% teacher training, 14% vocational and 15% said that their qualifications might not lead to a specific type of work. Currently, 48% of single mothers are in paid employment with 51% in full-time (30 hours plus /week) and 48% in part-time (under 30 hours/week).

Throughout this longitudinal study, single mothers scored high on self esteem measures, including for example: "I am satisfied with myself" (80%); "have a number of good qualities" (95%) and "have a positive attitude towards myself" (87%). Furthermore, single mothers continued to be hopeful about the future ,with 72% expecting it to be better, 25% to remain the same and 2% feeling it will get worse.

Caregiving is perceived by the majority of single mothers as their primary role; 97% describing themselves as homemakers. Thirty-seven percent of single mothers had one child, 33% had two children and 13% had three children living with them. Thirty-two percent of their children had left home which frequently meant a decrease in income for those on social assistance. Of those who did leave home, 61% were living on their own, 21% were in foster homes and 11% went to live with their fathers. Eighty-five percent of single mothers said they did not expect to have any more children. In addition to caring for their children, 34% were engaged in unpaid volunteer work, 29% had extra familial responsibilities with 74% caring for their aging parents once or twice a week. Anne is an example of the demands on the single mother: "I'm tired, really tired of having to do it all by myself. I wish someone would take care of me for once"(Anne, interview 3). Subsequently, mothers respond to daily pressures and supports by taking courses, working full- or part-time, caring for their children on their own and coping with poverty. In defining their current financial situation, 17% of single mothers said they managed with difficulty, 37% of the mothers said they managed but with not much money to spare, 26% found it very difficult to manage and 17% did not manage at all.

Coupled with having a low level of income is the stigma attached to being on social assistance. The humiliation is particularly felt by those whose children were older. One single mother reflected on differences in being on social assistance initially and now:

> It was a lot different when my child was a baby. Being on Family Benefits then was OK because society looked on it as OK. Now I am a 30-year-old, intelligent woman and my daughter is getting older, so even though I am actively job hunting, I feel embarrassed as though I shouldn't be on Family Benefits. It is humiliating now, where it was an unpleasant reality at the beginning (Mary Ann, Interview 3.)

The embarrassment for some emerged with the aging of the child, and for others it came at the end of educational upgrading and the search for a job:

> I'm more frustrated now about being on Family Benefits than when I first went on, because I thought it was going to be a temporary thing while I was at school. It seemed acceptable to receive it while I was preparing myself for a job. But now I can't find work! (Marj, Interview 3)

Table 24.2 suggests a negative correlation (gamma) between time on social assistance and self esteem, hopes for the future and anticipation of future income. The longer single mothers were on Family Benefits, the more likely they believed their futures would remain the same or get worse. Self esteem

Table 24.2: Impact of Time on Social Assistance on Selected Variables for the Mothers

	Time on Social Assistance*
Mother's self-esteem	-.39
Mother's hopes for the future	-.35
Mother's anticipated future income sources	-.44
Number of children at home	.04
Mother's educational aspirations	.03

* Gamma is used as the measure of correlation.

showed little measurable drop until after six years on social assistance. Subsequently there appears to have been a perceived period of grace, after which decline in mothers' self esteem was apparent. Being on social assistance while your children were young appeared more socially acceptable. As children aged, mothers are re-categorized from full-time care-giver to labour market entrants and pressures to successfully obtain full-time paid employment become significant. This comes at a cost for single mothers and renders past and future caring for children as invisible or not significant to the primary objective of diminishing welfare dependency through paid work.

The significance of mother-child interaction emerges when considering mothers' aspirations for themselves and their children and children's own aspirations. Two out of three mothers wanted their children to have a post-secondary education. Sixty-three percent wanted daughters and sons to complete university while 15% wanted daughters and 14% sons to complete community college. Most children agreed with mothers' aspirations for them. Sixty-eight percent of children wanted to complete a university degree, followed by 26% wanting to complete a community college diploma. The group that most frequently chose university were females 12–14 years, while the group that opted for community college were males, 15–18 years. Mothers also had other aspirations for their children such as:

> They will learn from me that they can survive, that they have confidence and can take care of themselves, that they love themselves and that they have a good relationship with me and that they will be financially independent before they have kids of their own. (Mary, Interview 3)

> I hope they will finish high school at least. Maybe become professionals. As long as they don't settle down too early. I love my kids but I missed my teen years and I can never get them back. I really don't want that to happen to them (Eileen, Interview 3)

Mothers' aspirations for children and for themselves may be linked to the child's future hopes. And perhaps the child's aspirations function as a continuing positive reinforcer of mothers' hopes for themselves and children. This dynamic of reinforcement between mother and child is apparent with a mother's perception of her own and child's health (Gorlick and Pomfret 1991). The mother's perceived health and her perceptions of child's health are closely linked. If a mother saw her child's health improving, her general health scores indicated an improvement. If a mother saw her child's health getting worse, her general health declined. Similarly if she thought her general health was bad, her mental and physical health scores were low. If a mother thought the child's health had improved, her mental and physical health was higher. If a mother thought her child's health had worsened, her mental and physical health scores were lower.

Defining and Responding to Poverty

Mothers clearly attempted to buffer the impact of poverty on their children, particularly younger ones. As a result, 76% of children interviewed perceived they were not poor. The older the child, the more visible the socio-economic markers of impoverishment, the more likely they were to feel poor. And this perception of poverty was more likely to be experienced by sons rather than daughters. Children who aspired to obtain a post-secondary degree, were less likely to feel poor. Furthermore, positive self perceptions and child's feeling poor were strongly linked. In addition, perceived positive maternal support was related to not feeling poor. "No I don't feel poor. My mum puts me ahead of herself so I can get what I need "(Cheryl, 15 years old). Subsequently mothers with few resources themselves are in the untenable position of attempting to isolate their children from the stigma of poverty.

Differences emerged in how children defined poverty. Some of the younger children based their understanding from media presentations of Third World hunger and deprivation, such as:

> The poor don't have lots of food and when they get rice, the person who is giving the rice takes out a whip and doesn't let the children have any. I watched a TV show and it was true and he had a big bowl of rice and everybody is grabbing it and when he saw a child taking some he whipped the child and the child died. (Charlene, 9 years old).

Often young children drew their understanding from school and friends:

> At school, people make fun of them. They say "ha-ha you're poor! You can't afford anything. You get your clothes from Goodwill!" The teachers probably give them lots more homework. They probably wouldn't have many friends because there could be rumours going around the school about them. They'd probably have torn-up clothes that were too small. (Corrine, 11 years old).

The younger the child the more likely they were to describe the severity of poverty in terms of homelessness, no food and so forth and the more unlikely they were to view themselves as poor. Some children articulated a fear of poverty. "Sometimes I am scared of being poor. Because sometimes I feel like we are going to get thrown out onto the street" (David, 9 years old). Older children defined poverty more in terms of material deprivation in relation to friends, about things they need like sports equipment, clothes, school trips and events. This was expressed by a male adolescent:

> I would love to go to football camp, but I have never asked to go because I know that my mother has a really hard time and these football camps cost $300-$400 to go. I did talk to my junior football coach once about going on a field trip, and the school spotted me the money and I did pay them back. I always pay back my debts. I don't know this time because it may be the senior coach who sends you to camp, and I don't know him as well. (Mike 16 years)

Although mothers attempted to divert concerns by younger children, older children felt the stigma of being poor. "The name welfare itself is a problem, because when you hear it in school, welfare sounds like you have lost hope, but I haven't" (Brad, 16 yrs old). Some were reminded in other ways that they were poor; for one it was a grandparent, "My grandma compares us to our cousins. They live in Kitchener and they have a big house and she thinks we should have the same thing" (Sheila 15 years old). Another youth noticed the shortage of food, "Sometimes just before Mum gets paid, we won't have a lot of food" (Ian, 14 years old).

Poverty perceptions interact with expectations in the context of opportunity structures or life chances. Equity themes and perceived moral authority run through many responses to the question: what would you do to change things for poor children? Younger children focus primarily on provision of adequate housing, enough food, decent clothes, while older children search for greater social equity:

> I would change the whole system. I would get rid of money completely. For me, if I could have everything in life free, I would work at a job, I would do my job, I would work in a factory or wherever, doing also volunteer work and then have everything in life free. And I believe that if everybody did that we would still have everything we have today, only we wouldn't have money, it would completely crush the crime system, you wouldn't need crime. Why would you steal from somebody? It would just be a whole sharing thing for everybody and everybody would be equal (Aaron, 16 yrs old).

> I would take money from rich people and give it to the poor. I think it is good how if someone doesn't have a job then they don't have to pay as much for rent. Because it's not fair for them to keep paying a whole bunch of rent when they don't have any money. I 'd give them more opportunity for jobs, because a lot of people are getting fired lately (Donna, 12 years old).

> Family Benefits should go up as the kids get older. We get the same amount of money now as we did when we were in public school and I think our costs are a lot more. Because there is a lot more things we need money for. I think the amount of money they give us is unfair (Jody, 17 years old).

And mothers spoke of the need to be independent from poverty:

> I don't want my daughter to remain in the cycle of poverty and the whole scene that accompanies it. I want her to have choices and be happy in whatever she chooses (Valerie, Interview 3).

> I hope my kids are well educated and independent. I want them to know that they can take care of themselves in every aspect. I also want them to be equally treated and for them to treat others that way. I also hope my son treats women as equals and my daughter doesn't experience chauvinism. If they have that independence they will be happy in their relationships (Pat, Interview 3).

Mothers' response to poverty is action in the form of educational upgrading and seeking employment. Nevertheless, by the third interviews there were significant concerns raised regarding retraining programs and future job prospects.

> Re-training was unrealistic because there are no jobs. I bought into the dream that was not based on reality and now I owe $5,400 and all I have is a boost to my ego (Elaine, Interview 3).

Finally, the frequency and extent of change is consistent to both mothers and children. Change in this study includes residential mobility, mother's

Table 24.3: Impact of Selected Changes on the Health Status of the Mother

	Mother's Health Status*
Discontinue social assistance	.36
Change residence	.33
Decrease in number of children at home	.08
Complete post-secondary programme	-.12
Complete technical upgrading	-.12
Complete technical upgrading	-.12
Complete educational upgrading	-.03
Obtain part-time employment	-.03
Obtain full-time employment	.30
Children's Health	.13

* Gamma is used as the measure of correlation.

marital status and employment, and school and friendship changes for children. Between interviews at time 2 and time 3, 15% of the single mothers had changed marital status through remarriage, 20% had experienced a decrease in number of children living with them (while 15% had an increase), and 56% changed residences. During this same period, 24% had discontinued social assistance, with 9% completing educational and 20% technical upgrading. Children identified residential, school and friendship changes. Ninety percent of children said they have moved residence (50% of whom moved 4 to 7 times) 79% changed schools (27% more than four times) and 65% said their friends changed. Some children (21%) remembered changes in child care arrangements.

Change also has an impact on perceived health. Correlations (gamma) between mothers' perceived health and other variables are presented in Table 24.3. Mothers perceived that their health worsened with discontinuing social assistance, residential changes and obtaining full-time employment. Single mothers hope to remove themselves from welfare dependency but stress increases when they actually discontinue social assistance and obtain paid employment.

> I am going off Family Benefits soon, because I have a job. But I am scared—really scared—that I may be taking too much of a chance for myself and the kids, because I'm not sure what the future will hold (Cathy, Interview 3).

In sum, the themes of voice and response by low-income single mothers and children include: conflict, coping, caring and taking chances. These themes are carried out in the context of ongoing individual, familial, income, residential, educational, health and employment changes. What might policy makers draw from the voices and responses of low-income single mothers and their children?

Policy Implications

Past child welfare policies suffer from program ambiguities and inconsistencies (Wharf 1993), inadequate policy assumptions (Armitage 1993) and systemic gender inequities (Swift 1991, Callaghan 1993). Although the sample size of this longitudinal effort is small and subsequently lacks generalizability, identifiable trends and challenges from the data might offer alternative and additional perspectives for child welfare program development.

Several provinces and the federal government are discussing various modifications and implementation measures of child income support programs as well as transition programs for single mothers exiting from welfare to paid work. Child income support programs are viewed as improving the child welfare system by providing a monthly cheque to low-income families with benefits decreasing as income rises. It is in this context that the voices and responses of low-income single mothers and their children would be useful. The primary advantage of a child income support program would be the de-stigmatizing of financial support by removing the direct "welfare" contact. Clearly, mothers' attempts to hide being on social assistance from their children and older children's negative self perception tied to welfare would be eased. Also, it might be assumed that these programs would lessen the impact of continued welfare dependency, leading to decreased mothers' self esteem, future hopes and income expectations. Would a child income support program de-stigmatize being on welfare? Perhaps, but without an adequate family income level and family supports it will not de-stigmatize or minimize the daily realities of living in poverty.

Accompanying a child income support program should be supportive family structures and processes. It is evident that mother and children are not independent units but closely linked through caring, perceived health status, educational and employment aspirations, future hopes, self esteem, and defining and responding to poverty. Also in the aftermath of marital separation and downward income mobility, mothers and children experienced significant familial, income, residential, educational, employment and health status changes. Age and gender of children impacts on their response to these changes with the older male being the most vulnerable to child welfare intervention. Throughout this period of change and stress, their mother was the most important and consistent adult in the children's lives. Subsequently policy initiatives should focus on the family as an integral unit.

Past child welfare programs were based on an understanding of low-income families as pathological with few resources. Yet strengths do exist in this family from which programs may be developed. One strength is the positive association with current and future education for both mother and children. The majority of children had positive past and current school experiences and were achieving academically; 73% of mothers had post-secondary education. Furthermore, most mothers hoped (and their children agreed) that their children would obtain a post-secondary education. Another strength is the high self esteem of mothers and children, and the mothers' commitment to breaking welfare dependency by furthering education and seeking paid employment. Paid employment as defined by low-income mothers is not an entry level position but a satisfying and income-sufficient job for a one income family. To achieve this goal, the mothers are willing to engage in a number of activities such as educational upgrading, skills training, full and part-time employment and volunteer work as well as combinations of these activities. Accompanying mothers' and children's education and employment plans is an overall positive view of the future, with 72% of mothers believing things will get better. Whether these mothers prove correct in their perceptions will depend on several considerations, many beyond their control. Thus, in addition to the strengths of low-income families, child welfare policy makers must also recognize that mothers and children are being asked to take chances in an unequal playing field of differing opportunity structures and processes.

Taking chances for these low-income single mothers and their children began with marital separation (or birth of a child) to residential, school, employment and friendship changes, to application for social assistance. Taking chances involves a variety of coping strategies in response to poverty from parent-child conflict, to buffering the impact for their children to the ongoing uncertainty and insecurity that poverty brings. Taking chances is the mother's recognition that a period of grace on social assistance exists. This period of grace is programmatically delineated as beginning and ending with child dependency (defined as age of kindergarten or primary/elementary school or adolescence) and the movement of mothers from primary care-giver to labour market entrant. The reality is that caregiving is viewed by 97% of mothers as their primary role whether in paid employment or not. Also, mothers expressed concern regarding the pressures to obtain paid employment fearing that moving too quickly would jeopardize exiting social assistance permanently. Taking chances leads to mothers' perceived health worsening through discontinuing social assistance, residential changes and obtaining full-time paid employment. Taking chances involves risking a family's hopes for the future. Children's perceptions of poverty were clearly linked to future aspirations, with those aspiring to complete a post-secondary education less likely to feel poor. For both mothers and children poverty perceptions interacted with expectations and understandings of life chances. Mothers' and children's educational and employment aspirations reinforce each other impacting on individual self esteem. To try, and fail, at achieving upward income mobility is to precipitate a chain of negative familial influences, frequently culminating in lost hope. Subsequently, policy initiatives must include the significance of time as experienced by low-income families.

In conclusion, child welfare policy should recognize that mothers and children play an active role in resisting, complying, interpreting and responding to child welfare initiatives. Within this context, they are also willing to take chances in participating in a program that improves their family's quality of life. Without a carefully planned, comprehensive, family-based child welfare policy incorporating family strengths and needed resources and their voices, the costs of taking chances for this family may be too great.

References

Armitage, A. (1993). The policy and legislative context. In Brian Wharf (Ed.), *Rethinking child welfare in Canada*. Toronto: McClelland and Stewart.

Callaghan, M. (1993). Feminist approaches: Women recreate child welfare. In Brian Wharf (Ed.), *Rethinking child welfare in Canada*. Toronto: McClelland and Stewart.

Gorlick, C. (1994). Divorce: Options available, pathways chosen, constraints forced. In A. Duffy & N. Mandel (Eds), *Canadian families: Diversity, conflict and change*. Toronto: Harcourt and Brace Canada.

Gorlick, C., & Pomfret, A. (1993). Hope and circumstance: Single mothers exiting social assistance. In J. Hudson & B. Galaway (Eds.), *Single parent families: Perspectives on research and policy.* Toronto: Thompson Educational Publishing.

Gorlick, C., & Pomfret, A. (1991). Responding to welfare: Single mothers in a Canadian context: Diversity, change and strain. Paper presented at the National Council on Family Relations 53rd Annual Conference, Denver, Colorado.

Hazzard, K., Christianson, J., & Margolian, S. (1983). Children's perceptions of parental behavior. *Journal of Abnormal Child Psychology, 11*, 49–60.

Kovacs, M. (1983). Child depression inventory: A self rated depression scale for school age children. Unpublished manuscript, University of Pittsburgh.

Swift, K. (1991). Contradictions in child welfare: Neglect and responsibility. In C. Baines, P. Evans, & S. Neysmith (Eds.), *Women's caring: Feminist perspectives on social welfare.* Toronto: McClelland and Stewart.

Wharf, B. (1993). *Rethinking child welfare in Canada.* Toronto: McClelland and Stewart.

25

Return Home as Experienced by Children in State Care and Their Families

Roger Bullock

This paper considers the process by which separated children return home. It concentrates on the experience as perceived and felt by those involved, particularly the children and their families. The findings come from an elaborate study of return home as experienced by children in state care (Bullock, Little & Millham, 1993). Qualitative research evidence is considered in a wider context that includes the return experiences and statistical findings about the frequency and duration of separation and reunion for the children.

Return is as fraught with stress as separation. The management of return is far from simple and, while the majority of reconciliations are successful, those that fail can have serious long-term implications for the rejected child. All this has to be viewed in light of the fact that in the United Kingdom, the majority of children in state care return home. An estimated 87% of those separated are back home after five years or are very likely to go there in the near future. Moreover, the probability of return remains the same, however long the child has been away; going home is statistically the most likely thing to happen to a child in care. For three-fifths of them, reunification takes place before six months have elapsed, and for one-fifth the absence is less than one week. The swift return of nearly 20,000 children each year is a largely unsung social work contribution to family welfare.

This success story should not obscure the problems of those few who linger. Indeed, the problems of reunion for those long-separated from home, usually adolescents, have excited particular concern; nevertheless they all maintain high chances of reunion with family members, even if they move from care to live independently. Naturally, some young people have more favourable prospects than others but return to home and community is always a likely outcome.

Twenty-four families, containing 31 children away in care, were studied from the point at which return home had become a possibility. Some returns were very likely and easy to arrange but other situations were merely plans to be implemented once difficulties had been overcome. A two-year prospective study of these children identified the difficulties intrinsic to the return process. The concepts of continuity, role, and territory were helpful.

Continuity

The concept that for satisfactory development, children and families need continuity, security, belonging and even a sense of history is implicit in much of the work on separation. Maluccio, Fein, and Olmstead (1986) open their study with the words "in order to grow up satisfactorily, children need to know that life has predictability and continuity. They need the reliability of knowing where they will be growing up." Continuity is also stressed by Kellmer-Pringle (1975) who writes, "a child is most likely to develop to a maximum level if he or she has an enduring relationship with at least one person who is sensitive to his or her individual needs and stages of development." Several writers have explained that families and wider social networks provide children with that sense of continuity and security from which to plan and help fashion their identity and sense of worth. Kahan (1979) in her perceptive study of young adults recollecting their careers as children in care comments that "families and what they mean to individuals not only as children but in adult life were of great significance to all, whether their families were related by blood-ties, by remarriage or by adoption." She also highlights young people's need "for a pattern and for that pattern to be an orthodox one, it is vitally important for the child that everything is done to avoid any thought of being different from any other child."

The value for the child of strong family links and the sense of continuity and belonging that these provide are all explored at length in recent studies (Millham, Bullock, Hosie, 1986; Millham, Bullock, Little, 1989). For most of us a sense of continuity is so omnipresent that it is taken for granted and hardly thought about; but for those without it, the past and its meaning become constant pre-occupations. Continuity and security are viewed as particularly important in satisfactory child development and any child who fails to enjoy such a birth-right faces considerable difficulty. As one teenager recalls:

> I had three foster home placements in the two years after I was taken into care and then I ended up in a children's home. I hadn't much clue as to where I came from and none about where I was going. Nobody seemed to care about me, they never asked me what I wanted or what I felt, never showed any interest in what I did, either in school, in sport or in anything. Unless, of course, you nicked something or kicked up rough, then there was hell to pay and everyone put their nose in.

Another boy comments:

> I was at an assessment centre for months waiting for a foster home but nothing came up, everyone needs to belong somewhere and to somebody. How can an observation centre replace your parents?

If continuity and a sense of belonging do not materialize, then children will create them and fantasize a past which usually bears little relationship to fact. Many observers have also commented on the value of possessions, photographs and other mementos to help maintain links with those absent and continuity with the past. Whitaker and colleagues (1986) comment that "while all concerned constructed explanations for events, for example why a child was in care, the children themselves had little life experience to bring to bear and sometimes accepted or ascribed blame inappropriately or held incompatible views." Thus, children comfort themselves with fantasy and myth:

> When I leave care I'm going to go back and find out exactly who my father is. Maybe he's a Duke or Lord or something and then everybody will be sorry and want to know me

Kahan offers us a most poignant example of a child seeking continuity and a sense of belonging:

> About three years after I went into adoption, I used to go down to the children's home, River-Side, to see if there was anyone there I remembered and took a big chunk out of the wall and I've still got it. In fact, I've heard the place is going to be pulled down, I think I'll get in first and ask for the name-plate. The chunk of wall is out in the shed somewhere, I wouldn't part with it.

But a need for continuity, a sense of belonging and the security that comes from a sense of place are not only needed by children; adults also seek to maintain continuities and to put separations and returns into context.

Continuity can be defined as that sense of meaning and order which we impose on a sequence of life events. These events may be unexpected or random, they may even be traumatic experiences such as a child entering care or the loss of a parent. A sense of continuity is a way of maintaining psychological health. One can also perceive different types of continuity. For example, there are expressive continuities, those that endure over time and change very little. Some of these have macro aspects, such as national and regional identities and perhaps religious, moral or political beliefs, but they also come in the form of feelings for those long departed or the rights of family over friendship. Second there are temporal continuities which do change over time. Indeed, such continuities may wither and be replaced by others such as changes in career or marriage. There may be conflicts between expressive and temporal continuities and return can cruelly expose these contradictions.

Two themes constantly emerge when asking children what going back is like. First, the complexities and difficulties in the resumption of roles and, second, the problems they encounter during the re-colonization of lost territory. Concepts of role and territory are part of the continuity sought by those who are separated, whether child or adult. The ideas that both separation and return are not discrete events, but part of a process, and that separation from home for the majority of children is negotiated with return in mind, are very important. The existence of strong links with family, particularly with the mother, is of great importance both for eventual return to home from care and for the success of any reunion. Will stressing these continuities to the absent child, highlighting continuities of relationships with family and neighbourhood, and emphasizing the likelihood of eventual return facilitate reunion and lead to a successful adjustment? On return, children's sense of continuity and security are likely to be much affected both by changes in the roles they are expected to make and by the space they seek to re-occupy.

Roles

Many years ago, we studied the Byzantine world of the English boarding school, a set of institutions which would have warmed the heart and stimulated the pen of Goffman, institutions beside which other asylums pale (Lambert & Millham, 1968). The relevance of boarding schools to the return of luckless children from local authority care might at first sight seem rather distant, but the complexity of the roles children played within the boarding schools, the demands made upon them and the skills necessary for adequate role performance stimulated great interest.

We classified roles in three distinct categories which may have some transfer value to the roles played by children within families (Millham, Bullock & Cherrett, 1975). First, there were instrumental roles, those concerned with acquiring skills and proficiency. Second, there were organizational roles, those concerned with oiling the wheels of the organization and keeping the show on the road. Third, there were expressive roles, those which were concerned with beliefs, states fulfilling in themselves, and which had a spiritual dimension. Children performed and moved between these roles swiftly, but not quite effortlessly. Their role performance often conflicted with others and there were tensions within a particular role-set. This classification of roles is not quite as complicated as it sounds. For example, a parent taking a cookery class might be part of an instrumental role; cleaning the kitchen floor an organizational chore, a role which hopefully prevents children from breaking their necks; and, third, counselling, supporting children and offering pastoral care are expressive roles. Neither should such a classification of roles be viewed as exclusive. For example, one may invest the balancing of accounts, the stacking of supermarket shelves, or even a gleaming kitchen floor with expressive dimensions.

Roles often overlap. In many role performances, instrumental, organizational and expressive dimensions are closely interwoven. One of the problems families and children face on return is that many apparently organizational roles within families, such as washing up, making the bed, cooking the chips, and taking the dog for a walk have expressive dimensions which pass largely unnoticed. Family members have expectations and investments in these roles which can easily be violated. For example, a mother comments on a returning daughter:

> I thought she would be delighted that I had got a second-hand dish-washer, because we used to row about whose turn it was to do the washing up. But she wasn't pleased at all, she moaned about being done out of her job and actually hardly ever used the thing.

Within families certain roles have considerable status and power, as anyone clasping the television's remote control well knows. Thus, on return, the child finds many seemingly trivial actions deeply invested with other significances; who lays the table, feeds the cat, turns on the fire, answers the phone, are each invested with rights and obligations, all forgotten or ignored at considerable risk. Conflict and tension are likely when organizational roles in a family are invested with the expressive dimensions. An armed services' wife said:

> A moment comes when I know that he is gone and that everything, kids, home, finance, everything is up to me. That realization comes last thing at night when I go round closing the windows and bolting the door, I hate it, I feel guilty and angry at the same time. It's his job and he should be here to do it, I say to myself, he should protect me and the children. In fact, locking up at night can easily bring on tears and then I feel bad and stupid and say to myself, "you wimp, without him you wouldn't have children to love or even a door to lock up."

Part of the management of return should be a keen awareness of the different dimensions operating within each role and that even the simplest of roles have expressive dimensions. It is also true that various family members, including the returning child, will have different perspectives on the meaning implicit in role performances.

Roles have different dimensions and can also have conflict. The holder of the television's remote control reminds others of the power dimension behind any role performance but he or she is likely to conflict with others when football coincides with "Coronation Street" or "Top of the Pops". The arbiter of the evening's viewing will be reproached with comments from others such as "well I bought the damn thing," "who paid for the licence anyway?", "I thought it was my Christmas present," or, deftest strike of all, "but Mum I'm supposed to watch 'Panorama' for my homework." The more key the role, the more derelictions in performance are noted. "It's never worked properly since you let the dog gnaw the damn thing."

There can also be conflict within role-sets, for example, between the parents' need to control, to be fair, and yet to encourage and empathize with their children. In addition, conflict can be omnipresent, built into roles. For example, the role of an adolescent or of a step-parent or step-child has built into it conflicting loyalties and difficulties in meeting the expectations of others. This glimpse of the complexity of family roles no doubt would encourage the socially sensitive to take refuge in the role of the recluse or anchorite. The gradual way in which roles are learned and changed and the loving environment in which performance takes place mean that most families are not arenas of endless dispute and tension. Nevertheless, the complexity of family roles illustrates how a child long separated from home will find reunion difficult and amply reinforces Winnicott's (1984) comment that "insecure children can have all the feelings they can stand within their families or within a few yards of the doorstep. "

Separation and return cause difficulties in any role performance. If absence is lengthy, children forget those signals which direct and reward appropriate behaviour. On return these signs have to be re-learned. While away, the child may adopt role behaviour very different from that expected at home and on reunion find an unappreciative audience. As one mother described:

> He came back from the assessment centre swearing like a trooper and throwing his weight around, that was at least until his father heard him and then gave him a belt.

Things have moved on both for children and their families, although separation tends to freeze the picture for those apart. The families of children who enter care display a wearisome procession of arrivals and departures, a turbulence and movement which make reunion difficult. The households from which children were removed may not be those to which they return; going back may involve them in reunion with siblings also separated by a care experience. During the interim, families may have welcomed new members or may have had lodgers thrust upon them. The passage of time means that there is a gap between the roles the children wish to take up on return and those that the family are willing to accord them. Their departure may have encouraged others to usurp their role and occupy their territory at home, thus resenting their return, particularly if the welcome proffered at reunion seems disproportionate to the trauma and reasons for the original separation. Children and adolescents, unprepared for the tensions and difficulties of return, will react aggressively and appear to the family to be recalcitrant and even less attractive than they were at the initial separation. As a thwarted adolescent girl illustrates:

> My new step-sister took the kids off to play group like some mother hen and Mum said "there, that Angela is really good with them. You never liked the job

and she does it without any fuss." Well there was a fuss 'cos I burned that little shit's bus pass and she had to buy a new one.

But there are ways in which the role conflict inherent in return can be managed and minimized. When counselled and assisted, separated children and young people can become more objective about the roles they and others play in family life and more accommodating to the needs of others. Distance encourages a cooler look. In the same way the arrival of step-parents and step-siblings, although initially threatening, can stimulate new interests in family members. Families can do much by their efforts to keep alive the image of the absentee member within the household, remain mindful of his or her preferences, and, where possible, seem anxious for the return and be instrumental in its achievement. A girl removed with her younger sister from a depressed mother comments:

> It was difficult when I was at home, I couldn't understand why Mum was lonely or depressed or what to do about it. She just used to sit in the pub or lie in bed. We used to row all the time. Being here makes me realize how little she has to look forward to while I and my sister have a lot, so now when I go home at weekends I try to be different to Mum. We go shopping together, watch T.V., sometimes it's quite a laugh. Now I'm looking forward to going home. Nicest thing is that Mum has been on to the social worker asking if we can go back.

In a similar way, a returning adolescent becomes reconciled to his new step brother:

> I didn't like the idea of a step-brother at all and things were a bit dicey at first. We both liked football and I was much better than he was. We go to matches and we have just bought a motorbike between us to go racing. Most of the time it's in bits but now we get on fine and Mum is over the moon about it all.

A lad returning from youth custody comments:

> Going back was easier than I thought. I felt bad about the trouble I caused everyone and they, I know, were none too happy at kicking me out in the first place. But when I went through the door everyone was smiles, my photo in the army cadets was in its old place and Mum had my favourite meal ready. My step-dad offered me a can of beer, so even he was trying hard. It's been like that now for a couple of months, I've got a job bringing in some money and they look at me different now.

Of course, what children find most distressing is inconsistency in parenting behaviour, a lack of forewarning, and unreliability in adult role performance. Re-negotiating a new set of roles on return may present problems; in addition, children also have to re-adapt to familiar places. In some cases they enter new households and other unfamiliar territories.

Territory

Territory and the personalization of space are of concern to children. On return, if having one's roles usurped is also accompanied by the seizure of one's territory, then tensions will quickly mount. As a mother swiftly learned:

> I thought he would be grateful the boy next door had looked after the rabbits. Well, he wasn't. He said he'd built the hut, the rabbits were his and nobody else would look after them properly

It is accepted good practice that separated children need to take something of home away with them, mementos and keepsakes, the loss of which can be very distressing. In the same way, during separation children's private places, their bed, cupboard, drawer, cluster of photographs and prized possessions should remain undisturbed and inviolate. Change can immediately be recognized and resented even after an absence sufficiently long to have contributed to forgetfulness. Age does not act as a filter to a sense of violation; adolescents are quite as sensitive to changed territories as younger children. Anyone managing return should explore the young person's expectations of what his or her territory is going to be like and what changes might have occurred in order to forestall disappointment. Bountiful additions, like a new chair or bedspread, may be welcome if the chance to retain what has gone before remains open, but the disposal of anything, varying from a pair of odd trainers to a pile of battered colour supplements, is fraught with risk. A naval wife copes with an upset child:

> I was amazed. Anne is only six and we had been in Gibraltar for three years. When we came home she was in tears because her bedroom was different. All that our friends had done while they stayed was to move the wardrobe and chest of drawers a bit. Anyway, she was inconsolable until we moved them back again. I didn't even realize they had been shifted, but Anne did and didn't like it one bit.

The gradual re-colonization of lost space is also a strategy to ease return, as a mother recalls the designs of her adolescent daughter in seeking reunion:

> I knew she was worming her way back in, each weekend she would leave more and more stuff behind, shampoo in the bathroom, clothes, magazines, anything. Gradually she took over the bathroom shelf and all my stuff went on to the window-sill.

The scattering of one's property not only helps regain lost territory but possessions themselves are symbolic of one's rights and place in the home. Possessions can be sacrosanct; the unauthorized borrowing of gear, however trivial, can allow tensions to focus upon the culprit. A returning adolescent girl comments:

> That scrubber my dad brought home had the cheek to borrow my skirt, then she complained it was too short, too tight and needed cleaning. "Wash it yourself," I said "then it will be even tighter for all your friends, like dad, with wandering hand trouble."

Winnicott (1984), slightly less acerbic, neatly summarized these issues fifty years ago as the dust of war settled on parents awaiting the return of their children. He reminded them that the child who came back would be different from the waif, brown label round the neck, that tearful mothers had seen off several years before:

> In two or three years of separation, both mothers and children will have altered, more especially the child out of whose life three years is a big chunk. After three years, he is the same person, but he has lost whatever characterizes the six-year-old because he is now nine. And then, of course, even if the house has escaped bomb damage, even if it is exactly as it was when the child left, it seems much smaller to him because he is now so much bigger. It must also be difficult to come back from a farm to a room or two in a block of flats in a big city (p. 47).

The re-occupation of lost territory is as important as the resumption of family roles on any return from separation. In addition, role and territory are often closely associated, sometimes they are invested with considerable expressive significance. So, it is not surprising that, after a brief honeymoon period, rows and tensions between family members and the returning child manifest themselves. Quarrels are likely to signify that reunion is on course rather than offering forebodings that rapprochement is not working.

Further Aspects of the Return Process

The significance of these issues becomes apparent when we trace the progress of each child. We did this by analyzing return in terms of episodes, defined as variable periods of time surrounding a particular phase of the reunion. This helps get away from a deterministic view of processes in which sequences follow automatically. It allows flexibility to include those families which miss an episode or enter the process late. As episodes are remarkable and dramatic to the participants as well as to the researchers, it enables us to understand the meaning and perceptions of the children and their family members as well as to wield control over the enormous mass of data assembled (Little, 1990).

Returns cannot be understood without knowledge of the separation that preceded it—the reasons for admission to care, the child's care career, and the quality of links between families and absent children. The child's entry to care and the separation that accompanies it is an outcome of a long and complex family history and much of what follows is affected by both the reasons for the child's entry to care and its style of implementation. The management of return has to be specific to each case and needs a thorough understanding of all the antecedents. Bitterness can endure long, as this poignant quotation from a child's letter to a dying father shows:

> I am sorry you are gone. I wish we could have had some more good times together. In some ways I am glad it is over. I wish you could have been a good adviser like the staff here. I have a lot of complicated feelings and I do not know how to put them. From your loving son, Dan.

Some families and children were far more prepared psychologically and culturally for separation than others. This anticipation had several aspects: in three cases, parents had been in care themselves and the pre-socialization took the form of inter-generational awareness:

> I and my sisters were in care six times. I think my gran was in an orphanage in Ireland as a girl as well. I was fifteen before I realized that every child did not have a social worker.

In another case, there was a cultural tradition either of private fostering or of high geographical mobility of wage earners and a sharing of care among female relatives:

> You must realize that in the Caribbean the family structures are different on different islands. In Jamaica, the men worked away and the women looked after the children.

As a consequence, preparations for care varied considerably. One mother shopped in Woolworth's as if her child was off on a school trip, while seven others claimed to have been neither consulted nor informed until the day of separation.

The ease and success of return are influenced by the quality of social work offered at the time of separation. Many parents are numbed by numerous anxieties not all associated with the loss of their children. Return will be less difficult when the problems leading to separation are perceived as likely to be ameliorated or resolved and the intervention is seen by the family as legitimate and in the best interests of the child. Reunions chill when the issue of return reopens unresolved difficulties. There is a great deal that social workers can do to obviate problems later on. By bridging the two worlds of the child and keeping parents involved in decisions, social workers can ease participants' sense of personal failure and reduce the likelihood of fantasy which can complicate reunion. Avoiding the sense of mutual loss is particularly important. This means helping relatives and children anticipate and interpret what the return will be like, for example, by getting parents to chart changes in their household and their consequences for the home-coming. The complexity of the negotiations necessary for a child's successful return home becomes manifest by looking at changes in circumstances while the child is away, the point at which return becomes an issue, the first days at home, the honeymoon, the row, and establishing a new modus vivendi.

Conclusion

Return is a process not an event. Indeed, it was sometimes difficult to identify the point at which return could be said to have occurred. Issues, beyond the problems of negotiating role and territory, became apparent as the process enfolds. In contrast to separation, fewer rites of passage marked reunions. Return also involves separation from things to which children and parents have become attached—substitute carers, life without children in the home.

Social work inputs, which feature strongly at separation, pale after the return. Social workers find it difficult to find a role once the child is back. Yet, this is a time when families actually need help—not only counselling and support to understand the return process but also financial support to feed another mouth. Families seek a revised modus vivendi, and clarification of the reasons for the initial separation and the meaning of the experience for the family. The anger engendered in parents and children by failures to live up to their own experiences has to be expressed. Older children have to establish new social networks at school, at work and in the community as well as negotiating roles and territories within their families. Preoccupation with return to the family should not encourage us to ignore the wider contexts of return. The stigma and insecurities of the past make these negotiations difficult for the young person, particularly if compounded by unease and tensions within the family.

Reconciliation involves facing up to one's personal responsibilities and failures. The fantasies which sustain every-day life have to be examined coolly. The past cannot be undone. Preparation, counselling and support as return takes place are not wasted efforts. Just as a shoulder to cry on is important during separation, so someone to catch the flying plates and interpret what is happening during a reconciliation is greatly to be valued. Greater awareness of the return process should enable social workers to prioritize cases and prepare contingency plans in those situations where reunion is likely to be delicate. Forewarned is forearmed.

References

Bullock, R., Little, M., & Millham, S. (1993). *Going home: The return of children separated from their families.* Aldershot: Dartmouth.

Kahan, B. (1979). *Growing up in care.* Oxford: Blackwell.

Kellmer Pringle, M. (1975). *The needs of children.* London: Hutchinson.

Lambert, R., & Millham, S. (1968). *The hothouse society: An exploration of boarding school life through the children's own writings.* London: Weidenfeld and Nicolson.

Little, M. (1990). *Young men in prison.* Aldershot: Dartmouth.

Maluccio, A., Fein, E., & Olmstead, K. (1986). *Permanency planning for children: Concepts and methods.* London: Routledge, Chapman and Hall.

Millham, S., Bullock, R., & Cherrett, P. (1975). A framework for the comparative analysis of residential institutions. In J. Tizard, I. Sinclair, & R. Clarke, (Eds.), *Varieties of Residential Experience.* London: Routledge and Kegan Paul.

Millham, S., Bullock, R., & Hosie, K. (1986). *Lost in care: The problems of maintaining links between children in care and their families.* Aldershot: Gower.

Millham, S., Bullock, R., & Little, M. (1989). *Access disputes in child care.* Aldershot: Gower.

Whitaker, D., Cook, J., Dunne, C., & Lunn-Rockliffe, S. (1986). *The experience of residential care from the perspectives of children, parents and caregivers.* University of York, Report to the Economic and Social Research Council.

Winnicott, D. (1984). *Deprivation and delinquency.* London: Tavistock.

26

Contributions to Resilience in Children and Youth: What Successful Child Welfare Graduates Say

Susan Silva-Wayne

The study of resilience in children and youth has a relatively short but dynamic history. This topic was first investigated as the logical extension of research which identified the factors, both personal and environmental, that place youngsters at high risk of emotional and behavioural dysfunction. Adversity in early life has long been associated with social and psychological difficulties in later life, and can be seen to be a risk factor. John Bowlby made the connections between deprivation of love and care in the early years and anti-social behaviour in adolescence and adulthood (Bowlby, 1951). The notion of risk in human experience connotes the hazard associated with an individual factor or experience, or a set of factors or experiences. Risk has been experienced uniquely by every research study participant, client, and individual. A factor or experience which places one person at high risk for damaging repercussions may "roll off the back" of the next person, based on differences among individuals with respect to how they perceive the experience or factor, their genetic predisposition, and the psycho-social environment in which they grow and live (Anthony, 1987, p. 4).

Risk research with respect to children has focused primarily on those at risk of experiencing the schizophrenic and affective disorders of their parents, and the socio-behavioural maladaptions connected with community disadvantage, family psychopathology and family and community criminality. Researchers who study children and youths exposed to biological risk factors and stressful life events have gone through several stages in their approach to understanding vulnerability. First, they emphasized the negative developmental outcomes associated with a single risk factor such as prematurity, or with a stressful life event, such as the absence of a parent. They then shifted from this main effect model of risk research to one that considered interactional effects among multiple stressors, such as the co-occurrence of parental dysfunction (e.g. alcoholism or emotional illness) and poverty. British epidemiological studies have identified a series of risk factors for children's mental health outcomes (Rutter, Maughan, Mortimore, Ousten, & Smith, 1979a; Rutter, 1979b). Contributory factors, including parental marital discord, father's low-skilled or non-skilled employment, familial overcrowding, paternal criminal behaviour, maternal mental illness, and the child's admission to out-of-home-care were seen to work together to produce poor outcomes for children. The child exposed to two or more of these adversities was at four times the risk of suffering childhood psychological distress; as the number of risk factors reached four, and the four had the opportunity to interact with one another, the likelihood of distress was projected to be ten times that of the child exposed to only one or none of the identified risk factors.

The concept of vulnerability has come to prominence in both animal and human studies, and relates to the tendency the individual or group brings, because of biological, perceptual, and environmental factors, to exposure to risk factors. The field of children's mental health has long focused on the topic of children's vulnerability to psychopathology. Bleuler's work, begun early in the twentieth century, explored the incidence and manifestations of schizophrenia in adolescents. His findings suggested a variability of outcome for the youngsters, leading to the position that each case should be studied individually for the purpose of learning what factors, genetic and social, had a bearing on the development of the disease (Bleuler, 1950). Research in this area has been on-going and rich in its complexity and variety throughout the century. Questions and data from the areas of genetics, family interaction, child development, childhood coping and competency, and others have illuminated a great deal about children at risk for the development of schizophrenia and other mental illnesses, as well as the more general areas of children's vulnerability to stress and struggles to achieve levels of competence and mastery. Extensive studies, undertaken over many years at the University of Minnesota, have indicated that the likelihood of youngsters' exposure to stressful life events, their intellectual functioning, general competency, ability to engage with others and with activities, and tendencies towards disruptiveness are all related to the socio-economic status of the child's family, and familial stability, cohesiveness, and organization (Garmezy, 1987).

The most recent phase of reported research findings in the area has been marked by a lessened emphasis on negative developmental outcomes and a greater focus on successful adaptation in spite of childhood adversity. Prospective longitudinal studies have fairly consistently shown that even among children exposed to significant risk factors it is unusual for more than half to develop serious disability or persistent problems (Werner & Smith, 1992). Youngsters subjected to adversity are not similarly or equally effected. Attention of the mental health community was directed to the topic of the invulnerable child in the early 1970s by Norman Garmezy:

> In the study of high-risk and vulnerable children, we have come across another group of children whose prognosis could be viewed as unfavourable on the basis of familial or ecological factors but who upset our prediction tables and in childhood bear the visible indices that are hall marks of competence: good peer relations, academic achievement, commitment to education and to purposive life goals, early and successful work histories ... To these children I have assigned the term "invulnerables" ... "Vulnerables" have long been the province of our mental health disciplines; but prolonged neglect of the "invulnerable" child—the healthy child in an unhealthy setting—has provided us with a false sense of security in erecting prevention models that are founded more on values than on facts. ...With our nation torn by strife between races and between social classes, these "invulnerable" children remain the "keepers of the dream." Were we to study the forces that move such children to survival and to adaptation, the long-range benefits to our society might be far more significant than our many

efforts to construct models of primary prevention designed to curtail the incidence of vulnerability (Garmezy, 1971, p. 114).

The term "invulnerable," which evokes visions of superior children or youth, impervious to the cruellest treatment and immune to the countless blows of misfortune, later gave way to the concept of the resilient young person. The resilient youngster suffers with both the short term and the long term effects of adverse experiences and relationships, but can incorporate these experiences into a coping core which may be strengthened by adversity. Some of the early ideas about resilience in children come from the work of child developmentalists who studied the coping behaviours of children from infancy through adolescence. One respected longitudinal study from the child developmental perspective showed that resilience in children is highly correlated with flexibility which allows them to break free from failures, avoid self-defeating repetitions, and try many different problem solving techniques in their efforts to cope with life's challenges (Murphy & Moriarity, 1976). Garmezy found that resilient children shared three categories of protective factors in almost all their experiences. First, the children themselves were easy to relate to, felt good about themselves, believed they were in control of their lives, and were self-reliant. Second, in most families, there was a warm relationship with at least one adult, the family felt close, and order and organization were in evidence. Third, in the neighbourhood or elsewhere in the community, there was a support system available to help the child move towards self-defined goals, and there were role models with whom the youngster could identify (Garmezy, 1983). Both Rutter and Garmezy, in their later work (Rutter, 1987, Garmezy, 1987), questioned whether there might be processes or mechanisms which took place in the lives of children and young people to make them more resilient. Rutter suggested four basic categories into which most of these resiliency-building experiences could be placed:

> The limited evidence available so far suggests that protective processes include those that reduce the risk impact by virtue of effects on the riskiness itself or through alteration of exposure to or involvement in the risk, those that reduce the likelihood of chain reactions stemming from the risk encounter, those that promote self-esteem and self-efficacy through the availability of secure and supportive personal relationships or successful task accomplishment, and those that open up opportunities (Rutter, 1987, p. 329).

The Study Of Resilience And Child Welfare Practice

The literature with respect to building resilience in child welfare practice has been limited. A large sample of young adult graduates of foster care in New York City had fared no better or worse than a control group of young adults from similar class background except with respect to education and employment, where the foster care graduates were at a disadvantage (Festinger, 1983). Festinger's findings did show significantly better outcomes for the youngsters substantially raised in foster family versus group home care. A British study with a much smaller sample of adult foster home graduates produced similar findings with 75% of the graduates manifesting largely satisfactory outcomes from their experiences in care (Triseliotis, 1980). The number of placements was significantly low for each young person in both samples. Both authors therefore question the degree to which the samples reflected the average youngster's out-of-home-care experience with respect to number of placements and consequent continuity of care.

Fanshel, Finch and Grundy (1990) conducted a retrospective, longitudinal study using information from closed case records as well as from direct accounts from subjects themselves. The study group was 585 graduates from placement in The Casey Family Program in Seattle, Washington. The program was specifically devised to provide high quality, planned, long-term foster care for children and youth with troubled behavioural and multiple placement histories. The goal was to stabilize and maintain the young people to the point of emancipation. Findings from this research indicate the importance of the program's commitment to trying again and again with the youngsters who require repeated placement changes. Graduates from the program often achieved a level of comfort and well-being in young adulthood which could not have been predicted from the adversity of their early experiences, but which were associated with increased well being at the time of emancipation. Minimizing not only physical abuse but all forms of corporal punishment in care had a positive effect on outcomes. Minimizing the numbers of placements also had a positive association with the condition of the young person at emancipation, which in turn had a positive association with important adult measures of well-being.

How youngsters integrate potentially damaging events into their world or life view may be a significant element in the building of resilience, and giving them repeated opportunities to develop an integrated view of their histories may be an important kind of therapy. In one study of female incest survivors, making sense of the incestuous victimization was positively correlated with effective adult coping, including less psychological distress, better social adjustment and higher levels of self-esteem than noted in those women less able to make any sense out of their experience (Silver, Boon & Stones, 1983). Understanding of one's own childhood history and one's lack of responsibility for the shortcomings or severe maladjustments of parental and family functioning are related to subsequent adult well-being where child maltreatment (Herrenkohl, Herrenkohl & Egolf, 1994) and parental mental illness (Beardslee, 1989) have led to family crisis and, possibly, family disintegration.

There are young people whose lives are transformed while they are in out-of-home-care and who, when leaving out-of-home care and in adulthood, seem to be reaching for self-actualization despite the serious disadvantage and dysfunction of their earlier experiences. What contributes to their success? What relationships and experiences will be remembered by them as helpful from before care, in care, and directly after? How much of their strengthening experience came from the people involved with providing foster care and child welfare services, how much will come from the educational world, and how much from the community and elsewhere?

Methodology

The study sample consisted of nineteen successfully launched graduates of foster care in Ontario. The definition of successful launching included those values directly related to youth who are developing their potential while excluding, as much as possible, those characteristics which distinguish people by class and culture, such as formal education and material wealth. The successfully launched young adults included in this research shared the following characteristics:

- Were between the ages of sixteen and twenty-six.

- Were in care within the previous five years.
- Had experienced three years, at a minimum, in foster or group care.
- Were working, attending school or training, or both, or were young parents providing for a child at home.
- Had a permanent address.
- Had at least one person with whom to share life's problems and joys.
- Had friends or acquaintances with whom to socialize.
- Developed interests, hobbies, or activities which animated them.
- Felt positive about themselves and somewhat in control of the future.
- Exhibited some self-reflectiveness and knowledge.

The two largest child welfare agencies in Metropolitan Toronto were contacted and asked to participate in a study of contributions to resiliency in recent, successfully launched young men and women. Interested workers, supervisors, and foster parents were asked to raise the possibility of being part of the study with the young adult being considered for referral. Each referred potential participant was then contacted, informed about the study, and an attempt to set up an interview appointment was made and held in an office on the campus of the University of Toronto, on site at Pape Area Resource Center (PARC), or at the home of the participant.

Each participant was asked a series of questions which attempted to engage him or her in talking about the history in out-of-home-care, the circumstances necessitating the care, the experiential, relational and cognitive elements which have added to the participant's feelings of strength and resilience, and self-assessment of adjustment to life today, as well as dreams about the future. Almost all of the questions were open-ended to allow the participant to follow a path, or share a narrative which seemed compelling. Interviews took from two to four hours each. Design of the study, the scope of the interview, and the analysis were congruent with the school of interpretive analysis (Geertz,1973; Denzin, 1978, 1989; Sullivan, 1984). Each participant was also asked to fill in an attributional style questionnaire (Seligman, 1984). This instrument measures the balance of optimism vs. pessimism in each participant's cognitive approach to the events in their lives. The fairly simple test was completed, in most instances, within the half hour following the interview. The taped interviews were transcribed, and the more than 500 pages were coded with respect to 53 distinct themes which were compressed into the more general concepts emerging from the data.

The Study Participants

Nine of the nineteen study participants were referred by PARC, a multi-service independence preparation and post-independence support center. The ten additional participants were referred by workers providing services to youngsters in out-of-home-care in agency branches across the city.

The participants' average age was twenty-one years, nine months. Their average time in out-of-home-care was about nine years. Eleven participants were born in Canada; the remaining eight came from the Caribbean, the Middle East, and East Asia. Five of those born outside of Canada were sent to Canada to find better opportunities for education and the establishment of a career. Two families sent their children away to protect them from the dangers inherent in growing up surrounded by war. Two youngsters came to Canada to reunite with a separated mother who had immigrated to Canada years previously; one participant was sent to the care of an unfamiliar father because caring grandparents had become unable, through age and infirmity, to continue raising the youngster. Seven participants were male; twelve were female. The numbers of placements experienced varied from one placement of twenty-two years enjoyed by one woman to more than eight placements, half of which were neglectful or abusive, in the history of one man. The average number of placements was three, including foster homes, group homes, extended family placements serviced and remunerated as foster homes, and independent living situations within the in-care system. Recorded reasons for requiring out-of-home-care included chronic neglect (4), abandonment (2), relinquishment shortly after birth (1), physical abuse (9), emotional abuse (7), sexual abuse (3), parental incapacity due to a chronic mental illness (5), alcoholism (4), chronic wife or spousal abuse (3) child living in Canada separated from caring adults (3), and death of a parent (1).

At the time of contact, eight participants were attending university full-time or entering a graduate or professional program. One young man and one young woman were entering their final Ontario Academic Credits (OAC) year and planning to attend university the year following. Six participants were enrolled in community college programs or had graduated from these programs in the recent past. Four participants had no formal education past the secondary school level; three of them completed twelfth grade despite being surrounded by stress, uncertainty and other major challenges. The women expressed the belief, however, that twelfth grade is not enough education to achieve their ambitions, and although two of them are mothers with small children, they all expressed a desire to return to school at a later date. The fourth participant without any experience with higher education is a Native Canadian man whose school leaving during the tenth grade was symptomatic of the many levels of chaos and loss in his life. He is seeking education and healing through the knowledge and traditions of elders in his community, and he intends to pursue formal education at a later date. All the study participants share the characteristic of social responsiveness which each displayed with an individual style, but which made interaction with all of them pleasurable and rewarding. Excellent social skills, represented variously as social sensitivity, cooperation, friendliness, and the tendency toward participation and emotional stability are displayed by resilient youngsters in studies from around the world (Garmezy, 1983, pp. 43–84).

Findings

Being a Foster Child is Perceived as a Stigma

Children who have lived in out-of-home care are doubly devalued, first by the circumstances which brought them into care, and then by the stigmatization attached to their foster status. Even when the out-of-home-care is good and sufficient, youngsters often report feeling devalued because of the stigmatization connected with living in families other than their own. The pervasive devaluation perceived by participants because they had been in out-of-home-care is the strongest and most surprising finding that emerges from interviews with participants. Negative feelings about having been raised in out-of-home-care were at least as prominent, in some respondents' accounts of themselves, as their feelings about most other adversity experienced in their young lives. Most of these young people have experienced crises with respect to who they are and what others think of them in the light of their growing up in out-of-home care. These experiences eclipse the significance of the difficult circumstances which resulted in their out-of-home-placements. All participants have, to lesser and greater extents, grappled with this double devaluation.

The self-devaluation is not, however, related to personal characteristics or behaviours. Rather, the negative and uncomfortable self-judgments relate to participants' social identification as people from dysfunctional backgrounds and people raised in out-of-home-care. Almost all these young people have, to a degree, accepted what they identify as a social stigma surrounding their life circumstances. Some have begun to face these feelings and have achieved some better sense of well-being as a result; they have had experiences, formed relationships, or used interventions which added value to their self-evaluations. Many attribute negative assessments of foster kids to others in the community. This phenomenon is manifested in a "people think" allusion, or an anticipated negative assessment or snub as in "I don't tell everyone about my background, only a few good friends. Most people don't understand."

Devaluation associated with out-of-home-care is clustered in three broad categories. First, participants report and display shame, embarrassment, self-doubt and hurt with respect to the perceived failings and insufficiencies of their natural parents:

> My mother is not that stable which you know. That's the easy way out kind of, you know, crazy, not as in psychotic. I don't know what her diagnosis is either. And even if I did know, other people don't even understand that so I usually wait for a reaction.... People want the details of how she, you know, she has all these problems. I don't know how you become a good father.... I grew up without a father.... I worry too much that I don't think I'll be a good father. I don't think I can offer all the right qualities to someone. Yeah, it's a question mark.

Second, just the fact of being a foster child is associated with shame and the anticipated rejection by others, at both the personal and the institutional level:

> Well, when I was a child I was a foster kid and other kids were normal kids. Normal kids, foster kids. That was the only... that's how I separated the two categories, you know. I didn't want to be around foster... everything foster. I wanted to be normal like everyone else.... Somehow I wasn't as good as everybody else cause I'm a foster child. That is exactly what I thought. Everyone else is better than me.

And finally, some out-of-home care graduates point to two areas, the inability to identify with characteristics of substitute caretakers and their families and the non-accessibility of personal and family history, when they relate difficulties in developing a strong and solid conception of who they are. This problem of identity building while in out-of-home care can be seen as identity deep freeze:

> Children's Aid is just a place to take care of your physical needs, right, while you are getting from childhood to adolescence to adulthood. Children's Aid is not a place where people develop culture, develop history.... It's not a developing place, right? And I think a lot of people who get into the Children's Aid too young don't know who they are, where they're coming from or just, you know, basically that...They have no contents. They have no ideas of themselves, right? They're void, they're empty.

The stigma associated with living in out-of-home-care tended to be ameliorated by life experiences establishing the young person's competence, acceptability, and worthiness. For some, exposure to other young people in out-of-home-care, even at an age approaching or following emancipation, helped them feel less stigmatized and alone. Some reported the enjoyable experience of meeting new people to whom one did not have to explain one's self. Several were involved, either as older youths in care or as recent graduates, in PARC programs and activities, such as committee memberships, advisory roles, or conference attendance which placed them in the position of experts, conveyors of wisdom, and advocates for the children and youth in foster or group care. Filling roles of this nature has had the potential to help change the young person's self definition from devalued victim to advocate, helper, advisor, and even system and policy analyst.

Successful Graduates Employ Role Models Extensively

The extensive use made of role models in the lives of study participants was a major theme emerging from the data. The dearth of positive role models in the family, in cases in which youngsters have been separated from inadequate or dangerous parents, has created a need for an even greater number and assortment of others to fill the void. The variety of role models includes:

1. Negative role models. Parents qualify largely as negative role models, that is, adults against whom participants fashion their lives; those who serve as models of what to avoid.
2. Occupational role models. One young man, who dreams of eventually becoming a police officer, was originally stimulated to think of his future in that occupation by an experience he had where a police officer came to the school yard and licensed children who displayed knowledge about bicycle safety. In that interaction the officer became an occupational role model. There were many examples of the use of occupational role models.
3. Path finders. Sometimes the role model makes a path through a particularly thick part of the bureaucratic forest, as happened when one participant, newly arrived in Canada and knowing very little about how to choose courses at High School, met a slightly older Caribbean-Canadian neighbour who served as a path finder by showing her how to choose secondary school courses which would make her eligible for University entrance.
4. Fictional role models. These serve an emotional and perhaps an analytical function in the lives of some young participants. The young person can express feelings vicariously or contemplate experiences in an objectified way through viewing or reading about someone with whom identification is easy.
5. Role models with respect to mastery, character, and behavior. Some respondents model their character, behaviour, or a particular kind of mastery on someone they admire. For example, one participant is understanding of the maternal line in her family; their personalities, their life choices, and their self-reliance seem to be mirrored in her own pattern.

Successfully Launched Graduates Belong to Many Communities

The young people were highly affiliative, belonging to at least one and sometimes many different groups, both formal and informal, and they spoke positively about their many communities. A few participants mentioned that each group represented some aspect of themselves, and sometimes the differing groups needed to be maintained separately. Some of the community experiences are fashioned by the professionals who understand the needs of these young people for belonging, for example the PARC informally gathered and formally goal oriented groups and activities. Other experiences are very individual, sought out by the youngsters themselves, and found in places the professionals might not have predicted. Participants discussed their feelings of belonging in their foster home or group home, and its familial and friendship network extensions, as well as finding a welcoming, validating community in a religion or a specific church community.

Participants name school groups, clubs, classes and programs as communities which stand for something important and which incorporate them as esteemed members. One participant's mother, before the child moved into out-of-home-care, but in the midst of stormy times when the two could not co-exist, had the foresight to have her child tested for the Board of Education's stream for gifted students. This effort served to shelter the child and provide her with a community of caring adults and long term friendships in the educational system, from elementary school through secondary school. Finding a sense of community in one's ethnic or cultural group was mentioned by most of the Afro-Canadian, Afro-Caribbean and Native Canadian participants but not frequently by the others, including those respondents who had immigrated to Canada from very different cultures. For these youngsters, association with their cultural communities offers an effective way to add to their strength through helping them develop a richer sense of who they are. Some of the young women find a sense of affiliation in the community of women to which they've been introduced through exposure to, and interest in, feminist ideas and feminist oriented activities. And, finally, more than a few respondents are either affiliated with the new family they are creating as spouses, in-laws and parents, or attempting to reconcile with their biological parents or siblings, sometimes where the last contact took place many years ago.

Respondents Name Experiences Which Raised Their Self-Esteem

Establishment and maintenance of self-esteem are linked with many of the relationships with role models, affiliative behaviour, and the willingness to take advantage of opportunities. Establishment and maintenance of self-esteem is singled out as its own process, both to underline its importance, and because some instances of self-esteem building (such as the recognition of a child's special qualities) are extremely significant to the child while being impossible to detect by the objective outsider, because it generally occurs outside of any formal program or treatment plan. Examples of the establishment and maintenance of self-esteem appear in the interaction between the child and a variety of others, including family members, professional helpers, foster family members, volunteers, friends and teachers.

For some participants, establishment of self-esteem took place in early childhood, perhaps with a grandparent or other caring adult who saw the child as special, gifted, and wonderful. At times of stress or when the young person's self-esteem is threatened, the mental evocation of the loving adult and her or his estimation of the youngster seems to be a process which helps the young person to cope. Foster parents, social workers, and others maintained youngsters' self-esteem when they supported youths' own goals, and contributed to their attempt to achieve these goals. Showing respect for the young person by inclusion and consultation also supports the maintenance of self-esteem. One participant cited very specific attitudinal and material advantages of one foster home over another when he talked about the contribution of foster parents to his success. He was sent to Canada, as an unaccompanied minor, to take advantage of the educational opportunities in Canada. His first foster home and parents' attitudes detracted from his ability to perform well in school; the subsequent placement, however, supported his efforts to excel as a student. In many cases the relevant other's recognition and positive assessment of the child helps to heighten or maintain the child's self-esteem. This particular phenomenon took place often in the classroom, where youngsters were fortunate enough to receive a positive message from a teacher:

> ...[J]ust a little bit of quality towards me... It was so small and so tiny it was almost invisible. It was almost non-existent to most people.... I guess a child from a functional type home wouldn't even realize that had an effect on your life at all. You know, they'd say "well that had nothing to do with it," right? To me though, it was huge. It was immense. It was incredible. It was powerful... It was wonderful. You know, it wasn't anything special, it was just special because it was something I didn't usually get.

One positive experience with foster parents can elevate self-esteem to a level which may carry a child through subsequent, sometimes difficult, experiences. One mature couple took a young woman into care for several years when she was a young teen-ager, had suffered the loss of her grandmother in Guyana, had been rejected and abused by her relations in Canada, and identified herself as a bag lady. Placements following the positive one were troubled and began to detract from her self esteem. This young woman attributes her hard-won sense of strength and self-confidence today largely to her years with these first foster parents who, above all, treated her with respect. The experiences which effect self-esteem do not necessarily take place in the earliest years. But some early experiences have long-lasting and helpful implications for a youngster. Those who want to intervene to raise or maintain a young person's level of self-esteem can be effective at many times and places in an in-care career, as long as personal contact with the youngster is established and recognition of her or his special qualities is communicated.

Successful Graduates Were Exposed to Opportunities

The child can only grow and develop to the extent that she or he is exposed to, and helped to make use of, opportunities and experiences. Children raised away from their families depend largely on those institutions responsible for their care and education to provide these possibilities. Opportunities are, as well, the presentation of a new turn in the road, a movement away from the predicted, and often a chance to circumvent disaster. An early teen-aged pregnancy without social support, for example, will probably confine the young woman to a life filled with the kind of adversity she already knows; a chance to be trained or educated for a job or career presented in the early teen years may delay pregnancy until the young woman is better prepared for parenting and can financially support a baby.

The public education system has the capacity to provide an avenue of social mobility for people of all circumstances. But the opportunities have been limited for some youngsters, adding to the list of hurdles thrown up by their life circumstances. Racism, sexism, and class bias in public education detract, in some respondents' narratives, from the system's ability to afford upward social mobility for children from disadvantaged circumstances. Young people shared their frustrations in the interviews that came from meeting these negative forces. The participants who had been involved with PARC reported that the program was central in their exposure to new experiences and opportunities, although this exposure occurred late in their in-care careers. Opportunities for friendship, learning employment skills on the job, getting work, learning how to do one's taxes, student aid forms, résumés and other necessary forms and papers, housing information, educational information, and many other categories of instrumental help were found in this setting.

Successful Graduates Exhibit Protective Thinking

Some habits of thought, or ways of viewing the self and the world, seem to have a protective quality which may contribute to the strength and well-being of the young adults. Examples of protective thinking are self-reliance, "keeping it all on the back-burner" (not thinking about the painful stuff), proving others wrong with respect to their low expectations of the young person, assertiveness, expressions of the real self, feminism, the experience of epiphanies, fantasies, unconscious motivations, and positive explanatory style. Some of these have emerged from the data in sufficient strength to be plausible cognitive aids in the formation and maintenance of resilience. Almost every participant in the study said something about the value of having been self-reliant, even as small children. Some said it in passing, others gave the concept a great deal of weight, and for some, the strength of self-reliance is paired with the problem of not being able to get close to others:

> I'm very independent, almost a loner sometimes. Even though I've lived with a foster family for six years and, I mean, I trust them and I like them and what not... it's as my foster mother said, like I really probably could... this is not necessarily a good thing, I really probably could when I go to university, go off and have very little contact with them and it wouldn't bother me that much. Partly because ...it's my emotional deficiencies when it comes to relationships.... But also because I know I could count on myself first. It's hard for me to depend on people and to trust them too much because well, because I've been let down in the past and I know that if I want something done, really the one I can always count on doing it is myself.

Concepts which have important meaning for some participants are assertiveness, self-expression, and feminism. For some, finding a voice has been linked with the ability to work towards goals, garner achievements, and break out of a world of negative self-evaluation. Although they may have mastered a great deal and feel satisfied in some areas, many of these young adults are aware of a lack of assertiveness within themselves. Not having one's own family is linked to a feeling of powerlessness, and from powerlessness comes lack of assertiveness. Also, these young people have felt the need to behave in certain ways and meet many expectations from others in order to have a home. This need to conform and be acceptable leads, in some, to a life-long pattern of being afraid to express the authentic self. Becoming able to take the risk inherent in authentic self-expression is a formidable challenge. For some of the women, there is a clear connection between exposure to feminist ideas, espousal of these ideas, and a growing assertiveness, expression of the authentic self, and positive self-esteem and self-confidence. The group attributional style questionnaire scores achieved by the participants matched the level of positive explanatory style exhibited by a large sample of psychology students at the University of Pennsylvania (Schulman, Castellon & Seligman, 1989). This evidence lends some weight to the idea that the ways children and youth learn to view themselves and their life experiences can be strengthening and protective.

Implications For Practice

Stigmatization of the Foster Child

Erving Goffman (1963) delineates three distinct conditions leading to stigmatization: 1) physical deformities, 2) attributed weakness of character arising from association with a record of mental disorder, imprisonment, addiction, etc., and 3) negative stereotypes associated with one's race, ethnicity or religion. The devaluation associated with out-of-home-care, seems to fall in the second category—a socially determined weaknesses of character arising from the record of being a foster child. Goffman lists three major adaptations to the stigmatized condition. First, the stigmatized person may try to correct the identified condition. Second, the stigmatized person may undertake to master an area of human behaviour or endeavour normally not feasible for a person in his or her category. Third, the person can break with the stigmatized reality and employ an unconventional assertion of his or her social identity. This third adaptation is illustrated by the young adults who have, largely through the intervention of PARC, moved their self-definition away from that of devalued foster child and marched toward a new self-definition as experienced foster care consumers, advocates for children and youth in out-of-home-care, and advisors to the policy and program shapers in the child welfare establishment. One participant appeared in various media to discuss and advocate for youth in care and has been a member of a committee to secure financial and community support for youth in care. Another's story of the birth of self-esteem and empowerment in late adolescence is welcomed and heard with interest in the media and at conferences on this topic. The story of a third youth is available and essential to policy makers in the area of Native Canadian child welfare, and a fourth, sits on the Board of a Child Welfare agency as a representative of the interests of children who are in out-of-home-care. These young people have been heard and understood, by being a part of a group made up of others with similar experiences. They have also been strengthened by learning they have a role to play in advising professionals and policy makers. They have been empowered in so far as each one of them has attained a position of respect and responsibility. They have been politicized when they have discovered the power inherent in the association of people with like interests, standing together to advocate for what they and others like themselves need and deserve.

The Use of Role Models and Path Finders

Every young person interviewed named other people in their lives on whom they have or would like to model their behaviour, style, career, character, gender-related role performance, family role performance, talents, or material status. Some discussed role models predominately from the negative standpoint; that is, they based decisions and goals on not reflecting the character and lives of feared, pitied, hated, or lost parents, parent-substitutes, or siblings. Some had a path in mind, and found people ahead of them on that path. Some chose a path based on the acceptance and friendship offered by a particular person, whose path became traversable because the individual was approachable and accepting. The many instances of role modelling named and discussed by these successfully launched young people leads to the conclusion that practice models need to incorporate role models in a planned way. Linking with role models should not be left to chance. The young people in this study were able to find and use a multitude of role models along their paths, but it is likely that these youngsters have an affinity, an ease, or an openness to the influence of others that other young people in similar situations, but not as canny at identifying influential others and making contact, may lack.

Mentoring programs have grown in recent years and can be helpful to youth in foster care. Mentoring programs can be made available for youngsters at all ages and on many different bases. Foster care graduates, for example, could be asked to help youngsters for whom the path through care and into adulthood is hazardous. Adults with specific career lines or talents could be matched with youngsters interested in these areas of future or continuing endeavour. Matches could also be made along any other lines, including political interests, artistic interests, the areas of sports or recreation and others. Older children in care could serve as path-finders and role models for younger children, not just in the same foster household, but in the same school, or geographic area. Older children in the community could also be engaged as role models for youngsters in care. A teen-ager, who practices gymnastics could be identified by a foster parent as a potential role model for the younger child in care who attends the same gym. Many ideas will emerge for the useful linking of youngsters in care with role models or path finders when the importance of the concept is emphasized in the culture of the agency.

Building Self-Esteem and Exposing Youngsters to Opportunities

Planning for a child's future is largely happenstance. Opportunities for exposure to jobs, for introduction to job training, and for planning with respect to avenues of education leading to careers should be addressed for each youngster far in advance of the last year before the young person leaves out-of-home care. Opportunities open doors and change paths. Agency practice might include regular exposure to music, arts, travel, recreation, community services, sports, theatre, crafts, and other areas of knowledge and expression that provide potential stimulation. Foster parents, group home parents, supervisors, social workers, and child care workers vary widely concerning their interests and activities, so that child welfare agencies need to formulate minimum standards and general expectations for the exposure of youngsters to opportunities and experiences.

The public educational system is the main avenue for mobility as well as an important site of socialization and development for children and youth. Liaison with the school system around the progress of every child and youth in care is a matter of great urgency. The young person's academic ability is only one focus for the agency-home-school communication. The school can provide opportunities for mastery, growth, and elevated self-esteem in the recreational, musical, social, dramatic, athletic, and stylistic spheres of life. When young people cope and feel adequate in one area of the school milieu, the confidence established will help them master other areas of endeavour.

Community Affiliation Meaningful

Child welfare practice can provide a variety of opportunities for community membership. Exposure to community life can be expanded to include not only what is familiar to a specific foster parent or geographic area, but also what within travelling distance. Linking a child or youth with the activities and communities habitually and most comfortably accessed for all children in the family is not as useful as linking the specific child with a community which would benefit her or him. An example was the attempt of foster parents to link a newly arrived Afro-Caribbean youth with the Boy Scouts organization. When the boy indicated his lack of interest in scouting, he was identified as a non-joiner and additional attempts to link him with communities did not happen. The young man believes he would have gained a great deal from an introduction to the Afro-Caribbean-Canadian community. Perhaps it is especially necessary, because of institutionalized racism, to link Afro-Caribbean, Afro-Canadian, Native-Canadian, and other visible minority youngsters with the strength in their communities.

Training Youngsters in Care for a Resilient Adaptation

Self-reliance, assertiveness, flexible optimism, and feminist ideas are among the patterns of thought and behaviour which may be associated with feelings of strength in young people as well as social responsiveness, or their ability to engage in mutually satisfying interactions with others. Protective thinking and protective interaction could be taught to youngsters in out-of-home-care. Practice with children in out-of-home care might include social teaching that would incorporate habits of thought and behaviour shown to be associated with high self-esteem and mastery. Assertiveness training, optimistic explanatory style training, and social responsiveness, if further exploration supports their efficacy, can all be conveyed, supported, taught, and practised. Girls and young women seem to benefit from exposure to the ideas related to the potential strength of girls and women and to the benefits to children of growing up in families where males and females are equal. Young women and men who have suffered abuse at home or grown in a family where their mother was subjected to assault and abuse by male partners benefit from awareness that there are nurturing men, that some men share in domestic labour, that men and women can live together as equals, and that women are strong and able, both individually and when united to attain their goals.

Conclusions

Being both real and good parents and rejecting minimalist interventions and formalized cut-off points, such as the designation of 18 or 21 years of age, are necessary to increase the number of out-of-home-care graduates who have a good opportunity at self-actualization or fulfilment of their potential as adults.

Creative energy and resourcing need to be focused on the de-stigmatization of the foster child role. Young people growing up in out-of-home-care require guidance and concern, but also a powerful adult presence and advocacy within the institutions that teach, train, enable, and open doors of opportunity. The children and youth also benefit as a group, and as individuals, when helped to rail against the institutions that raise them, demanding to be heard and to be given their entitlement. One of the child welfare system's primary functions *vis à vis* youngsters raised in out-of-home-care is to encourage and facilitate their organization and advocacy for positive and client-responsive changes to that system. The experiences of a small sample of young adults who are moving towards free and full development suggest that exposure to feminist ideas, knowledge of and immersion in their own cultures, awareness of their common experiences and interests, and being asked respectfully to find and use their voices have all contributed to this development, as have role models, community affiliations, opportunities, and cognitive habits which are protective. Helping interventions, by individuals in a variety of positions *vis à vis* these young people, have been of considerable influence, whether accomplished early or late in childhood, youth, or young adulthood. The opportunity to contribute to a youngster's resilience seems almost infinite in its possibilities and the commitment to do so is the greatest strength of helpers.

References

Anthony, E.J. (1987). Risk, vulnerability and resilience. In E.J. Anthony & B.J. Cohler (Eds.) *The invulnerable child* (pp. 3–49). New York: The Guilford Press.

Beardslee, W.R. (1989). The role of self-understanding in resilient individuals: The development of a perspective. *American Journal of Orthopsychiatry, 59* (2), 266–278.

Bleuler, E. (1950/1911). *Dementia praecox or the group of schizophrenias*. New York: International Universities Press.

Bowlby, M. (1951). *Mental care and mental health*. Geneva: World Health Organization.

Denzin, N. (1978). *The research act: A theoretical introduction to sociological methods (2nd edition)*. New York: McGraw-Hill.

Denzin, N. (1989). *Interpretive interactionism*. Newbury Park: Sage Publications.

Fanshel, D., Finch, S., & Grundy, J. (1990). *Foster children in a life course perspective*. New York: Columbia University Press.

Festinger, T. (1983). *No one ever asked us ... A postscript to foster care*. New York: Columbia University Press.

Garmezy, N. (1971). Vulnerability research and the issue of primary prevention. *American Journal of Orthopsychiatry, 41*(1), 101–115.

Garmezy, N. (1983). Stressors of childhood. In N. Garmezy & M. Rutter (Eds.). *Stress, coping and development in children* (pp. 43–84). New York: McGraw-Hill.

Garmezy, N. (1987). Stress, competence and development: Continuities in the study of schizophrenic adults, children vulnerable to psychopathology and the search for stress-resistant children. *American Journal of Orthopsychiatry, 57*(2), 159–174.

Geertz, C. (1973). *The interpretation of cultures*. New York: Basic Books.

Goffman, E. (1963). *Stigma: Notes on the management of spoiled identity*. Englewood Cliffs, New Jersey: Prentice-Hall.

Herrenkohl, E. C., Herrenkohl, R. C., & Egolf, B. (1994). Resilient early school-age children from maltreatment homes: Outcomes in late adolescence. *American Journal of Orthopsychiatry, 64* (2), 301–309.

Murphy, L. B., & Moriority, A. (1976). *Vulnerability, coping and growth: From infancy to adolescence*. New Haven: Yale University Press.

Rutter, M., Maughan, B., Mortimore, P. , Ouston, J., & Smith, A. (1979a). *Fifteen thousand hours: Secondary schools and their effects on children*. Cambridge Massachusetts: Harvard University Press.

Rutter, M. (1979b) Protective factors in children's response to stress and disadvantage. In M.W. Kent & J. Rolf (Eds.), *Primary prevention of psychopathology, social competence in children (Vol. III)* (pp. 49–74). Hanover, New Hampshire: University Press of New England.

Rutter, M. (1987). Psychosocial resilience and protective mechanisms. *American Journal of Orthopsychiatry, 57*, 316–331.

Schulman, P. , Castellon, C., & Seligman, M. (1989). Assessing explanatory style: The content analysis of verbatim explanations and the attributional style questionnaire. *Behavior, Research and Therapy, 27*(5), 505–512.

Seligman, M. (1984). *Attributional style questionnaire.* (Available from [Department of Psychology, University of Pennsylvania, 3815 Walnut Street, Philadelphia, PA 19104–6196]).

Silver, R. L., Boon, C., & Stones, M. H. (1983). Searching for meaning in misfortune: Making sense of incest. *Journal of Social Issues 39*, (2), 81–102.

Sullivan, E. (1984). *A critical psychology: Interpretation of the personal world.* New York: Plenum Books.

Triseliotis, J. (1980). Growing up in foster care and after. In J. Triseliotis (Ed.), *New developments in foster care and adoption* (pp. 131–162). London: Routledge & Kegan Paul.

Werner, E. E., & Smith, R. S. (1992). *Overcoming the odds: High-risk children from birth to adulthood.* Ithaca: Cornell University Press.

27

Looking After Children Better: An Interactive Model For Research and Practice

Sonia Jackson

Child welfare interventions are costly, time-consuming, and have life-changing consequences for the people involved. Their immediate purpose may seem self-evident: to prevent children from suffering harm, and in the last resort to remove them from families who are unable to provide a minimally acceptable standard of care for them. Family preservation has displaced rescue as the intervention of choice as evidence has grown of the risks involved in separating children from their families and communities. There is an implicit assumption, whatever the action, that it will lead to a state of greater wellbeing and better future life chances for the child.

This assumption is not usually challenged. Thus, the emphasis of research and evaluation tends to be related to the original trigger for the intervention or to the stated objectives of the service. The measure of success is that the child has not been abused again, or has been enabled to stay in the family, or that the residential or foster placement has not broken down. Yet these can only be intermediate aims. The intervention cannot be justified if the longer-term outcome for the child is no better—and possibly worse—than if a different decision had been taken. The effectiveness of a service for children must ultimately be judged by the extent to which it enhances the wellbeing of each individual child.

Why has this type of research been so slow to develop? One reason is that researchers tend to have easier access to service providers than to those at the receiving end, so that consumer research has always been the exception. More fundamental is the difficulty, both theoretical and practical, of defining and assessing outcomes for children. This chapter describes how some of these problems have been overcome in the Looking After Children program, a system of ongoing assessment which feeds directly back into practical action, in addition to providing data for evaluation and research. The scheme has been developed and piloted over six years by a team of researchers based at two British universities, Bristol and Swansea. It consists of three administrative documents: an Essential Facts Sheet, a Plan and a Review form, and six Assessment and Action Records, colour-coded by the age of the child. A computerized version is being developed together with an associated video and training pack. The Assessment and Action Records are the core of the scheme and the means through which its philosophy is expressed. They are designed as a method of recording and evaluating outcomes of residential and foster care and also provide a focus for collaborative work between all the people involved in the child's care, including the child or young person.

The program developed in parallel with the enactment and implementation of the 1989 Children Act (Department of Health, 1989). The Act required substantial changes in the way that services for separated children were provided and altered the vocabulary of child welfare in Britain. Children are no longer in care unless they are subject to a court order, but looked after by local authorities. This chapter discusses the theoretical basis of the scheme, its design, implementation and evaluation. It also considers the question of how far the principles of the scheme can be generalized to different national and cultural contexts and its potential for use in countries other than the United Kingdom.

Why Assess Outcomes?

The program originated in a meeting called by the government department responsible for child welfare and attended by most of the active UK researchers in the field (Jackson, 1989). The aim was to review currently available evidence on outcomes of public care for children, to identify gaps in knowledge, and to consider ways of measuring and assessing the impact of care on children's development. A number of factors coincided to give this issue high priority for politicians and administrators and to ensure continuous financial support. The most important impetus for a change of approach probably came from the government's ideological commitment to market principles in the delivery of social services. Cost-effectiveness, quality assurance, and performance monitoring were relatively new ideas in child welfare, but their impact had already been felt in other services. The climate was right for a focus on outcomes.

Research evidence of serious weaknesses in the child welfare system and of damaging consequences for children growing up within it was building. Children who did not return home within six months were likely to stay long, were in great danger of losing contact with their families and community networks, and were often completely alone on leaving care (Millham, Bullock, Hosie & Haak, 1986). Health and education, vital aspects of children's development, seemed to be overlooked both by researchers and by social workers (Jackson, 1987; Kahan, 1989). Other signs that the care system was not meeting children's needs effectively were the instability of placement (Berridge, 1985; Rowe, Hundleby & Garnett, 1989) and the inconsistency of planning and decision-making. Vernon and Fruin (1986) showed that there was a large element of chance in determining whether children remained in care or went home to their families. Similarly, Packman, Randall and Jacques (1986) found that the circumstances of children who came into care were little different from those who remained with their families. Research on outcomes tended to focus on continuity of placement, especially in foster care (Berridge & Cleaver, 1987). Apart from a few retrospective accounts (Kahan, 1979) there was a surprising lack of recent evidence on the impact of the care experience, positive or negative, on the children themselves. There were, however, worrying indicators. For example it was known that nearly a quarter of the adult prison population had been in care and 30% of homeless 16- and 17- year-olds had a care background. These facts suggested that the care system was failing at least some of the children for whom it was responsible. This picture has recently been confirmed by two official reports on children in residential care (Levy &

Kahan, 1991; Utting, 1991) and by follow-up studies of young people leaving care (Biehal, 1992; Garnett, 1992).

In 1989 there was almost no systematic information available about outcomes for children who had been in residential or foster care. Local authorities made no attempt to keep in touch with young people who had left care. Case records provided incomplete and often inaccurate information, and there was no generally accepted means of assessment or monitoring. A smaller group decided to take on the task of designing an assessment scheme which would be of use to social workers, carers, and managers, not simply to researchers. As a first step it was necessary to define the concept of outcome and to unravel the many complex issues which were raised as soon as the attempt was made. Roy Parker and colleagues fully describe this process (Parker et al., 1991).

Defining and Evaluating Outcome

Some of the dilemmas can be illustrated by taking a relatively simple example, such as placement of a child with foster carers following a substantiated allegation of abuse. Should this be seen as an outcome or a beginning? If the object of the intervention was to protect the child, has this been achieved? Or should we assess the impact of the whole experience on the child's development and functioning? If so, at what point should this be done? How do we evaluate this outcome? Ward (1994) has pointed out that it will look very different depending on whose perspective is taken. The outcome for the general public is that a child has been rescued. But it is not quite so simple for the service providers. A scandal has been avoided, but additional costs will be incurred. The child's social worker may be disappointed by the failure of her plan to support the child within the family, or relieved to have found an acceptable foster placement. The parents could see the outcome as good in so far as it relieves the strain on the family, or as punitive and stigmatizing. The child may welcome escaping from the ill-treatment but see separation from the family as a negative outcome, especially in the longer run. Some of these questions are resolved once it is established that placement of any kind is not an outcome but simply the context within which outcomes occur. The immediate protection of the child is necessary, but not sufficient, to result in a good outcome unless the intervention also has a beneficial effect on the child's subsequent development and life chances.

This leads to the question of when an outcome has occurred. In this case, should assessment begin from the time of first contact with the child care agency, when the suspicion of abuse was confirmed, when the child joined the foster family, or only after a period of settling in? And should it be continuous or take place at the point of leaving care? This might seem logical, but could be misleading if, for example, assessment coincided with a period of adolescent turmoil and disaffection. In any case, to postpone the assessment until then might provide some information on how well the care system had done its job but it would be too late to help that particular child.

The problem of different and possibly conflicting perspectives can be overcome once the decision is taken to focus on the individual child, in line with the principle that the welfare of the child is paramount. The aim must be to assess children's general well-being, not simply to consider if the immediate purpose of accommodating or looking after them has been met. Long and short term objectives need to be held in balance, just as parents try to do, rather than simply reacting to critical events. To improve practice, the assessment instrument needs to adopt a formative as opposed to a summative style of evaluation (Patton, 1978) and be suitable to monitor a child's progress at regular intervals. The weakness of most assessment scales, from the practitioner's point of view, is that they need to be administered and interpreted by an expert instead of producing information for direct use.

A further requirement was that the instrument should contribute to a better understanding of the connection between child care interventions and outcomes by establishing a theoretical framework in relation to which the outcome could be evaluated. Two theoretical perspectives which influenced the development of the Looking After Children scheme were the production of welfare (Knapp, 1984) and the notion of competence as a dynamic concept embodied in the work of Anthony Maluccio (Aldgate, Maluccio & Reeves, 1989). Both these models acknowledge the complicated interconnections between the factors determining a particular outcome, but stress the value of examining the intervening processes to provide relevant data on the strengths and weaknesses of services. Thus it is never possible to be sure that a particular long-term outcome for a child was directly attributable to a social work intervention, but a method of assessment which adopts an interactional perspective can determine how far the care or service offered contributed to the likelihood of success.

But what do we mean by success? What is the appropriate standard by which to judge the care provided for children by public bodies? In the past this was defined as providing for their physical needs at a level no better than that of children of a similar social background (Jackson, 1987). More recently, concern with their emotional experiences has claimed the attention of social workers, especially in Britain and the United States, but this has sometimes been at the expense of attention to more practical matters. The 1989 Children Act sets new standards related closely to what might be expected of an average parent. The intention is clear, although the definitions tend to be somewhat circular. Parental responsibility, a key concept in the Act, is defined as "a collection of powers and duties which follow from being a parent and bringing up a child" (HMSO, 1989). Earlier grounds for care and supervision orders are replaced with the question, "Is the child receiving that care which it would be reasonable to expect a parent to give?" This implies some consensus on what is reasonable parenting and assumes that the outcome will be the achievement of a satisfactory quality of life for children. It fits well with an interactional theoretical framework and with the idea of focusing on intermediate, rather than final, outcomes in designing a method of evaluation. This substantially reduces the difficulty of making connections between child care interventions and their effects. The extent to which a child care agency is successfully carrying out its responsibilities can be judged by the extent to which it mirrors the practices of the reasonable parent.

A Multi-Dimensional View of Child Development

Adopting an active view of child care as the promotion of welfare rather than the prevention of harm implies a move away from a one-dimensional view of outcome. Children's lives may be as deeply affected by the actions that child care workers fail to take as by what they actually do (Fisher, Marsh & Phillips, 1986). A comprehensive assessment scheme should cover all the aspects of development which are informally monitored and promoted by reasonable parents. Seven dimensions are incorporated in the scheme, all of which need to be assessed if the adequate fulfilment of parental responsibilities is regarded as the ultimate purpose of child care interventions. The dimensions are:

- Health
- Education
- Identity
- Family and social relationships
- Social presentation
- Emotional and behavioural development
- Self-care skills

The dimensions are self-evidently important, but in most cases research findings show that they are especially problematic for children in residential and foster care (Parker et al., 1991). Identifying the dimensions was the first stage in the process of constructing the assessment instrument. The population for assessment was decided into age groups, since it was intended to assess outcomes for all children and young people from birth to leaving care. The complete scheme comprises six Assessment and Action Records for age bands Under 1, 1–2, 3–4, 5–9, 10–15 and 16 and over.

The Looking After Children Model

The Assessment and Action Records follow a model that is set out in diagram 27.1. They start by trying to determine what the aims of a reasonable parent for a child of this age on a particular dimension would be . They then ask what would a reasonable, adequately resourced and well-informed parent do in order to maximize the chances of achieving those aims? This produces a series of quality of care questions. Each main question triggers a series of subsidiary questions. For example on the education dimension (for all age groups over 5) the aims are that "the child's educational attainments are average or above and that s/he acquires special skills and interests and takes a full part in school activities." Since school attainment is closely related to reading competence, one of the quality of care questions is, "How often does the child go to a library or bring a book home from school?" If the answer is less than once a week, the subsidiary questions are "what further action will be taken" and "who will take it?" The person completing the record is asked to explain lack of information (a "don't know" answer) or no action. Each section ends with the question of "have the specified aims have been achieved?" If not, this should lead to closer scrutiny of the preceding questions to see what more might be done.

Evaluating the model

This model has been evaluated in two stages. The first stage was a feasibility study designed to discover if the Assessment and Action Records would be acceptable to social workers and what impact, if any, they would have on their practice (Ward & Jackson, 1991; Ward, Jackson & Parker, 1991). Only 3–4-year-olds and over 16-year-olds were included in this study. Thirty-two social workers from four local authorities took part as well as staff in two residential units. The records were completely redesigned, and forms for four other age

Figure 27-1: What Do Good Parents Want for Their Children?

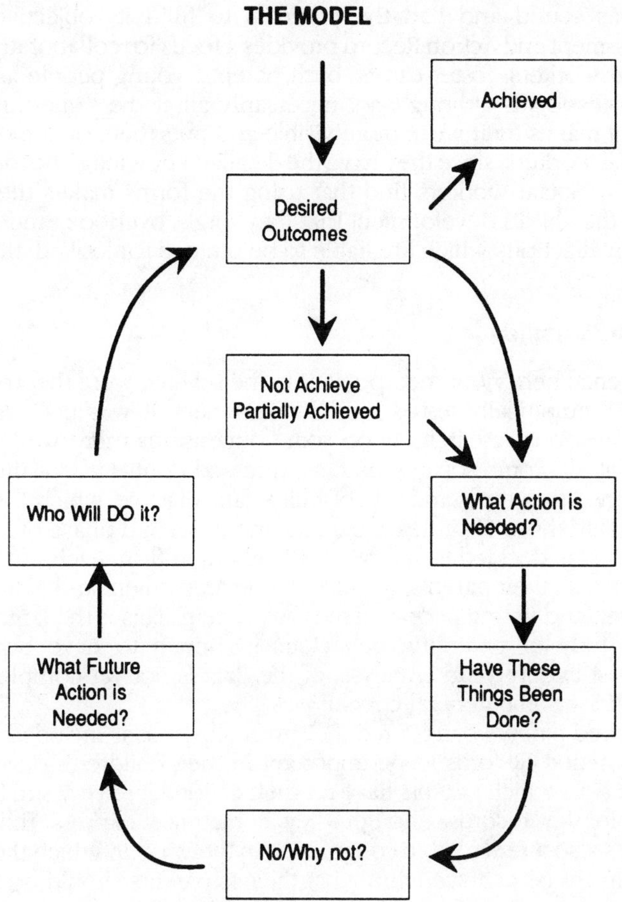

groups added on the basis of feedback and comments from the social workers, foster carers, and young people who took part in this exercise. In addition it was clear that there was little chance of the scheme being widely used unless it was seen as an integral component of child care practice in the locality. Three administrative forms were therefore added, a Basic Facts Sheet, a Plan, and Review of Arrangements. These, with the six Assessment and Action Records and Guidelines to their use, made up the package that was launched at the end of 1991 as a companion documents to the Children Act. All the materials were then available and could be used by any local authority or child care agency that wished to do so.

The second stage of evaluation had two main aims: to refine and improve the administrative documents and the Assessment and Action Records and to see if their use could be shown to improve child welfare practice and outcomes. There were many suggestions for improving the questions, but it was clear that the basic model was sound and had the potential to fulfil its objectives. Completing an Assessment and Action Record provides a focus for collaborative work between social workers, foster carers, birth parents, young people and sometimes other professionals although not necessarily all at the same time. Caregivers find that it makes their work more visible and puts them on a more equal basis with social workers, since they have the detailed knowledge needed to complete the form. Social workers find that using the forms makes them aware of aspects of the child's development that they might overlook, and of precisely those parental actions which are liable to be omitted for looked-after children.

Setting Standards for Parenting

The aims and parental behaviour incorporated in the scheme were theoretically derived and not empirically tested by the researchers. It was not even possible to rely on previous research, as on some dimensions there was no published evidence at all. Some social workers expressed doubts about their content on the grounds that the standards of child care practice which they implied were far beyond those of ordinary parents. In the second phase of the research, therefore, it was decided to interview 100 children from each of the four older age groups with their parents, using the same Assessment and Action Records as for children and young people in the care system. This is the largest and most detailed study of parenting behaviour in Britain to have been undertaken in the past twenty years. Analysis of the data is not yet complete but it is possible to draw some general conclusions.

First, all four hundred parents considered the seven dimensions included in the Assessment and Action Records to be important in their children's development. Second, the aims which parents have for their children are very similar to those specified in the records, though they sometimes express them differently. There was also a remarkable congruence in the ways in which they thought those aims might be achieved and what they as parents should do to make this more likely. Parents often considered that they fell short of the standards they set for themselves, but this was almost always due to lack of resources or other pressures, not lack of awareness. For example all those interviewed knew that it was important to read to young children, though not all were sufficiently well organized to do it on a regular basis. The questions about education and diet, that were often criticized by social workers during the evaluation phase as middle class, were not seen in this way by the working class families in the survey. The researchers found no evidence that the expectations about reasonable parental behaviour implied by the questions in the Records were unrealistic in any way. They were impressed by the efforts made by parents, including those living on low incomes in difficult circumstances, to do their best for their children.

Assessing the Quality of Care

The main purpose of the evaluative study was to refine the assessment instrument and to ensure that it was acceptable and useful to practitioners. The looked-after children in the core sample were drawn from five social services departments, selected to represent local populations with different characteristics. They included a socially and ethnically mixed inner-city area, a rural area containing several army bases with married quarters, a medium-sized town, and a large port with its suburban hinterland. The children were chosen for assessment by the social services departments in accordance with their own priorities, and cannot therefore be considered representative of all children in the British care system. However they do illustrate the way in which use of the Looking After Children scheme highlights unmet needs and points to necessary action if children are to be enabled to develop as well as possible. Altogether 202 children were assessed on one occasion, 73 twice, and 9 three times. They ranged in age from 9 months to 19 years. Sixty-nine percent of the children were in family foster care, 19% in residential establishments, 7% with parents and a small number with prospective adopters, or were older teenagers living independently. Fifty-three percent were boys and about 20% from a variety of minority ethic groups.

What can this study tell us about children in residential and foster care? The assessment system provides detailed and specific evidence about the quality of care provided for the individual and the impact of this on the child's development. It makes good practice more visible and pinpoints omissions and inconsistencies. It is thus an excellent instrument for quality assurance. Practitioners are aware of this, which can lead to resistance and defensiveness; we would all prefer not to have our shortcomings exposed. At best, use of the Looking After Children materials with this group of children led to more effective cooperation between those responsible for their care, including birth parents, and encouraged purposeful action.

The majority of the children assessed were found to be receiving a reasonable level of care, and this is an important corrective to the negative view conveyed by problem-focused research. In almost every case, however, there were opportunities to promote the child's development and well-being which had been overlooked, and these would certainly not have come to light as a result of the more generalized type of enquiry that social workers and supervisors typically make about children's progress. Moreover, on every dimension, there was a significant minority of children whose care was clearly deficient in some respect, and appeared to carry a high risk of an unsatisfactory outcome. In many cases the social worker and caregiver were stimulated to decide on some action to improve matters, but quite frequently the completed Assessment and Action Record revealed ignorance of children's developmental needs and a standard of parenting markedly lower than was found in the study of the comparison group.

Some examples of findings on different dimensions will illustrate how the assessment scheme directs attention to weaknesses in the service provided. There was ample evidence, on the health dimension, to support the finding of an official enquiry into residential homes for children that "the process of health assessment generally was haphazard" and that there was "little concern with prevention and health education" (Utting, 1991, p. 36). In two of the study areas, over a third of the children assessed had not had a medical examination, although this is a legal requirement. A number of children appeared to be seriously over or underweight for their height and age, but this was often not recognized by their social workers, who believed them to be eating well and growing within normal limits. Questions on health promotion revealed many significant gaps. Sixty-three percent of young people in residential homes smoked, compared with only 17% living with their own parents. Two-thirds of these were under the legal age of 16. Alcohol misuse was also common, and could be seen to interact with behavioural problems. Many children had a chronically low level of health, which must have affected their ability to function well at school and socially. Until the social worker, caregiver, and birth parent sat down together to complete the health section of the Assessment and Action Record, it might be that no one was aware of the overall pattern, so that each episode of sickness was treated as a separate occurrence. One ten-year-old boy, for example, in care for four years, was recorded over a period of six months as suffering from a heavy cold, worms, headaches, tonsillitis, and urinary and ear infections. The urgent need for a pediatric examination would not have been picked up without this assessment

The assessment revealed the extent to which children's schooling was disrupted by placement changes; some had experienced up to nine unscheduled changes of school. Twenty-one percent had moved placement four or more times. Some children were excluded from school, usually because of problematic behaviour. Forty-five percent of the sample were assessed as having special educational needs, but fewer than half of these were receiving additional help. This was brought into the open by use of the assessment scheme. Some children were performing at about average levels in school, but about half were markedly behind, particularly in subjects involving linguistic skills. There was little sign of social workers seeing it as part of their job to recognize and promote special talents or gifts. There seems to have been some improvement, compared with earlier research findings, in the numbers of young people taking public examinations and staying in education after the minimum leaving age of 16, but low expectations still prevail. Only one young person in the sample was planning to go to university. The generally passive attitudes of social workers in regard to education—some even suggesting that it was unfair to ask questions on the subject because so many looked-after children were not attending school regularly—contrasted starkly with the energetic concern of most parents in the comparison group. Few children in the sample had been helped to make career plans and sometimes their own aspirations were dismissed as unrealistic rather than being treated as an important source of motivation. It was painfully clear that these children often have to struggle through their school days without any of the support others take for granted, like encouragement to participate in activities and outings, or knowing that their close adults will be present at parents' evenings and school events.

The section of the Assessment and Action Records concerned with identity is designed to make sure that children have the opportunity to develop positive self-esteem and emotional well-being, to understand how they come to be living where they are, and to know something about their birth family and ethnic background. These are the kinds of issues with which social workers have traditionally been concerned, perhaps more than health or education. But here too practice had some way to go to catch up with theory. Ethnicity was often interpreted to refer only to black children. The legislation requires that due consideration be given also to religious persuasion and cultural and linguistic background but this had not happened in the majority of cases where the children were white. Seventeen percent of the children had no discussion with their caregivers about why they were not living with their parents. Fewer than half had a life story book either up to date or in progress. Low self-esteem is one of the factors most damaging to the development of children growing up in the care system. In answer to a question about whether the child receives loving approval, nearly one in five of caregivers stated that the child did not deserve praise or approval because his or her behaviour was too bad to merit it. The experience of a child subjected to this kind of treatment is painful to contemplate. There is good evidence, both from practice and research, that it is likely to produce a deteriorating spiral of behaviour and relationships, and one would predict that these placements are unlikely to endure. If the question had not been asked, would the social worker even have known, and what does it tell us about the selection and training of foster carers and residential workers?

The findings on Social and Family Relationships are particularly worth noting because they echo similar evidence from North America and continental Europe on the marginalization of birth families by the care system. Despite emphasis in the Children Act on working in partnership with parents and families, fewer than a third of children in the core sample were reported as having weekly contact even with a mother. Half the children had no contact with their fathers at all, and nearly a third had no contact with their mothers either. Questions about extended family showed a general lack of information on relatives other than parents. Forty-one percent of the children had no contact with grandparents, who potentially have much to offer as a source of continuity and knowledge about the family. A significant proportion of children (19%) had no continued contact with any adult during their lives. This was one of the main points of difference from children living in their own families, who were normally part of a wide network of friends and relatives on whom they could call for help and advice if necessary. This kind of alternative support can be vitally important, especially in late adolescence and during the process of moving into independence, a stage when conflict with primary caregivers is not uncommon even in well-functioning families (Jackson, 1992). Several leaving care studies have shown the prospects for young people without contacts with potentially supportive adults are fairly bleak (Biehal et al., 1992. Garnett, 1992). Thus, the action suggested by questions on the family and social relationships dimension of the Assessment and Action Records is for social workers and others to take active steps to rebuild links with extended family and friends.

How Relevant is Looking After Children to Other Countries?

The Looking After Children program has attracted international interest. Some parts of the administrative documents are country-specific, but the model is sufficiently adaptable to be applicable in many different circumstances. The materials are now being used in Canada, Australia, New Zealand, Scotland, Northern Ireland, Brazil, Belgium, Norway and Israel and have already been translated into Flemish, Norwegian, Hebrew, Croatian, Slovenian, and Ukrainian. These countries are diverse, and include some, like Norway, with well-established provisions for separated children and high aspirations for them. At the other extreme, other countries are struggling to set up a system of care to provide for basic needs.

Israel, for example, has a long tradition of good quality residential institutions for young people, and in contrast to many other countries, no stigma is attached to living in one. They tend to have stable, well-qualified staff groups and give great importance to health and education. However many Israeli child welfare workers and directors saw immediate possibilities for the Assessment and Action Records in their work. Some were shocked to find how many questions they were unable to answer about children with whom they had lived for several years, partly it seemed because the emphasis on the group and the value of collaboration and mutual support within it could lead to the needs of individuals being overlooked. Some group home directors have now set themselves a target of completing an Assessment and Action Record for each child in their care.

Not all the questions are appropriate in different national and cultural settings, but the developmental dimensions appear to have wide applicability. That does not mean that they have always been recognized as important. For example, in one institution a staff member remarked that she had never thought specifically about self-care skills. She had assumed young people just picked them up. On reflection, though, she thought that when children lived as a group, the competence of one or two might mask the incompetence of others, allowing them to leave residential care very ill-equipped for independent living.

Suggestions made by colleagues from other countries have exposed assumptions and values of which the team was not necessarily fully aware in constructing the assessment materials. For example, in Belgium it was suggested that greater prominence should be given to leisure skills by making them a separate dimension rather than splitting them between Health and Education. In Israel the questions relating to ethnic identity sparked off a fierce debate. The country's whole existence rests on the amazing survival, through centuries of dispersal, of the sense of Jewish identity. Is it thus desirable to encourage children to retain a potentially divisive attachment to a different identity? With successive waves of immigration from Ethiopia and Russia, including many unaccompanied children and young people, this is becoming an increasingly urgent question. Working through the Assessment and Action Record obliged the staff group to confront a crucial issue which they had previously either avoided or denied. It illustrates the point that we cannot always assume a consensus on what are desirable outcomes, but disagreement is brought out into the open.

In some countries, such as Brazil, where international agencies require programmes which they fund to be evaluated, there is interest in the capacity of the Looking After Children scheme to produce aggregated factual data on the progress of children as well as on the service being provided for them. In the United States and Canada it is being used to evaluate specialist programs, some of which involve high per capita costs. The scheme has the merit of producing a variegated picture, providing evidence of good points as well as weaknesses. It can demonstrate where there are strengths to be built on and which inputs are associated with good outcomes. It is therefore a more sensitive indicator than traditional types of evaluation and a more effective aid to the decision-making of funding agencies.

Conclusion

The Looking After Children program is an attempt to express an ethical position in practice. When it is necessary for a public body to take on the parenting role, either for a child's protection or because there is no one in the family able to provide care, that body acquires a responsibility to simulate as nearly as possible the behaviour of a good parent. In reality it is extremely hard to do this, and unintended consequences of child welfare interventions have often been worse than the harm they were intended to prevent. The present tendency to assume that children are generally best remaining in their own families will remain as untested as the previous urge to rescue them unless there is some reliable means of assessing the outcome over time in relation to the child's wellbeing.

The Looking After Children materials provide a way in which this can be done, not as a one-off research exercise, but as an integral part of the care provided for the child. The aims of the program are derived from those of ordinary parents and the outcome measures are designed to make explicit the way in which most competent parents informally monitor and guide their children's development. It attempts to ensure that vital aspects of development are not overlooked when the care of children has to be shared between their parents and a number of different professionals.

There is still no guarantee that the outcome will be favourable. Too many factors in the lives of young people in the care system are outside the control of caregivers or social workers. Evaluation of the use of the materials in practice, however, has shown that, if the model is used as intended, it is much more likely that problems will be identified and addressed at an earlier stage; the work of caregivers will be better valued, supported and guided, and communication between all the different people with an interest in the child will be much improved.

The program is still evolving, with a revised package due to be published in 1995. Further evidence will emerge from the use of the materials in practice, both in the UK and in other countries. There is scope for using them with different groups of children, such as those at risk or in need. The use of the assessment scheme for systematic study of parenting behaviour in the general population also offers intriguing possibilities for cross-national research. Present indications are that the model and the principles on which it is based are adaptable to many different circumstances and hold real promise of better care and better outcomes for children.

The Looking After Children: Assessing Outcomes programme is funded by the U.K. Department of Health and based at Dartington Social Research Unit, University of Bristol. Present members of the team are Dr. Harriet Ward, Sonia Jackson, Sue Kilroe, Sue Moyers and Anne Mason, with field consultants Hilary Corrick and Debby Jones.

References

Aldgate, J., Maluccio, A., & Reeves, C. (1989). *Adolescents in foster families*. London: Batsford.

Biehal, N., Clayden, J., Stein, M., & Wade, J. (1992). *Prepared for living: A survey of young people leaving the care of three local authorities*. London: National Children's Bureau.

Berridge, D., & Cleaver, H. (1987). *Foster home breakdown*. Oxford: Blackwell.

Berridge, D. (1985). *Children's homes*. Oxford: Blackwell.

Department of Health. (1989). *An introduction to the Children's Act, 1989*. London: HMSO.

Fisher, M., Marsh, P. , & Phillips, D., & Sainsbury, E. (1986). *In and out of care: The experiences of children, parents and social workers*. London: Batsford.

Garnett, L. (1992). *Leaving care*. London: National Children's Bureau.

Jackson, S. (1989). The state as parent: Assessing outcomes in child care. In J. Hudson & B. Galaway (Eds), *The state as parent: International research perspectives on interventions with young persons.* Dordrecht: Kluwer.

Jackson, S. (1987). *The education of children in care.* Bristol Papers, No.1. University of Bristol School of Applied Social Studies.

Jackson, S. (1992). Young people leaving care: Promoting networks and building competence. In J.D. Van der Ploeg, P. M. van den Bergh, M. Klomp, E. J. Knorth, & M. Smit, (Eds). *Vulnerable youth in residential care.* Leuven: Garant.

Kahan, B. (1979). *Growing up in care.* Oxford: Blackwell.

Kahan, B. (1989). The physical and mental health of children in care. In B. Kahan (Ed.), *Child care research, policy and practice.* London: Hodder & Stoughton.

Knapp, M. (1984). *The economics of social care.* London: Macmillan

Levy, A., & Kahan, B. (1991). *The Pindown experience and the protection of children: Report of the Staffordshire child care inquiry.* Stafford: Staffordshire County Council.

Millham, S., Bullock, R., Hosie, K., & Haak, M. (1986). *Lost in care: the problem of maintaining links between children in care and their families.* Aldershot: Gower.

Packman, J., Randall, J., & Jacques, N. (1986). *Who needs care? Social work decisions about children.* Oxford: Blackwell.

Parker, R., Ward, H., Jackson, S., Aldgate, J., & Wedge, P. (Eds.). (1991). *Looking after children: Assessing outcomes in child care.* London: HMSO.

Patton, M. Q. (1978). *Utilization-focused evaluation.* Beverley Hills: Sage.

Rowe, J., Hundleby, M., & Garnett, L. (1989). *Child care now: A survey of placement patterns.* London: British Association for Adoption and Fostering.

Utting, W. (1991). *Children in the public care.* London: HMSO.

Vernon, J., & Fruin, D. (1986). *In care: A study of social work decision-making.* London: National Children's Bureau.

Ward, H. (1994). The Looking After Children Project: Current perspectives. In B. McKenzie (Ed.), *Foster family care for children and youth.* Toronto: Wall & Emerson.

Ward, H., & Jackson, S. (1991). Developing outcome measures in child care: a research note. *British Journal of Social Work, 21*(4), 393–399.

Ward, H., Jackson, S., & Parker, R. (1991). *A feasibility study on the assessment of outcomes in child care.* Interim report to the Department of Health. Bristol: University of Bristol.

28

Inclusive Care, Separation Management, and Role Clarity in Foster Care: The Development of Theoretical Constructs

Kathleen Kufeldt

Why would services set up to protect children fail them? Why would a graduate of the system write a book entitled *Pain ... Lots of Pain* (Raychaba, 1993)? Why are young people who have been through the care system over-represented among runaway and homeless youth? The questions are disturbing, the answers not easy. Child welfare systems are plagued with problems that seem to be universal, to the point where one wonders if they are in fact endemic to the system. From time to time promising solutions emerge in the professional literature; solutions are applied but in turn produce unintended outcomes. Periodically, tragedies within the system raise serious debate with respect to government intervention in the lives of children (Howells, 1974). The debate has been intensified by individual tragedies as well as by institutional failures such as the Cleveland affair in the United Kingdom (Department of Health, 1988), residential schooling for Native children in Canada (Armitage, 1993), and child sexual abuse in institutions (Hughes, 1991). Discussion of problems and attempted solutions provides a backdrop to the presentation of findings from a series of research projects conducted in Ontario. The research explored the dynamics of substitute care in order to develop a theoretical basis for practice.

Unintended outcomes of child welfare intervention include: drift in care (Maas & Engler, 1959; Fanshel & Shinn, 1978); serious disruption of family ties (Steinhauer, 1983; 1993; Thorpe, 1980); separation of siblings (Aldridge & Cautley, 1975; Laird & Hartman, 1985; Timberlake & Hamlin, 1982); too many placements; too many changes of social workers; discontinuities and general instability of living situations (Fanshel, Finch & Grundy, 1990; Kufeldt, 1984; Thomlison, 1990); placement breakdown and disruption of schooling (Berridge & Cleaver, 1987; Cleaver, 1994); and the often traumatic effects of separation (Bowlby, 1979; Palmer, 1971; 1990; Steinhauer, 1983). But what are appropriate measures for the care of children in need of protection?

Permanency planning was the popular catch-phrase of the 1980s. The pioneering work in Oregon (Emlen et al. 1976; 1978) showed promising results. The meaning of the concept was not carefully translated into practice despite clear definitions by writers such as Maluccio, Fein and Olmstead (1986). Examples of poor practice included removing children from long term foster parents in order to be placed for adoption and children placed in closed adoption despite continuing ongoing contact with their own family. A new term, "adoption disruption," crept into the literature (Sachdev, 1984) as it became apparent that adoption as a permanent plan was not necessarily a panacea. Debates concerning the relative merits of in-home care, foster care, group care, and institutional care also affect determination of solutions. One belief system, for example, suggests that foster care is not suitable for teenagers although this notion is refuted by Hazel (1990). Young people themselves, if asked, will talk about the value of foster care (Allison & Johnson, 1981; Parker, 1989).

There is currently a philosophical shift towards prevention of reception into care. In some jurisdictions, this shift has been translated into legislative requirements to protect children by the least intrusive measure, which is broadly interpreted as leaving children in their own homes. Maintaining children in their own family and community is a laudable objective, and generally the procedure of choice. Nevertheless there are situations where home is not a safe place; some families are so burdened by multiple problems that they have little to give their children and little capacity to benefit from intensive in-home services. Too often there is a failure to provide resources and services that could contribute to the family's ability to care for its own children. Even where they are provided, the services may not necessarily prevent eventual reception into care. Wharf (1993) argues that child welfare resources should be targeted entirely to assisting and supporting parents. This would fit with the trend towards prevention of placement, in-home family support, and least intrusion. Relieving children and families from poverty might do much to reduce the child welfare intakes but income assistance and support services will not be sufficient for some families. A recent British study (Bullock, Little & Millham, 1993) noted the help that some overstressed families derive from temporary care of their children. Children and families have identified the necessity for care, and its ability to achieve positive effects for the children (Kufeldt, Armstrong & Dorosh, 1989). Research with runaway and homeless youth (Kufeldt & Nimmo, 1987; Kufeldt & Burrows, 1994) reveals the downside of least intrusion. Children are entering care older and more damaged as the result of failures of preventive efforts; some are turned away on the basis of age or fear of the deleterious effects of placement and end up on the streets (Kufeldt & Burrows, 1994).

A continuum of services for children and families is required. Foster care is the optimum approach where temporary removal is required, but it must honour the child's attachments and need for some manageable continuity. Treatment foster care (Galaway et al. 1990; Galaway & Hudson, 1989) and inclusive foster care (Blumenthal & Weinberg, 1984; Family Rights Group, 1986; Galaway, Nutter & Hudson, 1994; Hess & Proch, 1988; Kufeldt, 1991; 1994; Kufeldt & Allison, 1990; Pine, Warsh & Maluccio, 1993; Proch & Hess, 1987; Proch & Howard, 1984) are promising responses. Translation into practice is a more difficult undertaking because of the complexity of the undertaking, role ambiguities and uncertainties, and difficulty replicating in an institutionalized service the intense dedication of a caring parent:

> Typically, no one person has complete and comprehensive responsibility for the child's present care and future welfare in the way that is usually expected of a

> parent. Consequently, these children are dependent upon adults whose responsibilities are often ambiguous and who are themselves liable to be replaced. In particular, they are likely to feel uncertain and unsure about the future since it has no obvious or foreseeable pattern. As a result they may face particular difficulties in acquiring, or retaining, a sense of their identity. Often they can provide no answers for themselves to the questions: Who am I? Where do I belong? or Where am I going? They are, in every sense of the word, *vulnerable* children (Parker, 1980, p. 3).

This vulnerability may be exacerbated in a number of ways. While in care the effects of the earlier neglect and abuse as well as separation experiences may cause attachment problems or may trigger behavioral acting-out which is aversive to caregivers. On termination of legal childhood many young people have nowhere to turn but the streets (Conte, 1994; Kufeldt & Burrows, 1994; Shane, 1991). The necessity for creating models for practice that are conceptually well grounded was intensified by the findings of a recently completed study of runaway and homeless youth (Kufeldt & Burrows, 1994). The need to translate debate into theoretical understanding in order to design appropriate services and action is urgent.

Methods

The material presented in this chapter is derived from a series of research projects related to children in foster care. It began with a survey of children, their parents, social workers, and foster carers. The purpose was to engage in inductive theory-building based on reported experiences and opinions regarding child welfare services. This was followed by the use of the Family Assessment Measure (FAM) scales (Skinner, 1987) to ascertain children's ratings of their own and their foster families' functioning. The most recent project demonstrated a model for inclusive foster care in two Children's Aid Societies in Ontario (Armstrong, 1994; Kufeldt, 1994).

The survey sampled all children in the care of six Ontario Children's Aid Societies between the ages of 9 and 15 (children with developmental handicaps were excluded, as the instrument for the research was a structured interview). One hundred and twenty-two children were identified for the project, 92 were interviewed. Average time in care for these children was four years. Sixty-seven natural parents, 131 social workers (some children had two workers), and 104 foster parents were interviewed. Within these samples 45 *complete* role sets (the child, the natural parent, the foster parent, and the social worker) were obtained. For much of the data analysis the aggregates of each of these four groups are used but comparisons between role sets are based on the 45 complete sets only.

Forty children in the care of two of the Children's Aid Societies were selected on the basis of availability to complete the FAM scales (the second project). These 40 children provided measures of the functioning of their own family and foster family through the use of the FAM general scale. The Family Assessment Measure is a quantitative measurement of the strengths and weaknesses within a family system. It consists of seven sub-scales measuring task accomplishment, role performance, communication, affective expression, affective involvement, control, and values and norms. These sub-scales may also be combined into an average FAM score for a single measure of family functioning. The FAM includes two other sub-scales, defensiveness and social desirability, used as validity checks. A score of 40 to 59 is considered normal or healthy; a score of 60 or more falls into the problem range. Data were used to examine six hypotheses:

1. Inclusive care enables children to maintain a more positive attitude to their own family, as well as to the foster family.
2. Inclusive care is more likely to be supported by foster parents who exhibit role clarity.
3. Positive management of separation contributes to natural parents' role clarity.
4. When positive management of separation occurs, children and parents will report higher satisfaction rates with respect to child welfare interventions.
5. Experienced social workers and foster parents are more likely to support inclusive care.
6. Experienced social workers and foster parents are more likely to exhibit role clarity.

Inclusive Care

This construct represents the degree to which natural parents are actively involved in different aspects of their children's care while in a foster home. Responses were compared for all members of the role set to determine

- In which activities were parents most involved?
- What were people's belief systems or orientation towards inclusive care?
- Were there different perceptions of what the involvement of the natural parents really was?
- How congruent were the perceptions and orientations of the different groups?

Respondents were asked what they believe should happen in the ideal case (their orientations); this may not necessarily be what actually happened because different members may have differing levels of power to influence what does take place.

Only complete role sets were used for this analysis (a set is comprised of a child with the foster parent, social worker, and natural parent related to that child). Figure 28.1 displays orientations and perceptions of events. Support for inclusive care was much higher than actual practice and there were different levels of parental involvement in children's care. Only 5% of parents were being involved in setting rules for their children but 89% were involved in visiting. Also there is lack of congruence among members of the role set as to the actual extent of the parents involvement in the children's care. The most congruence was between children and foster parents. Other differences of note included:

- 84% of social workers thought that the parents were involved in making the decision about foster care. However, only 59% of the parents thought they had been involved.
- Only 59% of the natural parents thought they were involved in planning visits. Everyone else thought they were involved to a much greater extent.
- The natural parents thought they participated more in activities such as shopping for clothes, taking the child to the doctor, or going to parent-teacher interviews than did the foster parents. The natural parents thought

Figure 28.1: Parental Involvement in Children's Care Orientation of Members of the Role Set and Perception of Events (45 Role Sets)

	Orientation				Perception of Events			
	CH	NP	FP	SW	CH	NP	FP	SW
Decision to place in FH	I	I	I	I	I	I	I	I
Planning Visits	I	I	I	I	I	M	I	I
Overnight visits	I	I	I	I	M	M	M	M
Decision re return home	I	I	I	I	M	M	M	M
Involved in major probs.	M	I	I	I	E	M	E	E
Choosing foster home	M	I	M	I	E	E	E	E
Change of placement	M	I	M	I	E	E	E	E
Parent-teacher meetings	M	M	M	I	E	E	E	E
Visits to doctor	E	M	E	M	E	E	E	E
Shopping for clothes	E	M	E	M	E	M	E	E
Involved in minor probs.	E	M	E	E	E	E	E	E
FP visits NP home	E	M	E	E	E	E	E	E
Setting rules	E	E	E	M	E	E	E	E

I = Inclusion where two-thirds or more are in favour, or report occurrence
M =Mixed, between one and two-thirds are in favour or report occurrence
E=Exclusion where less than one third are in favour, or report occurrence

they were involved in resolving both minor and major problems of their children more than anyone else thought that they were.

The actual involvement of the natural parents fell short of what members of the role set believed should happen. This indicates general support for increasing the amount of parental involvement in every aspect of care. There were areas of care that members of the role set believed were more important for parental involvement than others. The majority of all respondents believed that the natural parents should be involved in:

- Deciding About Foster Care Placement
- Planning Visits
- Child Visiting Overnight
- Planning Child's Return Home
- Resolving Child's Serious Problems
- Choosing a Foster Home
- Deciding to Change Foster Home

Respondents also reported a high level of occurrence of natural parent visiting, phone calls, and discussing the child with the foster parents. Less than half of the respondents felt that it was important for natural parents to be involved in:

- Attending parent-teacher Interviews
- Taking child to doctor
- Shopping for child's clothes
- Resolving child's minor problems
- Having foster parent visit in natural parents' home
- Setting rules for child

A few discrepancies in the beliefs of the various members of the role set are worthy of mention. While three-quarters of the natural parents and social workers felt that the natural parents should be involved in choosing the foster home, only 36% of the foster parents believed that this was important. Social workers were more likely than any other member of the role set to think that natural parents should be involved in aspects of care such as clothes shopping, taking the child to the doctor, attending parent-teacher interviews, and setting rules. More natural parents thought they should be involved in the child's minor problems and foster parent visits to their home than any other members of the role set. Social workers and natural parents were more in favour of parental involvement in resolving child's serious problems and changing the foster home than were the foster parents. Fewer children believed that it was important for them to visit their parents overnight than did their parents, the foster parents, or the social workers who were all almost unanimously in favour of overnight visits.

The 10 activities that were believed to be the most important with regard to the natural parents' involvement in the child's care (i.e. the first ten of the thirteen activities listed in Figure 28.1) were used to operationalize the construct inclusive care. The more of these in which the natural parent is involved, the more inclusive is the care. Five activities or less were considered low inclusive care and six activities or more counted as high inclusive care.

Management of Separation

Seven variables addressed the matter of how the child's separation from the natural parents was managed:

- Did parents accompany the child to the Foster Home? (positive)
- Did the parents explain the need for separation to the child? (positive)
- Were parents advised not to visit at first? (negative)
- Did the child know when the parents would be seen again? (positive)
- Were definite visiting arrangements set out? (positive)
- Did the child bring favourite belongings to the foster home? (positive)
- Did the child bring family pictures? (positive)

In the ideal scenario, the parents would accompany the child to the foster home and explain the need for separation. The child would bring both family pictures and favourite belongings. Parents would not be advised against visiting; in fact, definite visiting arrangements would be set out and the child would know when the parents would be seen again. The child's separation was managed positively if all of these conditions were met. A count was made to determine how many of these separation management steps were taken for each child. Scores could range from a low of 0, where none of these steps was

Figure 28.2: Level of Inclusive Care and FAM Ratings

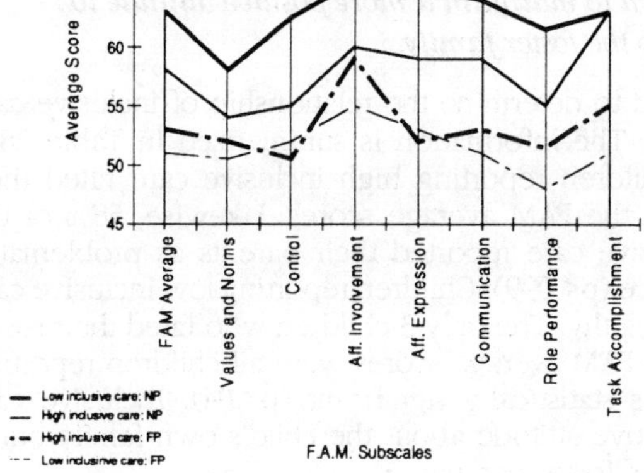

Reproduced from Kufeldt (1993)

taken, to a high of 7 indicating that all positive steps were taken to manage the separation experience.

The majority of both children and natural parents did not have a well managed separation experience. Only a few of the possible steps that could help ease the separation were actually taken. Of the 92 children, only 27% recalled good separation management (a score of four or more) and 30% of natural parents reported good separation management. Only 15 children and 5 parents reported that their parents actually accompanied children to the foster home. The foster parents and the social workers were asked how they thought the separation process should be managed (as opposed to what actually happened); 65% of the foster parents and 96% of the social workers were in favour of taking 4 or more positive steps to manage the separation. This is very different from what actually happened to children in practice.

Role Clarity

Role clarity was measured by four different variables:

- Who is a foster parent most like?
- What should a child call foster parents?
- How important is it for foster parents and natural parents to get to know each other?
- Who should matter most to the child in care?

A foster mother, for instance, who was clear about her role would not think that she was like the child's natural parents and would not think that she should be called "mom." She would see her role as more like that of a child care worker. She would believe that the natural parents should matter most to the child while in care. And she would believe that it was important for her to get to know the natural parents. The role clarity variables were also grouped in a composite variable using a simple count procedure. Those with 3 or 4 correct responses were considered to be clear about their foster parent role. Those with less than three were considered to be unclear about their foster parent role.

Results

Inclusive care enables children to maintain a more positive attitude to their own family, as well as to the foster family.

A crosstabulation was used to determine the relationship of inclusive care to the children's FAM scores. The information is summarized in Table 28.2. Sixty-three percent of the children reporting high inclusive care rated their parents as healthy, based on the FAM average scores. Likewise, 58% of the children reporting low inclusive care reported their parents as problematic. This was a significant difference (p<.099). Children reporting low inclusive care rated their foster parents as healthy. The only 3 children who rated their foster parents as problematic in the FAM average scores were all children reporting high inclusive care. This was statistically significant (p<.04). Inclusive care seems to be related to a positive attitude about the child's own family but is associated with lower rating of foster parents.

Inclusive care is more likely to be supported by Foster parents who exhibit role clarity.

Crosstabulations of the role clarity and inclusive care composite variables showed a definite trend, although not statistically significant. Foster parents who are unclear about their role have not participated in many inclusive care activities. In contrast, foster parents who are clear about their role are more likely to be in the high inclusive care category (p<.18). Each role clarity variable was examined in relation to inclusive care. Beliefs about ""Who a foster parent is most like," and "The importance of foster parent and natural parent getting to know each other" were both related to inclusive care. Sixty-seven percent of foster parents who thought that they were most like the child's own parents also reported a low incidence of inclusive care activities. However, 53% of those who thought that they were more like a friend or social worker reported a high level of inclusive care activities. This variation was statistically significant (p<.03). Seventy percent of foster parents who thought that it was not important for them to get to know the natural parents were in the low inclusive care category; 53% of foster parents who believed in this activity reported high inclusive care (p<.02). There was no relationship between "What a child should call the foster parents" and inclusive care. There was a slight inverse relationship between "Who should matter most to the child in care?" and inclusive care; 61% of the foster parents who thought that the natural parent or a sibling should matter most (the correct response!) were in the low inclusive care category (p<.20). In summary there is limited evidence to support the proposition that foster parents with role clarity are more likely to have been involved in inclusive care. Only two of the four variables that represent role clarity ("Who is a foster parent most like?" and "How important is it for foster parent and natural parent to get to know each other?") were found to have a statistically significant relationship with inclusive care.

Inclusive care was defined as the foster parents' perceptions of the actual involvement of the natural parents in the child's care. However, many factors might influence the amount of involvement apart from the inclinations of the foster parents; a foster parent might believe in many aspects of inclusive care but not be in a position to promote such activities. Thus foster parents' beliefs about inclusive care might be a better construct for use in examining the relationship between role clarity of foster parents and inclusive care.

Table 28.1 shows that more foster parents supported inclusive care activities in principle than had actually reported their occurrence. Using foster parents' beliefs, rather than experiences, produces a significant relationship between role clarity and inclusive care. Sixty-six percent of foster parents who were unclear about their role did not support inclusive care; 73% of foster parents who were clear about their role also supported a high level of inclusive care (p=.00). Relationships between the individual role clarity variables and foster parents beliefs about inclusive care were also examined. Three variables, "Who is a foster parent most like?," "How important is it for foster parent and natural parent to get to know each other?", and "Who should matter most to the child" were all significantly related to inclusive care beliefs. Seventy-three percent of foster parents who thought they were most like a friend or a child care worker believed that there should be a high level of inclusive care (p<.02). Seventy-one percent of foster parents who thought that it was important for them to get to know the natural parent believed in a high level of inclusive care (p<.04); 71% of foster parents who thought that the natural parent or a sibling should matter most to the child while in care believed in a high level of inclusive care (p<.07). There was still no relationship between "What should a child call the foster parents" and inclusive care. In summary there is a relationship between role clarity and inclusive care beliefs. Foster parents who are clear about their role as a foster parent are more likely to support the concept of inclusive care.

Positive management of separation contributes to natural parents' role clarity.

The way in which the separation experience was managed showed no relationship to the natural parents' beliefs regarding the importance of contact between them and the foster parents. Further, the way in which the separation experience was managed had the opposite effect to what was expected regarding the natural parents' understanding of the respective roles. Natural parents who experience positive separation management were more likely to believe that the foster parents were like themselves, were more likely to think that the foster parent should be called "Mom" and "Dad," and were less likely to believe that they mattered most to their child. In conclusion, positive management of separation does not appear to be related to role clarity of natural parents.

When positive management of separation occurs, children and parents will report higher satisfaction rates with respect to child welfare interventions.

Two variables measured satisfaction with respect to child welfare interventions. These were "Effect of care on child" and "Effect of care on family." The same questionnaire was used for each member of the role set to determine the different perceptions of the children, the natural parents, the foster parents, and the social workers. Eighty-eight percent of the children reported that foster care had been positive for them. The way in which the separation had been managed did not affect this rating. Overall, 57% of the children thought that their time in care had been positive for their families. However, when the separation was managed positively, 74 percent thought that their time in care was positive for their families ($p<.05$). The natural parents were slightly less enthusiastic about the effect of foster care. Overall, 51% felt that foster care had a positive effect on their child. When the separation had been managed positively, this increased to 60% although this was not statistically significant. Similarly, 49% felt that the time in care had been positive for the families. When there was good separation management, 65% felt that the time in care was helpful. This was a significant increase ($p<.09$). Ninety percent of foster parents thought that foster care was helpful to the child. Overall, 55% of the foster parents thought that foster care was helpful to the families. Their orientation to management of the separation experience did not have any effect on either outcome. Ninety-four percent of social workers believed that foster care was helpful to the children and 64% believed that the time in care was helpful to the families of the children. Neither result bore any relationship to their beliefs about the separation experience. In summary, the management of the separation experience does have some bearing on children's and parents' satisfaction rates regarding child welfare interventions. With positive separation experience both children and natural parents are more likely to think that the time in care was helpful to the families. Separation management does not appear to have any relationship to what they think about the effect of care on the child. For foster parents and social workers, there was no relationship between their beliefs about managing the separation experience and their thoughts on the effects of foster care.

Experienced social workers and foster parents are more likely to support inclusive care.

Experience as a social worker can be measured by the attainment of professional degrees or by the amount of work experience. Both of these variables were examined. A major drawback in this analysis was the lack of response by the social workers to the set of questions concerning the ten inclusive care variables. Eighty-four of the total group of 131 social workers failed to answer questions concerning their beliefs. The vast majority of the remaining 47 social workers believed in a high level of inclusive care; thus there was little variation on this variable. However, the social workers were divided into those with moderate beliefs (6–8 activities) and those with strong beliefs (9–10); 64% were strongly supportive of inclusive care and 35% moderately supportive. The trend was that professional education was related to stronger beliefs in inclusive care. Social workers with M.S.W. degrees supported more of the inclusive care concepts than those with B.S.W. degrees and the least supportive were those with other educational backgrounds. The differences, however, were not statistically significant ($p<.28$). There was no relationship between years of experience and beliefs in inclusive care. Social workers who had the child on their caseload for more than 18 months were less likely to support the concept of inclusive care. Workers' opinions may be influenced by the fact that children who are on caseloads for long periods of time are more likely to be from homes where inclusive care practices may not be practical or safe.

Experience as a foster parent could be a function of the foster parents' age, education, years of fostering, or experience with their own or other foster children. All of these variables were examined. Twenty foster parents did not answer the inclusive care questions and were excluded from the analysis. Forty-four percent of the remaining 84 foster parents showed high support for inclusive care (score of 8–10), and 55% had a low score (seven or less). There was a non-significant trend that younger foster parents (under the age of 40) were more likely to support inclusive care ($p<.36$). There was no relationship between education and inclusive care beliefs. The number of years fostering showed a curvilinear relationship with inclusive care beliefs. Those with less than 1 year of fostering and those with over 8 years experience were least likely to support inclusive care. Experience with other children does seem to have a bearing on inclusive care beliefs. Foster parents who did not have any children of their own were less likely to believe in inclusive care ($p<.16$). Similarly, foster parents who did not have any other foster children were less likely to believe in inclusive care (p.03). Foster parents who had other foster children or who had children of their own were more receptive to inclusive care beliefs.

Experienced social workers and foster parents are more likely to exhibit role clarity.

Data on all variables was available for only 47 social workers; 36% had all four role clarity responses correct. All M.S.W.s, 83% of B.S.W.s and 78% of those with other qualifications were clear about the foster parent role. However this difference was not significant. There was no relationship between years of experience as a social worker and role clarity. Foster parents with either 3 or 4 correct responses were considered to be clear about their foster parent role. There were 20 missing cases for a total of 64 valid cases. The age, educational background, number of years fostering and whether or not they had children of their own has no relationship to foster parents' role clarity. However, having other foster children is significantly related to role clarity in a foster parent. Those who have other foster children are more likely to be clear about their role than those who just have one foster child ($p<.03$). Foster parents who are experienced in dealing with many foster children are the most likely to exhibit role clarity.

Summary and Discussion

Inclusive care, separation management, and role clarity appear to be useful theoretical constructs in the task of conceptual analysis and theory building in child welfare. There is a relationship between inclusive care and children's ratings of their own and their foster families. However the relationship is complex. Palmer (1971, 1990) has been reiterating that management of separation for children coming into care is crucial; the findings in this study provide confirmation of this view. Separation from parents can have very traumatic short term effects. These findings suggest that how separation is managed may affect children and their families over the long term. The findings also suggest a relationship between inclusive care and role clarity on the part of foster parents. No relationship was found between the management of separation and natural parents' role clarity; rather, the findings suggested that when separation is managed well, natural parents may be more accepting of their children relating in positive ways to their foster parents.

The series of research projects of which this report is just one part confirmed that child welfare intervention is necessary, that inclusive care offers the most promising approach when substitute care is required, but, as Gambrill and Stein (1994) have demonstrated, a complex system is created.

The search for theoretical understanding must continue, and continue to include the voices of children, if the complexity of the undertaking is to become understandable, role ambiguities and uncertainties reduced and the interests of children and families well served.

The survey reported in this paper was funded by the Social Sciences and Humanities Research Council of Canada. The study using FAM was funded by the Laidlaw Foundation and by the Toronto Sick Children's Hospital Foundation. National Welfare Grants funded research with Runaway and Homeless Youth. The investigators acknowledge this support with gratitude. The author would also like to thank the Children's Aid Societies and respondents who participated, co-investigators Dr. J. Armstrong and Dr. M. Dorosh, as well as Carolyn Hursh who did much of the data analysis.

References

Aldridge, M. J., & Cautley, P. W. (1975). The importance of worker availability in the functioning of new foster homes. *Child Welfare, 54*(6): 448–453.

Allison, J., & Johnson, J. (1981). *Say Hi to Julie.* Calgary: Who Cares Society.

Armitage, A. (1993). Family and child welfare in First Nation communities. In B. Wharf (Ed.), *Rethinking Child Welfare in Canada* (pp. 131–171). Toronto: McClelland & Stewart.

Armstrong, J. (1994). Policy implementation and the quality of foster care. In B. McKenzie (Ed.), *Current perspectives on foster family care for children and youth* (pp. 48–58). Toronto: Wall & Emerson, Inc.

Berridge D., & Cleaver, H. (1987). *Foster home breakdown.* Oxford: Basil Blackwell.

Blumenthal, K., & Weinberg, A. (1984). *Establishing parent involvement in foster care agencies.* New York: Child Welfare League of America.

Bowlby, J. (1979). *The making and breaking of affectional bonds.* London: Tavistock Publications.

Bullock, R., Little, M. & Millham, S. (1993). *Going home: the return of children separated from their families.* Aldershot, Hants.: Dartmouth Publishing Company Limited.

Cleaver, H. (1994). An evaluation of the frequency and effects of foster home breakdown. In Brad McKenzie (Ed.), *Current perspectives on foster family care for children and youth* (pp. 132–144). Toronto: Wall & Emerson, Inc.

Conte, R. P. (1994). Homeless teenagers formerly in foster care: their stories. In B. McKenzie (Ed.), *Current perspectives on foster family care for children and youth* (pp. 145–161). Toronto: Wall & Emerson, Inc.

Department of Health (1988). *Report of the Inquiry into Child Abuse in Cleveland 1987.* London: Her Majesty's Stationery Office.

Emlen, A., Lahti, J., Downs, G., McKay, A., & Downs, S. (1976). *Barriers to planning for children in foster care.* Portland, Oregon: Portland State University.

Emlen, A., Casciato, J., Clarkson, D., Downs, S., Lahti, J., Liedtke, K., & Zadny, J. (1978). *Outcomes of permanency planning for children in foster care.* Portland, Oregon: Portland State University.

Family Rights Group (1986). *Promoting links: keeping children and families in touch.* London: Family Rights Group.

Fanshel, D. & Shinn, E. (1978). *Children in foster care.* New York: Columbia University Press.

Fanshel, D., Finch, S. J., & Grundy, J. F. (1990). *Foster children in a life course perspective.* New York: Columbia University Press.

Galaway, B., Nutter R., & Hudson, J. (1994). Birth parent participation in treatment foster family care. In Brad McKenzie (Ed.), *Current perspectives on foster family care for children and youth* (pp. 74–82). Toronto: Wall & Emerson, Inc.

Galaway, B., & Hudson, J. (1989). *Specialist foster family care: a normalizing experience.* New York: Haworth.

Galaway B., Maglajlic, D., Hudson, J., Harmon, P. , & McLagan, J. (Eds.). (1990). International perspectives on specialist foster family. St. Paul: Human Service Associates.

Gambrill, E., & Stein, T. J. (1994). *Controversial issues in child welfare*. Boston: Allyn and Bacon.

Hazel, N. (1990). The development of specialist foster care for adolescents: policy and practice. In B. Galaway, D. Maglajlic, J. Hudson, P. Harmon & J. McLagan (Eds.), *International perspectives on specialist foster family care* (pp. 43–62). St. Paul: Human Service Associates.

Hess, P. M., & Proch, K. O. (1988). *Family visiting in out-of-home care*. Washington, DC: Child Welfare League of America.

Howells, J. G. (1974). *Remember Maria*. London: Butterworths.

Hughes, S. H. S. (1991). *The Royal Commission of inquiry into the response of the Newfoundland Criminal Justice System to complaints* (Vols. 1 & 2). St. John's, Newfoundland: Queen's Printer.

Kufeldt, K. (1984). Listening to children—who cares? *British Journal of Social Work, 14*, 257–264.

Kufeldt, K. (1991). Foster care: a reconceptualization, *Community Alternatives: International Journal of Family Care, 3*(1), 9–17.

Kufeldt, K. (1993). Listening to children: an essential for justice. *The International Journal of Children's Rights*, 1, 155–164.

Kufeldt, K. (1994). Inclusive foster care: implementation of the model. In B. McKenzie (Ed.), *Current Perspectives on Foster Family Care for Children and Youth* (pp. 84–100). Toronto: Wall & Emerson, Inc.

Kufeldt, K., & Allison, J. (1990). Fostering children—fostering families. *Community Alternatives: International Journal of Family Care, 2*(1), 1–17.

Kufeldt, K., Armstrong, J., & Dorosh, M. (1989). In care, in contact? In J. Hudson & B. Galaway (Eds.), *The State as Parent*. pp. 355-368. Dordrecht: Kluwer Academic Publishers.

Kufeldt, K., & Burrows, B. (1994). *Issues affecting public policies and services for homeless youth*. Calgary: University of Calgary.

Kufeldt, K., & Nimmo, M. (1987). Youth on the street: Abuse and neglect in the Eighties, *Child Abuse and Neglect*, 11, 531–543.

Laird, J., & Hartman. A., (1985). *A Handbook of Child Welfare*. New York: Free Press.

Maas, H. S., & Engler, R. (1959). *Children in need of parents*. New York: Columbia University Press.

Maluccio, A., Fein, E., & Olmstead, K. (1986). *Permanency planning for children: Concepts and methods*. New York: Tavistock Press.

Millham S., Bullock R., Hosie, K., & Haak, M. (1986). *Lost in care*. Aldershot: Gower.

Palmer, S. E. (1971). The decision to separate children from their natural parents. *The Social Worker, 39*(2), 82–87.

Palmer, S. E. (1990). Group treatment of foster children to reduce separation conflicts associated with placement breakdown. *Child Welfare, 69*(3), 227–238.

Parker, R. (1980). *Caring for separated children*. London: National Children's Bureau.

Parker, S. (1989). *From foster care to independent living*. Unpublished MSW Thesis. Calgary: University of Calgary.

Pine, B. A., Warsh, R., & Maluccio, A. (1993). *Together again: Family reunification in foster care*. New York: Child Welfare League of America.

Proch, K., & Hess, P. (1987). Parent-child visiting policies of voluntary agencies. *Children and Youth Services Review, 9*(1), 17–18.

Proch, K., & Howard, J. (1984). Parental visiting in foster care: law and practice, *Child Welfare, 63*(2), 139–147.

Raychaba, B. (1993). *Pain ... lots of pain*. Ottawa: National Youth in Care Network.

Sachdev, P. (1984). *Adoption: current issues and trends*. Toronto: Butterworths.

Shane, P. G. (1991). A sample of homeless and runaway youth in New Jersey and their health status. *Journal of Health and Social Policy, 2*(4), 73–82.

Skinner, H. (1987). Self-report instruments for family assessment. In T. Jacob (ed.), *Family Interaction and Psychopathology*. New York: Plenum Publishing Corporation.

Steinhauer, P. D. (1983). Issues of attachment and separation: Foster care and adoption. In P. Steinhauer & Q. Rae-Grant (eds.), *Psychological problems of the child in the family* (69–101). New York: Basic Books.

Steinhauer, P. D. (1993). *The least detrimental alternative*. Toronto: University of Toronto Press.

Thomlison, B. (1990). Continuity of care: Family, developmental and attachment needs of children in long-term foster care. In B. Galaway, D. Maglajlic, J. Hudson, P. Harmon & J. McLagan (Eds.), *International Perspectives on Specialist Foster Family* (131–160). St. Paul: Human Service Associates.

Thorpe, R. (1980). The experience of children and adults living apart: Implications and guidelines for practice. In J. Triseliotis (Ed.), *New Developments in Foster Care and Adoption* (85–100). London: Routledge & Kegan Paul.

Timberlake, E., & Hamlin, E. (1982), The sibling group: A neglected dimension of placement. *Child Welfare, 61*(8), 536–544.

Wharf, B. (Ed.). (1993). *Rethinking Child Welfare in Canada.* Toronto: McClelland and Stewart.

29

Care Experiences and Outcomes of Child Welfare Services in a Scandinavian Context

Elisabeth Backe-Hansen

Scandinavia is a term commonly used to denote Norway, Sweden, and Denmark. Norway has about 4.5 million inhabitants, Denmark about 5.4 million, and Sweden about 8 million. Denmark is small and densely populated, whereas both Sweden and Norway are much larger, with many small and sparsely populated areas combined with some urban areas. Oslo, Norway's largest city and capital, has only 450,000 inhabitants. The Swedish and Danish capitals, Stockholm and Copenhagen respectively, have about one million inhabitants each.

The Scandinavian countries have lately experienced economic recession, increasing unemployment, and consequences of the changing demands on the labour force. But they are still fairly homogeneous societies with a generally high standard of living as well as fewer differences between various segments of the population than in Great Britain or the United States. This is partly due to the Scandinavian tradition of public responsibility for areas like schooling, medical care, old-age pensions, social security, and child welfare, as well as the construction of welfare states after the Second World War. The question of whether the Scandinavian economy can afford to keep the welfare state at its present level is being discussed, but most people have confidence in the state's continuing responsibility for citizens in several essential life areas. This is important when Scandinavian child welfare is compared to that of other countries. The threshold for intervention may actually be lower since the differences within Scandinavian societies are smaller, and the general standard of living higher. Poverty and marginalization do exist in Scandinavia, however, and child welfare services mostly deal with children coming from marginalized families with problems in many major life areas.

Child welfare services are predominantly a public responsibility. Each country has a Law of Child Welfare, which differs slightly from country to country, but the laws have been influenced by each other and have many common goals (Grinde, 1989, 1993). These laws specify under what conditions forcible intervention is sanctioned as well as how child welfare decisions are to be made. Each country has fairly elaborate rules for such decision-making, focussed on ensuring the legal rights of parents and children through the way cases are monitored, and through several routes of appeal. The private child welfare work (mostly in the non-profit sense) occurs when children and adolescents are placed outside their homes in foster care or residential care. These services are, however, subject to public sanctioning and control. The counties and municipalities pay most or all of the costs, thus imposing even more control. Preventive services while children continue to live in their families of origin is the primary goal of the child welfare services in all the Scandinavian countries, and such services serve the greatest volume of cases. In 1991, for instance, five Norwegian children were offered preventive services for each new child committed or admitted to care. Most child welfare services, whether preventive services or out-of-home placements, are received with parental consent.

Still, the system combines help and control in that parents may be forced to accept preventive services they do not want, or to have their child placed outside the home in spite of their protests. Adolescents may be forcibly removed from their homes and placed in institutions where their freedom is severely curtailed. Scandinavian child welfare workers and decision-makers face the dilemmas arising when the rights of parents to raise their children without state intervention seem to be in conflict with the rights of children to be protected when their care situation is below a minimum.

Five Selected Studies

It has been difficult to select the studies to be included in this chapter. The primary aim has been to include studies from all the Scandinavian countries, covering child welfare services from different points of view, but highlighting some important topics in the ongoing professional debate in Scandinavia.

Social Work With Small Children (Andersson, 1990)

This study was done in 1988, and concerns social work with 189 children between 0 and 3 years of age. The children lived in 10 different municipalities in Southern Sweden; the sample consisted of all children in the relevant age group whose families had been in contact with the social services (including the child welfare services) during one year. Data was collected through interviews with social workers. The processes were understood within a psycho-dynamic case-work tradition combined with the principle of family treatment. The study focussed on small children because these cases are thought to be the most difficult and emotionally taxing and because very young children often become invisible in this field.

The results point to the difficulties inherent in assessing children as young as this. The criteria for normality and deviance may be more fluid, and the workers may be more vulnerable for identification with their own parenting styles. There is no common standard in Swedish society for establishing without doubt which care situations are below minimum. Different professionals disagree among themselves, and the use of discretion is necessary because the law is not exact. The climate that is established between the social worker and parents is crucial. Services that are helpful to the children can be implemented if parents and social workers cooperate. If not, the outcome may be compulsory out-of-home placement. The development of this relationship interacts with the types of services that are offered and implemented.

Placing children and young people outside their homes. What can be learned from the families themselves? (Zobbe, 1993)

This was a pilot study to illuminate child welfare intervention by detailing the experiences of six children and parents. Data came from 30 interviews with children and parents. The six children came from one Danish county, were between 9 and 18 years of age, had a disturbed family background, and had different care experiences and outcomes. Data were collected in 1991. The interviews covered the period from when a problem was identified and the child welfare services were involved, through the actual out-of-home placement, to the children's situation at the time of the interviews. Results from the pilot study mirror central findings from larger Scandinavian studies concerning the situation in the families of origin, and the children's role as parents for their own parents. Also, the study points to problems in child care work concerning staff turn-over, undeveloped methodology, problems concerning interagency and interprofessional cooperation, and insufficient resources to follow up the children and their families after placement. The value of this pilot study lies in the way the parents' view of the processes was highlighted. The children were more difficult to interview.

Placing children outside their homes without parental consent (Ertmann, 1994)

The study included all compulsory placements outside the home in Copenhagen, Denmark in 1990, totalling 170 children between 0 and 18 years of age. Sixty-one were placed for the first time, the remaining 109 had experienced one or more former placements. Case material from all the cases was analyzed, and 12 families were selected for intensive study; both families and professionals were interviewed. The study had three aims—to describe the families and children experiencing compulsory placement, the kinds of services given to the families both before and after placement and formulating alternative social strategies for these families where the elements of positive development and continuity for children and parents were central. The study identifies a contradiction between a focus on continuity in relationships and a focus on meeting children's needs. The clinical documentation in the cases rested largely on child psychiatric and psychological assessments. In practice, professional discretion is used within a frame mainly influenced by social work practice and tradition. The legal element must be included following the rules pertaining to child care intervention against the will of the parents. Problems can be pinpointed in the way these cases are monitored. The reciprocal relationship between psychologists and social workers needs to be differentiated and elaborated as long as psychological assessments continue to be important in the decision-making processes. The casework shows weaknesses concerning methods and relationship with the parents. Access was severely curtailed and not part of an ongoing process in many cases.

The users' perspective (Christiansen & Brostrøm, 1994)

Interest has developed in using groups as primary preventive services for mothers and small children (Sandbæk, 1992). These groups are typically organized at a municipal level. This research is an evaluation of 24 groups in 16 different municipalities, situated in four different counties. One hundred and eleven mothers completed questionnaires concerning themselves and the group. In addition, twenty mothers were interviewed. The group work is based on social learning theory. The group leaders are non-professional women, who are supervised by a social worker. The groups have been meeting 1–2 times a week during day-time, with activities centring around social interaction, some activities, and some trips together with the children. Making of meals and eating has been central. Preliminary results of the evaluation point to the importance of the group leaders in the mothers' social network. Also, the mothers report that membership in the groups have extended their social networks to the other group members, as well as helping them to talk about problems and help each other.

Project Growing-up Networks (Ogden, 1994; Kristofersen, 1994, Sandbæk, 1994; & Backe-Hansen, 1994)

This is a prospective, developmental study including all children in the fourth and seventh grades (10 and 13 years of age) in one large, Norwegian municipality in the school year of 1992–93. The youngest cohort consisted of slightly less than 500 children, the oldest of about 550. A total of 912 children participated in the study, which will be replicated in 1994–95. The main focus of the study is children's social competence in context (Kristofersen, 1994; Ogden, 1994). Data was collected through the use of questionnaires completed by the children, their parents, and teachers. The study is based on an inductive model combining several theoretical approaches including the risk-protective factors paradigm and ecological theory. The part of the study concerning 10-year olds is being replicated in all the Nordic countries (Scandinavia, Finland, and Iceland).

Two in-depth studies are part of this project. In one, 140 children, at the same ages as the cohort children but who had been in contact with three central helping services for children and adolescents during 1992 were assessed by their workers/therapists. The workers completed a structured questionnaire for each child. The services participating were the school counselling services, the child psychiatric unit, and the child welfare services. The study aimed to analyze similarities and differences between the children who become clients in these services and the cohort children. One underlying question is whether the present organization of helping services for children is functional for the clients. The study aims to understand children's development of problems within the risk-protective factors paradigm. This understanding is contrasted with the development and dynamics of a sectorized system of helping services. The referral process provides a meeting-place between two different ways of looking at life. The results highlight the need to see each helping service as part of a larger context, as many of the clients move among the various services. Second, services for children need to be seen in a life-course perspective on the part of the services as well as from the children's viewpoint. Third, gender is important. Seven out of 10 clients are boys, yet there is little thought regarding what are suitable services for boys as well as girls. There may be a contradiction between menu-based services, where clients are offered what the services have because these are the only options, and a focussed approach where services are tailored to the clients' needs (Backe-Hansen, 1994).

The second in-depth study is a client study. Parents of children, and in some cases children, from the same client population were interviewed to elicit their experiences with the helping services (Sandbæk, 1994). A structured interview guide was used, with room for personal comments from the parents. This study focusses on the effect of social support on the families' situation over time. The effect of the contact with the helping services on the parents' feeling of autonomy is of particular interest. The families experienced themselves as in need of help, and the majority would have preferred more help than they received. Many families and children will need long-term help. The majority of the parents thought their and their children's situation had become better over time, although they did not expect the problems to disappear. They had clear opinions of the services they received. More knowledge about the problem on the part of the helping services, more concrete services, taking parents more into account, and offering services at an earlier stage were identified by parents as things that could have been done differently. Those in contact with child welfare became more positive than this service had thought. This might reflect a greater skepticism on the part of the parents at the outset. For the other two helping services, the change in opinion went the opposite way; more parents became more negative over time (Sandbæk, 1994).

Summary Across The Studies

The five studies addressed questions of how child welfare services are implemented, and how the clients themselves experience these services. The two Danish studies (Zobbe, 1993; Ertmann, 1994) focus on processes and outcomes when children are placed outside their homes; the Swedish study (Anderssen, 1990) focusses on how social workers approach all types of child welfare cases concerning small children. Both the Norwegian studies (Christiansen & Brostrom, 1994; Ogden, 1994; Sandbæk, 1994; Backe-Hansen, 1994) are concerned with child welfare services as part of a more comprehensive system of helping services.

The consumer perspective is present, to a greater or lesser degree, in four of the studies. In this context, consumer came to mean parents. The two studies aiming to include children in a systematic manner met with similar problems concerning the children's availability for interviewing (Sandbæk, 1994; Zobbe, 1993). Except for Zobbe's study (1993), the studies included are fairly large-scale for Scandinavian standards. Child welfare does not reach many Scandinavian children each year. Thus, studies of particular age-groups or samples with specific characteristics tend to be limited in size. The Norwegian project (Ogden, 1994; Sandbæk, 1994; Backe-Hansen, 1994), that included two full cohorts of about 500 children each in a large Norwegian municipality, had only 28 children receiving all types of child welfare services. Qualitative and quantitative methods were combined. Scandinavian child welfare research has a strong qualitative tradition. With some notable exceptions (Jonsson & Kälvesten, 1964), the child welfare research tradition is still young in Scandinavia and thus, the lack of knowledge has made more qualitatively studies necessary.

These five studies have highlighted deficiencies in the child welfare system concerning methods, monitoring, and the way clients are met. Parents voice frustration and feelings of not being heard or taken into account. On the other hand, both Christiansen and Brostrom (1994) and Sandbæk (1994) point to positive aspects of the intervention; when this is done within a context of preventive work, the interventions are perceived as helpful, and the parents' feelings of worth and autonomy are respected. Andersson (1990) points to similar phenomena when social work is seen through the eyes of the workers. Cases where out-of-home placement is a real alternative, whether the parents want it or not, constitute particular methodological challenges; an approach based on cooperation about change may not be sufficient.

Implications for Future Research

Far too little is known about preventive services and how they work, although by far the most child welfare money is spent on these services. In Scandinavia, much criticism has been raised about the way child care cases are monitored, particularly when they enter the legal system. More systematic knowledge is needed about approaches that are good both professionally as well as from a monitoring perspective. Consumers' views have been introduced in evaluative research during recent years, but knowledge of consumer views is sketchy. Finally, recent years have seen a plethora of development and trial projects, often initiated by State Ministries. These need systematic evaluation if they are to become more than short-lived experiments.

Research focussed on identified risk groups or problem groups introduce particular methodological demands because the numbers are low and sampling becomes difficult if the aim is to do more than describe the field qualitatively. Qualitative analyses become less significant as the general level of knowledge increases. One solution to this problem is to choose less rigorous sampling criteria, and allow for more variation in the samples to increase their number. On the other hand, this approach places demands on the analytic tools used. A fruitful alternative may to see child welfare services as part of more comprehensive services for children, young people, and their families. This makes it possible to study client groups as a whole, and see child welfare clients in this larger context. Epidemiological research suggests that 10–12% of the child population will have problems qualifying for some kind of professional help while they grow up. This makes sampling more manageable. Different client groups can be compared, and child welfare clients may be seen as part of a larger picture.

Children at risk may be contrasted with groups of children in general, thus investigating normal variance as well as more risk-specific situations. This requires prospective and longitudinal studies that are expensive and may drain money from research budgets that are already limited. In the Scandinavian context, with a strong investment in child care on the part of the state, one approach is to create separate programs for child welfare research. This has been done in Norway, in the shape of a program lasting from 1992–1996. More comprehensive child welfare research requires research programs that are more than responses to market mechanisms or personal motivation.

This issue becomes particularly important if services are mainly program-based, and funding depends on objectives that are liable to change with political priorities. When family preservation is the main goal, as it is in Norway, important objectives may be to reduce the number of out-of-home placements and the duration of such placements should they occur. But are such objectives necessarily the only valid ones, and do they imply that no child is better off growing up outside his or her family of origin? Seen in a wider perspective, family preservation is insufficient if it does not take into account the cases where such preservation is impossible for various reasons. Not placing children may be more detrimental to some children's development than placing them, and short spells in care may be more detrimental because they are too short for problem resolution. Thus, research on child welfare experiences and outcomes needs to have a lifecourse perspective, and outcomes need to be measured long-term as well as short-term.

References

Andersson, G. (1990). *Socialt arbete med små barn.* [Social work with small children]. Lund: Studentlitteratur.

Backe-Hansen, E. (1994). Hjelpeatjenestene og barna. [The helping services and the children]. *Report,* Oslo: The Norwegian Institute of Child Welfare Research.

Christiansen, K. U., & Brostrom, B. (1994). A groupwork approach to mothers of children assumed to be at risk: A preventive intervention. Oslo: Norwegian Institute of Child Welfare Research.

Ertmann, Bo. (1994). Tvangsfjernelser. [Compulsory out-of-home placements]. *Report,* Copenhagen: Kroghs forlag A/S.

Grinde, T. V. (1989). *Barn og barnevern i Norden.* [Children and child welfare in the Nordic countries]. Oslo: TANO.

Grinde, T. V. (1993). Child care perspectives—English and Norwegian views. *Report no. 2,* Oslo: The Norwegian Institute of Child Welfare Research.

Jonsson, G., & Kälvesten, A. L. (1964). *222 Stockholmspojkar. En socialpsykiatrisk undersökning av pojker i skolåldern.* [222 boys from Stockholm. A social-psychiatric study of school-aged boys]. Stockholm: Almqvist och Wicksell.

Kristofersen, L. (1994). Fjerde- Og Sjvendeklassingers oppvekst. [Growing-up conditions for 4th and 7th formers]. In press, Oslo: the Institute of Urban and Regional Research.

Ogden, T. (1994). Sosial kompetanse i kontekst. [Social competence in context]. *Report,* Oslo: The Norwegian Institute of Child Welfare Research.

Sandbæk, M. (1992). *Forebyggende barnevernsarbeid.* [Preventive Child Care Work]. Oslo: Universitetsforlaget.

Sandbæk, M. (1994). Foreldrene om 60 barn som klienter. [The parents talk about 60 children as clients]. *Report,* Oslo: The Norwegian Institute of Child Welfare Research.

Zobbe, K. (1993). *Anbringelse af børn og unge. Hvad kan vi lære av familierne selv?* [Out- of-home placements of children and young people. What can be learned by the families themselves?] Copenhagen: Akademisk Forlag.

30

Child Welfare Experiences and Outcomes: Themes, Policy Implications and Research Agenda

Kathleen Kufeldt and Evariste Thériault

The focus of this section is on child welfare experiences and outcomes. The initial summary, about what we know and what we need to know, is followed by discussion of the implications for Canadian public policy. After consideration of experiences and outcomes, the question of a research agenda is elaborated. The section on the research agenda includes coverage of issues relating to child welfare research as well as priority areas for research.

Themes

The impact of poverty on the capacity to parent can no longer be questioned. Adequate income is the most basic and powerful preventive measure; there is a range of means by which such an objective can be achieved. We know too that children need to have at least one adult continually committed to them (Bronfenbrenner, 1979). Bronfenbrenner also notes, as does Garbarino (1992), that children and adults affect and are affected by their ecological system. The implication is that the nested systems within the child's ecosystem must support and enhance healthy growth and development of the child as well as the capacity and ability of the adult to care. Kathleen Kufeldt's (1995) work illustrates this. Sociological theory helps inform understanding of family roles, who does what in the family and in society, as well as gender differentials and cultural issues. Considerations from sociology help shed light on the role and task of temporary caregivers, e.g. foster carers, and to differentiate them from that of biological parent. They also help in developing understanding and sensitivity to women's issues and to cultural biases that can impact on child welfare interventions.

Writers such as Hasenfeld (1977) and Blau and Scott (1962) provide understanding of how objectives can become displaced and process can take precedence over results. This knowledge supports Carolyne Gorlick's (1995) work on the importance of client perspective, the value of empowering clients, and the need for collaboration between services. Research focused on child welfare specifically has also increased knowledge. Fanshel's original identification of "parental visiting as the key to discharge" (1975) has been confirmed many times. If a child remains in care beyond 6 months, then care is likely to be extended. Children who remain in care beyond eighteen months have a very slim chance of return home, although Roger Bullock (1995) estimates that in the United Kingdom 87% return within five years. Young people who have been in care are over-represented among runaway and homeless youth (Kufeldt & Burrows, 1994) and, especially if they are boys, are at greater risk of becoming young offenders.

In this volume, Elizabeth Backe-Hansen, Roger Bullock, Sonia Jackson, Kathleen Kufeldt and Susan Silva-Wayne have discussed experiences and outcomes in child welfare. Experiences will affect outcomes, yet little research to date has focused on the link between the two. Service inputs and service outcomes displace attention to the real life experience of the child. A common element of this group of studies was the attempt to investigate and identify some of the qualitative aspects of service.

The Scandinavian studies presented by Backe-Hansen (1995) identify similar problems to those encountered in North America. Children are exposed to many different services and there is a tendency to refer on from agency to agency. Coordination and cooperation, as well as consideration of each service in the larger context of the child's life course, are all essential. Silva-Wayne (1995) drew on Festinger's (1983) and Triseliotis's (1980) examination of outcomes to affirm the need to strive for reduced movement in care and to establish a positive continuity. She also outlines the paradox that workers are located in static fashion in the system rather than being free to move and to relate in dynamic fashion with the changes in the child's life. Kufeldt's (1995) paper, part of a larger series of studies of experiences and outcomes as perceived by all participants, looks at inclusive care and management of the separation experience. Six hypotheses were examined in relation to these two crucial aspects of child welfare experience. Particularly interesting is the relationship between the way the initial separation is handled and satisfaction rates over time. Clarity with respect to the role of foster carers was also examined. Kufeldt identifies the need to take mementos of home into care and Bullock (1995) stresses the parallel need for prized possessions to continue to occupy territory in the children's own home. He illuminated the whole process of return; even where return is desired and longed for it will nevertheless involve further separation experiences. The reality of the child welfare experience is, sadly, careless rather than caring. More attention is paid to service arrangements than to the needs of the individual child.

Early adversity, abuse, traumatic separation, disruption and discontinuity in care all constitute high risk factors for children. Less is known about the factors that constitute opportunity and that can ameliorate negative effects. Silva-Wayne (1995) addresses this gap. Her relatively small sample allowed for intensive engagement with the graduates of care. These young people provided important insights into the experience (including a sense of stigmatization and insufficient attention to academic and other talents) with useful advice about what might help. Factors that contribute to resilience are effective role models, community affiliations, and opportunities for mastery, growth, and elevated self-esteem.

Jackson (1995) provides the most promising route to date to improving outcomes for children in care. She outlines the process of a central government sponsored initiative in the United Kingdom. A set of assessment and action instruments to monitor the experiences of the child in care has been developed. The approach has the potential to revolutionize the in care experience and yet its basic premise is hardly revolutionary. The design is based on the central question, "Is the child receiving that care which it would be reasonable to expect a parent to give?" Jackson acknowledges that children in care have special needs that demand more than "the ordinary reasonable parent would (or could) do" but reminds us that parents of special needs children usually do go beyond what normally might be done. The instruments developed focus on the day to day experiences of the child, across all dimensions of developmental tasks and needs. The theoretical basis is the contribution that healthy development and opportunity make to life course outcomes. This work is a positive response to the challenges posed by Silva-Wayne. Unlike most assessment tools currently used in child welfare, it contains action components to remedy any shortfalls discovered.

Implications for Canadian Public Policy

In North America, child protection and looking after children in substitute care are the two main functions of child welfare agencies. The law governing these services is based on the assumption that parents have the right, responsibility, and capacity to raise their own children without state interference. As a result, child protection agencies have to demonstrate that a child is in need of protection before they can intervene. Bala (1991, p. 359) suggests that the Canadian child welfare system is governed by two approaches, the interventionist approach and the family autonomy approach. Both imply that families who come within the purview of the system have deficits in their ways or capacity to raise children; the intervention is therefore geared to deal with this deficit. Failure in the child-rearing task is perceived as individual failure. No recognition is given to political, social, economic or other systemic forces that may render it difficult to maintain an adequate standard of child care. Little is done in terms of prevention, from state-mandated agencies or programs, to assist parents in their responsibilities of raising children.

Clearly child and family poverty affect child welfare intake (Backe-Hansen, 1995). Poor families are over-represented among families in contact with child welfare. In Toronto, 83% of the families who are involved with the Metro Toronto Children's Aid Society are poor and another 11% are just above the poverty line. Executive Director Bruce Rivers says that poverty debilitates and erodes parenting capacity and self-image. "One reason poor families are over-represented is because wealthier parents have access to more resources, such as alternate parenting programs—anything from camps to child care to private schools" (Scarth, 1993, p. 6). The state should be involved in developing programs and policies to ameliorate the financial situation of Canadians and to have an overall impact on the level of poverty in the country. Canada, compared to other industrialized countries, presents a poor showing with respect to the level of poverty generally, and that of children in particular. In a comparison of Canada, France, West Germany, Netherlands, Sweden, the United Kingdom and the United States, Canada ranks second (exceeded only by the USA) with respect to poverty. In the mid-1980s, 8.9% of all households, 9.3% of all families with children, and 9.4% of all lone-parent families with children were living in more severe poverty. (More severe poverty is defined as household income of less than 40% of the national adjusted median income.) (McFate, 1991, p. 2).

Baker (1994a) explores and compares the impact of social policy and programs on families in eight industrialized countries: Australia, Canada,

France, Germany, The Netherlands, Sweden, the United Kingdom and the United States. She considers a number of factors to explain differences among the countries under review. These include economic and political arguments, the importance of political ideology and types of government, structural constraints, demographics, social change over time, and mass support (Baker, 1994b, p. 129). She concludes that some countries have achieved much lower levels of poverty than others by a combination of direct services, social insurance programs, universal measures, and tax benefits. Countries have managed to maintain low levels of poverty by quite different social policies and social programs. France is a country with a family policy which is explicitly pronatalist and has an extensive maternity leave and public child care system (Baker, 1994a, p. 38). The Netherlands, on the other hand, has no explicit family policy and is essentially noninterventionist with respect to families. Its emphasis is on "autonomy, personal responsibility, and public education" (Baker, 1994a, p. 41). Sweden places its emphasis on full employment and labour market policies in addition to housing support and universal child allowances (Baker, 1994a, p. 43). Any policy reform should be based on a clear explication of underlying values including:

- Children are entitled to receive the necessities of life.
- Each child and family is unique and different.
- The response to poverty should be the provision of sufficient support, not removal of children.
- With sufficient resources and in a context of mutuality and interdependence most families have the capacity to nurture their children.

Policies related to income support and protection of children, as well as health and education, affect one another. Policies should respond to need rather than children and families having to fit policies. Child welfare policies, and indeed social policies that impinge on the welfare of children, must be informed by what we know. Umbrella legislation, rather than narrowly defined system specific legislation, is desirable. Such legislation could sanction the flexibility required for interdepartmental and interorganizational initiatives, with pooling of resources. It is incumbent on political leaders to allow public servants to re-organize departmental arrangements and service delivery in such a way that public response is geared to the needs of child and family, rather than the child and family having to fit some narrow definition of eligibility. The people-processing function (Hasenfeld, 1977) should be truly functional, not merely a structural arrangement. Prevention measures could be applied that would be conducive not only to healthy families and children, but also to a reduction in mental health issues, juvenile delinquency, and children in care. Better-fed school children would be able to perform at a higher level, to learn more effectively and to reach their potential. There would be less need for more expensive remedial and professional services; the immense costs of institutional care and incarceration of those whom society has failed would be enormously reduced. Such an approach to social policy development would allow policy makers and senior managers of service delivery to be more innovative and flexible. Their orientation should be towards community partnership.

The issue of public accountability, which is usually couched in terms of service outputs and service delivered, should be reframed in terms of achievements or client outcomes. Clear directives are required, such as those reported by Jackson (1995). Such direction has been lacking in Canada to date. Instead there has been an assumption that service inputs and documentation of service (as opposed to client) outcomes equate to fulfilment of policy directives. This assumption feeds into the scapegoating of recipients and/or direct providers of service when all does not go well.

It is clear that much is already known about how child welfare responses can and should be improved (Backe-Hansen, 1995; Bullock, 1995; Jackson, 1995; Kufeldt, 1995; Silva-Wayne, 1995). It is also clear that responses that are too narrowly targeted cannot raise the general level of well-being of children, nor reduce abuse and neglect in a significant way. The ecology of child abuse and neglect suggests that in only a small minority of cases can abuse and neglect be imputed to defective family and/or parenting and even here one should be cautious, since uninterrupted, intergenerational, defective socialization may well be the factor. Reform needs to be directed at the systemic factors that impact negatively on children, women, and some minorities to eradicate abuse and neglect of children.

The task of protecting children is further complicated by the fact that government arrangements for services for children are divided among many branches, i.e., education, health care, public health, child welfare etc. Federal legislation with respect to young offenders is limited in the extent to which it can attend to welfare needs. Despite the degree to which families are inextricably linked to, and interdependent with, government services in the business of raising children, children continue to be considered private endeavours. This translates into limited public concern until the children misbehave or offend, which in turn contributes to inadequate legislation. Nothing much has been changed since 1979 when the reminder was published that child welfare legislation focuses on what should not be done to children rather than what ought to be done for them (Task Force on the Child as Citizen, 1979). Children have to suffer damage (somctimes severe damage) before help can be provided.

The average family is subject to forces that effect it for good or ill. Most often strengths and resources exist within the family which allow it to overcome and to deal with the various ups and downs. If the state is to raise children well it must recognize that similar forces and dynamics affect it. In a sense its task is similar to that of a parent of children with special needs; to manage the task there needs to exist sufficient resources and access to special services as required. To be successful the state must understand parenting and the business of raising children. Such understanding requires active partnership between policy makers, researchers, practitioners, child carers, and families and children themselves.

Research Agenda

Several issues have emerged ranging from concern about assumptions to questioning what exactly is meant by child welfare outcomes. Also posed was the challenge to be clear about what actually is known. When researchers cannot be clear, policy makers are left without guidelines for designing services that will produce the best outcomes for children.

Issues

A number of issues require attention in the development of a research agenda. An important one is the assumptions (often undeclared) that have informed the particular project and its design and methodology. Flaws existing in research may well be related to faulty assumptions. Young people who have been through the care system are asking for a voice in order to provide authenticity. What were the views of the children? Is a particular process good or merely cosmetic? Is improvement in parents equated to improvement in the children's welfare? Is prevention of placement necessarily, or always, good? How should results be interpreted? Should (for instance in the case of Native adoption) a breakdown rate of 60% be considered bad or should the non-failure rate of 40% be cause for satisfaction? What are case breakdown rates really telling us, in foster care, or in adoption? We make an assumption that breakdown is a negative event, without paying sufficient attention to the quality of the placement and the child's experience over time. Is it negative if the child has precipitated the breakdown because of an abusive situation? What can those who refuse a particular program tell us about needs and services required? Researchers do not always ask why people did not want to be involved; this too would be useful information.

Another issue is that of task definition and the lack of clarity with respect to the task of child welfare. For instance, what is meant by family preservation? Is the intent to preserve the family at all costs, or should the intent be to ascertain the optimal placement for a child, as close to the family as is compatible with safety and security? In family preservation whose interests take precedence, parents' or children's? What is the task in foster care? Is it to provide a different family experience for the child, to work with the biological family for the child, to provide respite care, to provide treatment and therapy, or to engage in partnership with the social worker to improve prognosis for the future? What is the function of the state: to support families, to prevent abuse, to intervene only where abuse has happened? Can the state be a good parent? What is the task of parenting?

Theory development is closely related to the discussion of assumptions and task definition. Indeed solid theory building is the appropriate strategy for testing assumptions and defining tasks. Jackson (1995) related how she and her associates, in the absence of good predictors of outcomes, took as their starting point the established relationship between quality of parenting, children's developmental needs, and life course outcomes. Kufeldt (1995) compared a construct that made sense intuitively (inclusive care) to knowledge of child development and to sociological theory. Research must be informed by theory, theory becomes the clay to mould interventions, interventions (and thus theory) must in turn be tested in the furnace of experience. But there are some cautionary notes:

- Social constructs change over time.
- The same outcomes can be defined differently.
- Any situation evaluated is an outcome of something else.
- Can we define when an outcome can be presumed to have happened?
- Gaps in research agendas (e.g. reintegrating men into family life).
- Obscuring outcomes by terms used (e.g. family, step-parent).
- There is an inherent risk in basing policy changes on historical evidence that might be subject to obsolescence (a case in point is the changing face of adoption, from a closed to an open system).
- What services are required to support children's development?

- Should gender determine different intervention strategies?

Topics that related to service delivery and systemic issues are pertinent issues for research. They fall into two groups:

1. Variables for further attention:

- Gender as it affects outcomes
- Worker qualities that affect outcomes

2. System Issues

- Gaps between intent and service delivery
- Availability and accessibility of appropriate services and resources
- Obstacles to provision of service
- Obstacles to family contact
- Power differentials between consumer and worker and between worker and managers
- Power differentials in society, marginalization
- Resource implications of maintaining continuity of care

Research should be interactive and action-based. Decision making with respect to research agendas should be decided and prioritized through consultation among all parties in a specific jurisdiction. Timely feedback of results to the relevant stakeholders is as important as design and implementation of the research.

Much is not yet known. The long term outcomes of state care of children are still unclear, as is the question of whether the life chances of the children are better or worse as the result of such intervention. The majority of young people who have been in care return home, by design, drift, or desperation. The degree to which such return and reconnection is helpful is not known. Little is known about which parents might have a good prognosis or what might be the nature of chance occurrences that affect outcomes. A search for predictors continues to be of high priority. Good information about process is also needed. One-dimensional measurements of outcome are not helpful. Listening to children is crucial, and it is not helpful to generalize about all children in care. This implies that policies should be responsive to the individual child and yet interventions tend to be measured in terms of service outcomes rather than in terms of the effect on any given child.

Priority areas for research

What then are priority agendas for research? First and foremost is the consideration of outcomes. A serious problem is that projects are evaluated in terms of an intended outcome, but that objective itself can be a loaded assumption. The global outcome in any child welfare intervention should be the well-being of the child. In other words outcomes should be evaluated in terms of whether children have a better life as a result of actions taken. The Looking After Children Project (Jackson, 1995) decided very firmly that outcomes should be determined in terms of the individual child. The focus of outcomes should be on the needs of the child. Indicators of outcomes should be expressed in terms of the child and not the service. To pursue the study of outcomes effectively the following would need to be considered:

- Development of knowledge regarding community standards for parenting.
- Cultural and community variations.
- Measures of good parenting for children and youth in care.
- Young people's own perspectives on their experience in care.
- Importance of key relationships.
- Continuities in young people's lives.
- Regular opportunities for feedback from young people, including exit interviews.

Two areas for more intermediate research will contribute to Canadian child welfare. First, inter-provincial studies would allow for comparisons of the effects of different policy arrangements, sharing information, and pooling knowledge. This might help tease out what issues and problems are endemic to the task, and what might be avoided or ameliorated by policy change. Second is a study of leaving care in Canada. We could learn from consumers what aspects of the in-care experience were helpful/harmful and what contributes to good transition.

Two particular strategies will contribute significantly to knowledge building in the area of child welfare. One is the epidemiological approach which allows for comparisons to be made among naturally occurring phenomena. The other is longitudinal studies of children entering care and long term examination of the life history of graduates. Longitudinal research is essential if the cycle of intergenerational neglect and abuse is to be understood in order that it can be interrupted. A comprehensive national data base on children in care is an urgent need in Canada.

Clients have the right to effective intervention. An important question is what is the impact of research on policy? It is incumbent on researchers to share the knowledge derived from their work in order to inform policy and practice. Effective dissemination is dependent on reports that are written in clear and understandable language. It also requires the use of appropriate arenas and the creation of an atmosphere where practitioners will use research. There is a need to engage the media to further the interests of children as informed by the research. There is a need for partnership between policy makers, researchers, funders and practitioners. Interdisciplinary research is required that includes economists to determine, not only the real costs of a particular intervention, but also the costs of not intervening.

Finally, whatever the approach or research strategy used, it is essential that child welfare research is informed by good outcome measures that are in turn formed by the child's experience. If the child disappears from focus, the essential purpose of child welfare policies, programs and reserach endeavours is also lost.

References

Backe-Hansen, E. (1995). Case experiences and outcomes of child welfare services in a Scandinavian context. In J. Hudson & B. Galaway (Eds.), *Child welfare in Canada: Research and policy implications.* Toronto: Thompson Educational Publishing.

Baker, M. (1994a). Canadian family policies: Cross-national comparisons. Montréal: School of Social Work, McGill University.

Baker, M. (1994b). *Canada's Changing Families: Challenges to Public Policy.* Ottawa: Vanier Institute of the Family.

Bala, N. (1991). An Introduction to Child Protection Problems. In N. Bala, J. P. Hornick, & R. Vogl (Eds.), *Canadian Child Welfare Law.* Toronto: Thompson Educational Publishing.

Blau, P. M., & Scott, W. R. (1962). *Formal Organizations.* San Francisco: Chandler Publishing Company.

Bronfenbrenner, U. (1979). *The ecology of human development: Experiments by nature and design.* Boston, Massachusetts: Harvard University Press.

Bullock, R. (1995). Return home as experienced by children in state care and their families. In J. Hudson & B. Galaway (Eds.), *Child welfare in Canada: Research and policy implications.* Toronto: Thompson Educational Publishing.

Fanshel, D. (1975). Parental visiting of children in foster care: Key to discharge? *Social Service Review, 49*(4), 493–514.

Festinger, T. (1983). *No one ever asked us ... a postscript to foster care.* New York: Columbia University Press.

Garbarino, J. (1992). *Children and Families in the Social Environment* (2nd Edition). New York: Aldine DeGruyter.

Gorlick, C. A. (1995). Listening to low-income children and single mothers: Policy implications related to child welfare. In J. Hudson & B. Galaway (Eds.), *Child welfare in Canada: Research and policy implications.* Toronto: Thompson Educational Publishing.

Hasenfeld, Y. (1977). People processing organizations: An exchange approach. In Y. Hasenfeld & English (Eds.), *Human Service Organizations,* 60–71. Ann Arbor: University of Michigan Press.

Jackson, S. (1995). Looking after children better: An interactive model for research and practice. In J. Hudson & B. Galaway (Eds.), *Child welfare in Canada: Research and policy implications.* Toronto: Thompson Educational Publishing.

Kufeldt, K. (1995). Inclusive care separation management and role clarity in foster care: Development of theoretical constructs. In J. Hudson & B. Galaway (Eds.), *Child welfare in Canada: Research and policy implications.* Toronto: Thompson Educational Publishing.

Kufeldt, K., & Burrows, B. (1994). *Issues Affecting Public Policies and Services for Homeless Youth.* Calgary: University of Calgary.

McFate, (1991). Poverty, inequality and the crisis of social policy: Summary of findings. Washington, D.C.: Joint Centre for Political and Economic Studies.

Packman, J. (1986). *Who Needs Care? Social Work Decisions About Children.* London: Basil Blackwell.

Silva-Wayne, S. (1995). Contributions to resilience in children and youth: What successful child welfare graduates say. In J. Hudson & B. Galaway (Eds.), *Child welfare in Canada: Research and policy implications.* Toronto: Thompson Educational Publishing.

Scarth, S. (1993). Child welfare at the crossroads. *Perceptions, 17*(3), 5–8.

Taskforce on the Child as Citizen. (1978). *Admittance Restricted: The Child as Citizen in Canada Task Force.* Ottawa: The Canadian Council on Children and Youth.

Triseliotis, J. (1980). *New Developments in Foster Care and Adoption.* London: Routledge & Kegan Paul.

5

A RESEARCH AGENDA

31

The Directions for Future Research

Burt Galaway and Joe Hudson

The research reported in this book as well as the summary chapters by Madeline Lovell and A. H. Thompson, Suzanne Geoffrion and Sandra Scarth, Karen Swift and Lyle Longclaws, Christopher Bagley and Peter Gabor, and Kathleen Kufeldt and Evariste Theriault, suggest several directions for future research about the child welfare system.

1. A high priority is to reach agreement about the intended outcomes of child welfare services and measures of these outcomes. The fundamental question of what purposes we are trying to achieve with child welfare programs must be answered, along with related questions about the measures to be used in assessing results.
2. Research needs to be directed at clearly specifying and describing programs and interventions to gain clarity about what we are attempting to do.
3. Studies are needed of comparative approaches to organizing and delivering child welfare services. What are the costs and effectiveness of different organizational patterns?
4. Evaluations are needed of specific programs as well as program components, such as caseload size, within programs.
5. Research is needed on the process by which innovations that are found to be effective in demonstration projects can be incorporated into agency programs and practices.
6. Longitudinal research is needed about the nature of the experiences of children who enter the child welfare system.
7. Research needs to be conducted about the gatekeeping functions—the basis for decision-making in admitting children to the system, in moving children from one system to another, and in discharging children from the child welfare system.
8. Finally, research needs to systematically consider the possible unintended consequences of child welfare interventions.

A variety of research approaches can be used to carry out research in the child welfare system. Much of the research may need to be interdisciplinary, and will likely require collection and use of both quantitative and qualitative data. Research designs and the nature of data collected must flow from the research purposes and questions. Thus, the research questions must be formulated before matters of research design and type of data to be collected are considered. In this way, research questions drive the approaches used in addressing them.

Child Welfare Outcomes and Outcome Measures

Immediate attention needs to be given to specifying the purposes of child welfare services in terms of what is intended to be accomplished and to the development of measures to be used as indicators of the extent to which the purposes are achieved. A wide range of measures have been used to assess the effectiveness of family preservation (Pecora, 1995) and foster care programs. For the most part these measures have been case events, like return home, which may or may not have a direct bearing on the well-being of the child. Is keeping a child in an abusing home a successful outcome? The Looking After Children project in the United Kingdom may offer promising directions (Jackson, 1995). The project begins from the perspective of what good parents would want for their children and conceptualizes such multiple outcomes as meeting the children's health, educational, identity, family and community participation, social presentation, behavioral and social development, and self-care needs. Rather than defining outcomes as case events, they are conceptualized in terms of whether or not the child is receiving the type of care that a good parent would provide.

Determining desired outcomes for child welfare services will necessarily involve close interactions between policy makers and researchers. Determination of what the purposes of child welfare services are, and what outcomes should be accomplished to meet identified purposes, is a public policy decision. Once done, researchers can develop measures and procedures to be used to determine if the outcomes are being accomplished. These measures can most fruitfully be incorporated in administrative or management information systems providing for the on-going, routine feedback of information on program inputs, activities, and results. A key task, then, is the development of administrative systems that use common variables and values from one province to another, thus allowing for country-wide aggregation. The federal government should take responsibility for this type of initiative, placing emphasis on the provinces and territories implementing client tracking systems that contain a core, common set of data. The twelve jurisdictions would, of course, be free to collect additional, unique data to meet their individual needs. Without such a national child welfare data system, we will continue to lack the ability to provide time series data, to compare across and within jurisdictions, and to monitor and evaluate service trends.

Specifications of Programs and Interventions

Research needs to be undertaken to describe child welfare programs and interventions clearly, as well as specifying what resources are required to carry out each program or intervention. We lack precise definitions of child welfare programs and their components. This can be accomplished by collecting systematic information about how programs actually operate. This involves preparing structure and logic models and then collecting data to revise the models so they more accurately mirror program operations. It is impossible to know how well we are doing without a clear specification and description of what it is we are doing. Even with clear outcomes, a detailed understanding of program processes is critical for explaining program impact and effects.

Comparative Studies

Comparative studies are necessary to make informed decisions about the most cost effective way of delivering child welfare services. Several different types of comparative studies are needed, including:

1. Comparisons of the costs and effectiveness of services delivered by for-profit, non-profit, and public agencies.
2. Comparisons of costs and results of services delivered by different types of organizations such as community-based, feminist, and more bureaucratically structured organizations.
3. Comparisons of costs and effectiveness of different types of interventions such as foster care compared to institutional services, intense family preservation programs compared to less intense family support services, group services compared to individual interventions, and so forth.

By systematically comparing and contrasting the effects that different approaches have on standard outcome measures and by collecting accurate cost information, including capital costs, policy makers will be able to make more informed decisions about the most effective and cost efficient way to deliver child welfare services. The most effective services may not be the most cost efficient, but good quality comparative studies will provide policy makers with the information necessary to make decisions about trade-offs between efficiency and effectiveness.

Evaluations of Programs and Program Components

Once programs are clearly specified and outcome measures are determined, evaluation research can be undertaken to determine the extent to which various programs contribute to accomplishing the outcomes. Equally important, evaluations can be conducted as to whether various program components, if manipulated, make any appreciable effect on outcomes. For example, does caseload size effect outcome? Standards set by professional and trade associations often call for limiting caseload size without very strong evidence that smaller caseloads necessarily result in better outcomes for clients.

Institutionalizing Innovations and Research

Research needs to be undertaken to determine ways that innovative programs, once tested and found to successfully contribute to desired outcomes, can be integrated into existing institutional arrangements for delivering child welfare services. For example, Don Fuchs (1995) and Gary Cameron (1995) both report on demonstration programs which were tested and found to be successful at reducing child abuse by enhancing the social networks of child welfare families. But there are no indications that these innovations are being integrated into existing child welfare programs and practice. Research is needed to understand the barriers to integrating new programming concepts, the process by which change can occur within existing service delivery systems, and how practitioners may incorporate innovation into programs and practices.

This also applies to integrating research activities into child welfare agencies. How can we best organize and manage research to provide useful information that is used to improve performance? Organizing for research in agency settings requires thinking through and answering such questions as:

- Who are the intended users of the research?
- What are the set of agency programs to be subject to research
- What are agency priorities for research on the identified programs?

Answers to these questions will amount to an agency research plan that can help ensure that research is carried out in a purposeful way in the agency setting.

Longitudinal Studies

Longitudinal studies are needed of cohorts of children and families receiving child welfare services, the types and nature of services they receive over time, and the various courses which children follow in the child welfare system. Longitudinal studies are relatively expensive because they require a fairly large sample and data collected at multiple points in time. While they do not yield immediate results, longitudinal studies can provide a comprehensive picture of children moving through the child welfare system over time and can contribute answers to many of the questions raised in previous sections. Studies that rely only on cross-sectional samples of youth and families in the child welfare system at a point in time will likely produce inaccurate inferences about the larger population that comes into, through, and out of the system over a longer time duration. Some people stay longer in the system and, consequently, are more likely to be subject to cross-sectional studies, the results of which can be inappropriately generalized. Longitudinal studies can also follow children after the termination of child welfare services to assess the longer term impact that these services may have had.

Studies of Gatekeeping

Research needs to focus on the critical gatekeeping decisions that regulate the flow of young people and families into, through, and out of the child welfare system. How are key decisions made, what criteria are used in making these decisions, who makes key decisions, and what are the expected and unexpected effects of these decisions? Gatekeeping studies can also address the flow of cases between systems. Who decides when to shift a young person from the child welfare to the juvenile justice system or the mental health system, and on what basis are these decisions made?

Unintended Consequences

Research needs to explicitly focus on identifying potential unintended consequences of child welfare interventions. Are there conditions under which interventions worsen the conditions for children and families? What, for example, are the effects of responding to child abuse as a criminal justice rather than social service problem? Are there unintended consequences from cross cultural adoption or closed adoption? It is relatively naive to assume that good intentions lead to beneficial results. Researchers must be prepared to consider both the potential harmful as well as potential helpful effects of child welfare interventions in relation to the outcomes we are attempting to accomplish.

References

Cameron, G. (1995). The nature and effectiveness of parent mutual aid organizations in child welfare. In J. Hudson & B. Galaway (Eds.), *Child welfare in Canada: Research and policy implications.* Toronto: Thompson Educational Publishing.

Fuchs, D. (1995). Preserving and strengthening families and protecting children: Social network intervention a balanced approach to the prevention of child maltreatment. In J. Hudson & B. Galaway (Eds.), *Child welfare in Canada: Research and policy implications . Toronto: Thompson Educational Publishing.*

Jackson, S. (1995). Looking after children better: An interactive model for research and practice. In J. Hudson & B. Galaway (Eds.), *Child welfare in Canada: Research and policy implications.* Toronto: Thompson Educational Publishing.

Pecora, P. (1995). Assessing the impact of family-based services. In J. Hudson & B. Galaway (Eds.), *Child welfare in Canada: Research and policy implications.* Toronto: Thompson Educational Publishing.